Press On Regardless

The Story of the Fifth Royal Tank Regiment in World War Two

PRESS ON REGARDLESS

THE STORY OF THE FIFTH ROYAL TANK REGIMENT IN WORLD WAR TWO

by

Edward Wilson

SPELLMOUNT
Staplehurst

British Library Cataloguing in Publication Data:
A catalogue record for this book is available
from the British Library

ISBN 1-86227-217-4

First published in the UK in 2003 by
Spellmount Limited
The Old Rectory
Staplehurst
Kent TN12 0AZ

Tel: 01580 893730
Fax: 01580 893731
E-mail: enquiries@spellmount.com
Website: www.spellmount.com

1 3 5 7 9 8 6 4 2

Typeset in Palatino by MATS, Southend-on-Sea, Essex
Printed in Great Britain by
TJ International Ltd, Padstow, Cornwall

Contents

Preface

PRESS ON REGARDLESS does not claim to be a 'history' of the Fifth Royal Tank Regiment in any formal sense of that word. Such a book has yet to be written and would have to cover fifty-three years: from 1916, when the unit was formed, to 1969, when it was disbanded.

I have dealt with only six of those years: the period from Friday, 1st September 1939 to Tuesday, 8th May 1945. In other words, the years which my generation came to know as 'Hitler's War'.

Winston Churchill, shortly after becoming Prime Minister in 1940, visited his old school and there heard the boys singing about the 'dark days'. 'No!' Churchill thundered. 'These are not dark days. They are great days; the greatest days our country has ever lived.' What I have attempted to do is to tell, where possible in the words of men who served in it, the story of the part played by one Regiment in those great days.

The book is also my tribute to the men of whom their one-time Commanding Officer, 'Fearless Jim' Hutton (later to become Major General W M Hutton CB CBE DSO MC) said, 'the spirit of the Regiment was second to none in the British Army'.

All the available material – in books, in diaries, in letters, at Bovington, in museums and libraries, in learned societies and in private places – about the Fifth Royal Tank Regiment would fill a volume three, four, five times as long as this. I have had to be selective and can only hope that my selection meets with the readers' approval.

In The Fifth, a unit whose nominal strength exceeded five hundred officers, NCOs and men at any one time, and during a war that lasted nearly six years, over a thousand – perhaps over two thousand – men must have served. Only a few score of those men are cited here by name. I am only too well aware of how many others, including many famous Fifth Tanks personalities, are not mentioned at all. This is, in no way, a reflection on them.

Finally, I must explain that the words chosen for the title do not imply rashness or foolhardiness on the part of the men of The Fifth or their officers. They simply reflect – in a phrase which the men themselves so often used – an aspect of that spirit which Colonel Hutton commended: a willingness to get on with the job . . . a readiness to fight on against the enemy, whatever the odds and regardless of danger to themselves. They were, in fact, saying no more than an earlier generation of tank crews were saying, when they wrote BERLIN OR BUST on the sides of their tanks.

Edward Wilson
Sible Hedingham, March 2003

Introduction and Acknowledgements

There are some who claim, with considerable justification, that the origin of the 'tank' as a military weapon can be attributed to Leonardo da Vinci. A more practical genesis is to be found in a memorandum, dated in January 1915, from the First Sea Lord (a certain Mr Winston Churchill MP) to the Prime Minister which reads:

'It would be quite easy in a short time to fit up a number of steam tractors with small armoured shelters in which men and machine-guns could be placed, which would be bullet-proof. The caterpillar system would enable trenches to be crossed quite easily, and the weight of the machine would destroy all wire entanglements.'

Apart from the motive power, there you have the 'tank'.

The idea was developed, some say by, some say in spite of, the War Office and the High Command. Machines were constructed – and designated for security reasons as 'Water Tanks', with Mesopotamia as their destination. That there was always a strong Naval influence – the Royal Navy had armoured car detachments – can be seen in tank terminology. Why else do tanks have hulls and turrets?

Who was going to man and fight these machines?

The answer to this question has often reflected adversely on the sanity of the men who chose to do so! Be that as it may, almost exclusively we were volunteers. I was: in the Canadian Army in 1941. However, in 1944 I transferred to the British Army and, in due course, found myself with a letter of introduction in my pocket addressed to the Commanding Officer of the First Royal Tank Regiment. This took me, with great rapidity, as far as Belgium to a Forward Reinforcement Unit – which was also a staging point for personnel returning to their units. Here I got into conversation with two RTR types (Henry Osborne and Colin Messent) wearing mysterious red and powder blue flashes on their epaulettes. One of them, Colin Messent, was curious about my Canadian Medal ribbon and asked me what I was doing and where I was going. I told him that I was headed, I hoped, for the First. 'Oh,' Colin said, 'you don't want to go to that shower. You'd much better come with us!'

I did. Six hours later, I was posted to 'B' Squadron, Fifth Royal Tank

Regiment and, all my life, I have owed a great deal to The Fifth and the men who served in it. I hope that this book, in some measure, repays that debt

The business of writing any history demands much research and a lot of pestering other people for information. I received a magnificent response to my pestering from so many ex-Fifth Tanks members that it is impossible to name them all here. I would ask them to accept these few words as my most grateful thanks.

Research also means a large amount of reading. There is a separate bibliography of the many books and other sources which I have used. The core of this history is the Regiment's own War Diary. This (and I should add here that the Diary is reproduced verbatim with all the oddities of abbreviation, spelling, grammar and so forth produced, often under adverse conditions, by busy men) tells where the Regiment was and what it was doing. However, it is the personal accounts, provided by men who served in The Fifth, that tell what it was like to be there and what it meant to be doing those things the War Diary relates.

There are two essential sources of information without which no history of a Royal Tank Regiment could be written. The Public Record Office, to whom I am indebted for access to the Fifth Tanks' official War Diary, and the Library of the Tank Museum in Bovington which provided me with a wealth of information on every aspect of tanks.

It would be unfair not to add my personal thanks. The inevitable disruption of home life has been tolerated and I am duly grateful. I owe a debt of gratitude to Nancy Langmaid for initially niggling at me to write this book and then for coming frequently to my aid when I found myself in difficulties. To David Fletcher of the Tank Museum Library my thanks for letting me pick his brains and waste his time. To John Smith my thanks for his expertise in turning often inferior material into suitable matter for the illustrations and, finally, to John Newman for the cameo of a *Crusader* on the cover.

Picture Credits

Major D E Cockbaine (Private Collection): 3, 4, 5 & 16. Mr D Huett (Private Collection): 9, 11 & 13. The *Illustrated London News* Picture Library: 12. The Tank Museum, Bovington: 1, 2, 6, 7, 8, 10 & 14. The Author's Private Collection: 15.

Foreword

'When shall we five meet again?' This corruption of Shakespeare's famous question was asked repeatedly at Reinsehlen Camp on that famous day in 1967 when all five Royal Tank Regiments paraded in front of the Queen, their Colonel in Chief, on their Golden Jubilee. But no-one really needed to be given the answer, as everyone knew that the decision had already been taken to reduce the Royal Tank Regiment from five to only four regiments as part of the run down of the Armed Forces as we progressively withdrew from Empire. The decision to disband and amalgamate so many armoured and armoured reconnaissance regiments was a highly controversial one. Arguments had raged within Whitehall as to how the reduction in size of the Royal Armoured Corps should be undertaken. It is hugely to the credit of those senior RTR and cavalry officers involved in the debate that an equitable solution was found that was widely seen as fair, no matter how unwelcome.

Having decided that one of the Royal Tank Regiments should go, the next questions were 'Which?' and 'How?' The answer to the 'Which?' question was easy – the 'last in: first out' precedent had already been established. The Sixth, Seventh and Eighth had already gone and the next to go would inevitably be the Fifth. However, the decision to disband the Fifth rather than amalgamate with the Second was very controversial. The previous recent reductions had all been achieved through amalgamation. This ensured that the spirit and history of the individual regiments would continue into the future as part of the amalgamated regiment. Eventually the decision was taken to depart from precedent and disband rather than amalgamate the Fifth, on the grounds that it would disrupt only one regiment rather than two. The danger was, of course, that the history and spirit of the Fifth, and indeed of the Eighth with whom they had already amalgamated, would be lost forever.

These fears, however, proved to be unfounded. The Fifth, under the inspirational leadership of its last Commanding Officer, Dickie Lawson, threw itself into its last year of existence with a period of intense and highly successful training, culminating in a final glorious Cambrai celebration in Wolfenbuttel in 1969. I joined the Third in Wolfenbuttel a year later and many members of the Fifth had stayed on in that popular little town near to the East German border. The ex-members of the Fifth were something of a breed apart.

They brimmed with professionalism and self-confidence and clearly retained a sense of pride in their roots in the Fifth. Some of this pride came from their own early years with the Fifth but much of it was the product of the special spirit that a regiment possesses when it has a distinguished past and is able to pass that ethos on through successive generations. The Fifth was one of those regiments. Its performance in the Second World War was magnificent and gave the Regiment, in the decades of the Cold War that followed, unrivalled confidence in its ability.

The story of the Fifth throughout the war years from September 1939 to May 1945 is admirably told in this excellent book. It is underpinned by the factual accounts from the Regimental War Diaries but draws extensively on the narratives of those who were actually there at the time. It is, of course, the individuals that make a Regiment great and Edward Wilson – himself one of those individuals – charts their progress from a brief spell in France in 1940, through the major battles of North Africa with the Seventh Armoured Division (the original Desert Rats), a brief spell in Italy and then back to the UK to prepare for D-Day. The Regiment landed in France on D+1 and, after some intense fighting in Normandy, was one of the leading armoured regiments in the great sweep across Europe where it liberated Ghent. After crossing the Rhine, the Regiment finally ended up in Hamburg five days before the war ended. This is the Regiment of which its one-time Commanding Officer 'Fearless Jim' Hutton said, 'The Spirit of the Regiment was second to none in the British Army.'

This was the spirit that was so apparent in Wolfenbuttel twenty-five years later and the spirit that goes on to inspire the young men in our Regiment today. It is a story of professionalism, dedication, comradeship and courage that should be read by all who aspire today to join the Band of Brothers that is the Royal Tank Regiment. It is particularly poignant today. As I write this Foreword both the First and the Second are back in the desert with the Desert Rats, this time in Iraq. The weaponry and technology of today may have vastly changed, indeed changed beyond the wildest imaginings of those who fought in the Fifth in the Second World War years, but in spite of such changes much remains the same: the tanks are still only as good as the young men who crew them and victory will still depend on the quality and determination of their leaders.

The Queen, in her address to the Regiment that day in Reinsehlen in 1967, paid tribute to the part played by the Royal Tank Regiment in the fifty years of its existence.

> *Your contribution on the battlefield has been formidable and, on some occasions, decisive but perhaps the most important task in the defence of our country has been, and to a certain extent remains, the development and teaching of the armoured conception of warfare. We live in uncertain times but it is difficult to imagine the situation arising for many years in which the technical skills and*

expert training of the Royal Tank Regiment would not be required of the British Army

Times certainly remain uncertain and it is undoubtedly difficult to envisage the time when the personal qualities so clearly described in this book would no longer be vital to the Nation. No doubt the battlefield of the future will continue to be dramatically different from that of the past: we may have seen the last of the huge main battle tank of old but one thing will never change. We will continue to be inspired by the great deeds of our forebears and those who serve in our Regiment today will strive to live up to the standards that they have set.

Fear Naught.

Lieutenant General Andrew Ridgway CB CBE
Colonel Commandant
Royal Tank Regiment

Guide to Abbreviations

A/D	Accidental Death
Adjt	Adjutant
AFV	Armoured Fighting Vehicle
AP	Armour Piercing or Anti-Personnel – depending on context
APO	Army Post Office
A&Q	Adjutant General and Quartermaster General: the section of the Staff responsible for Administration and Supply
Armd	Armoured
ARV	Armoured Recovery Vehicle
A/Tk	Anti-tank
Bde	Brigade
Bn	Battalion
BEF	British Expeditionary Force – the Army in France in 1939/40, the name being taken from the British Army in Flanders in WW I
BLA	British Liberation Army – the Army in North-west Europe in 1944/45
Brig	Brigadier
BTO	Battalion Transport Officer
Capt	Captain
CCS	Casualty Clearing Station
Cfn	Craftsman
CIGS	Chief of the Imperial General Staff
CO	Commanding Officer
Col	Colonel
Coy	Company (of Infantry etc)
Cpl	Corporal
C-in-C	Commander in Chief
DCM	Distinguished Conduct Medal (decoration awarded to ORs)
D&M	Driving & Maintenance

Dis	Not strictly an abbreviation as there is no word 'diserviceable': same meaning as U/S
Div	Division
DoW	Died of Wounds
DR	Despatch Rider (Motorcyclist)
DSO	Distinguished Service Order (decoration awarded to field and general officers)
DUKW	Not an abbreviation at all. The initials stand for the manufacturer's model number of the GMC three-axle 2-ton amphibious lorry. Universally known as 'Ducks'.
ENSA	Entertainments: National Service Association
FAP	First Aid Post
FDL or FDP	Forward Defence or Defensive Line[s] / Position[s]
FGCM	Field General Court Martial
FOO	Forward Observation Officer
FOP	Forward Observation Post
GOC	General Officer Commanding
GS	General Staff: the section of the Staff, as someone once put it, responsible for getting on with the war
GSO	General Staff Officer
HE	High Explosive
i/c	in command [in charge] of
Inj	Injured (on duty)
IO	Intelligence Officer
KD	Khaki Drill (uniform)
KIA	Killed In Action
KO'd	Knocked Out
LAD	Light Aid Detachment
L/Cpl	Lance Corporal
LCT	Landing Craft Tank
LofC	Line[s] of Communication
LRDG	Long Range Desert Group
LRS	Light Recovery Section
LSI	Landing Ship Infantry
LST	Landing Ship Tank
Lt or Lieut	Lieutenant
MC	Military Cross (decoration awarded to officers)
MDS	Medical Dressing Station
MET	Motor Engined Transport
MG	Machine-gun
MID	Mentioned In Despatches
MM	Military Medal (decoration awarded to ORs)
MO	Medical Officer
MP	Military Police

MQMS	Mechanist Quartermaster Sergeant
MR	Map Reference
MRS	Medical Reception Station
Msg	Missing (in action)
NAAFI	Navy, Army and Air Force Institute, which provided canteens and shops for service personnel by land and sea wherever British Forces were stationed
NCO	Non Commissioned Officer (*ie* all grades of Sergeants and Corporals)
N/S	Not Stated
NTR	Nothing to report
OC	Officer Commanding (*eg* a Squadron)
OCTU	Officer Cadet Training Unit
OP	Observation Post
OR[s]	Other Rank[s]
PAD	Passive Air Defence
PCV	Passenger Carrying Vehicle
Pln[s]	Platoon[s] of Infantry
PT	Physical Training
QM	Quartermaster
Regt	Regiment
RHU	Reinforcement Holding Unit
RQMS	Regimental Quartermaster Sergeant
RSM	Regimental Sergeant Major
R/T	Radio Telephone
RTO	Rail Transport Officer
RTU	Returned to Unit
RV	Rendez-Vous
Sgt	Sergeant
SP	Self-Propelled
Sqn	Squadron
SSM	Squadron Sergeant Major
TA	Territorial Army
T&A	Test & Adjust
TDS	Tank Delivery Squadron [alternatively Section]
u/c	under command
U/S	Unserviceable
VRD	Vehicle Repair Depot [alternatively Detachment]
WD	War Department
WE	War Establishment
Wnd	Wounded
WO	Warrant Officer (*ie* Squadron/Company and Battalion/Regimental Sergeant Majors)

WOp [W/Op]= Wireless Operator

WS	War Substantive (with reference to rank)
W/T	Wireless Telephone

Regiments etc

ACC	Army Catering Corps
CLY	County of London Yeomanry
Greys	Royal Scots Greys
KDG	Kings Dragoon Guards
KRRC	Kings Royal Rifle Corps
LRDG	Long Range Desert Group
RA	Royal Artillery
RAMC	Royal Army Medical Corps
RAOC	Royal Army Ordnance Corps
RASC	Royal Army Service Corps
RB	Rifle Brigade
RE	Royal Engineers
REME	Royal Electrical and Mechanical Engineers
RHA	Royal Horse Artillery
RWF	Royal Welch Fusiliers

Corps are designated as *eg* XXXth Corps
Divisions are designated as *eg* 7th [Armoured] Div(ision)
Brigades are designated as *eg* 22nd [Armoured] B(riga)de
Royal Tank Regiments are designated as *eg* 5RTR, 44RTR
Individual Regiments are designated as *eg* 1 RB, 4 CLY, 5 RHA
Hussar Regiments are designated as *eg* VIII Hussars
Some Regiments are given their nicknames as *eg* the Cherry Pickers (for XI Hussars) or the Skins (for the Royal Innniskilling Dragoon Guards)

List of Maps

CHAPTER I

. . . *In the Beginning*

September 1939–June 1940

This is the story of one Regiment in the British Army during World War Two. The 5th Battalion of The Royal Tank Regiment, later The Fifth Royal Tank Regiment – 'The Fifth'[1].

Friday, 1st September 1939. Twenty years, nine months and twenty days after the end of 'The Great War' – the War To End All Wars – the country stood on the brink of yet another European conflict. Days, more likely hours, would decide the nation's fate. But no thinking man was in any doubt of the outcome. Since the mid-1930s, Hitler's rise to power had cast its shadow across Europe. Opinion in the UK had been ambivalent. There was a 'maintain the peace' and a 'prepare for war' faction. Gradually, popular opinion swung in favour of the latter. With Neville Chamberlain's last desperate, futile, effort at appeasement in September 1938, politicians and public awoke to the reality. War with Germany was inevitable.

Preparations for war had, it is true, belatedly been put in train. New ships for the Royal Navy: new planes for the Royal Air Force. Peace-time conscription had been introduced in April 1939 for the first time ever in Great Britain. One thing, though, had been neglected. Tanks.

In this context, one senior officer had something to say about the nation's lack of preparedness. According to him, the British Army was totally unfit to go to war in 1939. It was not, in some quarters in the late 1930s, even expected to do so. The 'Higher Powers' – veterans of previous wars – did not seriously contemplate the Army ever again fighting in mainland Europe. Containing Hitler could be left to the French: the British would, of course, support them but that would be the role of the Navy and the RAF. This senior officer commanded an Infantry Division in France in 1939 and 1940. He never saw a British tank there, in or out of action. 'And,' he concludes by saying, 'we were the nation which invented the tank and were the first to use it in battle in 1916.' Who was he? None other than 'Monty'[2]!

Friday, 1st September 1939. Perham Down. When reveille sounded, it sounded for a peace-time Army. Perham Down, the home of 5RTR, built in 1934 as a permanent tank centre, laid out to meet the special requirements of armoured units. Specifically, Royal Tank Corps units. On that Friday, 5RTR had two days left in their peace-time home.

What was life like in this still-just-peace-time Army? A Private Soldier's pay was two shillings a day – the decimal equivalent is 10p but, in early twenty-first century terms, more like £3.90 a day [£1,423.50 a year], 'all found'. Out of this fourteen shillings a week, four were deducted for an iniquity called 'barrack room damages', for replacement clothing and as a subscription for future membership of the Regimental Association: something being held in reserve against 'short leaves'. The remaining 'ten bob' was all for spending in the pub or the NAAFI or wherever the men liked but had to cover things like personal and kit cleaning necessities. Standard uniform in the RTR was the same as for other branches of the Army: khaki serge tunics with brass buttons and badges, khaki serge trousers with box crease, full length puttees and 'ammunition' boots – the only difference was the black beret. Another use to which pay could be put was saving to purchase a suit of 'blues' (available from Smiths Handy Stores in the village, on 'extended credit'). Whereas 'dress' uniform was obligatory for officers, other ranks could purchase it or not – depending, one suspects, on whether they fancied their chances with the girls better in blues than in regulation khaki!

Routine generally started with morning parade at 0800 hrs. This was followed by drill and something speciously called 'work on tanks'. Specious because more time was spent on cleaning and polishing than was spent on training exercises. Bert Hunt (or, more correctly Sergeant Major A Hunt MM, who joined 4RTC in 1937 but was later posted to 5RTR) remembers only one pre-war training exercise, that of driving the Battalion's tanks round the Essex countryside. This does not mean that the tank crews were not highly trained but it does mean that routine 'bull' occupied more of Private Thomas Atkins' time than that of his counterpart in the Wehrmacht. Afternoons were usually devoted to sport or some other 'manly exercise'. Evenings were theoretically free but, all too often, had to be devoted to kit cleaning for next day's parades or doing home work for one of the many courses which the Battalion organised.

Only the most senior officers, WOs and NCOs[3] were World War One veterans. Others, coming up to twenty-one years' service (he standard period for a full pension) were usually found in the depots or training establishments and not in the line units. Most older soldiers had, nevertheless, seen service in many different parts of the world – some in very active conditions. They were tough, loyal, competent, independent and utterly reliable.

Another indication of how different the peace-time Army of 1939 was from the happy-go-lucky fighting unit 5RTR became in World War Two is seen in the 1928 'Standing Orders of the 5th Battalion Royal Tank Corps', published (pursuant to Paragraph 1674 of King's Regulations 1923).

These 'Standing Orders' govern the duties of the Commanding Officer and the Corporal of the Guard – to say nothing of the good behaviour of the wives in Married Quarters. They also cover the dress and the rules of conduct of all ranks, on and off parade, on or off the station. In addition, they cover such privileges of Enlisted Men – at any rate, while stationed at Tidworth – as being allowed to own a motorcar or motorcycle but only, 'So long as', say the Standing Orders, 'Other Ranks' Cars and Motorcycles are kept in the shed behind the Officers' Mess and not in bunks, barrack rooms, ablution sheds etc.'

It is facile, seventy and more years later, to make fun of these Standing Orders but they speak very clearly of the high standard of discipline, training, sense of order and concern for the welfare of all ranks, which the British Army had established and was determined to maintain.

Another asset of The Fifth in 1939, apart from its prowess as a front-line fighting unit, was the skill and efficiency of all ranks which made it capable of absorbing drafts of civilians from every walk of life, with no previous or permanent desire for a military career, and of turning them into the war-wise unit which 5RTR undoubtedly became.

Unsurprisingly, the War Diary reports that, at 1545 hrs on that Friday, orders were received from No 1 Heavy Armoured Brigade to mobilise. By 1600 hrs work was underway; tented equipment being drawn and the pitching of the Battalion camp at Windmill Hill begun. At 1900 hrs, High Commands being ever-helpful, Major Farrington, one of the Battalion's most senior officers, was posted to a staff appointment.

By midnight, one Regular Army Reserve Officer, nine Supplementary Reserve Officers and thirty-three Supplementary Reserve Other Ranks had reported for duty.

A number of men who figure in this book were already caught in the net. Willie Dovey had joined the Army in April 1939 and had spent ten weeks of accelerated training for duties in the Royal Tank Corps, being considered fit to wear the black beret (in those days, his ambition in life) after basic training and six weeks' gunnery instruction at Lulworth Cove. Complete with his black beret, a leave pass and a travel warrant, Willie set off for home. Three days later, came the telegram, 'REPORT TO CAMP IMMEDIATELY'. End of leave but not end of story as Trooper Dovey W later joined 5RTR.

On Saturday, 2nd September work continued at 0900 hrs on pitching camp at Windmill Hill. This was interrupted at 1130 hrs by an all-ranks medical inspection. It speaks volumes for the health of that peace-time Army that only three ORs were found unfit for foreign service. At the end of the day, Battalion numbers had been increased by two Regular Army Reserve Officers, two Supplementary Reserve Officers and sixty-one Other Rank Reservists. This interesting balance – or imbalance – of fourteen Officers to ninety-four ORs shows the difficulties which units faced in mobilising for war. But, more significant and exciting than the arrival of reinforcements, was that of three tanks. These were *A13* 'Cruiser' tanks, despatched direct from Nuffields, their manufacturers. These, with the older *A9*s and the *Vickers Mark VI B Light* tanks, were the main armament which the Battalion took to France in 1940.

One of those sixty-one ORs who had been, in his own words, 'released after eleven months from my first, claustrophobic, civil employment as a progress chaser at the local aircraft factory' and 'recalled to the colours' was Leonard Coller (Len or, more usually 'Bing', as in Crosby: Len being renowned for his renderings of that popular crooner's numbers). Private Coller had served for six years in the RTC from 1932 to 1938. His first shock, on reporting to Windmill Hill in September 1939 was to discover that he was no longer *Private* Coller but *Trooper* Coller. Where, Bing wanted to know, were the horses? Where, for that matter, were the other eleven men who should be sharing a bell tent with him? On leave. They had been granted compassionate leave passes – to dig the potatoes, to mend the hole in the roof, their wives were pregnant. Or, as the Squadron Sergeant Major, an old mate of Bing's from their days 'east of Suez', rather more coarsely suggested, to get their wives pregnant.

Bing's tongue-in-cheek excuse for compassionate leave was to 'see my car': an excuse readily accepted by his Squadron Commander (another old acquaintance from India days). Bing and car duly reported back to Windmill Hill on 11th September with the tank full of petrol and the boot full of bottled ale.

But that is to anticipate. When Sunday, 3rd September dawned, no man in the Battalion could have doubted what he would hear in the broadcast the Prime Minister was to make at midday. And, sure enough, when Neville Chamberlain spoke to the nation it was to announce that, since 1115 hrs that morning, a state of war had existed between Great Britain and Germany. To generations brought up on memories of 'The War to End All Wars', the unimaginable had become the reality. Life, as Trooper Dai Mitchell commented philosophically over an early morning cup of char, would never be the same again.

Indeed it wasn't. By mid-afternoon, all ranks had, according to the War Diary, 'passed through gas chamber'. The next day saw the preparations for the move to the tented encampment at Windmill Hill. On the 6th, while preparing anti-aircraft emplacements, the Battalion was reinforced by a Medical Officer, another Reserve Officer and 'a deserter from 1RTR'.

The next two weeks saw intensive training, the arrival of requisitioned lorries, more Cruiser tanks – and 2/Lt AH Crickmay, who figures frequently in this account. It also saw 5RTR's first casualty of the war, when 7886135 Tpr Gliddon L was killed in an accident involving a light tank.

Training was interrupted in October by the weather. So much for moving out of proper accommodation and under canvas with no proper facilities. Officers and men came and went, still with a higher proportion of officers than men. By the end of the month, so the War Diary states, 'camp becoming very cut up and muddy'. Later it got still worse.

On Sunday, 29th October the Church Parade had hardly been dismissed before orders were received from Brigade HQ to be ready to move eastwards at six hours' notice. However, after a good deal of to-ing and fro-ing by advance parties, billeting parties and Battalion transport, 'orders were still vague' on 1st November. Some junior officers were posted away from the regiment: one of them, Arthur Crickmay, en route to Egypt. Next day, the billeting party left 'in two private cars and two trucks'. On 2nd November the move became a reality – except for two tanks which Movement Control contrived to leave behind at Perham Down.

On Guy Fawkes Day the tanks were being detrained at Stevenage where the men had arrived the previous afternoon for billeting in Harpenden. The Battalion had got as near to the enemy as Hertfordshire. November was spent settling into the strange new life in billets, in training and in endless conferences for Squadron Commanders and above. The weather changed from wet to fog and ice. Many December days are covered in the War Diary by the initials NTR, including Christmas Day. January 1940 brought no improvement in the weather but there were a few more Air Raid Warnings – or, rather, false alarms. Some reinforcements of personnel, tanks and soft-skinned vehicles trickled in. Gradually the unit was being brought up to strength.

By mid-January another move was in the air. So was winter, which hampered training. Despite this cold, the Battalion was ordered to move, and did so to the Salisbury area on 26th January. The move was carried out in what even the Navy would have called foul weather: rain, sleet, snow and bitterly cold wind. Notwithstanding these, the War Diary reports a successful move with all tracked vehicles running extremely well and the driving standard being high. The same, alas, could not be said of the new billets: many had no lights and most had no water (these were new speculator-built houses, requisitioned by the War Office before being completed). The next day conditions deteriorated, roads being ice-bound and movement being impossible. Despite the aid of the Police and the Town Hall, no alternative billets could be found. By 31st January a thaw had set in and so had a mood of desperation. Even the Brigadier 'expressed dissatisfaction with some of the billets'. Probably the only warm thing in them was the troops' language.

A brighter note is struck by the War Diary for 5th February: regular training patterns had become established and there is mention of 'normal work' being carried out, as well as PAD. On 12th February, the War Diary reveals the Commanding Officer's name. Previously, Lt Col EF Ledward had simply been referred to as 'the CO'. The brighter weather note dimmed on the 17th and stayed dim until 1st March: training, and Brigade conferences, continued unabated. On 2nd March, 'B' Squadron moved out of their Salisbury billets (the Victoria Hall, the Co-operative Hall and the Labour Club) into billets in Andover. For five days. Three junior subalterns were seconded to the RAF and the CO attended yet more conferences. A move to Linney Head was in the air but the War Diary is far from clear as to what actually happened. Easter came early that year, Good Friday and Easter Monday 'being observed as far as possible as holidays'.

The early months of the war had not, however, been without warlike activity. That Hitler was aware his invasion of Poland would bring Great Britain and the Dominions into the war, and that he was prepared for this, was shown by the U-boat sinking of the liner *Athenia* on 4th September – the first impact of the war on the civilian population. The RAF carried out a number of raids on Germany but, by the end of the month, there were two further blows. Russia joined in the partition of Poland: HMS *Courageous* was sunk with the loss of over 500 lives. In October, HMS *Royal Oak* was sunk with even greater loss. In November, Hitler gave further evidence of what was in store when he ordered Reichsmarschall Hermann Göring to prepare the Luftwaffe for a five year war against Britain. In the same month, Russia invaded Finland. December saw a swing in our favour with the scuttling of the *Graf Spee* after a trans-Atlantic naval chase. The pendulum swung in January 1940 with the loss of three of our submarines and a cruiser. The Royal Navy struck back in February with the release of 300 POWs from the *Altmark* in a Norwegian fjord. March saw Germany consolidating its position in Poland, and Russia consolidating its position in Finland.

Back with the Battalion, the weather again proved a major War Diary preoccupation, especially with a threatened move from billets into leaking tents. Apart from weather, conferences form the main items of the daily entries, with some light relief for all officers with a demonstration of 'wire-entanglement clearing by grapnels fired from a smoke mortar'. Heath Robinson was alive and well. Colonel Ledward must have wondered how to treat an order for his posting: it arrived on 1st April, as did the 2i/c's posting. Major HD Drew OBE MC became CO on 5th April. Two new *A10* tanks arrived; one from the Birmingham Carriage Company and one from Vickers. On the 26th, Major Drew was promoted Lieutenant Colonel. Dinham Drew had started his Army life in the Devonshire Regiment before being transferred in WW I to the Machine-Gun Corps and thence, through its Heavy Section, into the Tank Corps.

A particularly dull patch in the War Diary, just when the Battalion started the war in earnest, is conveniently enlivened by the recollections of Bing Coller. Shortly before the Battalion went overseas, it was stationed in West Harnham just south-west of Salisbury. 'Men's Quarters' at that time were large, inhospitable marquees with wall-board sides (modified by a series of holes bored in them about two feet six inches above the ground, just by the men's beds). Greatly to Bing's advantage, the Battalion tank park was next to the car park of the Swan Public House where the landlord allowed him to keep his car. Curiously the Squadron Officers never seemed to know how often Bing was on unofficial tours of weekend home duty.

Returning from one such tour in the early hours of 13th May, Bing found the camp in uproar and the tank park swarming like an over-turned ants' nest. Bing soon had the answer. 'Under orders for France, mate. Grab your Embarkation Pass at the Orderly Room.' Bing filled his tank (unofficially) and made the journey home (officially) for his Embarkation Leave.

Once again to return to the Battalion, a fairly detailed – and certainly accurate – picture of what happened at that time can be gleaned from Liddell Hart's THE TANKS: VOLUME TWO.[4] The account which follows for the months of May and June has been pieced together from this and a number of personal reminiscences.

However, before embarking on that account, a summary of events in Europe in the Spring of 1940 will be useful. Germany invaded Denmark and Norway on 9th April. From the Allies' point of view this move was doubly disastrous. It enlarged the Nazi grip on Europe while at the same time the immediate need to render some assistance to these latest victims of Hitler's megalomania distracted the British from building up our forces in France. Furthermore, the Allies simply did not believe that Germany could strike a second time within a matter of weeks. None-the-less, that is what happened. Belgium, Holland and Luxembourg were invaded on 10th May. France's 'impregnable' Maginot Line was rendered futile: it was bypassed. The Allies' flank was turned to the north, movement was rendered difficult – in some places impossible – by the floods of refugees, carefully shepherded onto the main traffic arteries by clever tactical strafing by the Luftwaffe. Effective liaison between the Allies was at an end: frequently the same was true of liaison within the British Army. While the main body of the French First Army and the BEF was withdrawing towards Dunkirk, the 3rd Armoured Brigade was landing at Cherbourg.

Len Coller, at that time one of the Echelon transport drivers, recalls how the crossing was uneventful and conducted in an orderly way. About the last thing that was. Bing was soon in trouble. Madame in the local village *estaminet* was generous with her raw red wine which soon went to the unaccustomed British heads, one of which was on Bing's shoulders. Sleeping off his potations at the wheel of his lorry, Bing fell forwards onto the horn button. What Bing didn't know, but the RSM soon told him in simple English, was that the sounding of horns was the official Battalion air-raid warning!

For the record: in 1940 5RTR formed part of 3rd Armoured Brigade, under the command of Brigadier Crocker[5], which in its turn formed part of 1st Armoured Division, commanded by Major General Roger Evans. The Brigade went to France in May 1940 (less 3RTR which had been diverted in an abortive attempt to reinforce Calais – an attempt entailing heavy losses), landing in Cherbourg on 23rd May. Here the Battalion encountered the first of the many problems which beset it during its brief campaign. The 1st Armoured Division was already cut off from the main part of the BEF (by then falling back on Dunkirk). By the time Brigadier Crocker reached Pacy, where he had been

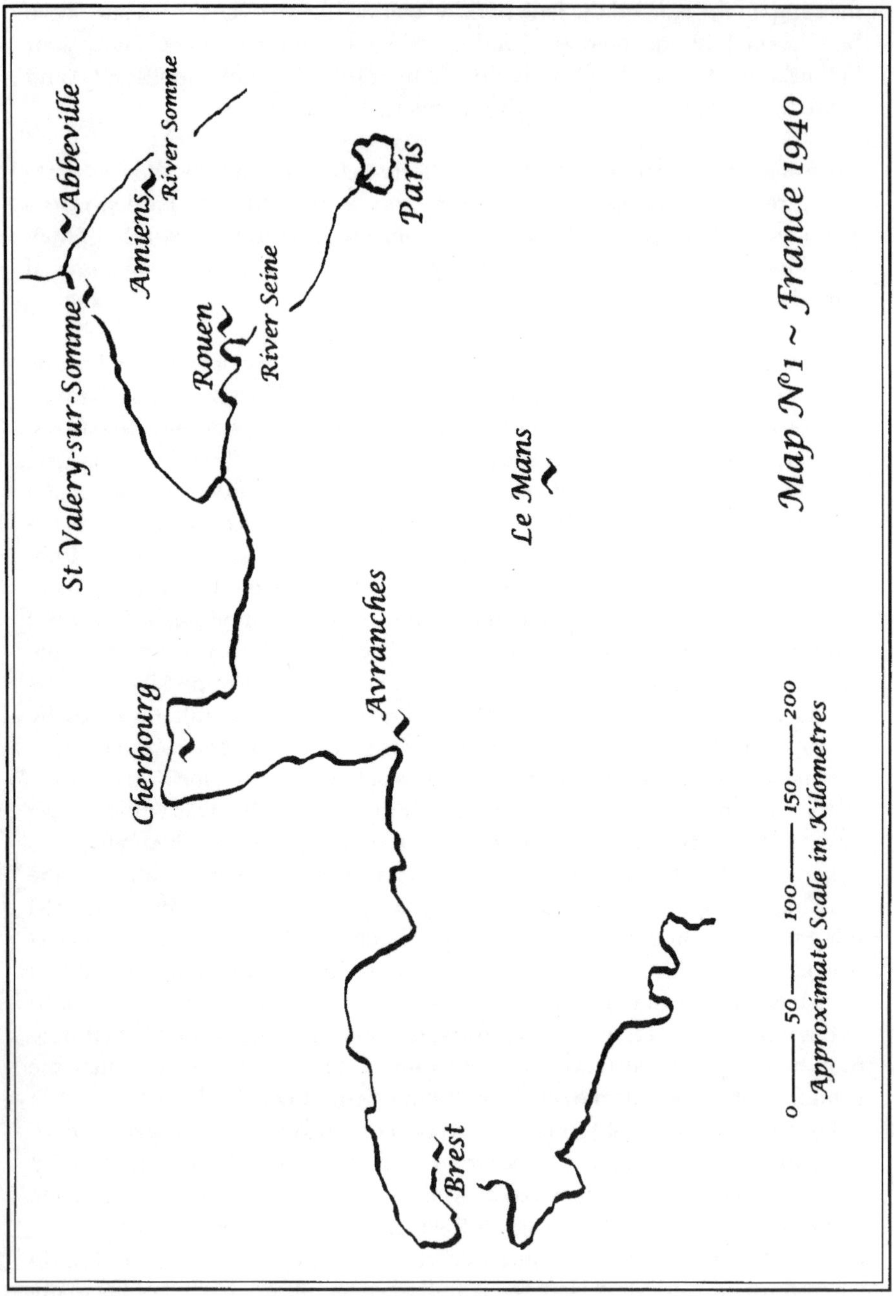
Map N°1 ~ France 1940
St Valery-sur-Somme
Abbeville
Amiens
River Somme
Rouen
River Seine
Paris
Le Mans
Cherbourg
Avranches
Brest
0 — 50 — 100 — 150 — 200
Approximate Scale in Kilometres

ordered to report, Divisional Headquarters had moved up to the line of the Somme with the intention of the Division's relieving the pressure on the flank of the retreating BEF, by supporting the French formations still in action in the area.

An excellent idea in theory. The only drawback was that the Germans had already reached the Somme – the line General Evans had been ordered to hold. It is worth recording, in view of later events, that one of those French formations was an armoured division commanded by a Général de Division named de Gaulle. In all probability, de Gaulle's handling of his division (eventually defeated by failure of supplies rather than enemy by action) saved 5RTR, along with the rest of the British 1st Armoured Division, from near-total annihilation. What exacerbated General Evans' difficulties was the inability (or unwillingness) of the French Tenth Army Commander to appreciate that 1st British Armoured Division was a mobile support force and not, therefore, suitable for frontal assault on prepared positions.

Whatever the High Command's ideas on strategy, Bernard Holder, who had joined 5RTR in March 1940, recalls that his Squadron Sergeant Major had a more pragmatic approach. During Bernard's first parade on French soil, the SSM said, 'The Germans are just over the hills and they will not pass except over our dead bodies.' Good Oscar-winning stuff for Hollywood but not historically accurate.

The Brigade was given orders to assist two French nominally Armoured (but, in fact, Motorised Infantry) Divisions in denying the enemy the Somme crossings. Orders came for the Brigade to join 1st Armoured Division in Pacy, some 450 miles away, on the River Eure and still something like 150 miles to the nearest point on the Somme. This forlorn hope was to be accomplished by train for the tanks and their crews and by road for the wheeled vehicles.

The Brigadier reached Divisional HQ only to find them on the move and with new battle plans. On 24th May, German armour had not yet crossed the Somme. It was hoped that, by swinging 1st Armoured Division north-west and operating in the general area north of Rouen, some holding operation could be effected.

After contact with the French 5th Light Cavalry Division on Sunday 26th May the Brigade was switched farther north-west and, for the first time since it landed, given precise orders. 5RTR was to advance from Le Tréport to St Valery-sur-Somme through largely enemy-controlled territory. The advance started at 0550 hrs. By 1135 hrs, the Battalion had reached the outskirts of St Valery, which was seen to be strongly held. On the right 2RTR, who had lost six tanks, reported that the outskirts of Abbeville were well-defended.

Poor liaison with (and, it was felt, worse co-operation from) the French created chaos on the Brigade front. After a Brigade decision to consolidate the armour and post French motorised infantry as outposts, 5RTR, in ignorance of this decision, launched an attack on St Valery. The attack was only moderately successful, being 'gallantly carried out but not supported by the French'. After getting lost on the way back to the Brigade harbour[6], the Battalion regrouped on the morning of 28th May. And counted the cost. Lt Thomson had been wounded and Battalion strength was down to five *A13* Cruisers, five *A9s* or *A10s*, eight Light tanks and six scout cars, the losses being mostly due to mechanical breakdown rather than enemy action. In spite of these losses and the set-back in front of the well-posted defence of St Valery, Colonel Drew probed the enemy defences, some of the Battalion's tanks penetrating as far as Boismont. Later that day, 5RTR with some French lorried infantry put in another attack on St Valery. This attack was carried out in Dinham Drew's ignorance of the frequently changed plans of the French Command. The French infantry, on the other hand, may have learnt of these changes, for they failed to support the tanks.

The general situation of the BEF was a good deal worse. A final attempt at a major counter-attack by British and French forces had been aborted by the capitulation of the hard-pressed Belgian Army. There followed one of the greatest feats in the history of the British Armed Forces. The Nine Days Wonder. The evacuation – *Operation Dynamo* – of 316,660 British and French troops from the beaches of Dunkirk.

It was, however, still considered that 3rd Armoured Brigade had a role to play. The 51st Highland Division, under command of the unluckily named General Fortune, had swung clear of the retreat to Dunkirk and was withdrawing to the Somme to prevent the enemy from sweeping round on Paris from the west and to deny them, for as long as possible, access to more Channel ports. What was left of 1st Armoured Division passed under General Fortune's command. Although the Germans were across the Somme in places, they were not yet across in strength. Two composite squadrons, one from 2RTR and one from 5RTR, were detailed to support the French by patrolling the area and containing the enemy. This they did with some success and were joined by elements of the Highland Division.

5RTR's new role made matters no easier for them: they were frequently under artillery fire or bombed and strafed by the Luftwaffe. By last light on 30th May, the Brigade and the main body of the Highland Division were on the line of the Somme.

On Friday, 31st May the Brigade received orders to withdraw to the Louviers area, south of Rouen and some 60 miles distant. The move was accomplished 'despite the non-arrival of the bulk of the tank-trains' in the early hours of Saturday, 1st June. In view of the Brigade War Diary's comments about artillery and air attacks on the railway network, it seems more remarkable that *any* trains were available, rather than that some were not.

In some respects the Battalion War Diary differs from the Brigade's. According to this, 5RTR was still in harbour between Le Tréport and Abbeville at 1550 hrs on 31st May. The few remaining tanks were ordered to entrain at two separate points later that night. The rest of the Battalion, including crews without tanks, were to go by road. This night march ended at

0630 hrs in St Aignan[7]. Orders were given for the men to find billets to rest in rather than sleeping in the open.

For the next five days life was without incident. The Battalion must have heard with relief that the evacuation from Dunkirk had been successfully completed on 4th June. No tank movement was permitted in daylight.

On 5th June, the Battalion suffered six casualties, due – so the War Diary states – to the men not having worn steel helmets on 'bathing [washing not swimming] parade'. Bing Coller was one of the bathers when an air-raid alarm was sounded. Not unnaturally, the men were naked and, in that state, ran for cover. What the low-flying German pilots – and some of the local inhabitants – would have seen was not that part of the men's anatomies normally covered by a steel helmet.

More seriously that day, the Battalion was put on four hours' notice to move. On 7th June this was reduced to half-an-hour's notice. At this date, the Battalion strength was reduced to eight scout cars (plus four in workshops), twelve Light tanks (plus five in workshops), five *A9M*s (plus two *A9G*s in workshops), three *A10*s and eight *A13*s (plus thirteen in workshops). Of the original Battalion strength, only five AVFs had been written off.

Because both 2RTR and 5RTR were so under-strength, each was ordered to form a 'Composite Squadron' and make up a composite battalion. The Squadron from 5RTR was designated 'Z'. This composite unit came directly under Brigade command while the rest of the Battalion was ordered to move farther south again 'to refit'. Another composite squadron was made up in a desperate attempt to form a unit strong enough to cover the withdrawal across the Seine.

Both the Battalion and the Brigade War Diaries mention the chaotic condition of the roads and of being forced to abandon their Centre Lines[8] because of the floods of refugees and the transport of disorganised French Army units. Nevertheless, the Brigade managed to move into defensive positions to cover the main Seine crossing at Les Andelys.

The 8th and 9th June were spent in sorting the Battalion out and in moving to a new harbour. The composite battalion withdrew back across the Seine, leaving one troop from 5RTR under 2/Lt Hinton (the War Diary says 'tank' in one place and 'troop' in another) to guard the approaches to the bridge at Les Andelys. This detachment was later reinforced by a skeleton squadron commanded by Major Pritchett.

'Any army can advance: only a good army can retire.' What followed showed the truth of this old saw. The Brigade, with the remaining elements of 1st Armoured Division, began an ordered withdrawal to the nearest Channel port – Brest. The Highlanders were less fortunate. Cut off and surrounded, they withdrew to St Valery-en-Caux, there to surrender to Major General Erwin Rommel, commanding the Wehrmacht's Seventh 'Ghost' Armoured Division. But not to surrender until the last rounds – as well as the 'Jocks' – were exhausted.

On 10th June a march of 120 miles was made on Normandy's grid-locked secondary roads. Any vehicle breaking down and not repaired in fifteen minutes had to be abandoned. In the event, only four tanks were left behind. Although Lt Hinton rejoined the Battalion, all contact with Major Pritchett was temporarily lost.

On the 11th new orders came from Brigade. All remaining tanks were to be grouped into a single Squadron – confusingly, also designated 'Z' Squadron – on 12 hours' notice to move. Major Winship was put in command of this. Major Pritchett re-appeared out of the blue . . . or rather the grey, as the weather had broken and rain had become the order of the day.

Major Winship's 'Z' Squadron left the Battalion on 12th June. Such tanks as remained were regrouped under Captain Harden on stand-by to reinforce 'Z' Squadron.

The 14th June proved that cleanliness might still be next to godliness but that it could also be hazardous. Another bathing parade was bombed and machine-gunned – this time without casualties. Perhaps they wore their steel helmets. The Battalion waited for orders. These came the next day but proved impossible to comply with. The orders were to entrain for Brest . . . but there were no trains.

At 0215 hrs on Saturday, 15th June the withdrawal got underway (at 0340 hrs for 5RTR), first by moving south-west to Alençon. Seventeen and a half hours and 275 miles later, the Battalion arrived outside Brest. The early part of the journey had been hampered by refugee traffic. General Evans painted a vivid picture of this. High, creaking, ponderous farm wagons drawn by teams of massive Flemish cart horses, bedecked with brasses and ribbons, with whole families aboard: cars, piled to the roof inside with adult passengers, crying children desperately clutching some treasured toy, luggage, shapeless bundles and striped mattresses on the roof: bicycles festooned with such worldly possession as the rider could not bear to abandon but which were of no earthly use in this massed, panic-stricken, Stuka-driven, exodus. Fortunately for The Fifth, traffic became lighter as the column moved westward into the Brittany Peninsula.

Len Coller's account relates what that westward movement entailed for the men of The Fifth. They had been informed that they 'were being withdrawn to England to re-fit'. This was an entirely probable statement as the Battalion had hardly any AFVs left and was certainly in no fit state to offer resistance to the invading Panzers. None-the-less, the 'withdrawal' was correctly interpreted as a retreat. Apart from the plight of the fleeing civilian population, what horrified Bing were the innumerable British Service vehicles which were simply abandoned in the fields or by the road side. When his turn came to drive his lorry into a field and park it, undamaged, nose to tail with the others, he could hardly believe his ears and seriously wondered whether the stripling Second Lieutenant giving the orders was really 'one of ours' or a Fifth Columnist, cunningly planted in the outskirts of Brest to ensure the Wehrmacht's future transport needs.

This doubt was somewhat allayed when the drivers were told they could remove the rotor arms from the distributors but was rekindled when the Subaltern effectively confiscated the cash, thoughtfully extracted by Bing from the Squadron safe, on the grounds that it might be needed to buy a boat to get back to England.

Bing, however, struck one blow for Britain. Near where he had abandoned his lorry was a petrol dump, apparently to be left intact. Bing punctured one of the cans, withdrew to a discreet distance and fired a verey light at the dump. He departed for the docks of Brest in a blaze of glory!

The men had only a few hours' rest before further orders came. At 0300 hrs on Sunday, 16th June the Battalion was transported into the centre of Brest. From there they marched to the harbour and embarked on SS *Manx Lass.* At first light, an enemy aircraft flew over but was seen off by Bren gun fire When the *Manx Lass* sailed at 1730 hrs, most of the men were asleep. Most but not all. Major Johnstone-Jones and 2/Lt Emden [or Embdon: two spellings are given] had been left behind in Brest with the Battalion's remaining transport. They had orders to destroy the vehicles by any means other than burning or gunfire. This they did with hammers and whatever other blunt instruments came to hand. This rear party, its work done, was able to embark on SS *Strathaird* which sailed at 1800 hrs. The *Strathaird* made Plymouth at 0700 hrs the following morning. This rear party was cared for by the Wiltshire Regiment until being returned to 5RTR on 22nd June.

The *Manx Lass* off-loaded her passengers in Plymouth at 0830 hrs on 17th June. In true British fashion, they were greeted with cups of tea. A picture of some of the men – looking astonishingly smart, considering what they had been through – appeared in a number of newspapers the following day. What the picture did not show was Bing's knapsack, full of cigarettes from an abandoned canteen truck.

After a five-hour wait, the Battalion, less one of its number, entrained for Warminster, which was reached after another five hours. From there, they were bussed to Longbridge Deverell Camp. Not a welcoming arrival: 'Difficulty in obtaining rations for men's evening meal' states the War Diary.

Bing Coller, meanwhile, decided to relieve the over-worked RTOs of the task of providing him with transport and to make his own way back to base. 'Base', as interpreted by Bing, meant home. He did this by suborning a cousin to come and fetch him on his motorbike, inadvertently leaving his cigarette-laden pack in the barrack room. Returning to that barrack room two days later, Bing found that his friends – and his pack – had been removed in his absence and transported to an unknown destination 'somewhere in England'. 'I might as well face a court martial for desertion as face the "Old Man" for absence without leave,' Bing thought and he persuaded his motorcycling cousin to take him home again. At this point, Bing's guardian angel put in an appearance in the guise of a mate from 'B' Squadron who told him where the Battalion was and where Bing should get himself as soon as possible.

Bing duly reported to Longbridge Camp and was promptly put under arrest. His Squadron Commander sensibly decided that Bing's transgressions were too serious for him and would have to be dealt with by the CO. Those who knew him in the Army knew to mistrust a look of sweet innocence on Bing's face. If Colonel Drew noted this expression as he listened to Bing's tale of the misfortunes endured in loyal endeavour to return to his unit and duty, he must have had great difficulty in restraining his smile.

With a straight face, however, and to the audible astonishment of the RSM, the Adjutant and Bing's escorts, the CO told him that he was the Battalion's most accomplished liar and that not one word of his story came within a mile of the truth and that one day of his pay would be stopped. 'Thank you, Sir,' said Bing. 'And please, Sir, may I have the Disembarkation Leave that I'm due?' 'Get this man out of here,' the Colonel said to the RSM. 'And keep him out of my sight until he has had his hair cut!' Nevertheless, Bing did get his Leave Pass and Railway Warrant and did have his two – this time, official – days at home.

However, it was not only the Brest rear party that had been left behind when the main body sailed. 'Z' Squadron had also remained in France. The movements of 'Z' Squadron are not recorded in the Battalion War Diary but something of their activities can be obtained from the Brigade Diary. Major Winship's command consisted of Squadron HQ with 2 *A9*s, an *A10* and an *A13*; two Troops of *Light Mk VI*s; two Troops of *A13*s; four scout cars and supporting transport.

In effect, 'Z' Squadron and Major Brown's Squadron from 1RTR were operating directly under Brigadier Crocker's orders. As his command had been separated from 1st Armoured Division, he found himself under frequently conflicting orders from both the French Corps Commander and detached British Infantry Divisions.

The true story of the last days of British armour in France in 1940 will probably never be known. Whether he was right or not, John Crocker stubbornly maintained that his prime duty was to withdraw the units under his command, with as much matériel as possible, in good order, so as to be able to fight again, rather than carry out various impossible tasks demanded by both British and French Commands. He was, by now, separated from the main body of his Brigade who were en route to Brest. The detached units of the Brigade withdrew to Cherbourg (a distance of some 180 miles) which they reached on 17th June. They embarked – with all armoured and 'essential' vehicles – on SS *St Briac* or SS *Manxman* at 1600 hrs on the following day, just as the German artillery started shelling the port. The ships docked in Southampton at midnight.

And Major Winship's 'Z' Squadron? As mentioned above, its full history is not recorded but two men's adventures with the Squadron are recounted by Dai 'Tweeny' Mitchell and Ron 'Titch' Maple.

Frederick James Mitchell had enlisted as a Private in the Royal Tank Corps in 1938. Being a Welshman, the barrack room re-christened him 'Dai'. Later his friends were to know him as 'Tweeny'. After his regulation thirty-six weeks' RTC training the question arose 'Which Battalion was he suited for?' This was the same as asking 'What sport is he good at?' Over the years, the RTC Battalions had become specialised: the Fourth, for example, was the soccer Battalion, the Fifth meant boxing and Rugby Union football. At 8 stone 4 pounds and barely enough inches to get him into the pre-war Army, there was no point in Dai's pretending to be God's gift to the Welsh RUFC. But Dai came of sound Welsh mining stock and wasn't afraid of a good turn-up with the gloves. Dai's destiny was sealed: the Fifth Battalion it was to be.

What Dai hadn't realised was just how dedicated to sport the Fifth Battalion was. There was no point in wasting a promising new member of the Boxing Team in a tank crew and, once Dai had proved himself, he was destined for Headquarters Squadron and the Transport Section.

However, Dai wasn't just a good boxer and a reliable driver, he had initiative and organising ability. Before long he was one of those mysterious but invaluable members of any Army unit, a Local Unpaid Lance Corporal 'In charge of .. '. It was never wise to enquire too closely what such a man *was* in charge of: there was always something that needed looking after and fate always turned up a Local Unpaid Lance Jack to look after it. In this case, Private (LULC) Mitchell FJ.

Thus Dai went to France with HQ Squadron. It was further his fate, as a Local Unpaid Lance Corporal 'In charge of .. ', to be selected as one of the drivers in Major Winship's 'Z' Squadron Supply Echelon. Like Mary and her little lamb, where 'Z' Squadron went, the transport and Dai went along behind, until one day the Major detailed him to return to Battalion HQ to collect some urgently needed equipment from HQ Stores. A route, a map reference, a shopping list for the QM Stores and off Dai set. The only trouble was that the Battalion had moved and hadn't left a forwarding address. After making a complete search of the area, Dai returned to what he knew to be 'Z' Squadron's last position. But, like Battalion HQ, Major Winship had upped-stakes and moved. Having no such luxury as a wireless link, Dai very sensibly set off for the nearest main town [probably Le Mans] as the likeliest place to find someone in Movement Control who knew the whereabouts of 5RTR.

En route, he was halted at a cross-roads by a solitary Military Police Sergeant to whom he explained his problems. The MP knew nothing of The Fifth but had been ordered to direct all retreating units and strays to Brest for embarkation. When Dai told him that he hadn't seen any troops, let alone tanks, for the past twenty-four hours, the sergeant admitted that he hadn't either! Dai offered him a lift but he refused, saying he had to stay on duty until he was ordered to remove himself. Dai drove off, thinking new, kinder, thoughts about the Military Police.

On his way, Dai collected two badly wounded French soldiers who were every bit as lost as he was. Dai's priorities now changed. Get these men to hospital and *then* find his way to Brest. Local medical help was not forthcoming, so he headed for the main hospital where he handed them over to a doctor. At this point, as Dai later explained, 'life got a little bit tricky'. On returning to his truck, he found the main gates shut and guarded by armed French soldiers with no intention of opening them. Dai 'created a bit of a fuss' and an officer turned up who firmly explained that, as France had capitulated, all members of the Allied Forces were considered to be prisoners of the German Army. 'Prisoner of War? Like Friday afternoon I am!' was Dai's reaction. He returned to his wagon, climbed in and started up. He reversed about 100 yards and then belted for the gate, slamming on the brakes and skidding to a halt within inches of them. When he realised that next time Dai wouldn't be stopping, the officer, so to speak, followed his country's example and capitulated. As Dai passed through the opened gateway, the officer wished him '*Bon voyage*'.

Brest is a level 250 miles from Le Mans. Dai metaphorically girded his loins and followed the signs which led him eventually to the port. Or nearly there, for he was stopped on the outskirts by an infantry patrol. Having satisfied themselves that Dai was what he said he was and not a forerunner of the Wehrmacht in cunning disguise, they told him to proceed. 'Follow this road into the town and, when you get to the bottom, turn right.' Unfortunately, when Dai got to the bottom, there wasn't a right turn. A sense of preservation rather than a sense of direction eventually led Dai to the docks. Where there was one ship. He was flagged down by an officer who told him to ditch his wagon and get on board.

'Ditch it, Sir? Where?'

The officer pointed to the quay-side. 'Get your kit and anything you can carry and drive it into the dock.'

Dai did as he was told and listened for the splash. All he was now 'In charge of .. ' was one small haversack with his shaving kit, a clean pair of pants, clean socks but not much else.

There was one further formality before the ship (Dai thinks it was the *Canterbury Queen*) could clear the harbour: even with the enemy pressing at the gates, the Harbour Master had to sign its papers. Minutes – each one seeming like hours – passed. A figure appeared and raced for the gangplank, puffing and blowing mightily. The gangplank was pulled aboard with the figure still on it. The propellers churned. The ship was underway. Outside the harbour, it was picked up by a British destroyer impatiently waiting to escort it to Plymouth.

Out of the organised chaos which was Plymouth in June 1940, Dai got despatched back to the Battalion, arriving there late on 18th June. The next day, after some – but not nearly enough – sleep, Dai was summoned to the Orderly Room. The Adjutant had a problem. Records had been lost: no-one was quite certain who had been with 'Z' Squadron, and 'Z' Squadron, like the records, was undoubtedly lost. LULC Mitchell was told to rack his brains and list the names of all the 'Z' Squadron personnel he could think of. LULC Mitchell was the Adjutant's only hope, as he was the only man from 'Z' Squadron to get back to the Battalion. The Adjutant spoke too soon. There was a clatter of tracks and a familiar rumble of tank engines. 'Z' Squadron had returned to base!

Another man who served in 'Z' Squadron and who recorded his experiences was Ron Maple – ironically, Dai Mitchell's companion in the lighter-weight sections of the Battalion Boxing Team. Ron was the youngest of six children, orphaned when first Ron's mother (when he was five) and then his father (when he was seven) died. Fortunately the family was well spread out and there was an elder sister to look after the young ones. Ron decided to leave school at fourteen (the then school-leaving age): this he did and went to work in the local cycle and wireless shop for 12/6d [62.50p] a week. However, his eldest brother, just out of the Army, arranged for Ron to go to work with him at the Bristol Aeroplane Company . . . for 15/- [75p] for a fifty-hour week . . . making Blenheim bombers. At home, Ron's admired Big Brother Jim didn't talk Blenheims, he talked Army. And Ron dreamt Army

Not surprisingly then, on 20th October 1937, still a beardless fifteen, Ronald Maple realised his dream and joined the Army – the Royal Tank Corps at the suggestion of the Recruiting Sergeant who did not bat an eyelid at entering Ron's date of birth as 5th August 1918, thereby adding three years to his age for the whole of his military career. In those days there was a bounty of five shillings for any serving, or ex-service, man who 'brought in' a recruit. The Recruiting Sergeant thought he was about to pocket the price of some dozen pints of beer for nobbling Ron. Not so Brother Jim who went off to tell the Recruiting Sergeant not that young Ron was still only fifteen but that the five bob bounty was his! Back home, the elder sister accused Jim of having sold her little brother to the Army for two measly half crowns.

Ron's first impression of the Army was one of devastating loneliness. He'd never really had a home and he certainly hadn't found one now: there he was, not yet sixteen, in Bovington Camp, told by an unsympathetic Corporal to take his kit into a bleak wooden hut on a bleak wind-swept plain. Ron didn't have any kit: only the clothes he stood up in! Fortunately for him, Ron Maple was a resilient youth and even, in the course of time, came to terms with his puttees. From early days, Ron found that he was most at home with D&M and managed to obtain the necessary educational and military grades to pass out at the end of his initial training. After a gunnery course at Lulworth, he was posted to the 5th Battalion Royal Tank Corps in the summer of 1938 at the age, so far as the Army was concerned, of twenty. He satisfied the high standards of The Fifth in D&M: he had worked in a cycle and wireless shop: he was obvious material for a driver/operator in a tank. He had an additional advantage for this position: small size. Which is why he became known in The Fifth as 'Titch'.

Titch was sent to the RTC Wireless School . . . and hated every moment of it. Nevertheless, he persisted (or rather, he was told brusquely to 'gerronwithit') and duly achieved the required expertise.

Titch found that The Fifth set great store by its renown for boxing. During the winter of 1938/1939, Private Maple found himself not just a member of the Fifth Battalion Boxing Team but Battalion Bantamweight Champion.

Although Titch had been mustered as a driver/operator and he was in a Tank Battalion, he had not so far learnt to drive a tank. That was the next stage: he became a driver/operator and all his many and varied later experiences in The Fifth stemmed from having this qualification.

Titch Maple has horrid memories of the wet conditions under canvas at Windmill Hill – 'almost like the Great War with the duck-boards sunk in the mud' – but happier ones of training in the Harpenden area and of the tea breaks taken at the Elephant & Castle, where the landlord and the locals soon got accustomed to seeing six or eight tanks standing on the forecourt. That winter was real 'brass monkey weather' with the tanks having to be started at regular intervals, day and night, and sometimes unable to move, as the tracks were frozen to the ground. Titch Maple reckons that the nearest he ever got to godliness in his service days was the night his Troop billeted themselves in a barn and he slept in a manger as the only warm place he could find!

May saw the Battalion preparing to go overseas – which meant to France – and being the subject of an unscheduled inspection by King George VI just prior to embarkation. Like so many others . . . from the High Command down to the tank crews . . . Titch never really knew what was going in the next few weeks before the French capitulated. Sometimes, he recalls, The Fifth was in action, suffering casualties and losing more tanks through mechanical failure than through enemy action, despite the attentions of the Luftwaffe's pertinacious Stuka pilots.

Titch Maple's tank was commanded by Captain Le Mesurier and was allocated to Major Winship's 'Z' Squadron. Detached from the Regiment, 'Z' Squadron finally received the message that they were to make their way to Cherbourg. The Squadron Commander studied the map, issued his instructions to the crew commanders and gave the order to his driver to advance. Fifty-six hours later, after driving almost non-stop, often under attack from the air – Titch received a minor head-wound when the column was machine-gunned – and always fighting for space on the roads with the pathetic columns of refugees, all the tanks in 'Z' Squadron reached Cherbourg, as did their support transport (less Dai Mitchell, off on that frolic of his). It was 0400 hrs on 16th June 1940: Sunday, but far from being a day of rest. There was no sign of the Navy but there were some transports. The orders were to abandon or destroy everything but the tanks and special vehicles, such as command vehicles, workshop lorries and wireless trucks. The 'Z' Squadron tanks were loaded, with a great deal of haste and rather less than good order, on what appeared to be the last ship to leave Cherbourg. As they cleared the harbour they were bombed but this was not enough to wake the men who slept where they dropped on the deck. Before they sailed, Captain Le Mesurier had told his crew that he had alternative escape plans of his own. He was a Channel Islander: his plan was, he told his men, to steal a boat and make their way to his home in Jersey and to safety.

The tanks and the still sleep-sodden crews were landed at Southampton. Here they were told to report to Warminster to rejoin their unit. Off Titch set only to have a track break en route, landing them in the ditch. Captain Le Mesurier wanted to 'abandon the damn thing' but Titch wasn't having any of that. It would have meant walking! He set to, split the track into sections, adjusted the idler and jockey wheels, connected the pieces up again . . . and drove the tank back onto the road and to Warminster.

What followed was a minor tragedy. After returning from his 48-hour leave, Titch found that *his* tank had been sent to a Training Regiment. And the tragedy? The crested, solid silver cutlery set that Titch had carefully hidden behind the wireless set had gone with the tank.

The third, but briefer, account of the last days in France comes from 'Charlie' Bull. Charles William Bull, born in February 1914, joined the Army in 1932 and served with 3RTC until July 1938. He was called up as a Reservist and posted to the Fifth Battalion. He went with The Fifth to France and, as he described in a letter written in late June 1940, was evacuated through Cherbourg – so he was also a member of Major Winship's 'Z' Squadron. After stating that the battalion only brought seven tanks back, Charlie continued by saying that they came away from Cherbourg and were probably about the last to leave. He added that the docks and the railway station were blown up after the unit left.

His letter concludes, 'When we were told that we had to get out of France we were about 200 miles from the coast and we kept going all the time, day and night, with the German planes after us nearly all the time. We were often bombed and machine-gunned but they didn't do any damage to us. I think we lost about 20 men in the batt[alion].'

THE OTHER SIDE

Contrary to popular belief and to the impression created as a result of the German invasion of Poland, the Panzer Divisions of the Third Reich were neither numerically nor mechanically superior to those of the joint Franco-British Armies.

For example, the combined Panzer units had only 625 PzKw IIIs (see Appendix 2 for details). The force of 2,000 other tanks under command were PzKw IIs (dating from 1934). Even with the addition of some 380 Czechoslovakian 38t tanks, the total strength was only 3,000 all types.

In 1939 the French had the same number of tanks, mostly the heavily-armoured and well-gunned Char B. Although the Char B dated from 1931, tank for tank, they were more than a match for the PzKw IIIs. In addition, the French had an unquantified reserve of older, if near-obsolete, armour.

Added to the strength of the French armour in 1940 were 640 assorted British tanks. (again, see Appendix 2 for details) The make-up of these 640 tanks was:

384 Light Tanks (approximately the equivalent of the PzKw II but faster)

100 Infantry Tanks (including 23 Matildas which, as the Germans admitted, were not only a match for the PzKw IIs but as good as [but for their 2-pdr main armament] the PzKw IIIs)

156 Cruiser Tanks (A9s, A10s and A13s, the latter being faster, better armoured and as well gunned as the PzKw IIs)

There are three reasons for the German success in 1940. Four if one counts the Blitzkrieg technique which had been brought to perfection over many years of planning and training, and the recent practical experience in Poland.

The first reason is a fundamental one. Ever since 28th June 1919, when the Treaty of Versailles was signed with the intention of clipping the wings of Prussian militarism, the High Commands in Berlin had but one objective – to achieve the German dominance in Europe which the Kaiser had failed to do. Inevitably, when Hitler commenced his programme of rearmament, German naval, army and air force personnel – from the highest to the lowest – set their sights on attack and conquest. All their training had these two aims and all their techniques concentrated on developing the killer instinct necessary to achieve these aims. War, in other words, was what they were meant for.

Conversely, the Armed Forces of the Crown were primarily intended for peace keeping, for preserving law and order, for 'showing the natives' the power and majesty of the British Empire. This does not mean that the Forces of the Crown were not highly trained, did not know the theory of war, did not exercise their brains as well as their muscles. But it did mean that, when those Forces went to war, they did not go with the single-minded purpose of smashing the enemy, of destroying his arms, of seizing his lands. This analysis is not a criticism of the men or their leaders; it is, rather, an explanation of the lesson which we had to learn and a reason for the time it took to learn that lesson.

The second reason is that the attack on the West had been planned as early as November 1939, even before the Polish campaign had been finished, and the troops employed had been rigorously trained for months in advance. Apart from the numerical weakness in armour, their equipment, preparedness, tactics and fighting zeal were well ahead of the Allies.

The third is a more general reason. An army with a clear-cut and well co-ordinated plan of attack, using the element of surprise, always has a strategic advantage over an army on the defensive, uncertain of when and where the blow or blows will fall.

Because of the success of the German attack and the erroneous tradition of attributing it to superior armour, it is not generally appreciated that the plan which was adopted was only agreed after resolving a major division in the High Command which was, in 1939, still largely composed of professional soldiers who were World War One veterans and not Hitler's Nazi henchmen.

There were two factions – a situation similar to that prevailing in the French and

British High Commands. One in favour of armoured warfare, one against.

Initially the pro-tank faction was overborne by the traditionalists who attributed the British successes at Cambrai in 1917 and Amiens in 1918 as much to the element of surprise as to the attacking power of the tanks. The anti-tank faction still preferred the intensive artillery bombardment followed by the massed infantry onslaught, beloved by the High Commands of both sides in World War One.

In the end, slight preference was, however, given to the pro-tank faction but only in so far as the use of Panzergruppen formed part of the master plan advanced by Field Marshal von Rundstedt's chief of staff, General Erich von Manstein. And it was a master plan. It combined using the experience gained in 1914 with an element of surprise that was as daring as it was original. The plan, which became known as 'the Sickle Plan' was only approved on Hitler's direct intervention in its favour. Hitler's intervention can be attributed to the results of the successful attacks on defensive positions shown to him by General Guderian in Poland. Hitler attributed these to the Luftwaffe: Guderian corrected him, saying, 'Not aircraft: tanks!'

In 1914 the German plan of attack on the West (code-named 'the Schlieffen Plan') was to strike not directly at France but through Belgium to the Channel ports. Von Manstein realised that to repeat this plan by itself would lose any element of surprise and, worse, bring the Wehrmacht into direct conflict with the superior French and British armour. His plan, which proved entirely successful, was to make a Schlieffen-style attack seem to be the main thrust but, in reality, to concentrate on an attack through Luxembourg and the Belgian Ardennes on the Allied right wing. He dealt with the Maginot Line by ignoring it (it was penetrated later but that had no bearing on his master plan), sweeping westward across its front and attacking the undefended frontier near Sedan.

It would be simplistic to say that the British fell for a 'sucker's punch'. It is, nevertheless, true that the Allied High Command reacted exactly as they were intended to do. The hapless Belgians had again been over-run as they had been in August 1914. Luxembourg had been swallowed in one bite. (The fact that Holland now formed part of a military objective was neither here nor there. The Dutch were pre-ordained, in Nazi philosophy, to form part of the new German Empire) What could the Allies do but move to the defence of their friends? And of the Channel ports?

The advance of German Army Group 'B' – their 4th and 6th Armies with four Panzer Divisions and supporting motorised infantry – on the Channel ports was, therefore, not the main thrust but it was the attack which the British had to move to meet.

The main attack by the German Army Group 'A' – their 12th Army with six Panzer Divisions, as in Poland, with supporting motorised infantry – was the left claw of the pincers which succeeded in bottling up our main forces with their backs to the sea in an area from which the only escape route was from the beaches at Dunkirk.

5RTR only became involved when the German Army Group 'A' had succeeded in its objective of investing the French coast from the mouth of the Somme north to Dunkirk. Having done this, Group 'A''s leading elements pushed south through the breach made in the Allied defensive line opposite 3rd Armoured Brigade.

In his book Panzer Battles *Major General F W von Mellenthin – a tank protagonist – states that the Schlieffen Plan part of the attack was meant to seem as formidable, and be as noisy and as spectacular as possible, whereas von Manstein's real attack was carried out, contrary to all military probability and tradition, through highly unsuitable and therefore thinly defended tank country. (The US Army found out just how unsuitable this terrain was for tank warfare during the winter of 1944/45)*

Because of Dunkirk and all that that means to us, we tend to think of the Schlieffen Plan attack through Belgium as being the principal reason for the fall of France. The reality is otherwise. What mainly decided the fate of France for the next four years was the second, unforeseen, element in von Manstein's 'Sickle Plan'.

THE WAR CHRONICLE

1939

September	03	Great Britain at war with Germany
	04	RMS *Athenia* sunk
	17	Russia invaded Poland
		– HMS *Courageous* sunk
	19	First broadcast of ITMA
	21	Heydrich ordered *pogrom* against Polish Jews
	22	Petrol rationed in UK
October	17	HMS *Iron Duke* torpedoed in Scapa Flow
November	18	IRA planted 4 bombs in Piccadilly, London
	23	Armed Merchantman *Rawalpindi* sunk
	30	Russia invaded Finland
December	17	German 'Pocket Battleship' *Graf Spee* scuttled in River Plate
	27	Earthquake in Turkey killed 30,000 people

1940

January	04	Bacon rationed in UK
	13	General Wavell appointed C-in-C Middle East Forces
February	06	IRA bombed Euston Station, London
	14	IRA planted bombs in Birmingham
	28	HMS *King George V* launched
March	11	Meat rationed in UK
	13	End of Russo-Finnish war
	16	First British air-raid victim killed
April	05	Income Tax increased to 7/6d in £1 (37.5%)

	9	Denmark and Norway invaded by Germany
	10	German Warships *Konisberg* and *Karlsruhe* sunk – Denmark capitulated
	11	German Warship *Lutzow* sunk_
	15	Enigma Code cracked
	29	Auschwitz Extermination Camp inaugurated
May	10	Iceland occupied by British Forces – Belgium, Holland and Luxembourg invaded by Germany
	11	'National Government' formed in UK under Winston Churchill
	15	Holland capitulated
	18	Marshal Pétain formed new French Government
	24	Allied Forces finally evacuated from Norway
	26	'Operation Dynamo' – the evacuation from Dunkirk – began
	28	Belgium capitulated
	31	Anti-invasion measures put in hand in mainland UK
June	04	'Operation Dynamo' completed
	10	Italy declared war on Allies
	12	First British encounter with Italian Army in North Africa
	18	General de Gaulle established Free French Forces in Britain
	21	Italy invaded southern France
	22	Last Allied Forces (British, French, Czechoslovakian and Polish) left France

NOTES

1 The Fifth, It is correct to refer nowadays to the Fifth Royal Tank Regiment. It was not until 1946, however, that this became the correct title. The Royal Tank Corps ('Royal' by command of His Majesty King George V on 18th October 1923) became part of the Royal Armoured Corps, being amalgamated with the mechanised Cavalry Regiments, in April 1939. At the outbreak of WW II, the correct title of the unit was the Fifth Battalion, Royal Tank Regiment, although official reports usually continued to use the old RTC title. Originally, the sub-units of the RTC Battalions were Companies, Platoons and Sections, and the Other Ranks were Privates. The change to Squadrons, Troops and Troopers was part of the amalgamation of Tanks and Cavalry. The changes were not popular in the RTC!

Because the various sources used in this book employ a wide variety of names, The Fifth is variously referred to throughout the text as 'the Battalion', 'the Regiment', The Fifth, Fifth Tanks or as 5RTR. Other Royal Tank Battalions or Regiments are simply called *eg* 7RTR

2 Monty is, of course, Field Marshal Viscount Montgomery of Alamein KG GCB DSO. Throughout the book, he is referred to exclusively as 'Monty'
3 Army terms. For an explanation of these initials and abbreviations, see the Guide to Abbreviations
4 THE TANKS: VOLUME TWO. Captain [later Sir] Basil Liddell Hart was, in fact, an Infantry Officer in WW I. After the War he became one of the champions of mobile warfare and, in particular, of modern tanks, using his position as Military Correspondent first of *The Daily Telegraph* and then of *The Times* openly to criticise the War Office and to advocate the up-dating of the RTC's equipment. His book, THE TANKS is the definitive history of the RTR
5 Brigadier Crocker. Afterwards General Sir John Crocker GCB KBE DSO MC, sometime Representative Colonel Commandant of the RTR. His nephew, Keith Crocker, served with 5RTR in North-west Europe.
6 Harbour. A collecting and resting place for an armoured unit, which made a temporary base. Harbours should be distinguished from the 'leaguers' which are mentioned later: these latter were purely extempore and mainly defensive in concept
7 St Aignan where the Battalion rested at the beginning of June 1940 is a hamlet some 15 km east-north-east of the outskirts of Rouen
8 Centre Line. This was the main route which a unit followed: it applied to all movement, whether in action or just moving from one place to another. It was referred to as the 'CL' or, using the then current phonetic alphabet, the 'Charlie Love' – a term which will appear frequently in this book. Many ex-army men still use that term to describe the route of their journeys

CHAPTER II

. . . Back To Square One

June–September 1940

Trauma-counselling and grief-therapy were unheard of in 1940 and, anyway, there were cogent reasons why 5RTR would have had no time for them. The Battalion simply went straight back to Army routine. The most cogent reason for getting on with the job, without time off for licking wounds, was that Britain was under immediate, serious, threat of invasion. The Battalion, as was the case with most branches of the Army, had gone to war ill-equipped and had come back from the first battles of that war without some or all of its equipment.

All that could be done, in the summer of 1940 therefore, was to get down to the business of rebuilding morale, training new recruits and hoping for new equipment.

Indeed, such was the state of the Battalion's equipment that the War Diary for 25th June states 'Four Light Tanks and seven Cruisers sent into Workshops. These are the only tanks left to this Battalion.' (The eleven tanks referred to were the ones from 'Z' Squadron brought back to England by Major Winship)

As for the men, a quarter of them and of the officers and NCOs were sent off with 48-hour leave[1] passes immediately the Battalion had settled into camp at Longbridge Deverell. When the first leave party returned, a second one was despatched, thereby missing two and a half hours in slit trenches during a night's air-raid alarm. Although not mentioned, presumably there were third and fourth leave parties as well.

Without tanks, training was confined to drill and individual instruction on Besas[2]. The next few days passed without incident: training continued; the weather was dull with some rain. This absence of incident, however, did not last long. On 29th June, at 1900 hrs, orders were received to move to Thursley Camp, near Hindhead in Surrey, the following morning. Fortunately, the Battalion had some transport: twenty-six 3-ton lorries had been collected the previous day. These, however, were for matériel and not for men. The main body of 5RTR marched to Warminster Station at 0815 hrs, entrained at 0945 hrs, arriving and detraining at Milford at 1308 hrs and then marching for an hour to reach Thursley Camp at 1420 hrs.

Life at Thursley was to prove very different. 5RTR was assigned an 'anti-invasion' role. Officers were sent out to reconnoitre and familiarise themselves with the area: motorcycle patrols were organised and the men set to preparing defensive positions. On 4th July, the first allocation of new tanks arrived. These were four *A10s*: one was reserved for HQ; the others went, one each, to the three Squadrons. Throughout the next weeks *A9*s and more *A10*s arrived until, by 24th July, the War Diary could claim that 'the Battalion had nearly all the Squadrons equipped with tanks'.

Following Regimental tradition, these tanks were all given names and the names duly recorded in the War Diary[3].

Tactical Exercises without Troops (TEWTs[4]) were held on a regular basis by the CO: the Brigadier lectured all officers on the recent campaign in France; the CO held a 'wireless exercise' and the Transport Section was put through its paces on the Rifle Range.

On the last day of July, a 'Party' left for gunnery practice at Lydd. The 'Party' returned on 3rd August and that seems to have been that. Throughout August there was a steady stream of new Second Lieutenants but no mention of recruits for the tank crews. After several more TEWTs, from Brigade level downwards, there were Squadron exercises, a Battalion exercise 'under control of the CO' [and who better?] and a Brigade exercise. In this, 5RTR acquitted itself 'satisfactorily' but the *A10*s did not, giving considerable trouble with their tracks.

The Battalion witnessed the Battle of Britain at its height. There were several Air Raid Warnings and a bombing raid on a nearby target for which no warning was given.

All in all, there were thirteen days marked as NTR in the War Diary for August, every Sunday being observed as a holiday. The only noteworthy fact recorded was the arrival of the Battalion's first new *A13* and the decision, when more of these arrived, to allocate them first to Battalion Headquarters, who would not have fought in them, rather than to the Squadrons, who would.

September saw the arrival in the Battalion, under canvas near Thursley, of Tom Chesterfield. Tom was in the Westminster Dragoons (22RTR [TA]) in 1939 and was called up on General Mobilisation. He was commissioned in April 1940 and, in September, was posted, as a Second Lieutenant, to 5RTR with five other Subalterns. Although not yet twenty and just posted to a Regular Battalion – and one very recently returned from having a rough time in France – he was given a warm welcome by both officers and men and not in the least made to realise that he was still 'wet behind the ears'. More than a little to his surprise, the four members of his first tank crew in 'B' Squadron were all under close arrest in the Guard Room, being released only during working hours to go about their regular duties while the invasion scare was at its height! As Tom recorded, 'It didn't seem to matter in the least and we all got on very well together.'

October started with a minor local excitement. Incendiary bombs set fire to nearby Cocksbury Common and the Fire Piquet was sent out to help extinguish it. The Battalion took part in a Brigade exercise the same day, with which heavy rain interfered, but presumably the rain must have helped with the Fire Piquet's problem. The next day rain interfered with the Brigade's wireless exercise. And the next day brought more rain. It also brought 2/Lt A Biddell [later to become famous for being caught 'in a bit of a dip'] as 2i/c HQ Squadron.

On 5th October 5RTR came under orders 'to proceed to a Tropical Climate'. This relieved it of its local anti-invasion role but there is no record of the unit's re-equipping for the change from the cold rain of England to anything remotely tropical. At the same time came orders for seven officers and 100 ORs to be posted away to form the cadre of 'the new Battalion'.

Over the next three weeks 5RTR felt the impact of the movement orders. The Battalion's B vehicles[5] left on 10th October, the scout cars on the 20th, the tanks being loaded on the 21st and 22nd, the baggage on the 26th and the main body leaving by night on the 29th. The plan – which was realised – was for the men to sail from Liverpool and the tanks from Glasgow. Titch Maple (who achieved every boy's ambition by making friends with the engine driver and completing the journey on the foot-plate) was one of the drivers. Jake Wardrop, who will shortly be introduced, was another.

The War Diary entry for 30th October has HIGH SEAS somewhat prematurely as a rubric. The actual events on that day were the arrival of the main body in Liverpool in mid-morning and its embarkation at noon on RMV *Stirling Castle.* With them were 3RTR and Brigade Headquarters. The next day was occupied with boat drill and on Friday, 1st November 1940 the *Stirling Castle* sailed in a five ship convoy with a three destroyer escort. On the Saturday the Liverpool convoy met the Glasgow fleet with the Brigade's tanks on board. As can be imagined, no-one – least of all the Battalion IO charged with keeping the War Diary – had a very clear notion of where the convoy was or what was going on for the next few weeks. Bernard Holder said that the convoy seemed to be heading for the Caribbean, it sailed so far west into the Atlantic. A submarine was reported to have been 'killed' by the escort. On the 14th the convoy hove to off Freetown. The Battalion soccer team, among others, was allowed on shore: the team beat one from HMS *Cornwall,* the escort cruiser, by 3 goals to 2. By a happy coincidence, the *Stirling Castle* crossed the Equator on Cambrai Day[6].

Cambrai Day is a good point at which to introduce Jake Wardrop. Apart from being one of the great characters of 5RTR, Jake is famous for the diary he kept (entirely in defiance of King's Regulations and Part One Standing Orders[7] for every unit). This starts on 31st October 1940, when Jake sailed from his native Glasgow on the SS *Clan Chattan* with the Battalion's tanks on board and ends on 4th January 1944 when his ship, with the homeward-bound 5RTR on board, sailed back into the Clyde.

John Richard Wardrop was born in Glasgow in May 1918, one of several children of an engineer father. After leaving school and some half-hearted attempts at routine occupations, Jake (he was never called anything else) took himself and his guitar off to the Recruiting Office and joined the Royal Tank Corps in 1937. Saying that Jake's career in 5RTR was chequered is a masterpiece of understatement. He was once described as being able to cause more trouble [in Cairo] in five minutes than the entire Royal Corps of Military Police could clear up in a month. Jake and trouble went together like steak and kidney but the trouble he enjoyed most was of being engaged 'at the sharp end'. By trade – and occupation, when not enjoying promotion – he was a tank driver; by nature he was a fighter and a leader. Qualities which were to cost him his life within a few days of the end of the war[8].

If life on board the *Stirling Castle* was 'bliss' according to one of Jake's friends, life on the *Clan Chattan* was 'smashing' according to Jake, who much appreciated an ample supply of beer, whisky and gin as well as the company of the crew who came, if not from Jake's native Glasgow, then at least from Scotland, which made them all 'great guys'.

From Freetown the convoy continued round the Cape – passing Cape Town twenty miles out at sea – and reaching Durban on 3rd December. Shore leave was granted to all ranks both from the *Stirling Castle* and the *Clan Chattan*. Jake met up with some of his friends and also with Nemesis, as he recorded in his diary. There being no other enemy in sight, they had 'a fine scrap' with some sailors. Jake 'remained unthrown but was sore for a week'.

On 12th December the convoy was back north of the Equator and on the 18th was off Aden where it broke up. *Stirling Castle* and two other ships went ahead and arrived at Port Suez on the 22nd. There then followed a rather shambolic movement which took the Battalion without proper transport or meals to Amirya, an encampment in the desert, south-west of Alexandria. In Amirya the shambles continued, the War Diary for Christmas Day reading 'Christmas Dinner held in evening as far as resources permitted.' In Titch Maple's view, those resources didn't permit very much!

The tanks had all been unloaded and moved separately, being sent direct to RAOC Workshops 'for desert modifications and painting etc'. 1940 ended with the arrival of Tom Chesterfield and the rear-party of fifty ORs, plus five new subalterns. As much as it ever was in the Desert, The Fifth was up to strength.

THE BACKGROUND

The external events affecting 5RTR in the months after their return from France had mainly been taking place in North Africa. Even before 'the Western Desert' became the centre-stage of the Western Allies' war against Nazi aggression, Wavell's campaigns had been fought with varying success since Italy had declared war on Great Britain and France on 10th June 1940. This declaration of war solves the question that is, to modern generations, a complete anomaly. Why were the Allies fighting the Axis in North Africa?

Benito Mussolini – Italy's dictator and 'Hitler's Jackal' – had, in the late 1930s, established, by military conquest and in defiance of the League of Nations, Italian colonies and military bases in both Libya and Somaliland. Britain had treaty obligations to defend Egypt and the vital Suez Canal, vulnerable to attack from Italy and known to be one of the Axis' targets. General Sir Archibald Wavell was GOC-in-C Middle East Forces – a somewhat hollow title, considering how few 'Forces' he had under his command. He certainly did not have the resources to defend both Egypt and British Somaliland. With a wary eye to Libya's proximity to the southern Italian ports and the greater strength of the Italian Army and Air Force there, Wavell concentrated his troops – the Western Desert Force – on the Libyan border. On the other side of this frontier, Marshal Rodolfo Graziani, the Italian C-in-C, had an estimated nine divisions in Tripolitania (Western Libya) and five more in Cyrenaica (Eastern Libya), giving him between 210,000 and 220,000 men, and some 500 aircraft.

Against these, and under General Maitland Wilson, Wavell had the 7th Armoured Division (not by any means yet fully equipped or prepared for battle), an Infantry Brigade (well trained but seriously deficient in supporting services, particularly artillery), the formidable 4th Indian Division and the indomitable, but still raw, Australian 6th Division and the New Zealand Division

Wavell didn't wait for an Italian initiative. Within days of the declaration of war, the 7th Armoured Division was on the offensive and advanced units started collecting their first 'bags' of Italian POWs. On 16th June the first tank-v-tank battle took place and was rightly counted a British victory. A stalemate then developed. Maitland Wilson was unable to capitalise on his early successes. He lacked transport (as the Army in North Africa nearly always did), his troops were thin on the ground: the wear and tear on his severely over-worked and obsolete armour was beginning to tell. A decisive factor was that the Italians had air supremacy.

The second stage of the war in Africa started with the invasion of British Somaliland by the Italians from their adjacent colony. This took place, with a fine touch of historical irony, on 4th August. By the end of the month, British Somaliland was evacuated and the Italians had penetrated the British Protectorate of Sudan.

Encouraged by this victory, although overestimating Wavell's strength as a result of Maitland Wilson's aggressive tactics, Graziani launched his expected attack on Egypt on 13th September. The attack came precisely as Wavell had predicted, with no element of surprise, thereby letting him withdraw strictly according to plan. There were 3,000 or more casualties on the Italian side and only 150 on the British.

What surprised the British High Command was the halt which Graziani called when the Italians reached the area of Sidi Barrani. Whatever Graziani's reasons, the halt allowed the British to suspend their withdrawal and prepare to go over to the counter-offensive, taking advantage of the reinforcement of men (III Hussars and 2RTR as well as two RHA regiments) and matériel. No small part of this preparation was the continual harassment carried out by the 'Jock Columns'[9] behind the enemy lines.

Another aspect of the British success was the poor quality of the Italian Army, officers and men frequently lacking the dono di coraggio. *In addition, neither the officers nor the men had proper training and the men – conscripts – had no desire to fight, certainly not with the poor equipment and lack of creature comforts provided for them. There were some notable exceptions but the average Italian soldier of the 20th century bore no resemblance to his Roman legionary forerunner.*

The main defect was, however, that of their High Command. By adopting a series of isolated strong-points with no proper means of communication or mutual support, the Italians laid themselves wide open to just the sort of tactics which the 7th Armoured Division and the Commonwealth Infantry Divisions had perfected for desert warfare.

The attack, launched with great secrecy on 9th December 1940, succeeded beyond all expectation, it being not unknown for a troop of tanks or armoured cars to 'bag' an entire Italian regiment. So great were some of these 'bags', that the British took to measuring them 'by the acre' rather than by the thousand!

Unfortunately it was for the second time impossible to follow up this success. Even if it had been possible to do it with full resources, this became impossible when scarce resources had to be sent to East Africa or were demanded by Churchill to support the Greeks' small Army in its valiant but unavailing fight against the invaders. To cap it all, Wavell now had to feed more POWs than his own front-line troops.

THE WAR CHRONICLE

1940

June	24	End of French Army resistance in France
	30	Channel Islands occupied by German forces
July	01	'Vichy' Government established in France
	03	Capture (or destruction) of French Fleet in Oran harbour by Royal Navy
	04	Italian forces invaded Sudan
	05	Romania joined 'Berlin-Rome Axis' – Sweden allowed passage of German troops to Norway
	08	Creation of the Local Defence Volunteers [LDV] afterwards the Home Guard . . . later still, 'Dad's Army'
	13	Italian aircraft raided Malta and Aden
August	04	Italy invaded British Somaliland
	11	First major aerial engagements in 'The Battle of Britain'
	19	British Somaliland fell to Italy
	20	Winston Churchill made his famous 'The Few'

		speech in Parliament
	22	Lev (Leon) Trotsky assassinated in Mexico
	24	First bombing raid on London . . . a mistake by the Luftwaffe
	26	Luftwaffe bombed London (on purpose). RAF bombed Berlin
	31	'Der Tag'. Scheduled date for 'Operation Sealion', the Invasion of Britain
September	06	The real 'Blitz' began, with London as main target
	09	Italian planes bombed Tel Aviv
	10	Italy invaded Albania
	12	Discovery of palaeolithic wall-paintings in a cave near Lascaux in the Dordogne (France) – Italian offensive at Sollum on the Libyan/Egyptian border began
	13	Italian forces advanced into Kenya
	15	Turning point in 'The Battle of Britain'
	16	USA introduced 'selective conscription' of single males over 21
	17	'Operation Sealion' put on hold by Hitler (until, in theory, April 1941)
	23	Institution of 'George Cross' and 'George Medal' by HM King George VI
	24	Gibraltar bombed by 'Vichy' France Air Force
	25	Planned invasion of Dakar (Senegal) failed
	27	Japan joined the 'Axis Powers' . . . in an as-yet-non-combatant role
October	03	Ernest Bevin joined the War Cabinet (in a combative role) on resignation of Neville Chamberlain – Warsaw Puppet and Vichy Governments stepped up 'pogrom' on Jews
	05	Japan warned USA that its 'Anti-Axis attitude' would lead to war
	07	German forces occupied Romania (nominally its ally)
	10	German occupation authorities in Luxembourg ran a Public Opinion Poll and discovered, to their immense surprise, that 97% of population wanted them out
	15	Mussolini ordered invasion of Greece
	20	Italian planes bombed Cairo
	21	Purchase Tax introduced in UK
	28	Italian invasion of Greece launched

November	05	The Armed Merchantman *Jervis Bay* saved convoy from attack by German Battleship *Admiral Speer*
	09	An industrial survey showed higher unemployment among women in UK than in September 1939
	11	Italian aircraft flew (unsuccessful) bombing mission against London
	13	Hitler ordered Göring to plan Luftwaffe attack on Russia
	14	Franklin D Roosevelt re-elected for third term as President of USA – Night raids on Coventry tore the centre out of the city and destroyed the cathedral
	25	First rumblings of Jewish determination to create an Independent State of Israel – Maiden flight of the Mosquito aircraft – 4,588 civilians killed and 6,202 severely injured in air raids during November, mainly in London, Birmingham, Liverpool and Southampton

NOTES

1 48 hours' leave. Although this was short enough, considering what the men had been through, it was not the same as a '48-hour leave pass', which simply permitted absence from the unit for 48 hours. The 48 hours' leave did not include travelling time but represented two days at home

2 Besas. The Besa was a tank machine-gun, adapted from the Czechoslovakian Bren [Brno] gun, which the British Army had adopted for infantry use in the late 1930s as a light machine-gun to replace the WW I 'Lewis' gun. Heavier in construction than the Bren and fed by a belt instead of a box magazine, the Besa used the 7.92mm rimless ammunition, common to the Continental armies (including the Wehrmacht). As a tank weapon, being air cooled, robust and mechanically simpler, it was a vast improvement on the water-cooled Vickers machine-gun. The Besa was developed by the Birmingham Small Arms Company – BSA spelling Besa, as every motorcycle enthusiast knows

3 Tank names. 'E' being the fifth letter of the alphabet, 'E' was the initial letter of 5RTR's tank names. The War Diary for July 1940 includes an Appendix giving the names of all the Battalion's tanks. Some of those 1940 names – Endeavour, Endurance, Eager, Excellent – were on the *Cromwells* and *Sherman Fireflies* that rolled into Hamburg in May 1945. When I took over an un-named *Cromwell* in 1944, I called it ESMERALDA

4 TEWTs could take many forms, and consisted of the lecturer postulating a situation and then asking for individual opinions as to how it should be handled. The most sophisticated, indoor, TEWT was the 'sand-table' exercise, where the situation was created by using sculptured sand to represent the chosen terrain. TEWTs could be very amusing, giving juniors a rare

opportunity to argue with their seniors. A good senior officer never minded such arguments

5 B Vehicles. For convenience, an armoured regiment's vehicles were divided into A – mainly the AFVs and scout cars – and B – the 'soft-skinned' vehicles *ie* the trucks, lorries, jeeps, staff cars etc which were not designed to be taken into action (although they often got there!)

6 Cambrai Day. November 20th, 1917 was the first day that the Tank Corps fought a planned, massed-armour, action. This was the Battle of Cambrai. Ever since then it has been the Regimental Day of the Royal Tank Regiment, marked (whenever circumstances permit) by a parade and a holiday for all ranks

7 Part One Orders. Under King's (now, of course, Queen's) Regulations governing all matter military, are Regimental Orders. Part One are 'standing orders' in that they remain in force, affecting all ranks, until replaced by new ones. Part Two Orders are issued to govern particular events or circumstances. ('Part Three Orders' are the most common – being the universal Army name for rumours)

8 Jake Wardrop's Diary. As mentioned in the text, 7888470 Wardrop JR kept a diary from late October 1940 to early January 1944. This diary was first published (with limited circulation for members of 5RTR) by another famous regular pre-war RTC soldier, Jackie Garnett MC. This version, called WARDROP OF THE FIFTH, is the one referred to in this book. For details of George Forty's admirable TANKS ACROSS THE DESERT, see the information given in the Bibliography. It is common knowledge in 5RTR that Jake continued to keep his diary right up to the time he died. George Stimpson rescued at least part of it from Jake's tank after Jake was killed in action and sent it home to Jake's family. No-one knows what subsequently happened to it

9 Jock Columns. These were named after Lt Col J C 'Jock' Campbell of 4 RHA whose idea they were. These units, which became part of the legend of the Desert War, were compact formations composed of armoured cars for reconnaissance, 25-pounder guns 'to hit where it hurts' and infantry 'to protect the guns by day and play merry hell with the enemy by night'. Highly mobile and acting on the initiative of the Column commander, their role was to penetrate deep behind the enemy's lines, attacking suitable targets, particularly supply columns and dumps, and lines of communication. Colonel Campbell not only devised the 'Jock Columns', he commanded the first of them. He was later promoted to Brigadier in which rank he was, for exceptional courage in command, awarded the VC to add to his DSO and MC. He was later promoted Major General and commanded The Desert Rats for a short time until killed in a car accident in February 1942

CHAPTER III

. . . War in the Desert: Italian Encounter – Rommel

January–April 1941

If one takes the 7th Armoured Division's move against the Italians on the Libya-Egypt border on 12th June 1940 as the start of the North African Campaign, and 12th May 1943, when Axis resistance in Tunisia finally ceased, as the end of the campaign, the Desert War lasted exactly two years and eleven months – more than three times as long as the campaign in North-west Europe in 1944/45.

The Fifth was not in at the start but it was in at the end, in all spending something over thirty-two months in North Africa.

January 1st 1941 witnessed the CO and Squadron Commanders making a reconnaissance of the training area allotted to the Division. It also started with a hangover for Jake Wardrop who had celebrated Hogmanay with the rum he had collared on the *Clan Chattan.*

Work went on meanwhile on the tanks and B vehicles to bring them up to 'Desert specification'. This was not always easy: none of the vehicles in service with the British Army had been designed with desert warfare in mind. Serious defects showed up in the air filters on the *A10*s and the radiators on the *A13*s. Problems were encountered with the fans on the Fordson lorries. Despite these difficulties, orders came pouring in for intended, delayed or – generally – cancelled moves. These delays benefited 'HQ', 'A' and 'B' Squadrons who were granted leave. 'C' Squadron was not so lucky: for unstated reasons, their leave was cancelled. Refreshed by their leave, 'A' and 'B' Squadrons were sent out for gunnery practice.

The Fifth had its first taste of what the Desert could do in making life uncomfortable when their camp was hit by a heavy sandstorm on 16th January. A prolonged storm was still being mentioned in the War Diary on 28th January.

After more work on the tanks and B vehicles (most of the trouble reported as having been due to damage sustained on the sea voyage) and further practice firing, the Battalion advance party left 'for the Front'[1] on 26th January. Pressure was on the remainder to complete the preparatory work. The reason for this pressure was that, having arrived in Egypt reasonably well equipped with *A9*s and *A10*s, the Battalion was ordered to exchange their *A9*s for 3RTR's *A13*s. This naturally delayed The Fifth's readiness to move which, in turn, changed The Fifth's role in the actions in the next four months.

The move started on 26th January (in the sandstorm) with the advance party going by road. They were followed on the 27th by the scout cars, also by road, and 'C' Squadron by rail. The War Diary indignantly reports 'superficial damage to tanks in loading' (the rail flat-cars were too narrow). The time would soon come when no-one bothered about the odd scratch on the paint-work! Rather more serious was the loss of two 'B' Squadron lorries on the 28th. Their destination, like that of the rest of the unit, was an encampment at Bir Sheferzen, some 30 miles south-west of Sollum (the end of the line for the Cairo, Alexandria and All Points West Light Railway). One lost lorry turned up on 31st January, 80-odd miles west of Tobruk: the other in Benghazi – nearer the enemy than anyone else in The Fifth!

By 5th February advanced units of 7th Armoured Division had cut across country over appalling terrain from a point west of Tobruk to the Cyrenaica coast in the Gulf of Sirte west of Sidi Saleh. This advance, one of the great feats of the Desert War, brought about the surrender of an Italian Army of 130,000 men, 400 tanks and 1,300 guns and was accomplished with a force of one Infantry and one Armoured Division, both depleted and perpetually short of ammunition, petrol, water and other essential supplies, and living and fighting in conditions seldom previously encountered.

Even before its departure on this advance, 7th Armoured Division was badly in need of reinforcements and 5RTR was originally destined to join the 4th Armoured Brigade in that role. Its orders were, therefore, intended to take it across country for this purpose. However, the speed of the Division's advance was such that it would have been impossible for The Fifth to catch up by following the Divisional Centre Line. The change of plan came on 5th February by which time the Battalion was at Bir el Gubi, about 100 miles almost due west of Sollum.

Jake Wardrop recorded that the march to Bir el Gubi had consisted of a two-day train journey followed by a drive of 40 miles towards Siwa 'to a place which some romancer had called Charing Cross.' Here the Battalion halted for two days and it was here that the orders were changed. Speed was no longer of the essence and the new route took the Battalion to an area 13 miles west of el Adem. It was well that speed was not important, as the weather changed from a heavy sandstorm on 6th February to heavy rain on the 8th and 9th. Rain so heavy that the men were glad to climb into the tank and sleep the rest of the night at their action stations, still in their soaking wet clothes.

On 7th February, the Brigadier had given orders for recces[2] to be carried out to find possible routes to Agedabia. This was another change of plan and meant abandoning the coastal route and cutting across country, more or less

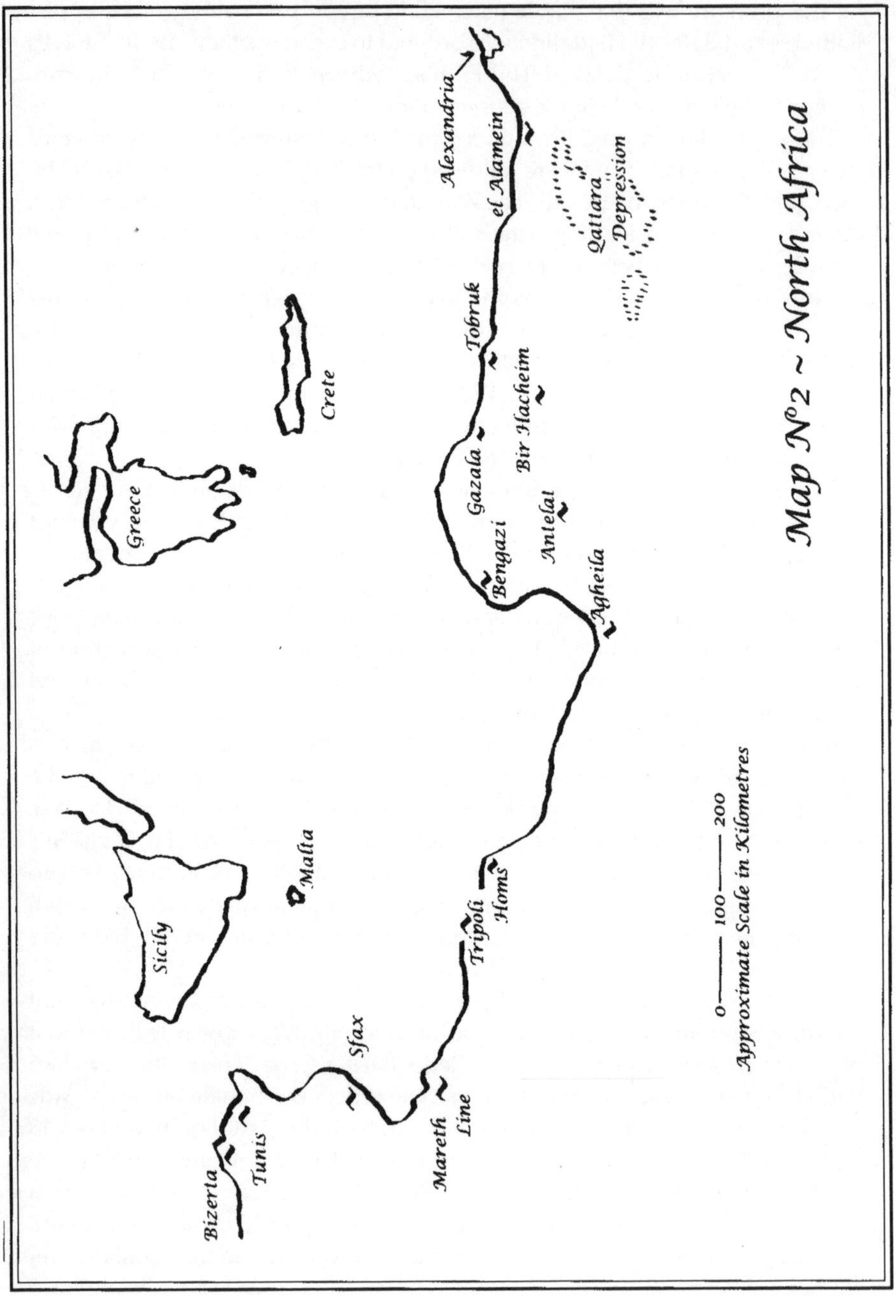

Map N°2 ~ North Africa

along the lines pioneered by the main body of Seventh Armoured. The recce party from 5RTR, consisting of Major Rash and 2/Lt DN Macdonald, set out, the unfortunate Deryk Macdonald getting himself and his party lost for four days. Major Rash was more successful but took another four days before making it back to base.

For 17th February a despairing entry in the War Diary reads, 'Brigadier returned from Corps HQ and gave verbal instructions about formation of a Brigade Group including all Brigade services but without 5RTR. 5RTR to remain el Adem area until receiving orders to move back to Egypt. No information concerning formation to which 5RTR is to be attached.' For the next three weeks, no-one quite knew what was happening. At the end of February, 'the 6th Battalion without vehicles or tanks' came, without explanation, under command of The Fifth, as did 1 RHA.

What happened between 17th February and 12th March, when the Battalion was put on one hour's notice to move, is described by Jake Wardrop.

Jake took the view that the line at el Agheila was on the thin side but that this probably didn't matter as the Italians were, at least temporarily, too disorganised to renew the engagement. However, in Jake's words, 'At that time a certain gentleman arrived in Tripoli with the Afrika Korps, Erwin Rommel, the bold bad policeman. I remember listening to a [radio] commentary about that time on some running battles which had been fought in the Med, in which most of the Italian stuff had reached Tripoli. It suggested that those ships had German troops: how right it was!'

Be that as it may, The Fifth continued at el Adem, taking advantage of the Australians' generosity – especially with their beer – and, in Jake's case, doing a lot of walking, trading WD-issue tea ration for eggs 'with the *wogs*', playing football and reading GONE WITH THE WIND. Before they left el Adem, the men were sunbathing.

On 12th March, five hours after being put on one hour's notice, one Squadron was ordered to join 3rd Armoured Brigade in the forward area 'immediately by normal marches'. At 1000 hrs next day, 'A' Squadron under Major Pritchett left with 14 *A13*s and 2 *A10*s. One tank had to be returned to Tobruk – where there were, in fact, no workshop facilities – with a partially seized engine. The War Diary notes here that the average recorded mileage of the *A13*s was 1,400, whereas the prescribed mileage between overhauls was only 1,000. The situation with regard to recovery of and running repairs to The Fifth's tanks was exacerbated by the complete absence of heavy recovery equipment within the Division and the fact that the LRS was right *forward* at Beda Fom.

'A' Squadron had arrived at Antelat on 15th March and by 1900 hrs on the 17th had leaguered[3] for the night near Agedabia. On the 21st the rest of the Regiment, sadly beset by mechanical problems, made a 260 miles cross-country march. When 'A' Squadron left the Regiment it had 14 *A13*s and 2 *A10*s. Three of these *A13*s had to be sent to the LRS . . . and were never seen again by The Fifth. The 2 *A10*s were handed over to 6RTR, which seemed to be collecting them rather as if they were playing a game of *Happy Families*. On the 21st when the rest of the Regiment moved, 'B' Squadron had 13 *A13*s and 2 *A10*s; 'C' Squadron had 14 *A13*s and 1 *A10*; 'HQ' had 6 *A13*s, of which two were described as being 'spare'. A total of 52 tanks. On 28th March the Regiment's tank strength was down to 28 *A13*s. Needless to say, 6RTR collected the remaining *A10*s – a common sense move, as they were not able to keep up with the *A13*s. Of the 28 *A13*s, some were in far from good health.

Then on 31st March 5RTR had its first clash with the enemy on African soil. This came about because 'Fit tanks of 'A' Squadron (6 *A13*s) went forward with the armoured car patrol of the KDG [experienced Desert fighters] in a supporting role. Half an hour later one *A13* became a mechanical casualty and by 1900 hrs another *A13* lost power and was sent back. The War Diary continues for 31st March, '0630 hrs 'A' Squadron encountered main force of enemy moving east. One tank of Squadron hit and turret jammed so withdrew from action. Remaining 3 tanks stayed in position of observation. Enemy casualties uncertain, probably about 3 M.13 tanks[4].' At 0900 hrs the Regiment was notified that the Codeword for the Day was 'Laxative'. Someone, somewhere, had a macabre sense of humour.

Jake Wardrop's account of this action reads rather more graphically. 'I don't know how it started, but one day we moved and it was the slickest bit of work we ever did. For four days the Battalion covered a hundred miles a day over desert that the *wogs* wouldn't go on. At the end of the trip we were facing the Agheila salt flats and it was 30th March. Out of fifteen tanks in 'C' Squadron, fifteen got there. The Major came and shook hands with all the drivers, it wasn't a bad effort. On the 31st we worked on the tanks and at night orders came round to pack up and stand by. A party of tanks of 'A' Squadron had been fired on that afternoon by none other than the blue-eyed boys of the Afrika Korps. They had got themselves sorted out in Tripoli and come whooping down the coast and were on the other side of the salt flats. We were silly boys to be where we were! They had the 15th and 21st Panzer Divisions and 90th Light, a pretty good motorised infantry division. The British front line at that time consisted of the 5th Tanks, the 3 RHA, the KDGs and 6 RBs[5].

'On the morning of 1st April, the fun began: a real how d'ye do it was! Stukas, Dorniers and a few thrusts by tanks. We came back that day and the next, until about four in the afternoon, when we reached Agedabia, where it was decided to have a dabble It was the quickest, deadliest duffy I've ever seen. We sat behind a ridge and waited until they came, then popped up and let loose. There seemed to be nothing in front but tanks coming on, but we kept on firing and they slowed down and finally halted and shot it out stationary. But they were feeling for the flanks and their Artillery had started to lob some 105s over. Well, there wasn't much else to it, we drew out slowly firing until it was dark. We had lost five tanks and there were casualties on some others.'

In spite of what Bert Hunt said about his lack of training 'in the field', the action was a classic example of carrying out, in the face of the enemy, The Fifth's training on Salisbury Plain. George Forty, in a footnote to TANKS ACROSS THE DESERT, quotes another great Fifth Tanks character, George Stimpson, as saying, 'As the Battalion withdrew, one squadron acted as rearguard and then leap-frogged through another which had taken up a defensive position to the rear. 'C' Squadron were rearguard and let the enemy come on until they were inside effective 2-pounder range (under 1,000 yards). Then, when the firing began, it was carried out in the well-practised manner of the hull-down shoot[6] – fire three rounds, reverse and come up in a slightly different position, then three more rounds and so on. This was instilled into us in our early training days and we scored countless hits without one of our tanks being damaged – undoubtedly this was the way to fight a tank-v-tank battle. However, just as we started pulling back some other tanks appeared, went forward over the ridge and charged the enemy, losing five tanks complete with crews – very heroic but definitely *not* the way to do it. If anyone learnt from this action, it was Rommel.' A very perceptive comment from 'Stimo'.

Jake Wardrop commented that this was the only serious attempt made to halt the enemy before Tobruk. From then on, all that the Regiment and the rest of the Brigade could do was to try to stay between the advancing DAK and the rapidly withdrawing Echelons and other supply columns. These were often forced to abandon their vehicles, complete with loads, whenever they broke down or ran out of petrol. This gave the retreating tank crews access to almost unlimited supplies – and they didn't pass up the opportunities! Jake added that the rammy[7] on the ridge seemed to have tamed the Boches for a bit, because the pace of their advance seemed gradually to slow and, for a while, they were seen no more. This was deceptive: what actually happened was that the Centre Line chosen for the withdrawal was being paralleled by Rommel, who struck the coast to the east of the Allies and, in fact, cut them off at Derna.

By this time, 5RTR had only six tanks left and these were hardly road-worthy, let alone battle-worthy, making 10mph at the most on the few-and-far-between surfaced roads. Although buckshee rations were plentiful, petrol was becoming a serious problem. The CO had sent two officers out in scout cars scouring the countryside for abandoned dumps. When the stragglers reached Derna, Jake's tank finally expired. There was nothing else for it but to get out and brew themselves a cuppa char. While they were enjoying this, a Liaison Officer arrived to warn them that the Germans had reached the top of the hill which they had just crept down and 'if they wanted to see their mothers again, they'd have to make a fight of it'. There were four other tanks and about a hundred men from the RBs. While these indomitable warriors went back up the hill to hold the fort, Jake and his crew finished their tea.

The easiest way to appreciate just what a madhouse an engagement of this nature could be is to read Jake's description of it. 'The plan was for the tanks to get up the hill, get into line and dash across the aerodrome, firing everything, and reach the road beyond, halt and see what developed, then let the RBs get away in their lorries. There seemed to be quite a number of faults in this. The big one being that nobody knew the Boche strength, but I wasn't looking for an argument and, in any case, it was a 'slap-happy' effort and it was our bad luck to be there. So off we went up the hill, the British war effort, four tanks that nobody but a fool would have given a bent thrupenny bit for! At the top we shook out into line, the Major waved a flag and we were off. There wasn't much there, a few anti-tank guns and some of the famous German Spandau machine-guns, but the charge broke them. They fired some shots and broke, one tank of ours was hit and stopped. We were next to them and picked them up as they baled out and they clung to the sides. At the road we halted and the RBs dashed up the road to Tobruk – it had worked. There were still ninety miles to do and, about fifty miles from home, mine and another tank flogged out. There wasn't a tow-rope between us and in any case, the remaining tanks would not have pulled the skin off a rice pudding: so the two crocks were blown up. There were four crews to be carried and we piled on to the last hope and off we went to Tobruk, fingers crossed.'

Jake reckoned that their mental worries, if not their physical ones, ended as they approached Tobruk and were cheerfully hailed by the Australian outposts. Once inside the perimeter, they surrendered what was left to them of tanks and joined the 'Tobruk Defence Force'.

Colonel Drew's supplement to the War Diary, compiled from two separate accounts, describes the next days as follows, 'It is impossible to get an accurate or complete description of the events of 2nd April, as at present none of the Tank Commanders or gunners of the surviving tanks is here: this resumé is based on certain Drivers' stories.

'On 2nd April the Regiment was withdrawing from an area 3 miles North of Fort Gtafia to a position on the track Agebadia–Saunnu, in accordance with a plan put in force on receipt of a code-word OXFORD, given to us at 0900 hrs that morning. By this plan, at about 1000 hrs, 3rd Armoured Brigade were to withdraw to a line North of Agedabia, with the III Hussars on the right [*ie* facing the enemy] of the Regiment. III Hussars had attached to them one squadron of 6RTR with [captured Italian] M.13 tanks.

'The timing of our withdrawal was regulated by the speed of A/E Battery RHA for whose protection we were responsible. Their speed was about 7 mph, compared with our 15 mph.

'The initial strength and disposition of the tanks in the Regiment was:

RHQ	4 tanks
A/B Squadron	6 tanks
C Squadron	12 tanks

'At some time during the action the Regiment had been still further depleted by 2 mechanical casualties to tanks of A/B Squadron and by one Troop of C Squadron (Lt Steevens) which had been detached to protect duties

1 RHA. The total strength of the Regiment during the action was, therefore, 17 tanks

'About 1300 hrs, considerable confusion was caused by a dust cloud created by part of 1 RHA which was withdrawing on the same CL. Sgt Clarkson in *Edgeworth* (11 Troop) mistook these for the enemy. Shortly after, an RHA Major who had become detached from his unit made the same mistake and nearly two hours elapsed before the confusion was resolved – fortunately without any shots being fired. About 1500 hrs the withdrawal was resumed but there were further delays due to mechanical breakdowns and to an order being given by Brigade and then countermanded. At approximately 1700 hrs – by which time it was getting dark – two of the petrol lorries caught up with the column and went round the tanks

'At 1730 hrs the CO and Squadron Commanders were at the rear link[8] tank standing by to receive important orders from 3rd Armoured Brigade. About 1745 hrs a runner came over to the CO's tank with C Squadron's first report, which was to the effect that there were 15 to 20 unidentified vehicles three or four miles away, some thought to be tanks.

'The CO then ordered OC C Squadron to return to his Squadron, which was doing 'Protection Rear', and to keep the column under observation and to report further.

'The second report, about 20 minutes later, estimated there were about 40 vehicles, a mixture of tanks and transport. At this time, the crews were reported to be riding outside the tanks. This report was repeated to Brigade who cautioned that these might be 6RTR. The second report came from 10 Troop to Lt Ramsey who wirelessed Major Winship's tank asking if the Squadron Commander had received the message – the one brought to HQ by runner. Major Winship then went to his tank and immediately wirelessed Ramsey 'Have you anything further to report about those vehicles?' Ramsey asked Sgt Wrightford who replied that he was still unable to distinguish them.

'Major Winship then ordered 10 and 11 Troops to take up hull-down positions on the ridge to the rear and to do 'Protection Rear' for the Regiment, saying that he would come up as soon as he could to see the position for himself. When our tanks started to move, the enemy tanks stopped behind a small ridge, some 5,000 yards away. Our own tanks took up the hull-down positions as ordered.

'From his hull-down position, Ramsey had a better view of the other tanks, bearing in mind the possibility that they still might be 6RTR or III Hussars. When he saw that the crews were riding outside the tanks and the tanks had no flags, he reported that they must be enemy, because they had wireless masts on the side.'

This account continues, 'When the enemy were 2,000 yards away, Major Winship gave the order, 'Stand by to open fire at 800 yards.' Information that Major Winship had given this order was passed to RHQ but not received by the CO, who had meanwhile ordered A/B Squadron to move to support C

Squadron. Major Winship again reminded his Squadron to be careful, in case the approaching tanks were from 6RTR. No sooner had he done so than heavy fire was opened on us by 47mm and either mortar or light artillery. Major Winship sent a message to the Regiment. 'They must be enemy as they have opened fire on us.'

'Within the first minute Lt Millar's tank was hit on the auxiliary petrol tank and set on fire. Lt Millar and his complete crew baled out and ran to take cover. They have not been seen since. Two RHQ tanks now reinforced the line held by 10 and 11 Troops. In spite of having to fire directly into the sun, we returned their fire effectively. The ranges given by the tank commanders varied from 900 to 1,500 yards and at least 8 enemy tanks are claimed to have been put out of action by our surviving gunners.

'Owing to the intensity of the enemy fire and our bad position relative to the setting sun, Colonel Drew decided to withdraw. He sent the coded orders which rallied the surviving tanks at about 1900 hrs. On receiving this order, Major Winship was overheard to say, 'Yes, it is getting rather hot.' Four tanks from A/B Squadron were then sent off to gain contact with III Hussars as previously ordered. The remainder of the Regiment moved back about another mile and waited for the A Echelon to be collected. At about 2000 hrs the remainder of the Regiment resumed the withdrawal to Antelat.'

The War Diary concludes its narrative by saying, 'The action was reported to 3rd Armoured Brigade and the casualties evacuated from the tanks. Major Winship's tank was hit as it was turning to come out of action and was set on fire; one man is said to have got out but there is no evidence as to where he went. Captain Clifford's tank was also set on fire, while none was seen to leave the tank. Captain Erskine was last seen waving the flag to signal for the advance and moving towards the enemy. Lt Ramsey's tank was seen to be hit early in the action and to be in flames. Eighteen Other Ranks were lost, plus an additional, unidentified, casualty in a tank that came out of the action.'

This story does not end there. Colonel Drew added a Post Script. 'The enemy force was eventually established to be between 50 – 60 tanks of Mk II and III and IV pattern, supported by a Battery of eight 47mm anti-tank guns. From a diary taken off a dead German soldier of this same regiment on 14th April in Tobruk, it was established that our enemy had been a Battalion of the Fifth Tank Regiment. A noteworthy coincidence. The same diary had an entry dated 3rd April worded as follows: "Yesterday we had a terrifying experience in action against British tanks near Agedabia. Our casualties were considerable although, thank God, I survived unhurt. After this I will give up drinking, smoking, and sexual intercourse for the rest of the war."'

In addition to this one unofficial and one official account, there is a very detailed version of the action. This was apparently produced by Colonel Drew some months later (it is dated Beni Yusef, 27th July). There are indications that this later version was prepared by Dinham Drew to repudiate some criticism of his conduct: this is not the only record in the Regimental archives which hints that he may have been unduly sensitive to criticism – expressed or imagined. This impression is strengthened by the number of references there are in the account to the Brigadier giving orders and then cancelling them. The surprising thing about the July account is the amount of detail in it which does not appear in any of the other records. Since the July account adds only detail and not substance, it is not included here: one or two points of interest, however, are reproduced.

Dealing with 1st April, Colonel Drew says that The Fifth saw no sign of enemy ground troops. As to this, see Note No 9. Colonel Drew's account confirms that communications were extremely difficult and largely unreliable when RHQ had to depend on R/T[10] which partly explains some of the confusion in giving and receiving orders. According to Liddell Hart, the whole Division was retreating to Antelat on 3rd April and it is presumably during this retreat that the Battalion was resting. Dealing comprehensively with the retreat, Colonel Drew said that the whole withdrawal was carried out in an extremely disorderly manner, transport being intermingled with some units' AFVs and that there was a general lack of control. As a result, he concludes, there was excessive congestion but luckily the withdrawal was molested by neither the enemy's land or air forces.

To add to the confusion, Dinham Drew states censoriously that one of the unidentified columns was from 6RTR 'who were not flying identifying flags'.

On the 4th the CO recorded that Battalion strength was down to ten tanks, of which one more was lost the following day, having to be destroyed.

At this stage the withdrawal was intended to be to Mechili but this was considered impossible as there were reports of enemy presence in Msus. Regima was given as the alternative destination . . . until the enemy was reported also to be occupying that town. The report on Msus proved incorrect and the Battalion was ordered to move there to hold it while the remainder of the Brigade passed through. Which, according to Dinham Drew, they took their time to do. The fact that Msus was occupied by 5RTR and not the enemy did not mean that the withdrawal to Mechili was to continue. Yet further orders were received to proceed Bir-el-Melz where the Battalion leaguered for the night of 4th April.

On the 5th the withdrawal continued, the Brigadier informing the CO that he had completely lost touch with Divisional HQ. To add to his worries, Colonel Drew lost touch with 6RTR. The only relief was that the petrol lorries, under Major Castle, arrived on 6th April.

Some indication of the strain on Dinham Drew is to be found in his account of the events of the 6th. Having been warned that any forces observed to the west were probably hostile, 2/Lt Chave of 'B' Squadron opened fire on what he took to be enemy armoured cars at 2,000 yds range. Not perhaps very wise with 2-pounders but not, surely, such a venal sin that the CO had to record in the War Diary that he reprimanded the unfortunate Chave. It was as well that Chave's guns did not score any hits, as the reported enemy proved to be 6RTR.

On 6th April the withdrawal continued, once more amid a degree of confusion both as to Brigade's orders (few intelligible ones were coming through to Brigade from Division) and as to the whereabouts of the Battalion's petrol supplies. Faced with contradictory information about enemy movement – to say nothing of the whereabouts of friendly units – and the increasingly acute shortage of fuel, the loss of tanks through mechanical failure was not surprisingly driving the CO frantic. Some relief came at 1800 hrs when Colonel Drew and the Adjutant discovered a petrol dump just in time to prevent its being blown up by Australian Engineers. By 2200 hrs that day the Battalion was able to resume its march to Derna.

For some reason, Dinham Drew thought it necessary to compile an even more detailed version of events for 7th April. This is too detailed to be included verbatim but the following summary will give a good idea of how hectic a day in the life of Fifth Tanks could be in the Desert.

The Fifth was the rearmost unit of the Brigade when a German force (estimated to comprise 12 armoured cars, two companies of Motorised Infantry with four anti-tank guns and two probably 100mm howitzers) was sighted. This force had captured the Brigade LRS and 5RTR's LAD at 1000 hrs: at 1200 hrs it attacked HQ 3rd Armoured Brigade and captured Brigadier Rimington and his 2i/c, Colonel Fanshawe

Seven *A13*s from 5RTR were involved, along with some eight A Echelon vehicles with the crews of the abandoned tanks. Reaching Derna they passed through a rearguard from the KRRC and a Platoon from the Tower Hamlets Regiment (holding some ruined buildings on the north side of the road but pinned down by enemy fire), two anti-tank guns and demolition parties of Australian Engineers, left behind to blow up the hill roads on both sides of Derna and dumps of stores in Derna itself, together with men from other units.

By 1200 hrs the remaining six – no longer seven – *A13*s of 5RTR were laboriously descending the Pass into Derna. While the CO was going ahead to contact Brig Rimington to find out his intentions, the road into Derna from the west had been blown up by the Australian Sappers. On the way, Colonel Drew's car came under fire, so he returned to the tanks and collected the OC's of the rearguard to carry out a recce. Although conducting this with great discretion, they came under concentrated fire which indicated that the crest of the hill was clearly under enemy observation and that any movement would draw down heavy fire. Dinham Drew gave orders for the KRRC to take up a position astride the road, with the Tower Hamlets in reserve and the remaining tanks of 5RTR hull-down on the left of the Riflemen.

By this time the road into Derna had been blown up by the Australian Sappers and only four *A13*s had been able to make the top of the Pass by 1600 hrs. During this time the enemy had developed their position and moved their infantry forward about 1,100 yards beyond the point from which Colonel Drew had carried out his recce.. They had taken up a position astride the road and were working round the flank with a mixed force. At the same time, they opened up with artillery, MG and A/Tk fire.

The KRRC took up their position as far forward as they could, with the A/Tk guns coming into action on their left: shortly afterwards 5RTR joined the action. The result of this engagement was that eight enemy armoured cars and an A/Tk gun were destroyed by the tanks and guns; in addition to which the 1 KRRC accounted for MGs and at least one enemy gun. Almost miraculously, The Fifth only had two men wounded by enemy shell-fire.

The enemy fire then died down, enabling 5RTR to make an opening on its left flank at 1730 hrs, through which this slender defending column passed with the loss of one lorry hit by gun fire and two expiring from overwork and overloading. The tanks were not so fortunate: they attracted most of the enemy's attentions and were either knocked out or, like their soft-skinned sisters, simply expired. According to the War Diary they more than evened the score by knocking out five German armoured cars.

Colonel Drew's account of the action ends by saying that the remaining transport, with the crews of the abandoned vehicles on board, eventually reached a RV[11] on the Tobruk perimeter at last light and without 'further molestation from the enemy'.

Part of the B Echelon was cut off and arrived at the approaches to Derna to find that the Australians had already blown up the roads, obstacles negotiated with the greatest difficulty and some inevitable delay. Nevertheless, Capt Sherley-Price reached Derna at about 2000 hrs, only to come under enemy fire. This was effectively countered with Bren gun fire. B Echelon eventually reached Tobruk and safety at 0400 hrs on 8th April.

There is a footnote concerning the misfortunes of the Regimental MO, Captain Kelsey. His truck was knocked out by shell-fire, the other occupants being safely picked up. For some reason, Captain Kelsey was not spotted and was abandoned: nevertheless, he managed to reach Tobruk on foot, much the worse for wear and after many adventures, a week later.

THE OTHER SIDE

Napoleon Buonaparte is reputed to have said of Italy that, as neutrals, they required three divisions on the frontier to watch them: as enemies, seven to defeat them: as allies, fifteen to rescue them. Hitler must have felt much the same thing when he viewed Mussolini's antics in North Africa

General Erwin Rommel, who had achieved the distinction of Pour la Mérite *(the highest, but curiously French-named, German decoration) in WW I, standing high in the good graces of both Hitler and the High Command for his conduct of his command in the defeat of France in 1940, was the obvious man to pull the Italian chestnuts out of the Libyan fire. He had additional advantages: he was a man who was free from pre-conceived ideas as to how desert warfare should be fought; he learnt very quickly from his own as well as his opponents' mistakes.*

There is an account of the North African campaign from the German point of view in Major General von Mellenthin's PANZER BATTLES. *Although von Mellenthin did not arrive in North Africa until June 1941, as part of a group of senior staff officers in effect sent to 'supervise' Rommel (if not quite to supersede him by purporting to provide him with an adequate staff structure), his account is extremely valuable.*

After the final defeat of Graziani's army, the German High Command decided to send Rommel and at least one Panzer Division to form the Deutsches Afrika Korps. In February and March 1941 the 5th Light Division (later the 20th Panzer Division) was despatched to Libya. With a fine disregard for the Italian High Command's views, Rommel immediately went on the offensive. Once again, the element of surprise was worth an army of soldiers. Reinforced by the 15th Panzer Division, Rommel was in a good position to counter Operation 'Battleaxe'.

Much has been written about 'The Desert Fox'. He was even made the hero of a film, played by James Mason. Von Mellenthin dismissed James Mason's film performance as altogether too polite! What seems to be overlooked in assessing Rommel's North Africa career is the extraordinary number of characteristics he displayed in common with his later desert adversary, General Montgomery. They both had incisive minds with a clear grasp of detail [12]. *As far as the officers under their commands were concerned, everything had to be just as they had ordered or very sharp rebukes were administered – even, heads would roll. As far as the men under their commands were concerned, they were both the genial, 'don't stand on ceremony', heroes of popular legend, with their respective,' have a cigarette', 'I'd love a cuppa' approach to Hans Schmidt or Tommy Atkins.*

THE WAR CHRONICLE

1940

December	02	General Franco 'guaranteed' Spanish neutrality
	13	Charlie Chaplin's film *Great Dictator* given London premier
	17	President Roosevelt inaugurated 'Lease Lend', later that month proclaiming the USA to be 'the arsenal of democracy'
	23	Anthony Eden re-instated as Foreign Secretary
		– 3,793 civilians killed and 5,244 injured in air raids in December, mostly in London
		– A plumber's daughter from East Ham first sang '*We'll meet again*'. (She is now Dame Vera Lynn)

1941

January	01	First broadcast of 'The Brains Trust'

	04	Combined British and Australian attack on Bardia netted 45,000 Italian POWs
	05	Amy Johnson, London-to-Sydney air ace, killed in air crash
	10	Germano-Russian Trade and Friendship Treaty signed – HMS *Illustrious* disabled by Stukas in Mediterranean
	16	Massive air-raid on Malta
	17	Final rupture between 'Nationalist' and Communist forces in China
	20	British offensive against Italians launched in Eritrea
	27	USA received – but ignored – categorical assurances that Japan meant war – Overnight tube shelters became an established way of life in London – Civil Defence became a compulsory service in UK for all civilians
February	03	German Battleships *Scharnhorst* and *Gneisenau* loose in Atlantic
	06	General Erwin Rommel appointed GOC of Afrika Korps
	07	Churchill directed Wavell to give priority to defence of Greece
	18	12,000 Australian troops reinforced Singapore garrison
	22	German forces moved through Bulgaria en route for Greece
	27	Martial Law declared in Holland
March	01	10,000 Greeks left homeless in Larissa as the result of an earthquake
	03	Larissa bombed by the Italian Air Force
	04	Pioneer 'Commando Raid' carried out on Norwegian Lofoten Islands
	06	Luftwaffe laid mines in Suez Canal
	07	British troops landed in Greece
	11	US 'Lease-Lend' came into effect – Halifax bombers flew first mission in raid on Le Havre
	15	Reichsmarschall Herman Göring carried out officially sponsored raid on French works of art
	16	Jam and marmalade rationed in UK
	19	Heaviest air-raid on London: more than 750 civilians killed

25/27 Anti-Axis riots in Yugoslavia after Government decision to join Axis
28 Discovery of 'plutonium 239' in USA
31 First British POW escaper made 'home run' to Switzerland
– Air-raid casualties for month: 4,259 dead and 5,557 wounded
– Women aged 20 to 31 registered for call-up in UK

NOTES

1 'For the Front'. 'The Front' was, in reality, an extremely fluid concept, seldom being fixed in one place for very long. The Troops had their own term for 'The Front' in North Africa. It was 'The Blue'. Thus, going to 'The Front' was always 'Going up the Blue'

2 Recce(s). Recce – pronounced recky – is short for reconnaissance. The word 'recce' was used for reconnaissance operations – 'doing a recce', 'go out on a recce' – just as the 'Recce Troop' was short of the Reconnaissance Troop. The word was extended to cover the 'Cherry Pickers' [XI Hussars] who were, from the start, the Desert Rats' 'Recce Regiment'

3 Leaguered. A 'leaguer' was a defensive position taken up by an armoured unit at night or during any prolonged stop in open ground. Basically it followed the pattern of the old Army 'square' and was formed by placing the AFVs on the outside of the camp, guns pointing outwards, and the soft-skinned vehicles or any supporting infantry or artillery on the inside. The larger the unit 'leaguering' the more formal the pattern. A squadron 'leaguer', particularly that of a squadron as reduced as 'A' Squadron 5RTR, would be more like the camp of 'Wild West' pioneers. The disadvantage of a 'leaguer' was that, being concentrated, it was more vulnerable to artillery or aerial attack than a more scattered formation

4 M.13 tanks. These would have been Italian tanks: see Appendix 2

5 Afrika Korps. It would be interesting to know where Jake got his information from. According to Liddell Hart, however, Jake's information was incorrect. In the Tank Museum Library edition of WARDROP OF THE FIFTH there is a copy of a letter from Basil Liddell Hart to the then Librarian. It is dated 18th November 1968 and reads [after the usual courtesies], 'Since I wrote to you, I have read the copy you sent me of WARDROP OF THE FIFTH. I am very glad that Sgt Jake Wardrop's diary (November 1940 to January 1944) should have been published in this way, *for it was one of the most illuminating diaries I have ever read – being both vivid and reflective.*' [Liddell Hart then points out some typographical errors that could with advantage be corrected in any subsequent editions] 'There are also a few factual errors that might well be corrected at the same time by editorial footnotes, *viz*: [Referring to the passage just quoted, Liddell Hart says] Wardrop is here mistaken about the strength of the Germans at the end of March 1941 (as well as about our own). The Germans only had the 21st Panzer Division at that time – the 15th Panzer and 90th Light did not arrive until somewhat later.' One must accept that, considering Liddell Hart's formidable resources as a researcher and historian, he was probably right

6 Hull-down. A tank is a fairly large target, most of that target being the hull. Common sense, and tactical training, dictated that the less you showed of your tank to enemy guns the better. There were two answers to this: the *turret-down* and the *hull-down* positions. In the *turret-down* position the crew commander could observe without any part of the tank being visible at all: observe, but not act. To act, the tank was moved up from behind its cover into the *hull-down* position, which allowed the turret- or sponson-mounted armament to be brought into action without exposing the more vulnerable hull

7 Rammy is a perfectly good Scots word, one meaning being a 'stand-up fight'. (Another meaning is a 'horn spoon'!)

8 Rear Link. At this date, each Brigade was on a wireless network. The Brigade Commander sent his orders to the COs of the units under command on the 'Brigade Net' and they were picked up by the 'Rear Link' and conveyed by the Regimental Rear Link Officer to the CO on an ultra-short-wave network. Under this system, the CO in turn passed his orders to his Squadron Commanders on the 'Regimental Net'. These were picked up by the Squadron Rear Link Officer and passed to the Squadron Commander on an ultra-short-wave Squadron frequency. On the 'big fleas have lesser fleas' principle, Squadron orders were sent to Troops and Troop orders were sent to tanks by the same method. As will be seen in Chapter VIII, Colonel Hutton of 5RTR was largely responsible for enormously simplifying this system and improving communications within units, thus making for far greater efficiency in action.

9 Saw no sign of enemy ground troops. But, according to Liddell Hart, 5RTR was far from seeing no sign of enemy ground forces on 1st April. In Chapter 3 of The Tanks: Volume Two, Liddell Hart categorically states that, 'On April 1 . . . the 5th Royal Tanks became engaged with the advancing enemy, who heavily outnumbered them, and in a short sharp fight lost five of their tanks – having five officers and eighteen other ranks killed. They claimed to have destroyed ten German tanks. Rommel says in his account that he lost three, pays tribute to his opponents here for the way they 'used a very effective camouflage in the form of Arab tents[13], which enabled them to come into action unexpectedly.' The 5th had to abandon two more of its tanks through breakdowns and by the time it halted for the night its strength had shrunk to twelve.' Liddell Hart could be wrong but, then, so could the War Diary

10 R/T. Radio telephone or, more simply, wireless. The point of mentioning R/T in the War Diary is to cover the receiver of the message against any faults in the transmission and to point out the orders were not sent by a Liaison Officer delivering the orders in person

11 RV. As in the general sense of a meeting place, the Army used RV officially to designate any meeting point

12 Rommel-v-Monty. According to the Personal Diaries of Field Marshal Lord Alanbrooke [from 1941, Chief of the Imperial General Staff] published in unexpurgated form in May 2001, Monty not only had a clear grasp of detail, he had an unhealthy preoccupation with it!

13 Arab tents. This is probably a reference to 'Sunshades', the practice of disguising the tanks as trucks

CHAPTER IV

. . . *Tobruk – Getting down to business*

April–October 1941

It is not surprising, at this point, that the War Diary became fragmented. That was precisely what had happened to The Fifth. As recorded in the last chapter, what was 'present and correct' of the Battalion was being converted into sub-units of the Tobruk Defence Force. The unlucky ones became unwilling infantry: a few lucky ones joined 'a little tank force.'

This 'little tank force', an amalgam of 'A' Squadron III Hussars and half of 5RTR, came under the command of Major Castle with Lts Steevens and Hemmings, 2/Lt Moss and 58 ORs. On 8th April all their tanks were in Ordnance Workshops. The War Diary spoke in the subjunctive of 'tanks which should be available tomorrow' but never in the present indicative of tanks being actually available. However, by 13th April the combined Squadron strength was seven *A13*s. One Troop was posted to the perimeter under Lt Steevens, the remaining tanks being in reserve under Major Castle.

Later that day the Squadron was put on five minutes' notice to move, enemy attacks being expected during the night. The attacks materialised and the outer perimeter was broken at some points. The Squadron, however, saw no sign of the enemy. On the 15th, 2/Lt Moss reinforced the Squadron with two more *A13*s from Workshops. After three days without incident, the Squadron, less B vehicles, was ordered to move (allegedly with III Hussars) against some Italian M13 tanks. The CO of III Hussars proved evasive and, when eventually contacted, told Major Castle that the operation had been cancelled. By nightfall on 19th April the Squadron was back in leaguer, having been heavily shelled during the day.

What followed during the next ten days belonged more to Fred Karno's Army than the Desert Army but that was the way things went. Men, sometimes with tanks, sometimes without, were shunted backwards and forwards between the Fifth and the First Battalions. Periodically the same fate befell the Echelons. The only consolation was that there was no shelling by the German artillery. From 25th April to 1st May the men were employed in filling[1] and digging.

Matters changed on 2nd May when it became obvious to everyone that efforts were going to be made to evacuate the Battalion from Tobruk. The War

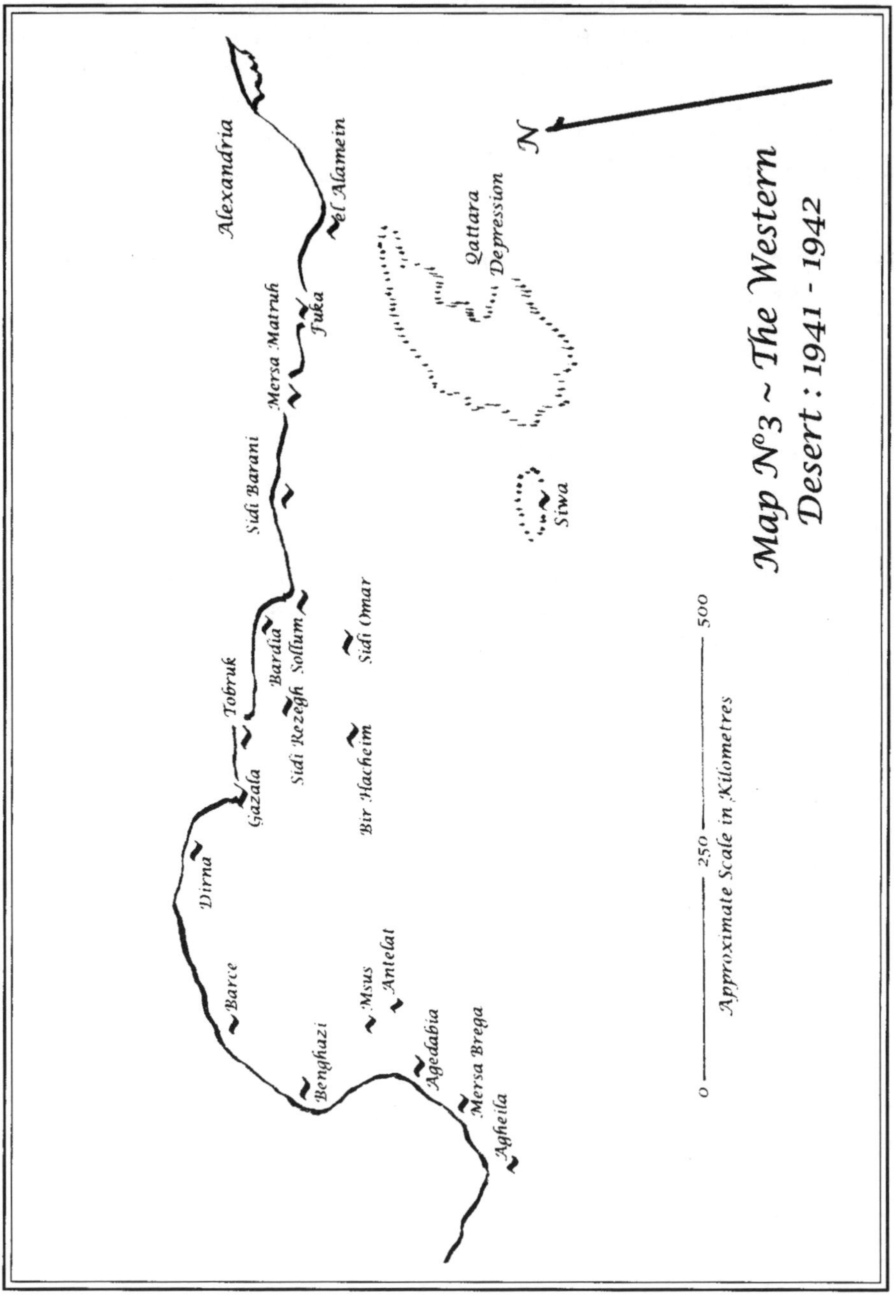
Map No3 ~ The Western
Desert : 1941 - 1942
N
Alexandria
el Alamein
Fuka
Mersa Matruh
Sidi Barani
Qattara
Depression
Siwa
Tobruk
Bardia
Sollum
Sidi Rezegh
Sidi Omar
Gazala
Bir Hacheim
Dirna
Barce
Msus
Antelat
Benghazi
Agedabia
Mersa Brega
Agheila
0
250
500
Approximate Scale in Kilometres

Diary entry for 5th May merely states 'Arrived Alexandria'. In the interval, however, the 'half that were given rifles' had become No 1 Mobile Infantry [MI] Coy, commanded by Capt Sherley-Price with its No 1 Platoon being made up of 'B' Squadron men under 2/Lt Tom Chesterfield. Altogether there were 4 Officers and 112 ORs with rifles, Bren guns and those most absurd of all infantry toys, the Boyes .55in calibre anti-tank rifles.

On 8th April these newly-converted foot-sloggers moved into dugouts and underwent a kit check to ensure they really were PBI [2]. The next day the Company received the first of many orders to move. Each time the Company did move, the first thing to be done was to dig in: the fact that the ground was mostly rock made no difference. No 1 MI Coy came directly under command of an Australian Brigadier. Better equipped and now considered to be proficient in infantry tactics, the Company was issued with 204 hand grenades and 115 Molotov Cocktails, which probably made them more of a danger to themselves than to any enemy.

The area initially covered by No 1 MI Coy overlooked the Bardia road but on the 14th orders were received to patrol towards el Adem to gather intelligence. This was successfully accomplished: some prisoners were taken and diaries etc recovered from abandoned enemy tanks. For the next two weeks, the Company acquired more infantry skills and found themselves on the receiving end of enemy shelling. Tragically, on 29th April, the day before orders came to report to the harbour for embarkation and evacuation, the Company suffered an air raid: one man being killed and three seriously wounded. Later that day the ship on which No 1 MI Coy was due to embark was sunk in harbour. At last light on the 30th the contingent was aboard another ship and by 2nd May it was in Alexandria. By midnight it was in Mustapha Barracks. The next two days were spent in refitting and the next five on local leave.

Tom Chesterfield, who found life in The Fifth tended to be a bit disorganised, recorded this account of events, 'The Battalion moved up to the Front in February and the Rear Party then became First Line Reinforcements. In March I was called forward with Lt 'Tubby' Clayton (later to be my best man) and went by sea to Tobruk. We arrived there in time to meet the Battalion which had managed, minus most of its tanks, to withdraw within the perimeter just before it was closed.

'The Battalion then took over 15 *A13*s from Tobruk Workshops and joined 1RTR, which had 22 *A10*s. Most of the other tank crews and tradesmen were evacuated by sea to Alexandria. The remainder of us were organised into a Mobile Infantry Company to support the Australians on the perimeter. I well remember joining them and immediately being ordered to dig in: as the ground seemed to be solid rock and we had no tools, this was not easy! However, with time and the encouragement of JU 87s and JU 88s[3] this was accomplished with some success. We were never actually engaged, most of our time being spent in our slit trenches watching dive bombers attacking the harbour or anything caught moving within the perimeter.

'After about a month we were evacuated. Not without incident. When we were on the quay and about to board a cargo ship, it was sunk by Stukas. The next day we moved to a beach on the other side of the harbour and were about to embark on two Infantry Landing Ships when we were bombed again. One of my men, Tpr Hartshorn, was killed. Eventually we rejoined the Battalion at Sidi Bishr, just east of Alexandria.'

In addition to Capt Sherley-Price's warriors there was another Mobile Infantry Company (No 2 MI Coy) made up from 5RTR; this was command by Capt G J Gilpin. No 2 MI Coy also came into being on 8th April and was intended to be organised, equipped and supplied with transport on the same scale. No 2 MI Coy. It had its own War Diary . . . whose author had a more refined literary talent. This Diary recorded that the men were very short of personal kit and only had weapons made up from spares etc. Endeavours to rectify this situation were, however, frustrated by orders to move, first to the 18th Australian Infantry Brigade (finding Brigade HQ presented quite a problem) and then to the 10th Infantry Battalion, which they reached at 1800 hrs in Wadi Marsa el Auda (minus two Troopers who got left behind, having dismounted at Bde HQ without orders).

For the next thirty-six hours the Company stayed put without seeing any action. Shortly after midnight on the 12th movement orders came, only to be cancelled. The Australian Battalion Commander kept the Company on one hour's notice. The time was occupied drawing and issuing small arms ammunition. The War Diary then somewhat cryptically records, 'Personnel becoming more settled, although disliking the job.' For some reason, the Brigade Commander decided that the Company would be better employed as Brigade HQ Defence: with this in mind, the Company moved 'down the Wadi'. On 14th April, there was an Immediate Stand To, as the enemy was reported to have launched an attack. It did not involve the Company but the threat had a tonic effect on morale. The Australians must eventually have decided that No 2 MI Coy was a fact of life, because weapon training instructors were sent to bring the Company up to scratch. This was a further boost to morale but it showed up serious defects and shortages in the Company's equipment.

Next, on 18th April the Company was switched to 20th Australian Infantry Brigade and came under command of the 15th Infantry Battalion. This move lasted only three days, as on the 21st the Company was moved again. And again on the 22nd: this time into the front line. On St George's Day the Company hit back at low-flying aircraft with Bren gun fire: hits were claimed but no aircraft were brought down. The following day, the Company was moved back into a reserve position and manned a [captured Italian] 100mm gun, two Vickers machine-guns, being also issued with bayonets. The Vickers were useless as they lacked essential parts. To add to the men's depression, there was a violent dust storm on the 26th. The next day the spares for the

Vickers arrived but so did the RHA to take over the guns. The same day orders were received from 3rd Armoured Brigade to prepare to be evacuated to rejoin the Regiment.

For the next few days, the story of No 2 MI Coy was very much that of No 1 MI Coy.

Bernard Holder can't remember whether he was in No 1 or No 2 MI Coy but he can well remember finding himself under an Australian Sergeant Major who had a poor opinion of Pommies who chose to fight the war in sardine tins. 'You wait till the blood comes out of your rifle bolt, then you'll know what fighting is!' was one of his favourite war cries. He wasn't the only man who liked to show up the 'tankies'. Lying out on the perimeter one night, reckoning he was 110% alert, Bernard nearly had a heart attack when he felt a pair of hands come round his neck and heard a soft Indian voice saying, 'OK, Tommy. You awake?' On another occasion, Bernard Holder was patrolling with Sgt Jack Ackroyd on a night when there was considerable aerial activity and a parachutist scare. They spotted a parachute coming down with something swinging underneath it. Jack Ackroyd said, 'Come on, Bernard, let's have this one,' and they raised their rifles to their shoulders. Just as they had the 'Jerry' in their sights, a gust of wind blew the parachute out over the bay. They lowered their rifles, deciding to let him drown and save their ammunition for another target. He didn't drown: 'he' was a landmine and might well have taken violent exception to being shot at by the two heroes. As Bernard Holder found out later in Normandy, a landmine explosion could be a very unfriendly affair.

Another man with vivid memories of 'garrisoning' Tobruk is Ron Maple. Bereft of his tank, he became one of those who, in Titch's words '.. contributed to the defence of the city by joining the Australian Infantry as anti-tank gunners with a Boyes Anti Tank Rifle. When firing from the prone position, these either (1) broke your shoulder or (2) drove your toes six inches into the ground or (3) both. Volunteers to fire a Boyes Rifle had to be detailed for the job. We were hurriedly placed in position about a mile inside the perimeter, where we dug ourselves in. As the ground was rock solid, this was quite a painful experience. About 300 yards behind us was a battery of 25-pounders: in front of us were some Aussies with machine-guns, well dug in. The plan was to let the Germans break through the perimeter and advance until their tanks were in point-blank range of the 25-pounders. This happened. The spear-head of the German break-through was closed by artillery fire. The Australians then attacked the Jerry infantry who were unable to return to their own lines. The attack failed, many Germans being killed. I am sure we actually hit a German tank. It didn't stop the tank but it did damage the paintwork.

'The Germans tried again a couple of days later and failed again. That was the last time they tried to capture Tobruk during the siege. Life in Tobruk was no picnic. At one stage we took over an area that had been used by the Italian troops. They had dug small caves into the side of the escarpment. They were full of fleas. Water – salty, distilled sea-water – was rationed to two pints per man per day. Those two pints were for drinking, washing, shaving. If you wanted a mug of tea, you had to give that amount of water to the cooks. No more than two men were allowed to go to the cook-house at any time: more than that normally brought enemy aircraft down onto your position. About a hundred yards from our position was a very large dump of Italian 210mm shells and, as our area was very often strafed, that dump didn't do too much for our peace of mind. We did manage to bathe in the sea on odd occasions but, again, with a limit on the number of people allowed to congregate, the odd occasion was not often.

'After about six weeks in Tobruk, we were told to prepare to leave by sea. We didn't exactly love Tobruk but the thought that anything moving in the harbour got bombed didn't encourage us to leave. We eventually left our position with all our belongings – which meant shaving gear, towel, mess tin, revolver and what we stood up in: not even a tin hat! As we moved round the west side of the harbour we were bombed and strafed by Stukas. My mate, Harry Johnson, lying alongside me was wounded in the arm. After the raid, we made our way to the dockside. In the harbour, by an extraordinary coincidence, was the *Clan Chattan* being loaded by lighters. This was the ship that was going to take us out of Tobruk and to safety.

'There was a German airfield at el Adem only about 20 miles south of Tobruk. True to form, the Stukas came over again. As they started their bombing dive, we took refuge in the nearby concrete bunkers. When we came out, we couldn't believe our eyes. Those Stukas had sunk *Clan Chattan*! At least we were luckier than the advance party who had already gone aboard. We moved back to our morning position. Two weeks later three Tank Landing Craft came in and tied up nearby. Each had four tanks on board, the whole ship being covered by camouflage netting. The tanks were unloaded and driven away. We were then told to board the LCTs. The hold was covered by a tarpaulin and battened down: there were about 120 men on board each craft. As we left we were yet again bombed by Stukas: the last craft was hit but not badly damaged and managed to keep going. It took three days to get from Tobruk to Alexandria. The LTCs were flat-bottomed and we sailed broad-side-on to the waves. How they rolled! Everyone was sick: there were only two seats in the latrines and we were always battened down in the heat of the day. The Black Hole of Calcutta would have been a picnic.'

From Alexandria, with a brief interlude of training on another RTR unit's *Matildas* (whose diesel engines 'smelt to high heaven' in the midday heat), Titch and his fellow members of the 'Tobruk Defence Corps' reached Beni Yusef Camp.

For the record, Jake's Diary should read April and not May in his account of manning Tobruk. Jake, along with the rest of the 'Tobruk Garrison' was back in Sidi Bishr by Friday, 2nd May. It was that night that he and Stan Skeels 'borrowed a pound and were sampling the beer in the Mustapha barracks canteen.'

By 5th May 5RTR consisted of 33 Officers and 517 ORs and was starting to re-organise itself – this time not as an Infantry unit but as an Infantry Tank unit. Most of May was taken up with training, training and yet more training on tanks, weapons and wireless. A number of new officers were posted to the Regiment, among them Lieut 'Paddy' Doyle who arrived on 17th May. The only variation in routine, and not a happy one, came at the end of the month when working parties were sent to Alexandria to meet personnel returning from Crete.

June saw 5RTR yet again in the melting pot. Following the debacle in Greece and Crete, tremendous efforts were made to reinforce Middle East Command with both men and machines. Pressure on the Royal Navy to run high-speed convoys through the Mediterranean was met with heroic results, while still maintaining convoys 'down under, round and up' via the Cape of Good Hope. The Fifth's part in all this was to absorb some of the men from the newly-formed 8RTR and the Territorial 42 and 44RTR. By 7th June 5RTR had five 'Infantry' Tanks Mark IIA – the famous *Waltzing Matildas* and not the earlier model of the same name[4]. However, this was not much to boast about as the entire AFV strength of the Regiment was:

2	*A9 Cruiser Tanks*
5	*Infantry Tanks Mk IIA*
6	*Light Tanks Mk VIB*
8	Troop Carriers [make not stated]

By the 9th of the month, the tank state had improved to:

2	*A 9 Cruiser Tanks*
14	*'I' Tanks Mk IIA* (of which 4 were *Mk IIA**)
4	*Light Tanks Mk VIB*
8	Troop Carriers

and to man these AFVs, the Regiment had 38 Officers and 556 ORs. Given that there were HQ vehicles to man and HQ duties to perform, that still meant that there were some 15 men available for each AFV.

These somewhat overcrowded conditions were considerably relieved by Sunday, 15th June when 5RTR got its marching orders. Tank state on that day was:

2	*A 9 Cruiser Tanks*
33	*'I' Tanks Mk IIA* (of which 9 were *Mk IIA**)
4	*Light Tanks Mk VIB*

1	*Light Tank Mk VIIC*
1	*Rolls-Royce Armoured Car*
8	Troop Carriers

making a total of forty-nine AFVs.

But having tanks, as Colonel Drew pointed out later, was but a small part of the problem. Getting spares was not merely difficult, it was impossible. There were no spares in the Middle East.

The marching orders were connected with Operation 'Battleaxe'. The objective of 'Battleaxe' was rather grandly defined as being 'to defeat the enemy troops in the Western Desert and drive them back west of Tobruk'. General Verney, in his book THE DESERT RATS very fairly disarms much of the criticism of Operation 'Battleaxe'. He points out the two major difficulties which confronted the forces on the ground but which Higher Command (and certainly, even more so, Highest Command back in London) took many months – years even – fully to appreciate. In the first place, the tanks with which the objective was to be achieved were seriously out-gunned. The 'two-pounder'[5] main armament of the new *Crusader* and *Matilda* tanks was ineffective against the PzKw Mk IV at any range over seven or eight hundred yards, whereas the PzKws' 47mm main gun could punch holes in British AFVs at up to 2,000 yards. This inequality put Seventh Armoured Division at a serious disadvantage whenever it faced the Afrika Korps' Panzer troops.

The other major difficulty was, admittedly, one faced by both sides. The very mobility of tracked vehicles in the Desert meant that they engaged in elaborate outmanoeuvring ploys, working round the opposition and taking it in the flank or rear. This meant that for every mile nominally advanced, the tanks and armoured cars sometimes manoeuvred ten, sometimes twenty or more miles. This created immense supply difficulties for the Echelons both in locating their forward troops and in avoiding destruction or capture by enemy armour. The first problem had to be solved by the Echelon Commanders (a race of beings too often under-valued by those 'at the sharp end') but the second problem frequently could only be solved by detaching quite strong forces of AFVs – sometimes as large as a squadron – to protect the Echelons and the supply dumps.

The main line of battle for 'Battleaxe' (in which 5RTR was not engaged) ran from Sollum roughly west-southwest through Ghirba to Sidi Omar. The Operation lasted only three days and can best be summed up in the concluding words of the Seventh Armoured Division War Diary. 'The presence of German armoured troops, active patrols and superiority in the air made us constantly on the alert, and the men withstood this severe strain in a spirit that is beyond praise. Our drinking water was at times undrinkable, NAAFI stores were non-existent and flies were very persistent.'

So what was 5RTR up to? Tom Chesterfield had the answer, 'In June the Battalion was equipped with *Matildas* which, because of the panic arising from the disasters in Greece and Crete, had been brought out at great risk through the Mediterranean, while the [RTR] Territorial Brigade was on its way round the Cape. The Battalion was taken by rail to Sidi Barani, then moved up south of Sollum and held in reserve. We did not see any action before we handed over our tanks to the new Brigade. After this we were moved to a camp at Beni Yusef, a short distance south of the Pyramids.'

The War Diary indicates a sense of urgency and it is obvious that the CO, at least, expected the unit would soon be in action. The entry for 20th June is headed 'Charing Cross', already mentioned in Jake Wardrop's Diary: here the Squadrons engaged in a variety of warlike exercises. Doom struck on 23rd June. The War Diary reads, 'Order No AQ55 Des received, warning unit that 44th Bn RTR are taking over complete and that this unit will return to Mena on a date to be notified later. Small advance party from 44 th RTR arrives.' Then, proving that big troubles always beget little ones, the Diary concludes by reporting, 'two 'I' Tanks Mk IIA sent to Ordnance Workshops with clutch trouble'.

The hand-over to 44RTR took place on 27th June and the following day the Regiment was entrained for points east. After twelve hours in the train, breakfast was provided at Amiriya and, by nightfall, the Regiment was in camp at Beni Yusef. The following day, a head count showed that 5RTR consisted of 37 Officers and 573 ORs. But no tanks.

With monotonous regularity for the first three weeks of July the War Diary reports 'Individual training under Bn arrangements.' There was a break for 'young officers' (drill under the Adjutant) and for all ranks (organised games under Paddy Doyle). On 21st July, individual training should have taken on a new twist – work on the guns and wireless sets of the new tanks about to be issued to the Regiment. However, neither guns nor wireless sets were forthcoming. The next day the Regiment received a warning order to concentrate at el Hammam by the 28th: more to the point, it received the first three of its new tanks.

These were American *M.3 'General Stuart'* Light Tanks which were known almost universally as *Honeys*[6]. With the promise of these tanks, specialist gunnery and wireless, as well as D&M, training should have begun in earnest. The contrary was the case, because, as the War Diary records, 'The policy of training for the month of July has been dictated by (a) the knowledge that the Battalion is to be equipped with the new America *M.3* tanks and (b) a complete lack of any kind of equipment. Until the 21st and the return of members of the unit undergoing courses on the new tanks, weapons and radio ['radio'? Could this be American influence?], general training only was possible. From 22nd onwards, instructors courses have been run on the one tank, radio and weapons that the unit has been issued with. These in turn have been completed but specialised instruction is still hampered by the lack of training equipment.'

A second *Honey* arrived on 2nd August and individual training continued, with a navigational Course for officers. The 21st saw the arrival of the first operational *M.3*s: by the end of the month the Regiment had 28, plus 3 training tanks.

On 16th September there is a rare entry in the War Diary, namely that Capt G J Gilpin (T/Major) had been awarded the Military Cross for Gallantry in Action. It is not that the award of Decorations to officers and men of The Fifth was rare; what is almost exceptional is to find any record of them in the War Diary.

For the rest of September, the War Diary is once again a tale of training, training and yet more training. Progressively, as the month wore on, this becomes more realistic with battalion exercises and battle practice being the order of the day. At the end of the month, 5RTR consisted of 36 Officers, 587 Other Ranks, 52 *M.3* tanks, 97 'soft-skinned' vehicles and 6 motorcycles. It was still commanded by Dinham Drew with Major RDW Uniacke as his 2 i/c. On 25th September a 'demonstration attack on transport by 'C' Squadron' was attended by General Auchinleck who had recently taken over from General Wavell the command of what had just become the Eighth Army.

Predictably, Jake Wardrop provides some light relief, being less concerned with administrative matters than with the business of living. Dealing with his time in Beni Yusef, Jake records how he once persuaded 'a few of the lads' to walk to Sakhare to see the pyramids and some ruins. Not only Jake's mates thought he was mad to go off hiking across the desert sands: the native population shared this view. The particular hike that Jake described was one of ten miles across the desert and in the full glare of the sun. Jake paid no attention to the fact that the native villages were out of bounds to the troops. He had a genuine fondness for the '*wogs*', amounting to an empathy which they understood and appreciated. Quite rightly, Jake thought that they were shamelessly exploited, working in the fields in the full heat of the day for little more than subsistence wages.

Jake's Diary states that the Regiment entrained at Gaza to go back up the blue on 15th September but this is not correct. Where his Diary is particularly valuable is less for the dates he gives but for the details he provides of who was who in his 'lot' ('C' Squadron), since this type of information is not recorded anywhere else. Jake was driving the Squadron navigator, a man he much admired – one of Jake's 'good guys' – in spite of his being small of stature. Dixie Dean, later Sgt and then SSM Dean, was driving Sgt 'Stooge' Alcock, also later an SSM. There were, Jake said in a rather disapproving manner, 'quite a number of changes all round.' The significance of the newly constituted 4th Armoured Brigade – consisting of 3RTR back from Greece, 5RTR and VIII Hussars, with 3 RHA[7] with 25-pounders, together with the 2nd Battalion Scots Guards – did not escape Jake. It was, as he said, 'an experiment in as much as previously there had never been tanks, guns and infantry all together like this'. By happy chance for The Fifth, the Brigadier was Alec Gatehouse, an old 5RTC man who had been at the Battle of Cambrai. His first job was to shake his Brigade down and get them accustomed to working together as a mixed force. He had also to learn to work under the Divisional Commander, Strafer Gott – who, as Jake rightly says, was later killed just before the Battle of el Alamein[8]. Jake continues this chapter of his diary by noting the composition of the other Armoured Brigade in the Division, which consisted of III Hussars, VII Hussars and 6RTR. To complete the list, Jake mentions the Artillery with heavier guns [in support of the RHA who had their 25-pounders]. It was, as Jake remarked, 'quite a Division' and, what is more, now bore the famous Desert Rats 'Jerboa' insignia.

THE OTHER SIDE

According to von Mellenthin, Rommel achieved his initial successes with 'weak German forces'.

This makes for good reading in an autobiography but the implication that Rommel was opposed to 'strong British forces' is hardly accurate. Both the DAK and the Eighth Army faced enormous supply problems: both depended upon the same Mediterranean supply route. For the Axis, it was the short trip from the southern Italian ports with the Royal Navy to avoid: for the British, it was the long haul round the Iberian Peninsula and then the length and breadth of the Mediterranean with superior German air power – to say nothing of the U-boats – to avoid. At the period covered by this chapter, the odds were still very much in the German favour. In the long run, the round-Africa passage (provided the convoys escaped the U-boats in the Atlantic) gave the Allies a critical edge.

As von Mellenthin points out, there were no major battles between June and November 1941, in other words, between the end of 'Battleaxe' and the engagement of 'Crusader'. Whereas Wavell had to consolidate his position and prepare for attack across many miles of desert, Rommel had the advantage of consolidating and preparing with very short lines of communication. At this stage, Rommel therefore had a double advantage and, being a good general, he made the most of it.

THE WAR CHRONICLE

1941

April	01	First use of 4,000lb 'block-buster' bombs by RAF – Pro-Axis coup put pro-Nazi Rashid Ali in power in Iraq – Eritrian capital, Asmara, fell to 5th Indian Division
	02	First flight by German jet-propelled aircraft
	03	Evacuation of Benghazi
	06	Piraeus harbour bombed, cutting off Allied

		supplies to Greece
		– South African troops captured Addis Ababa
	07	UK Income Tax raised to 10/- in £1 (50%)
	08	'Open City' of Belgrade devastated by Luftwaffe, followed by invasion of Yugoslavia by Wehrmacht
	09	Germans captured Salonika
	14	Australian Prime Minister Menzies threatened to pull Australian troops out of North Africa, claiming that they were being exploited – King Farouk of Egypt invited Hitler to 'liberate my country from British yolk'
	16	Allied forces ordered to withdraw from Greek mainland
	17	Yugoslavia capitulated
	20	Land Mines used for first time in air-raids on London
	23	Greek Government fled to Crete
	25	Worst-ever month for air-raids on Britain and for U-boat 'kills'
May	03	Renewed fighting between British and Italian forces in Ethiopia
	04	British and Indian troops tightened grip on Iraq
	10	Rudolf Hess landed in Scotland – Preston North End drew 1 – 1 with Arsenal in Cup Final
	11–13	Yet worse air-raids on London: House of Commons severely damaged
	15	The Whittle-engined Gloster *Pioneer* successfully tested
	18	German Battleship *Bismarck* escaped into Atlantic
	22	Germans invaded Crete
	24	*Bismarck* sank HMS *Hood:* only 3 men out of crew of 1,416 survived
	27	Royal Navy sank *Bismarck*
	31	Evacuation of Crete by Allied forces completed – Rashid Ali's Nazi-backed *coup d'etat* defeated in Iraq – Luftwaffe killed 30 and injured 90 in air-raid on Dublin
June	01	Clothes rationing introduced in UK
	02	Bizerta handed over to Axis by Vichy Government
	04	Ex-Kaiser Wilhelm II ('Kaiser Bill') died in exile in Holland
	11	Hitler 'put finishing touches' to *Operation*

		Barbarossa – the planned German invasion of Russia
	13	British and Free French Forces invaded Syria
	21	Allied troops occupied Damascus – Last Italian troops surrendered in Ethiopia – to native Ethiopian forces
	22	German invasion of Russia launched
	25	Finland drawn into war . . . 'Against Russia, not for Germany'
	30	Luftwaffe destroyed estimated 1,800 Soviet planes in one day
July	01	'The Auk' (General Sir Charles Auchinleck) succeeded General Wavell as C-in-C Middle East. Combined British forces became the 'Eighth Army' – Introduction of 'the Draft' in USA – General Chiang-Kai-Chek formally allied Nationalist China with Allies against Axis Powers
	03	Allied forces 'trounced' Vichy troops in Syria
	05	Wehrmacht penetrated 'Stalin Line' at Lvow
	10	. . . and reached Minsk
	16	. . . and reached Smolensk
	20	BBC introduced call-sign dot-dot-dot-dash ('V for Victory') in all broadcasts
	21	First Luftwaffe air-raid on Moscow
	24	Brest-Litovsk surrendered
	25	Vichy Government handed over French Indo-China to Japan
	31	Göring declared that *Einsatzgruppen* (the mass slaughter of Russian Jews) was not adequate to deal with 'the Jewish Menace' and introduced 'The Final Solution'
August	05	Smolensk 'obliterated' by Wehrmacht
	13	Japanese aircraft devastated Chinese city of Chunking
	17	Wehrmacht captured Nikolayev and Novgorod
	21	First Arctic Convoy of aid to Russia sailed from Iceland
	24	Vichy imposed blanket death penalty on all captured Resistance Fighters
	25	Combined Anglo-Russian force moved into Persia
	31	Estimated 15,000 Jews murdered by Nazis and 80,000 sent to Concentration Camps under Göring's 'Final Solution'

September	02	German forces within 20 miles of Leningrad
	03	Cyanide gas first used to 'eliminate undesirables' in Auschwitz
	07	German aircraft sank neutral American vessel in Red Sea
	10	Martial law imposed on Oslo
	11	*Typhoon* fighters commissioned in RAF
	16	First North Atlantic Convoy to be escorted by US Navy sailed
	19	British troops entered Tehran – German forces captured Kiev
	21	Total eclipse of sun seen in China
	27	Launch of first of many US 'Liberty Ships'
October	01	Chinese defeated force of 40,000 Japanese at Changsha
	08	Bad weather slowed German advance on Moscow
	19	American merchant ship sunk by U-boat
	24	Russian city of Kharkov fell to invaders
	31	SS Commander boasted that there were 'no Jews left in Estonia'

NOTES

1 Filling. The general sense here is that 'filling' was belt filling and the belts in question were the ammunition feed belts for the machine-guns. This was an on-going activity, as it was not always possible for the ammo belts to be delivered ready-filled. Ultimately it was the local or tank commander's responsibility to see that his guns had a full complement of filled belts. In the context here of 'digging', it may, however, have been sand-bags that the men were filling!

2 PBI. World War One slang for the Poor Bloody Infantry. Still sometimes used today

3 JU 87s and JU 88s. German light 'close-support, tactical' bombers

4 *Matildas*. See Appendix 2

5 Two-pounder. See Appendix 2

6 *Honeys*. There are various versions of the re-christening of *M3 General Stuarts* as *Honeys*. The version I favour is that they came to North Africa from the US Army with the reputation of being 'a honey of a tank'. Which, when one considers previous American tanks, is fair enough. And see Appendix 2

7 3 RHA.. According to General Verney, this was 2 RHA, not 3 RHA

8 Strafer Gott. There has been a lot of speculation as to when Jake Wardrop did actually write his Diary. It is known that he made what one might describe as personal notes in letters home almost every day. However, as General Gott was not killed until 7th August 1942, the extract referred to cannot have been contemporaneous with the events described. The origin of WHE Gott's nickname 'Strafer' goes back to WW I when the Germans adopted a slogan *'Gott strafe England'*. At that time, Gott was a junior officer

CHAPTER V

. . . *Operation Crusader*

November and December 1941

At this point in its history, when the Regiment had just been re-equipped with *Honeys*, it took part in Operation 'Crusader'. 'Crusader' was by far the most important, and the largest-scale, campaign yet planned in the war in North Africa. This was inevitable. The Eighth Army was faced not merely by a greatly reinforced Afrika Korps (with a not inconsiderable Italian contingent effectively under its command) but also by a General whose worth was acknowledged – if not fully appreciated – in Cairo.

The intention of 'Crusader' was two-fold: principally to clear Cyrenaica of enemy forces; incidentally to relieve Tobruk. What was to follow 'Crusader' was in the lap of the gods.

The Eighth Army by this time consisted of the largely infantry XIIIth Corps and the largely armoured XXXth Corps. The plan was for XIIIth Corps to hold a line from Halfaya [universally known, and not without cause, in the Eighth Army and the Press at home as 'Hellfire Pass'] – which lies south-west of Sollum and westward to Sidi Omar. This holding operation was intended to allow the New Zealand Division to move round the flank and pin the defenders down on a line running from Sidi Omar northwards to Sidi Azeiz. At the same time XXXth Corps was to move past the New Zealanders' left flank and head for Sidi Rezegh. This move by XXXth Corps was designed deliberately to engage Rommel's armour. If all went well, the garrison at Tobruk would make a sortie, attacking Rommel from the rear and linking up with XIIIth Corps in the region of Sidi Rezegh.

To a large extent the success of 'Crusader' depended on surprise. Achieving surprise in the Desert was extremely difficult where all ground activity was easily observed from the air. Deception was the answer and the enemy was deceived. Tom Chesterfield describes how this was done. 'Before Operation 'Crusader' began our new *Honey* tanks were fitted with framed canopies which gave them a profile similar to a three-ton lorry. These canopies were kept in place until the last possible minute and were discarded only on first contact with the enemy.' These devices were code-named 'Sunshades' and were used on many tanks other than the *Honeys*.

This element of surprise was especially necessary for the forthcoming engagement. Even though British tank strength was numerically superior to the DAK's Panzer units, the individual tanks were out-gunned by the PzKws by anything up to 1,000 yards. In open Desert terrain with little or no cover, this was a serious disadvantage.

Looked at now, the High Command's approach to 'Crusader' sounds unbelievably bombastic. The General Orders were larded with phrases like 'getting within killing range' [they didn't specify who was going to get killed], 'using our superior mobility' and 'our ability to out-manoeuvre the enemy'. Ominously, the Orders were silent on the conditions which the troops were going to encounter. If the days weren't as hot as an oven, then the nights would be as cold as a deep-freeze. Probably both. If it wasn't dry and dusty, it was likely to be wet enough to turn good solid tank country into a quagmire.

Furthermore, tank warfare in the Desert had its own special disadvantages – the presence of flies and the absence of normal amenities and the perpetual lack of water apart. Desert navigation was a major headache, there being few if any landmarks: wireless communication varied from being bad to being hopeless: identifying who was friend and who was enemy became a nightmare. Local conditions in a tank-v-tank battle were rendered hideous by burning vehicles, by exploding ammunition, by shelling and bombing, and by the dust clouds stirred up by vehicle movements.

And at the back of every mind was the anxiety. 'If we get out of this lot alive, will the Echelon ever be able to find us?'

Against this background, the 7th Armoured Division prepared for 'Crusader', 5RTR forming part of the 4th Armoured Brigade.

Coincidentally with the run-up to 'Crusader' Rommel had been planning an all-out attack on Tobruk. This attack was scheduled to start on 23rd November. Rommel was in Rome, getting the final approval for his plans, when 'Crusader' was launched on 18th November.

The Regiment pushed off at 0600 hrs on that day, reaching their first objective with little or no ground or air opposition. What Jake Wardrop described as 'The November Handicap' was underway. As far as Tom Chesterfield was concerned, the first two days were remarkable for the amount of motoring which the tanks did: something in the order of 150 miles. It came as a pleasant surprise to the tank crews to discover that supply dumps had been established for them on the far side of the wire[1]. These were the work of Major Robbie Uniacke who had gone forward forty-eight hours earlier to establish the Brigade dumps.

By midday, 5RTR had received a report that the KDGs were in contact with the enemy and their 'sunshades' had been discarded. The Fifth moved up in support with 'A' Squadron in the lead and Battalion HQ close enough behind for the Adjutant's tank to be hit, putting the wireless out of action but causing no injuries, when 'A' Squadron came under fire from what proved to be eight-wheeled armoured cars. Most of 'A' Squadron's tanks escaped damage.

The Regiment received overnight orders to do forward reconnaissance in force. However, as they approached their intended position, Brigade informed the CO that it was already enemy held. Paddy Doyle, then commanding 'B' Squadron, moved off to deal 'vigorously' with this enemy. This particular enemy turned out to be a group of our own guns with supporting infantry but the real enemy was not far away and both 'A' and 'C' Squadrons were soon engaged in running fights. An enemy armoured car and a lorry were knocked out but so was Lt Moss' tank, with resulting burn injuries for all the crew. There followed a lull of some two hours before the KDGs again reported the presence of the enemy and The Fifth was ordered up in support. Between then and last light there was some inconclusive skirmishing. Two of our tanks, which had been mechanical casualties, were recovered.

At first light on 19th November Brigade informed 5RTR that the enemy had leaguered only a few miles from the Brigade's own overnight position and the Regiment was to advance and engage. Discretion being not merely the better part of valour but a key ingredient in staying alive, 'C' Squadron, having advanced, took a close look before engaging. What they saw, some 3,000 yards away, was a large number of enemy tanks in leaguer. 'C' Squadron then advanced by fanning out and moving across the intervening, undulating, ground. As soon as they were sighted, a mixture of PzKw IIIs and IVs opened fire, supported by some concentrated fire from (probably) 105mm guns. 'C' Squadron used the undulating ground to get within 1,200 yards, at which range it was just possible for them to engage the enemy tanks.

The CO ordered 'C' Squadron to take advantage of the rising sun behind them and press ahead with their attack, while 'A' Squadron moved up to make a flank attack. The Brigade's supporting artillery was then brought into action. The enemy fire increased in volume but not in accuracy and 'C' Squadron was able to get within 700 or 800 yards. With an increased rate of fire, their ammunition began to run dangerously low, 'B' Squadron was therefore sent forward to allow 'C' Squadron to withdraw and replenish. However, flanking action is a game that two can play and enemy tanks were seen to be deploying on 5RTR's southern flank. This move was countered by switching the Brigade artillery to the new target.

Meanwhile, 'A' Squadron was running out of ammunition: it was ordered to withdraw to replenish, leaving 'B' Squadron somewhat isolated. In the event, within half-an-hour, 'B' Squadron was forced to withdraw, because of the threat to its left flank. About 0900 hrs VIII Hussars and 3RTR moved up in support and it became the enemy's turn to withdraw.

The rest of the morning was spent in replenishing and counting the cost which was, officially, five tanks destroyed and Lt Hawkins wounded. However, Tom Chesterfield doesn't agree with the official version of the cost. This engagement, according to Tom, started at first light on the third day but didn't, as far as he was concerned, last very long. While the enemy was still out of range of the *Honeys'* guns, Tom's tank was hit by a 70mm HE shell on the turret ring[2] and the turret jammed. In addition, the impact of the shot caused a lot of internal flaking and Tom lost the index finger on his left hand. Popular though the *Honeys* were, they were a bit primitive. Communication with the driver was supposed to be the latest thing in high-technology: Tom, as did many others, found that cords, tied to the driver's shoulders were far more effective. Pulling hard on both cords meant 'reverse'. So determined was Tom to back out of a battle in which he could no longer play an active part, that he nearly hauled the driver backwards out of his seat. When the unfortunate man eventually got the message, he couldn't reverse: the gear selector mechanism was jammed by empty shell-cases!

Tom's wound put him out of action for a couple of months.

According to the Squadron Commanders' estimates of this action, 5RTR had accounted for some twenty enemy tanks. This estimate was supported by the number of crippled tanks seen being evacuated on transporters, when the enemy withdrew next day, or found abandoned at a later date in the Gambut area.

The rest of the day's battle, according to General Verney in his book, started with a renewal of the main engagement of the previous day. A Panzer group was sighted moving across the Brigade's front and was engaged in a running fight. Although this was inconclusive, the Germans moved away out of range to the south. Perhaps mistaking withdrawal for defeat, the Corps Commander decided on the 21st that the time was ripe for a break-out from Tobruk. On the ground, however, it soon became apparent that the 15th and 21st Panzers were far from defeated, as they put in another appearance later in the day.

Jake Wardrop's impression of the battle was of being late to bed and early to rise, with breakfast in the middle of the afternoon. Late breakfast though this was, it had hardly been swallowed when the shells began to rain down and the reports of approaching tanks started to come in over the air. As Jake put it, the fun really began. 'We fanned right out and had a shufti[3]. Over the wireless came reports of ten tanks here, twenty tanks there and I sat where I was hoping that all these reports were of the same bunch of the Boche. No such luck. Each of these sightings was of a separate unit and we found ourselves taking on the 21st Panzer Division. And why not? Wasn't it 20th November – Cambrai Day. Only one order for that! 'Forward Five!' and we were off into the fray.'

Shortly before midday, Brigade ordered a renewal of the advance to a position north of Bir el Barrani, with The Fifth in reserve. At 1600 hrs soon after reaching Bir el Barrani, Colonel Drew was informed that 3RTR was being heavily attacked on their left flank. 5RTR was ordered to follow VIII Hussars in going to their support. The Fifth rapidly covered the intervening six miles, coming up on the left of 3RTR and finding themselves involved in a confused mêlée. 3RTR and VIII Hussars, one on either flank of The Fifth, were retreating 'rather quickly'. 'B' and 'C' Squadrons were immediately engaged with 'A' Squadron in reserve – a position they did not enjoy for very long. With their flanks exposed, 5RTR was also forced to pull back. Dinham Drew's report was flattering – and doubtless well-deserved. It reads, 'the Battalion withdrawal remained orderly and under full control, squadrons being alternatively leapfrogged whenever the withdrawal was forced on us. Throughout this very difficult action, all squadron commanders showed excellent coolness and power of command and, by 1700 hrs, the enemy advance had been definitely checked. The Battalion remained in action until darkness, when it rallied and withdrew one mile east.'

It was impossible to tell what damage had been inflicted on the enemy: the DAK remained in possession of the ground and were able to recover all their tank casualties. These were probably not numerous, as The Fifth had been shooting into the setting sun and conditions had not permitted them to move against the enemy's flanks. 5RTR lost one tank, Cpl Heathcock being killed and Cpl Noirmot and the crew missing. Capt Winney and 2/Lt Lester were killed.

When the Regiment reached its assigned leaguer position at last light, it was found that the enemy were only about 1,000 yards away. Too close for comfort! Brigade agreed that 5RTR could put another mile between themselves and what proved to have been the main body of the 15th Panzer Division.

Later that night, it was learnt that 22nd Armoured Brigade was leaguered close by and that the two Brigades would resume the advance.

Noises heard during the night were identified at the start of this advance as having been caused by enemy movement.. The capture of two abandoned PzKw IIs and a number of prisoners confirmed that the Germans were withdrawing rapidly in a general north-westerly direction. The Fifth, which was in the lead on the right flank, made visual contact about 0900 hrs with a column of tanks on tow or on transporters. One of these tanks, a PzKw III, was abandoned and suitably dealt with.

Half-an-hour later 'B' Squadron located a group of A/Tk guns about 2,000 yards to their front. The supporting artillery put in some accurate shooting, allowing 'C' Squadron to move in to the attack. While still over 1,000 yards away, they saw the position being abandoned and were able to bag three vehicles and some prisoners. 'A' Squadron also had a good bag, consisting of an A/Tk gun and some more prisoners, including an officer – all from 15th Panzer Division.

A large enemy column was seen moving away but 5RTR was told not to pursue, as 3RTR was encountering stiff opposition and had suffered some casualties on the left of the advance. Apparently 3RTR must have got themselves out of difficulty as the advance was underway again shortly after midday. Not, however, very far or very fast: by 1600 hrs rain had reduced visibility to less than 400 yards. In the end, a halt was called at 1630 hrs and the Regiment went into leaguer . . . much to the relief of OC A Echelon, whose supply vehicles were becoming bogged down.

Confusion reigned on the 22nd. At 0100 hrs orders were received that an enemy column had leaguered only five miles away and the Brigade, with anyone else willing to join in the fun, would attack the leaguer at first light. The attack was set up and launched . . . on an empty site. The birds had flown. However, by 0800 hrs an alternative target had been found. 3RTR had spotted an enemy column and was moving to the attack with 5RTR in support. These birds didn't fly: couldn't fly. The 'enemy column' was a collection of derelict German and British tanks left over from an earlier engagement.

The confusion continued. At 1100 hrs the Brigade was ordered to advance on a CL which would take them in the general direction of Sidi Rezegh. This CL was soon changed, a new objective being found – an observation position to the south-east of Sidi Rezegh. At 1500 hrs, the Brigade was ordered to advance as rapidly as possible to go to the aid of the Support Group which was heavily engaged there. The confusion was increased by a report of a column moving westward and therefore on 5RTR's right flank. It proved impossible to identify this column: it appears from the War Diary to have remained a mystery.

By 1600 hrs, The Fifth had reached a point about two miles south of Sidi Rezegh aerodrome. Here the CO was met, in 'a scene of tremendous smoke and dust', by the Commanders of both 4th and 7th Armoured Brigades. The [4th A/Bde] Brigadier ordered the CO to prepare to move against a force of enemy tanks and A/Tk guns on the north of the aerodrome, as the right tine of a two-pronged attack. The Brigadier added [rather unnecessarily, one would have thought] that The Fifth was to be careful of enemy A/Tk guns. 5RTR moved off sharply, 'A' Squadron leading, soon encountering those A/Tk guns and finding itself plunged into increasingly severe enemy shell fire from batteries of various calibre firing from a general northerly direction. Visibility, owing to increasing dust and smoke, rapidly worsened and heavy A/Tk gun opposition forced the Battalion to move farther to the west to avoid it. In so doing the Battalion was forced off its correct Centre Line and became mixed up with 3RTR. After a good deal of difficulty, but with assistance from the commander of the Support Group who spoke to the OCs of both 'A' and 'C' Squadrons, telling them where the aerodrome was located, the leading Squadrons moved forward. 'C' Squadron was able to engage enemy tanks and A/Tk guns: owing to smoke and dust, however, only intermittent and ineffective action proved possible.

Matters were not helped when, within a few minutes of going into action, both leading Squadrons were fired on by tanks of 22nd Armoured Brigade. The CO tried in vain to make contact with Brigade and sensibly decided to order the Battalion to rally back west of the aerodrome. Dinham Drew managed to contact the CO of 3RTR who took similar action and, later, to contact the Brigade Commander who approved the order.

Hardly had the two Battalions rallied to the west of the aerodrome, than the Brigadier informed their COs of a report that enemy infantry were advancing across the airfield and threatening the Brigade support guns. 5RTR was ordered to deal with this new situation. The crew commanders immediately found that, with failing light and continued heavy shelling, visibility was reduced to about 50 yards. In spite of this, the Battalion advanced across the airfield, being fired on by A/Tk guns on their right flank but finding no infantry. The A/Tk guns were dealt with. 'B' Squadron's advance then took them up to and through a large column of enemy tanks. The War Diary reports, a trifle laconically, that 'shots were exchanged' but, as it was by that time quite dark, the effect on the other side was not known.

At 1800 hrs the Brigadier called a halt to the evening's activities and returned to his HQ which was with 5RTR's A Echelon. He ordered 3RTR and 5RTR to return to their former rallying point and wait for further orders. Of the 40 tanks with which The Fifth had started the day, only 26 answered to the roll call at 1815 hrs. It was not possible to ascertain how many of the 14 missing tanks were battle casualties, mechanical breakdowns or simply lost sheep.

The evening's activities were not, however, yet over. As the Brigade Commander and his skeleton staff approached the A Echelon leaguer, he was informed by his IO that they were surrounded and being attacked by a large number of German tanks. Sgt Humphries displayed admirable coolness during this attack: he succeeded in extricating all but one petrol and one ammunition lorry and getting them to safety. Unfortunately, Lt Bullet and his truck were also found to be missing. Not unnaturally, the Brigadier decided to get back to the rallying point – which he did with the aid of a red verey light as a direction marker – and re-assess the position.

His re-assessment was that 3RTR had so few tanks that it was temporarily not a striking force and should remain where it was as a rallying point. On the other hand, 5RTR was in a position to relieve the HQ. There was no doubt where the beleaguered Brigade HQ was: it could be identified by the burning vehicles. There was no moon and this aided the Battalion to make its approach, which it did slowly in compact formation. So compact that the main danger was of the tanks running into one another. A final reconnaissance was called for within about a mile of the burning vehicles. This was made by Captain Doyle, who was ordered to take his tank forward to within two or three hundred yards of these vehicles and then signal back what he had found. A verey light followed by MG fire was to indicate soft vehicles: a verey light followed by the tank's 37mm gun was to indicate tanks. No sooner had the verey light gone up than Paddy Doyle's tank was seen furiously firing both MG and main armament!

Verey lights went up all round and, by their glare, a huge semi-circle of enemy tanks, guns and miscellaneous vehicles was seen drawn up opposite the small band of 5RTR *Honeys*. As soon as Paddy Doyle was safely back, The Fifth opened MG fire, with occasional 37mm fire when a suitable target was sighted. This fusillade lasted for five or six minutes without much response but, when the enemy did reply, they did so with light and not so light A/Tk fire. Shortly after the enemy began their retaliation, some of their tanks were seen working round the Battalion's left flank. These then opened fire, hitting several 5RTR tanks but, in spite of this, the engagement continued for another ten or twelve minutes.

The CO was now out of direct communication with the Brigadier who managed, nevertheless, to get a message to the Adjutant, ordering the engagement to be broken off and the Battalion to withdraw due south. Although all Squadron Commanders acknowledged the order, it was not received by all the crew commanders [many of whom did not, in fact, have operational wireless sets]. A high degree of confusion followed, as it was not known how many tanks had been knocked out. Eventually sixteen tanks rallied during the night and moved back under the CO to join up with 2 RHA next morning. Robbie Uniacke's tank was hit but was recovered by its crew and taken back to LRS. (Major Uniacke himself did not rejoin until 24th November) The tanks of Capt Jennings, Sgt Meyler, Sgt Ford, Sgt James, Sgt Hall and Sgt Frey rallied back with 3RTR and remained with them for the next two days. The Adjutant, Capt Coombes, was injured but came out on another tank. Capt Jennings and Sgt Hall rejoined with their tanks two days later. Sgts Ford, Frey and Green, with their crews but without their tanks – which had been knocked out – got back three days later. Sgt Meyler and his tank were never seen again: it was believed to have been knocked out when in action near the South Africans on the following day [Sgt Meyler was later reported to be a POW]. One way or another, these six tanks were all in action under Major Simpson of 3RTR on the morning of 23rd November.

On 23rd November, now mustering only sixteen tanks, the Battalion gained contact, somewhere out in the blue some 15 miles south of Sidi Rezegh, with 2 RHA, who had thirteen guns. Shortly after first light, the CO managed to contact the Brigadier who said that he was moving the Brigade to 'Point 175'[4] and meanwhile The Fifth was to await orders. In the middle of the morning, the CO was alerted to a danger facing the South Africans who were heavily engaged some 5 miles to the north-west. He contacted the Brigadier and asked permission to go to their aid. This was refused until more was known about a threatened attack from the south. Thereafter, to Col Drew's extreme frustration, the Battalion was three times ordered to go to the aid of the South Africans only to have the orders three times cancelled.

At 1630 hrs 5RTR linked up with Brigade HQ and the remnants of VIII Hussars. The Hussars then reported a sighting of enemy tanks, on which they opened fire, supported by 2 RHA. 5RTR was pushed forward to meet this threat . . . but could see nothing of any enemy or any threat. At dusk, the Brigadier ordered his force to rally and leaguer for the night.

It was altogether a day of frustration. From time to time during the day, it had been possible to make small sorties to destroy or capture straggling groups of German transport. Three vehicles were destroyed and 15 POW taken. At one stage, Major Sherley-Price was ordered to chase a column of 20 enemy lorries but the order was countermanded by the CO of 2 RHA who, quite contrary to Brigade orders, told him to go to the aid of the South Africans. By the time this nonsense had been sorted out, the enemy column had made off and only one laggard was bagged.

During the night of 23rd/24th November some stragglers from 3RTR and VIII Hussars, along with elements of Brigade HQ, joined the Battalion.

At 0900 hrs the CO received orders to move immediately to the aid of 22nd Armoured Brigade who were being threatened from the north. 5RTR was to come up on the Brigade's right flank and come under their orders. The move was completed at 0930 hrs. Fifteen minutes later the order was reversed: 4th Armoured Brigade was now under threat and needed the Fifth's support. As 4th Brigade HQ had moved, there was some difficulty in locating it, a difficulty exacerbated by random enemy fire. Before too much damage was done, it was discovered that 4th Armoured Brigade was exchanging fire with the South Africans whose columns had been identified as this new threat.

No sooner had this further nonsense been sorted out than VIII Hussars again reported an approaching enemy column. On advancing to meet this latest menace, the Battalion could find no trace of any enemy.

Major Sherley-Price, who had been unwell for some time, finally reported sick and was sent back to LRS with some mechanically defective tanks. At 1500 hrs he reported being fired on by an enemy column. Major Uniacke (in command while Col Drew was forced temporarily to give up command with an injured knee) gave orders for an immediate chase. This lasted for some 20 miles before the Battalion was able to come up and attack the enemy column on its right flank, the 3RTR tanks attacking on the left. This first attack was beaten off by anti-tank fire but a second attack got right in among the enemy, producing very satisfactory results, with about 40 vehicles being destroyed and heavy casualties among the lorry-borne infantry. 40 POWs were taken. Two of the Battalion's tanks were hit, that of Lt Gregor being destroyed; that of Capt Ward[5] being put out of action but recovered. Cpl Whitfield died of wounds and Lt Gregor was wounded.

This last statement is not as simple as it sounds. Despite being christened Cyril Thomas he was always known as 'Bob' Gregor – frequently as *Mac*Gregor. He was one of the unlucky ones to have his tank brewed up. His crew were killed and, technically, Bob fell into enemy hands. The German officer who found him apologised for *not* taking him prisoner as the DAK FAP was already full to overflowing. Bob accepted the apology and crawled to a safe distance from his burning tank. Fortunately for him he was picked up by his own side and lived to join the SOE. Bob died in 1999, his last words being 'that bloody 88 has got me at last'!

After leaguering overnight the Battalion was once more under orders at 0700 hrs. Fortunately it did not engage the reported enemy which – yet again – proved to be one of our own convoys. The next alarm was anything but false. As a result of the previous day's chase, the Battalion was now about 20 miles south of Sidi Rezegh. Information was received that the South Africans were in trouble in the area of Taieb el Essem and the Brigade was ordered to make all speed to their assistance. Making all speed meant lack of reconnaissance with the inevitable result that the Battalion nearly ran onto the German A/Tk defences. Fortunately the tanks turned away in time and withdrew to the only available hull-down positions, 1,200 yards away. Several attempts were made to close but each one was repulsed by heavy artillery fire. This was countered by 'some excellent shooting' by the Gunners and 5RTR's role for the rest of the day was to provide cover for the RHA guns. After dusk the Battalion withdrew and formed leaguer.

The next day, 26th November, what was left of the Brigade was ordered to move off north on a 25 mile march which soon turned into a chase when an enemy column was spotted. Most of the column escaped but the Fifth engaged a group of ten M.13 tanks, destroying two without suffering any damage. In leaguer that night the Battalion had a surprise addition to its strength of eight new tanks. This meant that, when Dinham Drew returned and resumed command, the Battalion comprised a two-tank HQ and two Squadrons each of eleven tanks.

At 1000 hrs on the 27th, the Brigade was ordered to pursue and engage an enemy column moving west on the Trigh Capuzzo. The Fifth caught up with the column at 1430 hrs when 'B' Squadron came under heavy A/Tk gun fire. An outflanking manoeuvre to the west was frustrated by fire from A/Tk guns protecting the column. One of these hit Paddy Doyle's tank, putting it out of action but fortunately not causing any casualties. The Battalion accounted for some of the A/Tk guns and soft vehicles. However, when orders came to go immediately to help 22nd Armoured Brigade, it found itself unable to move as the guns pinned it in position with enfilading fire. A group of some 40 tanks then moved to attack the Battalion's position. 5RTR counter-attacked and stopped the enemy advance. The action continued until nightfall, leaving the Battalion with some tanks out of action and Sgts Hart and Wilcox killed.

The A Echelon could not get through until first light on 28th November. When the tanks had been replenished, orders were received to resume the previous day's engagement. At first, the Battalion was held down in the same position but at 0730 hrs the Artillery came into action and kicked up enough dust to allow both Squadrons to close within effective range and 'get many hits on enemy tanks'. By what would normally have been breakfast time ammunition was running low and the Battalion was forced to pull back: the enemy followed for a short while but made no attempt to re-engage.

At 1000 hrs the Brigade, after picking up some stragglers from 22nd Armoured Brigade, moved west to take up a semi-circular position across the enemy's line of retreat. 5RTR was on the left flank, in an area totally devoid of any features to provide cover. Shortly after taking up this position, the enemy column appeared and, after being halted at 2,000 yards range by artillery fire, split into two to launch flank attacks. What ensued was a gun battle, first between artillery and tanks and then, spasmodically, between the tanks. Again the engagement was inconclusive, with both sides withdrawing when it became too dark to select targets. Col Drew estimated enemy casualties to have been heavier than the Battalion's, which were five in number – all capable of being repaired in leaguer that night.

The pattern of the war in the Desert was by now clear. Rommel was withdrawing his forces but with every move covered by A/Tk guns, onto which he continually tried to draw our armour. Earlier he might have succeeded: if DAK was learning fast, so was the Eighth Army.

The first action on the 29th was a case in point. At 0800 hrs an enemy column was sighted and the Battalion went in pursuit, only to be halted by the A/Tk guns which were, in their turn, engaged by the RHA. They withstood the Gunners' fire until their transport was out of danger and then themselves withdrew. The second action, however, was rather different. By 1500 hrs the Battalion was on a new CL but had been halted to identify a column seen moving about two miles to the west. 'B' Squadron found this column to be hostile when it came under heavy fire from 105mm and 88mm guns. 'B' Squadron went into action, supported by 'C' Squadron and a running battle ensued in extremely poor visibility. In spite of the intensity of the artillery fire and the (almost certainly) superior number of tanks at the enemy's command, 5RTR, with only some twenty *Honeys*, managed to prevent the enemy advance. The Battalion's casualties were fairly numerous but, except for Dickie Ward's tank which was destroyed (he was wounded), none of the damage was serious.

Col Drew reported that, by the end of November, nearly all the wireless sets were defective due to lack of maintenance or damage by gun fire. At the best, a squadron could count on three sets working; at the worst, only one. It must have been a relief when three new tanks with scratch crews reported at first light on the 30th.

These tanks, which gave the Battalion a strength of 26, were soon in action. A limited objective advance brought the Brigade into contact with a group of 30 enemy tanks which were immediately engaged – 'B' Squadron leading. The enemy, after losing only one tank, withdrew but took up a strong defensive position at the top of an escarpment. Before the main engagement commenced, the enemy tanks were identified as being Italian M.13s [which gave 5RTR a clear superiority of fire power and armour]. Covered by heavy artillery fire, The Fifth moved tanks out onto the enemy's flanks and, when the RHA lifted their guns, 'subjected the enemy to heavy and accurate fire' – so accurate that the enemy withdrew after only a few minutes, leaving twelve tanks and some soft vehicles destroyed but taking some badly damaged M.13s with them. 5RTR suffered no casualties but could not pursue as their line of attack was covered by A/Tk guns in the open valley.

No sooner was this action over than another likely target was spotted in the shape of a large transport column. This, however, was too well protected to allow the Battalion to get within range, one of The Fifth's tanks being hit by fire from an 88.

After rallying back to its start position, the Battalion reported two further enemy columns on the move. Unfortunately, due to a confusion between the Brigadier and the CO, neither of these columns was attacked. Nevertheless, an hour later, 2/Lt Vanes, out on patrol with his troop, observed 27 Italian tanks, with their crews in the open, in an exposed position at a range of only 800 yards. Although there were A/Tk guns in a position to cover these tanks, the CO gave Vanes the order for an immediate strike. His Troop crept closer and, at 600 yards range, opened fire with all their weapons, causing severe damage. This fire was maintained until the Troop was forced to withdraw when the A/Tk guns opened up on them.

The belief that relations between Dinham Drew and Alex Gatehouse were not cordial is given extra colour by one of Colonel Drew's 'supplementary War Diaries'. Both Gatehouse and Drew were RTC men, Alex Gatehouse having been commanding the Depot in 1939, while Dinham Drew was senior Major in The Fifth. Both held WW I Military Crosses. Nevertheless Colonel Drew saw fit to write that, 'It is most unfortunate no mention whatever of this action is made in the official history. The reason for this, I surmise, is because I became a casualty two days later and my Adjutant, Freddie Coombes, had become a casualty a few days before.

'In as much as Brig Alex Gatehouse was rather far from the action to appreciate what was happening, he appeared to take little interest: he never spoke a word of congratulation! I feel that perhaps the fact that we had no casualties was regarded as a matter of censure rather than praise.'

Dinham Drew followed this opening broadside with a closely detailed account, much along the lines of his earlier supplementary War Diaries. In fact, all this adds to the general picture is a great deal of detail, without pointing out any substantial differences between what the 'official account' had to say and what Colonel Drew had to say.

Whether they were prompted to do so by their Commanding Officer or whether their efforts were spontaneous, both Paddy Doyle (then commanding 'B' Squadron) and Emmin Hall (then a Sergeant but nevertheless commanding a Troop in 'C' Squadron) produced records of this action which indicate that they, too, felt praise rather than censure should have been the order of the day.

There is one postscript to add: the tale of an unlucky man – Arthur Medler. Arthur joined The Fifth in August 1940 shortly after the Battalion returned from France and sailed with it to Egypt as a member of 'B' Squadron. After the first sortie up the blue he had a spell working in the docks at Sidi Bishr. For a while his life back in the unit followed the routine pattern of the tank crews – Arthur's role being that of gunner in Sgt Hicks' *Honey* in 7 Troop – until 22nd

November when his tank was knocked out and he was taken prisoner. Like most POWs from North Africa, Arthur's first staging post should have been Italy. However the ship he was on was torpedoed and sunk by HM Submarine *Porpoise* in December on its way there. The unfortunate Arthur Medler landed back in 'German occupied' North Africa . . . and was not much more fortunate when he did finally reach mainland Europe and captivity, being passed from one prison camp to another, each one more uncomfortable than the last. His Army Pay Form R.16 (Release) shows that he received a War Gratuity in March 1946 of £35.10s, being 10/- a week for seventy one months service (about £1,180 in current terms).

December dawned with no respite, a message being received at 0430 hrs that the New Zealanders were being heavily attacked by tanks at Sidi Rezegh and the Brigade was to go to their assistance at first light. En route, yet another 'large column of enemy vehicles' was spotted and investigated by VIII Hussars. The Brigadier decided that this was too tough a nut – being in a well-defended position – to justify delaying their orders. By 0900 hrs, therefore, the Brigade was approaching the aerodrome. No sooner had Col Drew reported that the escarpment to the west was crowded with tanks and guns, than these tanks and guns opened fire. The Brigade ignored this fire and pushed on to the New Zealanders' position which was marked by a pall of smoke. The Brigadier then gave 5RTR some pretty sweeping orders: 'to push on to the NZ'land leaguer and make contact with the NZ comd – obtain all possible information and make a plan for an attack against the enemy tanks.' Easier said than done. The first hazard was the descent of the escarpment, which had to be undertaken slowly and in single file. The second was the increasingly heavy artillery fire. The third was the destruction of the two leading tanks by hitherto undetected A/Tk guns – which also accounted for several of the VIII Hussars tanks.

Col Drew ordered his 2i/c, Major Uniacke, to take command and rally the Battalion to a point farther east where there was some cover, while he went forward to locate the NZ HQ. This, like most of the day's activities, proved no easy task. When contacted, the NZ Commander explained that he had been driven off the airfield into a rather tricky position to the north where his men were coming under fire from German tanks – he estimated there were 40 of them – all in good hull-down positions 1,000 yards to the north. This fire meant that his men could find no cover from artillery fire being directed at them from the west. The New Zealanders were also worried about an Italian column, in sight but not in range, which had so far not engaged. With hope born of despair, the NZ Commander asked Col Drew to launch an attack on the German tanks. The only promise that the CO could make was that he would try. He felt bound to point out that it would be a costly enterprise, even if 3RTR were in a position to support him.

While conferring with the CO of the Third – which was in difficulties of its own from enfilading fire – word reached the COs that the New Zealanders had been ordered to withdraw in a south-easterly direction and that the two RTR units were to cover their withdrawal. However, neither of the COs could then make contact with Brigade due to wireless failures. Colonel Drew ordered Major Uniacke to remain in command of the Battalion while he acted as liaison with the New Zealanders. In spite of this lack of wireless links, the Brigade got orders through to Colonel Drew that the New Zealanders were to withdraw due south and do so immediately. Dinham Drew passed these orders on, pointing out to the NZ Staff Captain that it was imperative to follow the new, southerly, Centre Line to avoid coming within range of the waiting Italians. Notwithstanding having made personal contact with all the NZ units, Col Drew watched in despair as they wandered off their CL and into range of the Italian guns. Instead of correcting their line of withdrawal, the New Zealand units doubled back due north, acting on new orders of which Colonel Drew was unaware.

The Brigade reformed and moved to a new rallying point south of the escarpment and east of Sidi Rezegh, only to find they were now in range of the Italian artillery from the east and the Germans from the west. Capt Doyle took 'B' Squadron on a sortie against some unidentified tanks but no effort was made on either side to engage. During the afternoon, the remnants of the Brigade (3RTR, 5RTR and what was left of VIII Hussars) withdrew about 17 miles south, meeting up with their A Echelons on the way.

The Regiment had 2nd and 3rd December for maintenance and rest. The entry in the War Diary for 4th December is worth quoting as an example of splendid, phlegmatic, British understatement. It reads, 'Bde were in action in the el Gubi area during the whole day. During the morning 20 lorries and 2 m.3 tanks [*sic*: presumably PzKw IIIs] were destroyed by this bn. in an isolated action, but apart from this there were no incidents or actions worthy of note.'

Nothing really did happen on the 5th but the War Diary records that Major Sherley-Price, Captains Ward, Doyle and Hennings, Lt Moss, Sgts Hugget and Clay, Cpl Dixon and Tpr Mackenzie were recommended for immediate awards[6].

The next few days saw sporadic action, the Brigade being effectively prevented from moving from the el Gubi area by enemy anti-tanks guns. The morning of the 6th produced a bag of miscellaneous lorries and a dozen motorcycles and an unsuccessful sortie against an enemy column. The 7th was a repetition only, this time, it was the RHA who 'put in some good shooting' on enemy transport. The only variations on the 8th were heavier enemy shelling and a visitation by the RAF which luckily did no damage to their own side.

The 9th December brought a return of action. The Brigade was ordered to move with all speed in the direction of el Adem where a large enemy concentration of all arms had been located. It was, however, well-defended and direct attack was out of the question. Nevertheless, the Gunners had noticed that the enemy artillery and A/Tk guns were concentrated and suggested a combined onslaught. A frontal attack was not on the cards, even if the guns laid down a heavy barrage. 'B' Squadron was ordered to attempt a flanking movement to seize the el Adem escarpment. By clever use of ground, Captain Doyle accomplished this and was shortly after joined by Major Gilpin with 'C' Squadron. Further probing disclosed that, although the enemy position to the west was unassailable, there was no opposition to the north. The two squadrons made a dash for it 'first closing in on the enemy position and getting in some effective shooting'. When Brigade was told of The Fifth's intentions, the move was made into a general attack. This unfortunately failed, as the remainder of the Brigade became literally bogged down, leaving 5RTR in a very vulnerable situation. As luck would have it, the enemy delayed retaliation until 3RTR had struggled clear and come up on The Fifth's right flank. When the enemy did attack, there was a heavy engagement in which 5RTR lost one [un-named] officer wounded and one tank destroyed.

For the next week 5RTR was effectively out of things. Apart from engaging in one unsuccessful chase and again being strafed by the RAF, The Fifth went with the tide of war, following the retreating Afrika Korps. It was but a limited follow up, increasingly long lines of communication making our supply columns unacceptably vulnerable to enemy attacks.

Then, on the 19th came news even more exciting than that overheard on the air in the early hours on 8th December[7]. The Battalion was to be recalled to the Nile Delta to re-equip. 3RTR was to follow but, meanwhile, 9 tanks and 17 lorries were to be handed over with crews to the Third Battalion. The rest of the tanks were to be left, without crews, with the Royal Gloucestershire Hussars.

On Boxing Day the Battalion – now bereft of all but a score of lorries – reached the rail head. On the 27th they were at Beni Yusef. By New Year's Eve 1941, the Battalion was closed down and all the officers and men were sent on leave.

The War Diary and the official histories give one side of the picture. What all this meant to the men in the tanks emerges from the comments of some of those men men. One of these was Peter 'Carlo' Carlsson, a regular soldier but then a comparatively recent 'tankie'. Carlo Carlsson had long wanted to join the Black Watch but, when the Army finally accepted him, it posted him to the Buffs (Royal East Kent Regiment). Later, in typical Army fashion, it transferred him to The Fifth in time to be trained as a *Honey* driver and to take part in the Battle of Sidi Rezegh. But taking part in the Battle of Sidi Rezegh as far as Carlo was concerned could have been any battle anywhere. His overriding impression of all tank actions was that there was absolutely no way in which a driver could tell what was happening. It was bad enough with the driver's hatch open but, when closed down, it was a nightmare sequence of advancing, steering, stopping, advancing again, stopping again (and sometimes reversing) with the roar of the engine clearly to be heard despite the earphones and the banging of the main gun or the chattering of the machine-guns continually adding to the unfortunate driver's confusion. The driver's only consolation was that, ninety nine percent of the time, he was far too busy trying to do what his crew commander told him to bother about being afraid. By a cruel quirk of destiny, it was when Carlo was outside his tank and there was no battle going on that fate caught up with Trooper Carlsson, just four weeks from the end of the war.

Much of what Peter Carlsson felt was echoed by Willie Dovey (who had joined The Fifth from 22nd Armoured Brigade in May in time to get himself head wounds in an air-raid on Alexandria). Willie also recorded the disappointment felt among the tank crews that the *Honeys* were still no match for the DAK panzers – either when it came to hitting or being hit.

Personal impressions of battles seldom agree with War Diaries. However good or bad the *Honeys* may have been, Jake Wardrop certainly felt that The Fifth had been able to fight back at the best of the DAK and find themselves in possession of the field with as many brewed-up panzers marking the scene of action as *Honeys*. The great sorrow was always the losses which had been sustained, particularly those of friends. For Jake, such a one was Dixie Dean[8] who had been wounded in the morning and was, when Jake went to see him, 'looking awful bad'.

After a sort-out of crews, the pursuit began again but without getting a further sight of the enemy that day. Next morning their luck – and the weather – changed, with the capture of artillery, trucks and even the crew of a motorcycle outfit. At last light, contact was renewed but the action was inconclusive because of the heavy rain and the deteriorating 'going'. Many a crew member had the impression that his tank was in a 'particularly bad spot' – a sentiment doubtless shared by every other crew. The bad going, however, did mean that the Echelon vehicles became bogged down and the tank crews had to walk some distance to fetch the replenishments. Nevertheless, the famous Wardrop luck held good: there had been a huge rum issue that day and about an hour after Jake had drunk his, he felt he could have carried eight gallon cases of petrol[9] until dawn.

WARDROP OF THE FIFTH provides a splendid description of kipping-down for the night. As was common practice when sleeping rough – extremely rough most of the time – crews contrived what comforts they could. Kipping-down was a very democratic business: no suggestion of first-class accommodation for officers, second-class for NCOs and third-class for 'the men'. It was 'one for all and all for one'. The crew made up a sandwich of blankets with a topping of tarpaulin. At the given word, off came the boots and in under the selected layer of blankets went the bodies. Considering how cold the Desert nights could be, the selected layer of blankets was generally one underneath and the rest on top. This method had the added advantage that the bedding could be rolled up and slung on the tank. There was a *de luxe* variant of this

'Great Bed of Ware' technique: when nights were not so cold and a little air was appreciated, the bottom of the tarpaulin was pegged down and the top was lashed to the top of the track, with individual bed-rolls being made up and the night spent 'under canvas'.

The significant thing, as General Verney points out, was that the engagement on 20th November had made Rommel realise that the Seventh Armoured Division's activities were not simply reconnaissance in force but a full-scale attack on his position. Rommel therefore decided to concentrate his forces on Sidi Rezegh in the belief that the British would attack the airfield there and he would be able to meet them in strength and from a good defensive position. It was while the Panzer elements of the DAK were manoeuvring to take up this position that their move was detected and 4th and 22nd Armoured Brigades set off in pursuit.

The pursuit was in vain: although the German armour was slower than the British, its head start meant that all but the tail end of the columns got away unscathed. The chase became hopeless when the Brigade, and with it 5RTR, ran short of petrol and had to halt to wait for the Echelons to come up. Meanwhile other elements had launched an attack on the ridge overlooking the airfield at Sidi Rezegh. This attack, though costly, was successful.

It was on the next day, Saturday, 22nd November that 5RTR was embroiled in an action which started well, with a move at first light and an advance past columns of prisoners looking far from happy at their fate[10]. At midday, while the crews were snatching something to eat, stand-by orders came over the air to prepare for a move on Sidi Rezegh airfield where there was an unusually impressive state of chaos. This is hardly surprising, as both sides had become embroiled in a close engagement which, in non-military terminology, had got completely out of hand. The airfield was strewn with burning tanks and lorries. Some of the 'shots' which were being fired apparently at random were, in reality, ammunition exploding in the burning vehicles. On the landing strip itself, there were burning aircraft and the whole scene was covered with smoke and a fine cloud of dust. 'Nobody,' as Jake recorded in his Diary – surely the understatement of the day, 'seemed to have much idea of what was going on and we milled around for a bit.'

If the scenario had been envisaged by Sam Goldwyn himself in one of his more grandiose moments, what happened next could not have been more appropriate. In the middle of the chaos, Jock Campbell arrived and took charge. In an unarmed (and unarmoured) staff car, he set himself at the head of a disorganised cluster of tanks – including those of 5RTR – which was waiting to see where they could be of most use and shouted at them, 'Follow me!'[11] They set off round the airfield and after about a half-mile chase found themselves confronted by a defensive line of anti-tank guns and PzKw IIIs. There was no possibility of manoeuvre or taking up hull-down positions. The tanks halted and let loose with everything they had got, taking it in turns to fire and then pull out to replenish while others had their turn. As Jake said,

'Quite frankly, I was not so strong for this charging business, although we continued to do it until the next year at Knightsbridge[12], but off we went. We went storming in right up to these tanks, firing as we went, and then swung away a bit to go further on and beat up some artillery.' Not, however, the heavier guns, one of which took Jake's tank out of the action when a shell burst right in front of them and broke the left track. It was, by then, becoming dark and the guns were moving onto other targets. On getting out to examine the damage, Jake found that they had run on about twenty yards but that, in coming off, the track had ripped off the ration box in which . . . cruellest of cruel blows . . . there had been a bottle of whisky.

After showing this proper sense of the importance of things, Jake explained that their tank was rescued by another *Honey*, this time from 3RTR. The rescue was not completed until about 2030 hrs by which time it was quite dark and they were lost. HQ sent up a red verey light flare and the crew commander was able to home in on that. On return to the Battalion, 'Steve' Steevens, the crew commander, and Jake transferred to another tank and set off 'to sort out the Brigade Echelon which had got itself into a bit of a mess.'

The crew of the tank taken over weren't so lucky. They were captured later that night. As for the tank, when Jake revisited the scene of the battle next April, it was still lying where they had left it. Jake commented that – not for the first time – he had lost all his kit. That was nothing: there was plenty of kit about but there was only one Jake Wardrop and that man had his toothbrush, his money, his revolver . . . and his treasured blue sweater!

What Jake and his companions reached was 'quite a party' and consisted of a group of Boche in charge of a party of British prisoners. The arrival of the tanks from The Fifth soon reversed the roles and, before long there was a large number of German prisoners, guns and tanks and a fair amount of booty. This included rations and bottles of lime juice. In view of the Royal Navy's predilection for this beverage, it is curious that it was the Germans who had a lot of it, whereas the 8th Army never had any.

The night's activity was not yet over. At 0300 hrs the tanks refuelled and set off on a 30 miles drive towards Tobruk. The next day they reached the perimeter of the defences and, by a happy coincidence, the officer who came out to meet them in a tank was Colonel Willison[13].

Although the battles which made up 'Crusader' were far from over, the balance in terms of tank casualties was slightly in favour of the DAK. This was partly the superior fire power of the PzKws and their supporting anti-tank weaponry but was, in large measure, due to the more efficient recovery service which the Germans operated. Generally speaking, if an Allied tank was a casualty, it was written-off on the battlefield: conversely, if an Axis tank was a casualty, it had a 50% chance of being recovered, repaired and seeing further action.

Even so, the situation was not as bad as it was considered to be by General Cunningham, the Army Commander, who reported to General Auchinleck, in effect, that all was lost. Happily for all concerned, the 'Auk' did not accept this and flew up to the front to take personal charge. He also replaced Cunningham with General Neil Ritchie, his Deputy Chief of Staff in Cairo. At this stage, the 'Auk' assessed the position as being territorially in favour of the British, having regard to the advances made by the Eighth Army.

But, as already mentioned, 'Crusader' was far from over. If the various personal accounts make the engagements sound confused, they are only reflecting the views of the Divisional Commander. Our Island's history, from the landing of the Normans on the coast of Sussex in 1066, tends to be reported as a series of battles which 'we' either won or lost. Battles, for those involved in them, are never so simple.

An example of this is the story of the crew whose tank ran out of ammunition and petrol in the middle of a battle. They abandoned the tank and hid overnight, thus fooling the Germans into thinking that the tank had been knocked out. 'Came the dawn' and they contacted a passing Echelon – whose, they never discovered – and replenished, later sneaking back to rejoin the Battalion under the noses of the enemy . . . to find that the Battalion had not even noticed their absence! Of such confusions are battles made.

By this stage in the war, the co-operation between the tanks and the guns[14] of the RHA had developed from an occasional exercise into a regular feature of all actions.This could not have happened without the expertise of the FOOs from the Batteries. These Gunner officers had their own tanks and were seldom farther from the sharp end than the HQ of the Squadron they were supporting. From this position of observation, they passed back instructions to the guns and, almost as soon as the information had been given the guns started to shell the target.

To go forward in time, this close co-operation developed until it reached the stage at which individual tank Troop officers were trained to take over the role of FOO, once the Gunner officer had started the supporting shoot which had been called for.

The advantage of this artillery/tank co-operation was that it lifted the pressure off the tanks, as it gave the enemy something else to worry about. A technique was quickly developed whereby the tanks would profit from these artillery diversions to undertake out-flanking movements. So highly developed did this technique become that all the CO had to say was 'Give them left flank' and every tank moved smartly round to the left. As armoured units all too soon found out, this technique was really only feasible in the Desert with its unlimited room to manoeuvre: it could not be used in Italy or in the close 'bocage' country later encountered in Normandy.

Jake Wardrop summed the whole second Sidi Rezegh affair up in his Diary by saying, '.. at Rezegh there was a ding-dong scrap which lasted about five days: it was very tough. They had the high ground and all the advantages, but the infantry gave them the bayonet[15] until they had had enough.'

The Seventh Armoured Division was engaged for several days more in

'Crusader' but The Fifth only peripherally so. It seems probable that Rommel made the same mistake as General Cunningham, in believing that he had effectively eliminated the Eighth Army's armoured forces. On this assumption, he decided to drive almost due east with a view of cutting off XXXth Corps by reaching the coast at a point to the east of Sollum. So far as Seventh Armoured was concerned, this meant the Division was by-passed on the south. Rommel's gamble did not pay off: his lines of communication were over-stretched and he was forced to swing back west, after reaching to within 5 miles of Bardia on 27th November.

The DAK's return westwards brought them back along the line of the Trigh Capuzzo and into the neighbourhood of the earlier battle for Sidi Rezegh. It was here that 5RTR came back into the picture. The New Zealand Division was operating to the north-west of Sidi Rezegh and the 70th Division was operating out of Tobruk driving south-east. The task of the 4th Armoured Brigade was to prevent Rommel from getting back to Sidi Rezegh and to come to the relief of the 'Kiwis'.

That there are two sides to every question is shown in a quotation from Bayerlein[16] who said that, '.. on the morning of November 30 powerful enemy [*ie* British] armour and massed infantry advanced against our southern screen, but their attacks were unco-ordinated and we were able to repulse them all along the line.' Not surprisingly, the War Diaries of the 'powerful British armour' put matters rather differently. The Fifth, as already recorded, figured prominently in one of these actions. General Verney gives most of the credit to Paddy Doyle – although, as shown earlier in this chapter, Dinham Drew claimed his share! Of particular interest is that Jake Wardrop was, for much of his time in the Desert, Paddy Doyle's driver.

One record of the struggle on 30th November and 1st December says that fortune visited both sides . . . but not to stay. This is true: it had been a battle of attrition. Both sides were operating on long lines of communication, making supplies difficult. In this respect, the Allies had the best of the bargain: even so it is enormously to the credit of those concerned, from the A&Q staff in Cairo down to the hard-pressed RASC and Regimental Echelon troops on the ground that this was so.

On 5th December began what General Verney called the 'Third Round'. There were, after their defeat at Sidi Rezegh, very few Axis forces left east of Tobruk. The Allies started a rapid advance along the line of the Mechili track which was to push the Axis forces back, to the west of the Agheila salt flats. This was described by Jake Wardrop as 'the steeplechase', although he then spoilt the simile by saying that 'we ran rings round them'. A dominant impression of those days, for the drivers, was that of exhaustion. While the wireless operators could doze with their earphones on and the gunner sleep soundly and, even the tank commander drop off occasionally, the drivers had, especially at night, to fight numbing tiredness and concentrate on the job in hand.

Once, at Antelat, Jake's crew bought a sheep 'from a *wog*' for a bag of teas and some sugar. On reflection, Jake was rather proud of this: the owner could not have put up much resistance if the crew had simply helped themselves. Fresh roast meat must have been a great relief. Replenishments were short: no cigarettes and very little water [note Jake's priorities] but somehow or other, the men's spirits remained high.

If there was one thing plentiful in the Desert, it was dust. It didn't have to be a khamseen[17]; it didn't have to be an ordinary dust storm. Where there was desert, there was dust and the biggest producers of the commodity were tanks. It had its advantages and disadvantages: Bernard Holder discovered one of the latter when he was driving the Squadron HQ truck and following his Squadron Commander's tank in the happy belief that the enemy was nowhere near. In reality the enemy was very near: just behind the dust cloud. Bernard was lucky to get away with his life: he never saw his Squadron Commander again.

Conversely, water and privacy were the two commodities in shortest supply throughout the Desert campaign. There was seldom such a thing as a fixed 'water ration'. If there was water, it was shared out equally [although a very dry and dusty Bob Lay claims that he once found Paddy Doyle wallowing luxuriously in a canvas tub!] by the drop or by the bucket, according to the supply available. Sometimes, incredibly, there was enough to wash in: generally the priorities were the tank's need of a top-up for the radiator [in this respect, the American tanks with the air-cooled engines were a big advantage] and the crew's need of a brew-up. When water was in particularly short supply and the need for a clean pair of socks or pants became imperative, then the tanks' needs were subordinated to the crews'. After all, a tank could only go a few hundred yards on a pint of petrol: the crews' 'drawers, regulation, short (tropical issue) troops for the use of' could go for a whole week!

Privacy was a very personal matter. It is probably impossible for anyone who has not served in a tank crew to understand the intensity of the comradeship which existed among the crews. It was not necessarily a matter of liking one's fellow crew members. What mattered was that one trusted them, completely and implicitly. The 'living quarters' in a tank have been aptly compared with piling five well-grown men into a BMC Mini and then throwing not just the kitchen sink but all the kitchen equipment in after them. So, in addition to that trust, there had to be immense tolerance: give-and-take: respect. Certainly there were additional problems: what, in biblical terms, can be called 'wetting the ground at one's feet', and – in coarser terms – 'taking the shovel for a walk'. In a tank in action, one can't just get out and answer the calls of nature. So what? There were always empty shell cases, weren't there?

These were the conditions which existed during Jake's 'steeplechase' and, with them, went the hazards of war. Jake had two 'near squeaks' round about Merchili and 'poor old Steve[18]', his crew commander, was killed. Because it was necessary for the Troop Leader to be on a tank with a working wireless set, Lt Steevens and Jake had transferred to another tank when their set 'went dis'. Shortly after the transfer, the tank that they had left was hit and the driver wounded. The second near squeak was much worse. The wireless again packed up but, this time, only Steevens transferred to another tank. The next day this tank was hit, Steevens was wounded and died on the way to the FAP.

The Battalion got news that it was going back to Egypt for a refit. The men reached their destination on 30th December and were sent on leave. Not a long leave, as they were back with the Regiment by 5th January, on which day they had their Christmas Dinner. The Brigadier was cheered – not altogether respectfully – when he spoke to the troops and congratulated them on their record. Those who wanted to got very merry indeed but were later sober enough to attend, and be moved by, a service of Thanksgiving and Remembrance in the Cathedral.

After this, The Fifth moved to Beni Yusef to re-organise and re-equip.

For many, it seemed as though the war had fizzled out. Between the 11th and 27th December, Rommel had been shifted from his position – which was roughly a line stretching south of Gazala – and rolled back out of Cyrenaica to the position which the Allies had held in February 1941.

As the retreat went on and the pursuit followed, Rommel's supply lines got shorter and the Allies' longer. A situation was reached by Christmas in which there were not enough supplies reaching the front line to sustain the whole Corps. Nevertheless, Rommel's retreat had continued and on Christmas Eve an advance unit from the Support Group had re-entered Benghazi.

The 'bottom line' at the end of the day was [British and Dominion] 2,908 killed, 7,300 wounded and – perhaps the worst figure of all – 7,400 missing. Enemy losses were estimated at [all casualties] 13,000 Germans and 20,000 Italians. Tank losses were approximately equal: under 300 British and slightly more than 300 Axis.

One last word on Operation 'Crusader'. Ironically it was almost in the final hours of The Fifth 's last scrap at Sidi Rezegh that Dinham Drew was forced to leave his command. While he was watching with dismay the New Zealanders wandering into the range of the Italian guns, Colonel Drew's own tank received several direct hits from 20mm anti-tank rifle bullets. A splinter from one of these lacerated his hand, causing him excruciating pain and necessitating his evacuation to an advanced field hospital – and eventually to Cairo.

Aged forty-six and with some twenty-five years of active soldiering under his Sam Browne belt, Dinham Drew was not only wounded but completely exhausted. He appears again in the story of The Fifth but, in the last days of 1941, he handed over his command – a command which he assumed on 24th April 1940 – to his Second in Command, Major RDW Uniacke, who was then promoted Lieutenant Colonel and confirmed in command of The Fifth.

Colonel Uniacke, who was Adjutant of the Regimental Depot in 1939, was universally known in the RTR as 'Robbie'. He was, moreover, described by that mid-twentieth century genius of the camera and photographer of the famous, the fancied and the fashionable, Cecil Beaton, as 'the handsomest man outside the world of films'!

THE OTHER SIDE

Once again, an interesting picture of the Axis' approach to the events of November and December 1941 can be obtained from von Mellinthin's book PANZER BATTLES.

As mentioned in the text, Operation 'Crusader' coincided with Rommel's plan for an all-out attack to capture Tobruk. As a port, Tobruk was crucial to both sides: probably even more so to the Axis forces than to the Allies, as it would have enormously shortened Rommel's overland supply routes.

It is interesting, in the context of supplies, to note how important the German Naval High Command considered Malta to be. Grand Admiral Räder consistently urged Hitler not merely to neutralise the island by denying it supplies but to invade it and establish a base there before launching on the Russian campaign. With Malta in German hands and Tobruk as an operating port of supply for the DAK and directly threatening Egypt, it is difficult to see how the British could have maintained an effective presence in North Africa. Fortunately for the Allies, Hitler preferred to go ahead with the Russian gamble. This made the capture of Tobruk, in Rommel's view, absolutely imperative.

From the internal evidence, it seems that Rommel discounted the probability of the Eighth Army's launching an autumn offensive, although the Italian General Bastico (Rommel's nominal superior in Africa) was convinced such a campaign was what the British had in mind. Von Mellinthin produces some pretty specious excuses for the German Command's attitude but insists that Rommel's flight to Rome was specifically to impress on the Italian Chief of Staff the wisdom of his plan to capture Tobruk and the fallacies in General Bastico's assessment of the Allies' position.

Whatever the truth of the matter, the situation developed whereby Rommel was *almost completely prepared for a major autumn campaign, but an offensive one on his own terms.*

Even after Auchinleck made his move, Rommel aggravated the Axis problems by his reluctance – amounting almost to a refusal – to believe that his opponent was serious. He convinced himself (no doubt partly because he was not prepared to accept that the Italians were right and he, Rommel, was wrong) that the most the Eighth Army could undertake at the end of 1941 was a reconnaissance in force. Quite what he thought the Allies were intending to do after such a reconnaissance will never be known. Equally unknowable is what the result would have been if the DAK had been defensively prepared for 'Crusader'.

THE WAR CHRONICLE

1941

November	03	Russian City of Kursk captured
	08	Germans occupied Yalta
	09	Internecine warfare in Yugoslavia between Mihailovich's Chetniks and Tito's communist Partisans escalated
	14	HMS *Ark Royal*, after being sunk several times by Lord Haw Haw, definitively sunk 25 miles from Gibraltar
	21	Rostov was next Russian city to be captured by the German invaders
	25	HMS *Barham* torpedoed by a U-boat and sunk with heavy loss of life
	27	Last of the 'last' of the Italian Army surrendered in Ethiopia
	30	More than 11,000 people died of starvation in the besieged city of Leningrad in November
December	01	Axis planes carried out their1,000th air raid on Malta
	06	Britain reluctantly declared war on Finland
	07	Pearl Harbor, Guam and Wake Island attacked by Japanese
	08	Manila attacked by Japanese. USA 'at war' with Japan – Thailand invaded by Japanese – and surrendered
	10	HMS *Prince of Wales* and *Repulse* sunk by Japanese – Guam surrendered
	11	USA declared war on Germany and Italy – some claimed that it was the other way round
	14	Between 14th and 19th December, Britain lost HMS *Galatea* (cruiser), HMS *Queen Elizabeth* and *Valiant* (battleships), HMS *Neptune* (cruiser) as well as destroyers and supply ships in the Mediterranean
	19	TRHs Princess Elizabeth and Princess Margaret Rose performed *Cinderella* 'somewhere in England' before a selected (and no doubt select) audience
	23	Japanese forces landed in Sarawak
	25	Hong Kong surrendered to Japanese

28 Japanese landed in Sumatra
31 Orson Welles' film, *Citizen Kane*, voted 'Film of the Year'

NOTES

1 The wire. This term often creates problems for anyone studying the War in the Desert. In the first place, just as 'the blue' was the troops' name for the sharp end, so was 'the wire' their name for the dividing line between 'them' and 'us'. There were a few occasions when the 'wire' literally was a barbed wire entanglement separating the goodies from the baddies. Generally it was just the point one reached beyond which the shooting was likely to start. The original,1940, interpretation of the term was the border between Libya and Egypt

2 Turret ring. The circular opening in the top of the hull in which the turret rotated – 'traversed' in tank language. This was always a vulnerable point and many tanks were put out of action by jammed turrets

3 Shufti. Although Desert Rats are reluctant to admit it, this was originally RAF slang from the mid-1920s. More or less correctly taken from the Arabic, it simply means 'look'. 'Have a shufti' became the accepted way of saying 'take a look' and was used alike by GOCs and private soldiers

4 Point 175. This was on the 'Trigh Capuzzo' – the main road from the west, through Sidi Rezegh to Sollum. Point 175 was 4 or 5 miles east of Sidi Rezegh

5 Capt Ward. This was one of the many tanks that 'Tricky Dickie' Ward (later to become General Sir Richard Ward GBE KCB DSO MC) had shot out from under him. Indeed, he had the unenviable reputation of having lost more tanks in action than anyone else in The Fifth

6 Recommended for awards. The Officers mentioned were awarded Military Crosses and the Other Ranks Military Medals

7 8th December. The news being that, on the previous day, the Japanese had attacked Pearl Harbor. It was, in the nature of things, some considerable time before the full import of this news was felt by the men of the Eighth Army. At a higher level, the news that the Japanese had also attacked British bases in the Far East was to have far-reaching effects on the North Africa campaign

8 Dixie Dean. Sgt Dean recovered from this wound, only to lose his life near Foggia in 1943 a few days before The Fifth left Italy for England

9 Eight gallon cases of petrol. At that time – and for some time after – petrol was transported and delivered to the tanks in four gallon 'expendable' cans. For convenience, two cans were often packed together, hence Jake's reference to 'eight gallon cases'. Eventually, the powers-that-be recognised the superiority of the 20-litre re-usable cans used by the Jerries and adopted them instead . . . for all liquids, not just petrol. These expendables were notoriously inefficient. It has been calculated that, in the Desert, anything up to 30% of all liquids transported or stored in them was lost through damage or wastage

10 Prisoners. According to the Divisional account, their number was about 700 and was a mixture of Italians and Germans

11 'Follow me'. There are various accounts of Brigadier Campbell's arrival on the scene, all equally hair-raising. What seems certain is that he did arrive in his staff car and – in the glorious tradition of the Light Brigade at Balaclava – pointed to the enemy positions and gave the order to charge. When it was diplomatically suggested by the officers in local command that that wasn't

quite what was expected of them, Campbell cheerfully replied that what soldiers were for was – 'To die!' . . . and led the charge. As one of them later remarked, 'We were all one hell of a sight more scared of Jock than of the enemy – so we charged!'

12 Knightsbridge. Not London SW. See later for a description of the action at Knightsbridge

13 Colonel Willison. The 'Ant' Willison (WW I DSO MC) was at one time 2 i/c of 5RTR. Willison was then a Brigadier and commanding the 32nd Army Tank Brigade – known as 'The Tobruk Tanks' – in the beleaguered port. For a description (amounting almost to a eulogy) of Willison, see Frank Harrison's TOBRUK

14 'the guns'. At this stage in the war, the RHA did not have 'self-propelled' [*ie* guns mounted on a tracked chassis] artillery. The 25pdr guns that Wardrop is referring to were the conventional type, towed by some form of 'gun tractor'

15 'gave them the bayonet'. In Liddell Hart's letter referred to in the Notes to Chapter III, there is a comment by him on Jake's employment of this term. According to Liddell Hart, such use of the bayonet, even in fighting at close quarters, is one of the great myths of warfare. He claims that, only on two or three occasions in either WW I or WW II, was any action actually decided by the use of the bayonet

16 Bayerlein. This reference is to General Bayerlein whose Memoirs were published after the War. He was, at the time of the action described, a Colonel and Chief of Staff to Rommel

17 Khamseen. (Sometimes Khamsin) This unpleasant natural phenomenon is, according to the dictionary, 'a hot south or south-east wind blowing in Egypt for about fifty days from mid-March'. Anyone, however, who had been in the Desert would know that a Khamseen was no strict regarder of national frontiers or arbitrary time-scales

18 Poor old Steve. The 'poor old' is a term of respect, even of affection. 'Steve' was Lt P Steevens, an 'Officer under Instruction' at the outbreak of war but, by this time, an experienced and capable Troop Leader

CHAPTER VI

. . . Retreat to el Alamein

January–June 1942

The War Diary for 1st January 1942 is headed Pirbright Camp. But The Fifth had not been wafted back to England on a magic carpet. This Pirbright Camp was at Abbassia, and Abbassia was in Egypt!

All but the rear party was on leave and the rear party was busily engaged in making a home from home out of Pirbright Camp. The War Diary records that several un-named subalterns had been posted to the Regiment: that Lieutenant (Temporary Captain) Steevens had died of wounds: that Sgt Paice and Cpl Noirmont [Noirmot] both of 'B' Squadron and Tpr Hunt of 'C' Squadron were POWs: that Tpr Wattis had died 'in enemy hands': that the award of the Military Medal to Cpl Dixon T was confirmed. Battalion strength on 7th January was 29 Officers and 483 ORs. Not surprisingly, nothing was said about tanks. Once again, there weren't any.

Although 5RTR was not engaged in any of the actions in the Desert during the first three months of 1942, the various critical dates and actions of the war in the Desert are mentioned in parallel with The Fifth's story, to give a clear picture of events.

GHQ Middle East had intended to launch an offensive (Code Name 'Acrobat') in mid-February with the intention of driving the enemy back to Tripoli. Rommel pre-empted this offensive by one of his own. He had been reinforced at the beginning of January by the arrival of 55 tanks – bringing the DAK tank strength up to 111 – as well as other vital supplies. Rommel's decision was an on-the-spot one, prompted by air-reconnaissance reports of Allied weakness: like many of his decisions, it did not meet with the approval of his Italian nominal superiors. However, by the time the Italian C-in-C arrived to make his protest, Rommel's forces had already advanced over a hundred miles. As in other Desert operations, he had a particular advantage: whereas almost all the Allies' second-line AFVs and all their supply vehicles were four-wheeled (and not always with four-wheel-drive) the DAK relied on half-track or multi-axle vehicles. This gave the DAK the edge when it came to manoeuvring on the poor surface over which the advance was made.

By 23rd January the DAK had shattered the inexperienced Second Armoured Brigade and was thrusting eastwards. Rommel paused, but only temporarily, on the 24th when his Italian allies refused to go any farther: by the next day he had thrust even farther and reached Msus, destroying all but 30 tanks in the 1st Armoured Division on the way.

Not for the first time, GHQ Cairo misread the position . . . or was less than honestly informed as to the true position by the Field Commanders. Whatever the reason, Auchinleck issued the grossly optimistic order – 'hold and strike back'. 'Holding' might just have been possible but any hope of 'striking back' was fatally delayed, allowing Rommel to develop his own initiative. This he did by drawing off the British armour with a feint and driving straight to Benghazi, which he captured on 27th January. Fortunately for the Allies, this offensive had so over-stretched Rommel's lines of communication – he was 650 miles from base – that his eastward drive slowed to a stand-still.

Meanwhile, tanks at last got a mention in Pirbright Camp on 25th January when there was a 'Squadron Commanders and Representatives Conference – Subject: immediate re-equipment of Battalion. This to be completed in 14 days'. Next day, everyone got down to business – except Alan Biddell, who was sent on a junior officers' tactical course, at the RAC School next door in Abbassia. There were Driver Mechanics and Gunnery courses for the new American Medium M-3 *General Grant* tanks, ten of which were delivered on the 29th. These *Grants* (which are described in Appendix 2), whatever their disadvantages – and they had many – whatever one may think of them in retrospect, however late they came and however obsolete their design, were miles down the road by comparison with the out-dated, worn-out tanks in which The Fifth had fought in the Desert in 1941. The tank crews fell upon them as the Children of Israel fell upon the Manna . . . which, come to think of it, those Children of Israel first found not all that far from Pirbright Camp, Abassia!

The 31st January was an exceptionally busy day, including a visit from a Brass Hat and the shuffling of appointments among the Officers. Four subalterns and 130 ORs arrived. Major Jackson and Lieut Deryk Macdonald (who comes and goes on mysterious postings throughout the Regiment's WW II history) left 5RTR. Major Castle was promoted Regimental 2i/c: ex-Adjutant Freddie Coombes became acting Major and took over 'B' Squadron: Major Sherley-Price gave up 'A' Squadron to move to HQ Squadron: Dickie Ward assumed a crown and the command of 'A' Squadron: 2/Lt A Adams did a double jump and became A/Capt and Adjutant. 12 B vehicles were delivered . . . and so were 18 *Grants* – 8 of which were 'immediately transferred to 3RTR', as the War Diary glumly records.

In a way, this was the lull before the storm. However peaceful life in Pirbright Camp might have been, no-one had any illusions as to the seriousness of events away to the west, across the blue. The High Command, however, had seriously underestimated the cunning of the Desert Fox[1]. The cunning and the exceptional daring. That the High Command had made this mistake is recorded in a despatch from General Auchinleck – a man not given to being wrong: 'it seems highly unlikely that Rommel will be able to take the offensive again in the near future,' he wrote early in January. The details of Rommel's attack and the shambles which it created for the 1st Armoured Division and the gallant but weary 4th Indian Division must have been followed with dismay in The Fifth. Not for the first time . . . certainly not for the last . . . the mutter must have gone round. 'They ought to have sent for us!' Which is precisely the view expressed by the Brigade Commander, Rickie Richards, in a letter he wrote to his wife on 26th January!

On 1st February, Regimental strength was 33 Officers and 588 ORs. On the 2nd, AFV strength was enlarged by the arrival of 20 new (or reconditioned) *Honeys* and 3 more *Grants*. By the 5th, individual training was complete and, over the next week, the squadrons went out one by one to fire-in the guns on the *Grants*.

Out in the Desert, by 4th February, the position had stabilised on the Gazala Line[2], where it remained more or less stable until the end of April.

Again with the Regiment, tragedy struck on 15th February. Major G J Gilpin MC, the experienced and Desert-wise 'C' Squadron Commander, was killed in a motor accident. He was buried the next day at the Heliopolis Military Cemetery by Padre Warner. Paddy Doyle was promoted Major and posted to command 'C' Squadron.

By mid-February, Troop and Squadron training was well under way and Tom Chesterfield returned to the unit. To show that nothing was being taken at face value, The Fifth was used to carry out penetration tests on the new tanks. [Not as hazardous as it sounds; the target *Grants* were not manned!] There is no record of the test results, only that the tests were witnessed by the 'Auk' and Jock Campbell[3], the newly appointed Divisional Commander.

Sadly, there was a call for another Burial Party on the 25th February, when Cpl Waldron of HQ Sqn was buried at Heliopolis. And then, on 28th February, the War Diary reads 'CO and RSM attended funeral of Maj Gen Campbell VC DSO MC, Commander of 7th Arm'd Div at Old Cairo Military Cemetery.' 'Jock' Campbell, like The Fifth's Major Gilpin, had been killed in a motor accident.

At the end of the month, the Regiment's tank strength was:

'A' Sqn –15 *Honeys*

'B' Sqn – 13 *Grants*

'C' Sqn – 13 *Grants*

HQ Sqn – 1 *Honey* plus 2 on loan and 2 *Grants*

March started quietly, with nothing worse happening than Navigational Exercises for recently joined officers. On the 11th, a Warning Order came for the Brigade (4th Armoured), less VIII Hussars, to be ready to move 'to the forward area' on the 15th. There was hectic swapping of unfit tanks for fit tanks from VIII Hussars and 'Desert camouflaging' of all A and B vehicles.

Between the end of February and the beginning of March, The Fifth had moved from Abbassia to Beni Yusef. There is no record of how or exactly when this move was accomplished.

And on the 15th, another and bigger move began . . . with 5RTR having the greatest strength so far recorded in the War Diary: 30 Officers and 619 ORs. Between 16th and 20th March the Regiment moved from Beni Yusef, via Haqfet Uaar, Bugbug and Fort Capuzzo, to a new area north-west of Bir Hamarin and immediately set about intensive training 'in the field'. This training went through squadron level and battalion level to brigade level by 10th April. Promising though this progress in training may have been, the *Grants* were causing anxiety. At one time, 28 of them were in LRS being examined for excessive oil consumption. Conversely, all 18 *Honeys* were entered in the Unit State as 'fit'. On 14th April 5RTR was on six hours' notice to move to the 'battle areas' which the CO and IO had previously recce'd. In a way, this was a false alarm, since the next three days were spent on further recces – one of them described as 'offensive' [whatever that means] – involving everyone from Squadron Commanders up to the Divisional GOC.

The War Diary for 21st April depicts the 'home life' of The Fifth while waiting for the new, but long-expected, push: it reads:

1000 hrs. Conference down to Tp comds. Subjects:-
Operations order No 1
General
Bn strength: 31 offrs. 598 ORs
Tank state:- *Gen Grants* – 25 unfit, 10 fit.
Gen Stuarts – 20 (including 2 with RHA) fit
1400 hrs. Camouflage Competition
Winner: Tp commanded by 2/Lt Wilshaw, 'C' Sqn.

On 25th April the Regiment was put on immediate notice to move for 'Emergency Operations' at 1100 hrs: at 1200 hrs it moved and at 1800 hrs it arrived, only to be stood down at 1830 hrs. This state of on-off-on-off stand-to continued for weeks rather than days. On 28th April (except for Colonel Uniacke, Major Doyle, Sgt Clay with Cpl Banham who took time off to meet Lt Gen HRH the Duke of Gloucester) there were battalion sports held in the 'B' Squadron area. As the mid-day temperature two days later was 110°, one can only hope that the heat-wave came on suddenly . . . and after the sports were over.

When the Eighth Army lined up for the June offensive, it comprised two Armoured Divisions, each consisting of one Armoured Brigade and a Motor Brigade. In terms of Seventh Armoured Division this consisted of 4th Armoured Brigade (VIII Hussars, 3RTR, 5RTR,1 RHA and 1 KRRC [*ie* a mixed force]); 7th Motor Brigade (9 KRRC, 2 RB, 9 RB and 4 RHA [also a mixed force]); Divisional Troops (KDG, 102 RHA, 15 Light AA RA) and support troops (Divisional Signals, Royal Engineers, units of the RASC, RAMC and RAOC).

There were, in addition, four Infantry Divisions, two Independent Motor Brigade Groups and two Army Tank Brigades. In all, this gave Eighth Army a tank strength – on paper – of 850 *Grants, Honeys, Crusaders, Matildas* and

Valentines, with a reserve of 120 assorted AFVs in 'first line' and, theoretically, a further 300 tanks in Egypt.

Opposed to this, Rommel could muster three German Divisions, two of which were Armoured; one Italian Armoured Division, one Italian Motorised Division; four Italian Infantry Divisions (with a stiffening of German Infantry). All Rommel's units were under strength. He had about 550 tanks of which 280 were either Pzkw IIs or Italian M.13s. And no reserves.

GHQ assessed the matter by saying that the Allies were superior in [tank] numbers but inferior in quality 'despite the new American Medium tanks.' Liddell Hart (unlike General Verney) considered that the British 2-pounder and the American 37mm tank-mounted guns were more effective than the equivalent German 37mm and 50mm tank-mounted guns but less effective than the German 50mm anti-tank guns. The 75mm dual-purpose gun on the *Grants* was a new element, and an unpleasant surprise for the DAK, but had the inherent disadvantage of being side sponson-mounted (and therefore having a very limited traverse), as well as necessitating the whole of the upper part of the tank's exposure before the gun could be brought into action.

Other comparative factors were considered to be the superiority of the German gun sights, the inferiority of the Allies' ammunition and the indifferent reliability of their tanks. These may have been Headquarters' views: the crews would have added, as a major disadvantage, the ease with which both British and American tanks brewed-up.

There were, in reality, two other advantages on the Axis' side. One was tactical: the close conjunction of anti-tank guns *used offensively* with tanks. The Commanders of the British Armoured Brigades never learnt the advantage of this tactic and, what was worse, never appreciated that it would invariably be used against them. The other was the superiority of the 88mm high-velocity anti-aircraft gun, used as an anti-tank weapon. Had there been many more of these in North Africa, the position of Allied armour would have been precarious indeed.

On 30th April – that was the day when the mid-day temperature soared to 110°F – the unit stood to at 0600 hrs and remained at two hours' notice throughout the day. The three 'fighting squadrons' remained on two hours notice on 1st May but this was relaxed to six hours on the 2nd, 3rd and 4th. When a movement order came on 6th May, it was not to move to meet the enemy but to engage in a Brigade exercise! One way or another, preparation for this exercise, the exercise itself and the 'debriefing' lasted until 13th May . . . when the CO went on leave to Cairo. The next two weeks passed in conferences, in the studying of orders and in reconnaissance, before an order to get to grips with the enemy reached the Regiment.

When Battle Orders came on Wednesday, 27th May at 0330 hrs they were short, sharp and to the point. At 0750 hrs 5RTR, with B Battery 1 RHA under command, was engaged by the 21st Panzer Division with about 100 tanks manoeuvring to 5RTR's western flank and some 70 on its southern. The Battalion was engaged for approximately two hours and caused considerable damage to the enemy, although no precise details of this are recorded. What is recorded is that there were no losses. A good start to the day's work. On orders from Brigade, the unit withdrew to an appointed RV with 3RTR, VIII Hussars and Bde HQ – only to find that there was no sign of them. By way of compensation, 5RTR soon after made contact with an enemy column moving south. The War Diary speaks of 'considerable damage to the enemy' without losses to the Battalion. Scarcely had this, second, enemy column beaten a retreat, than a third column hove in sight. 'A' Squadron[4] made contact at 1400 hrs and, by 1420 hrs, the rest of the Battalion was engaged with it, inflicting yet more casualties and causing the enemy to withdraw in confusion. Again, The Fifth suffered no losses. At 1445 hrs, the Regiment learnt that some of the enemy, from the column sighted at 1420 hrs, had earlier got in among The Fifth's B Echelon and had captured some men and vehicles. Luckily, some of the personnel, with a few of the vehicles, took advantage of the confusion to escape and rejoin the unit later that day. Five trucks and a scout car were lost.

At 1815 hrs Bde ordered the Regiment to a new position and at 1900 hrs 5RTR engaged its fourth enemy column of the day. Again the enemy suffered casualties in men and machines, with The Fifth's tanks being unscathed. Not so the men: Sgt Hicks of 'A' Squadron later died of wounds received and L/Cpl Allan of HQ Squadron was killed in action.

The plan elaborated by Rommel, which brought the 21st Panzers into contact with The Fifth, was a typical example of the Desert Fox's cunning. He was never afraid to repeat one of his successful tactical moves when doing so suited his objectives and the terrain over which he had to operate. His intention, in broad terms, was to get back to Tobruk and capture the port. He realised that, with his numerical inferiority in AFVs, he could not achieve this by a frontal attack which would have involved the Allied armour. He therefore devised a small-scale version of von Manstein's 'Sickle Plan'[5]. Just as the Germans in 1940 repeated the Schlieffen Plan by cutting through Belgium while the main blow was struck by an outflanking move in the south, so Rommel feinted against the main Allied defences on the front between Gazala and Bir Hacheim, while his Panzer Divisions swept round the south of Bir Hacheim.

Rommel kept the DAK together under his command and deployed the Italian Infantry and Motor Divisions to attack the Gazala Line. Auchinleck, even if not quite so astute as his opponent, spotted the outflanking movement, and moved to counter it. However he misjudged its import, because he believed that Rommel's main thrust would still come in the centre of the Gazala Line. He was convinced that Rommel would try to split the Allied armour rather than roll it up from the flank.

As it was, the whole of Rommel's available forces, mustering more than

10,000 vehicles, swept round the Eighth Army's left flank, knocked out the 3rd Indian Brigade and overran the Seventh Armoured Division Headquarters[6]. Although, in Rommel's own words, 'the *Grants* tore holes in the Panzers' and slowed down his advance, both the 15th and the 21st Panzer Divisions were at Knightsbridge by nightfall on 27th May. Knightsbridge was, for all that, not his objective. This was to have cut through Acroma and to have reached the coast.

In his Diaries, Rommel admitted not only the damage the *Grants* caused but also that he would not have achieved what he did if General Ritchie had played him at his own game. Instead, his opponent had 'thrown his armour into the battle piecemeal and at different times', thus allowing him to make his own moves and make them in his own time.

At 0130 hrs on the 28th May 5RTR leaguered at 'Harry Fat' [or, to give it its proper name, Hareifat-en-Nbeidat]. Three hours later, they were on the move: nine hours later, they were under heavy shell-fire and in touch, but not engaged, with enemy units well placed behind an escarpment. At 1300 hrs the Regiment had reached el Adem and was receiving reports of intense enemy armoured troop movement, indicating that the Italian Ariete Division was on the move to reinforce the German armour.

At 1830 hrs The Fifth was showing off the prowess of their *Grants'* 75mm guns. This shooting match, in conjunction with the RHA, chased the enemy away to the south-west until 2005 hrs when contact was lost. Eventually, at 2130 hrs, the Battalion leaguered and met up with the A and B Echelons. 5RTR was still intact.

The time between 0500 hrs and 1330 hrs on 29th May was spent on maintenance. The Battalion then moved off, at five minutes' notice, being directed onto a new Charlie Love en route. At 1715 hrs the column was attacked by Stukas, Cpl Faveley (Lt G A Smith's driver) being killed and four other crew members wounded. However, at 2000 hrs enemy ground forces were contacted and a running battle ensued. This lasted an hour and a half, becoming a shooting match for the *Grants* with the RHA 25-pounders in support.

An overnight count of casualties showed that two enemy tanks, a 50mm and an 88mm anti-tank gun had been destroyed, along with a possible bag of 10 soft-skinned vehicles. In the Battalion, three *Grants* and two or three *Honeys* had been lost: apart from Cpl Faveley, five other ORs were wounded and ten were missing. Incredibly, Lieut Smith's tank was unharmed, in spite of the human casualties. Major Coombes was wounded; Tom Chesterfield and 2/Lt Wilshaw were missing.

Tom Chesterfield, it will be remembered, had been in dock as a result of losing a finger. 'After about two months in hospital,' he wrote later, 'I rejoined the Battalion which had come back to Beni Yusef to re-equip with *Grants.* After a while in camp, spent 'familiarising' ourselves with the new tanks, we moved up to the Desert where we were placed in support of the Free French at Bir Hacheim at the extreme southern end of the Gazala Line. We had several prepared positions to take up, if, as was expected, Rommel's attack came by way of a sweep round the Army's left flank. We were assured that we would be given at least 24 hours notice of such a move, as there was a Recce screen of XI Hussars, reinforced by the South African armoured cars, well out to our front. In fact, at first light on 27th May we were practically surrounded by the DAK's 21st Panzer Division! Inevitably we were forced to withdraw, first to el Adem and then in the general direction of Tobruk.

'In the next two days we covered a lot of ground, including one horrendous, moonless, night march in which it was a miracle that no-one lost contact for any length of time. Eventually we formed part of a large defensive 'box' south of Knightsbridge, where we hoped to halt Rommel's advance. Towards dusk we attacked a large mixed column which included some tanks and '88s' – these latter being so devastating that we decided to withdraw in what was, by then, virtual darkness. At this point, my tank was hit by an '88', which caused a lot of flaking [Tom's principal enemy] and started a small fire in the turret and another in my trousers! I remembered the fire extinguisher operating levers were outside the turret and climbed out to operate them. What I didn't realise was that my knee and leg had been hit as well as scorched and I couldn't stand. Result: I fell off the tank. Luckily for me, my W/Op (Trp Nuttall, sadly later killed in NW Europe) saw what had happened, came after me and helped me to walk. By this time it was completely dark and my Driver ('Taffy' Rees – later awarded an MM) bravely carried on and saved the tank which was still a runner. Nuttall and I spent a freezing night lying up somewhere between our forces and the Germans. Just before first light we heard some tank engines starting up nearby and a very English voice shouting, 'Are you on the air?' Nuttall ran across and found the tanks belonged to the Sharpshooters[7]. He contacted the Squadron Commander who sent him back to say that their MO would come and collect me. What was even more welcome – he sent a bottle of whisky!'

That is why Lieut Chesterfield TR was reported missing. Tom did not return to The Fifth until it was at Homs, when he became Assistant Adjutant, having, in the interval, been operated on in Tobruk Hospital, sent to the Naval Hospital in Alexandria, transferred to Ramla near Tel Aviv, thence to Suez and finally to Pietermaritzberg near Durban.

Jake Wardrop's Diary for 1942 shows his admiration for the new Divisional Commander, Jock Campbell, particularly the interest he took in the front line troops. Jake's admiration of the new *Grants* was not quite so unstinted: some of them, he remarked sourly, had already 800 or 1,000 miles on the clock and, by the time the shooting started again in May, were beginning to get a bit sluggish. This was the driver in Jake speaking: his glee that the new 75mm guns gave the 'bad boys' a nasty shock was quite another story.

Jake – and the rest of the Fifth Tanks – was back in action on 27th May. It is apparent from his Diary that this was another very scrappy engagement but one which seemed to be going well. There were some welcome pickings to be had from the various dumps they over-ran [Jake does not says whose dumps] to eat and to smoke and there was the welcome sight of seeing quite a few Allied troops, who had earlier been captured, making their way back through the line. While the tanks had been engaged in this ding-dong battle, a German column had worked its way round to the rear and attacked the Echelon: the column had been counter-attacked. In the end, Jake reckoned that, in terms of prisoners captured and set free, both sides ended up all square.

During the 29th the Regiment was bombed while on the move and one of Jake's friends, Pave[8], was killed. Under cover of approaching darkness, The Fifth put in an attack on a line of anti-tank guns. The action started by shelling the gun positions at near-maximum range for the 75s. However, when the tanks advanced, they discovered that they had not done as much damage as they expected. On the contrary, the crews were very much alive . . . and the guns were 88s. 'Very bad business' Jake called them.

And very bad business they were for the Wardrop crew, as their tank was hit twice. Jake saw that there was no-one in the turret [he would have expected to find the crew commander, the 37mm gunner and the wireless operator] so he took it upon himself to re-organise the remaining crew by getting the gunner[9] to take over as driver and the loader[9] to take over as driver while he clambered up into the turret to see what was going on. What he saw he didn't like: two of the Squadron's tanks on fire to his right.

Jake decided that, at that moment, his tank was not doing any good. He gave the temporary driver the order to reverse. Nothing happened: one of the shots had hit the driving sprocket [at the front on the American tanks] and the track was broken. Jake's fortunes changed: a tank commanded by his friend, Cliff[10] pulled up in front of them and towed them out of danger. By the time they had sorted themselves out, they found that they were not by any means the only tank casualty: among the crew casualties was another of Jake's old friends, Snowy[11], who had been badly hit. Jake – who felt his crew commander could have played a rather more heroic part in the incident – appears to have taken charge, next day collecting the crew's kit from the tank and hitching a ride in an ammunition lorry. The lorry's route took them through the scene of the previous day's action. Jake was pleased to note that, judging by the number of Boche wrecks, The Fifth's shooting couldn't have been too bad.

The Battalion was bombed during the night, causing some casualties, including one of Jake's crew who jumped out of the lorry when it started[12] and ran in the wrong direction.

The following morning, all the crews who had lost their tanks set off for a TDS near Tobruk to collect replacements. These were plentiful and were loaded onto new American transporters. A dust storm held them up for a day but they finally got going and, when they were near enough to the wire, the tanks were unloaded. The unloading point seems to have been badly chosen, as the officer in charge of the transporters didn't know where any of the units were. There was nothing for it but to camp for the night and set off again in the morning. By good luck, the tanks from The Fifth came across Divisional Headquarters and were put on the right track and reached the Battalion at about 1500 hrs. Here the men learnt that there had been a heavy engagement the night before with many casualties in tanks and men, including the CO[13] who had been killed. Among Jake's particular friends, Wag Fry and Topper[14] had been killed. Jake and Stan [Skeels] went to look for others of their friends and found that Wee George [Tpr George Carter, another 'C' Sqn driver] had baled out and lost all his kit but had collected a bit of shrapnel in his wrist. Inevitably there followed changes in the make-up of the crews. There were only about twenty tanks left. Jake found himself again driving the Squadron Commander, which pleased him.

Lieutenant Colonel RDW Uniacke was considered by at least one authority to be one of the most promising officers in the Royal Tank Corps. Unfortunately his courage in action prevented that promise from being fulfilled. Robbie Uniacke took great pride in his Corps and, even more so, in his command. On the evening of 22nd June, when the Battalion was withdrawing in accordance with Brigade orders, Colonel Uniacke's tank was hit, the steering being disabled so that the driver could not change direction. Robbie Uniacke saw that the tank was heading straight towards the body of a British soldier – though whether alive or dead, he had no way of telling. Despite the heavy shelling and to avoid running over the man, he halted his tank, dismounted and ran forward to remove the body. While doing this, Colonel Uniacke was himself shot and killed.

The following note was found by the Adjutant among Colonel Uniacke's effects after he was killed:

'I wish to thank all ranks for the first class performance they have put up during the last week. The performance of the three Squadrons on the night of the 28th May was particularly fine and the results of this battle have been most favourably commented upon personally to me by the Corps Commander.

'It is an obvious fact which gives the greatest satisfaction not only to myself but to Squadron Commanders that not one lesson taught during our training has been forgotten and I do feel that our teaching has been fully justified by results.

'I wish to take this opportunity to welcome all new arrivals and am confident that they will shortly have an opportunity to equal the performance of the old sweats.'

The message was signed RDW Uniacke and dated 2nd June 1942.

With the death of Robbie Uniacke, the Second-in-Command took over the Battalion. This was 'Jim' Hutton about whom a lot more will be said.

There are many authoritative histories of the part played by tanks –

particularly the Desert Rats – in the North Africa Campaign, written by historians (Sir Basil Liddell Hart is one such) or senior officers (Field Marshal Lord Carver and Major General Verney are two such). These give accurate pictures of the Campaign but they do not give an insight into the lives of the men who fought that Campaign in those tanks.

The rest of this chapter is, therefore, an attempt to redress that balance and to provide less a history of that Campaign and more of a story of life in those tanks. Broadly speaking, these accounts cover the period of the Campaign in the months leading up to the Battles at el Alamein.

I have quoted WARDROP OF THE FIFTH as frequently as the laws of copyright permit. For three reasons: it often gives greater detail than the official records; his language is graphic; since he was writing for private record and not general publication, he does not hesitate to describe incidents typical of Desert warfare – those of good men in a good Regiment being put to waste. On one particular day, for which he gives no date, The Fifth was on the move at 0500 hrs and went straight into action. It appears that no proper reconnaissance can have been carried out, as the advancing tanks approached a ridge behind which a strong force of German tanks and guns were concealed. Two tanks were hit and knocked out immediately, some but not all the crew members being picked up. Jake's tank was hit without being put out of action. The remaining tanks withdrew under cover of their own fire. Jake's comment was that it had all been a miserable failure.

5RTR was not the only member of the Brigade to find itself in a bad way: both 3RTR and VIII Hussars were in a similar condition. At this point in his Diary, Jake makes a remark which shows that his thinking exactly paralleled that of Erwin Rommel. He wrote, 'It seemed to me that if they [the High Command] had got a lot of kit together and had they made one big push in one place, we could have done something definite. As it was the units were just battering themselves to pieces in a lot of little scraps in which were getting nowhere.'

Jake's tank was again hit during the attack which the Brigade made to relieve the hard-pressed Free French in Bir Hacheim. The French had held out magnificently against almost ceaseless bombing and artillery bombardment: it was hoped that an attack on the besieging forces would allow the garrison to evacuate what had become an untenable position. Unluckily the initial attack went off at half-cock and this is when the turret of his tank was hit, injuring the crew commander, who ordered Jake to take the tank out of the action. Jake did this 'at peak revs' and then halted to survey the damage. The injury to the Squadron Commander [Jake's crew commander] was no worse than a superficial knee wound. However, the 37mm turret gun had been dismounted and was lodged on the floor of the tank, pinning the main gunner in his seat but without causing him more than shock and a few scratches. Out of action, the gunner was extracted from his predicament and the Major summoned his dingo[15] and went to take over another tank. There was nothing more for Jake to do that day than see that the gunner was evacuated and hang around for someone to rescue his tank: this was not pleasant as the scene of action was continually being shelled.

The Armoured Brigade failed in their objective but the infantry 'fought their way in with the bayonet' and Bir Hacheim was relieved. The Brigade then made a night move of some twenty miles, moving in three columns, led by the Navigating Officer. Apart from navigating, which was not the drivers' problem, the main worry of the crew was to keep awake and keep the tank in front firmly – but not too closely – in sight. Major Doyle, temporarily back on Jake's tank, helped him in his task. He sat on the mudguard, chatting to Jake, passing him lighted cigarettes and giving him directions and, crucially from Jake's point of view, sharing a bottle of whisky . . . which 'came the dawn' was empty..

When Jake later set off with the wireless operator to take his damaged tank back to workshops in Tobruk. Major Doyle took over another tank and the remainder of the crew went to the Echelon. But the latest German move had meant the workshop had been evacuated from Tobruk. Jake took the initiative and drove eastward along what passed for the main road out of Tobruk. It took him a day or two to find somewhere to dump the tank. No sooner had he found someone in authority to take the tank off him than he met a chap he knew with a big Scammel[16]. He was on his way back to his unit so Jake cadged a lift, although he had no obligation to do so since the whole Allied force was in retreat. Jake and his mate did not have far to go, joining the Regimental Echelon at Gambut. Here they learnt that the Regiment had been engaged the night before, so Jake hitched a ride with a replenishment lorry and found a tank which was short of a crew member ready to join in the scrap. Jake's enthusiasm was rewarded, as is explained by a line in his Diary which reads, 'We had a big rum issue that night.'

Leaving Jake Wardrop for the moment and going back a bit in time, there is another adventure to be found in a report by Major Ward, commanding 'A' Squadron. His report, rather fancifully entitled 'A Naval Occasion', was later stated, probably correctly, to be 'somewhat exaggerated' by both Gerald Verney and Liddell Hart. The 5RTR version must gain some credence from the fact that the War Diary, although differing in some detail, gives Dickie Ward credit for an even bigger bag than he claims. Dealing with events at the end of May and the beginning of June, Dickie Ward wrote. 'Rommel had failed in his first attempt to cut off the Desert Army west of Tobruk and had pulled back most of his forces into the Cauldron[17]. We had heard rumours that he was about to pull out completely and these rumours were, no doubt, responsible for the task I was given.

'I was told to take my squadron, then consisting of seven *Honeys,* round the south of Bir Hacheim, to thread my way through the masses of live and dummy minefields and to strike north and cause as much interference as I possibly could with the enemy's LofC during the following 24 hours.

'I got my orders about tea-time.' Dickie Ward wrote, after explaining that the previous evening the unit had been engaged in a minor attack, so that it was after midnight when the Regiment leaguered. 'My feelings on getting my orders were mixed. I had never been a member of any independent force and was not used to being deprived of the support provided by the rest of the Regiment. I was told that there were no other friendly troops where I was going, with the exception of Bir Hacheim which was still held by the Free French. No-one really knew where the enemy was, nor were we at all certain that all of his elements had withdrawn in the south. On the other hand, I was delighted to be sent on such a mission and given a free hand; I envisaged ourselves rounding up convoy after convoy and bringing them back to our lines.

'When we started we had about two hours to go before darkness fell. I had planned to stop soon after dark, just short of the minefields south-east of Bir Hacheim, where we would stay for the night, and set out again when there was sufficient light to enable us to find the path through the minefield. The first leg of our journey was almost uneventful. It was only enlivened when we spotted a vehicle on the horizon to the south-east of us, travelling westward as fast as it could go. We managed to head it off and it turned out to be a German recovery vehicle. We put it out of action and captured the crew but, as none of us spoke German, we couldn't discover what it was doing there all by itself. My 2 i/c's tank had developed clutch trouble, so I reluctantly had to send him back with our prisoners. So now we were six!

'The rest of that [day's] march was uneventful and we stopped for the night as planned. I was in a bit of quandary about what our guard arrangements should be. We had six tanks, which meant 24 men including myself. In the end, I decided to rely on getting early warning of approaching vehicles and kept only two men on guard at any one time, with strict instructions to call me if they heard *any* sound. In the event, I was only called three times and I didn't have to order a stand-to. We set off through the minefields at first light. There was a slight ground mist which I blessed.

'It wasn't until about 0700 hrs when the sun rose and cleared the mist that we saw Bir Hacheim towering up above us 1,000 yards to the north-east. The French reaction was quick and unfriendly[18]. They greeted us with a salvo of 75mm shells which burst all around us. I halted the squadron and frantically waved the splendid tricolour we had on board. Perhaps this made them doubtful of our identity, as they stopped firing and a Bren-gun carrier came tearing down the slope towards us. It stopped, obviously suspicious, about 50 yards from us. Perhaps our black berets and overalls were the cause. My incoherent protestations of friendship in execrable French must have upset the officer because, in a flash, he had turned the carrier round and was racing back to his fortress before we could lift a finger to stop him. We had no cause to linger longer and our fears about future treatment by the French were confirmed, as they recommenced shelling until we were out of range to the north. This was most annoying, as I had stressed to my commanders the need for stealth on our march northwards. We had kept down our speed to avoid throwing up clouds of dust and had maintained wireless silence and yet those infernal Frenchmen were drawing everyone's attention to us. Perhaps it worked out for the best as, had any Germans spotted us being shelled, they would have undoubtedly taken us for friends.

'As we made our way northwards, the ground rose gradually until, some miles north of Bir Hacheim, we were on a level with it and were able to see over a radius of five miles to the east and some 2,000 or 3,000 yards to the north and west. To the east we saw what we were waiting for. Several hundred vehicles, all of them looking grotesque and vertically elongated by the mirage, were clustered on the farther side of the Gazala-Hacheim minefield. They were obviously enemy; we therefore cautiously continued northwards, looking for the tracks used by their supply columns and, as luck would have it, we found their tracks in an ideal spot for an ambush. Looking back on it, it is fantastic to think that, in the Desert over the major part of which there is so little cover and visibility is frequently measured in thousands of yards, we were able to hide six tanks so that they couldn't be seen 100 yards away.

'The tracks which we found were running through a small depression on the plateau we had reached. Jutting out into this depression were a number of spurs sufficiently high to hide the tanks from the west. Some of us perforce were visible from the enemy encampment to the east but I considered that the heat haze would make our identification impossible. I called an O Group[19], gave each tank commander a position and explained my plan of action. It was now midday, very bright and hot with the heat haze shimmering all round us, so that objects beyond 1,000 yards took on the most fantastic shapes. I felt we were secure from ground observation and, as we had seen no enemy except for the encampment to the east, I was pretty sure that we had arrived unseen. I was slightly apprehensive only of a French sortie from the south and I hadn't really decided what we should do if they became aggressive. My plan was to remain concealed until the leading vehicles of the convoy reached my tank which was in the most easterly position. I was certain that their convoys would be escorted by some form of armour, probably armoured cars, but I didn't expect to find more than four per convoy. I hoped we would intercept a full convoy from the west rather than an empty one from the east. I told my commanders that no-one was to open fire before I did or, if there were no armoured cars in front, until I gave wireless orders. They were to concentrate their fire on the armoured cars and were to aim high as I did not want fires to tell the whole world we were here. Not one must be allowed to get away. The soft skinned vehicles were not to be fired on unless they did try to escape, and then only if we couldn't stop them by firing across their bows. I did not want to lose valuable stores and vehicles unnecessarily. I hoped, by knocking out the escorts, to catch a second convoy before the enemy knew that we were on his LofC.

'We settled down to wait and had a badly-needed cup of tea and some food. We didn't have long to wait. About 1500 hrs we saw our convoy coming. The vehicles were spread out in three columns and first appeared as huge rectangular objects seeming to float in the haze. As they got closer I estimated that there were about 60 or 70 vehicles but I couldn't pick out the escort. It was a most exciting moment. They seemed to be oblivious of what lay in wait. The escort consisted of three armoured cars, one at the front and two at the back. As the first armoured car drew level with me I opened fire. Pandemonium broke loose. The convoy tried to scatter but, finding us on all sides, stopped. The leading armoured car stopped dead when hit and the crew got out but we only got one of the armoured cars at the rear of the convoy. It was no-one's fault: the convoy was so strung out that the two rearmost armoured cars were only just within range of our westernmost tank commander. It took him three shots to stop the first of these two and that gave the second one time to get away.

'I knew therefore that we would have to work fast, as help in the form of tanks or aircraft would arrive within the hour, so it was no use hoping to collect another convoy. To make matters worse, the second armoured car was burning fiercely, so the enemy would have no difficulty in finding us. I then saw one of the most amusing spectacles of my life. The convoy was an Italian one and, when they realised they were in the bag, every man without exception leapt from his vehicle with his suitcase, stripped all his clothes off and changed his underclothes! They were obviously so well prepared for this sort of emergency that we could hardly contain ourselves.

'We now had to set about marshalling our capture for the return journey. We had the wounded from the armoured car crews to attend to and no Italian could or would understand our instructions. After much shouting and gesticulating, we finally got them to understand that we wanted them to get on the move again. All this had taken about half an hour but, before we were ready to go, my look-out tank reported five enemy tanks 3,000 yards to the north-west. I left my 2 i/c to get the convoy sorted out and went off to see what type of tanks they were. It was very difficult to identify them in the haze – they looked like tanks but might have been armoured cars. They appeared to be uncertain what reception they would meet with if they came any closer, so I told my look-out to do all he could to discourage a closer inspection and went back to get the convoy moving. About a dozen or so vehicles had refused to start, so we destroyed these, causing some wonderful fires, and set off with the rest. I saw now that my original estimate of the convoy had been on the high side and that it contained only about 50 vehicles of which we had had to destroy a dozen.

'Our march homewards was spectacular. One tank was in the lead, three far out on the western (enemy) flank and one brought up the rear with another acting as a sort of shepherd. The enemy AFVs had not come any closer, so I assumed that they were armoured cars. I wondered what sort of reception the French would give us as we passed round to the south of the fortress. Once again, it was most unfriendly. They shelled us the whole time we were within range. The shelling made our task no easier, as the convoy scattered to the four winds: a few were hit and more broke down, so it was a depleted force of some 30 captured lorries which finally met the Regiment just before dark. The convoy provided us with a good haul of provisions, including that nectar of the Desert – fresh fruit: oranges and lemons.'

But if, as he claimed, Dickie Ward thought this 'Naval Occasion' was going to bring him any prize money, he was doomed to disappointment.

An Appendix to the War Diary amplifies some aspects of Major Ward's account. And contradicts others! The first point is that his orders specifically stated that the Squadron was 'to cause as many casualties as possible': nothing about bringing home a bag. In addition to his tanks, Dickie Ward had an ammunition lorry and two petrol lorries. Now come the contradictions. The War Diary states that on 30th May, after taking up the positions described in 'A Naval Occasion', at 0645 hrs, 'The first movement reported was a column of vehicles coming from the west. This consisted of about 10 vehicles, a replenishing column, loaded with petrol and ammunition which walked straight into the party – on sighting, gave themselves up. One motorcyclist unfortunately escaped.'

The War Diary goes on, '0900 hrs: still no movement from the east. Another large column reported from the west consisting of 25 vehicles accompanied by 2 armoured cars which brought up the rear. Column, again loaded with petrol, ammunition and food, surrendered. Armoured cars fought: one was brewed up; the other, although chased for 3 miles, escaped. The Free French[18] then took a hand [The War Diary gives the same version of the party being 'inspected' by the French and then heavily shelled but places the incident in a different time-scale] One lorry had been hit by MG fire and fallen out 2,000 yards away. The crew had walked in. Suddenly a minute car appeared, dashed up to this lorry, set it on fire, and disappeared to the south: definitely Free French co-operation. Further trickles of vehicles came in during the rest of the morning until the bag rose to about 60 vehicles of all descriptions, 12 officers and 200 ORs.'

After giving the description of the Italian prisoners' change of underwear and the shambles of trying to get the lorry drivers organised, the War Diary concludes, '1230 hrs convoy at last got on the move as 3 Pzkw IIIs appeared 3,000 yards to the north-west. Still no movement from Gap. Convoy moved south: about a dozen vehicles broke down or wouldn't start and had to be brewed up. Long range 37mm fire kept the [enemy] tanks at a distance. Shelled by Free French again south of the fort. Convoy broke up but own armoured cars appeared on scene and helped to round them up. Convoy handed over to RBs.'

This Appendix to the War Diary is signed 'WM Hutton. Lt Col.'

This, therefore, is a good place to introduce 'Fearless Jim' who was certainly one of the finest Battalion or Regimental Commanders that any unit of the Royal Tank Corps or the Royal Tank Regiment ever had. And that assessment is made with unreserved acknowledgement of the peerless qualities of other officers who commanded units of the RTC or RTR. Jim – he came to The Fifth with the nick-name 'Gentleman Jim' but this was quickly changed to the even more appropriate 'Fearless Jim' – Hutton was born in May 1912 and in due course went to Sandhurst and was commissioned in the Royal Tank Corps at the age of twenty. At the age of twenty-four he won his first Military Cross in Palestine. During a skirmish, one of the vehicles in his Platoon broke down and was attacked by a force of Arabs who out-numbered his five men by at least ten to one. In the face of these overwhelming odds he held out for 12 hours until help arrived. His next three years should have been spent in peace-time soldiering as a Regimental Officer but, in fact, were broken into by the year he spent with a family in Egypt qualifying as a First Class Interpreter in Arabic. When war broke out, Jim Hutton was already in the Desert, going on to win his second MC while commanding a Squadron of 3RTR in the Gazala battle in 1942. The rest of Colonel Hutton's career with The Fifth is part of the Regiment's history and is told in the relevant places.

While all this action was going on at the front, there was plenty of activity in the rear. Mostly it was a matter of the Echelons shuttling backwards and forwards between supply depots and regimental dumps and between regimental dumps and the tanks in their forward position. An exhausting and unglamorous occupation for drivers and HQ Squadron personnel alike. Once in a while, however, something memorable did occur. One of those drivers, Dai Mitchell, wrote of such an event. A memorable event and an unforgettable character.

'Late one evening, motoring along in my Dodge 'one-tonner' I spotted a stationary staff car that had pulled over from the main dusty track. I made my way across to see if it was in any need of assistance. Lo and behold, as I neared the staff car, I saw a cross on the bonnet and I immediately knew it was the staff car belonging to our Padre, Geoffrey Warner.

'He greeted me with a large warm smile, telling me that he was returning from one of his trips to Cairo where he had collected a consignment of 'goodies' from the KUMANGETIT FUND. No mean journey – a good four hundred plus miles – and he and his driver, Tpr Carr, were pretty tucked out.

'Darkness was closing fast: we moved about 1,000 yards to the south of the track to bivvy [bivouac] down for the night. We placed the two vehicles about 12 feet apart with a canvas sheet windbreak at one end: total of four people – three to sleep behind the windbreak, with the Padre sleeping in his loved and trusty staff car.

'Knocked up an evening meal of 'bully stew[20]', then sorted out the 'stags[21]' for the night. Padre, the first turn, with me taking the last stag of the night. As we turned in for the night, he (the Padre) made a brew and added some of his KUMANGETIT goodies, with 'a drop of the hard stuff' in the mugs of char and, as we hit the sack, he gave us his blessing for the night.

'A relatively quiet night: growl of the heavy guns with the usual display of coloured light as ever in the sky. Just as dawn was breaking, in the half light, two Jerry fighter planes came screaming out of the blue, strafing up and down the column. Now fully alert, I started scanning the skies 360° around our vehicles. As I looked into the rising sun (this is mostly where they came from) I caught sight of two extra planes screaming down and heading our way. Banging on the bonnet of the staff car and yelling 'Enemy aircraft, Padre', the three of us legged it in opposite directions. I only made about 20 yards before hitting the sand. There was a roar of engines and the clattering of cannon shells: as I stood up, the other plane tore in from the other direction, causing me to kiss Mother Earth for the second time.

'I ran back to the vehicles, my heart pounding. The Padre had never made the open ground and was still in his staff car. Fearing the worst – how could anyone survive that onslaught of cannon fire? – it was with great trepidation that I flung open the door and the sight (which I will never forget) that greeted me was unbelievable. Sitting there, large as life, the Padre was putting on his socks. With a wry smile he said, 'Why do these chaps have to come at this unearthly hour making all this fuss?' This from a man who had missed death by inches!

'The KUMANGETIT WAGON was a big Canadian Ford station wagon, the type with a wooden body. On the back of the body, and fixed to the outside behind the mudguards, there were brackets for water cans. These had been blown away *on both sides of the car* by the cannon shells and there he sat on the back seat of the car between these brackets – in a space of 4 feet 6 inches at the most – cool, calm and collected. When I pointed out the great danger he had been in, he gave me another of his quiet smiles and he pointed to the cross on the bonnet. What can one say? I was speechless.

'The German pilots had concentrated on the staff car – no doubt about it – thinking, I suppose, that it was a prize target. The bravest fellow I ever met, the Padre!

'The fitters had welded the cross on his car and, when sometime previously, I had remarked on its stark simplicity, this was his reply, 'That cross is the icon of my faith and trust in God. It will ever be my shield and armour in these terrible days of war.'

'Padre Warner was truly 'a man of God': he practised what he preached. Courageous and compassionate, he was greatly admired and much loved by all ranks. It was a severe blow to us in The Fifth when he was taken from us on promotion.'

That was not Dai Mitchell's last encounter with Padre Warner. Some years later, in Normandy, Dai was not-so-quietly and very blasphemously swearing at life in general and all NCOs and officers in particular when he was fetched a smart clip on the ear from behind. Turning furiously round to do battle, Dai found himself confronted by a familiar, smiling figure. Padre Warner. After giving him a severe ticking off for taking the Name of the Lord in vain, Geoffrey Warner shared a brew-up with Dai and indulged in some reminiscences of the days when he had been with The Fifth. The Reverend Major Warner, as he then was, had chanced on some vehicles whose regimental sign he recognised and had stopped to see if there was anyone around whom he recognised. There was . . . and Dai still feels guilty when he thinks how it was that Padre Warner was able to recognise him from the back!

Another man who had adventures with the Echelons was Peter Carlsson. 'Carlo' had had a spell as a *Honey* driver but, like many another at that time, found himself without a tank to drive. However, on one occasion both a tank and the Squadron water cart were without drivers: Pete and another man were available; they tossed for it: 'Heads: *Honey* – tails: water wagon.' Pete called 'Tails'. Heading back to base, with a lot of traffic going the other way, the water wagon blew up under Carlo. He made a rapid and involuntary exit through the door – luckily, a canvas one – and hit the sands of the Desert a good few yards from where he had last been sitting. Whether the Squadron water wagon had run over the mine, or the vehicle passing it in the other direction had done so, didn't really interest Trooper Carlsson: getting back into the comparative safety of a tank did. He spent all but the last few weeks of his service with 5RTR as a tank driver. Water wagons were far too dangerous!

Bill Chorley saw the rough side of the Desert War without, at that time, seeing any tank action. Bill had joined the Royal Armoured Corps in June 1941 and had been filtered, through training as a wireless operator in the IV Hussars [Winston Churchill's old regiment], via a passage to Egypt and a 'holiday camp' at Bardia, into a spare crew for any regiment in need of trained reinforcements. This was a bad moment for spare crews as well as tank crews, as the Eighth Army was making a strategic withdrawal – in ordinary language 'being in full retreat'. He found himself in a *Honey* and assigned – in theory, at least – to 5RTR. However, what The Fifth wanted at that moment was not spare crews for tanks but spare tanks for crews. Bill with other 'spare crews' found themselves dumped at the side of the road and left to find their own way back. 'We managed to be picked up,' Bill wrote later, 'by a transporter which had been instructed not to proceed to Tobruk. Later some organisation was introduced in the retreat and trucks were found to take us towards Cairo. We had little food or water and became badly sunburnt. I had my twenty-first birthday somewhere near Bardia on the way back. We went via the Sollum Pass – a hair-raising experience. Finally we arrived at el Alamein where new American tanks, *Lees* and *Grants* were being issued.' Worse things, however, were later in store for Bill Chorley

Willie Dovey, who has a genius for seeing the funny side of far from comic things, recalls this period of the war as the 'Bad Bs' – bugs, bully beef, biscuit and battles. Willie was not alone in preferring the 'Good Bs' – such as baths, bitter beer and bints[22].

Harry Ireland built his account of this period of the Desert War round a personal diary – one, as Harry admits – somewhat vague as to dates, hence the reference to Day 2 etc. It is an invaluable account, being written by someone who saw it all from the inside of a tank. And by a man who is, incidentally, one of the few who can claim to have fired shots that knocked out Tiger tanks.

Harry joined 5RTR when the Regiment was stationed outside Cairo shortly after its return from the action at Sidi Rezegh. Many years later he wrote of his experiences. 'Settling in under canvas, I soon made new friends and managed a few drinking evenings in the 'wet' canteen. Being a regular Battalion, quite a few of the lads were hardened soldiers with experience in France and Desert warfare. The Regiment had been out in the Middle East for twelve months before I joined them, I felt a little embarrassed listening to their conversations about being in action and not able to join in, so I contented myself by trying to tell a little home news and made a friendship which was to last all through my service.

'About a fortnight later, a buzz went round the camp that the Regiment was to re-equip with the new *Grant* tank and going back up the desert. In the meantime I had been placed on spare crews and had a run out, shooting at targets on a range with good results. The unit had previously been equipped with American *Honey* tanks but, on listening to conversations by various ranks, I formed the opinion that they had been out-gunned by the more heavily armoured German tanks and lacked the punch that we hoped the *Grants* would have.

'The new tanks were already secured to flats at the rail head ready for the journey up the Desert. Transport for the crews was by road. Between them the trucks carried the necessary supplies for a regiment going into action; ammunition, rations, petrol, water trucks, trucks with stores and administrative supplies. I found myself, being spare crew, on an ammunition truck, weighed down and full to capacity. We moved in convoy along the coast road towards Amirya and made camp after pulling off the road into the Desert 60 miles west of Alexandria (In all we travelled from Beni Yusef, our first camp, 160 miles on the first day) I soon learnt in those first few hours that life in the Desert was hard going (those millions of flies) and the inconvenience of having to 'take the shovel for a walk' to relieve oneself and having my first army biscuit and corned [bully] beef for rations, sleeping under the stars for a roof. One way or another, we were all well equipped for this kind of life.

'Day 2: another 140 miles found us south of Mersa Matruh . . . and also with very sore backsides from a very bumpy ride.

'Day 3: still hugging the coast road where possible. Passed Sidi Barrani and camped in the Bug-Bug area – another 140 miles today.

'Day 4: on to Sollum, Fort Capuzzo, 'Hell Fire Pass': the fascination of the Desert and the scenery around Hell Fire Pass was electrifying and compensated for the rough ride. Camped 60 miles southwest of Sollum.

'Day 5: joined up with the tanks and prepared to function as a regiment ready for any eventuality. (Area Sollum) had my first shave but alas the water for both shaving and making tea was salted, which did not heighten my morale, likewise that of my fellow raw recruits!

'Day 6: was spent living around the tanks in defensive leaguer: in the afternoon a German reconnaissance plane flew over the camp. Our daily ration of water was 2 pints per person.

'Day 7: the day I was waiting for. Owing to sickness on one of the tanks, I was given the job of 'Driver Two' and found myself now actually on a permanent crew. So here I am doing a job which I have been training for for the last six months.

'Day 8: brought a bombing raid near to leaguer last night and you could hear the ack-ack and bombing in the distance. (Bardia – 18 miles)

'Day 9: at first light we moved off on patrol; (squadron strength) down south into the Desert just to feel out the German positions, if any, but to avoid engagement (Saw nothing and returned to leaguer)

'Day 10: began with a terrific sandstorm and no activity from either side and Day 11 was just the same, the storm making life miserable but we found that inside the tank was the best place to be – conversation, playing cards, making tea and eating bully. Little knowing about the future, I found things were getting boring but, observing the regular soldiers, I saw they took everything in their stride. The officers and senior NCOs [the tank commanders] were always busy being briefed by the Sqn Commanders or the CO on various map references, locations, both enemy and ours during the lull, so I guess we are in safe hands (I hope)

'This is where I forget the days on the Desert, each becoming just like another with the usual chores – gun cleaning, maintenance and waiting. Occasionally a single German plane would come over and drop a bomb and strafe some target in the distance but luckily not us.

'Next day: we move down to the area where the Regiment had its previous encounter in November last at Sidi Rezegh – burnt-out tanks and guns everywhere (for once I get the idea this war is no picnic). However, my turn will come

'After days and weeks of patrolling, following German tracks without success, first one way southeast [of] Tobruk, out near el Gubi 100 miles round trip, hearing one rumour after another, night navigating, day navigating, witnessing dog fights with planes over the camp, padre taking church service, reading a little mail trickling in from home, the Regiment moved south into the Desert on a 73 mile journey.

'Trouble with tank and had minor repair job at local mobile repair shop (3-ton truck with fitters and craftsmen in attendance). Found that Regiment had moved up and rejoined them southeast of el Adem (an aerodrome used by RAF). It is now May, considering we started out in late March, there has been little activity on the Regiment's front: I believe a few regiments including infantry, tanks and artillery have had minor engagements with the enemy but they are more forward in the battle area than us. Plenty of air activity all night and day, maybe a build up to a push. The Regiment is on 15 minutes notice to move to battle position (I believe the Free French and Indian Division went into action last night, so our turn could be soon)

'This is it! Moved up to form a battle line and German tanks can be seen on skyline. All guns ready. I take my appropriate position in the tank, the rest of the crew likewise. Tank commander in turret, scouring the skyline with binoculars for target to engage. The orders are now coming through the intercom to load the 75mm gun. Given the bearing of the target, the order comes through 'FIRE!' (I hear my first shot in anger) From now on it continues all morning – 'Load – Fire – Load – Fire – Load – Fire' with the occasional reply of 'Target!', meaning we've hit something (but not too often considering we've been firing all morning).

'Now the German tanks have got their sights on us and shells are bursting all round. (Uncomfortable but we are lucky. They are having the same difficulty as us, ranging on target) A sandstorm started and visibility is almost nil, so we halted for a couple of hours. Unfortunately, with all the manoeuvring, the clutch is bust: we have to evacuate the tank, leaving a skeleton crew behind (driver and main gunner), hoping the fitters will come along and take the tank away. Later in the day the sandstorm abated and the Regiment moved forward to attack. Myself and the rest of the crew came out of action and settled in with the spare crews. The Regiment fell right into a trap: unknown to our command, the Germans took advantage of the sandstorm and withdrew their tanks, leaving behind a screen of well dug-in '88's.

'The Regiment pushed on in pursuit but were met with a hail of fire from the guns and lost almost an entire regiment. The CO [Colonel Uniacke] was killed and lots of tank crews were killed, wounded or taken prisoner. I remember hearing at a later date one of my best pals I came out with from England was wounded and taken prisoner. I guess my first days in action were not pleasant: however, I now know what it's all about.

'Next day we picked up a new tank and formed up with the remaining tanks, moving forward to have another go at the enemy. This time, in with a different crew, I was the main gunner.

'(The skeleton crew which we left behind as I mentioned previously was over-run by the Germans but, although immobile, fought with great courage – the driver later receiving the Distinguished Conduct Medal for gallantry, the other member being killed.)

'This set-back in the Regiment seemed to have a demoralising effect on the men and I, in particular, began to doubt the effectiveness of our tanks.

Admittedly I had only been in action just over a week but the word 'eighty-eight' coming over the intercom had us all on edge. By now we were round the Knightsbridge area and settled down to some give-and-take with the enemy and seemed to have our confidence back once more and morale was high after the good reports we had had of the army's performance in general.

'We had lots of grub and the rum issue seemed to make life brighter, although the strain of long hours in battle – days on end – made one wilt a little. From first light around 0500 hrs until 2200 hrs was a very long day, especially hearing over the intercom the fate of some other crews. (In the confines of the tank, life sometimes could be very unpleasant, what with the heat of the day, the smell of the cordite fumes, hot empty shell-case and the flies, the poor visibility, hunger and thirst: these were just a few of the things we had to contend with, unable to get out because of the shelling and occasional Stuka dive-bomber attacks. The targets on the ground we could do something about but those Stukas were a dreaded foe).

'It is now June and we have been constantly in action on an average of five days at a time all month.

'Attacked an Italian column last evening with good results. Down south in the Desert the French forces at Bir Hacheim have been over-run and we are trying to relieve the remnants with slight success. After what appeared to be a holding action and everything ready for a break-through in the enemy defences, the whole front on our side cracked up (don't ask me how or why) but all we could see was a massive German column approaching from the south – tanks, guns, armoured cars, trucks, all sorts of vehicles – a marvellous sight if you didn't know what it meant. They were trying to cut the entire army up.

'The Regiment swung round to meet the threat but were so out-numbered that for the rest of the day all tanks were slowly reversing and engaging on the move backwards. We were holding them up so all our transport would not fall into their hands. Casualties on our side were numerous, we have been out-gunned, out-manoeuvred, out-generalled: in other words, led up the garden path. From now on it was a matter of survival and all the army was in full retreat (but the Army Commanders call it a 'Strategic Withdrawal'!)

'After handing over the remainder of our tanks to another battalion, all remaining crews were transported on the long haul across the Desert back to the Nile. Passing through the wire boundary into Egypt you had to think to yourself 'What went wrong?' After three and a half months it was back to square one.'

This is not, by any means, the last of Harry Ireland's narrative nor is it quite his last word on this stage of the Desert War. He has already made some pungent remarks on the subject of the High Command. He cannot have been the only man in the ranks of the Eighth Army to have felt that 'we had been out-gunned, out-manoeuvred and out-generalled' (although it was probably seditious, and contrary to King's Regulations, for him to have said so!). But

Harry has this to add. 'Let me try to analyse the last few months. We had started out as a well-equipped Regiment [here Harry is really contradicting himself: if 'we' had been well-equipped, 'we' would not have been out-gunned], well trained, good administration, very good officers and NCOs, plenty of experience in tank warfare in the Desert. It boiled down to one thing, the enemy had out-gunned us with superior armament and fire-power, plus a few bad decisions by the High Command. It was like seeing your favourite team reaching the Cup Final and getting licked 6 – 0! Well, we must just try again.

'However, although back in Egypt and the enemy pushing down on us with all the might he could throw at us, the army managed to fall back in an orderly retreat. The main defence line became known at a later date as the 'Alamein Line'. To rub salt into the wound, Tobruk fell. It had held out against all odds in the last ten months and had been a morale booster for the army. The garrison were all taken prisoner.'

Philosophically, Harry concludes this part of his 'Diary' with the words, 'I believe a few top rank generals have been replaced. It could never happen to us. Imagine the tank crews getting the sack and being told to go home; we don't need you any more.'

At the risk of pointing out the obvious (and of repeating myself), I must reiterate that this book does not purport to be a history of The Fifth Royal Tank Regiment in the Liddell Hart sense of the word where everything is slotted into its correct time and place. What the book is meant to do is to tell the story of the unit as it was seen by those who played their part in The Fith in those World War Two years. This means, inevitably, going backwards and forwards in time to include the personal accounts of as many people as possible.

This time-warp is the case with the account that follows.

At this point, Len 'Bing' Coller returns to the narrative. Len was born in 1916 and, as the old country saying goes, 'wen 'e wor borned, a imp wor borned along of 'im'. Bing's imp of mischief was, generally speaking, a benevolent imp: although it led him into at least one very tight spot, it led him out again with a whole skin.

In June 1942 Len Coller was a Sergeant tank commander in 'C' Squadron. He recalls the events of 11th June starting with the voice of the CO on the wireless alerting the Regiment to the presence of an unknown quantity of enemy tanks and guns advancing on them from the south-east. Len continues his account by reporting the CO's orders that the unit was to form battle line two miles to the west. 'Slowly we move to our allotted positions. Six and Seven Troops left: Eight right. There is no need for any further orders. Every man knows his job – we have done it so often before. Any fold in the ground is taken advantage of, especially if it offers a hull-down position. We are in battle line by 1630 hrs and now comes that period of waiting which is so hated by everyone. However, eventually we hear the familiar whistle of our own guns throwing 25-pounder shells over our heads. As yet we cannot see what they are firing at but I can see the Gunner's FOO some 1,000 yards to my front, sitting on top of his *Honey* with his binoculars to his eyes, looking every bit as though he were about to view the 2.30 at Newmarket!

'I remember thinking that the large number of derelicts to my front were going to make identification of the enemy very difficult and that they would certainly give him opportunities for concealment. At last I can see the bursts of our shells – though, as yet, no targets for me. Then, away on my right front – range about 2,000 yards – appear three black dots. Looking through my binoculars, I identify them as Pzkw IIIs or IVs: not much for me to worry about as we have friends on that flank. But now to my front and in the vicinity of the derelicts tall shadowy shapes are moving. They look fantastic in the haze: I think they are probably guns, but are they in range for me? A ranging shot from my [side sponson-mounted]'75' will decide that, so down over the intercom go the orders to my gunner, '75 [load with] HE – enemy transport to our front – range 3,000 [yards] – one round fire.'

'The shell seems to take hours to get to its objective – in reality, it takes some six seconds for my gun to sling a shell 3,000 yards. Our burst is well short of the enemy, so for the present I will have to leave that target to the field guns. Unfortunately though, they just happen to be engaged elsewhere. This is going to be a very big party. By now shells are falling pretty thick and fast around us as the enemy batteries get our range but, so far, all his stuff is HE which we have learnt to treat with contempt.

'Away to my extreme left there is a sudden terrific barrage amongst the light tanks which are giving us 'Protection Left'. They will obviously not be able to take that for very long. It means, too, that Jerry has got quite a lot of guns with his tanks. Except for the shelling things are pretty quiet in our sector but I learn from the wireless that those friends on our right are having a good shoot, even though they appear to be outnumbered. Next, away to my left front definite shapes are becoming visible. Tracers from AP shot are whizzing about: shots are tearing up the ground in front and on both sides of my tank: others are sizzling over my head: God knows where they are landing. But this is no time for admiring the view. At last I can get a shoot of my own in! Visibility for us is very bad, though we must stand out nicely for Jerry who has the setting sun behind him. His machine-guns are adding to the racket. Evidently he is trying to make us keep our heads inside the turrets: he won't succeed at that game though.

'But the left flank is having trouble. It is being forced back by the enemy fire power. That's pretty ugly for us, too, as it means that Jerry will soon be able to enfilade us with flanking fire. We can't move over to help our friends because by now we have quite enough on our hands dealing with the enemy to our front. God! There must be about 80 or 90 of them! Brother Boche is trying to concentrate his fire on both our flanks. If he succeeds in forcing our 'Protection

Left' back, we also will have to fall back to keep the line straight and – even more important – to prevent their guns getting at the vulnerable, thinner, side armour on our *Grants.*

'Now all hell is being let loose. Off to my right two tanks are blazing, with great columns of black smoke going up to show their petrol tanks have already blown up. Hope the crews are safe. But we are not the only ones who are 'keeping the home fires burning': At least three Panzers are burning in the Jerry lines. All this time our Gunner FOO has been out there but now he has been spotted and will catch it if he doesn't move pretty quickly. At last he does move but only very slowly, about 500 yards further out of danger's way.

'An HE lands and seems to explode smack under my tank. I wonder if it has broken a track, so I reverse about three yards to find out. All is well. Then – wham! – definitely an AP hitting my tank on the side. It must have been a present from the Panzers who have driven our left flank back. If I turn my tank to face them, then the blighters to my front will be able to shoot me up. Inevitably now we must withdraw to keep line and so we do, reversing very, very slowly. This seems to be the signal for every gun in the Afrika Korps to open up – everything comes at us, AP, HE, even smoke! As we reverse, so he advances: with his superior numbers, he's not going to give us any time to re-form. To my left, one of our crews has baled out of a burning tank and Jerry is trying to get them with HE and machine-gun fire. A *Honey* dashes forward and picks up four men even as the turret is blown sky-high by the exploding ammunition inside it. There were six men in that crew – only four baled out.

'We halt again and prepare to make another stand but ammunition is running low and it's impossible to replenish with this barrage beating down on us. Now my Troop Commander's tank is reversing back – have I missed something? No. He is signalling me to conform and, after reversing for about 200 yards, he gets out carrying the cleaning rod. He must have an empty case stuck in the breech and pluckily he is dismounting to try to push it out from the muzzle end. He evidently succeeds because, when I look again he is back on my left. Good: we certainly need every gun!

'We are being forced to reverse again: the sun is sinking in a most appropriate burst of red flame. Visibility for us, with that glare straight in our eyes, is very bad indeed. If only we can hold out a little longer, the coming darkness will allow us to re-form but I have to use my ammunition very sparingly now. Our Gunners must be firing their 25-pounders at very short range. Later I heard that their last rounds were fired at only 800 yards. Fine fellows the RHA! We are still reversing and I am only able to fire my [top turret-mounted] 37mm gun, though there isn't much hope of penetrating Jerry's hide with it. Nevertheless, we have learnt from previous 'meetings' that to keep firing anything at him, even if you don't do him any damage, makes him stop a bit and think. As it gets darker we are able to rally round, protected by our Anti-tank guns, and withdraw a few miles to replenish. By the time we have all filled up with petrol and ammunition it is quite dark. In the distance the burning tanks, British and German, light up the battlefield with their funeral pyres. It is now too late for any more fighting but not too soon for a few hours rest!'

That is not quite the end of the Bing Coller story. Another incident took place 'somewhere in the Desert' only a few weeks later. Bing did not recount it but his local Bristol paper did. This is what the BRISTOL EVENING POST had to say under the heading BRISTOL HERO IGNORED NAZI ADVANCE, 'Sergeant Leonard Coller (26) of 67 High St., Easton, Bristol, coolly exposed himself to the advancing German tanks in Libya and extinguished a fire in his own tank started by a direct hit. He later continued to engage the enemy. As already announced in the EVENING POST he has received the Military Medal for his gallantry. The official citation says: 'On the morning of 16th July the unit was engaged in a sharp tank-v-tank battle on the Ruweisat Ridge. Sgt Coller was commanding a tank in 'C' Squadron. During the action the front of his tank received a direct hit by a HE shell. Three of the crew were wounded. Some kit on the front of the tank and the canvas muzzle cover of the 75mm gun caught fire. Sgt Coller then showed the very highest standard of coolness and courage. In spite of being in battle line and being engaged by on-coming tanks, which were firing both AP and HE, he dismounted and, standing in front of his tank, by use of the fire extinguisher, got the fire under control.

''He then withdrew his tank to where the battalion had taken up a new battle line and continued to engage the enemy. The enemy were beaten back. This very brave deed undoubtedly saved the tank and, as every tank in the line was of the utmost value in the engagement when the enemy had the initial surprise, this NCO's magnificent example was worthy of the highest praise'.'

Len Coller is always at pains to point out that the Editor of the BRISTOL EVENING POST, in choosing the words 'coolly exposed himself', did not, in 1942, mean quite what he would have meant today! Now such an action might have meant the appearance of Len's name in the Sex Offenders List: then they meant the inclusion of his name in the 'Honours and Awards' columns of the LONDON GAZETTE.

Keith Treasure had a different view of life in the Desert at this time. Keith had joined up in May 1941 and was theoretically trained as tank crew and assigned to the RTR. In theory only: he claims [rightly, although it sounds incredible nowadays] that he never touched a tank until he landed in the Middle East and was posted to 5RTR in Beni Yusef. Even after joining The Fifth, he did not immediately become a tank crew member but found himself in the Echelons. Nevertheless, this is what he has to say of his posting. 'Not enough words in the dictionary to say how very proud I am to have been a member of The Fifth. Comradeship from the top and through all Squadrons was tremendous. Not only 'was' but 'is' to this day. Being number five in a family of six – with three elder brothers to keep me in order – what I felt was not that I had joined a

Regiment but that I had a new family. When I was called up, I was a very junior Technical Assistant with Blackpool Corporation Transport. This stood me in good stead. My job with The Fifth was always Transport – in due course becoming Transport Sergeant for the Regiment.

'With the Regiment I found myself, to start with, co-driving a 3-ton Chevrolet wagon with some 1,000 gallons of high-octane petrol on board. The other driver was 'Titch' Mellor. In March, April and May, he and I alternated between the Chevvy and training in the tanks. I can't remember where 'Titch' went but I found myself in charge of one 3-tonner with L/Cpl Jimmy Trousdale (who had a Long Service and Good Conduct Medal[23] and a six or seven inch waxed moustache). When Rommel came our way on 27th May and everything and everybody scarpered in all directions due to unexpected AP and HE coming from *their* direction, there was L/Cpl Jimmy T, standing on the running board, directing me down a blind escarpment, through a minefield until we ended up somewhere between el Adem and Tobruk. The following day we 'found' The Fifth again, having been posted as missing! During the following weeks there was only one word for it – chaos! Not the best of conditions when driving around in a wagon with a highly lethal load.

'When what was left of 5RTR had returned to base for re-equipping etc, I didn't return with them. A fellow Trooper – one 'Ace' Cornwall – of 'A' Squadron was missing at the time and I was chosen (if that is the word for it) to replace him with an 'expedition' under the command of Major Dickie Ward. Only he knew where and what the expedition was all about – at least, we hoped he did. We thought it was some sort of rear guard action but it mostly consisted of harrowing night marches, nose-to-tail. Blessed be he that can navigate by the stars. One night our column was sandwiched between two German columns, all travelling in the same direction. I suppose 'they' each thought that 'we' were their parallel column. After lying doggo for a long period, with instructions not to strike a light or make a sound on pain of instant death or worse, we eventually managed to skedaddle pretty sharpish.

'Around that time I celebrated my 21st birthday – with a tin of 'meat and veg' between two of us and a water bottle with only a few drops left in it. Eventually I returned to 'C' Squadron. All the SQMS (I think it was 'Knocker' Knight) had to say when I reported for some new kit was 'An' where've you bin, then?' He didn't even wait for an answer! It was all a rough old do. We lost our CO [this was Colonel Uniacke] and I lost a lot of members of my new family. Great chaps all of them.

'A place named 'Stuka Valley' sticks in my mind[24]. Not a nice place to be at certain times of day and that's when I always seemed to be there!'

To return for a moment to Titch Maple's account. After briefly recording that, 'Captain Doyle was awarded the MC and I was awarded the MM[25]. On return to Cairo I was promoted Lance Corporal', Titch casually mentions that he was wounded. However, the main burden of this part of his account concerns the difficulties of navigation in the Desert. As driver of the 'B'

Squadron navigator's tank he undoubtedly knew something of the problem.

His *Honey* had a compass fitted between the driver's legs [so convenient for the crew commander who actually had to do the navigating and was accommodated in the turret!]. 'This was very inaccurate and most of the navigation was done off the tank and with a hand-held compass. The business of navigating was not just a nightmare for the tank crews, in many ways it was worse for the echelon lorries as the smallest error could mean that the replenishments ended up not in their own side's leaguer but in the enemy's. The only consolation was that it happened to both sides.'

Titch commented on the rapid and unpredictable changes in temperature and climate. Scorching days followed by bitter cold nights; blazing sun followed by torrential rainstorms. These storms, as Titch philosophically points out, could be tiresome when the crews were nearly drowned while sleeping alongside their tanks in the bottom of a wadi[26]. After a few nights like that the troops were not amused by an Army Order stating that anyone suffering from sunburn would be charged with having a self-inflicted wound.

However – and, as a driver, Ron Maple knew what he was talking about – it was not only the crews that were suffering. Whoever designed the American *'General'* range of tanks – *Stuarts, Lees, Grants* and *Shermans* – any more than the British tank designers – never envisaged that they would be used to fight a war in a desert. Wear and tear on the tracks and the engines was appalling. Whenever possible, which wasn't often, maintenance halts were made at hourly intervals. This frequently meant covering only 10 or 12 miles – sometimes less – but there was always something to be done to keep the tanks going for the next hour or two.

The final break-down of a tank was a bitter blow to its crew. Often, in spite of the best efforts of the LAD fitters, the tank had to be abandoned. This entailed off-loading all the ammunition, the wireless set, the rations and water, the crew's kit and dumping it all into a truck or, if none was available, into the already over-loaded fitters' wagons. On one occasion though, the loss of his tank proved to have compensations for Titch. On reaching their temporary base, the crew picked up a spare three-tonner and an Italian lorry, and headed back to where they thought the Regiment was. They didn't find the unit but they did find an abandoned NAAFI which some Arabs were in the process of looting. Having seen these gentry off, they proceeded to load the lorries with all the food and cigarettes they could get on board. However, the clutch on the Eyetie lorry wasn't up to the job and started slipping. Titch set his passenger to dribbling sand through the top of the clutch cover. They made it back to the unit!

All the personal accounts of this period have emphasised the prevailing chaos, the frustration of not knowing what was happening and the near-despair at the attrition which the Regiment was suffering without, in real terms, anything to show for it. This is reflected in the War Diary, starting with the record for 1st June 1942 and dealing with some of the ground already covered.

On Monday, 1st June The Fifth was on one hour's notice to move at 0800 hrs but at 1300 hrs this situation was changed by orders for a move to take up battle positions to repulse an attack from a force of 120 enemy tanks in the area of Acroma. At 1415 hrs, the Regiment had moved and at 1600 hrs was in its battle position. Nothing further, however, happened that day. The Regiment broke leaguer at 0530 hrs on the 2nd, being put on five minutes' notice to move at 0545 hrs. At 0645 hrs there was a move to a new position and at 1030 hrs there was a report from Brigade that enemy tanks had been sighted. 'A' Squadron was sent on patrol but could see nothing due to poor visibility. At 1500 hrs Lt Lyon-Williams reported that he had three German POWs 'but no further reports from him and he did not return'.

At 1700 hrs, some enemy guns were located and the Battalion Group was ordered to move out to engage them. Almost simultaneously, a group of vehicles – quickly identified as enemy tanks – was sighted and the Battalion Group moved to engage this new target. This group proved to be some 25 tanks, attacking from the front and eight or ten moving to attack the unit's right flank. Confining itself strictly to facts, the War Diary then states, 'Heavy engagement took place.' Later, the Diary records that enemy losses were put at 20 Pzkw IIIs and IVs, with some Mark III special tanks being seen. 'Own casualties – 9 *Grant* tanks. 3 *Honey* tanks. Also 4 *Honey* tanks evacuated. 2 *Grant* tanks evacuated.' But then one comes to 'the bottom line'. 'Bn strength – 8 *Stuart* Tanks. 1 *Grant* Tank. Own personnel casualties:- [*KIA*] CO Lt Col RDW Uniacke and 5 ORs. *Missing*: Lts Beckett, Lyon-Williams, GA Smith and 42 ORs. *Wounded*: Capt Adams and 8 ORs.'

On the following day (3rd June) Major Castle took over command of the Regiment which moved to a new position at 0800 hrs. In mid-afternoon 12 new *Grants* arrived and crews were reorganised, all hands setting to to make them battle-worthy. On 4th June, The Fifth took up a new position and had a sighting of enemy armour but no engagement with it. Reveille on 5th June was at 0400 hrs. This was to be the prelude to a Brigade assault on enemy positions: 5RTR was on the left flank and was not engaged until 1700 hrs when it put in an attack. The enemy withdrew from their position but counter-attacked The Fifth on both flanks, causing it to withdraw. When the unit leaguered at 1900 hrs the state of play was 3 or 4 enemy tanks destroyed; 3 *Grants* lost and 1 *Honey* evacuated. *Missing:* Lt Laing and 2/Lt Wilshaw and 5 ORs. *Wounded:* 2 ORs.

On 6th June what was left of the unit took up observation positions but was not engaged. On the 7th The Fifth came under temporary command of 22nd Armoured Brigade, was heavily shelled at 1700 hrs and withdrew into leaguer at last light . . . without replenishments. The unit was ordered to return to 4th Arm Bde but 22nd Arm Bde ordered the unit to stay where it was! By 1730 hrs The Fifth was back where it belonged and amalgamated with 3RTR under Major Castle's command. Late on 8th June 3/5RTR became part of a mixed force with a Company of KRRC and an RHA Battery, whose purpose was to try to relieve the pressure on the beleaguered Free French in Bir Hacheim. On the 9th this mixed force was in contact with an enemy position but was unable to attack due to the appalling visibility which obscured the position of the heavy guns which were pinning the *Grants* down. At 1900 hrs, orders came for the mixed force to co-operate with 7th Motor Brigade in making a demonstration[27]. It seemed that this demonstration was only partly successful. The unidentified vehicles with which they came in contact withdrew but the guns which were supporting them stayed in position.

The 'demonstrators' did not get their heads down until 0100 hrs on the morning of 10th June and then only had five hours' rest before they broke leaguer to replenish from B2 Echelon. Then followed another five hours of unease and uncertainty, as no movement was possible before 0950 hrs, due to heavy ground mist. During the day, the Group staged another demonstration and got fired on for their trouble, luckily without material damage. From 1100 hrs to 1700 hrs the Group and the enemy engaged in inconclusive skirmishes. At 1730 hrs orders came through that the Group was to form part of a decoy column designed to draw the enemy away from Bir Hacheim, from which the Free French were due to break out at midnight. This order suffered an all-too-common fate: it was cancelled. After leaguering overnight and replenishing at sparrow fart[28], the Group was again unable to move until 0930 hrs, due to the ground mist. When it did move, it was to come under direct 7th Armoured Divisional orders and to take up a defensive position against an attack which did not materialise. At 1730 hrs, 3/5RTR, less 'A' Squadron, which stayed with Seventh Armoured, was returned to 4th Armoured Brigade. In spite of much exhausting manoeuvring, there were no engagements on 11th June. 'Battalion strength' is recorded as being 22 Officers and 515 ORs. Nothing is said about tanks.

The 12th June saw another early start with 'A' Squadron returning to the unit . . . which, at 0930 hrs acquired a new Commanding Officer – Major (Temporary Lt Col) JP Archer-Shee of X Royal Hussars. According to the War Diary, Colonel Archer-Shee had only been in command for 15 minutes before 3/5RTR was in action. The action, which lasted until 1630 hrs, was against a mixed force of tanks and 88mm guns. There were no losses but, when the order came to withdraw, the enemy followed close on the Group's heels. This order appeared unnecessary, as considerable chaos, if not damage, was being caused in the enemy ranks. 'Some doubt as to the reason for this withdrawal was felt,' the War Diarist noted. At 1730 hrs, the withdrawal was halted, to allow other units to fall back.

As The Fifth later learnt, these orders to fall back were part of the 'Strategic Withdrawal' of the whole of the Eighth Army. The withdrawal continued on the 13th when the 4th Armoured Brigade formed part of a mixed force that was ordered to 'demonstrate' in the Knightsbridge area to relieve pressure on the Guards Brigade which was still holding the 'box' there. Throughout 13th and 14th June, these 'demonstrations' turned into intermittent, sharp, encounters with enemy armour. On 14/15th June, 3/5RTR moved through the night to yet another new position.

However, not all movement was towards the Egyptian border. On 16th June the unit was back in the area of Sidi Rezegh and the *Grants* were again engaged with enemy armour. On the 17th, the unit broke leaguer at first light and spent most of the day carrying out maintenance or resting. At 1745 hrs, B Battery 1 RHA, who were in advanced positions, reported the arrival of enemy tanks. Once again, the *Grant* squadrons moved out to the attack. By 1900 hrs, their position was hopeless: the enemy was in overwhelming numbers and the unit had 'suffered some losses'. Brigade ordered a withdrawal. Effectively this was the end of the Regiment's part in the campaign. On 18th June what was left of 3/5RTR moved again. On the 19th, 'the remaining fit tanks were handed over to other units within the Brigade and Bn awaited orders to move east the following morning.' On 20th June the unit crossed the Egyptian border and formed harbour, from which they sent out patrols on the 21st: patrols which had nothing to report. Between the 22nd and the 24th 3/5RTR had worked its way to a position 15 miles south of Mersa Matruh. By 27th June the unit was in the el Imayid staging camp. From the 28th to the 30th there was leave for some of the men.

Charlie Bull wrote home at this time. After lamenting the lack of fruit in the Desert after its cheap and easy availability in Cairo, he wrote graphically of the sand. 'I'm sitting inside the tank writing this as it is a bit windy outside. It's cooler now than what it was two months ago. The only trouble in the desert is that you get those dust storms sometimes. That is when it tries you. The sand gets everywhere no matter where you go. If you wear goggles, it still comes through. Gets in your food too, so you eat it, drink it and sleep in it. It's certainly a tough life in the desert. No matter were you go there's always millions of flies, add a few scorpions and snakes, not forgetting the desert rats and you can imagine how nice it is.

'I think we are getting some pay today, though it's not much good as it is only now and again we can buy anything. A lorry went into Mersa Matruh yesterday and came back with some stuff but the sugar has been cut down before we could get as much as we could afford, at about 3d a lb, but this time they couldn't get any, so we shall have to go easy on the tea now.

'We've got plenty of tea and milk, we have been brewing up 4 or 5 times a day, but I don't like tea without sugar. We have about 5lb of sugar but that is emergency rations but I'm afraid the bag will develop a leak very soon!'

It was not surprising that Charlie Bull complained about the lack of sugar: he had been brought up in the shadow of the Nestlé condensed milk factory in Tutbury, Staffordshire, where his father was a sugar boiler. Interestingly, Bull goes on to say that he had been a tank commander for two months and that, as he had completed eight years 'colour service', he was being paid another 3d a day. This made his pay up to £2.1s.0d a week [approximately £80 nowadays]. He went on to ponder what to do after the war. '.. whether to get married or buy a car. I don't know which is best.' He had a macabre sense of humour: in another letter, written near Christmas, he speculated on the Regiment's Christmas fare. 'Probably bully stew but I saw a dead camel yesterday a few miles down the road, so it might be a nice big steak.'

That there was another aspect of life in the Desert emerges from a book, published in 1944, entitled PRISONER FROM ALAMEIN[29]. This is by Brian Stone who, according to his Preface, found that, 'For a young man war was usually a series of exciting and possibly pleasant adventures, and so it was with me. France and a year and a half in the Desert with the Fifth Battalion Royal Tank Regiment gave me much excitement and pleasure.'

Brian Stone's own particular interpretation of 'pleasant' and 'pleasure' will emerge in the next chapter.

The first mention in the War Diary of 2/Lt BE Stone is not with the Regiment in France but is on 18th May 1941 when he was reported as being 'admitted to hospital and posted to X (II) List and struck off strength.' He re-appeared on 20th June 1941, not from hospital but after completing liaison duties with Brigade.

However the book gives some of his earlier history. Brian Stone (after being a near-contemporary at Taunton School with Tom Chesterfield) joined the Westminster Dragoons as a TA Trooper, was commissioned and posted to 5RTR in March 1940. He went with the Regiment to France and was still with The Fifth when it arrived in Egypt.

Although PRISONER FROM ALAMEIN mainly tells the story of his experiences as a POW, Brian includes a long retrospective chapter which covers the period from March through to June 1942. Much of what he records, in terms of the unit's engagements, is covered by existing accounts: much, however, is new and is recalled in an individual and often amusing manner. What follows is taken from his book.

For a start, Brian Stone and Titch Maple appear to be unique in commenting on one of the Desert's most surprising aspects. Spring, 'when the Desert shall rejoice and blossom as the rose'[30]. At the end of March, with the Regiment 20 miles South of Capuzzo, both Brian and Titch recorded a week of heavy rain which caused the Desert to be mantled with a marvellous profusion of grasses and flowers, surviving in every shallow depression for weeks after the rain had ceased. Even when these 'huge pastoral stretches' were crossed and recrossed by the tracks of the unit's new *Grants*, it was still possible to smell the flowers.

But this rural idyll never lasted long. At the back of every mind was the ever-present fact of war. There was only one question, really: who would be the first to start it going again? Us or them? Could the DAK be ready so soon after the last show? Surely not. But then . . . could our side be?

By April the flowers were fading, only blooming briefly in the dew of night.

To make up for that, those same nights were becoming more and more enlivened by the distant patterns of tracer as the respective artillerymen exchanged compliments. The days were becoming hotter: the realities of life in the Desert were becoming more and more pressing.

One of the harshest realities of Desert warfare, Brian reminded his readers in the UK, was lack of water. Fortunately for his Squadron – which was 'A' – one of the transport drivers had an uncanny 'nose' for water, making him a sort of long-range water diviner. This was Corporal Kershaw who had also an uncanny sense of direction and an ability to drive in straight lines across uncharted tracts of Desert. With a primitive compass, his 'nose' and a reluctant passenger, Cpl Kershaw would set off early in the morning in his three-tonner laden with empty captured jerricans and return nearly every evening with them full. Not, by any means, always full of drinkable water but usually with a bigger and better supply than that available elsewhere. Any evening that Cpl Kershaw returned empty-canned, saw him glum of countenance and off even earlier and ever more determined the following morning.

It was a rule [more often honoured in the breach than the observance] that any newly discovered sources of water should immediately be reported to Brigade. One day Kershaw discovered a well of quite unsurpassed excellence: a well known only to him and quite capable of supplying the whole Regiment. The well was soon named after him. The Regiment rejoiced but, as Regiments do, The Fifth moved on: it would nevertheless be nice, Brian Stone remarked, to think of subsequent generations of Bedouin or Senussi, miles from nowhere, watering their weary camels at Bir-el-Qershau!

PRISONER FROM ALAMEIN contains a heart-felt description of the Khamseen. Brian comments on one peculiar aspect: although, at its peak, it brought all the fighting – indeed, all activity – to a standstill, the southerly Khamseen did not pick up as much dust and sand as the prevailing westerly winds at gale-force level. The worst feature of the Khamseen was its paralysing heat: an unexpected – but welcome – feature of the countervailing storm which blew the Khamseen away was the clear air which it left, albeit fleetingly, in its wake.

One of the chief aspects of this period of waiting, Brian found, was the unprecedented efficiency of the 'Q' department. Everyone from the Quartermaster General in Cairo down to the Storeman in the Squadron Quartermaster's Stores seemed to have nothing better to do than issue lavish rations and other creature comforts.

For all the generosity of the 'Q' Department, the months of April and May 1942 were months of serious and realistic training with the new *Grant* tanks. Training interspersed with stand-to orders and false alarms: also interspersed with entertainment and relaxation. It used to be said of the British Army that it only needed two Other Ranks and a football to produce two Regimental Football Teams and a Regimental Sports Officer! The Fifth was no exception but sometimes there were more enterprising events than Desert football with tanks for goal posts.

One such event appears to have been an 'A' Squadron 'gymkhana'. This had nothing to do with horses but included an inter-troop scavenging hunt, judged on the variety and originality of the objects collected in the forty-eight hours preceding the judging – which was the Squadron Commander's privilege. The troop that won this particular 'hunt' included a live rabbit[31], a prime selection of the best Egyptian 'feelthy pictures' and 'an article of ATS personal issue attire'!

So liberal were the rations at one stage that another gymkhana included a 'bully beef eating contest'. Probably, however, the most popular event of all, for the spectating troops, if not for the participating officers, was a wheel changing contest for teams of subalterns. This had to be carried out in the heat of day on a three ton lorry, without a jack and against the clock!

Not surprisingly, when there was an alcohol issue – in whatever form – there was a party. One of the benefits of such parties was the way they fostered friendships. The intimate relationship of crew members has already been mentioned: Brian Stone found that such parties, with the inevitable 'letting down of hair', enabled all ranks to get to know one another better. Certainly the 'A' Squadron officers felt they could hardly live all their lives in awe of their Squadron Commander after seeing him swinging by one arm from the lorry superstructure [which served as the Officers Mess], stamping his feet – slightly out of time with the music – and joining raucously in the choruses of bawdy songs!

But Dickie Ward's exuberance was not confined to his musical repertoire: he had a great deal of energy left for welding his Squadron into as perfect a fighting machine as limitations on practice ammunition and training mileage would allow. These limitations challenged the officers to devise schemes to entertain their men. Possibly the greatest enemy of Service morale is boredom and the Desert could provide plenty of that if it were not diligently kept at bay. 5RTR personnel became surprisingly proficient in French, basic Arabic and interpreting enemy documents, to say nothing of acquiring a vast amount of frivolous general knowledge, such as the fact that Nell Gwyn was King Charles II's favourite mistress and the mother of the first Duke of St Albans.

The CO himself, Robbie Uniacke, established prizes for limericks in which the first line was to end with the name of some well-known, but by no means well-loved, Desert landmarks. No prizes were awarded: Rommel unsportingly started the war again before the date-line was reached. Colonel Uniacke also instituted bigger and better gymkhanas. The first Regimental one included a long-distance spitting competition: an event which, Brian Stone remarked, 'brought to light several people who had never before shone in Regimental sporting activities'. Apart from a fancy dress parade (a Gandhi in deep meditation, a ranting Hitler, an Arab street vendor of Egyptian 'exotica' – a reader of Brian's book in 1944 would be expected privately to substitute 'erotica' – two seductive young offerings from a well known Cairo establishment [Out Of Bounds To Troops] and a Luftwaffe Officer complete with a genuine Iron Cross), the *pièce de résistance* was an event 'for loud-voiced private soldiers and officers with a good sense of direction'.

This simple and harmless diversion consisted of an obstacle course to be negotiated by the officers on the shouted instructions of the private soldiers. The officers, carefully blind-folded, stood at the start line; the private soldiers stood at the finishing line. On the word 'Go!', under cover of the troops' enthusiastic yells of encouragement, the obstacles were deftly removed. Subsequent orders for the circumnavigation of the non-existent obstacles by the hapless officers were left up to the fertile imaginations of the loud-voiced private soldiers. When, that is, they could be heard above the roars of laughter. It is not true, as the story went after the event, that one officer was last seen heading for the skyline, sent into the setting sun by the instructions of his brass-lunged tank driver.

The Regiment was reminded that the war still had its serious side by the capture of a German staff officer. He proved to be 'a hectoring, unpleasant fellow' but not proof against proof spirits. In his cups he revealed some useful information about the war on the Russian Front, from which he had just been transferred, and gave, with the voice of authority, the date for Rommel's next offensive. The 24th May.

To what extent this information made GHQ revise their idea that 9th June was the probable date is not known, The captured officer's forecast was pretty near the truth: Rommel launched his attack on 27th May.

In these reminiscent chapters, Brian's is the authentic voice of the Fifth Royal Tank Regiment speaking . . . but it does not all make pleasant reading.

'On the day Divisional Headquarters was over-run.' Brian wrote, 'I was up with Brigade HQ with a detail of petrol and ammunition lorries and we had to sit up on top of a bare escarpment for two hours before the transport was sent on down. On the way down a shell landed on the lorry nearest to me. I went over and heaved out the two men, who were hit so severely that their bones crunched when I lifted them, but the lorry itself was completely unharmed and was driven down the hill with its load of ammunition by another of the lads (a batman by profession) who was with me in the car. At the bottom of the hill, the two men died and we put them in an old slit trench and covered them with earth, saluting them in the absence of a padre, and getting an exact location so that they could be buried properly later on. I did not like throwing earth on their faces.'

Again, he wrote, 'On the third day the Brigade was sent round to the South side of the 'Cauldron' and the Regiment took over a position, sitting opposite a well dug-in Jerry position. After a brief reconnaissance the Colonel decided to attack at once, although the CO of the unit we took over from told him it was madness. The battle which followed was a demonstration of the efficiency and power of the Regiment. Twenty guns – much more powerful than anything we had on the tanks – were knocked out for the loss of three tanks.

The best performance of a day of high valour was that of the driver of one of the Troop officers. When they were charging an '88', the gun fired at them from about 100 yards range, hitting the turret, putting the crew out of action and killing the crew commander. Finding himself with no instructions from his commander, the driver simply accelerated and ran over the gun with its ten or eleven man crew.'

Brian gives an account of the time that Dickie Ward was wounded by 'metal splash'. Shortly after he baled out he was joined by the Adjutant, 'Stinker' Adams, who had a flesh wound in the neck. The best policy on these occasions was often to lie low and wait to see what happened next. Major Ward and Captain Adams adopted this policy but were found by a German who ordered them off to the POW collecting point, telling them to wait until medical assistance arrived. However, neither Major nor Adjutant was wearing badges of rank and, when the German doctor arrived, it was a case of Officers and NCOs first, private soldiers last. Dickie Ward and Stinker Adams found themselves among the rank and file and discovered there were advantages in this loss of rank. No-one paid much attention to them, so they did not pay much attention to what they were told to do and simply 'sloped off', lying up over-night (watching the Germans blowing up their damaged tanks) and rejoining the unit next day.

Nobody who ever knew Padre Warner spoke of him with anything but admiration: Brian Stone was no exception. In the thick of the fighting – any fighting, anywhere – the Padre's frail, wooden-bodied staff car could be seen, touring the battlefield to enable Padre Warner to pick up men he found left on the ground. He was, so he said, only once defeated. He encountered two men who, although physically uninjured, were so 'shell shocked' that they refused to be helped, insisting that they were better off where they were. What happened to them in the end, Padre Warner never knew.

The fate of being taken prisoner was, quite naturally, something to be avoided. And there were some incredible avoidances. Immediately after Bir Hacheim fell, the Germans bit off rather more captured transport than they could chew. In their 'bag' was a column from The Fifth which included Major Freddie Coombes, who had no ambition to spend the rest of the war as a POW. As column commander, he was put through interrogation at the HQ of the 90th Light Panzer Division. Then, by the simple process of removing his crowns, one captured Major became just another Trooper and mixed with a lorry load of his men. The Germans searched vainly for the missing Major among the fifteen swaddies waiting in a lorry guarded by a large and aggressive Boche private soldier. At the critical moment, the small-sized 'Trooper' Coombes manoeuvred himself into a tactical position in front of the guard and kicked him hard where a man least likes to be kicked. With the guard out of action, Freddie Coombes leapt into the lorry and drove off at speed. The Germans opened fire with everything they had and wounded two men but they did not prevent the lorry from escaping back to the unit.

That was not the only lorry-load which escaped as the result of initiative and courage. Sergeant Humphries, the Battalion Transport Sergeant, and his driver, Trooper Johnson, also won their share of glory. They had been disarmed and were standing near their lorry which was being guarded by two armed Germans. The Germans beckoned them over. A nod of understanding was exchanged between Humphries and Johnson. They obeyed the order but Humphries went round one side of the lorry and Johnson went round the other. As they converged they leapt on their guards. One guard's rifle went off harmlessly as Johnson knocked him out. Humphries' opponent was bigger than the Sergeant and he was getting the better of the fray until Johnson joined in and helped to over-power him. They decided that taking a prisoner was better than being taken prisoner, so they threw the larger of the pair in the back of the lorry. Sergeant Humphries drove off with Johnson in the back, keeping the prisoner quiet with the aid of a heavy spanner.

There were, fortunately, many others who escaped that night without quite so much drama, because the Germans 'did a flap' and pulled out in double-quick time without rounding up all the prisoners. Even so, many who had chosen the quiet life of clerks, cooks and storemen found, in those twenty-four hours, that life in the Desert was full of adventure

Brian Stone's book shows that the man he admired most was his driver, Ryder, who 'embodied the virtues both of saint and soldier.' In 1941 Ryder was already in his late thirties, married and with four children. No-one would have thought the worse of Ryder if he had arranged to be relegated (along with the other older, married men with families to support) to the transport echelons or even farther back. Not for Ryder: he was in this war to fight: the only place to do that was in a tank and driving was his trade and pride. He had driven a tank in every action in which the Regiment had been engaged: driven it and maintained it. He was always the last to finish work and the first to be ready for the new day's assignments. He saw to it that his – and the crew's – mess kit was clean . . . and ready for the char he could produce quicker than anyone else in the Squadron. As a driver, Ryder had a genius for not merely obeying orders promptly but for anticipating them. In action or out, he never missed a gear and always selected the right one: he was able to pick out the best route before he was even told where to go. Ryder was appreciated not just by Stone. His nick-name 'Pop' was not a cheeky reference to his years, it was a mark of respect for a man who was an often-needed 'father' to the crew.

THE OTHER SIDE

The myths surrounding Rommel and his success in North Africa may have been enough to make him a hero in his homeland and a bogey-man to the Allied commanders but it did not make him universally popular with the High Command in Berlin. Probably the man who placed least value on Rommel was Colonel-General

Franz Halder, at the time of the Desert War, Chief of the Army General Staff.

Halder scorned any plan to turn the Mediterranean into a major theatre of war and dismissed any argument in favour of capturing Egypt and the Suez Canal. Perhaps this blinkered vision was not altogether surprising in a man who opposed von Manstein's brilliantly successful plan for the invasion of France through the Ardennes in 1940.

Rommel probably made matters worse for himself. When the question arose of reinforcing the Italian position in Lybia by appointing him and diverting Panzer units to North Africa, Halder scathingly asked Rommel, 'Even if we had such forces to spare, how would you supply and feed them?' To this Rommel replied, 'That is your problem: not mine!' Not a good answer from a man who had already referred to his superior officer (Halder was seven years older and ten years senior to Rommel) as a 'Dummkopf' *and publicly asked what Halder had ever done in two wars but sit on his arse in an office.*

Tarred with the same brush as Halder were Field Marshal Wilhelm Keitel (who, in Hitler's opinion 'had the brains of a cinema usher') and General Alfred Jodl (who was said to have had brains but never to have used them). These three men were – fortunately for the Allies – entrenched at Headquarters and, however popular Rommel may have been with Hitler and the German people, were in a position to ensure that North Africa did not, until too late, escalate into a major front.

Against this unpromising background, it is not surprising that, in 1942, Rommel had two German Divisions in North Africa whereas the Generals on the Russian Front had some two hundred.

Rommel's campaigns perhaps, therefore, should be seen as never having had any serious chance of ultimate success. The Allied High Command in Cairo (as did Churchill and the CIGS in London) saw the defence of Egypt as vital to the whole war effort. That Rommel effectively made the whole North African campaign an open running sore and a continuous drain on Allied resources is enormously to his credit.

On the ground, tactically, the Afrika Korps benefited from Rommel's leadership. In the round, strategically, the German High Command did not. Rommel – to take one example – saw the immense importance of Tobruk. Berlin thought otherwise. When Rommel was initially repulsed by the Australians, he did not get the reinforcements he so desperately needed: instead, he got a reprimand.

Just how important to the Desert War Rommel was considered to be by the nerve centre in London can be judged by the fact that, in November 1941, the British launched a Commando raid on his Headquarters at Beda Littoria near Cyrene. The purpose of the raid was, quite explicitly, to capture or kill Erwin Rommel. The raid proved abortive. The building attacked was not, in reality, Rommel's Headquarters but that of his 'Q' Staff. The Desert Fox had his lair in the Desert near Derna. And, anyway, on the night in question, Rommel was in Rome

Without in any way belittling the courage and fortitude of the Eighth Army under appalling conditions, what happened in the summer of 1942 was inevitable and Rommel almost certainly knew it. He advanced, daily stretching his lines of communication which – without the vital support which Berlin was denying him –

were becoming less and less elastic. He was becoming progressively more vulnerable to attack by land, sea and air. His men and his matériel were being steadily worn out. And he was well aware that, as he grew weaker, his enemy grew stronger.

THE WAR CHRONICLE

1942

January	06	'British Restaurants' instituted. Average meal price 1/- (5p but, say, £2.00 by present standards)
	12	Japanese captured Kuala Lumpur
	14	Russian troops recaptured Kirov
	15	Airey Neave DSO MC (later MP and murdered in the Palace of Westminster by the IRA) made first 'home run' from Colditz
	19	3,650 Allied troops captured at Tong Peng in Malaya
	29	First broadcast of 'Desert Island Discs'
	31	Siege of Singapore – from the landward side – started
February	09	Soap rationed in UK
	12	German warships *Gneisenau, Scharnhorst* and *Prinz Eugen* escaped from Brest
	14	Japanese captured Singapore
	15	Japanese soldiers bayoneted 150 bed-ridden patients to death in Singapore Military Hospital
	20	Australian mainland port of Darwin bombed by Japanese naval aircraft
	23	Mainland USA shelled. Japanese submarine attacked Santa Barbara in California
	25	Rift in Cabinet. Stafford Cripps, lately appointed Minister of Aircraft Production, severely criticised Bomber Harris over build-up of Bomber Command
March	01	HMS *Exeter,* (cruiser) sunk by Japanese Navy
	03	*Lancaster* bombers flew first operational mission
	09	Java fell to Japanese after capture of Rangoon
	11	HMS *Naiad* sunk by U-boat in Mediterranean – Introduction of 'national wheatmeal loaf' in UK
	28	U-boat pens at St Nazaire successfully raided by Royal Navy and Commandos
April	01	First Arctic convoy reached Murmansk

	06	Japanese aircraft bombed east coast of India in Bay of Bengal
	09	HMS *Hermes* (cruiser) sunk off Trincomalee (Ceylon [Sri Lanka])
		– Some 80,000 US and Filipino troops forced to surrender in Bataan
	14	Sharp increase in UK taxes on tobacco and alcohol
	15	Introduction of 'utility' clothing in UK
May	01	Japanese captured Mandalay, Burma
	02	HMS *Edinburgh* (cruiser) scuttled by Royal Navy, after crippling bomb damage
	04 to 09	The Battle of the Coral Sea (the 1939-45 War equivalent of the Battle of Jutland) left both US Navy and Japanese Imperial Fleet with heavy losses but with the moral victory going to the USN
	06	US garrison forced to surrender at Corregidor
	15	HMS *Trinidad* (cruiser) scuttled by Royal Navy, after crippling bomb damage
	31	*Mosquito* aircraft flew first operational sorties
		– First 1,000 bomber raid on Cologne
June	01	Japanese midget submarines attacked shipping in Sydney Harbour
	03	Japanese staged 'hit and run' raid on Alaska
	06	US Naval bombers, flying from aircraft carriers, sank a Japanese aircraft carrier off Midway Island
	08	Sydney Harbour shelled by Japanese submarines
	10	SS Stormtroops massacred all the inhabitants of the Czech village of Lidice in revenge for the assassination of 'the Hangman' Heydrich
	20	Japanese submarine shelled Vancouver Island
	21	. . . and the State of Oregon

NOTES

1 The Desert Fox. Just as both sides (so it is said) sang '*Roll out the Barrel*' and '*Lili Marlene*', so both sides called Erwin Rommel by this name. The Afrika Korps with whole-hearted, the Eighth Army with reluctant, admiration. An amusing story – quite likely to be true – relates that Rommel, during one of his lightning advances, was told by a junior Panzer commander that his unit was running out of petrol. 'Well,' replied Rommel. 'The British have plenty. Go and get some of theirs.'

2 Gazala Line. This ran from Gazala on the coast to Bir Hacheim, about 40 miles almost due south, and consisted of a belt of wire and minefields interspersed

with 'boxes' (of anything up to brigade strength and mixed arms). Militarily speaking, the Gazala Line was a better springboard for attack than a defensive position. The War Cabinet seems to have been unaware that this put the Eighth Army at a serious disadvantage. Nevertheless, faced with the situation in the Far East, the Mediterranean and in Russia, Churchill's buzz word at the time was 'Attack'

3 Major General Campbell. No-one can doubt 'Jock' Campbell's genius as a commander of the Desert 'flying columns' or his quite incredible personal courage – after all, the inscription on a Victoria Cross reads 'For Valour' – but there are, in retrospect, considerable doubts as to whether his approach to tank actions would have made him an altogether suitable commander for an Armoured Division whose antagonist was 'The Desert Fox'. A comparison between Rommel's approach to the tactical use of, and defence against, tanks and that of General Campbell, tends to the conclusion that it might well have been the Desert Rats who got the bloody nose in the ensuing scraps. Whether those doubts are right or wrong, the death of 'Jock' Campbell, the man, must be regarded as one of the war's pointless tragedies.

4 'A' Squadron. The reason 'A' Squadron was so frequently the first to make contact with the enemy goes back to Royal Tank Corps practice. 'A' Squadron was traditionally the 'light' squadron whose duties were reconnaissance and observation rather than engagement. Thus, Battle Orders frequently gave the Order of Advance as: 'A' Sqn < RHQ < 'B' Sqn and/or 'C' Sqn following next. When 5RTR acquired *Grants*, 'A' Sqn retained its lighter, faster *Crusaders* to continue this role. Later, with the introduction of a separate 'Recce Troop' and re-equipment with *Shermans* (even later, with *Cromwells*), this practice was abandoned and 'A' Squadron joined 'B' and 'C' as a 'Fighting Squadron'

5 The Sickle Plan. As to this, see the comments in Chapter I

6 Seventh Armoured Division HQ. As a result of General Campbell's death and General Lumsden's wounds, the Desert Rats had been taken over by Major General Frank Messervy at very short notice. Messervy had commanded the 4th Indian Division with distinction but he was not well up on tanks and tank warfare. His interpretation and giving of orders was consequently slow and not always sure. Partly as a result of this, 7 AD HQ was overrun. In addition to the GOC, the GSO I, II & III and the CRA were all captured. Frank Messervy's orders may have been slow but his wits certainly were not. When the HQ was overrun he was caught 'at his ablutions' and out of uniform. He made the most of this and managed to persuade his captors that he was only an elderly batman ('You're a bit old for this, aren't you?' his interrogator asked. 'Yes,' Messervy replied. 'A Reservist: they didn't ought to of called me up.') and, of course, had no idea where the General was. As a result, Messervy was not properly guarded. Later, during the night, he slipped off with his three GSOs and made his way on foot back to the British lines and to the command of the Division

7 The Sharpshooters. The County of London Yeomanry: in this case, 3 CLY.

8 Poor old Pave. This was Corporal Pavely, also of 'C' Squadron

9 Gunner: loader. These would have been the gunner and loader of the 75mm main gun mounted in the side sponson in the hull above Jake and to his right.

10 Cliff. Sergeant Clifford Fishwick – who subsequently lost a leg at Villers-Bocage, in Normandy.

11 Snowy. Sergeant 'Snowy' (any girl would have envied his blond locks!) Harris. He recovered from this incident and survived, only to be killed in Germany, like Jake, about three weeks from the end of the war.

12 When the lorry started. As noted earlier, defensive leaguers were always vulnerable to air attack and artillery bombardment. Standing Orders – and the men's automatic reactions to such attacks – were to disperse immediately.
13 The CO. This was Lieutenant Colonel RDW 'Robbie' Uniacke who was killed on 22nd June 1942.
14 Wag Fry and Topper. 'Wag' was Sergeant Fry, one of three brothers who all served in the RTR. 'Topper' was Sergeant Brown.
15 Dingo. This was a scout car, a lightly-armoured four-wheel-drive vehicle. It was not unusual to find the Squadron dingo in close attendance on the Squadron Commander, for him to use in just such emergencies or if he wanted to carry out a reconnaissance for which his tank was not suitable
16 Scammel. Scammel lorries were the 'tugs' for British tank transporters. Unlike the later American transporters which towed the tank on a separate trailer, the British ones were semi-articulated, thus severely limiting the rear axle pay-load. The first American transporters were heavy-duty Mack EXBX trucks (originally destined for the French Army before German intervention) with a high centre of gravity, and consequently a steep ramp which made loading very difficult, as well as making them top-heavy and unstable when loaded [See Illustration No 5]
17 The Cauldron. This term was well used to describe a general area of the Desert, some 20 miles in diameter, which – if regarded as a clock face – would have had Knightsbridge at one o'clock
18 The Free French. This hostile attitude on the part of the French was ironic as well as unfortunate. The Free French (mainly Foreign Legion) contingent in Bir Hacheim was nominally under the command of Seventh Armoured Division!
19 O Group. 'O' is for Orders. Any group at which the senior officer gives his subordinates their orders
20 Bully stew. The popularity of bully stew over plain bully beef may need some explanation. In 100° plus temperatures, corned beef does not come out of its tin in a convenient form for cutting into nice crisp slices. It emerges, first, as a trickle of sickly-coloured and greasy liquid and, secondly, in a series of unattractive gobbets of reddish matter with bits of grey gristle attached. It is perfectly wholesome but a good deal less unappetising if heated up and mixed with biscuit or tinned carrots or anything else handy
21 Stags. A very old, but no longer common, term for 'watches' or spells on guard duty
22 Bint. Originally taken, quite properly, from the Arabic by soldiers stationed in Egypt in the late 1800s and meaning simply 'a girl'. Later, soldiers being what they have always been held to be – *ie* brutal and licentious – the term sometimes reflected adversely on the girl's virtue
23 LSGC Medal. Awarded to Other Ranks who had served for twelve years with an unblemished record. Less kindly referred to as being awarded for twelve years' undetected crime
24 Stuka Valley. According to THE DICTIONARY OF SLANG AND UNCONVENTIONAL ENGLISH, this was 'the plain around Souk-el-Khemis'
25 Awarded the MM. Ron Maple was awarded the Military Medal for outstanding courage and devotion to duty. The Citation records how he three times escaped from tanks which had been knocked-out and followed his crew commander to take over another one during the course of a single action
26 Wadi. The Arabic word for a river bed. A term which causes some confusion as it has various uses. There is usually the sense of a major valley [as in the

Battle of Wadi Akarit] but the word was also used to describe a gully. Essentially a wadi was dry . . . but not always!

27 Making a demonstration. This was not a demonstration in either of the modern senses of the word. No student riots and no sales pitches were involved. This particular demonstration would have been intended to confuse the enemy as to the Allied forces' intentions, with the possible additional advantages of making him show himself or think that the Allied forces were stronger than they really were

28 Sparrow fart. Naively – if somewhat vulgarly – substituted for 'Cock crow' in the belief that by using this term for First Light, the enemy would not know what was meant. Used throughout the war and for many years afterwards

29 PRISONER FROM ALAMEIN. The Introduction to Brian Stone's book must be read with some reservation. It speaks of Brian's having escaped from France *with the Regiment from St Malo.* This is factually incorrect: the history of 5RTR's evacuation is covered in Chapter I of this book. Nor does there seem to be any evidence for the claim that *Brian brought the only remaining tank in the Army back to Tobruk.* These errors are, it must be emphasised, not those of Brian Stone but of Desmond MacCarthy who wrote the Introduction

30 The Desert .. shall blossom. Isiah. Chapter 35, Verse 1

31 A live rabbit. It is a well-known fact that there are *no* rabbits in the Desert: only hares

CHAPTER VII

. . . No Let Up: el Alamein

July–October 1942

For some reason (nobody who fought in the Desert can understand why) there was in the UK in 1942 – and there still is in many minds today – a belief that July, August, September and October (until the 23rd of that month, at least!) represented a period of peace and tranquillity in North Africa.

Nothing could be farther from the truth.

As far as the story of the Fifth Royal Tank Regiment is concerned, the 'Desert Interlude' opens a new chapter, in that material for this story is, with the possible exception of 'The Italian Idyll', more and more freely available. What is more, the personal diaries and so forth are more narrative in form and less episodic.

But for the moment, back to the War in the Desert.

Throughout late May and early June, engagements, from the Allies' point of view, had become more and more fragmented. As always, Rommel was single-minded and able to co-ordinate his attacks – as far as his supplies of men and munitions of war allowed him. Nevertheless, the withdrawal to the el Alamein Line was a matter of retreat, retreat, retreat and was a battle as much against exhaustion as against the enemy.

The retreat was, first, to the Tobruk[1] perimeter but, after the fall of Tobruk, to the prepared 'lines of defence' west of el Alamein. These were not 'lines of defence' in the historical sense (such as Wellington's Lines of Torres Vedras in the Peninsular War) being, in reality, a series of individual strong points, each able to give support to the others.

Some modern war historians in their 'quest for truth' claim that the retreating troops brought back with them a distrust of the other arms and a disgust of their senior commanders. This is, at best, a gross exaggeration, for all that some senior commanders were, one by one, replaced. Men who were the 'orphans of defeat rather than the fathers of victory' could not possibly have put up the magnificent resistance in the first Battle of el Alamein which not merely stopped Rommel dead in his tracks but sent the DAK reeling back.

What probably gave rise to this alleged 'distrust' was a fundamental mistake on the part of senior officers who had never, during their education as commanders, been made properly aware of the *limitations* rather than the *use* of tanks. Too much Army thinking on the need for and use of tanks was a Great War legacy: the infantry mentality (leave it to the PBI to slug it out on the ground): the cavalry mentality (a mobile force to break through and exploit the breach). In the first scenario, tanks were merely to support the PBI: in the second, the tanks *were now* the cavalry. Therefore, Army reasoning went, there should be two sorts of tanks: infantry support and another sort to make and exploit the break-through. This, in itself, is a sound theory. Like most theories, however, it required sound practical development and this is where the powers-that-be failed the British Army. 'Infantry' tanks and 'cavalry' [*ie* 'cruiser'] tanks were developed – albeit late in the day and badly. Leaving aside the joker in the pack (which was the power of an anti-tank gun which could make the use of all armour ineffective), the fault in the Desert was that, even when there were enough tanks to play their proper roles, they were frequently not used in those roles. The infantry tended to think all tanks could always protect them and blamed the armoured units when this was not so: the armoured units tended to blame the gunners or the sappers when their paths were not cleared for them to make their break-through. The word, if one is necessary, might perhaps more properly be 'misunderstanding' rather than 'distrust'.

Whether it is true or not that the men on the ground had developed a disgust of their senior commanders, it is certainly true to say that the Top Brass in London decided to take a close look at them.

Following the news of the fall of Tobruk, Churchill returned to London from America at a good round pace. This return was only partly dictated by events in the Middle East. An equally powerful incentive to return was a political one. A motion 'that this House has no confidence in the conduct of the war' had been tabled in Parliament and was thought to have a large measure of support. The support melted 'like snow in the fire of Winston's eloquence and the blaze of his anger' and the motion was defeated by 475 votes to 25.

Having disposed of that threat, Churchill flew out to Cairo on 3rd August accompanied by the CIGS (General Sir Alan Brooke) and Air Chief Marshal Sir Arthur Tedder, to be joined there by General Wavell from India and Prime Minister Jan Smuts from South Africa. The upshot of this meeting and Churchill's visits to Advance Army Headquarters (and some RAF and Army units – *including the Fifth Royal Tank Regiment*) was the decision to relieve 'the Auk' of his command and replace him with 'Alex' (General the Hon. Sir Harold Alexander) as C-in-C and to relieve Ritchie of his command of the Eighth Army in favour of 'Strafer' Gott[2].

Fate, however, intervened. As Gott was flying back to Cairo (from his command of XIIIth Corps) his plane was shot down. Gott was machine-gunned on the ground while helping other passengers out of the wreckage and died almost immediately.

This was a serious blow to Middle East Command since there was no-one in North Africa with sufficient seniority to take over command of Eighth Army. Urgent instructions were sent to the War Office to chase out the man with the requisite qualifications and seniority. The result was that, five days later and on the personal selection of the CIGS, Lieutenant General Bernard Law Montgomery[3] landed at an RAF airfield 'somewhere in Egypt'. 'Monty' had been one of Alan Brooke's Infantry Division Commanders in France in 1940. According to his Diary, 'Brookie' had a very high – but not unqualified – opinion of Montgomery. He said he was a difficult mixture to handle: a brilliant commander in action and trainer of men but liable to commit untold errors, due to his lack of tact and inability to appreciate other men's ideas and opinions. For the sake of simplicity, the new Eighth Army Commander is referred to only as 'Monty' throughout this text.

As one of Monty's most experienced opponents in the Afrika Korps remarked, 'Nothing was ever the same in North Africa after Montgomery arrived. The War in the Desert ceased to be a game.'

The War Diary for June 1st to 3rd, records that 3/5RTR moved to Amirya Camp – familiar territory to the older hands – and started to re-equip with one 'light' squadron and two *Grant* squadrons. By night-fall on the 3rd, the 'light' squadron and one *Grant* squadron were equipped. These, according to the War Diary, belonged to The Fifth, properly so called; the yet-to-be-equipped squadron being really what was left of 3RTR. On 4th July, Jim Hutton took over command of the combined Regiments from Col Archer-Shee. During the afternoon the squadrons with tanks moved to the forward area under Col Hutton, leaving the 3RTR squadron, under command of Major J Granton, to complete their re-equipping. On the 5th the two advanced squadrons came under 2nd Armoured Brigade in the vicinity of el Aguri Tomb.

On 6th July the Battalion took over a position of observation from 1/6RTR. The War Diary then reads, 'During the morning one of our forward patrols spotted a 50mm A/Tk gun which was thought to be isolated. It was decided to send out a troop to destroy and capture the gun. This was only partially successful as the gun was covered by other A/Tk guns. The gun was destroyed but only one tank returned from the attack. Bn stayed in position for the remainder of the day and was withdrawn at last light. Casualties – Killed – 1 Officer and 1 OR. Wounded – 3 ORs. Missing – 1 Officer and 7 ORs.'

This is the action which gave birth to PRISONER FROM ALAMEIN, the book Brian Stone wrote after his repatriation from being wounded and taken prisoner. As mentioned in the last chapter, Brian had a variety of functions in 'A' Squadron but, at the beginning of July 1942, he was commanding a Troop of two light tanks. The account that follows is taken from his book and tells, in graphic and very human detail, the full story behind the brief factual entry in the War Diary.

Before dawn on Monday, 6th July Brian moved out of leaguer to take up an observation position with his troop of *Honeys*. On the way he collected a couple of German prisoners who had obviously got themselves lost in the prevailing mist. The nearest known enemy position was the anti-tank gun which he had set out to destroy: the two stragglers indicated that this might be near-by, so he advanced with great caution. When he arrived at the spot where he had carried out forward observation the previous evening, he found the FOO from the RHA already there. The 'hardy artilleryman', as Brian described him, was interested in some Germans occasionally visible through the mist on a ridge at a range of about 2,000 yards.

Brian left his other tank to maintain observation and went to join the FOO to discuss 'how best to annoy Jerry'. The ridge under observation ran from north to south with the Afrika Korps to the west and the Eighth Army to the east. However, the position was not equally balanced: the baddies were dug in on their side, whereas the goodies had open ground in front of them – open ground covered by German artillery placed to enfilade anyone rash enough to try to cross Tom Tiddler's Ground. There was little Brian's tanks could do but the FOO could enliven things with a few rounds from his 25-pounders whenever, in Brian's words, 'Hans decided to get out of his slit trench and go and talk to Karl'.

After deciding nothing could be gained from chatting to the gunner, Brian moved off to patrol the rest of his beat before his friend, Geoffrey Rawlins, arrived to relieve him at 0900 hrs. With his thoughts on breakfast (he had acquired four eggs from an Arab at el Hamman a few days ago – but not long ago enough for the eggs to have gone off) he motored slowly off to the south. After about half a mile he noticed that an insignificant fold in the ground was, in reality, a re-entrant going towards the German position. What was more, it was deep enough to conceal a *Honey*. He moved up the re-entrant with all the stealth possible in something as large and as noisy as a tank. At the point where the cover ran out Brian found himself staring at a 50mm anti-tank gun with its muzzle pointing straight down the re-entrant but with its crew relaxing some 15 yards away. He took a very close look: all seemed well to the front and left but he had a suspicion there might be something hostile over on his right flank[4].

Before backing out, Brian gave the area a good dose of machine-gun fire without being sure how much damage he had done. It seems from what Brian himself admits that he had disobeyed orders in loosing off with his Browning, as his orders were to observe but not to take any offensive action. Nevertheless, after discussing the position with the two FOOs (another gunner had materialised to join the first one) it was agreed that the opportunity of capturing or, at the worst, putting a 50mm A/Tk gun out of action was too good to be missed..

Brian then called his Squadron Commander [Richard 'Dickie' Ward] on the wireless, and asked for orders. Major Ward asked the Colonel who was also 'in favour of a little party.' Promptly at 0900 hrs Geoffrey Rawlins arrived with his troop. It didn't take long for the two of them to decide the more there were in this party the merrier. Just how much more and how much merrier soon became evident when the Squadron Commander came on the air to say that the party was not to start without him.

The OC arrived a few moments later and Brian assembled the crews to tell them what was to be done. Both Rawlins and Stone, having only two tanks each, commanded very limited fire power, as Dickie Ward was only to play a covering role. On the other hand, there would be two troops of 25-pounders to give cover when the *Honeys* broke open ground. The plan was simple: Brian was to make straight for the gun and deal with local opposition while Rawlins hitched his tow rope to the gun and towed it away. The Squadron HQ tanks would give protection right and left.

Everything started well. The tanks moved carefully up the gully, creeping along slowly to avoid raising the dust, until they reached the end of the cover offered by the re-entrant. At a given signal from Major Ward, the tanks raced across the intervening 200 yards, firing their machine-guns. Brian arrived first, about 50 yards in the lead, before disaster overtook them. Stone's sergeant's tank was the first victim, being hit and going up in flames. A moment later his own tank was hit and Brian felt his legs go numb. Nothing moved in the turret, including Brian's legs. He pushed himself up on his hands and dropped onto the back of the tank and from there onto the ground behind the tank. 'I saw that one of my legs was shot off below the knee and the other had three holes in it, one of them on the shin bone and another on the side of my knee.' Before he could move away – his main fear was that the tank would brew-up and the rear doors of the engine compartment would burst open on top of him – the tank was hit again.

Geoffrey Rawlins arrived in his tank and jumped down to pull Brian clear. Before he could do any more, Rawlins' own tank was hit and he had to leave Brian to go to the aid of his gunner. The disaster was not yet complete. Rawlins' sergeant's tank was also hit and was ablaze, with two of the surviving crew members being taken prisoner. The third member was wounded but Rawlins managed to carry him to shelter.

By this time, seeing four of the tanks out of action, the Germans had returned in force and were engaging the survivors with small arms fire, despite the attentions of the RHA's 25-pounders. Armed only with his tommy-gun, Geoffrey Rawlins threw himself in front of his burning tank and fought off the counter-attack until he too was killed.

All that remained of 'the party' was the Squadron Commander in his covering role. Dickie Ward had little choice but to withdraw to fight again another day.

It had all gone tragically wrong but, in some ways, the worst was still to come for Brian. A German soldier came up, not to rescue him, but to relieve him of his binoculars. The RHA kept up their fire (but were probably shooting blind due to the smoke from the burning tanks). A German officer crept up to Brian, at considerable personal risk, to explain that they could not get a stretcher-party forward because of the shelling. 'It is not fair,' the officer said in flawless English, 'it is not fair.' 'You're telling me it's not fair!' Brian replied.

He then goes on to say, 'By this time I was interested only in my own salvation and, as the Germans seemed to offer me the best hope, I put my trust and faith in them. I was in no pain and fully conscious. The fact that my right leg was not there worried me not at all; indeed, I remember thinking of it lying in the tank and the waste of a brand new desert boot on it which I had bought in Alexandria a few days before.'

He was wrenched out of these thoughts by noises indicating that the German gunners were trying to get their gun back into action to take a pot shot at Dickie Ward who had just then reappeared. Brian was lying right in front of the gun and, if it had been fired, the flash would have killed him. He shouted loudly but in vain: fortunately for him, the gun had been damaged and was jammed and, anyway, Ward's tank had disappeared. Brian lost consciousness for a while, his next recollection being of drinking a water bottle full of ersatz coffee. This, he realised, could only be German and that reminded him that he would soon be, if not dead, then a prisoner . . . either way, he would be searched and he had the day's wireless codes in his note book. He was sufficiently awake and aware to rip out the sheets and tear them up, letting the pieces drift away in the breeze.

This first loss of consciousness can only have been momentary: when he looked at his watch he saw it was just after eleven. The whole 'party' had barely taken fifteen minutes! Brian was woken from a second loss of consciousness by the approach of a stretcher party under a large Red Cross flag. An orderly put a tourniquet on his stump and tied dressings on his other wounds. That was, however, all they could do: whenever they tried to move the stretcher, the 25-pounders opened up again. The gunners could see the movement in their target area but they were unable to distinguish the Red Cross on the flag. 'Oh, well,' Brian thought as he blacked-out yet again, 'It will stop the perishers from salvaging the tanks.'

In fact, by this time, Brian was delirious from the heat, the creeping pain and the loss of blood. He was vaguely aware of another German soldier running over to his tank to collect a water can to bring him a drink and wondering if the man enjoyed Beethoven's Ninth Symphony and whether they could sing it together. And of another soldier who crept over to him and begged his identity bracelet from him as a 'Talisman'. Brian let him take it, wondering what the man would make of the word 'Ludwig' [Brian was a fanatical lover of Beethoven's works] scratched on the back. At four o'clock, now appreciably weaker and thinking definitely in terms of death rather than a POW camp, he saw a second party approaching under a Red Cross flag. This time they were more successful but Brian had a moment of delirium: the truck to which he was carried was a British Army pattern Morris Fifteen-hundredweight. But no: those were Wehrmacht markings, sure enough. The truck, like Brian Stone, had been captured. Later, but how much later he could not tell, there was a German MO and a needle and a jab in his bottom and blissful oblivion.[5].

Meanwhile, life in the Regiment went on. On 7th July it rested in reserve in the same area: it was joined by the remaining squadron under Major Granton and this added 12 *Grant* or *Lee* tanks to the AFV strength: the unit strength being 23 officers and 487 ORs. On the 8th the Regiment was still in reserve but on the 9th it moved some 4,000 yards and took up battle positions facing west. There was no tank activity but a healthy amount of artillery fire. At last light the unit moved again and went into leaguer where it remained until first light only to move back to their previous positions. Once again there was no tank activity.

The 11th saw The Fifth in action by 0530 hrs when they were attacked by heavy artillery and anti-tank fire. This was repulsed and the enemy withdrew by late afternoon, leaving behind 1 Pzkw III, 1 Pzkw IV, two armoured cars and two half-track personnel carriers. Two 5RTR *Grants* were damaged. At 1930 hrs a New Zealand Infantry Brigade moved through the Regiment's lines and consolidated a defensive position in the depression to their front. By last light, the Regiment had moved to a new leaguer, once again within range of the German guns. As a result of shelling, one OR was killed and three ORs were wounded.

The 12th, 13th and 14th saw much moving around but no action. Matters looked up on the 15th when the Regiment moved off at first light. As 5RTR advanced to its new position, the tanks encountered a screen of anti-tank guns: the Regiment changed direction right and moved to meet and support the Indian Division in their attempt to secure a key position. The meeting was successful and together they captured the position. This produced a good bag: about 700 Italian prisoners and several guns. The New Zealanders, on the other hand, had not been so fortunate: they had initially captured their objective but had been 'pushed off' by a strong force of armoured cars. The Fifth saw these off the field after a brisk exchange of fire which cost the life of one OR and left two wounded and one missing. This action by The Fifth, according to Liddell Hart, 'drew the sting out of the enemy's thrust.'

The Regiment stayed in position overnight and at 0530 hrs engaged some anti-tank guns who were in a position to enfilade the New Zealanders. At 1000 hrs the enemy attacked with tanks and more A/Tk guns, causing the loss of two tanks destroyed or severely damaged. The CO had no choice but to order a short withdrawal, covered by our own A/Tk guns. The enemy renewed the attack with a force of about two dozen tanks and a heavy barrage. This time, it was 5RTR's turn: the enemy was driven off with an estimated loss of 8 tanks but without further loss to the Regiment. During the action a squadron from the CLY came up and took over flank guard, allowing the full strength of The Fifth to be engaged. In spite of the tank casualties, at the end of the day only one OR was unaccounted for.

The next two days saw the Regiment in fixed position with patrolling activity, mainly by 'A' Squadron. Throughout this period incessant enemy artillery activity caused two officer and two OR casualties. The 19th and 20th followed much the same pattern, with the addition of two Stuka attacks. There were, however, no casualties.

The 21st July was quiet – if one discounts the trauma of watching the RAF relentlessly bombing the unfortunate New Zealand Division – until 1800 hrs when there was a CO's conference for 'Operation Eliza'.

There is no mention of 'Operation Eliza' by Liddell Hart or General Verney and it is impossible to tell from the Desert map references in the War Diary exactly where this action was taking place. Some clue can be obtained from the mention of the engagements of the Indian and New Zealand Divisions. 'Mike' Carver, in his Short History of the Seventh Armoured Division, places these units at Abu Dweis and Qattara respectively at this time 'with 7 Armoured Division operating on their southern flank'. A more precise location is given a few paragraphs farther on in Harry Ireland's Diary. There is, moreover, nothing further said about 'Operation Eliza' in the War Diary as the pages between 22nd and 31st July are blank!

Whatever the Operation was or wasn't called in higher circles, Jake Wardrop always had something to say about life in the Desert. In this case, that it was rough, they were continually being shelled and receiving calls from those unwelcome visitors, the Stukas. Jake's tank received another shell hit, destroying the crew's precious water supply, smashing the periscopes and leaving some impressive scars on the barrel of the gun. He recounted one specific action when the Regiment beat back a night attack by about thirty tanks. In Jake's opinion, the enemy would not have been so successfully repulsed if it had not been for the calm voice of Fearless Jim[6] in his men's earphones, telling them to hold their fire until he gave the command. When he did, the results were devastating, leaving half the approaching tanks disabled or in flames. Colonel Hutton then turned the action into a shooting match, encouraging the crews to pick off individual tanks, particularly one which was flying a blue flag. They did! As usual on these occasions, Jake described the action as 'a great scrap', going on to say that this action set the pattern for the summer, although they were by no means all good days, as the Regiment suffered considerable losses.

Harry Ireland's diary for this part of the el Alamein battles reads, 'It is now late July, we have new tanks and a new Commanding Officer [Jim Hutton]. After a brief spell of relaxation we are ready to go back in the line in a defensive role. (It is now a matter of survival: if we crack the whole of the Middle East will fall).

'We take up our battle positions after being briefed by the CO – a very impressive man and a fine commander. We learned at once that this man was a winner. The clarity of his voice over the air, giving orders and directions, was an inspiration to us all. The first few days in action we knew that we could hold back the Germans and the Italian armies . . . at least, from our front. The enemy put everything into trying for a break-through, Stuka raids, very heavy shelling, infantry attacks, tank battles[7], but the line held.' Harry goes on to give his version of knocking out the tank flying the blue pennon in the engagement already described by Jake Wardrop.

'There were very heavy casualties on both sides. With the hot weather in July the stench of the dead was sickening and the flies in their millions were everywhere. It was a static position for everyone in unbearable conditions. Another instance I remember was the very frightened voice of a wireless operator coming on the air and repeating over and over again, 'What shall we do? My tank commander's been hit.' He was answered by a very irritated Squadron Commander saying, 'Get off the bloody air – and keep off!' understandably committed to the job in hand. As soon as things quietened down, he came back on the air and sympathetically ordered the operator to withdraw the tank out of action for assistance to the tank commander.

'The front on which the Regiment had been operating in the last week was known as Ruweisat Ridge, a feature with very good defensive capability. One morning while on the ridge, I'll always remember, in the heat of battle out of nowhere, running straight across all the lines of fire, was a very nervous and rare gazelle which ran – and escaped – across the front. At that very moment all guns stopped on both sides and complete silence fell for a minute or two until it disappeared from view. Everyone was completely taken aback. A voice – the CO's – came on the air, saying 'What a beautiful sight!' then BANG! BANG! BANG! off we went again. Makes one think: what's it all about? Friend and foe cared about that gazelle.

'Both sides developed a certain amount of respect for each other and it was known that all prisoners and wounded were treated with humanity on both sides[8].

'The Alamein Line in a way was to our advantage: after coming off the vast desert it thinned out into a narrow corridor about 20 miles or so wide. To the south were soft sands [the Qattara Depression] making it impossible for mobile warfare[9]. This concentrated the army into a compact unit, enabling us to help one another, whereas, on the vast Desert, we seemed to fight as isolated units and effectiveness seemed nil. Because of the heavy concentration, we were easy targets for bombing raids. One particular area was known as 'Stuka Valley'. Days on end, even when relieved from the battle area for a brief respite, we were harassed continually. The bombs would crunch among the tanks, taking the breath out of you: a funny sensation, a feeling of being punch-drunk. (Shrapnel clanging on the tanks, making a sound like a giant bell). Fortunately there were few casualties: strange; it takes an awful lot of bombs or bullets to hit a target, even in action. One wonders as to how we survive, but we do and carry on the war game.

'Winston Churchill had been on the Desert and had decorated the Commanding Officer and a few Other Ranks in recognition of their deeds in the Regiment. But the defence of Alamein still goes on. One day, taking up battle line on a ridge, in the distance you could see about twenty or so enemy tanks. They started to roll forward in an all-out attack to break through our lines. Still coming on with all guns firing, us returning heavy fire. We had been engaging, on the tank commander's orders, various targets with good results.

'As we fired the 75mm it recoiled with the breach block open, bringing down the barrel a torch of flame which lit the inside of the tank and I felt the heat of it on my face. We had been hit by an armour-piercing shell on the gun ring: it did not penetrate the tank, although it stopped the gun from traversing left or right.. The driver immediately opened his visor, shouting 'We're on fire. Bale out!' I never waited for a repeat order and, with the crew, baled out of the side hatch into blazing sunlight. Running away from the burning tank, we were fired on by a machine-gun. I could see the spurts of sand as the bullets hit the ground and dived for cover into a vacant slit trench previously dug by the infantry. The driver kept on running. Clinging to the ground, I looked back at the tank, about 20 yards away. To my surprise, there was the tank commander[10] by the side of it in full view of the enemy with the fire extinguisher putting the flames out. (In the meantime, one of the other Squadron tank commanders had spotted my predicament and drew his tank broadside on to the slit trench and took me on board).

'My tank commander (although by now the Squadron was withdrawing and the enemy tanks coming on) climbed inside our tank and drove it out of action. He had been slightly wounded and was evacuated to base. (We live to fight another day!) At a later date, my tank commander was decorated for this action. Later we had a new tank commander: 'Mad as a Hatter' but I guess he knew his job[11].

'We had drawn back 1,000 yards ready for a new brigade of tanks [three regiments] to take over our positions. It was straight out from England and had not been in action before. Within a couple of hours we were going back into the line. (What had happened was that the new brigade had tried to make a limited advance but, unknown to them, the enemy had laid several mine-fields, with the result that they ran smack into them and lost almost two regiments of tanks. So now we were filling the gap. What a cock-up!')

Liddell Hart, quoting from the History of the Fourth Indian Division, sums up the serious reverse which Rommel suffered and then adds, in rather more stately prose than Harry Ireland or Jake Wardrop employed, that, 'The 5th RTR, under Hutton's leadership, played an important part in the infliction of this costly repulse – its tally of tank 'kills' was eight in this second fight, without any cost to itself.'

Because the War in the Desert had taken a new turn for the Eighth Army – concentrated and continuous defence and counter-attack on a narrow front – serious anxiety was felt in medical circles over the ability of the tank crews to survive the conditions in which they were being forced to fight. The Medical Research Section of GHG MEF produced a report which summarises the typical life of a tank crew.

Thus, 'Turn out at 0500 hrs: break leaguer and go on patrol or take up battle positions by first light. Actions are usually in the early or late hours of the day, the intense heat of mid-day making accurate fire impossible. These hours are, however, spent in alert wakefulness and hours of expectancy can be much more exhausting than battle periods. It is unusual for any member of the crew to be able to leave the tank. Engine noise and fumes, fumes from the guns and the wearing of head-phones add to the fatigue.'

The report continued by pointing out that, as the opposing side seldom withdrew before 2100 hrs, the crews had to wait until then before, possibly, a drive of two or three hours to night leaguer. In leaguer, there followed refuelling and ammunition stowing as well as carrying out essential maintenance. Only after all this could the crews expect to feed – which first often entailed preparing uncooked or 'raw' rations. Thus it was rarely before 0030 or 0100 hrs that the men were able to sleep.

The medical experts also noted, 'There are numerous occasions when replenishments do not arrive as expected or at all and there are numerous occasions when rest is impossible due to shelling or the threat or fact of night attacks. Combinations of these circumstances can mean that the crews go without sleep for 48 or even 72 hours at a stretch and that units are in action for continuous periods of as many as 18 or 20 days.

'In spite of the exhaustion suffered by these crews, senior officers have stated their belief that such men fight better and give a better account of themselves than fresh, but inexperienced crews newly arrived in the desert.' No-one who served with The Fifth in the Desert would quarrel with that report.

The only things that the report does not mention are the flies but then they were not exclusive to tank crews.

General Verney records that August was a month of re-organisation and re-equipping with, at the front of everyone's minds, the need to strengthen the defensive positions. Not just those at the line: there was, if not panic, among the staff in Cairo, then a very strong sense of impending danger. The hitherto unarmed 'nine-to-five' desk-bound warriors found themselves being armed, drilled and turned out in war-like order at all times of the night and day. If there was not quite panic in the staff in Cairo, the same was not always true of the citizenry. As one senior officer remarked, the only thing that stopped them running away was that there was nowhere to run to!

Rommel's advanced units were only sixty miles west of Alexandria and 5RTR was in an area to the east of Himeimat and very much in a state of re-organisation and re-equipping. To begin with, on 1st August, The Fifth was assigned to 22nd Armoured Brigade, under the command of Brigadier 'Pip' Roberts, with 1RTR and 3/4 CLY and the 'Greys' for company. On that day, the composition of the Regiment was still something of a hotch-potch: the separate squadron made up of personnel from 3RTR returned to their own unit but a squadron from the 2nd Battalion Royal Gloucestershire Hussars [RGH] came under command. The composition of the unit – which the War Diary despairingly says was '*at the moment* 5RTR' – was two *Grant* squadrons from The Fifth and a light squadron from 2 RGH. The Regiment moved its position on that day, as it did again on 2nd August. Lieuts RG Goodyear, DJ Browne and HL Potter were promoted A/Capts.

At 0700 hrs that day the CO and IO went on a Brigade recce to scout out possible battle positions. While the CO's back was turned 'F' Squadron 2 RGH arrived and relieved 'A' Squadron 5RTR. The War Diary does not say what the RGH relieved them of but it does record that the strength of the new squadron was 15 *Crusaders*[12], 5 Officers and 104 ORs. The despairing note in the War Diary proved justified: on the 3rd it states, 'Bn now known as 5RTR/2RGH.'

After a recce by the CO, 2i/c and Squadron Commander in the morning of the 4th, the unit was visited by the Divisional Commander [Major General JML Renton] in the late afternoon. Had he done a head-count, General Renton would have found 26 Officers and 576 ORs in charge of 18 *Crusaders*, 17 *Grants* and 1 *Honey*. On Wednesday, 5th August the CO, 2i/c and Squadron Commanders carried out another recce first thing in the morning and, at noon, nine *Grants* of 2 RGH joined the unit. As also did 3 Officers and 42 Enlisted Men of the US Army (Tank Corps) on attachment. And if that wasn't enough, Major Biddell came back to claim 'B' Squadron from Captain Chave. On the 6th the Regiment did a practice turn-out for Operation 'Partridge' and on the 7th the CO, Squadron Commanders and all Troop Officers carried out a recce of battle positions in the area of Deir el Ragil and later that day attended a post-mortem on the previous day's practice turn-out. The report on the unit's strength seems to show that another officer as well as Alan Biddell had joined the Regiment but that 102 ORs had left[13]. The 8th August saw further recces and the arrival of Lt DH Skinner from Base Camp. The degree of preparedness of 5RTR can be judged from the daily reports in the War Diary. Recce parties were a regular feature (including one carried out in conjunction with the 2nd New Zealand Division's forward positions), as were all-officer discussions of 'battle formations' and the search for a site for a practice range. A suitable range at Samaket Gaballa was found and firing practice was carried out on 11th August. On the next day the immediate future shape of what had by now become very much a 'composite unit' was decided. It is difficult to work out what the precise tank strength of the Regiment was from the decision, 'to form one *Grant* Squadron under Major King of 2 RGH, consisting of 2 RGH [personnel] and the American crews, and another *Grant* Squadron under Major Biddell, consisting of 5RTR crews.' Eight *Grants* for Major King and nine for Alan Biddell? And what about the 18 *Crusaders*? Four for RHQ and fourteen for – presumably – 'A' Squadron, as the 'light' squadron? Later that day this 'composite outfit' came under orders for Bde Operation 'Grouse'. Which could have been well-named.

After moving and practising and standing-to and standing-down and exchanging 'Grouse' for 'Snipe', 5RTR/2RGH received new movement orders on 15th August because an infantry attack was going in on the New Zealanders' positions. Nothing came of this nor of Operation 'Pheasant' on the following day, which was only a 'dry run' for the benefit of the Army Commander. The 17th and 18th must have been frustrating for Colonel Jim as, after yet more reconnaissance parties, he learnt that the agreed battle positions had been deemed unsatisfactory and new ones had to be found. Having decided that enough game birds had been started, some humorist at HQ dreamt up 'Twelvebore' as the code word for the next operation. August 19th predictably brought more recces and more discussions but no-one, with an imminent battle in mind, could have predicted the events on 20th August. A Parade – with a capital 'P' – for a Very Important Person – also with capitals. None other than the Right Honourable Winston Leonard Spencer Churchill, His Majesty's Prime Minister. 'Winnie' duly came, inspected the chaps, pinned a well-earned medal on the Colonel's chest, had a few words to say and departed in a pleasant aroma of Havana tobacco. There seems no reason to doubt the rumour which circulated after this visit that Churchill was much struck by what he saw and told 'Pip' Roberts that The Fifth seemed to him to be a very impressive body of men.

Whereas Damocles had a sword hanging over him, 22nd Armoured Brigade still had Operation 'Twelvebore' hanging over them. The thread snapped, so to speak, at 0530 hrs on 22nd August and the Regiment moved up to its allotted position and thence to alternative positions. And back again. And again. Operation 'Twelvebore' was not, however, merely a blank cartridge: it had its purpose. The next few days were spent in still further recces, familiarisation with the position of supply dumps and minefields, and the exploration of possible new positions in the el Raqqas area.

On the last day of August, it all came together: Rommel made his expected move and 7th Armoured Division received the code-word 'Pepsodent' at 0200 hrs. By 0220 hrs 5RTR [teeth, no doubt, shining] was on the move and at 0400 hrs it was in position. The next five hours were spent listening to reports and speculating as to where and when the action would commence. 0900 hrs provided the answer with a report of a concentration of 150 enemy AFVs in the vicinity of Deir-el-Ragil. The 'light' squadrons of both 5RTR and 4 CLY were sent out on patrol at 1030 hrs but it was not until 1745 hrs that the Brigade was ordered to launch an attack on a force estimated to consist of 70 tanks.

What followed is best understood by giving the details recorded in the War Diary. The engagement was, in every respect, typical of War in the Desert as fought between the Afrika Korps and the Eighth Army.

August 31st 1942

1750 hrs	Bde artillery commenced putting down concentration of fire

1800 hrs	Orders for Bn to form up for an attack. 'A' Sqn protection front. Bn moved out.
1805 hrs	Ordered to return to former posns as the enemy was forming up facing NE, at the same time being surveilled by 'A' Sqn
1820 hrs	'A' Sqn ordered to withdraw
1845 hrs	'A' Sqn reported enemy moving round to left of our posn and they are ordered to repel
1900 hrs	'C' Sqn report they are engaging 8 enemy tanks followed by a large column of MET, guns and inf. 'A' Sqn forced to withdraw in fading light to left flank of Bn posn. 6 enemy tanks penetrated left flank and reached a point behind our guns and 1,000 yds from Bde HQ. They were halted by darkness and remained stationary all night.

September 1st

	At first light these tanks were stalked by 'A' Sqn assisted by A/Tk guns. One enemy tank destroyed. Remainder withdrew hastily. 6 enemy tanks attacked 'C' Sqn front during night. One destroyed, remainder withdrew. Own casualties – 1 *Crusader* destroyed. Enemy – 6 tanks destroyed: 1 SP gun captured.
0145 hrs	Enemy guns shelled our positions
0620 hrs	150 vehicles facing the Battalion position which is heavily shelled by enemy guns
0640 hrs	'A' Sqn reports that the enemy are outflanking us on the left and that they are engaging. Enemy advance held
0650 hrs	The Bn is heavily engaged on the left flank. Assistance arrives from 4CLY who are guided into position by 'A' Sqn. No further advance by enemy.
0705 hrs	'B' Sqn reports that there are large quantities of A/Tk guns to their front and that tanks are moving round to the right flank
0725 hrs	'B' Sqn push forward one troop to engage enemy tanks on right flank
0740 hrs	Replenishment of ammunition by sub-units
0800 hrs	'A' Sqn hands position over to 4CLY and returns to reserve after replenishing
0835 hrs	'B' Sqn reports 30 enemy tanks to their front
0900 hrs	10 Armd Div operating in [nearby] area are coming in to engage the tanks on our left from the rear
1030 hrs	10 Armd Div attacked and inflicted casualties to the enemy on our left flank causing them to withdraw but

were held up by A/Tk screen covering the withdrawal. The Germans during the morning had put in two or three strong attacks on our position but failed to reach his objective and was forced to withdraw

1430 hrs 70 enemy tanks to our right flank turning north and appear to be attacking the NZ position

1545 hrs Heavy concentration of fire put down on enemy A/Tk screen to give 4CLY a chance to operate, we were to assist if good target offers

1650 hrs 23 Armd Brigade on the right of our Brigade are engaged in an infantry battle and the 1RTR were being attacked by tanks; guns to our front are still being engaged

1720 hrs Brigade Artillery put down concentration to assist 23 Armd Brigade

1840 hrs German bomber (Ju 88) shot down in front of Bn position. Intense air activity for 10 minutes. Until last light another attack on our position seemed imminent with 40 MET, Inf and approx 20 tanks. During the night the Germans recovered tanks, our own parties being unable to get there first. Inf patrols were sent out but otherwise quiet night.

Casualties. 1 Officer killed. 1 USA Officer wounded. 2 ORs wounded

September 2nd

At first light there were numerous vehicles on our front including 2 groups of 40 tanks and a group of 15 moving west. There was no action except for intermittent shelling by both sides

0830 hrs 4CLY to our left were trying to contact 10 Armd Div to our north east

1030 hrs A patrol of 'A' Sqn reported that a group of 10 tanks sighted were believed to be friendly

1035 hrs Tank busters destroy 4 Pzkw IVs, 1 Pzkw III Special and damaged one

1050 hrs 'A' Sqn is ordered to push patrols out as far south as possible. Patrols remain in contact with enemy throughout the day as he gradually withdrew west. There was also intermittent shelling by both sides.

Tank state: *Grants* – 17 . *Crusaders* 10

For the next three days, life became very much less hectic, as the enemy was believed to be withdrawing from their main positions. As usual, the DAK did not make things easy: their withdrawal was covered by one anti-tank screen after another as they leap-frogged back through the Allies' eastern minefield. During this withdrawal, 5RTR was in contact on and off with the enemy but there were no engagements. On September 5th the War Diary was able to state, 'No further events'.

That is how the engagement looked from the point of view of 5RTR but what about the view of the man next up in the command chain? In a few lines, this is what that particular brush with the enemy on Wednesday, 1st September 1942 looked like to Brigadier GPB Roberts DSO MC. '.. the enemy are edging forward .. and meanwhile some of them have started to work round our flank and the 5th RTR are in action. And now in the centre the enemy is edging forward again. The artillery is the only thing I have available to stop them, so we bring down all we can, and again they are halted. And then the Greys come over the crest from the north ['Pip' had been waiting anxiously for their arrival]; they are quite clear as to the hole they have to plug and they go straight in. The light is beginning to fade and the situation in the centre seems to be stabilised. But there is a little trouble on our left; some of the enemy have worked round the 5th Tanks' position and are now coming onto our 25-pdr gun lines. Accordingly, since the centre is now a little congested with the Greys in most of the CLY's position, I order the CLY – what remains of it – to move round to the left and cover the gap between 5th RTR and the 44th Division's defences. As darkness falls flashes and tracer are to be seen on the left flank: the CLY have to meet the enemy but have halted them so we seem secure at any rate for the night.' 'Pip' Roberts' use of the 'historic present' in telling the story gives it an immediacy which no War Diary can ever achieve.

Among the mass of new material mentioned earlier in this chapter, a contribution which ranks very highly is that of Sydney Storer who joined The Fifth from 6RTR at the beginning of August 1942. Syd, unlike Jake Wardrop or Harry Ireland, did not keep a diary at the time: however, he did write a detailed account of his experiences in the War at the request of his family. The rest of this story of The Fifth in World War Two will include many extracts from that account.

After being told that he was being posted to the Second Battalion, Syd learnt that he had just enough time for a Christmas shopping expedition in Alexandria before the wagon left . . . for the Fifth Battalion! On arrival, he discovered that he was to be the 75mm gunner on a *Grant*. This surprised both Syd and the Sergeant crew commander, since Syd was a wireless operator by trade. 'Next morning,' Syd wrote, 'I was transferred to another tank, this time in 'B' Sqn where a gunner had been put to wireless operating by mistake. Now, for the first time, we were given some idea of what our movements were to be; previously it had been impossible for crew members to know the area or objective of any attack. I recognised our area: we [6RTR] had made a small counter-attack there before we were withdrawn. The CO explained our position and the enemy dispositions as far as they were known. He told us Rommel was expected to make a big push for the Delta: our job was to stop him. The attack was expected any time after 25th August when the moon would be full. On being given the code-word, we would take up prepared positions and 'create as much havoc as we could amongst the enemy armour'.'

Syd found himself for the next few days taking part in a deception exercise – manning a squadron of dummy tanks [and repairing them after they had been shot-up by the Luftwaffe] – or patrolling, on foot, through the gaps in the newly laid minefields. When the day of Rommel's expected attack arrived, the men suffered another disillusionment, as it was not until the fifth night that they were ordered to stand-to when the patrols reported signs of enemy movement. Nothing dramatic happened: the crews packed up, the W/Ops clamped on their head-sets and then they all settled back to watch the pyrotechnics while the RAF bombed a column of soft vehicles. The crews soon had reason to become more alert when the enemy started shelling and reports came in of troops advancing to try and clear passages through the minefields.

'Then,' Syd wrote, 'we got the order to take up our positions at Alam el Halfa which we did in bright moonlight. Next morning word came from the General, 'No withdrawal and no surrender': Rommel had begun his push for Cairo. As the day progressed the RAF bombers kept up a shuttle service. Inside the tank it got hotter and hotter.'

In the late afternoon, the expected enemy advance began but the action became confused by a sandstorm before either side could engage seriously. Some tanks from the CLY went forward to try to ascertain the enemy's intentions and were rather roughly handled but they did ascertain that the enemy force consisted of about a hundred tanks. All The Fifth could do was to sit tight in their hull-down positions until ordered to pull forward. The panzers came within about 1,000 yards before The Fifth moved forward to draw attention to their presence. This had the expected effect, as the enemy formed up for an attack. With about an hour of daylight left, the Germans opened fire first on the CLY and then on 5RTR. The tanks retaliated and the RHA 25-pounders and 6-pounder A/Tk guns opened fire. Syd Storer could hear but not see what was going on and had the unhappy experience of having to sit listening to reports from the unit's tanks which had been hit. It was a sharp engagement, dying out with the dying light but leaving everyone with the feeling that the Boche would resume as soon as the moon rose. However, this was not the case: they withdrew to replenish overnight. The Fifth Tanks ruse of drawing attention to their presence looked like being successful when the enemy returned to the attack at first light, because their line of advance led them into range of the tanks which had been concealed on The Fifth's right flank. As soon as these opened up, the panzers withdrew, leaving several of their kind behind them in flames. For the rest of the day – except for being stood-to just as the crews were preparing their midday meal – the battle was continued by the Gunners and, farther off, by the RAF in the area of [Deir el] Ragil, where the German soft vehicles were getting bogged down in the poor going.

Syd Storer concluded this account by saying, 'So ended the first day of September but the bombing continued in the Ragil and farther west. It was heartening to have the RAF at last in control, instead of being constantly under attack from Stukas. With this constant attention from the Air Force, the enemy continued to withdraw: other Allied forces continued to push them back until they eventually retired to the position from which they had originally started.'

The account in Jake Wardrop's Diary is substantially the same, although he gives the range of the action at 2,000 yards rather than 1,000. Whatever the range, Brother Boche chose to hit Jake's tank and to contrive to break one of the tracks in doing so. Jake, with good reason, felt himself to be an expert on broken tracks and must have exasperated his crew commander by saying, 'I told you so!' The Squadron Commander did not accept that this was an excuse to be hauled out of the battle and told Jake's crew commander to shoot it out as long as possible. This proved to be but a short possibility and, within five minutes, Jake was reaching for his haversack and revolver and his blue pullover . . . and 'was jumping again'. Jake's legs took him back over a ridge and into a 25-pounder emplacement where he was made welcome and given a cuppa. The 'ding-dong' went on for about three days, at the end of which Jake went back to find that, although hit several more times, his tank hadn't brewed up and could be recovered. It was and, by last light, it and Jake were back with the Echelons.

These diarists, as well as Harry Ireland, go on to remark, each in his own way, that 'we had a new Commander-in-Chief – Montgomery.' But, before dealing with his arrival and the changes he wrought, there is time for a fuller review of the overall situation. It is summed up by Liddell Hart who said that during 2nd September the enemy was seen to be thinning out and columns started moving westward. However, Monty refused to allow any follow up, knowing quite well that Rommel still had enough bite left to cause the Eighth Army unnecessary waste of armour. On the other hand, Monty did order a limited-objective attack on the southern flank to be launched on the night of 3rd/4th September by the New Zealanders. In the event, the attack proved a near disaster and, in spite of some brisk action by squadrons of 46RTR and 50RTR, the Afrika Korps was able to pursue its retreat in its own good time. Rommel continued to pull back until he reached positions which it would have been too costly to assault. On the one hand, Rommel had gained something by being left in possession of the field. Against this, he had lost 2,900 officers and men, 49 tanks and armoured cars, 400 other vehicles [many of them British], 17 field artillery pieces and 38 anti-tank guns. British and Commonwealth losses were fewer in men and guns but almost equal in tanks, at 1,750 all ranks, 15 guns and 54 tanks.

Essentially, what followed for the rest of September and the beginning of October was the same for The Fifth as for all units of the Eighth Army. The War Diary gives as good an account as any of these weeks but it is worth mentioning that there were a number of changes within the Desert Rats.

The Division was re-organised into two Armoured Brigades: the Fourth (Light) Armoured Brigade, which consisted of:

The Royal Scots Greys
VI Hussars – with one Squadron of VIII Hussars
XI Hussars[14]
2 Battalion Derbyshire Yeomanry
1 RHA
1st Battalion the King's Royal Rifle Corps

and the Twenty-second Armoured Brigade, which consisted of:

1RTR
5RTR
4 CLY
4th Field Regiment RA
97th Field Regiment RA
1st Battalion the Rifle Brigade

and was commanded by Brigadier 'Pip' Roberts.

Taking up the story again from the War Diary at the point on 5th September when it reports 'No further events', as it does for the next three days, there was a break for the CO, the Adjutant with Captain Baillie and his men from the US Tank Corps, when they 'went to Brigade to meet Mr Wendell Wilkie[15].'

The next few days were occupied with sorting out personnel [The Fifth was still inextricably mixed up with 2 RGH] and tanks and other equipment. On 12th September Major Taylor, who has not been mentioned before, went on sick leave and Capt Maunsell took over 'A' Squadron. On the same day, the American contingent left the unit 'for the Delta prior to returning to the USA'. By 20th September the hand-over of tanks and 'controlled equipment' [whatever that may have been] to 2 RGH was completed and The Fifth was once again known as 5RTR. If most of the entries in the War Diary from this point until the end of the month are taken literally, one would assume that 5RTR, along with other units in the Brigade, had either been sent back to study their primers or someone higher up the line was busy 'teaching grandmothers to suck eggs'! The truth is rather otherwise: all the lectures, conferences and exercises led up to a Corps Scheme on 8th October, summarised in the War Diary as, 'entailing movement of an attacking force through own and enemy minefields at night, adopting quick battle positions and attacking enemy strong-points'. In other words, a full dress rehearsal for the break-out from the el Alamein Line.

The Regiment had, in fact, been visited and addressed by Monty on 24th September and by the new Divisional Commander on 10th October. This was Major General AF Harding CBE DSO MC who had recently taken over from General Renton – who was returning home after some twenty years of almost continuous foreign service. On a more domestic note, Dinham Drew – now a Brigadier – paid a visit to his old command on 17th October: an Army Catering Adviser paid a visit on 9th October and Capt RE 'Bob' Maunsell MC was posted to 5RTR from 2 RGH – this time officially.

Among others figuring in this account who joined The Fifth at this period and in time for the 'Battle of Alamein' were Lieutenant Eric Wilde, Troopers 'Pete' Petersen and Willie Dovey. Each has a story to tell and merits a short introduction.

Bob Maunsell claims that he only joined the Army because (1) he was idle at school and (2) he was 'sports mad'. Be that as it may, Bob joined the ranks of the Fifth Battalion RTC in 1933 and was on detachment in Egypt with the rank of Sergeant when the war broke out. According to Bob, he only accepted a commission because there were better opportunities for sport as an officer and the accommodation at away matches was better. There was also the matter of the pay! For his commission, Bob was sent back to England and, once commissioned, was posted to the First Battalion Royal Gloucestershire Hussars, a Territorial regiment that had just been put on war-time footing. After a period as adjutant, he was back in North Africa as a Troop Leader with 2 RGH. In this capacity he won his first Military Cross for rescuing his Squadron Commander under fire. He started his integration into The Fifth when the two units were combined and completed it in time for the Battle of el Alamein.

Eric Wilde, on the other hand, was already headed for a career as a soldier when he arrived in Egypt in the summer of 1942. Being, on his own admission, the worst technically educated and least technically minded officer in the RTR with no interest in gunnery, wireless operating or driving and maintenance, it was a bit of a shock when he found he was expected to do a two month technical course at the RAC Depot at Abbassia. However, a navigation course was being run and he volunteered for that. Not only did he find it 'great fun' but it led to his posting to The Fifth. 'This,' Eric wrote later, 'was the greatest piece of luck I had during the war. I could easily have been posted to one of the newly arrived, inexperienced units. Instead I went to a regular battalion which was then at the peak of its efficiency. It was battle-wise, having fought in France in 1940 and in the Desert since early in 1941, playing some part in all the Desert campaigns. One of its great strengths lay in its senior NCOs who were experienced and battle-hardened. They were all capable of taking command of a Troop if the Troop Leader became a casualty – and frequently proved it in action. Above all there was the inspiring example of the Colonel, 'Fearless Jim' Hutton.' Eric here makes the point that so many others have made, namely, Colonel Jim's steadying and quietly encouraging voice over the regimental wireless net.

It happened that, when Eric joined The Fifth, the Desert Navigating Officer was about to return to the Depot in Cairo. The CO offered 'young Mr Wilde' the job and 'young Mr Wilde' jumped at the opportunity. 'When one is young one is full of self-confidence even though, in reality, one is very ignorant. I was saved,' Eric admits, 'because I had the good fortune to inherit an absolutely first class driver in the person of Corporal Legge. A pre-war regular, he was experienced in Desert warfare and in coping with the hard Desert conditions. He was also a highly trained mechanic and kept his vehicles on the road in the most adverse circumstances. In addition to all these virtues he had one outstanding gift: a born sense of direction.

'Our vehicle was a Dingo. For day navigation we had a sun compass and for night navigation one of the ordinary hand-held WD-issue ones. In the Desert there were virtually no distinguishing features, no roads except the one from Alexandria to Tripoli, tracks made by the pads of camels and the tyres of trucks – which shifted and, in any case, were not marked on our maps – so that Desert navigation resembled the ocean variety.

'As Regimental Navigating Officer my position was right next to the CO's tank, so that I was immediately available to carry out his orders, to ferry him back to the Brigadier or up to the forward elements of the Regiment or across to the other units in the line. Above all to go ahead of the Regiment in the approach to contact the enemy, to indicate their correct Charlie Love. This, of course, only until contact was made, after which I would rapidly scuttle back to the Colonel. The most stressful part of my duties was to guide the supply echelons up to the Regiment at night. Once the Brigade had settled into its scattered night-time leaguer positions, the supply lorries had to be brought up to replenish the tanks. To do this, each regiment had to send back its navigator to the Brigade Assembly Point. I would be told by the Adjutant where this would be – a featureless point on a featureless map – in relation to our own position – another featureless point in the middle of nowhere on another featureless map. So off I would set on the compass bearing between these two points and travel the required distance. Somehow we always found the Assembly Point, fetched our rations and set off on the 'reverse bearing' that would take us back to the unit. This is where Cpl Legge's great gift bore full fruit. He could sense, far better than my reliance on the compass, where we had to go: and he was always right. He saved my bacon on so many occasions and stopped me wandering off into the night with a full convoy of lorries behind me. I cannot describe the overwhelming relief I felt when we came across our night leaguer. How I blessed Legge.'

At this point in his narrative, Eric Wilde gives the following precise description of a Desert Night Leaguer. 'A Night Leaguer ensured that 'all were safely gathered in' and reduced as far as possible the danger from tank hunting patrols. It also made replenishing simpler and safer as the supply echelons only had one rendezvous to keep. It was essentially a 'box' in the form of a square. 'A' Squadron stretched in one long line on the forward face with the OC's tank in the middle. On each wing and at right angles to 'A' Squadron, 'B' and 'C' Squadrons formed the side faces of the box. The RHQ tanks formed the fourth face. All tanks faced outwards with their guns traversed forwards. In the centre of the box, drawn up in orderly lines, were the guns of the Support Artillery, the lorries of the Close Support Infantry, the RHQ soft vehicles (the MO's truck, the fitters' wagons etc). Within this box, replenishing, routine maintenance, 'O Groups' and so forth could be carried out with the minimum waste of time and effort. By tradition the officers slept separately from their crews. This had nothing to do with class distinction but was simply a practice followed so that the officers could be woken for 'O Groups' without disturbing the men unnecessarily. As soon as dawn broke the unit would move out into 'open leaguer' *ie* dispersed into squadron formation. Also by tradition, cooking was carried out as soon as the sun rose far enough for its rays to hide the light of the Desert Cookers [which consisted of a cut-down expendable petrol tin, filled with sand – there was plenty of that around – soused in petrol and ignited]. Frequently this luxury had to be foregone, because orders to break leaguer came before first light. Not a luxury but, in any well-officered unit, an unbreakable rule was the insistence that, whenever water supplies made it possible, all ranks washed, shaved and cleaned their teeth. Not only did this save life in the event of wounding but it was an immensely important factor in a unit's morale.'

'Pete' Petersen signed on for 'Seven Years Hard' in July 1940 and was in danger of becoming a 'donkey-walloper' until Fate switched him, via a good dose of spit and polish [Pete had a different word for it], into a bunch of reinforcements headed for North Africa. Here, Fate's fickle finger pointed him to 6RTR and some pretty strenuous and hazardous Desert warfare until that Battalion ran out of tanks and Pete, along with others, ended up in The Fifth. Pete landed on his feet: he was assigned, as 37mm gunner, to a *Grant* which had Sgt Bing Coller MM as Crew Commander, Cpl Steve Barton DCM as driver, Harry Ireland as the 75mm main gunner and Frank Tring as the W/Op. When he joined it, 5RTR was in Stuka Valley. Pete agrees with the others who spent time there that it was not a comfortable place: 'not as dangerous as the Luftwaffe would have liked to believe but tiresome, as their visits were noisy and disturbed our card games'. In a less light-hearted vein, Pete acknowledged that there was serious business ahead but that The Fifth were ready for it and had every confidence in the man at the helm both of the Regiment and the Army.

Willie Dovey, that newly qualified 'tankie' whose first home leave was interrupted by the outbreak of war, was far from being a novice when he came to The Fifth. In the Desert since January 1941, Willie had seen plenty of active service with 22nd Armoured Brigade. He joined 5RTR as the wireless operator on a *Honey* when the Regiment was still within jaunting distance of Cairo. A place, Willie claims, he only visited to further his education. Quite possibly but one may be forgiven for wondering just what it was that Willie learnt there. After a spell across the wire, Willie was sent on an advanced wireless operator's course and returned to his Squadron to find that he was now the operator on a *Grant*. More room, thicker armour and a better gun. Thicker and better but still not good enough.

Willie states, in summarising his experiences between July and October 1942 that 'we were now equipped with *Shermans*.' This is not reflected in the War Diary which is still giving *Grants* and *Crusaders* in the Tank State as late as November 1942 and only mentions *Shermans* for the first time on 19th January next year. There is, however, evidence that The Fifth did have *Shermans* before that date. In the 'Summary of Log of Composite Sqn of 'B' and 'C' Sqns.' kept by Captain E Whitty and dated November 1942, there is an entry for18th November which reads, '1130 hrs Collected 12 *Shermans* .'

All of which brings the story up to Friday, 23rd October 1942.

THE OTHER SIDE

On the day Brian Stone met his nemesis, Major General FW von Mellenthin of the DAK admitted that Rommel's position was perilous. Only in terms of artillery did he feel there was any room for confidence. It was true, he said boastfully, that Panzerarmee Afrika might only have a few guns and a few rounds for their own guns (15 Panzers had only two rounds for each gun) but they had plenty of 25-pounders and a large supply of recently captured ammunition.

On 4th July Auchinleck had given orders for an all-out attack, which Rommel would scarcely have been in a position to resist if it had been pressed home: but, for one reason or another, it was not. One would not like to think that the reason for this was, as claimed by von Mellenthin [surely one of the Wehrmacht's most arrogant senior officers, to judge him by his own words], 'that a few shells from an 88 usually sufficed to deter their tanks from any serious assault'. But, whatever the reason, Rommel must have thanked his stars that there was no serious assault.

It is interesting to note that von Mellenthin describes the Battle of Alam Halfa as the turning point of the war [in the Desert] and that, 'our [that is the Axis] presence at el Alamein was producing tremendous reaction by the Anglo-American war machine.' He remarks, in passing, that the Panzerarmee was paying the penalty, in August 1942, for the Axis failure to capture Malta. To excuse himself in the eyes of posterity, rather than in pursuit of strict historical accuracy, von Mellenthin claims that 'as a matter of sober military appreciation, the General Staff of the Panzerarmee did not believe that we could break through to the Nile'. He generously admitted that the British excelled at static warfare. A curious claim in the light of subsequent events.

At this point, Rommel's DIARIES *and von Mellenthin's* PANZER BATTLES *exhibit several contradictions. Both Rommel and his General Staff are recorded as admitting two factors which made further progress to the Delta impossible: diminishing supplies, which showed but little hope of increasing, and the strength of the Eighth Army's position at el Alamein.*

As far as supplies were concerned, the capture of Tobruk had not made the significant difference on which Rommel placed such reliance. The Royal Navy had command of the Mediterranean and the Royal Air Force had almost overwhelming superiority in the air. Tobruk, one way or another, had not proved good value for Rommel in terms of men and matériel.

As far as men and machines on the ground were concerned, the Panzerarmee lacked adequate supplies of both to make the irresistible flanking thrust that would bring them round on the left of the Eighth Army's position and then encircle the main Allied forces by turning first north and then north-west to the coast by el Alamein itself.

As far as the strength of the Eighth Army's positions were concerned Rommel was badly served by his Intelligence Section.

Nevertheless, trusting in promises of essential petrol supplies, made by no less an authority than Field Marshal Kesserling [the C-in-C of all German forces in the Mediterranean and the Luftwaffe's senior ranking officer] and needing the full moon for a planned night attack, Rommel launched his final thrust on the night of 30th/31st August.

On Rommel's own admission, the key factors in which he placed his trust were the effect of surprise and the gaining of sufficient ground to make it impossible for the Eighth Army to regroup. 'Had there been a quick break-through,' he afterwards wrote, 'the British would have needed time for reconnaissance, for decision-making and for carrying out those decisions. But we lost the advantage: the British knew where we were. Their tank forces were assembled[16] ready for immediate action. In the event, the offensive failed for three reasons. The British positions (contrary to our reconnaissance reports) had been completed in great strength: the RAF kept our forces pinned to the ground: the promised petrol did not arrive.'

Von Mellenthin, as ever a master of excuses, adds a sandstorm to the chapter of misfortunes and tells, from the Axis' point of view, the story of the 'going-map' which British Intelligence planted and which indicated good going where only the worst was to be found but which DAK accepted as authentic . . . to their cost.

It should be said parenthetically, when discussing Rommel's difficulties, that in the summer of 1942 he was an extremely sick man. Wasted by neglect of incessant attacks of the usual desert diseases, physical sickness cannot but have clouded his judgement. If, which is reported to be the case, he felt that he ought personally still to be at the peak of performance, he undoubtedly felt that the same should be true of his army. In neither case was this true.

Rommel, who was exceptionally clear-sighted, must have found it hard to comprehend, for example, why battle-equipped Wehrmacht Divisions should remain unnecessarily stationed in France when he needed them in North Africa: he could see quite clearly that there would be no invasion of the Continent of Europe in 1942.

Perhaps Rommel's tragedy was that, no matter what he did or said, no-one in Berlin really cared two pfennigs for the War in North Africa.

THE WAR CHRONICLE

1942

July	03	End of Soviet resistance in Crimea
	07	Disastrous Arctic Convoy PQ17. 23 out of 36 ships sunk by U-boats
	26	Sweets rationed in UK
	29	Ernest Bevin announced post-war 'Pensions for All' Scheme
August	06	General Alexander appointed C-in-C Middle East. General Gott appointed C-in-C Eighth Army
	07	'Strafer' Gott killed by enemy action
	11	HMS *Eagle,* Aircraft Carrier, sunk in Mediterranean
	13	German Army reached the gates of Stalingrad
	15	Monty took over as C-in-C Eighth Army
	17	USAAF 'Flying Fortresses' made first daylight raids on France
	18-20	Allied raid on Dieppe. 6,100 Canadian and British troops staged disastrous attack, losing two-thirds of ships, men and aircraft
	25	Both US and Japanese suffered heavy losses in fighting on Guadalcanal
	26	HRH Duke of Kent, HM the King's youngest brother, killed in an air crash. – 'Daily Worker' back on the street after an 18 month ban
	29	Soviet aircraft stepped up bombing of Berlin and Danzig
September	04	Open clashes between police and IRA gunmen in Belfast
	10	British and South African forces took control of Madagascar to stop Vichy Government aiding Japanese submarines
	11	Churchill warned Congress Party in India to cease 'revolutionary activities'. – RAF bombers went on the offensive in Burma
	15	Major USN Aircraft Carrier *Wasp* sunk by Japanese submarine
	18	British Arctic Convoy PQ 18 largely successful in bringing aid to Russia
	23	'Go-ahead' to plans for the 'Atomic Bomb' given in the USA

	30	Battle of Stalingrad reached stalemate through September
October	02	RMS *Queen Mary* accidentally rammed and sank HMS *Curacao* in Atlantic
	13	US Marines succeeded in Guadalcanal offensive
	16	A cyclone killed 40,000 in Bengal and seriously disrupted the Burma supply lines
	23	The end of the beginning

NOTES

1 Tobruk. Everyone in the Desert knew the vital importance of Tobruk: for the Allies to hold; for the Axis to capture. In one of his rare lapses – acting more like Adolf Hitler than Winston Churchill – the Prime Minister issued an order that Tobruk was to be held 'at all costs'. General Klopper, the Australian Garrison Commander, might just have had the resources to obey but he lacked experience to give the necessary commands and the wherewithal to transmit them. Churchill was with the US President in Washington when news of the surrender reached him. On hearing the news, Roosevelt asked what he could do to help. 'Tanks and guns, and ships to get them to Suez,' was Churchill's reply. Roosevelt's offer had not been an idle one. He put in hand instructions for the immediate despatch of 300 *Shermans* and 100 anti-tank guns (which the US Army could ill spare) on a fleet of six of the fastest ships available

2 'Strafer' Gott. See Note 8 to Chapter IV

3 B L Montgomery. Before he adopted his faithful Humber Snipe staff car, Monty used to pay his visits in a jeep with the letters BLM emblazoned on the side. This caused some merriment to tank crews, particularly the gunners, since the initials BLM stood for the main gun's 'Breach Loading Mechanism' – a term which had all sorts of improper interpretations

4 Something hostile. In the clear light of wisdom after the event, one can see that Brian and, indeed, Dickie Ward may have fallen into one of DAK's favourite traps. The 50mm A/Tk gun could well have been a lure. This possibility is given some colour from the speed with which the 'right flank protection' tank was knocked out . . . by something hostile over on the right flank?

5 Brian Stone. Brian's capture inevitably finished his part in the story of The Fifth but it did not, luckily, finish Brian. He was cared for as well as possible by the Germans but had the misfortune to be handed over to the Italians whose casualness with regard to treatment and hygiene nearly killed him. He was repatriated through Lisbon in late 1943, recuperated and became a schoolmaster. He died in 1995

6 'Fearless'. The CO, Colonel Hutton, was 'Fearless Jim' or sometimes just 'Fearless' to all ranks in 5RTR. In one man's view – Jake's – 'he must have been one of the greatest guys who ever joined the Army. The lads would have done anything for him and gone anywhere with him – if he said we were going to make a frontal attack on the gates of hell, they would have been off like a shot.'

7 Tank battles. Estimates scarcely vary as to the number of tanks left to Rommel at this stage of the War. The lowest (Rommel's Chief of Staff) was thirty five:

the highest (Liddell Hart) was thirty seven. As far as the Eighth Army was concerned, they still seemed pretty numerous, ubiquitous and aggressive!

8 Treated with humanity. There was a period in the Desert when this was not the case and the British were entirely to blame. Some Senior Commander misguidedly issued an order that prisoners were not to be fed until they had been interrogated. The intention was that, if questioned while still in a state of shock, they would be more likely to 'come apart' but that, if comforted by food and water, they would have had time to gather their wits. A copy of this order, according to Brigadier Desmond Young in his biography of Rommel, fell into German hands. The DAK (and the Italians) not unnaturally took the order to mean that prisoners were not to be fed until they *had* 'come apart'. For a while, until the misunderstanding was cleared up, Allied prisoners were not allowed food or water until they were considered to be softened up: a process which, on occasion, took thirty six hours or more

9 Qattara Depression. Not quite impossible to cross, however unsuitable for mobile warfare. The infallible belief that the Depression could not be crossed was shattered when a certain Major the Hon R Plunkett led his Squadron of Guides Cavalry armoured cars across it

10 The tank commander. This was Sgt Len Coller. His account of the action was recorded in the previous chapter. Sgt Coller, it will be recalled, puts the incident firmly in June

11 Mad as a Hatter. Sgt 'Stooge' Alcock. Even Jake Wardrop thought him a bit eccentric – so did the MO when it was reported to him that 'Stooge' was seen baling out of a brewed-up tank holding his tin helmet over his bottom. Later became SSM of 'C' Squadron

12 *Crusaders.* These were the new *A15* British Cruiser tanks (see details in Appendix 2) The *A15*s were the successors of other, even more useless, cruiser tanks, whose only virtue was their Christie suspension. The waste of time, money and material in developing the *Centaurs* and *Covenanters* (which never saw front-line service) was incalculable. It meant, among other things, that the *Cromwell*, which might have been of some use in the Desert – 88mm anti-tank guns always excepted – did not see active service until June 1944

13 102 missing ORs. The new figure of 474 ORs is probably a typing or transcription error if the earlier figure of 576 is correct

14 XI Hussars. This is according to the version produced by Mike Carver. General Verney puts the XI Hussars (the 'Cherry Pickers') in with the Divisional Troops, which seems more likely as they had been, as early as June 1940 (and they were as late as May 1945) the Recce Regiment of 7AD

15 Wendell Wilkie. Republican candidate for the American Presidency in 1940. Despite the difference in political ideology, Wilkie acted as President Roosevelt's roving but unofficial ambassador

16 British tank forces were assembled. This is not strictly correct but may only be a quirk of translation. The various armoured units were not so much 'assembled' as strategically placed in precise anticipation of Rommel's attack

CHAPTER VIII

. . . el Alamein: 'The End of the Beginning'[1]

October–November 1942

Apart from its military significance, the October 1942 Battle of el Alamein was the first occasion of which the appropriate authorities appreciated the value of propaganda, or even simple publicity. His critics say that Monty was responsible for el Alamein being the first battle ever to have unrolled before the cameras. No doubt Monty enjoyed the coverage but he did not generate it. The first time that the British got near to successful Public Relations for our war effort was the recording of the Battle of el Alamein.

And rightly so. As an operation, the launch of the el Alamein offensive was a PR showpiece as well as a military set piece.

In the background of the background to The Fifth's part at el Alamein was the 'clean sweep' that Winston Churchill had made in the High Command and the quite phenomenal speed with which those changes produced results. General Alexander only became C-in-C MEF on 11th August: Monty took over Eighth Army on the 15th (a day in advance of his appointment) and, in very short order, Lt Gen Sir Oliver Leese took over XXXth Corps and Lt Gen Brian Horrocks took over XIIIth Corps. More firmly in the saddle, and unaffected by Winnie's changes, were Maj Gen 'John' Harding, GOC Seventh Armoured Division, Brigadier 'Pip' Roberts of Twenty-second Armoured Brigade and, to complete the trio of those with nicknames rather than given names, Lt Col 'Jim' Hutton of The Fifth.

Liddell Hart remarks that armoured fighting changed its form at el Alamein: 'a more cautious form of action and a slower tempo'. He goes on to say that this was the pattern for the rest of the war. [He seems to have forgotten 'The Great Swan' and that hell-for-leather charge across the Central German Plain!] However, there is a great deal of truth in his statement that the commanders of armoured units at last learnt that isolated 'concentrated punches' were both ineffective and costly against tactically positioned anti-tank guns.

Monty's original plan for the Battle of el Alamein had been to launch two simultaneous attacks, one on each flank, and then, once breaches had been made, to let loose the Xth (Armoured) Corps on Rommel's supply lines, leaving the infantry to mop up its opposite numbers.

Monty changed his plan for two reasons: firstly, to catch Rommel on the hop by adopting an entirely new strategy: secondly, because he thought that there were still shortcomings in the standard of training of the Eighth Army as a whole.

The strategic change was a complete reversal of previous desert warfare. Instead of first destroying the opposition's armour and then 'dealing with the rest of his forces', Monty decided to go for 'the rest' first and then deal with his armour. The plan was subtle. By adopting it, he forced Rommel to use his armour in counter-attack: in other words, on ground of the Eighth Army's own choosing.

His criticism of the standards of training cannot have been popular among those who had been on the blue any time the last two years. There were, however, two aspects of this criticism. Everyone in the Eighth Army was not battle-hardened and, anyway, Monty's tactical use of his forces in the Desert was going to be different from that of his predecessors. Many who doubted his wisdom or experience were unaware that Monty *had* been in the Desert. He served in Egypt in the 1930s and did so under an exceptional senior officer: exceptional if only because he believed in the value of the night attack, particularly in the Desert.

Even allowing for the soundness of Monty's strategic thinking, Rommel still felt justified in commenting after the Battle of el Alamein that, 'The British attacked again and again with separate bodies of tanks and did not, as might have been expected [for which read *as I would have done*], throw into battle the 900 tanks which they could have employed.'

According to Liddell Hart, Rommel's figure of '900 tanks' was an under-estimate. On 23rd October 1942 the Eighth Army had 1,441 tanks of which 270 were *Shermans* and 210 were *Grants.* The DAK had 173 Pzkw IIIs (of which 88 mounted the up-graded 50mm gun) and 38 Pzkw IVs (of which 30 had the long 75mm gun), with 38 Pzkw IIs and 22 assorted tanks in the workshops.

From the general, then, to the specific ... and nothing could be more specific than the 5RTR War Diary, on this occasion anyhow, which reads:

23rd October

0900 hrs CO's Conference for all officers. Subject – Final orders for Operation 'Lightfoot'.

1. Information

   (a) Enemy. The enemy is holding a line running north and south from west of el Alamein to el Mreir, Deir Munassah, Deir Alinda to Qarat Himeimat with positional troops, keeping in reserve his armour and mobile forces

   (b) Own Troops. We have been in positions in touch with the enemy since 4th September and, during this time, have regrouped, re-equipped and reinforced

2. Intention. The German Afrika Corps and the Italian Libyan Army will be destroyed.
3. Method.
(a) 10 and 30 Corps are attacking north of el Mreir
(b) 4 Ind Div and 50 Div are harassing in the Central Section
(c) 13 Corps, less 50 Div, are attacking on the general line 256 Northing Grid
(i) 22 Armd Brigade will advance along 256 Northing Grid and establish battle positions 3 miles west of the February Minefield. Later moving north towards Deir Alinda
(ii) 44 Div will attack 500 yards to our north and on the same axis and later take over protection of Bridge Head on the February Minefield
(iii) 1st Free French Brigade will make a silent attack, under cover of a smoke screen laid from the air on Qarat Himeinat at 0300 hrs 24th
4. Intercommunication. Wireless silence until 1800 hrs 23rd and then normal
5. Administration – normal
Bn Group consists of:- 5 RTR. 378 Bty, 97 Fd Reg RA. H Troop 250 Anti/Tank Battery 65th Anti Tank Regt RA. 'I' Coy 1 RB
Tank State:- *Crusaders* – 18. *Grants* – 24

1700 hrs Bn formed up in four columns facing south, 1 mile south of MR
1800 hrs Bn. group moved in 2 columns through May, June and Nuts minefields to concentration area
2000 hrs arrive in concentration area. Artillery programme commences. An advance party advances to clear gaps in January Minefield.

24th October
0300 hrs [Map ref] Clearing of gaps held up by small arms fire: only one and two gaps clear so far
0305 hrs Orders to pass through minefield and take up battle positions to the right of the Greys
0400 hrs Arrived in position and engaged by enemy anti/tank fire
0445 hrs Carriers of attached infantry attacked an enemy anti-tank gun position, over-running it and killing its crew. At first light took up positions facing north and north-west and were heavily engaged by enemy artillery fire
0815 hrs ORDERS:- Bn is to push north 1,500 yds keeping close to western edge of January Minefield. Greys to our left are to push south. Our task was not practicable without suffering heavy losses, owing to intense artillery and anti-tank fire, so were cancelled and instructions given to engage with accurate fire on A/tank positions to our front
1000 hrs The Greys had some success and gained contact with minefield north of Himeimat

1130 hrs The crews of the A/tank guns to our front surrender and 200 prisoners are taken. 7 – 50mm A/tank guns captured
1315 hrs A patrol of 'A' Sqn and a section of carriers pushed forward to the ridge 1,200yds to our north. Our position is still being heavily shelled by enemy artillery
1400 hrs Some tanks of 'A' Sqn run on mines scattered in front of minefield to our north. During the afternoon *Grants* remain in same position and heavy shelling continues especially in area of minefield gaps through which we advanced early this morning
1745 hrs 16 tanks reported on our front, 10 moving north, 6 moving south
1810 hrs Information that there were 30 tanks on Brigade front moving west to east. All tanks believed to be west of February Minefield. Up to last light no attack developed but enemy A/tank and artillery fire continued
Casualties:- 1 Officer killed. 1 Officer died of wounds. 3 Officers wounded. 1 OR died of wounds. 5 ORs wounded. 200 POWs captured

25th October
Attack by 1/5 and 1/6 Queens was successful in so far as they reached February Minefield and one gap was made, through which 4 CLY advanced but were knocked out. The rest of the Brigade advanced and took up positions east of February Minefield, were shelled (not so intense as yesterday) took up Battle positions and continued to snipe enemy positions. More prisoners (about 250) were taken during the morning.
1500 hrs 'B' and 'C' Sqns are continuing to snipe enemy positions. 'B' Sqn are ordered to send [out] a patrol covered by fire from *Grants* and Gunners
1525 hrs Patrols get to [within] 100 yards of point and confirm A/tank gun knocked out earlier and stacks of mines around minefield. On turning to come away, tank was knocked out. Bn stayed in position until 2000 hrs when they were withdrawn
2230 hrs Bn arrived at [designated position] and leaguered.
Casualties:- 2 Officers wounded.1 OR killed. 1 OR died of wounds. 1 OR wounded
[Enemy] 2 – 50mm A/tank guns destroyed, 1 SP gun destroyed and 1 88mm gun destroyed
26th October
Bn rested.

Mike Carver[2] notes one positive and one negative feature of the advance not remarked on elsewhere. Clearing of the minefields was aided by the use of *Scorpions*,[3] the first time they had been used in action: penetration of the first minefield was impeded by soft going which had not been indicated to the Brigade.

However, the most remarkable feature of the Battle of el Alamein was the hour at which the attack was launched. Last light: just when all sensible Desert

Warriors were thinking about withdrawing to leaguer for the night, replenishing, doing a spot of maintenance and getting in a bit of shut-eye. This was one of the lessons Monty learnt from 'Tim' Pile (later General Sir Frederick Pile RTR) during his 1930s tour of duty in Egypt.

There are several accounts of the Battle of el Alamein by members of the Regiment. Some are just of incidents, others are detailed recollections. They are introduced by alphabetical order to avoid playing favourites.

Bill Dovey claims that he only remembers the battle for the noise made by the artillery, which, he said, was still ringing in his ears fifty years later.

Bing Coller recalls it for the Personal Message[4] he received from his GOC-in-C. This was the first of many which Monty issued. It is dated 23.10.42 and is curious for its incidental contradiction of an earlier GOC-in-C's Army Order. 'The Auk' had specifically forbidden saying 'Rommel' instead of 'the enemy'. The Army was not, he pointed out, fighting a myth called Rommel, it was fighting the German and Italian Armies and Air Forces. Not so Monty. The first paragraph of his first message reads, 'When I assumed command of the Eighth Army I said that the mandate was to destroy ROMMEL [Monty's capitals] and his Army and that it would be done as soon as we were ready.' Prophetically, he went on to say, twice, that the battle would be the turning point of the war. That was, he admonished his readers, if every officer and every man did his duty and did not surrender as long as he could fight. He continued by saying, '.. we have first-class equipment, *good tanks* [*not* Monty's italics], good anti-tank guns ..' Most crews in those tanks would have taken leave to differ. Better; yes, but not good.

Harry Ireland gives a rather fuller version, starting with 'Jim' Hutton's detailed explanation of what was in store, then skipping to 2200 hrs which, 'brought the biggest barrage of artillery guns I had ever witnessed, (lighting the sky all around to almost daylight – what a sight and the noise – thunderous continuing for about an hour or so). Within the hours that followed we had been guided through the first enemy minefield and spread out so that, at first light the following morning, we were in the battle line.

'At some time during the night the driver and myself had got out to stretch our legs and 'take the shovel for a walk'. We heard moaning near the tank; on looking round we found a very badly wounded Italian soldier in a near-by slit trench. We approached him; he was asking for water and calling 'Mamma, Mamma.' We gave him water and some morphia tablets out of the First Aid kit but could not get him evacuated because the Italian guns were shelling the only gap open in the minefield. We hoped he'd be picked up come daylight by our medics.

'Next day my companion driver transferred to the Squadron 2i/c's tank and was killed in action. The fighting was very hard going night and day, catching a few hours sleep in the tank, but the tank commander standing in the turret, always on the alert. I don't know how he keeps going (dedicated to the job like all the officers and Senior NCOs). Plenty of prisoners are coming over now but we still cannot break through the second minefield.

'Taken out of Southern Sector and moved north, maintenance and replenishing.

'Organising with infantry for the final assault, the break-through came after twelve hours hard slogging. Out we rolled taking everything before us, thousands of prisoners, trucks, guns – some of it our own the enemy had captured on the run down the Desert. What a feeling!'

Titch Maple, among others, comments on two changes in wireless procedure which were introduced at this time. The first concerned the regimental wireless net and was one for which Colonel Hutton was largely responsible. Although Titch, as one of the leading wireless luminaries in The Fifth was closely involved in this change, it is left to Jake Wardrop to describe it later in this chapter. The second change was the introduction of a new Phonetic Alphabet[5]. Titch Maple remembers this vividly: it was his job to teach it to the wireless operators!

In his personal 'Diary of a Desert Rat', Syd Storer recalls that his run-up to el Alamein did not start propitiously. His *Grant* developed the habit of bursting into flames when it was started and eventually had to be taken back to TDS. No immediate replacement was available and the crew spent the next few days living in a petrol lorry and away from the forward concentration area. This provided a relief from sandstorms and the stench of burning vehicles and flesh, to say nothing of flies which were everywhere in their millions. 'They walked,' Syd wrote, 'on your face, bathed in your tea and shared each meal. This caused an epidemic of Gyppy tummy which made everyone who caught it terribly ill. By the beginning of October it suddenly began to rain. We were astounded for we had never seen rain in the Desert before. It rained in spells for the next few days, with an especially heavy storm during the night of the 9th October.'

There are some contradictions there. Harry Ireland, for instance, talks of rain storms at the beginning of November – as does the War Diary – but does not mention the storm on 9th October.

On 15th October Syd's crew still had no tank when they came under battle orders. Activity increased everywhere, with almost daily enemy air raids and resultant dog fights overhead. The Regiment moved south-west, closer to the front line and in between Ragil and facing the Himeimat position, with only the Free French farther to the south, nearer the Qattara Depression. The whole area was being protected by minefields.

On the afternoon of 21st October the men were called on parade in a corner of a small wadi. There, complete with maps, Colonel Jim told them, as promised by Monty, about the forthcoming attack; where it was to take place and what the objectives were. They learnt that there would be no reveille on the morning of the 23rd – no sleep during the night, for that matter – and that they were to move through the artillery barrage at 2130 hrs. On the 22nd there was still no tank but the canteen came up for the last time so that the crews could purchase all they needed. Syd and his crew placed their purchases with their rations and personal kit, so that everything could be loaded quickly They knew there would be plenty checking for them to do if the tank arrived in time to move off with the Squadron.

In the best tradition of 'spaghetti westerns', relief was delayed to the last moment. 'At 2000 hrs a tank transporter arrived with our tank – one and a half hours before the push. It was quickly unloaded,' Syd went on. 'Our kit and rations put on, water cans filled. Then each of us checked our equipment and reported ourselves ready, except the gunner who had no chance to test and adjust his guns but it was agreed to carry that out at some future time and hope for the best.

'We completed a long march through our own minefields in brilliant moonlight and were a little ahead of time when we approached the start line just short of an enemy minefield, code-named 'January'. As the barrage opened up it was difficult to hear anything at all but we saw the gapping parties working ahead to clear the minefield and admired the way in which the MPs coolly placed the marker lamps along either side of the gap. Four gaps were to be opened but, due to some blockages in the southern two, we were switched to pass through the northern two gaps and, once we had reached the open area, we moved to the right of our friends, the Greys. Through the night there was only a limited amount of heavy enemy gun fire[6] but plenty of small arms fire.

'By daybreak most of the battalion were on small pieces of ground between 'January' and 'February' [minefields]. The area was very congested and dawn showed how exposed our positions were. Supported by the infantry we proceeded to clear the ground of all enemy troops who had stayed in their foxholes. These were sent back through the gap. However, while we were occupied with this task, we failed to notice an enemy anti-tank gun being placed in position on the high ground to our front. The Baker[7] tank of our troop was just taking up position to our left when there was a loud explosion and smoke and flames poured from it. The commander and turret crew climbed out of the top, the side door of the *Grant* opened and the gunner and a badly wounded driver crawled out. They carried the driver to shelter behind our tank as we radioed for the MO: there was no sign of the wireless operator as the tank burned in the early morning sunlight. The MO arrived in his jeep and took away the driver and some of the crew: the remainder of the Squadron quickly ranged on the anti-tank gun and knocked it out.

'With the dawn the full barrage opened up again and the gapping parties began to work on 'February'. Their numbers had been depleted on the previous day and, in the face of devastating small arms fire, it was decided to withdraw from the minefield until later: we stayed in position, picking up any target that presented itself.' Syd then recounted how, in these uncomfortable conditions, he and the main gunner managed to provide the crew with a good strong brew of tea and some food, which improved morale as well as alleviating hunger. When the message came that an attempt to break through 'February' was to be made at 1730 hrs, the crew 'felt ready for anything'.

Once another heavy artillery barrage had been put down and reinforcements had arrived, the gapping parties of engineers moved forward to remove the wire surrounding the minefield. It was, however, soon evident that the enemy's forward positions had been reinforced during the quiet period and the engineers were pinned down, unable to work in daylight. In spite of several requests for covering fire, The Fifth was not allowed to move forward to give close support. Despite the heavy casualties to the men in exposed positions, the order had gone out that the tanks were not to risk sustaining unnecessary losses at this stage of the battle.

Syd Storer again. 'In the Desert the sun sets very quickly and, as the sun disappeared over the horizon, the gapping parties were recalled. And, instead of our support, it was decided that the infantry would concentrate on any enemy infantry that remained in between 'January' and 'February'. That night we were withdrawn into reserve and took up firing positions along the edge of 'January'. We received a welcome midnight visit from the cookhouse, instead of cooking inside the tank: some lovely bully stew and biscuits which greatly improved our outlook on life. On the previous evening prior to the barrage we were given a rum issue. I had always previously refused this but I decided, unwisely as it turned out, to drink mine. Instead of giving me extra courage, it upset my unaccustomed stomach so badly that I spent most of the night outside in a slit trench, despite the enemy fire.

'As the sun rose next morning the sky was full of our fighter planes raiding enemy targets. This aerial activity continued all morning. After midday, we were told to move up to a new position. We travelled a few miles and then leaguered up for the night, after replenishing and receiving some mail. We were told that things were moving in the northern area as planned and that we were to move northwards and be prepared to assist in the final breakthrough and to take advantage of it when it occurred.'

This carries Syd Storer's very detailed account up to the point reached by the War Diary.

Keith Treasure's recollections are typical of the man. When asked what he remembered of the el Alamein Battle, he replied that he recalled motoring through the white-taped, lantern-lit gaps in the minefield following the tanks on the night of 23rd October – as always with a load of over 1,000 gallons High Octane Petrol [not the most comfortable travelling companion]. There were, he commented laconically, no 'cats' eyes' in the roads in those days. Even more insouciantly he added, 'When the MO came along, he removed a sliver of shrapnel from my left eye and said, 'You're a lucky blighter, Treasure!'.'

Jake Wardrop starts his version of the Battle of el Alamein by telling how The Fifth Tanks changed the face of British military history. In fact, 5RTR really did do so in a small but significant way. What happened was that someone – or perhaps several people – on Monty's staff felt that he needed to be shown that things were done differently in the Desert from the text book manner of the Home Command. An important aspect of this was the 'regimental net' for tank units. It was not by any means pure chance that The Fifth was selected to demonstrate the 'one frequency' method On Colonel Hutton's initiative, The Fifth had pioneered and adopted it.

Monty is reputed not have believed that this new method was possible or, even if technically possible, capable of giving the commanding officer and his squadron commanders effective control of the battalion. The method, that of having every tank on the same frequency with equal access to 'the air', did require good wireless discipline. Perhaps this is another reason why the Fifth Tanks were chosen? Whatever the reason, 5RTR put on a battle demonstration with Monty and his senior staff listening on monitors. As Jake Wardrop said, it was a 'piece of cake'. The exercise went perfectly and, after confirmation of the feasibility of the method by his Chief Signaller, Monty directed that all tank and assimilated units should use it. The text books were accordingly re-written. 'Good old Fearless!' was Jake's comment.

After covering the same ground as Syd Storer, Jake went on by recalling that the opposition had their two old enemies, the DAK Panzer Divisions, such old 'friends' as the 90th and 164th Divisions, sundry veteran gunners and assorted Italian Armoured and Infantry Divisions. So much did Jake and his pals regard the 90th Light as friends that they said they were going to invite them to join a Victory Party in Tripoli after the war. That didn't mean that they weren't 'out to fix them now: they have been in our hair long enough'. Jake was not the man to underrate his opponents but he felt that, with the RAF, the Allies had their measure in the coming battle.

When it came to the battle, Jake, Stanley and George were on the Major's tank, as was a bottle of Gilbey's Spey Royal. There was little or no sleep for the crews and they were on the alert when the order to advance came at 0400 hrs. One or two tanks were caught by gun fire on the way through the minefields but most of The Fifth got through safely and out into the open ground beyond. Here they opened out into a semi-circle and continued to push on until being held up by another minefield, which caused some casualties. They stayed in position and engaged some guns on high ground to their front: these found their range as the sun came up behind the advancing Eighth Army and gave The Fifth 'a lacing with everything they had.'

To the left, on the high ground at Himeimat, the Free French Legionnaires from Bir Hakeim were advancing against strong opposition. The worst part of the 'lacing' was the air-burst HE, to which the turret crew were particularly vulnerable. A splinter from one of these got Paddy Doyle, causing him nasty – and certainly bloody – injuries. There was no hope of the MO getting up to the tank, so, after patching him up, Jake pulled the tank back to the nearest cover he could find, which was only a slit trench. Major Doyle wanted to get into the tank and get back into action which put his crew in a dilemma. Jake solved this by disobeying him and going across to some near-by infantry to ask for help. Here he found a much-decorated KRRC major who was calmly organising a brew-up for his men. He couldn't help either but recommended Jake to pay no attention to orders and take the wounded man back to wherever help was available. Jake did this and, in due course, got Paddy Doyle into an ambulance, depriving him of his State Express 555 cigarettes and bottle of Johnny Walker, for the very good reason – or so Jake thought – that he wouldn't be doing much smoking or drinking in the next few days. In fact, Major Doyle didn't rejoin The Fifth until the summer of 1943 in Tunis.

George Stimpson added a word to Jake's version by recounting how near Paddy Doyle came to losing his life. It was sometimes prudent, when the air-bursts were coming over thick and fast, to 'close the hatch' and imitate a tortoise by pulling one's head in under cover. Even so, the head had to come out at times to have a shufti. For this, some tanks had a steel helmet handy for the crew commander. However, the combination of beret, headphones and a tin hat did not sit easy on the head. Correct procedure was to slip the headband of the head phones down onto the back of one's neck [hoping the perishing things didn't fall off and end up eight feet below one in the bilges of the hull or become inextricably entangled with the strap of one's binoculars] whip off one's beret and clamp the helmet on one's head. On this occasion, when 'Stimmo' shouted to Paddy Doyle not to forget his helmet, Paddy said a rude word but did clamp the helmet on top of beret, headphones and all. Just as well he did. The helmet was struck by a fragment of the air-burst shell: this is what knocked Doyle unconscious. George Stimpson agrees with Jake Wardrop that, when Paddy Doyle came round, they had the devil's own job in preventing him taking the tank back into action even though he was bleeding like a stuck pig through the towel with which George had bandaged his head. Not for nothing did Major Doyle end the war with a DSO and a bar to his MC.

Stewart, the wireless operator, took over the tank and brought it back into action where the infantry had managed to push through the mines, 'beat up some guns and come back with a lot of prisoners.' That night there was a counter-attack which was beaten off but served to keep the crews awake at their posts in the tanks for the rest of the night and through the heat of the following day.

The last of these personal recollections to fall into place here, before reverting to the War Diary and the official histories, is that of Eric Wilde. It is not really a very personal recollection, as Eric makes no mention of himself. All Eric says is that, 'The Battle of el Alamein was a very hard time for us. On the first few days alone, the Second in Command of 'A' Squadron and all his Troop Leaders were wounded, as were all the Troop Leaders of 'B' Squadron and the OC 'C' Squadron. In addition, all the officers in our Infantry Support unit, 'I' Company 1 RB. But thereafter we seemed to have a charmed existence. We missed the very heavy tank battle round Tel el Aqqadir and, after that, the advance to Tripoli provided very few casualties.' Eric makes no mention of his own activities at el Alamein but it is a matter of history that he was one of the first officers in Seventh Armoured Division to be awarded a Military Cross for his part in the Battle.

On the 26th the War Diary has only a map reference and the words 'Bn resting' to say for itself.

Rest was also the order of the day on Tuesday 27th October until 1400 hrs when the CO went to Brigade and came back to call a Squadron Commanders' Conference at 1500 hrs. This was effectively an O Group to pass on new orders, the first of which was to move the Regiment into a new position with 1RTR on the left and 5RTR facing west. Further orders were to (1) observe and harass the enemy in the area of Samahet Gaballa (2) counter-attack any enemy penetration east of the 'January' minefield and (3) prevent enemy occupation of Qorel Labun. From the following day's entry – 'No event' – there can have been no counter-attack and there was no activity until 1700 hrs when the Regiment shifted its position and went into Divisional Reserve to be prepared to counter-attack any enemy penetration from south-west to north-east.

The shuttling around and taking up various positions in readiness for a counter-attack continued for the next two days and ended with the entire Brigade going into Army Reserve on the last day of October. These moves in fact took the Division well behind the line, some 15 miles east of el Alamein. While there, the composition of the Division was changed and took on the format which lasted, with only minor changes until the end of the war. For the Battle of el Alamein, the Division had comprised the 4th Armoured Brigade and the 22nd Armoured Brigade with the 131st (Queens) Brigade on attachment. As from 1st November 1942 the core composition of 7AD became 22nd Armoured and 131st Lorried Infantry Brigades.

Although the Battle of el Alamein has rightly been considered a great victory, it was – as the Duke of Wellington said of the Battle of Waterloo – 'a damned near-run thing'. At one point at the end of October, Monty ordered contingency plans to be drawn up to discontinue the advance and consolidate on the ground captured. The advance had not gone entirely according to plan; the tank losses were much heavier than had been expected with a 6-to-1 balance in Eighth Army's favour (General Lumsden, the Corps Commander, was slated by Monty for this and, later, expressed the view that the COs of some battalions had still not learnt their lessons. A criticism which can hardly have applied to the three battalions in 22 A Bde). Principally, and with Rommel back from hospital in Germany, the DAK could not be dislodged from what they called 'Hill 28' and we called 'Kidney Ridge'[8].

Rommel had risked everything on a nearly successful strategic move. He had weighed up Monty's plan, decided that the main Allied thrust really was in the north and positioned the 21st Panzer Division and the Italian Ariete Division on his left flank. He knew all too well that, if he had miscalculated, he simply did not have enough petrol to shift his armoured divisions from north to south. It was this opposition which the Eighth Army was encountering and it was this opposition which was to be cracked by Operation 'Supercharge'.

5RTR's situation was that, at 1230 hrs on 1st November, the unit moved to a new position, always facing west, and at 1700 hrs the Brigade received orders for the following day. The plan was that, during the night, infantry under command of Xth Corps [as was 7AD] were to put in an attack between the positions held by 15th and 21st Panzer Divisions. Gaps would then be made in the minefields in the area of Tel el Eisa, with 9th Armoured Brigade forming a bridgehead. It would then be the turn of 1st and 10th Armoured Divisions to move up and engage the enemy armour. When the enemy forces had been split, 22nd Armoured Brigade would pass through the gap, striking westward and then turning north to Ghazal with the object of cutting off the 90th Light Division. Whoever drew up the plan agreed with Jake Wardrop: the 90th Light had been 'in our hair long enough'.

On 2nd November, at first light, the Regiment moved up into position ready to pass through the minefield. By 1430 hrs the infantry had taken their objectives and established the bridgehead. The two British Armoured Divisions were engaging the enemy as planned and The Fifth was warned to be ready to move during the night. It was yet another cancelled stand-to. It was not until 1600 hrs on 3rd November that Colonel Jim got his orders. The Brigade was to be ready to move at 1730 hrs: the enemy was withdrawing and it was thought that the original Brigade plan would be put into operation. Possibly, but not that night. The Regiment moved up into yet another new position 'and leaguered facing west in five columns as it was possible that a night move might be made.'

The Regimental IO must have sweated both over the details of the orders which the CO spelt out at 0100 hrs on 4th November and the recording of the events on what proved to be a very busy day. At 0130 hrs there was to be a concentration of artillery fire on enemy positions until 0300 hrs. This concentration was to be followed up by a battalion of infantry from 51st Highland Division who, in turn would be followed by 22 Armd Bde with 1RTR leading, then a Coy of 1 RB, 5RTR, 4 CLY and the Gunners, with all groups in five columns. The route was laid down and the start time given as 0245 hrs. But at 0230 hrs the operation was postponed until 0615 hrs . . . and an unwelcome, thick ground mist held things up even further. At 1000 hrs the Regiment was again held up, this time by a screen of anti-tank guns and 22 Italian M 13 tanks. By 1120 hrs the remainder of these tanks and guns were forced to withdraw and The Fifth was on its way again. For ten minutes. This time the opposition was heavier and included some SP guns, spiced with heavy artillery fire. At 1350 hrs the Brigade had advanced to the area of Sidi Hamid and from 1500 hrs was again in contact with the enemy until last light. There was no exact tally of enemy guns and tanks destroyed but the day's bag, when the Regiment leaguered at 1800 hrs, included 250 Italian POWs.

On Guy Fawkes Day the Regiment was really on the move. The advance towards Ghazal started at 0630 hrs, swung west to a point 10 miles south of Fuka where a minefield caused another change of direction, this time to the south to skirt the minefield and enable the westward chase to be pursued. There was no major contact with the enemy by the time the tanks leaguered but many stragglers, both Italian and German, were swept up 'plus several odd guns and vehicles'.

A start on the 6th at 0630 hrs enabled The Fifth to cover 17 miles north-west to engage a German column, which they did very successfully at 0830 hrs, capturing three half-tracked vehicles, two 25-pounders, plus 17 lorries and about 100 Italian and 50 German POWs.

It is interesting to note that the War Diary does not mention anything about running out of petrol on 6th November, whereas General Verney states very specifically that 22nd Armoured Brigade's operations during the morning were seriously hampered by petrol shortage. 1RTR's attempt to cut the enemy off ran out impetus when the tanks ran out of petrol, as did an attempt of 4 CLY. *'Soon after 1100 hrs 5RTR were also grounded by lack of fuel'*. It is difficult to believe that an incident so contrary to Colonel Hutton's impeccable preparedness for action would have escaped remark in the Regimental record. In fact, The Fifth was in trouble on 7th November when 'the Battalion was held up as a number of vehicles in the Echelon were stuck' and 'there was no contact with the enemy during the day'.

Although the War Diary for the next few days, as will be seen, tells of one advance after another and brings into play so many names with which the older Desert hands were all too familiar, other factors took a hand to delay the victorious advance of the Eighth Army. One of these, it has to be said, was Monty. Unaware that Rommel could have counted the number of serviceable tanks left to his Panzerarmee on his own fingers and toes but all too well aware of his adversary's power to turn back on his attacker, Monty decided that the advance must be restricted to the speed at which the supplies could keep up with the main body, this speed being drastically reduced during the days and nights of the 8th, 9th and 10th by torrential rain in the northern, coastal 'cloud belt'. Logistically the rain delayed the wheeled transport which found itself wallowing in glutinous mud: physically it made life for the men in the slit trenches and the chaps in the tanks or with the guns sheer unadulterated hell. If, as someone bitterly remarked, 'hell can be wet.'

But the advance did go on as The Fifth's history shows.

Bob Lay was sent back to collect a replacement tank. Along with Bill Chorley and a 'Cumberland farm boy', Bill Walker, whose ambition in life was to settle his parents on their own piece of land [an ambition he did not achieve; he was killed when his tank was hit by an 88] they collected a very second-hand *Lee* which they immediately christened the 'Pepper-pot', its turret being so generously covered with welded-over shell holes. Bob relates how, 'We drove back with a replacement officer: as it got dark the barrage started up and the sky was alight. We arrived at the unit, drove through two minefields to the bridgehead. [Sgt] Henry Hall popped his head in the turret and, when I asked him what that green tracer was, replied, '88s.' I learnt that my tank commander had been killed. Paddy Doyle had been struck by shrapnel (and subsequently had a silver plate in his head, ultimately returning to us in Italy). We pulled back from the minefields as the attack in the north took over. We were scheduled to go in reserve and re-equip.

'Some days later we moved north past dummy tanks and lorries and went through the gap in pursuit of Jerry. Our crew were temporarily in 'B' Squadron. We were in the 'Pepper-pot': it had an obsolete wireless with separate head-sets for inter-com and for transmit-and-receive. Our officer grovelled on the floor when we were faced with a small Italian A/T gun. In leaguer we complained and saw no more of him. Back to 'C' Squadron; Joe Lyons was our tank commander. The pursuit continued until torrential rain bogged us down but all squadrons fired at maximum range as the last Jerry train headed away to the wire. Later we broke down in a wadi and were left behind. We were out of R/T range and I transmitted our position by morse. Nobody replied. Later I spoke to the CO's operator and reported what had happened. 'Oh,' he said, 'so you were the one who was transmitting?' Why the blazes did he not read me!

'*Shermans* arrived on transporters. Only drivers had been made familiar with them. They were mobile but the rest of the tanks were solid with hard, dark brown shipping grease. I was transferred to Henry Hall's tank in 11 Troop. We got aboard and, while on the move, stripped off most of the grease and got the tank in shape. We had trouble with the release mechanism for the turret machine-gun. I eventually found that wiping off the rest of the grease had obliterated a spring-loaded plunger.

'We became part of a composite squadron with 1RTR and were sent across the Desert to Agedabia to cut the road from Benghazi to the west. We are on trailers behind Diamond-Ts [US built 4x6 wheeled 'tractors' which were every bit as brutally powerful as they looked] but were constantly dropped off to tow the tractor out of the sand. It was finally decided to continue on our tracks. We had a day firing HE consistently. I loaded three complete complements of the stuff and eventually passed out, overcome by the fumes. I came round on the floor of the turret soaked in water.'

This sousing had an unfortunate result for Bob. Unlike the others who had been issued with battle-dress, he was still in KD and had no overcoat. He suffered intensely from the cold, particularly as the radial aero engines on the American tanks were partially cooled by air drawn through the turret. Bob recalls that the Composite Squadron was sometimes supplied by RAF air-drops, with 'supplementary rations' found in an abandoned German cookhouse lorry.

Jake Wardrop recalls the rain. But first he recalls that, once 'the bugle had blown' the only thing they seemed to stop for was to investigate the stream of prisoners trudging dispiritedly back into the hinterland of the Eighth Army.

If some prisoners ended up short of a watch or a pair of binoculars as a result of these little investigations, well, that's war for you. And, anyway, the chaps at the sharp end could put such things to rather better use than a lot of 'base wallahs'.

After four days of rain, mud became the main enemy and was the cause of The Fifth's missing what would have been the prize to end all Desert Army prizes. Rommel. Or so Jake thought but whether this is true or not is hard to decide. Certainly, The Fifth pursued a column consisting largely of captured British equipment – *Honeys*, 25-pounders, Ford lorries and so forth, but just failed to catch it and, certainly, Rommel was reported to have been travelling in just such a column. But . . .

Many of the men recalled listening to the BBC at nights on the tank wireless sets. The news was good, with reports of Italians and the Germans being captured in thousands. The men were always amused when some particular incident was described: they would look at each other and say, 'That's us!'

One incident in the follow-up particularly tickled Jake's sense of humour. 5RTR had crossed the wire near Sherferzan and swung north towards Capuzzo and, in Jake's opinion, met the man to whom Casey Jones was as nothing. As the Regiment drove north, they approached the east–west railway line and saw, standing outside a lonely railway-man's hut, a small and rather dilapidated diesel engine, hitched to some even more dilapidated wagons. As the tanks came into sight, a figure emerged from the hut and rapidly uncoupled the wagons. With a derisive toot of the whistle, the engine departed on full throttle, belching out an impressive, protective smoke screen. 'I think,' Jake wrote, 'he was giving us the Heidelberg raspberry, but good luck to him.'

The advance on Tobruk began to speed up. El Adem aerodrome was captured, with twenty-five Me 109s and such of the Luftwaffe personnel who came out quickly enough with their hands up. Those who were too slow or looked to be offering resistance paid dearly: the tank crews were in no mood to show mercy to the men who had made their lives uncomfortable or, worse, had bombed their families back home. The capture of the aerodrome brought a pleasant, and surely unexpected, bonus. A cooked meal. It was all ready, waiting for the Luftwaffe personnel: it got eaten, amid mocking shouts of, *Hoch, Hoch* and *Heil-you-know-who*, as welcome liquid refreshment went down desert-thirsty throats.

Willie Dovey, at this time W/Op to Brian Beresford, had one of those chance encounters which the war provided, meeting his brother, George, who was in another unit operating near 5RTR Willie's main impression of those days was 'that the enemy was always retreating and we were always advancing.' It could almost have been a number from a Bob Hope and Bing Crosby 'Road' film, 'We're off on the road to ..'

Harry Ireland, like Jake Wardrop, remembers the rain. 'Early November: the advance was brought to a halt with the first rain I had seen in the Desert; but did it rain – by the bucket full.' Here, Harry's memory telescopes events, as he says that the rain ceased within twenty-four hours: it didn't but, nevertheless, '..we were off again and mobile. We were coming up to the old names, Fuka, Mersa Matruh, which we never thought at one time that we would ever see again. Off to Capuzzo 150 miles, through the wire at Gap 68. Now north-west [of] Capuzzo. There was a shortage of water: the supply finding it hard to keep up with us.'

Which is, of course, just why Monty put the brakes on the advance.

'Ran into a German column in full retreat but found it hard to keep up with the speed it was going and the head start it had on us. (Still I'm in no hurry at this moment). We were enjoying motoring along, sitting outside the tank breathing fresh air but by the end of the day feeling exhausted. All caked in sand, faces looking like we had all had a face pack (sweat-and-sand mix). With the nights drawing in it was cold when the sun went down and we would pull our bed rolls off the back of the tank and fully clothed, boots off, go fast asleep, knowing the enemy was going away.'

'Titch' Maple had a near escape when the Regiment was racing towards Bardia. The W/T broke down and the tank commander, Captain Chave, told 'Titch' to wait until the Signals crew repaired it and then catch up. 'Titch' waited until the Signals Instrument Mechanic arrived. This was 'Pooky' Rees, the Squadron Fitter Corporal and, at 5'2", probably beating Titch as the smallest man in the Regiment. He arrived in one of the Marmon Harrington armoured cars, this one without a gun turret. The repair took about half-an-hour and, when it was completed and there was no-one in sight, 'Titch' set off again to catch up with the Squadron. Out of the blue three ME 109 fighters arrived flying in low. 'Titch' goes on, 'I shouted to the crew to close down and waved to the Signals before dropping to the turret floor. The three 109s opened fire with cannon and hit us a number of times. When they had gone, I looked out and saw that the armoured car was stationary. I ran across and, as I did, 'Pooky' Rees stood up with his face covered in blood. His driver had been hit in the back and was dead. Our tank had been covered in shrapnel: the bedding rolls were like lace work.'

At this point, some new members of The Fifth come into the picture. First, Harry Beacon. Harry experienced one of the more bizarre incidents in the war but that was not until much later. Harry reckons he should never have been invited to join in the war at all. By the time Hitler started the whole business, Harry was twenty-seven years old and, as a school master, was in a reserved occupation. [A lot of school masters – and school mistresses – thought that: they didn't read the 'small print'. School teaching was only 'provisionally reserved'!] Anyway, in November 1940, Trooper Beacon started his military career at Perham Down and, early in 1942, arrived in North Africa as a qualified tank driver without having ever driven anything bigger than a Bren Gun Carrier. With this qualification he spent some time as an echelon driver in 6RTR before fetching up in 'C' Squadron 5RTR driving a *Grant*. Not a lucky

Desert Warrior: his tank was knocked out on the great westward gallop – he was uninjured – but, before he could rejoin, he contracted jaundice and didn't see The Fifth again until the day before Tunis surrendered.

Another man involved in a bizarre incident later in the war was a Yorkshireman, George Johnson. He arrived in Egypt in August 1942 and, after kicking his heels in Abbasia Barracks was sent up the blue where, in George's words, 'Sgt 'Pluto' Ellis got me as his driver in 'B' Squadron'. Trooper Johnson had the good fortune to have one of The Fifth's great characters as a tank commander and the way he was welcomed into the crew as a new boy and made to share in the comradeship of the Regiment made an impression on him which lasted the rest of his life. The fact that Pluto Ellis was a fellow 'tike' may, of course, have had something to do with it!

Syd Storer's tale of events gives an almost hour-by-hour account of life on the blue. Recalling the great westward gallop, Syd's lasting impression was of the speed at which events moved and the efforts which the men had continually to make to keep up with them. Sometimes the Regiment was in reserve with time to replenish and carry out maintenance which, in the Desert, was made more important by the frequent dust clouds that quickly clogged the air filters on the engine. The men were informed regularly of the situation to the north but, even so it was difficult for them to have a clear, overall picture. Syd recalls that on the evening of 29th October the Regiment was put on stand-by and later moved off slowly northwards, passing through the lines of reserve trenches where some of the infantry were preparing to move.

Here the Squadrons were put on an hour's notice but were able to rest and have a midday meal which consisted of meat and vegetable stew with tinned fruit to follow. The main skill, Syd pointed out for the benefit of his family reading his Diary many years later, was not in eating the food but in replacing the billy-can lid between each mouthful before the millions of flies settled on it. The crews rested during the heat of the afternoon in what shade could be found and, by 1600 hrs, were on stand-by to move. A new attack had begun which The Fifth was to follow. As soon as the sun had gone down the tanks moved off slowly, to create as little dust as possible. They moved through new gaps in the minefields, made the night before, but came under heavy artillery fire. Apparently the infantry had not advanced as far forward as the CO had been led to understand.

There followed a night with fire, chiefly small arms, being exchanged with the enemy infantry who ran forward and tried to climb on the tanks or lob hand grenades into the turrets. These brave but foolhardy attacks were repulsed and the Regiment eventually reached the position from which the attack was to be launched. As dawn came the supporting artillery barrage opened up and the Regiment advanced. The enemy in their trenches, who had given so much trouble during the night, promptly climbed out with their hands raised. They were waved behind the tanks where the infantry took care of them. A short engagement followed during which The Fifth disposed of several tanks before being ordered to withdraw.

At this point, Syd recounts one of the misunderstandings which occur in any war. 'We pulled back into our position of the previous evening and were then directed to move about a mile to the north. We passed once more through the minefields and went straight in with the support of the infantry. The effect was most startling for, as we charged forward, hundreds of Italians climbed from their trenches with hands aloft, shouting and pleading. It was more than the infantry could do to gather them together. As we moved on, a bunch of about twenty Eyties ran forward, unfortunately one jumped on the tank and our commander shot him. The gunner, thinking that it was a trap to capture the tank, opened fire with his Browning and shot them all.

'More enemy tanks then appeared to try and close the gap we were making and, after a short, sharp battle, during which time we disposed of 14 of their tanks for the loss of two, they withdrew westwards. Orders then came over the air to turn south. For the next hour or so we created havoc as we moved through the enemy rear, shooting up his transport vehicles and cutting off the supplies. We were then ordered to push on as fast as possible, ignoring prisoners. This we did, destroying everything we saw. By nightfall we had covered 70 miles. A halt was called at 2030 hrs to enable the Echelon to catch up and replenish the tanks. We hadn't had a brew or a meal all day, only eating the issue chocolate. While we awaited the arrival of the replenishment vehicles, I prepared a bully beef stew. This was followed with some Ovaltine which I had received in a parcel from home.'

Not surprisingly, when one remembers how few and how sketchy the meals had been in the last seventy-two or even ninety-six hours, Syd Storer's next paragraphs include descriptions of what were, for the Desert, gourmet meals. 'We were again standing-to well before dawn and, as there was wireless silence, I cooked a breakfast of tinned bacon and army biscuit which was quickly devoured. We then moved forward, meeting no opposition in the area, and were ordered to speed up our advance and head north-westwards. By 0900 hrs we had caught up with the tail of the retreating Axis forces. These were chiefly Italians, as the DAK had commandeered all their transport and they were having to walk. Most of them seemed very pleased to be put in the 'bag'. While we awaited for the infantry to take away the prisoners and the captured guns, we made a meal of tinned stew with our ration of bully beef added. By 1300 hrs we were once more on the move. The enemy now had no stomach for a fight, so guns were knocked out as quickly as we spotted them and more and more prisoners poured in, delaying us much to the disgust of HQ who continually urged us to push on towards Mersa Matruh.

'As darkness fell we formed night leaguer south-west of Fuka, having travelled another 80 miles during another very hectic day. We were pleased indeed to see that the Echelon had brought along a cookhouse. So, as soon as the tanks were refilled with petrol and ammunition, we were refilled with some hot 'bully stew' followed by mugs of strong tea. Around 0200 hrs we bedded down while the Echelon troops mounted guard. We moved off as dawn broke with no stand-to and soon overtook a convoy of troop-laden enemy lorries which were about to move off westwards. These were encouraged to turn round and move off eastwards by a few well-placed HE shells. These, however, had the effect of alerting another similar convoy which began immediately to speed away from us across the Desert. We gave chase but, as they had about a mile start on us, our shells were dropping just short. For the next hour we sped over hard and soft sand, through stony areas which tended to hold them up and, by 1230 hrs, as we had them well within range, they stopped and showed a white flag. Again we re-directed them eastwards and the order was given to brew up and have breakfast. [Note the hour for 'breakfast']

'We were now ordered not to go to Mersa Matruh but to head westwards towards Sidi Barrani. As we were streaming in open formation across the Desert, we were attacked by an enemy rearguard which had been positioned at the top of an escarpment. While we took them on from the front, our 'C' Squadron moved round to take them in the rear but they were aware of the move and made a quick getaway to the north-west.'

An exactly similar incident is described by Liddell Hart [see p238 of Volume II of THE TANKS] which is attributed to 8th Armoured Brigade on the Allies side and to Rommel's former ADC, Hauptmann Voss, on the Axis side. This is not a misattribution but an illustration of the delaying tactics that Rommel employed to cover his retreat. As everyone found in numerous encounters, these Desert escarpments frequently provided commanding positions from which it was very difficult to dislodge the enemy or from which to be dislodged.

Syd next gives his version of the blinding rains which suddenly descended and, for a while, brought both sides to a stand-still. 'By this time the skies had, for the first time since I had been in the Desert, become heavy and black: soon torrential rain was pouring down and sleeping outside for the night was out of the question. We sat through the night, realising as time passed by that tanks are not waterproof. As dawn came we proceeded to mop up the inside of the tank and prepare a little breakfast but the word came from the B Echelon wagons which should have replenished us on the previous evening that they were completely bogged down to the axles, as water had swept down the wadi in which they had taken refuge. So we were sent back to use our strength to drag the lorries back onto dry ground.' Then, as Brian Stone had earlier done, Syd Storer noticed how the Desert suddenly bloomed after the rain, '.. little flowers appearing everywhere and the small bushes that we had thought dead and occasionally used for firewood had burst into life with leaves and flowers and looked beautiful.' But war is war and '..we stayed with the echelon until 1400 hrs and then left to try to catch up with the Regiment but by night fall we had only reached 'Charing Cross' and, though we were able to report to the Regiment that we were on our way and to get their map reference, we – that is our tank and the other one which had been rescuing the stranded lorries – had to form our own leaguer and mount our own guard. Fortunately the sun had returned during the latter part of the afternoon and we were able to get the worst of the wet out of our blankets on the now hot sand.

'We moved off early in the hope of catching the Regiment before they broke leaguer. As we moved across the Desert, we met a company of infantry which was marching a long column of 7,000 prisoners back eastwards, the result of the previous day's bag which we had missed. By 0800 hrs we caught up with the Regiment and travelled on without much opposition. At 1000 hrs a halt was called for breakfast and time to get the rest of the damp out of our blankets. Our tank commander, who had suffered a wound in the side of his shoulder during the short action two days earlier was not too well and appeared very flushed. He saw the MO who was travelling with us and was immediately evacuated to the FAP for treatment. As it happened, our 2i/c had lost a track running over a mine, so he, Capt Adams, took over as our tank commander. We moved off again at noon and travelled 60 miles, seeing no enemy. We leaguered up on a cold winter evening south of Sidi Barrani.'

One of the men in the crew of the second tank that helped unplug the B Echelon lorries was Pete Petersen. He summed the situation up by saying that '.. we all got bogged down but the Echelon lorries worse than anyone else. We had to help haul them out.' Seven monosyllables to describe seven hours hard labour!

Back-tracking to the War Diary and 8th November, it is possible to pick up the plan for the movements which have just been described. This was for 22nd Armoured Brigade to attack Fort Capuzzo from the south-west while the 4th Light Armoured Brigade was to attack Sollum and 'Hellfire Pass' from the east. The third prong of the trident was that of the 1st Armoured Division, currently re-organising at Charing Cross, which was then to advance, via el Adem to take Tobruk. However, it is not possible to follow the exact Charlie Love, since the War Diary traces the Regiment's movements by a series of map references which, without the map, serve no practical purpose. Nevertheless, there are some essential details and these are given in chronological order.

On 10th November, the Regiment was 'on the wire' waiting for the minefields to be cleared: there were casualties resulting from the attentions of the Luftwaffe: 1 OR killed and 5 wounded. It was on the 11th that the Regiment caught up with the enemy at the railhead at Fort Capuzzo. On the 12th the tank state at last light was 14 *Grants* and 5 *Crusaders*.

On 13th November the Regiment had advanced to el Adem without contacting the enemy but had gained another *Crusader* tank. No events were recorded in the War Diary for the 14th, 15th and 16th but the news had reached the Regiment that Tobruk was once again in Allied hands. The truth of this news was proved on 17th November when, at 1000 hrs, all the tanks were handed over to Workshops in Tobruk, with the crews remaining with their tanks. On the 18th Major Maunsell, with 4 Officers and 90 Other Ranks left with 1RTR for Agedabia. Except for the unfortunate OR mentioned on 21st November, it is hard to believe that there was a war on for the rest of the month. The War Diary reads:

19–20 November	No event
21 November	Major ERS Castle leaves unit for Staff Course at Haifa Bn moved: Route: el Adem, thence Axis Road and Derna–Tobruk Road. 1 OR wounded by enemy air activity during night
22–23 November	No event
24 November	CO to Bde HQ
25–28 November	No event
29 November	Bn sports day in leaguer area
30 November	No event. Tank state: 6 *Grants,* 3 *Crusaders.* Strength: 12 Officers & 462 Ors

On the other hand, a completely different story is told by the 'Summary of Log of Composite Squadron of 'B' and 'C' Sqns.' kept by Captain Whitty[9]. This is the group of four officers and ninety men which left under the command of Bob Maunsell to join the First Tanks.

The Log indicates that it was this Composite Squadron which got The Fifth's first *Shermans,* as they collected twelve of them at 1130 hrs on 18th November, along with one *Grant* and one *Lee* from 1RTR in an area south west of el Adem. This party then travelled on transporters to a point south-west of Bir Hacheim – a distance of 90 miles '10 of which were done on own tracks due to soft going.' The composite Squadron was also a highly mobile one, as it covered another 90 miles in moving to the forward area at a point 25 miles south of Msus on the 19th. On the 20th they again made an early start and covered 73 miles to reach a camp six miles north-west of Antelat. They found this camp very wet and swampy. The next day things began to warm up and the names become even more familiar, 'enemy being located to our north front along road to Agedabia'. On 22nd November the Squadron left Agedabia at 0640 hrs and engaged the enemy at 0730 hrs and continued to do so until 1800 hrs in the hills to the east of the town where the opposition was dug in along the main road running from north to south. One of the tanks – that of Lt Harris – was damaged by 50mm fire, the Troop Officer being wounded and evacuated. Harris' tank and one that ran on a mine were the only casualties for the price of two 88's and two 50mm's (certain) and one 50 mm (probable) with a quantity of MET. Next day things began to go less well: two tanks were KO'd on mines and the enemy was located on high ground either side of the road to Mersa Brega. Nothing positive happened on either the 24th or the 25th except for 'much enemy air activity'. The 26th saw some success when the Squadron 'had a shoot at enemy in hills north of road and destroyed an 88, a 50mm and an ammunition lorry.' But, says the Log, 'Got stuck in swamp when moving back to leaguer. *27th November* Stuck in swamp all day. One old Scammel failed to pull us out.' However, two fresh Scammels appeared and did the trick next morning. By the end of that day the Luftwaffe had wreaked severe damage among the Echelon vehicles and caused some casualties. For a reason which is not given Major Maunsell's tank was evacuated, thus reducing the effective strength of the Squadron to six tanks. The next two days were spent on maintenance and, on 1st December, the tanks were handed over to the Greys.

It would be too much to expect that a frolic of this nature could have taken place without at least one old hand taking part. It didn't and it will be no surprise to find that that old hand was Jake Wardrop. There is no date given in the Diary but Jake states that, after staying in el Adem for two days, a convoy of transporters arrived bearing *Shermans*. It was from these new arrivals that the composite Squadron was created: in very short order for they were on the move within the hour. Jake was driving Bob Maunsell. According to him the Composite Squadron had with them a Squadron from 1RTR, some RBs and 5 RHA. All these units came from Seventh Armoured Division side and were under Lt Col 'Teddy' Mitford, known as 'Long Range Mitford' and a cousin or brother of Unity[10]. Mitford had an enviable reputation as a Desert traveller: it was said of him that if he left his hat in the middle of the Desert he could go back twelve months later and find it.

Jake wrote in praise of the A&Q organisation. Whether by good luck or good judgement the transport planes came into Msus aerodrome with supplies just as the Fifth Tanks went past. Jake gave A&Q the benefit of the doubt. They were now some thousand miles from Alexandria and this was the point, Jake reflected, where previous pushes had come to a halt. Would Monty do any better? The answer was affirmative and the Highland Division and the New Zealanders, with massed artillery and the support of 2nd Armoured Brigade, continued to push along the coast. There weren't many pickings for The Fifth: the Royals had advanced so quickly that there weren't many prisoners to 'bag' or loot to collect. This – the area round Agedabia – was familiar territory to the old hands: the Regiment had been there in April 1941. On 6th December The Fifth handed their tanks over to the Scots Greys: the crews boarded lorries and headed east 'to a place called Morasses.' Their next stop, they learnt here, would be Tripoli

Going back briefly to November, someone somewhere prepared a document entitled '5th BN. ROYAL TANK REGIMENT: BATTLE DRILL'. As a manual for a tank regiment coming into the forward area for the first time it is a masterpiece of lucidity but, at first sight, it may seem a surprising document to discover among the papers of a unit which had already been on the blue for months rather than days or weeks. On reading it some sixty years later, one can understand its value. For the old hands, yes, it did tell them what they already knew but it set it all out with crystal clarity and spelt out its message in no uncertain terms. Speaking as one who joined the Regiment as a 'new boy' somewhere in the Low Countries nearly two years later I can only say that I wish I had been handed a copy of this manual and been given a couple of quiet hours in which to read, mark, learn and inwardly digest its contents.

To quote the introduction is to explain what I mean:

'Section One

The three vital essentials for the operation of an Armoured force are:-

(a) CONTROL
(b) RECONNAISSANCE
(c) CONCENTRATION

Without CONTROL it is impossible to operate. Without good RECONNAISSANCE it is impossible to make a plan and the danger of surprise is great. Without CONCENTRATION, tanks will be destroyed piecemeal

1) Of the three, CONTROL is the most important. It means rapid, fluid and simple drill and manoeuvres, with every man in charge of a sub-unit or vehicle knowing exactly what to do and where to go, with the MINIMUM of orders.
2) This Battle Drill is designed to provide the essentials required to achieve this control. It MUST be familiar to every officer and full-rank NCO in the Battalion.
3) The pamphlet is based on an Armd Regt of three Sqns, one of which is used for reconnaissance. At least one Sqn is presumed to be equipped with tanks which have some form of large calibre HE weapon as the 75mm on the Grant.'

Except for the details of the make-up of the battalion and the weaponry, everything in that introduction made sense then and makes sense now. What follows in 'the pamphlet' are the details which cover such things as Movement in Line Ahead; Open Formations; Protection Right/Left; The Fire Fight and the Attack; Leaguering; The Echelon (including details of vehicle loading); Guard Duty and Wireless Discipline. Nothing, if not comprehensive.

And returning to the Regiment on the ground, it will be recalled that the War Diary for 13th November said that Tobruk was reported as being once again in Allied hands. The report was true and, not surprisingly, since the Desert Rats were sniffing round the port, it was a troop from the Cherry Pickers which went into the town and found that the enemy had fled.

If 'the bad policeman', as Jake Wardrop calls Rommel, had any hopes of making a stand east of the el Agheila Salt Marshes, those hopes must have died when he had to abandon Tobruk.

THE OTHER SIDE

On 24th October 1942, when the news of the concentrated attack on the DAK's positions between el Alamein and the Qattara Depression the previous night reached Rommel, he was in no position to react.

He was lying 'on a bed of sickness' in hospital in Zemmering and Zemmering is in Germany. At noon, Rommel was wanted on the telephone. 'Rommel,' the voice at the other end of the line said. 'There is bad news from Africa. The situation looks very black. No-one seems to know what has happened to Stumme [11]*. Do you feel well enough to go back and are you willing to go?' As the caller was Hitler, it is hardly surprising that Erwin Rommel said, 'Yes' to both questions.*

He would have said 'Yes' anyway. Where the Afrika Korps was, there was Rommel's heart and he was back in Africa within thirty two hours of receiving Hitler's telephone call. Back in Africa but too late to affect the battle that was raging: it was already lost . . . 'lost before it was fought,' according to General Johann Cramer . . . even though the dispositions taken up under Stumme's command were those laid down by the Desert Fox himself.

When it came to the battle, Stumme's greatest concern was the reliability of the Italian Divisions. He bolstered them with parcels of German infantry or paratroopers but to no avail. Under the hammering of more than a thousand guns, the soldati *gave way and opened up the first gaps in the defences.*

However, this was not the only weakness. The Germans had one of their own. Their Intelligence Service. Not only was their information frequently wrong, their assessments of the situation were almost invariably at fault. By the time Rommel had made his own appraisal of Monty's plan of attack, all his reserves had been committed and he did not have the resources effectively to counter it.

That, of course, did not stop him from trying. When he failed, he planned his withdrawal with all his old flair: but of what use are the best laid plans in the face of orders from on high? On 3rd November Rommel received an order from the High Command in Berlin. It read, 'The position requires that the Alamein defences be held to the last man. There is to be no retreat: not so much as one millimetre! Victory or Death.' The order was signed 'Adolf Hitler.'

Even though he knew this to be nonsense, Rommel circulated the message to all ranks. General von Thoma, then GOC DAK, shortly after asked for permission to withdraw from Fuka to Daba. Mindful of the order, Rommel refused. Von Thoma withdrew: Rommel turned a blind eye. He would have done better to have turned a blind eye on his Führer's edict.

He did not, and his vain attempt both to obey his orders and to save his Army cost that Army dear. Nevertheless, Rommel fit or Rommel sick, Rommel was still a genius on the battlefield.

He turned his attention to withdrawing in good order.

THE WAR CHRONICLE

1942

October	29	Stalemate reached in the battle for Stalingrad
	30	Revised 'Enigma' code captured in a sinking U-boat
November	01	Development of FIDO [Fog Intensive Dispersal Of] allowed more night raids on mainland Europe
	08	Hitler claimed that Stalingrad had capitulated
	10	Monty became Sir Bernard – Operation 'Torch'. Allied forces landed in Algeria to fierce French opposition
	11	Australians went on the offensive in Papua – French forces, in North Africa, sued for an armistice
	12	. . . and came over to the Allies
	13	Stalingrad devastated and over-run but had still not 'capitulated' as Hitler claimed
	19	Investment of German besiegers of Stalingrad began
	22	Stafford Cripps eased out of War Cabinet and replaced by Herbert Morrison
	27	French 'matelots' scuttled French Fleet in Toulon
	30	German forces besieging Stalingrad encircled

NOTES

1 The end of the Beginning. Winston Churchill described the turn-around in our fortunes evidenced by the Battle of el Alamein as being, 'Not the end: not even the beginning of the end but perhaps the end of the beginning.' He later said that before el Alamein we never had a victory but that after el Alamein we never had a defeat

2 Mike Carver. Strictly, when those words were written, they should have read 'the late Mike Carver' as the paragraph was drafted four days after the death of Field Marshal Richard Michael Power, Baron Carver GCB CBE DSO MC RTR. The fact is not relevant to the story of 5RTR in WW II but is mentioned as a passing tribute to the Royal Tank Regiment's most senior officer

3 *Scorpions.* These were *Matildas* fitted with a forward-mounted rotary flail, the chains on which thrashed the ground as the tank advanced, thus exploding both anti-tank and anti-personnel mines

4 Monty's messages. These became a feature of the advance from el Alamein to Tunis. Whether they were more effective in boosting the troops' morale or Monty's ego is a subject which has been hotly debated over the years

5 New Phonetic Alphabet. See Appendix 1

6 Heavy enemy gun fire. General Stumme [see Note 11 below] had been forced

to restrict his artillery, due to lack of ammunition, even though he knew the likely consequences of doing so

7 'Baker tank'. This designation was common to other regiments. The Troop Leader's tank bore the Troop number (later with the addition of 'Sunray'), the Troop Sergeant's tank was 'Able' and the Troop Corporal's tank was 'Baker' (In North-west Europe, with four tanks in a Troop, the *Sherman Firefly* was 'Charlie')

8 Kidney Ridge. Liddell Hart points out that both these definitions were wrong. The kidney-shaped feature was actually a depression in the ground, even though the general level of the Desert was rising at this point

9 Capt Whitty. More, and more personal, details of Ted Whitty are to be found in the next chapter

10 Unity Mitford. The reference to Unity Mitford is to one of the much publicised, 'society' and literary daughters of the eccentric 2nd Baron Redesdale. Unity was an avowed Nazi and either tried to be or succeeded in being Hitler's mistress. The story goes that she once took a large, framed picture of her hero back to her – eminently prim and proper – old school. Her former house mistress took one look at it and said, 'Yes, dear; very nice. I should leave it in the cloakroom.' Colonel Teddy Mitford was not Unity's brother: that was Tom

11 Stumme. General Stumme took command of the DAK when Rommel was invalided back to Germany. He Did not survive long, dying of a heart attack shortly after the el Alamein offensive was launched

CHAPTER IX

. . . *The TT: Tobruk to Tunis*

The First Lap: December 1942–March 1943

Reading the Fifth Tanks War Diary for the first part of December 1942, a student of history might well wonder how any unit of the Eighth Army ever guessed what it was supposed to be doing. Taken in isolation, the Regiment's own account would be very confusing and the 'official' histories do not tell one much.

The anonymous Divisional history is frankly no help at all and Mike Carver's DILEMMAS OF THE DESERT WAR gives no details. The former skips over the period from 25th November to 12th December by detailing Command and administrative changes which did not in any way affect 5RTR. Moving on to General Verney's DESERT RATS . . . one finds exactly the same thing: with the possible exception of the claim [contradicted by the evidence] that the whole of 22 Armd Bde had been re-equipped with *Shermans*[1]. Go to Liddell Hart . . . but he provides no details, beyond saying there was a further two weeks' pause while the Eighth Army brought up reinforcements and built up supplies.

Go to the top – one of General Alexander's Despatches. From this one learns Alex's explanation. With the enemy withdrawing through the Jebel, it was a great temptation to imitate the Army's previous strategy by pushing a force across the Desert to cut off Rommel in the Agedabia region. However, in view of Monty's determination not to take any chances, especially in view of the difficulties of the maintenance situation, Xth Corps had been instructed to push forward only armoured-cars by this route. Later, when it had appeared that the enemy's retreat had actually been brought to a temporary standstill by lack of fuel, Xth Corps had been given new orders to strengthen, if possible, the outflanking force. General Alexander concluded by saying that this, unfortunately, had proved impracticable in the existing circumstances.

What it comes down to in the end is seeing what the War Diary has to say and then reading it between the lines against the general background of the War in the Desert.

The War Diary says 'No event' for the first three days of December. On the 4th there appears to have been another example of that well-known Desert Party Game, namely 'teaching one's grandmother to suck eggs'. In this case,

'0930 hrs CO, Officers and NCOs attended a demonstration on the location of enemy anti-tank guns.' At 1630 hrs Major Maunsell and Capt Whitty rejoined the unit from Mersa Brega. December 5th saw nothing more exciting than a CO's Conference for which the Subject was 'the agenda for a further conference on training'. The 6th saw the return of Capt Chave and the tank crews from the Composite Squadron: it also saw another CO's Conference: this one being on . . . Training. The 7th brought news that the Regiment was to be re-equipped with a mixed bag of 30 *Grants* and 22 *Crusaders*. This must have been a bitter disappointment to all concerned in the knowledge that the relatively superior *Shermans* were being issued to other units. No time was lost between being told about the 'issue' of tanks and the collecting thereof. The BTO left at 0800 hrs to examine them and Capt Browne left with the tank crews at 1400 hrs to collect them and ferry them to workshops. The same day the Regiment got a warning order that it was to be ready to move in ten days' time: it also got 12 3-ton and 5 15-cwt lorries. Lt Hammond, the Signals Officer, was off early in the morning of the 8th to establish wireless communication with the Area Command and at 1730 hrs Brigadier Roberts visited the unit. No events occurred for the next two days but sickness seems to have struck on the 11th, when three officers, including the MO, were evacuated for health reasons.

Although no event was recorded for 10th December, Colonel Hutton had gone back to Alexandria: the reason for this trip became apparent over the next few days. As recorded in the War Diary and in Eric Wilde's recollections, the Battle of el Alamein had taken a heavy toll of the Regiment's officers. Replacements were urgently needed, particularly those who had already had battle experience. Some such were available from the units which had had to be broken up as a result of their losses in the Battle. Between the 13th and the 16th a number of new names appeared on the nominal roll. Major WGG Watson was appointed as Second in Command and Lts B Beresford, PC Burt, DE Cockbaine and Daniels were taken on strength; three of them being posted to Squadrons, Dennis Cockbaine becoming a Liaison Officer.

Brian Beresford's name has already appeared and will be met with again. Dennis Cockbaine needs a little more introduction. He joined 'D' Squadron of the First Battalion the Royal Gloucestershire Hussars as a Territorial Trooper in 1938. He was called up in 1939 when the TA was mobilised and commissioned in 1941, joining 41RTR while it was still in the UK. He went with the Forty-first to North Africa and saw action there as a Troop Leader. Dennis, in the earlier stages, was one of the luckier ones, his tank being hit on several occasions without its being disabled. However, his luck ran out during the el Alamein Battle when he was wounded, if not critically, at least badly enough to land him up in hospital in Cairo. While there, 41RTR 'temporarily ceased to exist' and Dennis went on the unemployed list. On coming out of hospital he was sent to Alexandria where he found himself being interviewed by Jim Hutton who was in need of 'likely lads'.

Many years later, Major General Hutton, as he then was, told me that he thought Dennis was a 'very promising officer and that he was very pleased to have got him'. Lt Cockbaine, in his first employment as a Liaison Officer was, like Eric Wilde, supplied with a Scout Car and became at the CO's beck and call. Most probably, the Scout Car driver would have regarded himself as 'having got a new officer'.

In addition to the new postings, there were some other changes. Capt Goodyear left the Regiment to go to Brigade as IO, his place in 5RTR being taken by Lt Partridge. Brian Beresford was appointed HQ Troop Officer. Not only did new officers reach The Fifth at this juncture; eight more tanks arrived. On 17th December, Capt Chave went to Bomba to 'examine and select tanks and scout cars'. On the 18th there was a talk by Pip Roberts 'to all officers and WOs in Brigade in 1 RB's tent' [which gives one an odd idea of how well the Rifle Brigade lived in the Desert; there must have been over 150 bodies to accommodate!]. Later that day Capt Browne returned with 31 mixed tanks from Charing Cross and, later still, the tanks left on transporters for the forward areas. The CO, 2i/c and Adjt left for the forward area on the 19th and Capt Chave arrived with a selection of 10 mixed tanks (including some Brigade *Crusaders* and *Grants*).

By 20th December the Regiment was definitely on the move. The B Echelon left that day and was followed by the rest of the Regiment on the next. On 22nd December 5RTR was at Marble Arch and on the 24th learnt it would be remaining there for Christmas. What is more, Christmas promised well: Major Watson had visited a mysterious organisation called DIDS and had returned with Turkey, Pork, Christmas Pudding and Beer. The Colonel addressed all ranks at 1400 hrs on Christmas Day and at 1630 hrs 'men had their Christmas dinner'. Boxing Day was marked by a visit form 'Lt Gen Denvers US Army *etc*'. Whatever that 'etc' meant, it seems to have had a cathartic effect as, at 1330 hrs, the Regiment left for a new leaguer. This was at Merduma. No events here until 30th December when Monty visited the Regiment at 1000 hrs.

Nothing in the routine for the next week indicates that the change from 1942 to 1943 had any dramatic significance for The Fifth, nor are any Hogmanay celebrations recorded by Jake Wardrop. There was an intensive training programme, coupled with shoots for all tanks 'on the range', lectures for all tank commanders on mines and gunnery, sand table exercises not only for 5RTR officers but also for the senior ones of the RB and the supporting Field Regiment RA and a 'reconstruction of the Himeimat and Fuka battles'. If there was a change in routine, it was on the 3rd and 4th when everything was brought to a standstill by heavy sandstorms. At 1100 hrs on Friday, 8th January the CO gave a 'Griff Talk[2] to Bn' and at 1200 hrs held a Squadron Commanders' conference on the impending move to the new area.

When the move started it was on the blue, being in various westward stages, first to a point 12 or 13 miles west of Sirte, then 32 miles farther west until it swung north 16 miles to reach Battalion leaguer at 1930 hrs on the 11th.

It must have been some relief to all concerned to discover that their tanks were there waiting for them. The next two days saw a series of conferences, the one on the 13th being labelled 'The Coming Battle for Tripoli'. It also saw the arrival of a new MO, Captain MC Fulton MC. On the 14th the Regiment began to move into battle positions but, at 1830 hrs, true to form, learnt that there had been a change of plan.

It is obvious from the War Diary that, even without The Fifth, the War in the Desert was going forward. The most significant change was that the Eighth Army was not simply chasing the DAK ever farther westwards: it was driving it back into the approaching Anglo-American First Army which had landed in Algiers in November. Monty's plan of action in the lap of the race which took his Army from Tobruk to Tripoli was for 7th Armoured Division, with the New Zealand Division, to advance across country, while the 51st Division continued to chase the DAK along the coast route. The initial attack in the south was by the 8th Armoured Brigade and was met by determined resistance. As expected, Rommel had used the lull in the fighting to strengthen his defensive positions and had used all his old tactical skills in doing so, maximising his limited resources of tanks and guns.

The expression 'advance across country' was used literally. To allow the infantry access to such roads and tracks as there were, the armoured elements were operating in open country and the going was often very bad indeed.

The Fifth had its first contact with the enemy in this stage of the battle on 15th January when 'A' Squadron was sharply engaged at 1030 hrs. On the 16th the Scout Troop of 'A' Squadron rescued an American pilot who had baled out and sent him down the line with the MO. The following day 5RTR found itself in the lead of TAC Army rather than only of 7th Armoured Division. The 19th was spent in leaguer doing maintenance on the 15 *Crusaders* in 'A' Squadron, 4 RHQ *Crusaders* and on the 12 *Grants* and *Shermans* which both 'B' and 'C' Squadrons had. On the 21st the Regiment leaguered 5 miles west of Homs but at 0735 hrs on 22nd January things really began to happen. The War Diary takes on narrative form and reads:

'22 January. Continue advance to Tripoli, Order of march: TAC Army – TAC Brigade HQ – 5RTR Group. Coast road blown up in many places, necessitating detours through difficult sandy country hardly suitable for wheels. At Gasr Garabulli aerodrome 5RTR Group takes over to lead coastal drive on Tripoli. Towards late afternoon Bn. is held up owing to A/tank and mortar fire. About 1,000 yards short of Tripoli Perimeter road was blown up; high bank on left and mined on right. Railway embankment running at land side of road was also blown. As REs started to clear mines the leading troop of 'A' Sqn reported defensive positions and people walking about. 'A' Sqn then deployed left. No 5 troop 500 yards south of road and forward of the block. No 8 troop 1,500 yards south. As soon as No 5 troop showed themselves over a ridge they came under mortar and MG fire. Three tanks of 'B' Sqn were then ordered up in support, taking over No 5 troop positions who then moved

300 yards south along ridge. The enemy were in close country among shrubs and dunes, just west of two deep A/tank ditches. 300 yards south of the road a wood ran away to the SW for 2,000 yards. 'A' Sqn located 2 – 50mm and 1 – 75mm also several heavy mortars. A 'Snipe' shoot was started by the *Sherman* tanks and inflicted casualties on enemy. Situation remained like this until dusk. Just before the light failed, 'A' Sqn reported a good shoot on some MT in a small Wadi, but when the *Shermans* got there it was too late, visibility being insufficient.'

In the evening there was a maximum-range shoot by the 25-pounders of 111 Field Regiment RA, the gunners not being able to get any closer because of the state of the roads. At 1900 hrs the Regiment went temporarily into 'close march order leaguer'. While there, Lt Burt, who had received a scalp wound, was evacuated. He was the only casualty. At 2200 hrs the unit was on the move again, the War Diary cheerfully stating, 'Object:- Forinace Gate, Tripoli by first light (5RTR leading 22 Armd Brigade). Progress was rapid in spite of two A/tank ditches with bridges blown and road demolition. The enemy thoughtfully left a good supply of railway sleepers which facilitated the job.' At 0430 hrs the Regiment had reached its objective. At 1200 hrs, Fearless Jim had joined the Brigadier to make a recce of the situation: their party constituted part of the first Allied military presence in Tripoli.

Apart from a Squadron Commanders' conference on 27th January and a rehearsal for a Church Parade on the 30th, nothing happened until the last day of the month when – and there is photographic evidence to prove it – the notoriously Scruffy Fifth [its Tank Corps nick-name was something less polite] showed what it could do. Sixty immaculately battle-dressed men, led by Major Biddell and supported by Lt Gordon, marched past the GOC of the Eighth Army for the first British Church Parade to be held in the former Italian 'colony' of Tripolitania[3].

In most ways, life in Tripoli was a rest cure for battle-weary Desert Rats: there was no event on the 1st and a Welfare Cinema Show on 2nd February. There was plenty of activity the next day, as all the 'Tripoli Garrison' made ready for the Occasion – with a capital 'O' – due to be held on 4th February. How better to describe this than in the orotund prose of the Right Honourable Winston Leonard Spencer Churchill MP? 'We[4] had another two nights in Cairo and then flew to Tripoli where Montgomery, a victor at the end of his historic march, awaited me at the airfield. The enemy had been pushed forty or fifty miles west of the city. I spent two days in Tripoli and witnessed the magnificent entry of the Eighth Army through its stately streets ... Spick and span they looked after all their marching and fighting. In the afternoon I inspected massed parades of two divisions. I stayed in Montgomery's caravan. I addressed about two thousand officers and men at his headquarters. I spoke to them about Yet nightly pitch our moving tent a day's march nearer home[5]. But they were still a long way from home, nor was their route to be direct.'

With justifiable pride, the War Diary adds that the Regiment had a position of honour in Castle Square and that the CO was presented to the Prime Minister. There was more work for Colonel Jim: he had to attend a conference later that day in the Muddan Hotel. However, there was one man who did not get a position of honour for the Great Parade. Two young Fifth Tanks officers went on a bit of a bender the night before the parade and one of them at least had a 'spot of bother' – like falling into a disused quarry and marring his manly beauty – on the way back to wherever it was that the young officer should have been getting his beauty sleep. Next morning a very sorry sight, cuts and bruises and an arm that should have been in a sling being the most visible, met the Colonel's eye. 'That man,' the CO said, 'is not going to be seen in public.' Result? Lt Cockbaine appointed Camp Duty Officer for the day! Colonel Jim, being the man he was, nothing more was ever said.

One result of the conference in the Muddan Hotel was another one for Squadron Commanders the following day to discuss 'promotions and other matters'. At 1600 hrs on 6th February 5RTR was told to be ready 'to move at 0900 hrs tomorrow'. It didn't: it moved at 0730 hrs the following day to Zuara – not so far farther forward that the CO was unable to attend yet another conference in the Muddan Hotel at 1500 hrs on the 8th. There was a two day conference, addressed by Monty, in Tripoli which the CO and Adjutant attended on 9th and 10th February and a move of some 30 miles south to Uotia on the 11th. The next day, Lts Ridley and Robinson accompanied the IO on a 'going' recce to Sidi Toui and on the 13th the CO held another 'Griff Talk Parade' for all ranks.

Saturday, 14th February was another historic day. The Regiment, along with the TAC Brigade Group crossed the frontier into Tunisia. On the 15th it moved to Taghemit and on the 18th it moved to Neffatia, where 22 Armd Bde took over from 8 Armd Bde. The Regiment also acquired 3 6-pounder *Crusaders* and 1 *Sherman* from the Staffordshire Yeomanry. On the 20th it was back in action. As part of 'an advance in five bounds' with the object of cutting the Medenine–Mareth road, 5RTR led the Brigade on a right-flanking move via the Pass at el Aine. This was accomplished between 0815 hrs and 1000 hrs when the Regiment came under slight shell-fire. At 1020 hrs, this fire had intensified to such an extent that the advance was halted. At 1040 hrs 5RTR was moving round some wadis to the right of the Centre Line in order to try to get out of range and locate the source of the shelling. Unfortunately the move led it into even heavier fire and 'A' Squadron was temporarily halted. 'B' Squadron was sent up to try to neutralise the enemy gun position with an HE shoot. Luckily the Squadron was able to find some good hull-down positions. This was the beginning, at about 1100 hrs, of a major engagement.

From its position, overlooking the main road, 'B' Squadron ranged on the enemy gun position at 2,000 yards and succeeded in silencing one gun and engaging some MET. At 1130 hrs an 'A' Squadron patrol had pushed on about two miles to the west of the 'B' Squadron position, thus extending the

Regiment's front to about 5 miles. The remainder of the Brigade was still over 4 miles in the rear and the CO asked for assistance in cutting the road, his Squadrons being too widely spread out to do this but having a good chance of capturing some of the enemy. At noon 'B' Squadron knocked out a half-track towing an 88 and chased off some enemy tanks which had shown themselves briefly. These departed in a south-easterly direction. At 1340 hrs matters were getting out of hand. An 'A' Squadron forward patrol reported MET streaming away down the road in a north-westerly direction but was 'at the limit of its tether' and could not stop them. Brigade was again asked to send assistance. This was not immediately forthcoming and there was a resultant disaster. At 1426 hrs the Scout Car patrol of 'A' Squadron came on the air to report taking prisoner a group of 23 German officers and men with 5 vehicles and to ask for support. OC 'A' Squadron attempted to get help to the patrol but was handicapped by already being dangerously thin on the ground. One troop of [two] tanks made a determined approach but came under fire from an 88 screen and lost one of its number. The other tank got to the road too late to assist the patrol which had been overpowered. The officer commanding the patrol was Douglas Lowe and he did not remain a prisoner for long. For some reason his captors forced him to strip, presumably thinking that he would be less likely to get into mischief in his underpants. Thinking him safe, they took their eye off him . . . and soon learnt that they had misjudged their man. Clad – or rather unclad – only in underpants, socks and boots, Dougie Lowe took off into the desert and duly reported back to the Regiment. For this and his general indifference to danger, he was awarded an MC.

At 1435 hrs, the unit was still shooting up any movement on the road and hit two lorries and some men. The Light Squadron of 4 CLY came up on the left of 'A' Squadron and, with the aid of a detachment from 1 RB, helped to cut the road. Nevertheless, most of the enemy got away, although a few POWs and some MET were captured.

By 1600 hrs enemy resistance was decreasing and by 1900 hrs, when the Regiment leaguered, ceasing altogether. In addition to the POWs and MET, the enemy 'bag' was reckoned at only one half-track and two lorries. Our own casualties had been more severe. The Fifth lost 3 ORs killed and 1 OR wounded with 1 Officer and 1 OR missing. In addition, the unit had lost 2 *Crusaders*, 1 Scout Car and 1 lorry.

After the events of the 20th it was a relief to spend the 21st 'in observation all day'. The next day was even quieter with nothing to report. On the 23rd, 5RTR swapped leaguers with 1RTR. Nothing startling about that but what was surprising was the demand – instantly met at 1100 hrs – to send '2 Sgts and 10 ORs experienced *Sherman* crews to 1st Army by air'. First Army evidently needed heavy reinforcing: at 2200 hrs a further two drivers were despatched! A move was ordered on 24th February for the next day but was cancelled at 2030 hrs and not restored until three days later. In the interval, a 'training exercise' must have made the 'A' Squadrons types feel pretty smug on 26th November. In the succinct words of the War Diary '1400 hrs. 'A' Sqn demonstrates concealed position of observation to all tanks Comds.' As it happened, the move on 27th February was only one of position and preparation for further moves, the first of which was of one mile and took place on 1st March. This was described as being 'to a more favourable site for taking up an immediate battle line position known as 'Moore' at 15 mins notice'. Famous Peninsular War commanders must have been the key to the coding of orders in March, since the next move was to 'Wellington' late on the 2nd.

On 4th March Capt Whitty acquired 2 *Shermans* and 10 *Crusader* tanks which were added to the strength, already reinforced by the arrival of 6 new Scout Cars, four of which were equipped with No 19 W/T sets. On the same day, Lt Burt was promoted Captain and posted as 2i/c 'A' Squadron. Regimental strength was 33 Officers and 555 ORs. No activity is reported in the War Diary for 5th March but there are rather cryptic entries for the 6th, 7th and 8th. The entry for the 6th read 'Stood to all day, prepared to move to any of battle positions. Reports come in over Rear Link set of German tanks and Inf attacks to the W and SW of Bn positions on our Inf FDLs. Reported bag of 37 German tanks.' That for the 7th reads, 'No event. Received Army Commander's message re giving enemy a 'Bloody Nose'. This appears to have been achieved.' And that for the 8th reads, 'CO meets Army Comd on Hill (E 6688) which Army Comd said would in future be known as 5th Royal Tanks Hill having been captured by the Bn on Feb 20th when Medenine was taken'. Cryptic as to the 'bag of 37 tanks' and 'giving the enemy a Bloody nose' but very flattering as to 'Fifth Royal Tanks Hill'. Fortunately the tide of war was flowing in the Allies' favour and no-one ever had to come back to fight over it again.

Following what would nowadays be called an 'over-view' for unit commanders by Monty on 9th March, Colonel Jim gave an all ranks 'Griff Talk' on the 10th. This was followed by three days of training, including a day on the ranges and more of the inevitable conferences. On this date The Fifth had 34 Officers, 553 NCOs and men, 16 *Crusaders*, 19 *Shermans* and 9 *Grants* and was under command of Xth Corps. During the next five days the Regiment went on three hours' notice. Lieut General Brian Horrocks, the Corps Commander, visited the Regiment on the19th in the morning and at last light it moved out to take over protection of 201 Guards Brigade from the CLY. The tank crews must have enjoyed obeying their orders at 0430 hrs on 20th March, as these were to break leaguer making as much noise as possible between 0445 hrs and 0500 hrs. This was 'for diversionary purposes', although who else was being diverted is not made clear. After being briefed by the CO at 1400 hrs the Regiment moved up to battle positions at 2300 hrs but did not reach them until 0400 hrs. It had been a long day's night. Although on stand-by all day, there was no indication of what was in store for The Fifth until 1800 hrs when warning orders came through to be prepared to act as independent support for either 50 Div or 4 Indian Div.

At 1000 hrs on 22nd March the CO took the Brigadier on a recce and to liaise with 151 Brigade. It was just as well he did for, at 1300 hrs, the enemy launched an attack on 151 Brigade. An hour later, the CO got orders to take the Regiment forward to reinforce the bridgehead made through the Mareth defences by 50 Div. At 2300 hrs RHQ and the two 'fighting Squadrons' moved to a position north of 151 Brigade. Their immediate role was somewhat out of the ordinary: it was proposed to hitch 6-pounders onto the back of the *Shermans* and tow them across the gap in Wadi Zig Zou[6]. [And see later what Eric Wilde has to say about this] The Regiment, less 'A' Squadron, was on the move at 0500 hrs on the 23rd and was soon in action on the Chet Meskine Ridge. At 0900 hrs 'A' Squadron joined the others and everyone came in for very heavy shelling, mortar, MG and A/Tk fire. What must have been nearly all the Panzerarmee's strength in PzKw IVs – some two dozen of them – were sighted in an area of high ground. It seems that they were not engaged but one of the 'C' Squadron *Shermans* was hit – probably by a 105mm shell – and brewed up with the resultant loss of 1 OR killed with 1 Officer and 2 ORs being wounded. The following day 1RTR took over the tank position, and 154 Bde of the Highland Div took over the infantry position from 50 Div.

On 25th March the Regiment moved back to the 'Wellington' position but remained under immediate notice to move to reinforce any part of the Mareth Line which came under counter-attack. There was an all-ranks briefing at 0900 hrs the next morning, with Liaison Officers going out to contact all the Brigade's holding positions on the Mareth Line. In the event the Regiment was not called upon and had two days' effective rest. Eleven Other Ranks joined the Regiment but there was still a shortage of one Officer in 'C' Squadron. On the 30th, the Regiment was on the move again, this time to the Gabes area: a move made with an inflated 22 Armd Bde. So inflated, as things turned out, that congestion in the forward area caused the Regiment to halt and leaguer at 1500 hrs while still seven miles short of its destination. On the last day of March it took two hours to cover the seven miles to the correct leaguer position. Here, at 1600 hrs, Fearless Jim gave the Regiment its orders for the forthcoming Battle of Wadi Akarit.

After spending some time with those 'great guys', the tank transporter drivers, Jake records a period of relative inactivity, which gave him time to approve the advance being made by some other 'great guys' – the men of the Highland Division – advancing along the coast road. He also had praise for the Kiwis, whose action had enabled The Fifth to cross the Wadi Zem-Zem unopposed. The farther west they got, the less like the Desert the men found the terrain, recording olive groves, trees and fields which were actually green. For all this, the terrain did not improve from the tanks' point of view. The advancing units frequently had to send out reconnaissance parties to find suitable routes and, when they did, these routes all too often led to demolished bridges or impassable craters in the roads and tracks.

As always, when chasing Rommel, The Fifth encountered DAK rearguards, always well sited to cause the maximum delay with the minimum danger to themselves. On these occasions, the tank crews much appreciated the verve with which the Riflemen from the RBs threw themselves into the attack. A point which the War Diary does not mention, but the men registered with appreciation, is that, at nearly all the obstacles – blown bridges, road craters – the Sappers had not only to repair the damage, they had to sweep the area for, and clear the area of, mines before they could start work or the tanks could advance.

Eventually, after a night move, the forward elements of The Fifth had their first sight of Tripoli. Much though the men in the tanks would have liked to see The Fifth driving into Tripoli at the head of the Eighth Army, they gave unstinting credit to the Gordon Highlanders who rolled into the city, riding on the *Valentines* of 40RTR.

Everyone found life in Tripoli very much to their liking: there was legitimate loot ('rations and army kit, sugar, tins of butter and things like that') to be had and there was brandy to be bought and there were friends to be made.

Jake Wardrop's Diary records the great pride the men took in the part played by the Fifth Tanks in the Victory Parades in Tripoli – even if it is more than a bit caustic about the Cherry Pickers having the honour of leading Churchill's car for the Prime Minister's review.

However pleasant the break in Tripoli was for all ranks and all regiments, there was still a war to be fought and that meant the assault on the Mareth Line. From a tactical point of view, the key to the situation was less the Mareth Line itself than the ridge which lay to the west of it. The Fifth had the role of attacking this and did so after a night march of some thirty miles. Somewhat to their surprise the tank crews found the Boche 'must have been a bit jittery', as the opposition wasn't as fierce as they had expected and, when the enemy did break, they streamed away from their positions, leaving rich pickings for their opponents in the way of men and weaponry. The ridge referred to in the reports is the one which Monty said would be called Fifth Royal Tank Regiment Ridge.

One of the interesting – and valuable – aspects of the individual accounts [and not just to the author of this book] is the manner in which they record incidental aspects of the war and set such events in their proper context. For instance, at this point in his Diary, Wardrop describes the arrival of the 17-pounder anti-tank gun – to complement the 6-pounders which, he says, 131 Brigade had towed all the way from el Alamein but never used! Having made this point he then resumes with a description of the German counter-attack . . . using one of his favourite expressions to do so – 'a great scrap' It was not quite as great in one way as Jake thought: his description of the 'bag' indicates that the Boche lost more tanks than they were ever able to put into the battle.

Jake's favourite 'Major' was Paddy Doyle, already the holder of a Military Cross. While resting at this point, news came through that Major Doyle had been awarded a DSO. It was then still rare for anyone below the rank of Lieutenant Colonel or not holding the equivalent command to a battalion to be so honoured. Paddy Doyle is also on record as having the highest opinion of Jake Wardrop as a driver and as a fighter, although he was far from blind to Jake's occasional lapses from virtue. However, the Major whom Jake was to be driving in the next stage of the battle was not Paddy Doyle [who had been wounded] but Ted Whitty, who impressed Jake not just for his size but for his aristocratic bearing and his connections, being evidently on hand-shaking terms of familiarity with the Divisional Commander.

An aspect of the war in the Desert which showed that, in many ways, nothing really changes was the manner in which the tanks in 1943 negotiated the deep wet ditch of the Wadi Zem Zem as their forefathers had negotiated the trenches in World War One . . .with big bundles of sticks[7].

In a sharp engagement at el Hama on 23rd March the Regiment was held up in the same spot under very heavy shell-fire and had made the acquaintance of the 'Moaning Minnie'[8]. It appears from the accounts that the Germans had several of these in this engagement: one salvo knocked out a *Sherman*, brewing it up and killing the driver: others played havoc with the forward gun crews and worse than havoc with the infantry in the open. So much so that some men from the Durham Light Infantry started to run for it, until rallied by an unknown hero. The opposition melted during the night when the Highland Division went in. 'Next morning,' Jake wrote, 'there were no Germans east of the Gabes Gap, except stiffs and prisoners.'

Jake's description of the remainder of March is largely confined to such interesting military subjects as the number of hens – or cocks if the buyer, or more probably pilferer, was not a poultry expert – to be found on each of the Squadron tanks; the changes in the High Command [General Alexander had gone to the First Army to be General Eisenhower's right-hand-man] and the arrival in North Africa of the PzKw VI – the dreaded 'Tiger'. The High Command's recommended method of dealing with them unfortunately overlooked the fact that it could only be employed after the *Shermans* had been within range of the Tiger's main armament for some 1,500 yards!

Eric Wilde, now a 'B' Squadron Troop Leader, also had something to say about these Fifth Tanks days. He later wrote, 'Shortly after the fall of Tripoli the Division was pushed to the west, to join up with the British and American forces fighting in Tunisia. In front of us was the Mareth Line, the pre-war French frontier defences against the Italians. The Germans were conducting their usual skilful withdrawal and held the line in strength. When we closed up to the German defences, The Fifth was on the extreme southern flank. We were warned to expect a heavy German counter-attack, the Americans having already suffered a severe defeat in the Kasserine Pass. We occupied excellent hull-down positions and, because we knew that we would be conducting a static defensive operation, we filled the tanks with additional 75mm shells.

My tank had 150 rounds on board; twice its normal capacity. In the event, the German counter-attack was delayed, our Division was relieved by two Infantry Divisions with additional artillery and so the attack when it came was bloodily repulsed but, even so, they penetrated beyond the position which we had held.'

Eric goes on to describe the Wadi Zem Zem action, noting particularly the fate of 50RTR which ended the battle with a tank strength of four runners, having had their CO killed in the action. Following the German counter-attack, elements of 22nd Armoured Brigade were lined up in support. Eric's account continues, ''B' Squadron was the leading squadron and we were lined up in lanes made through the minefield to the east of the Wadi, ready to attempt to cross it. Suddenly we were told that we were to tow the [131 Queens Brigade] 6-pounder anti-tank guns across the Wadi to help hold the bridgehead. I had never heard so stupid an order. How were we to attach the guns? Both sides of the Wadi were so steep and so cut up by the tracks of the 50RTR tanks and we were continually being shelled and mortared. All the time the poor gun crews would be exposed to artillery and machine-gun fire and would certainly be swept off the back of the tanks. And somehow we were to get across the Wadi, still towing the guns [with drastic loss of manoeuvrability] and would then have to disconnect the guns in the open and under shell-fire before we could get on with the business of fighting. I was convinced, for the one and only time in the war, that I could not possibly survive the coming battle. In all other dangerous situations there was always some prospect of surviving but on this occasion I was convinced that we were all doomed. However, having spent some frustrating hours attaching the guns to the tanks, the order was cancelled and we were told to free ourselves of the guns. Never was an order more happily carried out! Eventually we were moved up to the back of the Wadi, the survivors of 50 Division were pulled back through us.

'That part of the Mareth Battle petered out and a wide flanking movement made the Germans continue their retreat. We then had to pull back from the Wadi and I remember that it was the most difficult movement we ever did. All the tank crews were absolutely exhausted, having been without sleep for over three days. We all had great difficulty in keeping awake. I sat on the front part of the hull beside the driver's head, sticking out of his hatch, and I was tied to the gun to ensure that I would not fall off the tank if I fell asleep. Every time we stopped, which was often in a long column of tanks moving over difficult terrain, be it for a few moments or several minutes, the driver fell asleep, so I beat his head to rouse him. And all the time we were in a fog of dust kicked up by the tanks in front of us. The Mareth Battle caused us very few casualties but it was one of the most stressful and exhausting times I ever had in the war.'

Eric next recounts an incident of a rather less stressful and very different nature under the title 'Ethel'. No, not the Girl from the NAAFI: quite a different bird. 'One day,' the story goes, 'we had advanced through an area which had obviously been the abandoned site of an Arab tribe which had wisely decamped. Suddenly we spotted a scrawny chicken, evidently not worth taking along or too stupid to have made its escape. Out jumped the co-driver, grabbed her and was back in the tank before you could say 'Jack Robinson'. When we finally stopped for the day, we gave it a feed of biscuit and tied a very long piece of string to its leg and let it roam around the tank. Soon it didn't require to be held by the string and very quickly learnt to fly onto the tank and get in by the co-driver as soon as it heard the tank start up. It fed regularly on biscuit, got noticeably fatter and actually started to lay an egg on average every two days in a snug blanket-lined nest by the shell racks. True to the tradition of The Fifth, all of whose tank names began with an 'E', we called her Ethel. She flourished happily for some time until one day we were in action a very great deal of the time and the tank became absolutely full of fumes. Poor Ethel died quietly in her nest. We did, it must be admitted, think of cooking her but our finer feelings prevailed and we buried her during the night.'

Bob Maunsell's experiences around the time of Tripoli were farther from the Front Line but one of his responsibilities proved equally onerous. He had had the misfortune, while scanning the horizon through his binoculars, to be hit by a fragment of an air-burst shell which pierced his hand, missing his head by a matter of two or three inches. The wound was sufficiently seriously to require hospital treatment. This was administered in what was known as a 'mixed ward'. 'Mixed', not in the modern sense – no-one had that much luck in the Desert – but in the sense of being for all ranks. Bob was the senior man in the tent which constituted the ward and, as such, was told that he was in charge. His task was to assure Matron or any visiting medical staff that all were present and all was correct, any empty beds being accounted for. Under cover of this assurance and with Major Maunsell's presence in the entrance to confirm the fact, the tent immediately emptied and the various casualties took themselves to a neighbouring tent. Which just happened to be the New Zealand Ward where booze was plentiful. Bob never did get to visit those New Zealanders.

Another man who had been away from the Regiment, although in his case it was his tank that was disabled not him, was Harry Ireland. His return to The Fifth had been marked by an incident which haunted him for a long time. As they were driving down a track just off the Coast Road, Harry saw the fully-clothed corpse of an Italian soldier lying in the sand, sunken eye-sockets, bony fingers and all. Sand storms must have uncovered his last resting place and left him exposed. Harry said a little prayer to himself, thinking about the number from his side – his comrades even – who might well have suffered a similar fate.

Harry continued on a more cheerful note by describing a Rifle Brigade Concert Party which 'entertained the lads'. After his time in the Desert, 'the lads' were 'the lads' to Harry: it will be remembered that, earlier, he was respectfully referring to them as 'the men'. Other relaxation included swimming parties, good nights' sleep and – above all – plenty of fresh water. But, too soon, it was, 'Off we go again. *Sherman* tanks, the Regiment brought up to strength with some new officers and other ranks. The Highland Division had broken the el Agela Line, we were on our way to exploit the success. Our Xmas goodies had come up by now and we celebrated Xmas Day. Beer, turkey and all the trimmings: a marvellous effort by our cooks and Quarter Master's staff. Monty visited the unit on December 30th, near Marble Arch, telling us about the push to Tripoli.

'At times we were held up by strong rear-guard action, sand storms, booby traps and had to go carefully. A month of slow progress, by January we found ourselves in the Grass Belt 30 miles off Tripoli. What a delightful change of scenery, looking at a corridor of green, lush, cultivated land about five miles or so from the sea into the Desert. (The Italian colonists had done a marvellous job here) Now on the coast road about ten miles before the City of Tripoli, the Infantry pass through us and enter the city. Tanks are not allowed in, maybe street fighting so we stand back for once. Our first major success. There had been set-backs in the early part of the year, but now a complete change around. We heard that an Anglo-American landing had taken place in the Algiers area so now the enemy had to cope with two armies (the 8th Army and the 1st Army) trying a crushing and final blow.

'At times we were able to tune into the BBC Home News from England on our tank wireless set. The news was good, Russian offensive, Japanese halted, bombing raids on England slackening. Could this be a turning point in the war? At least we are going in the right direction – West. To celebrate our capture of Tripoli (January 31st), a big parade was held in the city. A march-past of infantry, pipe bands, Colonial troops [who was Harry daring to call 'Colonials'?], artillery, we with our tanks lined the route, I was elated, standing in the turret, Churchill, Alexander, Montgomery, all the top brass of all the services on the saluting base. I hope this keeps up, even King George VI came out to see us later.

'I had lost a good few pals on our way up the Desert, the price of success – what a price, their graves scattered over the Desert. God Bless. The rum issue was doubled although I hated the taste of it, it helped to forget the bad times, They say it takes ten men in administration to keep one man in action (What about a swap? No, I don't think I would want it.)'

For one enthusiast even the acquisition of a *Sherman* did not provide the excitement he craved. Pete Petersen wrote '.. at this time our old battle wagons ran out of steam and they decided to give us something faster. We were equipped with *Sherman* tanks, a much better proposition than the *Grant*, with a 75mm gun in the turret. I became [what is] known as a lap gunner[9] with a 30-calibre Browning next to the driver in the hull. Much to my disappointment I didn't get a chance to use it: I had visions of charging in among the enemy and carving my initials on their backsides but all I saw was mirages. We pushed on past Benghazi and into Tripolitania across the border and halted at a place called Marble Arch and here we Christmassed for 1942.' However, all was not disappointment. 'The beer wagon caught up with us and we managed a few bottles and it did wonders for our morale. Then came the orders to press on. The nights were cold and we stood around in our great coats. It was still 'Westward Ho! The Wagons' and we had a few skirmishes: one at Homs which the Highland Division took care of. We kept pressing on but, within a few miles of Tripoli, we got blown up on a mine on the coast road: not too much damage, just the right-hand track. It was coming up to sunset so we decided to have a brew – the morale booster on all occasions.

'Next morning after a good night's kip alongside a noisy road, we set to after another brew to repair the track. We had to be very careful where we walked; the place was littered with mines. However, we managed to finish the job by midday and proceeded west to catch up with the Regiment, which we did within a few miles of Tripoli where they had come to a halt. We were there for a couple of hours so we took advantage to have a brew and a bite to eat. Our marching orders came and we moved to an area south-west of Tripoli and leaguered . . . which turned out to be for a week or two. During this period our old friend Mr Winston Churchill held his Victory Parade in Tripoli in which we had a part to play. We had never looked so smart for years!'

Pete left the Regiment at this point for what he described as a four month involuntary vacation with two other members of the crew, so there is a break in his narrative.

It will be remembered that Syd Storer's account of the War in the Desert ended where Capt Adams took over his tank. His narrative continues here in November, with a comment on the crews' scruffy condition and, which worried him as a WOp, the condition of the wireless batteries. When replenishments did arrive they included a cookhouse wagon and a water bowser, so the crews had a good wash and a good meal. What was supposed to be an early start turned out to be a move at 1430 hrs, which gave everyone some extra rest. The move took them over the border into Libya and, unfortunately, into the range of the Luftwaffe, who luckily caused only one slight casualty. The next early start was the real thing and the Regiment set off at 0500 hrs in pursuit of a large enemy column. The Fifth caught only the tail end of the column, taking 167 prisoners, while the remainder ran for Bardia. The support infantry caught up at this point and launched a frontal attack on the town, while 5RTR worked round the back. This pincer movement produced a bag of some 600 POWs.

The next few days in which, as Syd remarked, the Regiment had covered over 350 miles entailed a number of chases, culminating in the capture of el Adem aerodrome. Syd includes in his description that the planes they captured could not take off due to lack of fuel. After el Adem, Capt Adams took over the Squadron, which meant that Syd Storer became Squadron Operator. Syd continues, 'On Friday 13th we again moved off early and, after 31 miles without contacting the enemy, halted for breakfast. We were now due south of Tobruk and were ordered to stand by for further orders. Supplies were now coming up through both el Adem and Tobruk, so we were able to have a good wash and change of clothing. With constantly wearing headphones in the sand-laden air, my ears were causing problems. I managed a visit to the MO while Cpl Maple maintained wireless watch. I was amazed at the amount of wax plus sand which was removed from my ears.'

Syd's tank was used by Capt Chave in the Composite Squadron, so that the prospect of a couple of weeks in Tobruk for maintenance was abruptly ended when aerial reconnaissance reported a large enemy column moving along the Derna coast road. Chave's orders were to cut south-westerly across uncharted Desert to cut this column off at Agheila or Agedabia. This Squadron, consisting of 20 tanks, was assembled by Wednesday 18th and was to be carried as far as possible on transporters but, as already mentioned, reached the point where they could move faster on their tracks. Unfortunately Chave's tank developed engine trouble and was taken back to the transporters' leaguer where mechanics worked on it during the night. In vain: it was declared unfit. The crew took over a spare tank in the morning without having time to check the equipment but, nevertheless, with orders to speed up to make up for lost time. They covered 100 miles under their own power despite a slipping clutch. It was not a good replacement: the wireless set was 'dis' as were several headsets so, when they leaguered up at dusk just south of Msus, the fitters took over once more.

Whoever got any sleep that night, it was not the fitters. By working hard, they managed to keep the squadron up to strength and next day, with an early start, the Squadron was 100 miles nearer its target. However, the fitters had to condemn Syd's replacement tank so the crew found themselves on a new diesel-engined type. By dawn on the 21st they had caught up with the tail of the enemy column near Agedabia. Unfortunately the main part of the column had already got clear and, as the Squadron was short of fuel, all they could do was to play havoc with any soft vehicles within range. Overnight replenishment allowed the Squadron to catch up again with the rear of the column. This time the enemy took up positions around Agedabia and there followed a day spent in constant action – lorries set on fire and guns knocked out – with the Squadron gradually closing in. At dusk Capt Chave decided to pull back to leaguer, knowing the enemy would probably withdraw during the night and that he would be unable to manoeuvre the Squadron round and cut the escape route to the west, as the Boche would undoubtedly have laid a minefield.

Syd's narrative: 'When we entered the village at first light the following morning we found several guns, many damaged, and some destroyed vehicles: also some enemy troops who had either not been told to withdraw or had been unable to get transport to do so. The going was now different: besides the stony areas which we had earlier encountered, there were areas of very soft sand and large patches of damp boggy ground. For this reason and the possibility of more mines, the advance was continued along the main road but, even then just after 0900 hrs, there was a loud bang as we hit a mine which blew off the left track and the front bogey. The remainder of the Brigade had now joined us and the fitters worked all day to carry out the repair while we walked around looking at the result of the previous day's fighting. By evening we were off again under our own power, joining the remainder of the Regiment in leaguer by nightfall only 8 miles further on. True to form, we were on the move again early next morning, to try to maintain contact with the enemy whose practice was to withdraw through the night. We covered 10 miles before our forward troops reported contact. Then, however, came the welcome order to brew up and the rumour that we were to be relieved.'

The pattern was repeated on the 25th by which time it was obvious that more infantry was required as the opposition stiffened. Nevertheless, the enemy did not make a stand at Mersa Brega which the Squadron entered at midday. This relief was short-lived for, almost immediately, the leading tanks ran into heavy shelling as they approached a bottle-neck in the road. They took up hull-down positions around the area and orders were received to 'harass and observe' only. The following morning the Squadron was relieved by 2nd Armoured Brigade and returned to Mrassas[10] to re-equip with new *Sherman* tanks. After a two-day journey, Syd Storer had to report sick and it was not until 11th December that he was fit to report back for duties.

'Late in the evening of 16th December,' Syd's narrative continues, 'we were told that the tanks had arrived at the rail-head. The crews were selected and I became operator on a *Sherman* with Sgt Cooper. The *Shermans* had, among others, an important advantage over the *Grants*. A cupola was provided in the turret so that the WOp could share the look-out with the tank commander. On the 18th we loaded once more onto transporters and at 1800 hrs we began our journey 'back to the front', this time using the coast road. We travelled mostly at night to avoid attention from the Luftwaffe who had been very active during our refit in Tobruk. At 1500 hrs we stopped and were told to bed down: we had covered 85 miles to Matuba. We were on the move by 0700 hrs and spent the day travelling through some lovely scenery. At midnight we halted near Barce, having travelled 101 miles. The night march was to avoid the Luftwaffe whose reconnaissance planes had located our movement. Another early reveille did us no good as we had to wait till 0900 hrs to allow a convoy of supplies for the front to go ahead. We then passed through Barce, eventually stopping in a green area 10 miles from Benghazi. We had covered 87 miles and were told to bed down immediately as we would be on the move much earlier next morning. But before last light the expected air attack took place, though little damage was done. However, no sooner were we bedded down, than another attack took place and seven men were wounded.'

Syd was right: it was an early start. The Convoy was on the road at 0400 hrs and through Benghazi before a breakfast halt at 0900 hrs. There was only one short stop before Agedabia was reached as light was fading. The day's run was another 90 miles. There were no interruptions to the evening meal. After a quiet night, there was another early start on the 22nd. This did them no good, because the road ahead was jammed with every sort of vehicle, all going the same way. Efforts to overtake these were liable to end with the transporters getting stuck in the sand as they attempted to pass, so it was decided to slow to the pace of the traffic. The convoy passed through Mersa Braga, where The Fifth had had its last short action before the refit, and continued to el Agheila where the men had a roadside picnic lunch. Traffic was lighter in the afternoon and Marble Arch was reached at 2045 hrs. Here the tanks were off-loaded and formed leaguer. The day's journey had been 105 miles so, after their evening brew up and a meal, the men were very ready for bed.

The following morning, 23rd December, was spent in cleaning the tanks, adjusting the guns, netting [*ie* tuning in] the wireless and loading with ammunition and fuel. The day was cheered by a welcome visit from the canteen which enabled the tanks to be stocked up well with tea, sugar, milk and sweets. Also welcome was a generous supply of water. After stand-to next morning and an order to move, new orders came through that the Regiment would not be moving for two days.

Christmas Day started with the usual stand-to but, at 0745 hrs, the order came to stand-down for the day. Arrangements had somehow been made for central messing and a beer issue arrived at 1000 hrs. Colonel Jim gave a talk during the afternoon on the progress up at the front and about the future plans. In the early evening dinner was served, the officers (as is the Army custom) serving the men. There was plenty of beer for those who wanted it. The others on Syd's tank did and, as night and heavy rain began to fall, Christmas Day 1942 ended for Syd Storer with his dragging the crew, one by one, back to the shelter of their tank and putting them to bed.

That was one side of the coin. On the reverse side, the enemy was strengthening his position around the town of Buerat. As the old year ended, The Fifth moved forward and made contact with the enemy rearguard at Wadi Chebir, only to see it withdrawing to the main defensive line. However keen the men might have been for renewing the battle, orders were received not to push on for the time being but to maintain contact while newly-equipped reinforcements were brought into position. The final concentration was to be left as late as possible for reasons of secrecy. As earlier explained, the general plan was that, while the Highland Division with armoured support would try to clear the coast road, Seventh Armoured, with the New Zealand Division were to do a flanking movement directed towards Sedada and thence to Tarhuna to cut off further retreat. On 13th January The Fifth moved shortly before last light and leaguered just north of Wadi Chebir, staying in position there during the day. At last light the Regiment moved off along a marked and lighted route which enabled them to avoid the areas of treacherous sand and reach the Bir Ngem road by midnight. At first light the lead tanks crossed the road towards the Wadi Zem Zem and immediately came under intense fire. The following tanks took up positions and gave support. The enemy guns were in sight south of Gheddahia.

At this point there was a hitch. The New Zealanders had swung northwards to carry out the flanking movement but they had soon run into soft sand which slowed them down and restricted their movements. The Fifth was then ordered to abandon the original plan and assist in a frontal attack against the entrenched enemy.

'In the battle which lasted the whole afternoon,' Syd continued, 'we knocked out several guns and a few tanks but, in our slow advance, we also lost several tanks There appeared to be a minefield on the approach to the wadi which held us up. As night fell infantry recce patrols went forward but they returned to report that the enemy had withdrawn. The XI Hussars went forward at first light and by 1000 hrs reported the wadi clear and that the minefield was a dummy. We were then ordered to advance – no breakfast: just a brew and some army biscuits and chocolate in the tank. We encountered only patrols until late in the afternoon, as we were approaching Sedada, when we ran into a screen of anti-tank guns in position near the bridge over the wadi. We engaged them and destroyed several guns before the light faded. The enemy then withdrew, pausing only long enough to blow the bridge over the wadi. This caused inevitable delay on the morning of the 17th as we had difficulty finding a way down the escarpment and across the broad sandy wadi beyond but, once we had crossed, the going was very good and we moved on fast, reaching the small village of Beni Ulid before the light failed. The RAF reported a heavy concentration of enemy vehicles north and east of the village: our anti-tank gunners were sent forward and created great havoc with their 6-pounders.

'The advance continued the next day, again over extremely bad, stony going, intersected by small wadis. We found 13 tanks, abandoned due to lack of fuel, and caught up with the tail of a convoy some ten miles south of Tarhuna. We made contact with the enemy again six miles to the south of the village but, as our forces were badly strung out over the stony ground, we were ordered to await the arrival of more help before going into action. Very few tanks could be seen in the enemy's defence line but we were certain that there were still some there. As we waited for our reinforcements, General Harding, the Divisional Commander, came up to look at the position. While he was observing from the top of the Brigadier's tank, a shell landed nearby and blew him off the tank, wounding him in the left arm and leg. Our Brigadier [Pip Roberts] took over temporary command but there seemed to be no way of out-flanking the position that had been chosen: beside this we were now subject to constant visits from Stukas, despite the fact that we had RAF cover. The RAF bombed the road west of Tarhuna during the night of the 19th; we could not see what the results were but found on the following morning that the enemy had withdrawn into the pass through which the road to Tripoli descended into the plain of Gefara. Here he was completely concealed but seemed to observe every move that we made. It was decided to put in a night attack, the infantry going along the ridge to try to get to the foot of the pass while we made an attack straight down the road. The whole effect was an anti-climax as our attack coincided with the enemy's withdrawal. But, as they went, they blew great craters in the road down the pass. This caused some delay but fortunately some South African Engineers who were in support had an extremely large bulldozer which was brought forward and did magnificent work, so that by first light on 21st we were at the foot of the pass. We pushed on as rapidly as we could and by midday we were engaging the enemy rearguard around Castel Benito. The country was very close, the ground on either side [of the road] was very soft and [they had] an anti-tank ditch to their front to protect them. We could see the gates of Tripoli. It was decided to bring forward the Queens, our supporting infantry. This was difficult as there was so much traffic on the road. Everyone was ordered to pull to the side to allow the infantry carriers to pass and by 1730 hrs all was ready and the attack went in at 2200 hrs but the enemy, who had been nearly cut off by the tanks, had withdrawn and Castel Benito was found unoccupied.'

Here, Syd Storer's account differs from others. 'At first light on Saturday, 23rd January, led by the XI Hussars, we drove into Tripoli unopposed, accompanied by the Highland Division who had come along the coastal route.' But he remarks, as nobody else does, 'it was three months to the day since the opening of the Battle of el Alamein.'

Monty was now faced by major logistical problems, especially those created by the thirst of the armoured units. For the time being, therefore, it was decided to let the infantry push forward with only light armoured support. The main delays were caused more by blown bridges over the wadis and the terrain than by rear-guard activity. Some bridges were easily replaced, others were more difficult. The main hazard soon proved to be the wide expanse of sand dunes between the escarpment and the narrow strip of fertile land by the coast. This was passable by jeeps and light vehicles but the tanks were soon in difficulty. This made it impossible to outflank the enemy by any local move. This hold-up was turned to good advantage by The Fifth, who used the enforced idleness to carry out some much-needed maintenance.

Syd Storer includes at this point his description of the Victory Parade held in Tripoli, going on to say that, after heavy rainstorms on 5th February, the Regiment eventually moved off again on the 7th. The move did not take The Fifth very far, as the rain had washed out the work of the Sappers at a bridge near Assa. As a result of this, 5RTR swung across country to take el Utia by a flanking movement. This manoeuvre attracted the Luftwaffe's attention until an airstrip at Assa was cleared to let the RAF get the upper hand once more. As soon as the Engineers had finished their causeway – it was that rather than a bridge – The Fifth crossed on 14th February, followed by the rest of the Brigade and then the Division. Faced with this renewed threat, the enemy wisely withdrew.

No matter how close on his heels The Eighth Army was, the Boche used every slightest delay to improve his position. He was short of most warlike matériel but not of mines and these he strewed liberally in the path of the advance. While the infantry made straight for Ben Gardane, the armour made slow progress due to the inevitable delays of mine clearing and negotiating soft sand.

Syd continues with a description of the difficulties encountered. 'Our fellow tank brigade now stopped for a refit as they had only 12 battle-worthy tanks left. Our patrols advanced right up to the edge of Medenine while the divisional engineers repaired the road near the town. We were handicapped by a thick mist which covered the whole area: it showed no sign of lifting and reduced visibility to under a mile. Recce patrols meanwhile found crossings over the wadis north of the road. The enemy, we knew, was digging in at Metameur and in the Tadjeras hills. These would have dominated the whole area if the visibility had been good. On the night of the 18th we made a limited advance which brought us about 3 miles east of Medenine. In support we had the RHA and the Queens infantry [131 Brigade]. Then at dawn on 19th February we took advantage of the mist to cross the wadi north of the road and cut cross-country north of the Tadjeras to Mareth. We succeeded in reaching the hill (later known as Fifth Tanks Hill) which overlooked the road just before 1000 hrs as the mist began to lift. When the mist lifted we found ourselves completely overlooked from the Tadjeras and came under heavy and accurate artillery fire. We wirelessed back for assistance and were quickly supported by the rest of the brigade, 4 CLY and 1RTR who came up on our right and left.' Syd Storer finishes this, his version of the events of mid-February 1943, on a gleeful note, saying that the Regiment took cover and destroyed all the vehicles that tried to get away up the road, in the meantime taking a large number of prisoners. He goes on, the same happy strain, to recount how the pursuit was continued by the infantry entering Medenine and closing on Metameur as fast as the mines could be removed.

'That night the enemy withdrew into the hills to the east of the Mareth Line.'

What follows in The Storer Diary is an account of the assault on the Mareth Line. As this has already been fully covered, only one incident from Syd Storer's account is given, as it illustrates the hazards which threatened front line troops when in action. 'We then had an unfortunate accident when we were instructed to withdraw to take up positions elsewhere. We started up the engine and began to reverse from our position when we became aware of shouting from the infantry. We found that one of them had been sleeping under the tank and we had run over his arm. We knew that, if we moved forward, we should be exposed to enemy fire but it had to be carried out within the limited distance of the edge of the escarpment. Under instruction of the commander, the driver moved forward so that the soldier could be released. The driver then swung the tank round sharply to the right and began to pull away down the slope when a shell hit us in the middle of the engine doors. Luckily the angle was too sharp and it shot into the air, leaving us with a gaping hole in the engine doors. It was fortunate that we had a diesel engine for there is no doubt that a petrol engine would have been set on fire.'

Elaborate plans were made for an all-out assault on the Mareth Line. Before this was launched, el Hama fell and the DAK withdrew, leaving the Desert Rats out of contact with the enemy for the first time since el Alamein.

THE OTHER SIDE

Rommel's retreat from el Alamein must be seen in the context of Germany's overall position at this stage of the war.

The Wehrmacht had enormous forces engaged on the Russian Front. It had to 'garrison' countries as far apart as Norway, France and Greece and it had to contend with that running sore which afflicted it on the southern shores of the Mediterranean. In addition, there were the Kriegsmarine and the Luftwaffe, both being forced from the offensive to the defensive.

In the winter of 1942/43 things were not going well for Hitler who had, so to speak, painted himself into a corner. There was no single part of his 'Empire' on which he could relax his grip: a single collapse would have had a domino effect throughout the whole. Hitler had promised the German people an 'Empire which would last for a thousand years' – an Empire gained by the invincible sailors, soldiers and airmen of the Third Reich. Whatever the German people may have thought of this promise, Hitler believed it: it was a cornerstone of the Nazi credo. It would be, consequently, unthinkable for him that one millimetre of the territory acquired by conquest should be ceded back to the conquered.

The result of this was his disastrous policy of demanding from his commanders in the field that they should not withdraw from any position, no matter what pressure they came under.

In North Africa, the DAK had reached the el Alamein Line. It was, therefore, axiomatic that the whole of the North African coast must be held. There must be no retreat: Hitler had said so.

This put Erwin Rommel in an impossible position. Given a free hand, it is conceivable that he could have made a lightning turn-about and raced back to the Tunisian Peninsula where a strong defensive front could have been established – and supplied – before the slower-moving, more cautious Allies, with their ever-lengthening supply lines, could catch up with him. Even when the Allied advance became bogged down in the rain (and it seemed that the 'Lord Mighty in Battle' was not on Monty's side, after all) this was never an option for Rommel. The orders from

Berlin and Berchtesgaden were quite specific: 'No retreat'. Time and time again, Rommel was forced to interpret this order as 'a fighting retreat'. Faced with enormous superiority of men and matériel, this was a recipe for disaster. And the proof of the pudding was *disaster.*

From the military point of view, the reason for this is obvious. The Axis' success in the Desert – and the DAK had known plenty of that – depended on the correct deployment by Rommel of his forces in their role of mobile, armoured warfare. This was what the Panzer divisions were designed for, what the men were trained for, what the DAK's dwindling resources were capable of. Mobile armoured forces are never so successful in defence. As the Allies had learnt. Save for one factor, the Panzerarmee was ill-equipped for retreat.

This factor was in part matériel and in part tactical. It was one which the Wehrmacht never lost from sight. Simply the offensive, as well as the defensive, use of anti-tank guns. Had it not been for the persistent tactical use (as well as the marked technical superiority) of the German anti-tank guns, the race for Tunis could have been over in weeks rather than months.

Nor was Rommel's conduct of the retreat helped by a summons from Hitler and an interview in which he was told that he and all his soldiers were cowards, and that he deserved to be shot for suggesting an immediate withdrawal of the Afrika Korps from North Africa to Italy – which Rommel correctly assumed would be the Allies' next target.

It seems that, next day, Hitler had simmered down and realised the pertinence of Rommel's question, 'Would it be better to lose Tripolitania or the Afrika Korps?' Too late, Der Führer conceded Rommel's urgent request for reinforcements and ordered Göring to ensure that Rommel had everything he needed.

The Reichsmarschall promised the earth – and provided air: hot air. Disillusioned, Rommel returned to his men.

THE WAR CHRONICLE

1942

December	12	'Cockle-shell Heroes' Commando raid on Bordeaux
	15	Venereal Disease declared a greater menace to the civilian population than enemy air raids
	20	Japanese aircraft raided Calcutta by night
	24	Admiral Darlan (French Naval Chief and Vichy vice-premier) assassinated
	25	Leningrad 'celebrated' fifteen months of siege by the Wehrmacht
	31	Japanese began evacuation of Guadalcanal – 'Cultural Highlights' of 1942 were 'Mrs Miniver',

with Greer Garson; 'In which we Serve' with Noel Coward; 'The First of the Few' with Leslie Howard; Vera Lynn's 'White Cliffs of Dover' and Dmitri Shostakovich's 'Seventh Symphony' – but not necessarily in that order.

1943

January	02	Papua captured by combined Australian and American forces
	14	Winston Churchill and Franklin D Roosevelt met in Casablanca
	18	Relief of Leningrad started
	21	Armed Jewish uprising in Warsaw
	31	All German forces under Feldmarschall Paulus surrendered in Stalingrad
February	03	Russian forces go 'on the offensive' at all points on the Eastern Front
	05	Count Ciano, Mussolini's son-in-law, sacked as Foreign Minister, after holding the post since 1936
	08	'Chindit' Offensive launched in Burma – Russian forces retook Kursk
	18	William Beveridge introduced the 'Welfare State' plan
	28	Commando raid on German 'heavy water' plant in Norway
March	03	Tragic accident killed 178 Londoners at Bethnal Green Underground Station
	05	First flight of the Gloster 'Meteor' jet-engined fighter
	10	Attack on Goa Harbour caused four Axis merchant ships to be scuttled
	13	Plot to assassinate Hitler failed
	14	HM Submarine *Thunderbolt* (the ill-fated *Thetis* which sank on trials in 1939) torpedoed and sunk
	15	German forces re-captured Kharkov – Chindits crossed the Irrawaddy River in Burma
	23	Troopship *Windsor Castle* sunk
	24	Chindits withdrawn from Burma

NOTES

1 *Shermans.* The Fifth suffered the same fate in North West Europe when other units (including the Fifth Royal Inniskilling Dragoon Guards in the 22nd Armoured Brigade) were issued with *Comets* in place of the well-worn but little-loved *Cromwells.* 5RTR was not equipped with *Comets* until October 1945

2 Griff Talk. Surprisingly, griff, a WW II word for genuine information or 'pukha gen' dates back at least to 1830

3 Church Parade in Tripoli. It is, perhaps, a pity that the photographic evidence also shows Alan Biddell out-of-step with the rest of the Fifth Tank's contingent

4 We. This included General Sir Alan Brooke (the CIGS), General Sir Harold Alexander (C-in-C MEF), Air Chief Marshal Sir Arthur Tedder and, exceptionally, Winston's son, Randolph

5 'Moving tent'. The quotation is from the poem, *At Home in Heaven*, by the early nineteenth century English critic and poet, James Montgomery

6 Wadi Zig Zou. This place causes some confusion. Liddell Hart spells it Zigazou, as does Syd Storer, but neither Mike Carver nor Gerald Verney mentions it at all

7 Bundles of sticks. Fascines – nothing new about these: they were frequently used in the Great War to help the tanks cross the trenches.

8 Moaning Minnie. A 150mm mortar launcher with six barrels. 'Moaning' from the noise it made (the six barrels fired at 2 second intervals) going off: 'Minnie' short for its German name, Minenwerfer – 'Mine thrower'. Introduced in 1941 and in common use by 1942, they were derived from the Russian 'Stalin's Piano'

9 Lap Gunner. There are various descriptions for this member of the crew and, indeed, he did have various functions. He was, in both *Shermans* and *Cromwells,* the 'front seat passenger'. The lap gunner sat alongside the driver and was responsible for manning the secondary Browning or Besa machine-gun. Lap gunners were often treated as a spare member of the crew: this was true but, as he might at any time be called upon to take over as driver or as main gunner, he not infrequently had other functions nearly as important as brewing the char

10 Mrassas. Already encountered in Jake Wardrop's version as Morasses

CHAPTER X

. . . *The TT: The Finishing Flag – Tunis*

April–May 1943

'No event' reads the War Diary for the first two days of April 1943 nor was there any Regimental action on the 3rd when the CO, 2i/c, Adjutant and Squadron Commanders went to a 'demonstration of 'I' tank work by 1RTR'. On the 4th 'B' and 'C' Squadrons had their turn on a range and 10 'heavy' tanks arrived from workshops: these meant the Regiment tank strength became 18 *Shermans*, 12 *Grants* and 18 *Crusaders*. Next day at 0800 hrs the CO and Squadron Commanders went to a Divisional conference while 'A' and HQ Squadrons had their turn on the range. At 1500 hrs the CO gave another Griff Talk concerning the attack on Wadi Akarit which was to be launched next night. At 1000 hrs on the 6th the CO issued Operation Orders and at midday the Regiment moved forward on the prescribed CL only to be told to push on and protect the flank of Xth Corps – an order which was changed later on the march and brought The Fifth into a different leaguer from the one originally ordered.

The Order of the Day, 'WHIPS OUT!', arrived at 0630 hrs on 8th April: this had 5RTR in reserve. In reserve, yes, but not above receiving '300 Italian POWs with 2 x 105mm, 11 MET and much SA [small arms and ammunition].' During a march, interrupted by numerous long halts, the Regiment 'took 4 POWs from Panzergruppe 115 who were part of a unit scattered by the RAF bombing the previous day.' After leaguering for the night, the Regiment moved at 0600 hrs to form protection right front, with1RTR on the left. At 0800 hrs the unit 'bumped enemy [anti-] tank guns, probably 20 and 50mm. Took several POWs from 164 [German Infantry] Div. One gun brewed up.' More serious opposition was encountered at 1715 hrs when the Regiment 'bumped' another line of enemy guns. However, these were dealt with when 'B' Squadron made a right-flanking movement, rolling the enemy up and capturing 12 more prisoners from 164 Div, destroying a 75mm gun, 2 lorries and 2 cars, and bagging 2 trucks. They also left a number of the enemy dead: all without loss. In spite of extremely bad going, fighting enemy rearguards and being shelled until last light, the unit advanced 35 miles before forming night leaguer. The Fifth was on its way again at 0600 hrs next day, continuing its advance through close country until attaining its objective of cutting the

Sfax–Tenioui road. Having attained this, scout car patrols were sent out on recce and came back to report the road blown in several places.

The entries for 11th and 12th April are succinct: they read respectively, 'Carried out much needed maintenance' and 'No event'.

The Divisional Commander's visit on the 13th was cancelled because the Regiment was on the move, ending up 6 miles south of Kairouan at 1230 hrs. What they did in the afternoon is not stated but the following day was devoted to maintenance. At 1130 hrs on 16th April 5RTR was sent off by itself in support of 131 Brigade, leaguering in their area and establishing a permanent LO with 131 Bde HQ. In the afternoon the CO and Squadron Commanders carried out 'forward recce', then – as if recording the weather report – the War Diary states that there was 'light shelling' in the afternoon! Over the next two days, this 'light shelling' becomes 'slight shelling'. Which did the men find worse? Light or slight?

Regimental state on 17th April was one *Crusader* fewer since the last count, with 34 Officers and 557 ORs on strength. April 19th was a busy day with the Colonel going to a Brigade Conference at 0700 hrs. At 1130 hrs the Regiment got marching orders for an attack with four separate, and unusually-named objectives, Rachel, Naomi, Rahab and Ruth[1]. These were four points on the left flank of 131 Brigade, which in turn was doing protection left for Xth Corps. The Regiment moved up into position at 1400 hrs and – a nice exotic touch, this – 'leaguered among the cover of cactus and olive groves.' Reveille on the 20th was at 0400 hrs followed by an O Group at 0415 hrs and a move into position at 0445 hrs, reaching Rahab at 0530 hrs with 'A' Squadron pushing on to Ruth with orders to remain in observation all day. The others came under intermittent shell-fire, Capt Whitty being a victim with a head wound. Without any reported action, 5 more German 164 Division POWs were taken. At 1730 hrs 3 tanks or guns and 6 men were sighted. What they were doing or what happened to them is not recorded. The enemy cannot, however, have been far away, as close leaguer was ordered for the night.

The 21st was another early day, especially for 'A' Squadron which was again sent out to take up observation positions, taking advantage of the low profile of their *Crusaders*. The CO carried out a recce of the unit's right flank. The enemy's attentions to the A Echelon area unfortunately caused the death of one of the fitters and wounded the MQMS. 'A' Squadron was deployed on observation for a third day, being able to push forward to command a good view over the road running from Saouaf to Sidi Dhrine. On Saint George's Day 'A' Squadron was again well up and able to act effectively as a Gunners' FOP. One troop of *Crusaders* was pushed forward onto a 'prominent feature from which they had drawn fire the previous day, making themselves conspicuous with the object of finding out if the enemy had withdrawn his guns. He had NOT.'

Willy-nilly the Regiment made an early start on the 24th when shots were heard to their immediate front. There was a hasty stand-to at 0340 hrs and shortly after that a report from a Queens infantry standing patrol that they had opened fire on some enemy attempting to infiltrate their position by coming up a wadi on their left. The fire had been returned and the Sergeant Patrol Leader had sustained slight injuries – to his beauty and dignity. A scout car patrol was sent out to chase off the enemy, only to find that they had already withdrawn. A dawn patrol went forward and discovered that the enemy had taken up a defensive position in the area where 'A' Squadron had established their OP the previous day. Before first light 'A' Squadron plus a troop of *Shermans* went out to regain this position: they succeeded but lost a *Sherman* on an enemy mine laid during the night. The remainder of the day was quiet.

'A' Squadron was back again next day in its previous OP position, spotting for the guns of 5 RHA. A number of patrols were also sent out and 'came under a good deal of accurate enemy artillery and SA fire.' On 26th April the Brigade played 'General Post'; 5RTR being relieved by 1RTR and taking over the Sharpshooters' position, while they moved in where 1RTR had been. There was a 'No 1 Party[2]' at 1430 hrs and another one at 1440 hrs the following day before the Regiment moved to a new leaguer at 1645 hrs. There are 'No event' entries in the War Diary for 28th and 29th April with a head-count of 34 Officers and 563 ORs and a tank-count of 11 *Shermans*, 7 *Grants* and 10 *Crusaders* of which 3 now had 6-pounder main guns.

The War Diary does scant justice to the events of 30th April. There is an entry which records the visit of the Divisional Commander, Major General GWEJ Erskine DSO, at 1000 hrs and the arrival of new tanks, making the unit strength up to 32 'heavy' tanks (*Shermans* and *Grants*) and 17 *Crusaders*. There is then a totally inconsequent entry which states '2100 hrs Bn A Echelon leaves for 1st Army front. Route – Div axis – Kairouan – Ousseltia – Siliana – Le Krib. Driving all night. Tanks to follow on transporters next day'. It is, of course, not the part of any Regimental War Diary to map the course of the war but these twenty-eight words are all that is mentioned of the dramatic change of plan which took The Fifth, among others, out of the Eighth Army and into the Eisenhower/Alexander Anglo-American First Army, so that they were not, after all, to enter Tunis at the head of the Eighth Army, as they had been expecting – indeed hoping – for nigh on three years.

A full analysis of the Axis situation is given at the end of this chapter in *The Other Side*: all that needs to be said here is that the Allied Command was faced with a strategic problem very different from the one envisaged at the time of el Alamein. And with a new DAK Commander – Colonel General Jürgen von Arnim[3].

So far as 5RTR was concerned, the scene of action changed dramatically when General Alexander ordered the transfer of the Seventh Armoured and Fourth Indian Divisions from the Eighth to the First Army. This choice of two of the most experienced Desert Divisions was agreed between the two Army Commanders and was a compliment to the men serving in them. As the entries in the War Diary show, this transfer was accomplished with great speed and efficiency. Its result, in a matter of weeks, spelt the end of Axis activity in North Africa.

The first day of May found The Fifth on the move, led by the A Echelon with the tanks following on transporters. On the 2nd the Echelon had arrived at Le Krib at 1200 hrs and leaguered 'leaving room for the tanks to come later.' Evidently at least some of the Regiment arrived safely, as at 1000 hrs, Colonel Jim went on a recce with the Brigadier and visited Pip Roberts who was then commanding 26th Armd Brigade. At midday the old tanks arrived in leaguer, to be joined by enough new tanks to bring the strength up to 32 'Heavy Tanks' and 17 *Crusaders*. The reference to visiting Brigadier Roberts of 26th Armd Brigade needs some explanation. Pip Roberts, after taking temporary command of Seventh Armoured Division when General Harding was injured, had been posted back to the UK (to take over the Eleventh Armoured Division which he later commanded with distinction in North-West Europe): on his way home, however, he was 'borrowed' to command 26th Armd Bde which was temporarily leaderless. The other Brigadier referred to was WRN ('Loony') Hinde of the 15th/19th Hussars, recently promoted to replace Pip.

On the 4th at 0945 hrs the Colonel held a Battalion Group conference on tactics: this included the Gunners – field and anti-tank – and the Infantry COs. There was another conference at 1700 hrs for the CO and Squadron Commanders at Division. A No 1 Party was held at 1000 hrs on 5th May: here, Colonel Hutton outlined the plan of campaign for the capture of Tunis. At 1230 hrs the Regiment moved up to its 'kick off' position where, at 1830 hrs, the CO addressed all tank commanders. The operation started at 0500 hrs on the 6th when the Battalion Group moved up to their FDLs. From these the unit took up protection front and, in about two miles, passed through a line of *Churchill* tanks which were supporting the 4th Indian Division. The advance was temporarily held in check and the Regiment ordered to keep to the left of the CL. None the less, at 1530 hrs the first objective was reached after encountering spasmodic resistance, while 'A' Squadron pushed on to the second objective, engaging enemy patrols on the way. By 1700 hrs several pockets of resistance had been cleared up.

It was a profitable start for 5RTR: their bag for the day included 2 Italian M13 tanks, one half-track and 2 x 75mm guns destroyed, plus 10 MET, with a 150mm, an 88mm and a 20mm gun captured, and a 25-pounder gun and a White half-track [armoured truck] being recovered. Altogether the bag of prisoners totalled 76, of which two were officers. On the debit side, one NCO and his driver were killed when their scout car was hit by anti-tank fire and one OR was wounded when an HE shell hit the back of his *Sherman*. The scout car was recovered during the night by the Troop Leader. The next day started early with a move at 0415 hrs, the objective being to seize the high ground above St Cyprien. A certain amount of opposition was encountered on the right front, where enemy anti-tank guns, concealed in small woods, fired on

'B' Squadron. This cannot have been too serious nor does it seem to have produced any casualties, since the War Diary reads, 'the high ground on the left was reached without much difficulty and various groups of prisoners were taken besides some enemy equipment. Two half-tracked vehicles were brewed up.' The Luftwaffe flew one of its last sorties in North Africa at 0730 hrs when 6 ME 109s unavailingly bombed and machine-gunned the Regiment. The 5 RHA guns in the Battalion Group had a successful shoot, knocking out two 88s.

At noon the leading elements of 5RTR must have felt 'like stout Cortez when with eagle eyes he stared at the Pacific[4].' They were looking down on the City of Tunis. The Fifth was halted here, no doubt feeling doubly pleased with their achievements, as they had knocked out no fewer than six 88s during the morning's advance. At 1430 hrs Fearless Jim sent a composite force of *Crusaders* and *Shermans* with some infantry under Major Ward into the City with strict orders to go no farther than Bardo Station. They arrived there half-an-hour later, thus being the first British tanks and infantry to enter Tunis. It was not an easy ride, as 'this group met with quite a bit of opposition in the way of sniping and street fighting, particularly from upper storeys of houses. One private car full of Germans who shot at one of the leading tanks was brewed up.' Rather in the manner that an ambitious Colonel Buonaparte quelled his opposition with a 'whiff of grape-shot' so did The Fifth quell theirs with 'some 75mm HE fire on houses in which the enemy were holding out.' At 1530 hrs the remainder of the Battalion Group advanced into the town. By 1800 hrs 5RTR had taken up to 2,000 prisoners. The advance encountered some unexpected difficulty; as the War Diary says. 'The street fighting was not facilitated by the cheering local populace trying to mount tanks and throwing flowers.' The overnight leaguer was close to Bardo Station

On 8th May – when The Fifth still had two years of war before it – the Regiment was sent across the city to clear up any remaining opposition and to secure the high ground north of Ariana and the adjacent aerodrome. Once again, and although it was only 0500 hrs, 'progress through the town was slow owing to the thousands of cheering civilians who persisted in climbing onto tanks.' Something over 100 prisoners were taken: these were sent back along the Regimental axis without escort [but probably more in need of protection than guarding]. On the outskirts of the city, the Battalion Group divided into two; one sub-division following Colonel Jim on the northern route directly to Ariana and the other successfully securing the high ground. Not content with achieving this, a Troop of *Shermans* and a Motor Platoon were despatched to clear the dock area. This party bagged a large number of POWs. It was still only 1100 hrs when the CO handed his party over to Major Aldridge (the 2i/c) to go over to see how Dickie Ward was getting on with his 'A' Squadron group. Dickie reported one expected and one unexpected problem. Expected: his group had met with fire from a determined party armed with 20mm Bredas and small arms – 'C' Squadron had joined him to help deal with this.

Unexpected: an appeal for help from the infantry who could not cope with the flow of POWs, pouring in and overwhelming their positions.

There had been a false alarm earlier in the day when Brigade had ordered Fifth Tanks to act on a report that a ship, laden with German troops, was pulling out of the harbour. A Troop from 'C' Squadron went to investigate but found nothing to substantiate the report. This Troop did, on the other hand, return from Carthage with some 1,000 more prisoners. It would have been hard for a lesser man than Colonel Jim to keep track of what his Regiment was doing: it had been divided into small packets and sent hither and yon – returning from nearly every expedition with yet more prisoners and laden with the spoils of war. At 1200 hrs 'A' Squadron had reached the coast at Cap Gamard where they collared some prisoners who were waiting hopefully for boats. By 1400 hrs, the whole of the Carthage Peninsula had been cleared of enemy. The haul from this part of the action was in the order of 5,000 men (mostly Wehrmacht but with some Luftwaffe personnel), an 88 and a 20mm A/Tk gun: it included 'some hundred lorries driven by enemy drivers into our cages.' But this was by no means all. Also captured or cleared of enemy were two airfields, one with about 100 damaged planes and another with five intact, a petrol dump, a transport vehicle park and a hospital, complete with 150 bed patients.

When Major Aldridge accounted to Colonel Jim on his return, the CO found that his Second-in-Command had been far from idle. He had carried out a sweep of his surrounding area and could lay claim to an Italian hospital with 200 wounded, 4 officers and 118 ORs from the German Signal Corps, one aerodrome with 250 A/A personnel and 12 multiple 20mm guns and range-finding equipment, to say nothing of about 50 stray POWs, rounded up by the civilian population or the support infantry, and an even larger petrol dump – safely under guard of the A1 Echelon. It was a relief to all when close leaguer was established outside the city at 1900 hrs.

The following day the Regiment moved to a Brigade leaguer on the other side of Tunis and was joined by the B Echelon. On 10th May the first leave parties were let loose in Tunis but otherwise, as with the 11th and 12th, there was nothing to report. That may have been true for 5RTR for that third day but it was hardly the case for the Top Brass, as Wednesday, 12th May was the day on which General von Arnim formally surrendered and all Axis opposition to the Allies in North Africa ceased. It was estimated at the time that a quarter of a million men were taken prisoner[5] in those last few days: no estimate was ever made of the amount of equipment, apart from one report which stated that it was 'enormous'. On that and the following day, two signals were despatched: one, sent to Berlin, saying that the Afrika Korps had fought itself to the point at which it could fight no more; the other, sent to London, simply telling Churchill that his orders had been carried out and the Allies were now masters of North Africa.

There followed days of movement, idleness, daily PT and swimming: then

Squadron Parades and organised sports. Lt DE Cockbaine was appointed Brigade Sports Officer. Although the War in the Desert was over, 5RTR was still part of a Division and an Army with a task to accomplish. This being the case, it was subjected to lectures – from Monty downwards – and inspections, down to and including one by the Brigadier who took his fine-tooth comb to every tank in the Regiment and expressed himself satisfied with what he saw. Fearless Jim had a few days' well-deserved leave and nothing worse disturbed the peace than an unfounded rumour of German Paratroops being dropped in the areas of the Benghazi and Castel Benito airfields.

May slipped into June, the roll-call showing that there were 35 Officers and 591 ORs. The entry for 19th June records that these Officers and Men had a surprise in store for them. '1845 hrs. No 1 Party. CO gives orders for road move to a point west of Tripoli for coming inspection of [it would have been more polite to have said 'by'] HM the King.' At 0700 hrs the following day the Regiment left in 30 lorries, with three cook-houses, for the site chosen for the Parade, arriving and leaguering at 1700 hrs. At 1500 hrs on Monday, 21st June 478 WOs, NCOs and Men, with 22 Officers, of the Fifth Royal Tank Regiment lined the route of His Majesty's inspection. At 1620 hrs Lieutenant Colonel WM Hutton DSO MC was presented to the Colonel in Chief of the Regiment who was given the traditional 'three cheers' by the assembled men.

At 0400 hrs the next day the contingent arrived back in camp in Homs. This is the first mention of Homs and is the point at which to leave the War Diary for the time being and to return to the personal accounts of this stage of the Desert War. Before doing so, however, it may cause some amusement to hear a true story about Homs. Some fourteen or fifteen years after The Fifth was at Homs, an ex-Fifth Tanks member went on a package tour to a place an easy passion-wagon-ride from Homs. As often happens on package tours, outings were laid on and these tourists were told one evening's entertainment was to be held in – and here the tour guide lowered her voice – a former brothel. On arrival, the ex-member noticed, without particular surprise for the colours are common in Arab countries, that this former brothel was decorated in brown and red and green. However, on being shown into the salon where the goods had one time been displayed and the assignations arranged, his worst suspicions were aroused when he observed that this most important of chambers was decorated exclusively in powder blue and red.

Going right back to the point where his narrative breaks off to introduce the War Diary, Syd wrote, 'We were in support for the attack on Wadi Akarit which was carried out by the infantry divisions, 5RTR being at the rear in case of counter-attack. The country was very close, pleasant to look at but with too much cover for sniping. Several tank commanders were lost to snipers hidden in the olive groves. Owing to the soft going and the time taken for mine removal, we only moved 10 miles through the Akarit Line by nightfall on 7th

April. We came unexpectedly into contact on the following morning west of Skhira, when we saw our first Tiger tank, but it withdrew before coming into action. Later in the day the forward patrols of the 11th Hussars captured a 'live' but broken down Tiger. We had a quick look over it and decided that they were best kept at a distance.

'We were now approaching a small place called Achichina and, as we attempted to enter it, were fired on from the high ground to the north-west. We took up firing positions and the New Zealanders came up to attack. Together we pressed the enemy back until last light. Once more in the morning they were gone and we made rapid progress with only a short skirmish north of Chahal. But the resistance began to stiffen as we approached the high ground in front of Agareb at about 1400 hrs. The fighting conditions were strange to us: olive groves everywhere made observation difficult and the low boughs of the trees created a hazard to the turret crews. Near here we surprised some enemy as they were preparing to dig in, capturing 20 prisoners and two anti-tank guns. We followed a few who escaped and came upon another rearguard on a ridge two miles from the town. This was stronger, consisting of field and anti-tank guns supported by tanks, placed there to protect their soft-skinned vehicles which were attempting to escape. We could not get close but opened up at long range while others got in among the vehicles, capturing prisoners and doing great damage. The action went on until last light when we entered the edge of the village. Those of the enemy who escaped sped off down the road towards Sfax: meanwhile we went cross-country to a point north-west of the town without seeing any opposition.'

The Fifth was then told it would not be needed and would probably be stationed near Sfax for a fortnight. The Army's advance up the road towards Sousse, after a temporary hold-up at Chebba where a bridge had been blown, was going according to plan. This fortnight's rest proved to be a myth and, on the morning of the 12th, the Regiment was on a long urgent move through Triaga and La Fauconnerie to join the rest of the troops at Karouain. Here The Fifth made its first contact with the First Army and took over part of the front next to the Fighting [Free] French. Syd continues, 'We continued to edge forward slowly but surely, pushing the enemy back into the foothills north of Djebibina. In the meantime the New Zealanders had taken Enfidaville and Takruna. Most of this time we fired our [main] guns very little, a few rounds of small arms fire causing isolated rearguards to retire. On 28th we were given orders to move to the area of Enfidaville where we were to carry out an attack up the coast road with the object of capturing Bou Ficha and, if possible, advancing to Hammamet. Once again we had no sooner arrived than the plans were changed, due chiefly to the success of the First Army which had at last captured Medjez el Bab. On the night of 30th April we loaded our tanks onto transporters for a long haul through Kesserine to Le Krib which we reached on May 2nd after a journey of 300 miles.

'A few days were spent reconnoitring the recently captured ground east of

Medjez. On the afternoon of the 4th we moved up to the front on a road clogged with traffic taking supplies to the Indian Division whom we were supporting in the attack. Once more a silent attack (ie with no artillery preparation) was decided on, chiefly to allow the Gurkhas to move silently in during darkness and remove the opposition before anyone realised that the attack had started. The attack began at 0300 hrs, we followed on at dawn and saw the havoc created by the kukris of the Gurkhas. By 0700 hrs we were safely on the high ground and the artillery opened up on the final objective. The Indian Division had attained both their objectives and, according to plan, we concentrated on the open ground to their front. When the artillery shoot lifted at 1100 hrs we advanced with a little opposition. A short halt was made on some high ground overlooking Massicault and we got out to make a quick brew. As the mugs were handed round the enemy opened up with HE. We jumped into the tank just as a shell landed immediately in front of us. Three of us got inside safely but Geoff, our commander, was less lucky. A shell fragment took his left ear cleanly off and he fell to the bottom of the tank spurting blood. While one of the others put an emergency bandage[6] over the wound, I tried to radio for the MO but our aerial had been shot away. I ran across to the nearest tank and asked them to call the MO while we reversed down the hill to meet him. The MO's 'mercy wagon' took Geoff away. Unfortunately in the rush, my small kit went with it. Our driver was senior to me, so I took over driving and he became crew commander. We continued to advance and took Massicault and Djebej by 1600 hrs. Then we pushed on to the outskirts of St Cyprien. We leaguered in a very wet olive grove and sat out a night of rain in the tank.

'Sgt 'Pluto' Ellis had come at first light to take over our tank, having lost his on the first day. We advanced seven miles, meeting 15 tanks, one of them a Tiger. By midday we were in control of the high ground north of St Cyprien. We were then ordered to push on with the Queens and take the high ground overlooking Tunis. There were several 88s on the ridge but our arrival caught them by surprise and they were quickly dealt with. By 1500 hrs we in the Fifth, with 1RTR on our right and 4 CLY on our left, were looking down on Tunis. Our appearance was a complete surprise to the garrison, just as the enthusiastic reception by the French population was a surprise to us. The mass of prisoners who came forward proved a real embarrassment to movement as did the several pockets of resistance which we encountered. We went to La Bardo where some SS refused to surrender until we put a few HE into the houses they had hoped to defend. The Queens were brought into the city to collect the prisoners and we moved north-east to Carthage where the Luftwaffe were still trying to get aircraft away: as we approached the airfield, the last aircraft took off. We opened up with machine-guns on some figures we saw behind piles of baggage. Too late, we realised they were Arabs doing some looting. Next, about 40 Luftwaffe personnel came marching out of the hangars and gave themselves up. There was a mass of anti-aircraft guns and assorted equipment on the airfield, so we had to remain overnight to guard it.

'We had now travelled 2,000 miles from el Alamein in six months and we were proud to be the first troops to enter Tunis.'

Syd Storer then gives a picture of the unreality of life in Tunis after the liberation. Leave parties were organised from the leaguer near Matur and the French population made their liberators very welcome . . . as far as their limited resources allowed. This sense of unreality lasted until 12th May when the tanks were loaded onto transporters for an early start the following morning. Syd remarked that the men were able to cope with this artificial peacetime life because, just as when they were in action, more orders were cancelled than were ever carried out. Eventually The Fifth moved 75 miles to Bou Taid where it stayed until the18th, giving the men an opportunity to trade with the local Arab population for fresh eggs.

In Syd's words, 'Again, on the19th, an early start prefaced a continuous move through Le Krib, Le Kef and the Kasserine Pass, on to Gabes and Mareth, covering 100 to 120 miles each day. Whenever we stopped for meals, we examined wrecks and knocked-out tanks. By the 23rd we were back in Tripolitania. Once, when we halted for a midday meal, we looked over the Roman ruins at Sabratha. After passing Tripoli we suffered a series of punctures: we also had to make several detours, some bridges not being able to take the heavier vehicles. On 26th May we unloaded at Homs in a sand-storm and took the tanks down near the seashore where we were told we were to stay. It was a disappointing sight after all our expectations; nothing but miles of sand and sand dunes. Only the sea, with the prospect of swimming, offered any joy.

'After settling in we completed the maintenance on the tanks – they had to be cleaned and polished inside and out for a Divisional Commander's [the War Diary says Brigadier's] inspection. After this, on 8th June, we were warned to keep the tanks and equipment in good condition as a further inspection was to due to take place. On the 16th we left for Tripoli where, amidst all sorts of rumours, we were given beds in a rest camp for a week. Who would be inspecting us this time? Churchill again, perhaps? He had been out to us after the fall of Tripoli. Most bets were that it would only be Monty. However, the 19th proved us all wrong. We paraded that day in the streets of Tripoli as a welcome party for King George VI. On the 21st the King took the salute as we paraded with our tanks through the middle of the city. We returned to Homs during the night and were given a day of rest.'

'Carlo' Carlsson was doubly fortunate when he was let loose on Tunis. Not only did he meet a very charming French family, who took him in and befriended him, it turned out that the head of the family was a dentist. When Carlo laughingly remarked that he could do with a replacement tooth as the Army Dental Service was not equipped for such refinements, Monsieur did not hesitate. With a speed which would have left our present NHS gasping for breath, he whipped Pete into the chair and provided him with free service in gratitude for his City's liberation.

Another account of these days comes from Dennis Cockbaine in which he pays his personal tribute to the CO, saying, 'In mid-April 1943, 5RTR found itself about 1,000 miles west of el Alamein, having taken part in many battles, notably Medenine, the Mareth Line, Wadi Akarit and the fall of Tripoli. It had been a very long haul and our CO had commanded us brilliantly. He had already earned himself the title 'Fearless Jim' and he also rightly earned the respect and admiration of all ranks.

'It came as a surprise to us when, as we were lining up for an assault on Enfidaville, we were loaded onto tank transporters and taken southward and then westward through the Desert towns of Kairouan and Le Klef until we joined up with the First Army at a place called Madjez el Bab. The whole 7th Armd Div, together with 4th Indian Division, were being switched to this area in order to carry out the last attack of the North African campaign on the city of Tunis. Our two Divisions formed the left flank and 6th Armd Div with 46th Infantry Div formed the right flank of First Army.'

It had already come as a surprise to Lt Cockbaine that, instead of the comparative security of a tank, his 'battle wagon' was again to be a scout car, since Colonel Jim had appointed him as a Liaison Officer. Dennis described his first task in this new capacity after the switch from Eighth to First Army by saying, 'The Colonel held the customary O Group the evening before the attack and, at the end of it, said that we might have heavy casualties. This was very unusual for him. He then said that I was to go forward with the Gurkha Brigade to liaise with them as they were leading the infantry attack. I was not too enthusiastic about this mission but, in the event, the attack was notable for the low casualties involved and I was able to relay what I hoped was interesting news to 5RTR HQ. As day dawned I saw several groups of Gurkhas sitting around in the captured ground – smiling as always – having achieved all objectives.

'When 7th Armd Div, led by The Fifth on the left flank and 1RTR on the right, advanced, progress was rapid against fading opposition. Our main problem arose from the consistent attacks we suffered from 'friendly' aircraft. Every orange smoke canister[7] was used but still the fighters gave us their attentions until dusk. However, there were few casualties in the advance and the entry into Tunis was greeted by the inhabitants with rapture. In the following days we rounded up thousands of prisoners, captured ex-enemy HQ sites and airfields (even shooting down a German plane taking off in an attempt to escape). It was pleasantly chaotic and a great tribute to all of those who had suffered so much in the Desert battles in previous years.

'Before we entered Tunis, the CO had ordered me to take a look at a huge white building perched half-way up a hill about a mile or so on our left front. I approached the building carefully and, with pistol in hand, climbed the ornate steps up to the front door. It was flung open and a stream of uniformed Italian officers lined the steps and handed me their weapons. One of these spoke English: he informed me that I had captured a Field Hospital!

'After all the festivities, parades and palaver, we fondly imagined that we would be given leave in Cairo or with the Delta flesh-pots. This was not to be and we ended up on the Mediterranean beach at a place called Homs where we spent many weeks combining leisure with training for our next battle, which was to be the landing at Salerno in Italy in September. It was here at Homs that I was posted to 'B' Squadron – the happiest posting of my life and the start of an association which has endured to this day.'

Bob Lay had an adventure of a similar nature. This illustrates something that nobody else mentions, namely that there were a lot of strange troops around or, worse, a lot of troops around behaving in a strange way. Bob wrote of this, 'The next day we went through Tunis. The crowds at the roadside were very quiet; they did not know what to make of this queer lot. We stopped and I spoke in French to some people standing staring at us. I said, 'Nous sommes la huitième armée britannique – les jerboas.' They went mad! The whole street lit up as the news went down the road. As we moved on we collected bottle after bottle of wine . . . even some genuine German beer. Out on the other side of the town we sent streams of POWs back down the Charlie Love. There was a striking building with big double doors. I banged on them and out came a motley lot of Germans and I obtained the key from one of them. I learnt later that this was the Royal Palace. A little further on I noticed movement behind a hedge. I went into a field full of, I suppose, a squadron of Spahis or equivalent. I told them to stack their arms. Officers appeared and I requested their pistols: they got excited and ordered their men to recover their arms. Rapidly I retreated and we came back with the tank. They formed up, and down the road they went. A kindly elderly couple insisted that I went with them into their bungalow. Inside was a young Luftwaffe pilot whom they had befriended. Out he went, and down the road with the others. Later on, the crew had a trip to an almost deserted Bizerta. We swam off the pier, changing in the entertainment hall.'

It will come as no surprise to learn that another man who had something to say at this time was . . . Monty. The day after the Axis surrender in Tunis he issued the last of his North Africa 'Personal Messages'. This one was addressed 'to all his soldiers' and told them how intensely proud he was of all that they had done. He pointed to the contrast between the miraculous escape of the BEF at Dunkirk and the total surrender of the DAK in Tunisia. He then rather dampened his readers' enthusiasm for their victory by saying in the plainest possible language that they weren't finished yet and they weren't going home yet. Not happy reading for men who had been two, three or even more years in the Desert. Equally, it was a clear hint that the next stop was going to be Italy – that being the only place for them to go if they weren't going home: the only place that they would see Monty's 'good hunting in the battles that are yet to come and which we will fight together'.

Not surprisingly, with 'Time's wingèd chariot hurrying near', memories of those days have become fragmented and only odd – but, mercifully, usually amusing – ones stand out. This is the case with Keith Treasure, last heard of having a sliver of shell fragment removed from his eye. Keith had been remustered and had ended up in HQ Squadron under the kindly eye of RSM Mick Fern (and the even kindlier one of Jock Gordon). Being one of the Echelon drivers, Keith was kept pretty busy and reckons that he still holds the record – three days and three hours – for the 1,300 road/track/desert miles from Homs back to Cairo, or the other way around, in his faithful three-tonner. Tunis had one pleasant surprise for him . . . and one reminder that the Army is always the Army slice it whichever way you will. In Tunis Lance Corporal Treasure encountered his eldest brother, Major Treasure of the Royal Corps of Signals. A happy reunion as they had hardly even heard of each other, let alone met, for what would nowadays be called 'yonks'. But still an Army occasion, as L/Cpl Treasure, 5RTR of the Eighth Army, was reminded when he was given a dressing down [not the word that Keith used] by his brother's Sergeant Major for not standing to attention when addressing Major Treasure, RCS, of the First Army! However, blood is thicker than water and Big Brother 'kept' Little Brother for his three days' leave, and did so on better rations than Keith had known for quite a while.

Another fragment of memory is supplied by Harry Ireland by way of an excerpt from his Diary. One of the blessings of being 'out of the line', Harry recalls, was not simply the arrival of mail from home but having the time to reply to one's letters. Another blessing was the appearance of the 'Sally Ann' canteen with its cornucopia of goodies. 'Real' cigarettes instead of the standard issue of the abominated 'Victory V's, tooth paste, tooth brushes, sweet biscuits, sugar, note paper and pens: much, if not most, of it free. Many a man in those day ended what passed for his nightly prayers with the words, '.. and God bless the Salvation Army.'

Jake Wardrop, of course, had a lot to say about those days: unsurprisingly he includes many incidents that no War Diary would . . . or tells of them in a manner that no War Diary could. Of the time that the Regiment was sitting outside Enfidaville, and expecting to have to take the place by frontal assault, Jake recalls that a German mine-laying party came out one night into what they thought was no-man's-land only to find it already claimed by the RBs. The two sides had a lot to say about that, but it was the familiar although unwelcome voice of the Spandau that got the tank crews out of their bedrolls and into their tanks. Law and order was restored when some more RBs turned out. Jake's description of the countryside does not dwell on green fields and olive groves but on the surrounding hills. These he commends for being as high as Ben Lomond[8] but condemns for being thickly provisioned with unfriendly Boche guns. The tame hen on Jake's tank celebrated Easter by laying an egg on Easter Monday, causing the crew to 'dash about like proud fathers'. Having found out how to lay them, the hen was equally proud of itself and laid an egg a day for several weeks. On 28th April the crews had some surprising orders: to repaint the tanks olive green and disguise their Desert Rat signs. The next day they loaded up onto transporters.

As Jake records, it was a three day journey but he did not, as Willie Dovey did, see one of the tanks break loose and part company with its trailer. On the other hand, Jake did see, and no doubt joined in the whistling at, *les demoiselles* in the villages through which they passed, in the same way as he joined in the scrounging for rations from the wayside dumps which they encountered en route. One of these produced luxuries unknown to the Eighth Army, provoking one of the crew to comment that it wasn't surprising the First Army couldn't fight: they were too well fed. A remark typical of the not-altogether-friendly rivalry that existed between the two Armies. In Le Klef they passed a number of refugees from Tunis and Bizerta, whose joy at seeing the Desert Rats was only equalled by the men's excitement at seeing the girls. On 1st May the tanks were unloaded . . . and Jake found himself as crew commander of a *Grant*. Jake was pleased: he'd spent enough of his life hauling on steering levers or changing gear; he had a good crew, all of whom knew each other and had worked well in the past. This was a glorious moment for Jake. That very evening there was an O Group for all tank commanders – and he, John Richard Wardrop, a few days before his 27th birthday, was one of them!

Jake goes on to describe the next actions much as do others but adds a note of admiration for the thoroughness with which 'the Indians' [by which he actually meant the Gurkhas] did their work. This may sound somewhat bloodthirsty of Jake. Certainly the Afrika Korps were worthy opponents but there was a lot to be said for the only good German being a dead German. Which was how the Gurkhas generally left them. Jake hoped that they, and the New Zealanders, would be with them in England for the next show. Jake seems temporarily to have forgotten his unstinted admiration for the Aussies. That morning, Jake passed some of the Gurkhas, calmly making chapattis, amid the carnage and wreckage of 88s and 105s which they had wrought.

Things went well – apart from being bombed by the USAAF – and the advance allowed the newly-promoted Jake to claim two trucks with two shots and a half-track with one short dose of Browning. Jake's report of their first night leaguer shows that they had indeed left the Desert behind, for the crew found themselves near a farmhouse. Jake and his friend, Stan, investigated this and discovered the people were still there. They were invited in and, in no time, were sharing out cigarettes and some biscuits for the children [trust Thomas Atkins, whenever or wherever he is, for that] and being pressed to accept some wine.

Next morning the advance continued, The Fifth only stopping to engage, and eliminate, some guns which they spotted on breasting a ridge. They paused here but not for long: the Brigadier and Fearless Jim came up in their scout cars, held a short discussion and sent The Fifth down the other side of the ridge and into the outskirts of the town.

Jake's description of 'entering the outskirts of the town' and of the milling civilians and the occasional resistance (put a stop to by 'the odd 75 through the window') tallies exactly with all the other descriptions until his tank reached the Bey's Palace [Jake said he thought it was just another school]. Here they found the civilian population taking firm charge of the defeated Germans. The tanks were surrounded by a huge, rejoicing crowd and all was going along splendidly until someone opened fire from the Palace on the left. Captain Chave [the Squadron Commander] took this seriously and silenced the opposition with some HE from the 75s. This brought out more prisoners but it also brought a warning from a bystander that one of the buildings housed some Allied POWs. These were released with the aid of the RBs who then found that the building also housed the German Consulate. The Consul claimed that he could not be taken prisoner as he had diplomatic immunity. What answer he would have received from the Fifth Tanks is not known: the answer he received from the First RBs made it painfully clear to him how wrong he was!

The released prisoners, Americans and First Army men, had armed themselves with captured rifles which they were very ready to use. This they did on some of the Consulate staff who unwisely showed signs of resistance. The sight that Jake enjoyed most was that of an elderly French woman, armed with a pistol and a *Tricolor*, bringing in her private bag of fifty very subdued prisoners and handing them over to an RB officer.

The population's reception was doubly welcome. There was the wine, of course, but there were golden opportunities to wash off at least three days of accumulated grime. Some return was possible: the men thought it not unreasonable to return their thanks with some of the articles they seemed to have been collecting over the last few hours. After all, their late owners would have no immediate use for them.

The night was spent on the pavements by the tanks and, even though the men made an early start, the local population was out and celebrating before the first brew had been swallowed. Soon, the crews had more to swallow than their early morning cuppa: fresh bread, fruit, wine and sweetmeats were theirs for the having. The Regiment moved off through the town but Jake's tank was reluctant to keep up and soon it was an SOS over the air for the fitters when it sputtered to a stand-still. The tank was immediately surrounded: the main question shouted at them was, 'When comes *le brave Général Montgomerie*?' In the midst of all this rejoicing, celebrating, bathing and what-have-you, the fitters got the tank going again, shared some of the benefits and sent Jake on his way.

Jake's joys were not yet at an end. He found someone with a guitar.

On a more practical level, another Desert Rat pointed out that these times more than made up for the Retreat to Dunkirk: the equipment captured in

North Africa was far better and far more modern than anything the Wehrmacht got hold of in France!

'That was the end of the trail,' Jake reflected. 'We did not fire another shot in anger in Africa. It had been a long trail and taken two years and five months and it was fitting that it should finish the way it did, with the Desert Rats Division hammering through and ringing down the curtain on the North Africa campaign. We had fought in the blazing sun and in the pouring rain, in sandstorms and mud and blazed the trails across the blue, where even the Senussi would not venture. We had lived on salt water and bully and biscuits and done long stretches in the tanks and once it had seemed that we were beaten. But we were never licked. We had fought and run, but the spirit had always been there and when the time was ripe we showed them and we shall show them again.'

Jake then describes visiting a family in Tunis that he had got to know and know well. His tales were not of war but of his mother and sisters and the beauty of Loch Lomond. Like so many tough, seasoned servicemen Jake was a softie at heart when it came to family. His or those of his new-found French friends.

Jake had a lot more to say about those days but it is mostly about Jake Wardrop and not about The Fifth. The whole of Jake Wardrop's Diary of the war in the Desert and in Italy can be read elsewhere: he will be met again when he has something to say about life in Homs.

Of the Fifth Tanks' arrival at this notorious seaside resort, some wag suggested that the original Order had been SEND THEM HOME but that the Signallers had got it a bit wrong and the message came out as SEND THEM TO HOMS.

THE OTHER SIDE

The event which triggered Hitler's fury in the early spring of 1943 was not so much the news that an Anglo-American force had landed on the north-western coast of Africa as the news that the French had surrendered to it. Surrendered and gone over to it. His first reaction was to order that all France was to come under direct German rule. His second reaction was to realise that his policy of regarding events in North Africa as a diversion intended to save the face of his futile Italian ally had – as Rommel had all along warned him would be the case – proved disastrous.

His fury must have been increased by the knowledge that he only had himself to blame. Those who like to 'point the finger' seldom enjoy seeing one pointed at themselves.

In this case his demand for immediate action met with better results than he deserved. In Italy, Feldmarschall Kesserling (the 'Supreme Commander South') had anticipated just such an eventuality and had already assembled a scratch force of reinforcements. Fortunately for him, some of these men were trained airborne troops and a fair-sized pool of armour was available. No sooner had he received the orders than Kesserling started to despatch these reinforcements by air, whenever possible, or by sea to Tunis from Sicily. The mechanised part of the contingent included a battalion of Tiger tanks.

The objective of these reinforcements, which totalled some five divisions, was to form an enceinte of the Tunisian Peninsula. This would have had Enfidaville at its south-eastern corner, run some 40 miles west and then swung north to Medjez el Bas, thence north-north-west to the coast a few miles on the Bizerta side of Cap Serrat. Although time was short, the consolidation of these forces within the enceinte was helped by the rather more than somewhat erratic advance of the First Army from their landings 400 miles to the west in the Algiers area. This erratic advance was due principally to the fact that the troops in the Anglo-American First Army were new to warfare whereas the German troop arrivals very soon included the battle-hardened Fifth Panzerarmee. *Initially, even with inferior logistic support, these experienced troops were more than a match for the newly arrived Allies.*

The ironical situation then arose that, while Rommel was being pushed west by the Eighth Army, the First Army was being pushed west by General von Arnim. This, however, did not last long and a second ironical situation arose – this time in the Allies' favour. All this last-minute reinforcement of men and matériel, which could later have been used to much better advantage in Italy by Kesserling, fell into Allied hands, without having had any effect whatsoever on the North Africa Campaign, thus enormously enhancing the value of the Allies' victory. Genuinely, Winston Churchill's 'Turn of the Tide'.

THE WAR CHRONICLE

1943

April	12	Fourth wartime Budget further increased taxes on tobacco and alcohol (1/3d a pint on beer) and increased to 100% Purchase Tax on 'luxuries'. Income Tax stayed at 50%
	17	Katyn – mass grave of 4,000 Polish Officers murdered by Russians uncovered after a tip-off
	18	RAF dominated Tunisian skies after major defeat of Luftwaffe – Admiral Yamamoto, Japan's No 1 War Lord, shot down and killed over the Solomon Islands
	19	Renewed uprising in Warsaw ghetto
	30	Publication of Official Statistical Report stated that more [147,500] people killed or injured in road accidents on the roads of the UK in previous 12 months than total Armed Services casualties [145,000] in first two years of war. Most road

accidents were blamed on the 'blackout'
– British Intelligence pulled off 'Operation Mincemeat' [Duff Cooper's 'Operation Heartbreak' filmed as *The Man who Never Was*] misinformation stunt to mislead the Axis as to the date and place of the invasion of Italy

May 01 Dover shelled for 45 minutes

02 Darwin in the Australian Northern Territory bombed by Japanese

07 German technicians started television broadcasts in Paris

08 Full- or part-time work made compulsory in UK for all women aged from 18 to 45

13 Formal surrender of all Axis forces in North Africa

NOTES

1 Rachel, Naomi, Rahab and Ruth. All worthy women in the Old Testament

2 No 1 Party. This type of 'get-together' was for the purpose of bringing the officers and, sometimes, crew commanders up-to-date on the situation rather than for giving out orders. Apart from putting into effect Monty's instructions that everyone was to be kept in the picture, they saved an enormous amount of time at O Groups, because everyone knew the background to their orders

3 von Arnim. Colonel General von Arnim was withdrawn from the Russian Front and succeeded to the command of all the Axis forces in North Africa after Rommel returned to Germany on 9th March 1943. He held his command for 35 days before surrendering to the British in Tunis on 12th May

4 Stout Cortez. The quotation is from John Keats' *On first looking into Chapman's Homer*. It is not known by what criterion Keats measured Cortez' girth

5 POWs. According to some authorities on both sides, many of the German soldiers taken prisoner in the 'Battle for Tunis' never fired a shot in anger, having been despatched too late from Sicily to be formed into any organised units capable of putting up resistance

6 Emergency bandage. All ranks carried one of these First Field Dressings, either in a pocket of their uniform or in their small haversack. It consisted of a sterilised pad attached to a length of bandage. One clapped the pad over anything but the most major wound and wrapped the bandage round the head or limb or even body as tightly as possible. First Field Dressings were extremely effective even when they were past their 'best by' date as a result of spending many months in a none-too-clean environment

7 Orange smoke canisters. Orange, or yellow, smoke canisters were carried in some form by all Allied ground troops. If there was any danger of confusion, likely to result in attack by 'friendly' forces, orange smoke was let off to indicate 'We're on your side down here'. It was, however, not always as effective as it should have been: the worst example being when some bright spark in the Gunners used orange smoke to indicate a target for his guns

8 Ben Lomond, The cairn at the top of Ben Lomond, a few miles to the north of Jake's native Glasgow, stands 3,192 feet above sea level

CHAPTER XI
. . . *Holiday Camp – Homs*

June–September 1943

Before joining the Fifth Tanks in their rest camp in that much vaunted seaside resort at Homs, there is one last glimpse of what War in the Desert was all about. This takes the form of extracts from a letter which Len Coller wrote home to his family, a week after the Axis surrender in Tunis. The first sentence tells a great deal of the reaction, not only of Len, but of so many others like him. The war was over and yet the war wasn't over: not by any means . . . but no-one seemed to be doing anything about it. Len wrote:

'Tonight I find myself awfully bored. It gets dark out here about 6 pm and, after that, if we're not on operations, there's Sweet Fanny Adams to occupy one's time. So I'm going to try to describe our life when we're in action – I hope you won't be bored or, what is worse, think I've suddenly started to 'blow my own trumpet.'

'You must have often wondered just what life in the Desert is like. You read in the local press so-called 'actual' accounts but many of them are very much unlike the actual story.

'Perhaps you'll be surprised to hear we don't all 'hate' the Desert. I don't – neither do any of my present crew. We hate it no more than any other place we might be stationed, so far from home. On arrival, one certainly curses one's fate at having been sent to such a bleak, uninteresting, melancholy, monotonous country. It's such a change from 'built up areas' and the normal countryside of Europe. Mile after mile of sand covered with small and large stones – but surprisingly seldom without some vegetation, though it's only tough camel-scrub.

'It's not flat either, although in some place one can see for 20 or 30 miles. Usually there are folds in the ground – just like huge corrugations – these our tank people are very glad of . . . but more of that later.

'It's easy to wander off a few yards and become completely lost – then woe betide the man who sets off in the direction he *thinks* he came from. He's never right. The Desert is so vast and faceless that treating it with contempt is more than one's life's worth. Every mile travelled must be carefully noted for, even after doing the same stretch a dozen times, heaven help the man who thinks he knows his way about. The Desert, like the Sphinx, just smiles . . . and leads him miles further astray.

'Sometimes, after an exceedingly long trip by track – *not* the Coast Road which, for hundreds of miles, is the only sign of civilisation – we wonder if it's ever going to end. Recently we travelled for eight days continuously and all we saw was sand, scrub and rock. What makes this country worth all this fighting? On the ninth day we were rudely awakened by a Boche rearguard: they didn't think it worth fighting for either and it wasn't the country they were worried about so much as their precious retreating transport. I'm afraid they paid the price of all 'suicide' rearguards.

'What's life in the desert like? Would you like to join my crew and find out?

'There are good things and bad things. First of the good things are letters from home. Then there is the very occasional (very, very occasional!) bottle of beer. Enough water to have a really good wash all over. The delight of cooking some special dish in our desert oven, such as jam tart or pancakes: that makes us pleased to feel that we've somehow been able to get one up on the army diet – which, I hasten to say, is quite adequate though somewhat monotonous.

'Some of the bad things. NO LETTERS: chief complaint of the Eighth Army. It suddenly rains unexpectedly and, although we've been praying for a drop, it always rains when we're unprepared for it – and, never expecting any, we're *never* prepared for it! You'd be surprised how hard it can rain, though, when it does and it's either freezing or feels like it. Then, as soon as one's had the first good wash for days, someone finds a job which covers your hands with oil and dirt. Or, after being on biscuits for weeks, getting a bread issue and dropping your piece in the sand – always margarined side down. These are some of the small things new crew members must get used to.

'What are you going to be? Driver, gunner, loader, wireless operator, machine-gunner? Whatever you decide, you've got to be darned good at it, because we can't afford to have a useless crew member when we're having a go at Jerry.

'You're in the crew and we get the good news. The 'do' is shortly going to start. It's always better being on the attack than being on the defensive.' Here, Len rather misled his imaginary recruits by saying that they had, at last, got the 'right equipment'. This new equipment might have been better but Len, Recruiting Sergeant Extraordinary to the Coller family, was stretching the truth more than a little by suggesting it was superior to anything that Jerry had.

'In the last few days we've checked and double-checked everything about the tank: Guns, ammunition, engine and wireless set must all be in perfect working order. We were sure it was but we went over everything again. Once action is joined, it might be weeks before we have another chance to do any real maintenance.

'There is a conference for tank commanders. We know that within the next twenty-four hours we will be testing the enemy's mettle.

'Orders, orders and more orders. Formations, distances, times, map references, codes and call-signs for the wireless – and the plan.

'We're to go in tonight. The enemy is well dug-in, with the usual minefields, anti-tank traps and guns – with 21st Panzer Division (our old 'playmates') in reserve in the rear. It should be pretty easy going for us at first, because, of course, the minefields are mainly the infantry and Engineers' pigeon. That part was very easy. It's very cold though.

'Hell's Bells! What's that? Suddenly our barrage, fired by hundreds of 25-pounders and 4.5in guns, goes down on the enemy infantry. All we see is the continuous flash of the guns: all we hear is the shells going westward, enemy-bound.

'What a barrage: one wonders how anything can possibly live in it. We can see nothing to our front but we know the infantry and the Sappers will be there – probably catching the enemy's counter-barrage but still going on with their job of clearing lanes to let us through. We wait for hours – until we begin to think there must be a hitch somewhere.

'Our night bombers join the fun. We can see bomb after bomb exploding about four miles ahead – that's as well as one can judge distances in the dark. How we could do with a brew of tea!

'At last the order to start up has come over the air. Now for it: the gap has been made and we are going through it . . . for what?

'Slowly we wind our way along – not too far apart in single line ahead. Now we can see the lights with which the Engineers have marked the lane through the mines. There isn't much of a moon left but we can make out the infantry, walking past the tanks – rifles slung, lit cigarettes in mouths. I wonder what sort of a time they've had these last few hours? Pretty bloody, I'll bet. In more ways that one!

'They pose a bit of a problem, the poor old footsloggers, because we're prepared for an infantry attack on the tanks – I have the tommy-gun ready – but how the heck, in this light, will I know who's friend or who's foe? After all, Brother Boche is quite clever enough to sling his rifle and light up a fag before chucking his bomb at me.

'We're now moving through the gap itself. It's largely up to the driver here to find the path and not get us blown up. Strangely enough there's no heavy fire coming down. I thought this would be one of the stickiest parts of the job. Wrong again. In front, I can make out the silhouettes of tanks which have got through the gap and have fanned out the other side. They're coming in for a lot of heavy machine-gunning but are returning just as much. Presumably it's infantry they've met. The red and green tracers of the bullets look very frightening – though, of course, they won't worry us very much inside our steel box. Must remember my darn head's outside!

'We're through the gap and now change formation to meet any counter-attacks. We take up a rough line facing where all the fire's coming from.

'The enemy certainly know we're here. Vicious red tracers from armour-piercing shells are flying around us. The enemy's really getting warmed up now and I begin to wonder who's going to be the first to get hit. The annoying thing is that, although we can see the small flashes from the anti-tank guns, we can't fire back, because observation's nil in the dark and we can't get the range. Roll on the dawn when we can see what's happening.

'There is little or no cover here but I try for a hull-down position but the space I choose is already occupied. Never mind: they'll move out later.

'The message comes over the wireless to 'disperse' as it is becoming lighter. I take a look around and feel like saying, 'Yes: but where the hell to?' because every available bit of ground I can see is already occupied by one of 'us' . . . or one of 'them'. I stay put. With the dawn comes the enemy's big stuff. Great crashing shells bursting among us with sheets of flame and shells bursting alarmingly a few feet in the air. But it's 'eyes front' now as the light improves. If the enemy is going to counter-attack, it's most likely to come now and, anyway, I'm longing to take a crack at the fellows who've been firing at me half the night.

'Reports come in from our forward screen: these will give the 'higher-ups' a picture of our situation. They tell us the whereabouts of another minefield; of concealed anti-tank and artillery pieces. I can now see the defence lines to our north, some 2,500 yards away stretching all the way to the next minefield. We can see occasional movement and this gives us our long-awaited chance to fire *our* 'big stuff'. I get several direct hits on the enemy trenches but fail to silence a machine-gun post which is worrying an infantry first aid post tucked away in a small wadi to my right.

'Enemy shelling is now reaching out all round us. One of our lorries is on fire to my rear, great sheets of flame coming from its load of exploding ammunition. It amazes us that many more haven't similarly 'bought it'. To add to everything, three Boche fighter-bombers fly low over us but our very efficient and formidable AA defences cause them to shy away and 'lay their eggs' harmlessly. Later in the morning two more try it out: one falls victim to our Bofors and goes smack into the ground about 2,000 yards to my left – burns for a few minutes only.

'I am able to do some useful machine-gun work but, eventually, the gun jams. To clear it, I shall have to go over to my Troop Officer's tank and borrow his cleaning rod. Getting out of the tank calls forth several bursts from that darned Spandau I haven't been able to pick off. On arriving at his tank, I am amazed to find he has been wounded and already evacuated: the Troop is now commanded by the Troop Sergeant.

'It's very much of a ding-dong battle during the remainder of the morning. Eventually I run low on ammunition and receive permission to pull out to the replenishment area. To do this I have to pass back through last night's minefield. There are very visible signs of the tough fight the infantry and Sappers must have had to make the gap.

'If you want to see people hustle, just watch us when we reach the ammunition and petrol lorries in the Echelon. Personally I'm always glad when we've finished replenishing and are on our way back: I always dread being caught 'with my slacks down' there. But replenishing does give one a few minutes away from hours of action.

'On the way back the engine catches fire: we must have spilt some petrol while filling up and, once the engine warmed up, it must have ignited it. We have some anxious minutes wondering if the [built-in] extinguishers are up to their job. Luckily they are and we carry on.

'On arriving back, we find the situation very much as before: we have some new friends on our right and the enemy seems to be 'copping it proper'. I join in and, very shortly after, a white flag flies from their position. This makes me think they're not Jerries but Eyties: when they come out, hands held high, they do turn out to be from an Italian Parachute Division. They provide very welcome additions to the 'bag'. For Italians they have fought exceedingly well: later on when we occupied their positions this is proved by the number of 'dead uns' lying around.

'For the rest of the day, it's mostly an artillery action. Some big stuff occasionally drops uncomfortably close, filling the tank with dust, HE fumes and small pieces of stone. This is all perfectly normal and, about four-thirty, we get out and risk a brew. Very, very welcome, too. This, with a biscuit sandwich of cold sausage, is our first food or drink since five o'clock yesterday, remember? That's life in a tank for you.

'While we are dining *à la désert*, our forward screen reports enemy movement which suggests a possible counter-attack with tanks. Well, that's what we're here for, so we form up for battle and I manage to get a reasonably good piece of ground cover. A sharp increase in shelling rather convinces me the attack is coming off but, apart from the odd appearance by a couple of Mk 3s [PzKw IIIs], nothing happens. These, I'm glad to see, hurry off when one of us fires at them at about 3,500 yards. It proves they must be rather nervous. The enemy, I mean.

'As darkness falls the battle becomes one of small arms fire, as both sides bring infantry forward for night protection. When it gets completely dark around 10 o'clock we get orders to leaguer. [Here, Len Coller explains to his family what a leaguer is] Into leaguer we go, steadily and watchfully, because the possibility of an infantry attack is always there. Once in leaguer we all start to work: each to his own job. Even after that's finished we can't all go to sleep because of course we have to find guards. We're lucky if, on occasions like this, we get as much as four hours sleep.

'As I'm settling down the guard reports there's a badly wounded Italian soldier lying in a trench about ten yards away. Investigation shows he's so badly wounded that all I can do is to give him morphia: we cover him with a blanket and lay him among his already-dead comrades. I know he won't live.

'Reveille is at 3 am. That'll be about two hours sleep – if I'm lucky! But our artillery is firing a barrage and I find sleep impossible.

'That, then, is twenty four hours in our life – repeated again and again: you have a battle – again and again: you have an advance – again and again.

'Again and again . . . then – victory!'

Len concluded by saying that he didn't know about his family reading his letter, but he was ready for bed.

What Len Coller wrote to his family recounted a life all too familiar to Desert Rat tank crews. A normal day in a normal life. It must, on the other hand, have been more than a little horrific to Len's family when they received it in the UK and to anyone to whom they showed it.

Understandably, such Desert Rat tank crews deserved a rest and this is what Homs was initially supposed to provide for 5RTR.

To any member of The Fifth who was at Homs or had served with the Regiment up to that time, the name of the place is synonymous with the bitterest blow to strike the Regiment in those three and a half years of war. This chapter is divided into two sections: the time when Fearless Jim was still with his men and the time after his men had lost him.

The first section begins on Saturday, 22nd June when the Regiment arrived back in camp. The next day the CO went to Brigade for a 'conference on tank questionnaire'. Unfortunately the War Diary gives neither questions nor answers: some of the latter might have been unprintable. On the same day, 'Some Bn officers interviewed by Div Comd with a view to Staff Appointments'. Again, no record of the results.

On the 24th The Fifth said 'goodbye' to its *Crusaders*. Probably not so touching a farewell as that in Caroline Norton's *'An Arab's Farewell to his Steed'*[1] but doubtless a nostalgic moment for those who had served in these somewhat obsolete and thin-skinned AFVs. By way of exchange the next day, ten *Shermans* arrived from 46RTR 'who brought them up from Cairo'. You win some, you lose some: in this case the loss was of ten *more* Jeeps and an 8cwt truck 'to Corps for operations'. What, one wonders, was wrong with their innards that called for operations.

On the 26th Colonel Jim went to Eighth Army HQ, with Major Aldridge assuming temporary command. His was the unpopular task of instituting a training programme which started with the inevitable conference on the 27th. Just as well he did, for the next day the Divisional Commander visited the Regiment to inspect training. This training was for real: 6 *Shermans* arrived from 1st Armd Div on the 29th 'for training purposes' and there was a Battalion Conference on the subject at 1100 hrs.

On 30th June Colonel Jim returned from Eighth Army HQ and left again immediately to go to hospital for an operation on his foot. He left behind him a full complement of 37 officers and 605 ORs.

The first ten days of July were spent in training, with a day on the ranges for each of the 'fighting squadrons'. On 11th July all officers and WOs were given a 'Griff talk' by the Corps Commander, General Brian Horrocks. This confirmed the long circulating 'Part Three Orders' that Seventh Armoured had been retained in North Africa to take part in the forthcoming invasion of Italy – an invasion of the mainland to be preceded by landings in Sicily.

It was hardly surprising, therefore, that the Colonel gave a Griff talk to all ranks the following day on this same subject. What was surprising – and, in truth, shattering to all his hearers – was his news that he was to leave the Regiment.

Because of absence of detail, it is not possible, from the War Diary alone, to keep track of all the men who moved in and out of the Regiment as a result of wounds, postings and other hazards of war. I can only record such movements when I have been informed of them by the individuals concerned. One such person to reappear is Tom Chesterfield who came back to The Fifth, restored in mind, body and soul to face the rigours of Homs.

Most members of The Fifth have little good to say about Homs. There is the impression that, as a rest camp, it was not regarded as a success: there are a couple of favourable comments on the 'Jerboa Club': there is a discreet silence about any other places of entertainment. As for training, well, most members of the Regiment felt they could give the authors of Training Manuals ninety-nine yards start in a hundred-yard race and still beat them to the tape with one leg in plaster.

They very soon realised, however, that this was not a matter of Training Manuals. It was true that there was not much The Fifth – or the rest of the Division – could be taught about Desert warfare but they soon realised they were lacking in experience of landing in their tanks on a defended enemy shore from Tank Landing Craft. And this, the Corps Commander told them, would be their next task. They also soon learnt that the Regiment was not going to be re-equipped with shiny new tanks and smart new support vehicles straight out of the showroom but was going to have to make do with reconditioned *Shermans* and the same old wheeled vehicles that had ground their way backwards and forwards from the Delta. What was more, much of that reconditioning was going to have to be done by the men themselves. Even the vehicles which were new to The Fifth – the Bren Gun Carriers for the newly-created Reconnaissance Troop – had had other people in them

The Division would have been in an even worse state if it had not been for the devoted efforts of the Corps Commander who cajoled (bullying was not his *métier*) such matériel as was available out of the base depots. What was more to the point was that he ensured that transport was allocated to fetch it over the 1,700 miles from Alexandria – still the main supply base for North Africa. In spite of our mastery of the North African shore, sea routes were by no means free from assault and much of the sea transport that might have otherwise been available was already ear-marked for the invasion of Sicily.

Against this background, Jake Wardrop had plenty to say. In Jake's view there could have been worse places than Homs. [He gave Devil's Island as an example] With a population of about two hundred whose livelihood appeared to depend on growing lemons, palm trees and water melons, there was nothing to interest the men except a few villas and the neighbouring Roman ruins at Leptis Magna or the occasional concert[2]. After including a mini-Baedeker guide to Tunisia, Jake got down to details of life in the camp at Homs. Unusually, although each Troop was centred on its tanks, there was a central cookhouse and the possibility for those with initiative [by which Jake meant people like himself] to 'build themselves shacks' in the best beach-comber tradition. Jake added that, despite the central cookhouse, the men ate sitting on the sand 'like *wogs* in the sun'. Later, this shack complex was developed into something far more sophisticated, with a proper officers' mess and somewhere for Jake and his mates to eat their meals off a table like civilised people.

With the sea so near, it wasn't surprising that Jake and some others decided to try their building skills in the making of a raft. It proved to be more fun in the making than success as a sea-worthy craft.

Jake's description of life in Homs continued with one of the eight-day leave trips which were run into Tunis by the Regiment. He points out that the eight days included the journey time and reckons that The Fifth held the all-time record for the 700-odd miles at 25 hours. Not bad, as he points out, for a Fordson three-tonner well past its first youth and with fifteen men in the back. He does not record the comments of those passengers: presumably Jake always had the front seat. Jake finished this section with the return of Paddy Doyle, 'none the worse for the donk on the head'. Paddy Doyle had been in India and Syria, as well as in hospital, since he was wounded. What Jake could never have known, as it was written after his death, was that Paddy Doyle wrote a letter saying how glad he had been to see that Jake was still alive and kicking – kicking up trouble, being understood – when he got back to the Regiment in Homs and resumed command of his old Squadron.

Most COs had been concerned about the health of their men after so many months or years of desert warfare. Every branch of the service felt that it had had the roughest time but no-one denied that life had not been easy in the tanks. There was probably some sympathy, therefore, for the COs of long-serving armoured units who expressed the view that their units should be sent home and replaced by troops which had not so far left 'Blighty's shores'. Sympathy, perhaps, but not much else: there was no transport available and experienced troops were going to be required for the Italian campaign: and then, after that was launched, the same troops would be required for the 'Second Front' – then, but not before, they would return to the UK.

Jim Hutton was among the COs who were worried about their men's health. There were too many cases of ulcerated desert sores, lingering gyppy-tummy and skin complaints for his liking. If there was no prospect of going home and no chance of the Regiment's being sent back to the Delta where there were proper facilities for 'health-care', then the Fifth Tanks were going to enjoy what relaxation was possible in Homs. Colonel Jim decided that three days' complete freedom from all duties, formalities and any threat of 'training' was the best that he could do for his men. It was a pity that the Brigade Commander decided to choose the third of these rest-days for a visit to the Regiment. He must have known that the Divisional Commander had only a few weeks previously carried out a formal inspection and had expressed himself completely satisfied with the turn-out of both men and equipment in the Regiment. Their fighting efficiency could not possibly be in doubt: there was, therefore, no reason to put on a 'bull parade' for the Brigadier's benefit.

Unfortunately the Brigadier thought otherwise and considered Fearless Jim's attitude to be unpardonable insubordination. The Brigadier had not held his command of 22nd Armoured Brigade for very long and appears not to have known the extremely high opinion which his predecessor, Pip Roberts, had of Colonel Hutton nor of the high regard with which he was viewed in the Royal Tank Regiment. Insubordination, real or imagined, in Service philosophy, means the officer is not fit to hold his appointment and must therefore go. Brigadiers are two rungs up the ladder from Lieutenant Colonels so philosophy became reality. How Brigadier Hinde ever justified Fearless Jim's dismissal to the Divisional Commander remains a mystery. One can only suppose that the unlucky General Erskine – also fairly new to his Command – felt that, if he had to back one man against the other, he had to support the Brigade Commander against the Battalion Commander.

Whatever the reason, Fearless Jim's departure from the men he had led so brilliantly [he had been awarded the Distinguished Service Order for his command of the Regiment in the chase from el Alamein to Tunis] was an emotional moment not only for him but for the men who had followed him so devotedly. They lined the route to salute him as he drove away, many with tears in their eyes. They cheered him to the echoes and, down on the shore, three *Shermans* fired a farewell salute[3].

If The Fifth had been unhappy about the departure of Lt Col WM Hutton DSO MC*, they were not happy with the appointment of Lt Col RN Wilson [not related to the author] as his successor. There could be no comparison between the two men.

But before returning to the War Diary, there is one incident of this change-over of command to be recorded. We left Bob Maunsell in charge of a mixed tent of walking (and drinking) wounded somewhere in the Delta. Possibly as a result of his successful command of this unit – his men's drinking habits were never detected – Bob was given a Staff appointment in the Cairo area. He had, incidentally, added a Bar to his MC but that stemmed from his Desert and not from his Delta soldiering. This Staff appointment did not suit Bob, as the sort of work he was engaged on was writing things like Fire Orders . . . and finding his own name at the bottom of the Distribution List. One day, gazing out of his office window, he saw a three-tonner with 5RTR markings on the outside and a sergeant he knew on the inside. Bob managed to stop it and, after chatting to the sergeant, found himself being tempted. How better to deal with temptation than to yield to it? He sent the sergeant off to his quarters with instructions to pack everything up and load it onto the wagon, then come back and collect him. He cleared his desk, climbed into the three-tonner and said 'Let's go!'

On the way to Homs, they met the 5RTR CO's staff car coming in the opposite direction and stopped to exchange news. Bob was not unnaturally shattered by Colonel Jim's information but was considerably mollified to be told that the sooner he got to the Regiment the better, as he would be badly needed there. Bob reached Homs and reported for duty. Shortly after his arrival he was in the Orderly Room when a signal was received from HQ Cairo asking if the Regiment knew what had happened to Major Maunsell. Without hesitation, Bob despatched a reply which read. 'Major RE Maunsell MC has returned to duty as Second-in-Command Fifth Battalion Royal Tank Regiment' and signed it 'RN Wilson – Lt Col Cmdg 5th Bn RTR'. An appointment which the War Diary duly acknowledged on 2nd August.

The War Diary from 15th July for the rest of the month makes pretty dull reading, the only break from training and lectures and conferences came on the 30th when 'tank crews practise loading of tanks on LCT' which they did again the next day. The Regiment was now at its greatest recorded strength with 40 Officers and 670 Other Ranks. On 1st August, Major Aldridge left to take up an appointment as a GSO II with Eighth Army in Sicily: the following day Capt Whitty was promoted Major and given command of 'A' Sqn and Bob Maunsell officially became Second in Command of the Regiment. The War Diary also noted, '2/Lieut Stiddard joined the Bn.'

There is no doubt that the unit's training and practical exercises were becoming more and more realistic. Emphasis was laid on such subjects as 'action of forward body immediately after landing' and 'working in semi-enclosed country', with the lectures and TEWTs being nearly always attended, or given, by officers commanding units of other branches. This training was soon to be followed by practical exercises of landing from LSTs. At least this was the case for HQ personnel: the rest of the unit had their turns postponed because of bad weather . . . and, so far as can be seen from the War Diary, that postponement was indefinite.

On the 10th of the month the War Diary takes on a new, more up-market tone with the entry, '1230 hrs CO had lunch at Bde to meet Corps Comd Lt Gen Horrocks.' On the 14th and 15th the whole Division took part in exercise 'Dry Shod'. This seems to have been aptly named as it took place some miles inland in the Desert: it was designed to co-ordinate the movements of the tanks with their supporting Echelons, groups of tracked and wheeled vehicles being sent off hither and yon and then being required to meet up again at fixed points. The War Diary notes [one hopes with pleasure and not surprise] that 'as far as Bn was concerned all movements and timings went according to plan'.

The next day was the turn of the Battalion Gas Officer (Eric Wilde). He put all ranks through the gas chamber to test respirators. The exercises which took place on 18th and 19th August were much closer to reality and represented situations which The Fifth was shortly to meet. The Diary describes them as 'action of forward body of troops on meeting opposition in the nature of a small rearguard of enemy troops' and they were carried out in conjunction with 1RTR and a Coy of 1/7 Queens. In view of everyone's familiarity with meeting 'small rearguards of enemy troops' in the Desert, it must be presumed that the area chosen for these exercises represented 'close country'.

At this point there is an intriguing entry in the War Diary which reads, '19 1800 hrs Bn does 2z171 miles route march'. What amazing jamming of keys on the Regiment's faithful old Remington type-writer produced that? Or did the Orderly Room Clerk know something that we don't know now? How far is 2z171 miles and when did the men get back if they didn't start until 1800 hrs?

That was an intriguing entry: the next day's was a tragic one. '1000 hrs. Funeral of Lt Lowe.'

This hides the story of a remarkable officer whom one of his colleagues described as being 'as mad as a hatter' and of whom another said, prophetically, that he would either win a VC or get himself killed. Douglas Lowe joined the Regiment after Tripoli and was made Liaison Officer when Eric Wilde was posted to 'B' Squadron. After his return to his unit in un-dress uniform Douglas continued in HQ Squadron and formed one of a group of young officers who enjoyed the swimming at Homs but were always in search of other entertainment. Three of them, Eric Wilde, Geoff Smith and Lowe himself, decided that not only would fishing be fun, it would also add variety to the Regiment's diet.

The decision to become fishermen would have been harmless enough if Lowe had not combined it with one of his other interests – demonstrating explosive devices. Among Douglas' party tricks was showing the use of fused detonations. One of the ways he did this was by setting a fuse to a slab of HE, lighting the fuse and then walking into the sea holding the HE above his head. On shore, someone would call the time. He would then throw the charge as far out to sea as he could, swim inshore, wait for the bang and go back to collect the catch. This is where he made a tragic mistake. He miscalculated the burning time of the fuse and the charge exploded before he could get clear, killing him instantly.

Earlier in the month there was mention of the Brigadier and Divisional Commander visiting The Fifth to inspect 'new infantry telephones fitted on back of *Sherman* tank.' This experiment in armour/infantry co-operation was carried a step further on 24th August with a demonstration of a platoon of infantry being carried on three *Shermans.* It is easy for those of us who served in armoured units, and were consequently intimately familiar with tanks – riding in them, riding on them, climbing all over them at rest or in motion – to forget that many men, brave soldiers at their own game, were most unwilling to have anything to do with tanks, let alone having to ride in or on one. A demonstration of this nature would thus have served as a useful indoctrination course. At any rate these men from the Queens had their own back when, later the same day, they showed dismounted tank commanders from The Fifth what it was like to attack an enemy strong-point in close country.

Another interesting exercise for all tank crews was the visit to the concrete mock-up of the proposed landing site on the invasion beach: this gave the men some idea of what they were to expect.

There is an entry on 23rd August to the effect that 'the Brigade Swimming Gala contest was won by 5RTR.' Organised, no doubt, by the Brigade Sports Officer, Lieut DE Cockbaine.

Between the 26th and the 29th the Regiment got underway and moved to an Assembly Area near Tripoli. Here everyone set to and carried out the waterproofing of the tanks. Some of the officers had seen a demonstration of *Shermans* going through 5ft of water and most of them had decided that that was about 3ft too many. Now they learnt that the difference between being watertight and not being watertight could be the difference between life and death. At the end of August the Regimental state was 41 officers and 598 ORs with a complement of 52 *Shermans* – all now given suitable 'E' names. The baptismal roll has, unfortunately, been lost.

The first nine days of September were spent on waterproofing in the Assembly Area, varied by an introduction to the Support Artillery's new 'Priest' guns[4] and a series of lectures by the 2i/c and the MO on such varied subjects as security, hygiene, loot and malaria. On 10th September the move started that was to take the Regiment to Salerno, with the unit's transport going on board LSTs in the port at Tripoli and the tanks being whisked away to the quay side on transporters. Here they stayed until the 12th when, after being checked over by REME personnel to make sure that the waterproofing was waterproof and not interfering with any essential parts, the tanks were embarked for Italy.

Life in Homs had to go on even without Colonel Jim and even though, as Syd Storer said, his departure left everyone upset and depressed. Syd goes on to say that '.. the following day we played football again. This particular match was against the Notts Yeomanry, which we won by a goal.' Which should have cheered the men up, although a 'coming together' left Syd in the MO's care with a badly sprained foot.

'There were quite a lot of sand-storms at this time,' Syd Storer continues, 'and it was very hot as we sat listening to lectures on waterproofing tanks. We had now begun to paint our tanks with a new type of camouflage we should have had in the greenery of Tunisia but never had time to put on. The sandstorms continued into the beginning of August. On the 10th [the War Diary placed this on the 20th and 22nd] we had an early reveille and were taken to see a model beach: we were told that our next battle would entail leaving the LSTs and landing on a beach, this model being laid out exactly as we should see it. For several days we went into Tripoli where we loaded onto the LSTs which then transported us along the coast and we practised leaving the ship and landing on the beach.'

Syd Storer recounts that, at the end of August, the green envelopes[5] were withdrawn which was a sure sign that a positive move was impending. This came on the 28th with an order to move off at 1130 hrs. After travelling for 40 miles the Regiment leaguered by the roadside and was away again after an early reveille the following morning. On reaching Tripoli, The Fifth pulled in beside the Lancia works. Permission was granted for the men to attend a service and concert arranged by Padre Lewis in the English Church. The following morning was free and the men wandered around the area and were surprised to find a considerable number of American troops camping among the orange and lemon trees. The Americans had a portable cinema with a nightly showing, the film that evening being *Holiday Inn*. A lot of men went and spent an enjoyable evening with an invitation to see another film next day.

'Over the next week,' Syd continued, 'all the waterproofing on the tanks was inspected and tested and everything declared ready for whatever was to take place. The area was so packed with troops of all kinds that it was difficult to find any free space. The number of flies increased rapidly. On the morning of 2nd September we were given the 'Griff' about the move and told that the Eighth Army were about to make their move to invade Italy. A few days later, we were to land at a different point: the Americans had requested British tank support, so we were to become part of the US 5th Army. We stood by day after day, watching the American films in our spare time, until on the 9th we wireless operators were called and given the netting frequencies and the codes. We were told that things were going very well in Italy. On the morning of 10th September we moved down to the docks to load as the LSTs arrived. At 0930 hrs on the 12th we were all loaded up and ready to go but did not sail until 0630 hrs on the 13th. The sea fortunately was very calm. By evening we passed the coast of Sicily. The calm weather continued through the night but, as dawn broke, our LCT broke down. It was quickly repaired but immediately broke down again. Repaired once more, we caught up with the convoy as land was sighted.'

Before sighting Salerno with Syd Storer, we must go back a bit in time to see how life had been treating Jake Wardrop and his pals. The answer, of course, was very well. The irrepressible Jake had been on leave in Tunis with one of his 'C' Squadron mates. They stayed with Simone – one of the family that Jake had fallen in with immediately after the town's liberation. Jake never gave any details of the family nor disclosed what Simone's age or vital statistics were. From Jake's description, it seems unlikely that he would have fared better if The Fifth had been sent back to Cairo, for there were picnics and even, one day, the hire of a car to go swimming at the seaside. In spite of 'the old man's eye on them they sneaked off and had some sessions'. They ended by swearing eternal friendship and vowing to meet again in Paris *après la guerre*.

Back at Homs, Jake found things much the same. The July weather was consistently fine and everyone was so brown that getting browner was impossible while their hair and KD got ever paler. Jake and company enjoyed the concerts at Leptis and, when the spirits ration arrived, had an all night session when 'we drunk [*sic*] a lot of gin in the fitters' shack'. Jake confessed that, without lime or lemon juice, drinking gin was rather like drinking Brylcreem but that, 'after a bit, nobody cared'. To complete his euphoria, Jake had his guitar. Next morning was not so bright but an afternoon swim did help.

Although he was unashamed of his 'high days and holidays' there was a very great deal more to the soldier in Jake than a boozy old sweat who didn't care a damn for anyone or anything. Inter-unit boxing competitions were in the air and those Jake took seriously. With Stan Skeels he went on the wagon and started serious training; road-walking in the morning, PT in the evening, 'knocking one another about with the gloves' for practice. Jake and Stan upheld the honour of the Brigade, although the finals – which were held in Tripoli – were won by the Queens Brigade. Shortly after this there was an inter-battalion swimming gala for the Brigade. There were five teams, 1RTR, 5RTR, 4 CLY, the Royals and 5 RHA. This time, 5RTR were the winners . . . with some help from Jake Wardrop. The British Army's genius for improvisation was witnessed by the use of four LSTs to mark the boundaries of the water polo 'pitch'.

Jake gave rather more details of the invasion preparations than Syd Storer but, perhaps this was because Jake's crew won an informal shooting match with what Jake called their 75 pounder[6]. The crews of the *Shermans* with really high mileages to their credit were relieved when these were taken away and slightly newer ones supplied in their place. There must have been some doubts in the minds of all the tank crews about the efficacy of the water-proofing measures, because a demonstration was laid on to show that the tanks could be safely submerged right up to the level of the turret ring. Not only submerged passively, but driven into, in and out of the sea. The watching crews, like the ranks of Tuscany, could scarce forbear to cheer when the test *Sherman* lumbered out of the water.

Finally, Jake and the others who could find time and cash to do so laid in supplementary provisions, 'sausages, tins of steak and kidney and all sorts of stuff like that.' Jake Wardrop, at least, after one or two farewell parties, was ready for the fray. As a farewell gesture on the part of the African Continent, the Division was treated to a fireworks display when there was a fire in the harbour and a couple of barge loads of ammunition went up. They were tied up just in front of the Miramare Theatre and Jake hoped that the shells bursting on the roof might have shaken some of the bugs out of the seats.

The Divisional Commander held a 'Griff session' for all officers and gave them an outline of what was to come next as part of the American Fifth Army They learnt that the campaign would be under the command of the American General, Mark Clark. Many people in the Regiment regarded Mark Clark 'as a bit of a dark horse', since nobody knew very much about him, other than that he had arrived in North Africa and done some 'cloak and dagger' diplomacy before the Americans and First Army landed[7]. Jake reckoned it would be a change and 'maybe we'd get some of these pansy American rations'.

The wait for embarkation orders allowed some relaxation of routine. This was hardly surprising, as there was hardly space for eating and sleeping, let alone training or daily routine. The conduct of the waiting crews was a source of puzzlement – sometimes amusement – to the native population. One of the men, Coutts, was fluent in Arabic and possessed of a good singing voice. On several occasions he broke into the Arabian love song, *Igri, Igri, Igri,* giving immense pleasure to his listeners who joined uninhibitedly in the choruses. But, if the troops entertained the natives, the natives could return the compliment. This was the case when a troop of Swahilis came into town and performed their war dances, 'shields, spears and great long drums: all the trimmings'. The Swahilis were, it is true, hardly native to this part of Africa: they were there because, in the daytime, they worked as gangs mending the roads and bridges.

Jake's last reflections on leaving North Africa and setting sail for Europe were to wonder how long it was going to take him to get to Calais and a boat for Dover and a train for Glasgow – and a bus to Clachan's or Dow's!

To Bob Lay being at Homs meant, 'being in a very small town with little to offer and back on Eighth Army rations, bully, biscuits, a tin of pilchards, jam of suspect content, soya links and oleo-margarine – very oleo. There was one addition; there was belated concern about desert sores, so we had dried cabbage which we called 'dried gas-cape'. We also had mepacrine tablets to fight off malaria. They were so revolting that we had to swallow them on parade.'

Bob recalls two incidents on the way to Homs. Like others, he was astonished by the way in which nature reasserted itself after rain and by the vivid primary colours of the flowers which bloomed almost as one watched them. The other incident was not so pleasant. Kipping down at the roadside one night, he noticed that the ground was peppered with small holes. A little petrol poured down one of them, followed by a lighted match, and 'out scampered scores of scorpions'.

'On board the tanks,' Bob goes on, 'we had pets: we had chickens, another tank had a goose; someone had a dog. We sold our chickens to the Sergeants Mess: they were much too scrawny for us! We had our first ENSA Concert. The previous entertainment had been in Shafto's Cinema at Amirya in a tent constructed from carpets. The concert took place in the arena at Leptis Magna, a magnificent Roman arena. There was a female in the cast: you needed a pair of binoculars to see her. One of the lads knew her and invited her to the mess. We all had to be decent for the daily swim, our only pastime. The ingenuity was a hoot. Climbing back up the beach after a swim was a terribly exhausting business. This was the consequence of dehydration, a process in which the cookhouse meals did not help.'

Most of the other comments and recollections about Homs are in the same vein. Bitter disappointment that it was Homs and not home or even the Delta: appreciation of the understanding shown by Jim Hutton for the men's problems. The disbelief and despair at the news that 'their' Fearless Jim was to leave them. Even, as Bob Lay said, a talk by General Horrocks, the Corps Commander, who spoke more as if he were addressing his grandchildren than the soldiers under his command. No-one who was at Homs will ever forget it. No-one will ever recall it without a groan.

THE OTHER SIDE

In 1943 Hitler was still driven by the German fantasy – Lebensraum. *This 'living space' was not, however, exclusively a matter of increasing German elbow-room at their neighbours' expense. The countries which Hitler wished to annex also offered Germany nearly all the material resources – oil, minerals, agricultural produce – which would make Germany either completely self-supporting or so powerful that other countries with products which he required (one example being raw rubber) would be anxious to trade with the Reich. The* Lebensraum *dream did, on the other hand, have one aspect which was of advantage to the Western Allies.* Lebensraum *was essentially a Continental mainland aspiration. Hitler and his Nazi party were but little interested in acquiring overseas territory, such as the British Empire, or in defeating the USA for the sake of gaining land in North America.*

If the Lebensraum *dream had an advantage for the Western Allies, this was not the case for Russia. The acquisition of Russian territory was just as much an aim for the Nazi party as the defeat of Communism at source. Hitler's dream of power included annexation of Austria, Bulgaria, Czechoslovakia, Hungary, Poland, Romania (by then already achieved) and ultimately Russia, leaving such sweepings of Eastern Europe as Albania, Greece and Yugoslavia to his jackal, Mussolini. Belgium, France and Holland would naturally be retained as part of the German Empire, along with Denmark and Norway, because these bordered on the Atlantic and, as such, were bulwarks against the 'Anglo-Saxons' (which was Hitler's rather odd term for the Anglo-American Alliance).*

What was happening in the Mediterranean was not, however, merely a tiresome distraction from the military point of view vis-à-vis Hitler's Russian Campaign. Part of Hitler's overall strategy was the annexation of the countries at the eastern end of the Mediterranean; first Greece and then Turkey. This would expose Russia's southern flank and also greatly enhance his prospects of striking yet farther east through Syria to the oilfields of Iraq and Persia. A great deal depended on Turkey's neutrality. Essentially distrustful of Britain's Middle Eastern aspirations since the Dardanelles Campaign of 1915, Turkish neutrality originally listed towards the Axis. However, the unqualified success of the British and Empire forces in North Africa swung the balance against Germany. Any move after the summer of 1943 to sweep up the eastern Mediterranean countries and cut off Britain's access to India (as well as outflanking Russia) would have to be made in the face of a hostile Turkey. Too late Hitler and his High Command realised that they had thrown away their chance of making the Mediterranean, at one and the same time, a moat to protect the southern flank of the Axis and a barrier to cut Britain off from her Asian interests. Too late, Hitler and his High Command did their arithmetic. When they had added up their sums, they found that the bottom line read: Axis losses – Manpower, nearly one million casualties: Aircraft, nearly 8,000: Tanks, nearly 2,500: Guns, nearly 6,000: Transport, nearly 70,000 vehicles: Shipping, nearly 2,400,000 tons. With losses of this order, the word 'nearly' does little to soften the blow, nor does the realisation that the land losses are greater than those suffered at Stalingrad.

One man was aware of the gravity of the situation, even if his Führer was not. Doctor Göbbels. At the end of July 1943 he wrote in his Diary that it was simply shocking that a revolutionary movement which had been in power for twenty-one years could be liquidated in such a way. The Pope, wrote Göbbels, was intriguing against Germany; Stalin was claiming that the Wehrmacht's summer offensive had failed; reprisals against England had been delayed because of the beating the Luftwaffe had taken in Sicily; a former Prime Minister of Bulgaria had openly dared to criticise the Reich. There was even criticism in Germany itself. 'Why,' people were asking, 'does Herr Hitler not visit the bombed areas? Why is Göring nowhere to be seen?' Above all, 'Why doesn't Der Führer talk to the German people and explain the present situation?' One worry after another was piling up and no-one knew how to meet them.

Life on 'the other side' was not easy.

From the military point of view in the summer of 1943 opinions in the German High Command were divided. Guderian urged the regrouping of all the Panzer Divisions from the Russian front to form a strategic reserve – an 'instant reaction force' – available for the Eastern Front, or for the threatened 'Second Front' (the cross-Channel invasion) or for the actual second front (the invasion of Sicily and the inevitable landings in Italy). There were, however, insufficient tank forces to follow this strategy. Despite this insufficiency, General Keitel ordered one of Guderian's finest Panzer Divisions, instead of one of the far more practical Mountain Divisions, to the Balkans where the Partisans were becoming increasingly active – thereby, Guderian complained bitterly, demonstrating his continuing ignorance of armoured warfare.

Having been on the receiving end of three times the tonnage of bombs in the first three months of 1943 that London had received in the entire 'blitz' months, the High Command had to admit that the Luftwaffe no longer ruled the German skies. An admission, incidentally, which confirmed Hitler in his belief that the 'V' weapons could be made to do to London and the 'invasion ports' what the Luftwaffe could not.

Interwoven with this was the collapse of Mussolini's Fascist Empire. The collapse started in mid-July when Hitler issued Mussolini with an ultimatum which required the complete hand-over of military power in Italy to the German High Command. Mussolini blustered . . . but yielded. However, the Fascist General Council, at its first meeting for three years, decided that all military – in fact, all Il Duce's dictatorial – powers should revert to the King and the Council.

Mussolini's amazement on hearing that decision was nothing to what he felt the following day when King Victor Emmanuel endorsed the Council's decision and Il Duce found himself under arrest.

Marshal Badoglio – a life-long anti-fascist although a life-long colleague of Mussolini's – took over the reins of government. Badoglio might have been too clever for Mussolini to dismiss him but he was also too clever for his own good. In one breath he announced that Italy would fight alongside her German allies until the last invader was driven from Italian soil. In the next he opened secret negotiations with Whitehall.

Such diplomatic duplicity ended in disaster and would have done so of its own accord without military intervention in the form of the US Fifth Army's landings at Salerno. Badoglio proposed an armistice and found the terms were being dictated by the Allies rather than negotiated with him. They included the laying down of arms by all Italian ground and air force personnel on being approached by the Allies, the evacuation of the Italian Fleet and its surrender to the Royal Navy in Malta, and the handing over of all Allied POWs to the Allies and not to the Germans. All this was agreed by the Armistice which was signed on 3rd September. The Germans, who had suspected some sort of treachery from their ally, took their own measures. It has to be admitted that, in order to obtain the surrender of the Italian fleet, Whitehall had promised more than it knew it could perform. Duplicity was not entirely an Axis prerogative.

What the British regarded as the most important military aspect of the Armistice was achieved – if one discounts the sinking of the battleship Roma *by the Luftwaffe en route – for, on 11th September, the Italian battle fleet was under the guns of the Royal Navy in Malta. The King and the Italian Royal family, together with Marshal Badoglio and his entourage, were wafted to safety in the South of Italy.*

Hitler's first reaction on hearing of his 'partner's' overthrow was to order that a picked Panzer division be sent hot-foot to Rome to arrest the King, Marshal Badoglio and everyone else in sight. He overlooked, in reacting like this, the fact that every available Panzer unit was already fully committed by his abortive offensive against Kursk and such an order could not be obeyed.

In Sicily the Allies' initial assault had gone badly for the Axis; airfields had been captured – in several cases, complete with the aircraft; Italian resistance had been overcome and German counter-attacks repulsed.

The lack of adequate sea-going landing craft and of assault vessels which prevented the Allies from rapidly following up the initial successes in Sicily was put to good use. The Italian mainland was heavily reinforced by trained Wehrmacht and Luftwaffe detachments.

THE WAR CHRONICLE

1943

May	13	Final surrender of Axis forces in North Africa
	17	Successful attack on Moehne Dam by RAF 'Dam Busters' using Barnes Wallis' 'bouncing bombs'
June	03	French Resistance achieved massive burn-up of tyres at the Michelin plant – Film actor, Leslie Howard, presumed killed when the civilian plane in which he was flying from Lisbon was shot down by the Luftwaffe in the mistaken belief that Winston Churchill was a passenger
	08	Japanese abandoned Pacific Island of Kiska
	10	Mass bombing raid by Russian planes on German-held Kursk
	11	Himmler ordered 'liquidation' of all Jewish ghettos – Mediterranean island of Pantelleria yielded to Allies by Italy
	12	RAF Sergeant pilot, out of fuel, landed on Mediterranean island of Lmpedusa, which promptly 'surrendered' to him
	13	Luftwaffe used 'butterfly' anti-personnel bombs on civilian targets, causing heavy casualties
	14	Mediterranean Island of Lampioni yielded to Allies by Italy
	25	Black American troops engaged in gun fight with Military Police in Lancashire
	30	Anti-invasion measures (removal of sign posts etc) revoked in UK – 'Music While You Work' was praised for increasing the productivity of munition workers, who earned a average of £7.10s [male] and £3,10s [female] per week
July	02	Australian and American troops joined forces in New Guinea
	04	General Sikorski, Polish GOC of forces in exile,

killed in plane crash
10 Invasion of Sicily started
13 Russian massed counter-assault at Kursk succeeded
17 With landings in Sicily, AMGOT (Allied Military Government of Occupied Territory) came into operation
– First of many disagreements between Monty and US General George S Patton
21 Sicily came under effective control of the Allies
25 Mussolini deposed and replaced by Marshal Badoglio
31 Over 2,000,000 Chinese either died of or forced to flee from famine in Hunan Province
– Up to 50,000 civilians killed and 800,000 rendered homeless by Allied bombing of Continental Europe
– Hedley Verity, former England cricket captain, died in an Italian POW camp
– Hamburg rendered 'useless' as an industrial town by Allied bombing

August 01 The US Patrol Boat on which the future President, John F Kennedy, was serving sunk by a Japanese destroyer
05 Sweden revoked the 'licence' permitting passage of German servicemen and war material through its territory en route to or from Norway
07 Wehrmacht arrived in Italy to take over military control of the country
04 Russian troops recaptured Bielgorod
15 Italy started negotiations for a separate armistice with Allies
23 Kharkov recaptured by 'Red Army'
25 Mountbatten appointed Supreme Commander in South-east Asia
29 Increasing resistance activity in Denmark reported to tie-up 50,000 German troops on 'occupational duties'

September 03 Allies seized Reggio Calabria
07 Corsican populace attacked occupying forces and seized capital, Ajaccio
08 Italian surrender
09 Allied landing on Italian Peninsula with attack on Salerno

– Italian fleet surrendered
10 German forces evacuated Corsica
– German paratroopers occupied Rome
12 Mussolini 'snatched' from captivity by SS Stormtroopers and reunited with his 'friend', Adolf Hitler
15 British captured Greek Island of Kos

NOTES

1 An Arab's farewell. A legitimate analogy, since the departing steed was told, 'Fret not to roam the desert with all thy wingèd speed.'
2 Occasional concert. ENSA had by this time arrived in North Africa and had sent 'Concert Parties' to all the forward troops that they could reasonably reach. ENSA concerts varied enormously in content but very seldom misjudged their audiences when it came to the 'tone' of their performances. Sometimes, however – and this happened at Homs – they did not realise quite how long the men had been away from the UK, so that the jokes, and even the popular songs, meant nothing to the audiences. For the men stationed at Homs, ENSA set up shop in the Roman ruins at Leptis Magna
3 'Fearless Jim' Hutton. Lieutenant Colonel Hutton is far too important a man in both 5RTR's and the Royal Tank Regiment's history to be left driving away from Homs, never to be mentioned again. Colonel Jim was posted to the Staff College at Haifa as an Instructor for a short while and then went to Italy to command 40RTR in 23rd Armoured Brigade. He returned to the UK at the end of 1944 and became the last Commandant of the RAC OCTU at Sandhurst. From there he went to the Specialised Armour Development Establishment until going, as a Brigadier, to be Chief Staff Officer to Glubb Pasha of Jordan's Arab Legion. When Glubb was given the order of the boot, Brigadier Jim became Director of Administrative Plans at the War Office and then, in 1961 as a Major General, Director General of Fighting Vehicles. He retired in 1966 and became Home Bursar at Jésus College, Oxford. Here, in recognition of his outstanding qualities, he attained the rare distinction of being made a Fellow of the College. After some years in Spain, he retired to Cornwall, where he died in March 1994, at the age of 81. It is said that 'If' is the most potent word in history. 'If' Colonel Hutton had not had his career so abruptly and unjustly interrupted in June 1943, where might he not have gone? Who knows? But surely far, far farther than he did
4 Priest guns. At last the Seventh Armoured Division was getting self-propelled artillery. Not yet exactly what it wanted but in the form of a Canadian *Ram* tank 'chassis' with an American 105mm gun mounted, facing forward with a limited traverse. The *Rams* were Canadian-built Mark I *Shermans* with a Wright instead of a Continental 9-cylinder radial engine. Unlike the welded hull of the *Sherman*, the *Ram* had a cast hull but was otherwise similar. Later, when the Sextant arrived, the Gunners were better pleased. The Sextant was based on a later version of the *Ram* and had the 25-pounder gun mounted. Give a Gunner of WW II vintage a 25-pounder to play with and he was a happy man. Rightly so, as it was probably the best front-line artillery piece in any WW II army
5 Green envelopes. These were issued to the troops when they were 'on active

service' but not 'in action' so that the men could send letters home which did not have to be read by an officer from the writer's own unit by way of censorship. The men had to sign a declaration that no secret information was included. Green envelopes were enormously valued by married men (and by men who wanted to marry their correspondents) as it represented their only chance for intimate communication. Green envelopes were subject to random Army censorship but this did not have the same inhibiting effect on a husband or young lover as knowing that *eg* his troop officer would read what he had written . . . possibly even about him!

6 75 pounder. No way! This is a slip on Jake's part. The main gun on the *Shermans* had a calibre of 75 millimetres and fired HE shell or AP shot weighing approximately 14 to 16 lbs. A shell weighing 75 lbs would be up in the heavy artillery category

7 General Mark Clark. He did indeed 'do some cloak and dagger diplomacy' before the 'Operation Torch' landings. See, for example, FM Lord Alanbrooke's War Diaries

CHAPTER XII

. . . *An Italian Idyll*

September–December 1943

If, which it does, the word 'idyll' means a 'scene of happy innocence', then one can be reasonably certain that not many readers who took part in the Fifth Royal Tank Regiment's Italian Campaign are going to agree with that chapter heading!

Salerno[1] was the destination of the flotilla which set out from Tripoli and which, on landing, disgorged the Seventh Armoured Division into the American Fifth Army's waiting arms.

The War Diary for Wednesday, 15th September 1943 reads: '1915 hrs 5RTR lands on Italian soil on Sugar Beach in Salerno Beachhead.' It then proceeds to contradict itself by saying that disembarkation did not start until 2300 hrs and that, immediately on landing, the crews set about 'dewaterproofing', after which they got one to two hours sleep. At 0200 hrs on 16th September, the CO went to 131 Brigade HQ to get the latest information. He learnt that The Fifth had come directly under command of 131 Brigade and was to move into leaguer in their area. This it did at 0500 hrs. At 1000 hrs Col Wilson went on a recce of the area, sending OC 'B' Sqn out to recce the Alfani Road and OC 'A' Sqn to liaise with Brigadier Lyons, commanding the neighbouring 169 Brigade.

At 1100 hrs, the LST which had been delayed at sea arrived at the disembarkation point. It was here that one of Jake Wardrop's greatest friends, Trooper Stanley Skeels, was killed when he was trapped between two tanks which shifted together on the impact of beaching. Two other men were injured in similar incidents. At 1300 hrs the CO reported on the results of his recce but there are no further entries until 2300 hrs when an order came through for two Squadrons of 5RTR to be detached under direct command of 23rd Armoured Brigade. This affected 'B' and 'C' Squadrons who moved, with their A Echelons, at 0615 hrs on the 17th. There was obviously a certain lack of cohesion in command at this stage of the landing, as RHQ 5RTR and 'A' Squadron came under command of the Divisional AA Regiment (who had no guns) and became the Corps reserve, held against the possibility of a counter-attack. The Regiment suffered more casualties when three fitters were injured by air-burst.

If anyone hoped that 18th September would clarify what The Fifth was meant to be doing in Italy, they would have been disappointed. At 1100 hrs, RHQ and 'A' Squadron moved to join 'B' and 'C', the Regiment being relieved by the Greys [from 23rd Armd Bde], and again coming under the direct orders of OC Queens Brigade. From then until 26th September, the Regiment saw no action, only holding No 1 Parties, doing recce work (or nothing at all) and maintaining contact with the three Queens Battalions.

So what had been going on? To start with, the situation in Italy had changed dramatically between the time that Xth Corps (Seventh Armoured Division and Forty-sixth and Fifty-sixth Infantry Divisions) embarked and the time that it landed. On 8th September, as already recorded, Italy had thrown in the towel. This led the majority of men in the American Fifth Army to look forward to unopposed landings, a view shared by many in Xth Corps. However, the Germans had acted with the promptness to be expected of trained troops commanded by Kesserling. They had simply elbowed the Italians out of the way – not all that gently – and taken over as many of the prepared defensive positions as they could. One result of this was that, although 5RTR's beachhead was not manned in strength, it was under continuous and at times heavy artillery fire. Another enemy was the mosquito and the resultant risk of malaria, as the Divisional concentration area was in only partially reclaimed marsh land. So far as the armoured elements of Xth Corps were concerned, their future lay in the moves ahead when they passed through the perimeter of the bridgehead and linked up with the main body of the Eighth Army which had been advancing up the central and eastern parts on the 'ankle' of the peninsula – in the latter days of their advance, covering some 300 miles in just over a fortnight. In this waiting period, 7th Armd Div was being held in reserve.

The move should have started on 27th September but, as the War Diary says, 'Very heavy rain made fields muddy and wheeled transport was bogged until midday.' Nevertheless, the tanks got going at 1100 hrs, with 'A' Squadron linking up with 1/7 Queens to form an advanced guard.

'A' Squadron, it will be remembered, was no longer the 'Light' Squadron in the Italian and subsequent Campaigns. It had surrendered this traditional role to the newly formed Reconnaissance Troop and, now equipped with *Shermans*, was one of three 'Fighting Squadrons' each composed of five Troops of three tanks. This arrangement was far more suitable for the close country which was, in effect, encountered right through to Hamburg. This Recce Troop (or Section) was, in Italy, equipped with Bren Gun Carriers. The Section was commanded by Arthur Crickmay with Brian Beresford as his 2i/c. In Italy each of the fighting Squadrons frequently had a patrol of the Recce Section detached to work with it.

Mike Carver paints a graphic picture of the conditions which the Seventh Armoured Division was now encountering. Fortunately the tank commanders had experienced a small foretaste of these in the close country in

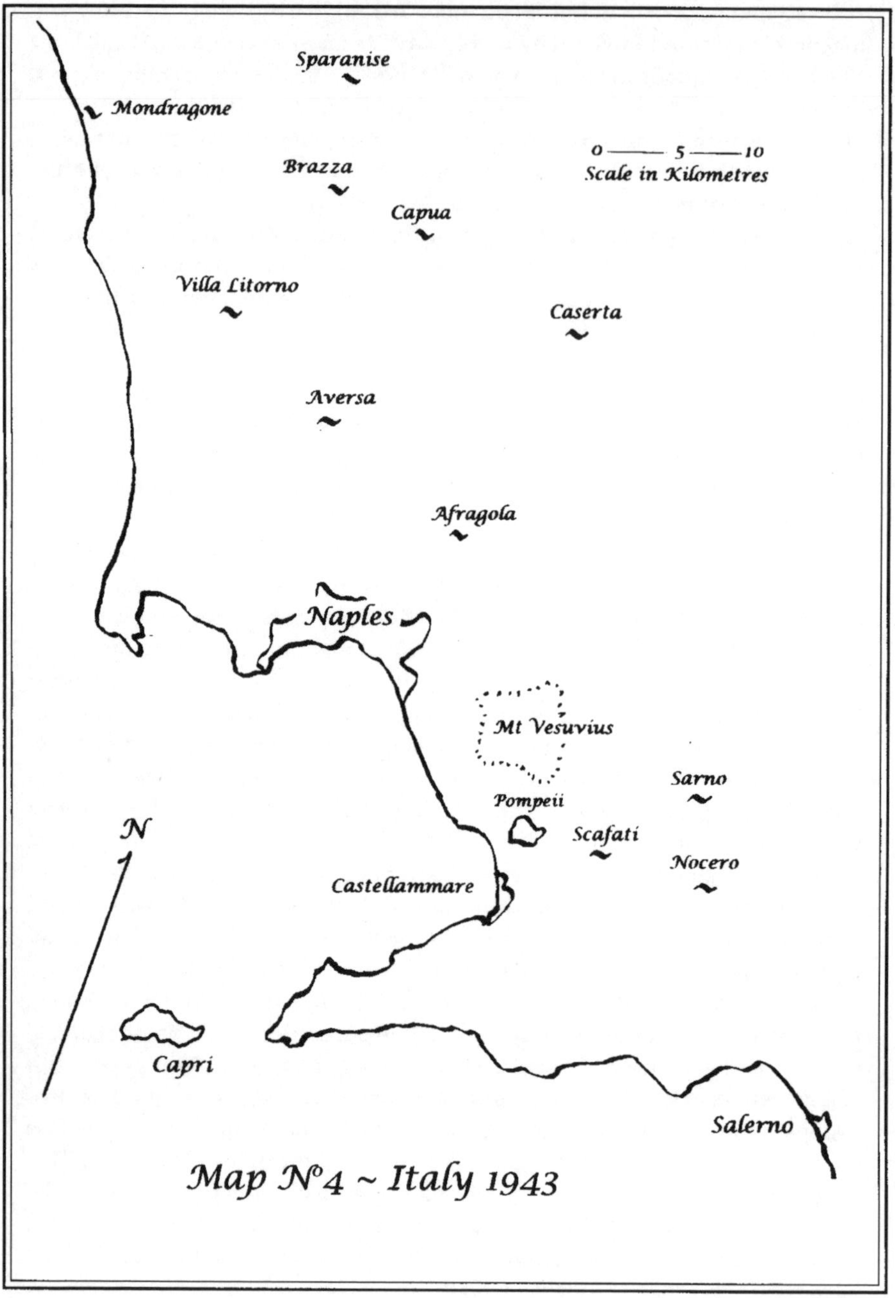
Sparanise
Mondragone
0 — 5 — 10
Scale in Kilometres
Brazza
Capua
Villa Litorno
Caserta
Aversa
Afragola
Naples
Mt Vesuvius
Sarno
Pompeii
Scafati
Nocero
N
Castellammare
Capri
Salerno
Map N°4 ~ Italy 1943

Tunisia. Had it not been for this, crews coming direct from open Desert conditions would have been at an even more serious disadvantage than they were.

The terrain on much of the run-up from Salerno to the Volturno[2] crossing was hilly, interspersed with streams or rivers (nearly every one of which had to be bridged, as the Germans had blown or mined the bridges and culverts). Italian vineyards may have sounded romantic, when the troops were kicking their heels in Homs, promising unlimited *vino*, but the reality was very different. Southern Italian vineyards were unlike the French or German variety with neat, clipped and cultivated rows of vines. The Italian variety were more like Kentish hop-fields, with the vines growing frequently so high that a tank commander, standing on the top of his *Sherman*, could hardly see over them. Supporting infantry was equally handicapped when they had to move through fields of maize standing well above head height.

These conditions made the German defensive role simple and effective. With the advantage of knowing, having retreated along them, the likely lines of approach, they could – and did – site and conceal their tanks, their SP and their A/Tk guns with the greatest effect. This was so much the case that the Recce Section's patrols frequently failed to detect the enemy's exact whereabouts and the advancing armour had no warning of what was in store.

The War Diary for 28th September reads, '0630 hrs 'A' Sqn and 1/7 Queens having taken over from 46 Div forward troops continue advance and attain first objective – Camerenne – with little opposition. Troops of 'A' Sqn block all side entries into the Div axis. Two of the Troops had small actions with small German recce sections.

'0900 hrs 'B' Sqn with 1/6 Queens pass through 'A' Sqn with objective Scafati Bridge over River Sarno and doing recce of villages of Nocera and Pagani on the way. They made extremely good time and recce section of 'B' Sqn reported Germans laying mines on Scafati Bridge preparing it for blowing. A 'B' Sqn Troop was rushed up to the bridge and saved it from being blown. Both the Recce Section under Lt Beresford and the tank Troop under Lt Wilde were fired on by snipers and an A/Tk gun covering the bridge. Lt Wilde was wounded and evacuated. By last light 'B' Sqn and 1/6 Queens A/Tk guns had blocked all main road junctions leading into town. 'B' Sqn recce section in advancing down the main road to Pompeii lost one carrier which was brewed up by a German tank from 800 yards range. Lt Beresford and his crew managed to get clear. The main opposition had been three Pzkw III tanks, considerable infantry with mortars and some artillery. Enemy counter-attacked during the night to re-capture the bridge. All attacks were repulsed. Bn (less 'B' Sqn) leaguered on road Nocera – Pagani. 'C' Sqn tank hit on gun-mounting. 'C' Sqn lost two tanks, one while attempting to recover A/Tk gun from 1/7 Queens hit by SP gun and burned out. The other hit on driver's hatch and complete loss. Driver killed. Co-driver and officer burned.'

These reports in the War Diary highlight one of its main shortcomings, namely the totally illogical way in which casualties are recorded. Why, for example, is Eric Wilde reported as having been 'wounded and evacuated' but the unfortunate 'C' Sqn driver who was killed, or the co-driver and officer who were burned – an injury which surely qualifies them as having been 'wounded' – are not named?

"'B' Sqn and 1/6 Queens,' the War Diary continues for 29th September, 'in the course of the morning cleared Scafati and continued advancing along Div axis up to the Boscoreale Road. 'C' Sqn with 1/7 Queens passed through Scafati and advanced up to Striano Road by nightfall. 'A' Sqn remained in reserve and were responsible for the defence of approaches to Div axis in Piscane area. 'B' Sqn in area Passanti. Cpl Harvey, 'C' Sqn, killed: 2 officers and 1 OR injured. One 'B' Sqn tank knocked out by SP.'

The advance continued next day with 'B' Squadron on the S Guiseppe road by noon and 'C' Squadron in the area of Poggiomarino where they had encountered tanks and infantry and had been shelled. Later in the day, 'B' Squadron met further opposition in the form of tanks and infantry but chased them off: not however, without casualties as Sergeant Thomas was killed and one of the men injured. At the close of the day, Regimental strength stood at 37 Officers and 571 ORs. There were 48 *Shermans* and 10 Bren Gun Carriers.

Progress was maintained throughout 1st October against steady rearguard action. By last light 'A' Squadron with its attendant 1/5 Queens had reached the area of Prison: 'B' Squadron and 1/6 Queens were in the Somma Vesuviano area and 'C' Squadron plus 1/7 Queens were near S Gennaro. RHQ leaguered at S Guiseppe. Two replacement tanks arrived from Brigade. On the 2nd 5RTR came back under command of 22nd Armd Bde and went into reserve, regrouping with RHQ and leaguering for the night near to Somma Vesuviana. The order of march is then stated to be 'Now 'A' Sqn, RHQ, 'C' Sqn, 'B' Sqn.' It depended on the CO how big the gap was between 'A' Squadron and RHQ. Which calls to mind the classic Fifth Tanks' Italian Campaign story of the CO's voice on the wireless querulously asking for clarification of a report from one of the forward troops and the very determined voice (of Paddy Doyle) coming on the air saying, 'If you got a bit closer to the sharp end, instead of being five miles back, you'd bloody well see for yourself what was happening!'

The Diary for 3rd October reads, '0630 hrs Bn moved on in rear of 22 Armd Brigade. 1 Troop from each Sqn acted as right flank protection on roads leading in from north east towards Div axis and 22 Armd Brigade TAC HQ situated just outside Afragola. Recce Section carried out recces for 22 Armd Brigade.' The next day the Regiment moved off at 0830 hrs, following 1/5 Queens up the Divisional CL, bypassing Afragola and leaguering for the night west of Atella Di Napoli. On 5th October, 'A' Squadron was called on at short notice to relieve one of the 1RTR squadrons with the objective of guarding a bridge. No other activity is reported for that day.

On the 6th there was more activity, although this is not very clear from the

War Diary. In fact, it takes The Fifth up to the Volturno. It was not a comfortable day for 'A' Squadron as their position 'was shelled and Nebelwerfer[3] was put on most of the day and also during the night. 'C' Squadron did not fare much better: their position guarding a cross-roads was also shelled all day. Less one Troop which was left guarding a canal, 'C' Squadron was pulled back for the night to Luigi Razza. There is no report of casualties from either of these Squadrons but a Recce Section officer and his driver were injured when their scout car was blown up on a mine while out reconnoitring a bridge. On 7th October The Fifth acted as mobile reserve, supporting 1/5 Queens against possible counter-attack.

The 8th October saw a slight departure from the normal duties of an armoured regiment. At least this was the case for Lt Haywood and his two Troop Sergeants. Haywood was the Troop Leader of the 'C' Squadron Troop which had been left out overnight guarding the canal. The War Diary reports the incident quite dramatically enough not to need elaborating. It states '0700 hrs. 'C' Sqn troop which guarded canal reported all ammunition dumps in area left by Germans fitted with charges and time clocks set to go off on the 18th day. Lt Haywood and his troop Sgt removed about 8 'ticking' clocks from 8 different dumps. 1 dump had in addition a pull ignition fuse and charge.' End of story, yes: but who knew when those 'ticking' clocks were going to reach the end of their 'shelf life'?

The rest of the entry for the same day is rather an anti-climax. At 1400 hrs there was an O Group at Brigade for the CO and Squadron Commanders to outline the plan for the coming attack on the Volturno Line. Later in the day 'B' Squadron took over a position from 40RTR[4] and 'A' Squadron was withdrawn: not without incident, as the unlucky Sgt Birch lost a foot on an AP mine.

On 9th October 'B' Squadron and RHQ were pulled out into a rest and maintenance area on the main road from Aversa to Capua at 1600 hrs. This was not a comfortable spot, as it was shelled frequently, particularly during the night. One member of the opposition gave himself up during the night to a Troop of 'B' Squadron, having become separated from the rest of his four man patrol. One member of The Fifth was injured during the night by the shell-fire. Nothing except shell and mortar fire is reported for the 10th.

At 0700 hrs next day the CO went on a Brigade TEWT. During the day the Regiment handed over its positions to 4 CLY. The entry for next day reads rather ominously, 'Normal Regimental routine commences.' On 13th October the CO took all tank and Recce Section commanders on a TEWT. Apart from recording the Regimental state at 35 Officers and 535 ORs, with 59 *Shermans* and 9 Carriers, there was nothing else to report for the rest of that day or on the 14th and 15th.

Regimental routine reached a new dimension on 17th October with an Adjutant's Parade – the first one recorded since 1st September 1939! Back to normal next day, as at 0530 hrs 5RTR, minus its Echelons, moved to the

Divisional Concentration Area. Or would have done if it had not been 'grid-locked' in traffic trying to get over the only available bridge. It was still there on the 18th. 'No Event' is reported for 19th October but, presumably, the Regiment had by then reached the Divisional Concentration Area.

Nothing happened the next day until 1630 hrs when the CO went to Brigade to get new Battle Orders. These he relayed to a No 1 Party at 1730 hrs. The Battle Plan was for an assault on the high ground to the north of Francolise and Sparanise by 56th Infantry Div with 22nd Armd Bde on the left flank. On the 21st the Regiment moved off at 0530 hrs and crossed the Volturno at 0600 hrs by the first (pontoon) Bailey Bridge to be built by the REs under enemy fire. The day was spent in reserve until moving up at 1500 hrs to take over positions from the Greys and going into leaguer for the night, except for two Troops of 'C' Squadron which spent a lonely night guarding a river crossing over the Del Lanci.

The War Diary for 22nd, 23rd and 24th October reads, '0530 hrs 'C' Sqn crossed bridge and Recce Section went forward to recce roads (1) to Francolise, (2) to Sparanise, (3) road running SW to S Andrea. Patrol to [S Andrea] were fired on by 88mm and SA fire. Patrol to Sparanise entered town. Patrol to Francolise held up by blown road. 'C' Sqn sent one Troop forward to watch where road was blown. 'A' Sqn moved up to try to get across railway leading to Sparanise. 'A' and 'C' Sqns leaguered for night forward of bridge. Scout car blown up on mine in 'A' Sqn leaguer. Cpl Rossiter and Trooper Clarke evacuated. One 'C' Sqn tank blown up on a mine, one track blown off. No-one injured. 'C' Sqn held up by A/Tk ditch 300 yards short of objective. 'A' Sqn pushes on towards Sparanise, one Troop round to the right of Sparanise and one Troop just behind it. Major VE Whitty wounded and evacuated. 'B' Sqn sent patrol to S Andrea to contact 131 Brigade.' Continuing the narrative for the 23rd, ''A' Sqn HQ in Sparanise. All Troops went forward up valley to right of Sparanise. Met opposition of Spandau MG posts and these were cleared up by Recce Section and No 1 Troop of 'A' Sqn. Recce took 5 prisoners. In afternoon two carriers and one tank lost a track each. At night enemy infiltrated towards these vehicles. Defensive fire brought down by 'G' Battery 5 RHA and enemy withdrew on high ground. 'C; Sqn pushed on down Francelles road and gained objectives on high ground south of Sparanise. 'B' Sqn established firm base south of Sparanise. Carrier hit mine. Lt Payne wounded, driver killed and operator died of wounds.' Then, for the 24th, 'A' and 'C' Squadrons get most of the credit, with 'A' Squadron, 'cleaning up two Spandau MG nests and moved forward into final objective of high ground. Enemy had withdrawn during the night. 'C' Sqn sent two Troops forward to support 1 RB who were to capture high ground south of Sparanise by Francolise. Objectives were captured. 'A' Sqn moved back to support left flank of RB south of Sparanise. 'C' Sqn moved north of Francolise.'

At the end of October the Regiment had its last brush with the enemy until 7th June 1944. The Division had been moved to the coastal area near Regi

Agnena – a move rendered extremely difficult by the state of the roads and by bridges which could only be crossed at snail's pace and by one tank at a time. The main enemy position in front of Seventh Armoured was on Mt Massico on the coast: from here they commanded the whole coastal plain down to Mondragone and the line of the Volturno. Reconnaissance showed that there was a stretch of the river, fordable by tanks, down near the beach. Although the river was fordable, this area was heavily mined. One Squadron of the Fifth was sent on ahead to force this crossing while the remainder of the Regiment supported a battalion of the Queens in an attack of Mondragone. The attack on Mondragone was launched at first light and proved entirely successful. One official record rather callously says that 'a few tanks were lost on the mines' but does conclude by saying that the whole operation went according to plan and the high ground on Mt Massico was occupied at small cost. The same record then points out one of the great advantages of motoring instead of marching to war. While the infantry spent an uncomfortable night in the open waiting for their rations (which often never arrived) the tank crews had only to unpack their picnic hampers, put the kettle on and, in due course, unroll their bedding and have a good night's sleep!

There are only scanty entries for the rest of the month and, indeed, for November and December. One of the main items being that 40RTR had arrived and, by 26th October, had taken over from The Fifth. The Regiment's next main task, confusingly, is stated to be 'the move across Volturno to protect 46 Div left flank'. Confusing because the Regiment had already crossed the River Volturno at 0600 hrs on Thursday, 21st October. In the last two months of 1943 Seventh Armoured Division was withdrawn into reserve behind the Monte Massico feature, except for a thin khaki line of some 4,000 yards which was 'held' by 1 RB, a Squadron of 5RTR and XI Hussars [a role which can hardly have pleased the Cherry Pickers!]. Luckily, the Germans did not even move to probe this line.

As for the rest of The Fifth – indeed, the rest of the Division – they were dumped in the Sorrento Peninsula and left to their own devices. These soon included 'day trips' and longer leave to Naples, to the Isle of Capri by courtesy of the Royal Navy, and to Pompeii. However, goods, the presents to take home – *mutandini, sotani, calze di seta, reggipetti* – and entertainment were very expensive (and there were certain risks attendant upon some of the latter) so that the day trips became a way of relieving boredom rather than enjoying oneself. And, sleeping or waking, everyone dreamt of being home again.

One military duty, however, did remain: that of handing over the tanks, carriers, scout cars and soft vehicles to the relieving formation. This was the Fifth Canadian Armoured Division, one of whose regiments, the British Columbia Dragoons, was destined to receive the Fifth Tanks cast-offs. I had been in 5 Cdn Armd Div and had trained with the BCD shortly before they sailed for Italy and remember how we were all told we would be leaving our ageing *Ram* tanks behind in England, along with everything else, and how we would be equipped with brand-new *Shermans* and an up-dated version of the *Stuart*, to say nothing of soft vehicles galore sent on specially in advance from Canada. Much later, I met a friend in the BCD. Great had been their fury when they saw those Fifth Tanks' cast-offs with which they were expected to win the war. Shades of The Fifth at Homs.

However, that was their worry: The Fifth's was when . . . or rather, how soon . . . they would sail for home. The answer came when they embarked in Naples on the *Cameronia* on Saturday, 20th December 1943, with the prospect of Christmas on the High Seas and Blighty early in the New Year.

There are a number of private records of the active part of the *Italian Idyll* – some mere anecdotes. A favourite example of these is probably apocryphal. A particular tank commander, who may have been clueless but who *was* keen, was in a unit struggling forward and heading for Naples. Three times, as he followed up the Charlie Love, he came on the air and reported the sighting of smoke over to his right. On the third occasion his Squadron Commander himself came on the air. 'Smoke over on the right flank? Yes – and there has been these forty million or more years. That's ruddy Vesuvius you're looking at, man!'

These private records cover some eight weeks during which the Seventh Armoured moved about 85 miles up the Italian Peninsula. As the crow flies it might have been 85 miles, yes, but that sort of distance could be, and often was, covered in manoeuvring, leaguering, demonstrating, re-organising, taking up battle positions, reconnoitring and replenishing, without even coming into contact with the enemy. In reality, then, those 85 miles of crow-flight were a long hard slog against determined opposition, often in appalling weather conditions, on roads which varied between inadequate and annihilated, across rivers that had no crossings, in terrain where observation was a matter of luck rather than judgement, through towns and villages which had been all but obliterated. If there was one redeeming feature it was that 'the natives were friendly': not just pleased to be liberated but actively helpful, often sheltering wounded men or strayed patrols, pointing out mines and defended positions, helping clear obstacles and, of course, providing *vino*.

Willie Dovey had one of his many close calls. But his main impression was not of the war as fought by the British Army but of the rations as eaten by the American Army. Like nearly everyone else, he was pretty sure in the first hours after the landing that they were going to be pushed back into the sea and that a beach-head could never be carved out against such determined opposition. His immediate concern was that the Bren Gun Carrier, on which he was Brian Beresford's operator in the Recce Section, did not afford as much protection against the incessant shelling as the proper tanks he had been used to. His consolation was that they had a good driver, Garry by name. Or so Willie thought until Scafati when Garry failed to find a much needed reverse gear. Out on recce in front of 'B' Squadron, as they turned a sharp bend at the end of the town, a large and unfriendly shell whistled past their noses. 'Driver reverse,' came the order: Garry muffed the gears and the crew baled out. Just in time, for a second and third shot followed in short order and their Carrier was no more. The Tiger, as they saw when they had a shufti round the corner, was only about 200 yards away.

'After a lot of hard fighting,' Willie went on, 'we pushed along the coast road. Then past Naples as far as the Garigliano River. Then some good news: we were being relieved and moving back to Sorrento. This was towards the end of November. It was not exactly a holiday resort but still nice to be back to civilisation. I sampled some of the local *vino* plus an organised trip to Capri. By the middle of December our move started. We were on our way home.'

There is a fleeting reference, found in a Metropolitan Police Staff Magazine, to a Trooper DG 'Boxer' Brown who landed at Salerno as a *Sherman* driver, having previously driven a *Honey* across the Desert with 3RTR. Boxer Brown was not a lucky man: after a few days in Italy he was wounded but recovered sufficiently to come back with the Regiment to train for D Day. Which he did, only to be captured on 4th August and spend the rest of the war in 357 Krugs POW camp.

For Keith Treasure – by then Corporal Treasure – the memories of Italy are always cast in the shade by Stanley Skeels' tragic death and the absence of Fearless Jim in command of his men. Nevertheless he survived the action and, the bright spot, went to Naples on a 'Passion Wagon' from Castellammare, where the Regiment was based on the Sorrento Peninsula. Here, after witnessing the famous 'punch up' in which 'Carlo' Carlsson was involved, he encountered a Private in the Signals. He asked this man if he knew a Major Treasure and was told that the man certainly did, as he was the Major's driver. Once again Keith was united with his Big Brother . . . and had yet another free meal off him.

Peter Carlsson's punch-up was on the grand scale. Not content with tangling with the Military Police, he chose to take a swipe at one of their RSMs. Nothing less than a Court Martial offence and to a Court Martial it duly went. Here, however, Carlo's fortunes changed. His Defending Officer was his unit's Second in Command, Bob Maunsell. Bob was not content with getting his man off the charge: he went the full length and got the charge thrown out. There had been no reason, Bob argued, for the RSM to have interfered: the matter should have been left in the hands of his men, who were quite competent to deal with it and, in due course, lay a charge of good old-fashioned 'drunk and disorderly' which the accused's CO would have dealt with. If the RSM hadn't been officious he wouldn't have been struck and no charge of striking a superior officer would have arisen. The two most surprised people in the court when the charge was dismissed were Bob Maunsell and Carlo Carlsson!

*

Dennis Cockbaine's account of the *Italian Idyll* gives some interesting details. He wrote, 'Having landed in the Salerno area on 15th September 5RTR found itself in unusual territory. Gone were the Desert wastes where visibility could extend for miles and gone were the days of open coastal plains of Libya and Tunisia. We soon discovered that life and death depended on who saw each other first when going round the corner of a hedge-lined road. The battles that followed were sharp and nasty. We found ourselves fighting in villages and towns, being stonked by German Minenwerfers.

'By-passing Naples, we had major problems at rivers – the Volturno, for example – and always there was Vesuvius simmering on our right. It was excellent preparation for our next role – landing in Europe – although we did not know it until we were suddenly pulled back in November to go into reserve. We were then told that, if things continued to go well in Italy, we would be going home. This was on 10th November and we commenced pulling right back, eventually stopping at Castellammare on the coast of the Bay of Naples. We started preparing the tanks for hand-over to the Canadians almost immediately and then we had to wait for a boat home.

'In the following weeks many trips were organised to places like Pompeii, Sorrento, Ravello and the Islands of Ischia and Capri. One adventure was to go to the top of Mount Vesuvius which was getting ready to erupt (and did so just after we sailed for home). The RTR Band visited us and played 'Selections' in an old tin-can factory. The evening's concert was conducted by the famous Trooper Nat Gonella and his RTR Rhythm Section which brought the house down.

'During this time 'A' Sqn was involved in embarking into a LST to act as a decoy to the Germans who were about to be subjected to the big landings at Anzio. It was all very hush-hush but I believe their LST was attacked, though any casualties were never made known to us.'

Dennis' account of the Italian campaign finishes, as do others, with embarking on the *Cameronia* and sailing from Naples on 20th December 1943.

Fortunately there is a first-hand account of the exercise in deception which Dennis Cockbaine mentions. It is written by Ronald Leonard who joined the Regiment in Homs, and whose first recollection of The Fifth was witnessing Douglas Lowe's fatal accident. Writing about the sea-borne expedition, Ron Leonard recalls, 'The Americans, in the meantime, suspected a leak of information from their Army HQ, so we were asked to withdraw a squadron of tanks, waterproof them and run them in and around Naples for everyone to see. We then loaded the tanks on the decks of four landing craft. The LCTs then sailed line ahead out of the Bay of Naples. I was on the Commodore's ship – first in the line. Our look-out spotted a floating mine ahead of the ships and signalled to the following craft. The leading three were able to avoid the mine but it went under the bows of the last one and exploded under its stern. The mine completely demolished the engine room and crew's quarters but left the LCT still afloat with four tanks on the deck. The tank crews leapt into the sea and were rescued. What was left of the ship was beached: the crew had been blown to pieces.

'The diversionary exercise continued out to open sea and then turned south to Castellammare. Whether the Americans ever solved the mystery of the leak of information we were never told. We returned to Naples and shortly afterwards were on our way home.'

There are two accounts of the campaign in Italy and there is a great deal of detail available from Syd Storer's Diary [which contradicts some of what others had to say] as well as some interesting sidelights.

Syd Storer's account starts at about 1700 hrs on 15th September when the men in the LSTs first sighted land and the Luftwaffe first sighted them – 'coming in like flies in the Desert'. Luckily for Syd, his was not the first tank to land. The sailor responsible for making the sounding confused fathoms with inches and sent the first tank into the water well over turret height. Neither the tank nor the crew were ever seen again. An officer then took charge and ordered the ship another four or five cables in shore, where the rest of the load beached in not more than four inches of water.

Syd went on, 'We moved up the beach as quickly as possible. Shells were landing everywhere but the MPs calmly directed us to our concentration area for dewaterproofing and testing our guns. We were ready by midnight and hoped to get some sleep. But at 0400 hrs the enemy made a strong counter-attack and, though we did not find many targets, we were kept dashing from one part of the bridgehead to another to make believe there were more tanks on the beachhead than actually were. 5RTR was the only tank battalion there at the time. We sheltered in an orchard during the day just behind where the Americans were dug in: each night we moved out round the front, revving our engines each time we halted. We had been warned of the mosquitoes but were surprised by the number that came out as soon as darkness fell. We had to be issued with mosquito nets for those few occasions when we got a chance to sleep.

'At 0500 hrs next morning we had an air raid, followed by a sharp attack and were ordered back to protect an MDS which was threatened by a breakthrough. Our gunner, George Tracey was the first mosquito victim, being so badly bitten he had to go to hospital. By the 17th we heard that the Eighth Army was getting nearer which considerably improved things for us. The enemy had withdrawn from some hills overlooking us but, each time we attempted to move, he reminded us of his presence. On the19th we moved forward and contacted some Americans, who were dug in not quite in the front line: we found this when we were shelled a mile further on as we attempted to cross a narrow bridge.'

Syd digresses briefly to dilate on the welcome crop of grapes and of the plum tomatoes which he fried up for his crew with their breakfast [tinned] bacon rashers. On the debit side was the continual rain and the slow progress made because of bad roads. He describes how, moving cautiously through a pass to try to reach the open plain, 'The road was narrow with a steep drop on the right side and, as we edged round each bend, an enemy gun would open up from across the valley. On the night of 27th September, despite the rain, we moved through the pass out onto the plain where eventually all the Division gathered. We slept by the roadside, with reveille at 0430 hrs, and advanced on Nocera [Inferiore] without much resistance. Things were much too quiet as we approached Scafati. Our infantry climbed on top of the houses overlooking the square and reported a gun in the middle of it.' What then happened is later described by Eric Wilde.

When Syd's tank did get across the bridge it was involved in a most unfortunate incident. There was a Tiger concealed in the village. The Troop Leader did not know this but, nevertheless, called the infantry forward to have a look. However before they arrived, Syd's tank was spotted and fired upon. The infantry was warned of this, so that they carried out their recce with great caution . . . and spotted the Tiger. Its presence was reported to Squadron HQ who, much to the crew's relief, told them to stay where they were. A short while after this four War Correspondents arrived, having heard news of the Tiger. One was the BBC's Frank Gillard with three photographers. They were warned of the danger when they said they intended to cross the road to get a picture of the Tiger but they ignored the warning and ran across the road to where a shell from the Tiger had already blasted the front of a house down. But, before they could get into position for a picture, the Boche fired again and killed all three.

Predictably, the enemy launched a counter-attack to try to recapture the bridge. What was not predictable was the method of the attack. They came over the tops of the houses, firing down on the crews and dropping hand-grenades onto the tanks. The support infantry retaliated by climbing onto other roofs and engaging in a scrap that went on all night. During one of these fights, Sgt Fearnside, the crew commander was slightly injured. He stayed on duty but the pain made him restless and he was spotted out of the tank by the Squadron Commander who, not knowing the circumstances, gave him a most unmerited dressing down. The sort of incident, as Syd commented, that was all too likely to occur when nerves are at full stretch.

By first light, after a night of rain, they saw that the Tiger had gone.

It was shortly after this that 'B' Sqn encountered members of a Hermann Göring Battalion and caught some of them napping by pushing down a wall and taking them unawares. One of their number was found carrying explicit instructions to destroy all bridges, railway stations, water points and electrical installations. It didn't do this particular lot any good: in fact, they lost an SP gun to The Fifth. Like everyone else who fought under these conditions, Syd retains a vivid memory of the tactics the Germans employed to hold up the Allied advance. Roads mined and blocked by felled trees, carefully sited A/Tk guns, Minenwerfer aimed to drop a continuous fire of mortar bombs on the very spot where the advance would have to halt, an armoured car waiting to warn of the tanks' approach and then fade out of the picture. He also retains vivid memories of the wildly enthusiastic Italian peasants, cheering the arrival as liberators of the very people who had only a few weeks ago been officially regarded as the enemies of their country.

Syd Storer again, 'One night we managed to get some sleep, in spite of wet blankets, in the square of Pasanti. The night guard had been provided by the Anti-tank Gunners who had pushed to the edge of the village to give us cover. We roused at 0430 hrs and were quickly reminded of the dangers of any area vacated by the Germans when Frank Tring, the wireless operator on the tank nearest us, stepped on an anti-personnel mine which blew off part of his right leg. Having seen Frank despatched to the rear, we found we had little enjoyment in our own breakfast. It was our morning for lead tank, which was always the worst position, especially under the prevailing conditions and terrain. To make matters worse refugees, driven by an irate Italian, trying to stop them eating his grapes, flocked down the road. We chased him away and told the fugitives to get off the road for their own safety. We then continued without any trouble to Terzigno. In front of the village was a long straight street which could have been laid by the Roman army many years before. It was all very quiet as most of the inhabitants had left. There were houses on either side with vineyards behind them. We took what cover we could, hugging the side of the road, and were halfway up the street when all hell was let loose. Mortar fire on the infantry who were walking behind the tanks, shell-fire on everyone . . . and then we were hit by AP. This blew our left front driving sprocket and track off. Fernie shouted 'Bale out!' on the inter-com. We did, and moved sharply into the nearest house. We explored and found a large cellar with about 50 men, women and children sheltering in it. Shell and mortar fire continued as the following tanks, backed by the Queens infantry, edged their way along the street towards the level crossing at the far end. We lost two more tanks but, by nightfall, we held the village. The villagers had been very helpful, showing us ways through the vineyards and giving us information on the whereabouts of enemy strong points. However, all the information had to be checked as there were still some men around who sympathised with the Germans.'

Syd thought that this partisanship was the cause of a catastrophe which overtook the Queens later that day. Their cookhouse had arrived after the fighting had died down about 2000 hrs and the Queens were having a well-earned evening meal in an olive grove when a barrage of Minenwerfer rockets crashed down in the exact place where the men were eating.. This continued for about ten minutes. The tank crews were helpless to do anything about it and, when the barrage eventually stopped, there were dead and wounded everywhere. The Squadron stood-to for the next hour in case of a counter-attack but there was no further enemy ground activity but shell and mortar fire continued throughout the night.

Syd then had an unpleasant half hour. Just before dawn the Squadron

Commander arrived and ordered Sgt Fearnside to take over another tank where the crew commander had been lost through sniping. He then asked Syd if his wireless set was in working order. Syd said it was and was ordered to unship it and transfer it to another tank whose set was useless. A somewhat reluctant Syd waited for a quieter moment, then dashed across the road and climbed into the tank. Dismantling the set was no problem; getting it out of the tank and back across the road without being spotted, was. With caution, careful observation and a good deal of luck, both Syd and the set got back where they were wanted.

The advance was renewed later in the day and, after the rest of the Squadron had moved through, the fitters arrived, shook their heads and called for a transporter. This took Syd and the crew into the newly liberated Naples, where, despite the fact it had fallen only a few days earlier, a workshop had already been set up. The tank took two days to repair. The crew spent the time having a good bath and a change of clothes, and looking round Naples. What they saw revolted them. It was in a filthy condition: no refuse had been collected; it had been dumped in the roads; the smell was terrible. The Military Governor was doing his best but organising Italians, Syd commented wryly was never easy. After two days of solid rain, the crew left again on 7th October and reached the reserve Squadron at 1700 hrs. Here they replenished and pushed on to reach 'B' Squadron as light was failing. They found the Squadron in a virtual swamp after all the rain but managed to find some shelter in a nearby farmhouse. This was at a small village called Villa Literno and across their front was a canal with all the bridges blown. The REs worked hard during the night and erected a Bailey bridge as well as repairing the roads, thus enabling the tanks to move nearer to the stretch of the Volturno on their front between Capua and Cancello.

An Italian officer, who had deserted from the German Army and given himself up, provided a lot of useful information about the lay-out of the opposing forces. He also disclosed that the Boche had been told the bridges *to their rear* would be blown and they would have to cross the river as best they could. This proved to be correct. All bridges were blown well before The Fifth reached them. The support infantry were not best pleased to find that, in most cases, the banks were very steep, making the work of crossing very difficult. The Fifth had the task of trying to convince the enemy that they were about to cross the river near Grazzanise and above the blown bridge. There had been an attempt here by a patrol a few nights earlier to see if the Germans had the area covered. The patrol did not get very far: the enemy suspected a real attack and opened up with all guns on the crossing point. The Gunners gave supporting fire and the patrol withdrew. Then, using the same crossing place, the Queens made an attempt under a combined artillery and tank barrage but this again brought down heavy fire, including air-burst, and the attack was postponed for three hours. Much to the surprise of the tank crews, this attack succeeded, being met only with sporadic fire. The following night jeeps and

A/Tk guns were ferried across, followed by the REs who started to build a bridge to take the tanks across. Either by good luck for the Germans or by their good water management, the water level fell, which made the REs work very difficult. But luck, like Janus, is two-faced. The drop in the water level disclosed a place where tanks could cross, so a bulldozer was brought up and 4 CLY got a squadron of tanks across without loss.

At this stage, another Roman god intervened: Jupiter Pluvius[5]. The weather rendered off-road tank movement virtually impossible, so close-contact work had to be left to the infantry; in this case, the 56th Division. The Fifth went due east cross country and then turned north to where a crossing, strong enough to take the *Shermans*, had been made over the Volturno. 5RTR diverted to clear Capua from the north-west, while the rest of the Brigade went due north on Highway 6. As the withdrawal continued it was the same story of demolished bridges, mined roads and constant skirmishes with 88s and mortars from rearguards, usually supported by artillery. The Fifth was held up for a while by concentrated fire from the mountains around Sparanise and Francolise on the morning of 22nd October. The Fifth side-stepped to Sparanise and found it abandoned. It was occupied and patrols were sent into the mountains beyond but found no trace of enemy. By the 26th the area above the Volturno was cleared and the Regiment was on the banks of the River Savone. At the end of October the tanks moved to Regi Agnena. Things had not been too bad in Syd's opinion: casualties had been light, when the conditions and the pertinacity of the opposition was considered.

And there were, as Syd remarked, lighter moments. 'Fortunately one of our drivers was a butcher in Civvie Street for, a little way down the road, we had seen a farm with a number of piglets at the back. Leaving the infantry on guard, we went to try out our pidgin Italian on the farmer while Trooper 'Butch' Lovell went round the back. But, when the farmer heard the squealing at the back of the house, he ran away and left us. We returned to our tank to find a small pig hanging from the tree and already partly dismembered. Most of the meat was disposed of with army biscuit and a cup of char.

'Despite being heavily shelled, we pushed on next morning, the infantry leading, and cleared the area between the mountains and the sea. A day or so later we captured Cicola after a sharp fight and moved on towards Sessa Aurunca, where we met the 46th Division who had come over the mountains. The Germans had now retired behind the Garigliano and Monte Cassino line, occasionally sending out fighting patrols which the RBs dealt with. On 6th November the great news became official: we were to return home as soon as ships were available. It was difficult to realise it: everyone was in excellent spirits as we packed the tanks and made our way back to Aversa. A period of cleaning and polishing followed as we prepared the tanks for handing over to the Fifth Canadian Armoured Division. When they were ready, we had to move them. For the hand-over, the beautiful clean tanks were lined up in several inches of mud!'

Syd Storer's account then becomes a highly personal one, written for the benefit of his family. Nevertheless, some parts of it are of universal interest showing, as they do, what life was like at the time. Syd enjoyed the 'sight-seeing tours' which were arranged, particularly the one to Pompeii: also a shopping expedition to Naples. Had he known of the shortages on the 'home front', he felt he would have purchased much more acceptable presents for his family. A visit from the mobile laundry was much appreciated, as was the issue of angora shirts since the weather was becoming decidedly chilly. Not so much appreciated were the billets – the floor of a far-from-spotless laundry building – in Castellammare.

The account by Syd Storer's Troop Officer, Eric Wilde, of his curtailed Italian Campaign reads, 'The Division landed as a follow-up to the two Infantry Divisions making the assault in the Bay of Salerno. It was they who had the very difficult and costly fighting and had already blunted the German counter-attack by the time we arrived. The Germans started a methodical withdrawal along the valley road leading to Naples and 'B' Sqn led the Regimental Group. We were soon faced by the small village of Scafati with a vital road bridge: the Divisional Commander personally came up to my tank (which was in the lead) to urge us to make all speed. The village was held by German infantry who were believed to have mined the bridge. We had a small fight in the outskirts of the village and in the street leading up to the bridge which was situated at right-angles to the road: we could not therefore see if it was mined or covered by A/Tk guns. So I got out of my tank to do a foot reconnaissance. There appeared to be no mines so I started crossing but, as I reached the middle of the bridge, I was hit by a bullet which went through my chest. When I picked myself up and turned to make my way back to my tank I could see two Germans sheltering behind a wall below the level of the road. They again fired their pistols but missed – pistols are notoriously inaccurate, to my good fortune – and I was able to crawl round the corner to the safety of my beloved tank . . . and to speedy evacuation to the Advanced Surgical Unit. My driver, Corporal Onions, took over command of the tank and his subsequent actions won him an outstanding Distinguished Conduct Medal

'After my wound had been treated I was told that I would be flown out of the bridgehead. There was no proper airfield, merely an emergency landing strip which had first been used by the Germans and subsequently by the RAF. The planes used for medical evacuation were those old, reliable, war horses – the Dakotas. It could not carry Red Cross markings because, on the inward flight, it carried essential stores and personnel. At this time the Germans held local air superiority. Their bases were close at hand, whereas Allied planes had to fly up from Sicily and could only stay over the gulf [the Bay of Salerno] for 15 minutes at a time. The Germans thus had very free play to strafe our lines of communication, the beaches and the landing strip. Medical casualties were moved up to the landing strip and placed under the wings of knocked-out aircraft to await the arrival of the Dakotas, which also waited until a German strafing run was over. Then the stretcher cases were rushed to the waiting Dakotas which took off immediately they were loaded and flew very low until well away from Salerno. While flying so low and so near to the front line, the atmosphere in the plane was very tense.' It was not improved in Eric's case by a fellow casualty suffering from loudly and repeatedly expressed hallucinations.

To go back to the bridge at Scafati, George Onions, the eleventh of fifteen children, joined 5RTC in 1938 and saw service with the Regiment in France and the Desert. He missed the later stages of the Italian campaign, being unwillingly side-lined to teach others how to drive tanks. He rejoined The Fifth as a Sergeant *Firefly* commander in time to land on D+1. George was badly wounded on 14th July 1944 and eventually invalided out of the Army after a year in hospital. The citation for George Onions' immediate DCM, signed by the CO of 5RTR, Brigadier Cmdg 22nd Armd Bde, GOC 7th Armd Div and General Sir Harold Alexander C-in-C 15th Army Group, reads, 'His Squadron had been ordered to seize a bridge over the river at Scafati, which was known to be the only bridge left intact. Onions, then a Corporal, was driving his Troop Leader in the leading tank in the Squadron and, as they approached the bridge, the Troop Leader was wounded and evacuated. Cpl Onions then took over the command of the tank, crossed the bridge and took up a position on the enemy side from where he held off many counter-attacks which were put in at last light and all through the night. He was shelled by enemy tanks, sniped by many enemy who were in the houses round him, yet he stayed in position without any support, as no anti-tank guns could get across the bridge. During the night he ran short of ammunition, so organised a party of infantry who were in the house parallel to his tank to help by going back across the bridge to fetch the necessary supplies. He was under intense enemy fire throughout the whole period, the streets being illuminated like daylight, as a vehicle on the bridge had been set alight by enemy shelling. By his bold and resolute action, his initiative and utter disregard of his own safety, the bridge, which was vital to 5th Army, was kept intact throughout the night and safe from numerous enemy counter-attacks.'

Another stalwart who wrote about the Italian Expedition was Harry Ireland. Harry starts his account by saying how he, '.. noticed all around the way the Regiment has changed in my time. Apart from a new CO, we had new officers, new NCOs and other ranks. Many of the new faces are Territorial Army. All were well-meaning men but lacking the expertise of regular soldiers. My own tank commander, for instance, a regular soldier, six years in India before the outbreak of war, trained in mobile warfare, knowledge in all departments; mechanics, gunnery, map reading, tactics, compass and above all – guts. Quite a few of these men who had given their all to the Regiment fell by the wayside. I now became mellowed and the zing and zip of inexperience had faded. However, old soldiers carry on.

'The best part about the Salerno landing was the rations. We had never seen so much grub: what a change from bully beef and biscuits! Coming under the American Command meant all our supplies were Yankee: Spam, tinned fruit, mixed meat and veg., chocolate – the lot. We were getting fattened up for the killing.

'The landing was a spectacular affair; we spent the last four days travelling across the Med, passing through the Messina Strait at night. The bridgehead had been established by the Commandos and infantry under the fire power of the Navy, with their Cruisers' 16inch guns, and Air Force cover. We approached the beaches and, after dewaterproofing, we quickly pushed up into a very thinly-held shore line, about one mile deep. (Churchill said afterwards that it was touch-and-go: how right he was) From the time we hit the beaches we were attacked and nearly thrown back into the sea. Luck was on our side; the weather was good and reinforcements came pouring ashore. The bridgehead held. Next day we were able to spread out and attack our objectives with reasonable success and few casualties.

'Now it was a different kind of war. Compared with the Desert's vast spaces, we now operated on a Centre Line only a few miles wide; country lanes, hedgerows, orchards, anti-personnel mines, tank traps, road blocks, snipers. All something we had to get used to . . . and quick.

'The going was hard but we were making slow progress. We heard that the Eighth Army had linked up with the bridgehead in their push from the Messina landings but we have, on our front, two mountainous passes which we must break through before we can reach our objective – Naples. After very hard fighting, we approached the Vitre Pass where the American Rangers and our Commandos take over, also a division of infantry. It took five days before the Pass had been cleared of enemy, the infantry casualties were high, the American Rangers doing a fine job clearing the high ground while the infantry fought in the Pass. By now there are plenty of refugees coming through our lines, making a very confused situation. Civilians in war: something only very few us – those who had been in France in 1940 – had experienced before. A pitiful sight, poverty and hunger although we couldn't do much about it. They went on their way through our lines to be dealt with by the Military Government officials. The Italians had surrendered and we are now being hailed as their liberators . . . but the Germans still carried on. After the Regiment pushed through the Vitre Pass, incurring a few casualties, we branched off the Centre Line and travelled round the back of Mount Vesuvius, to Nocera, Scafati: very hard fighting all the way.

'My crew commander left our tank and we had a new one: new to us and new to the game. He didn't last long: he had us cleaning the gun and I was in the turret with the breach block open, waiting for the brush on the end of the cleaning rod to appear. Instead, there was a loud explosion and I was peppered with gravel and dirt from the road. Looking quickly outside, I saw the tank commander lying seriously wounded alongside the tank. He had

1. *A13* tanks of the British 1st Armoured Division after being off-loaded from a 'dirty British coaster' at Cherbourg in May 1940

2. The 'A' Squadron *A10* tank ELISSA posed 'somewhere in North Africa' early in 1941

3. Rallying point for one of the 5RTR MI Companies in the Tobruk Perimeter, May 1941

4. Major Freddie Coombes and two of his crew pose by their *Honey*, which had the doubtful distinction of being the first 5RTR tank to be hit after 'crossing the wire' in Operation 'Crusader'

5. 'B' Squadron Cookhouse – Desert style. No complaints for the Orderly Officer

6. One of the 5RTR's *Crusaders* gets a piggyback ride [*See Note No 16 to Chapter Six*]

7. The crew of a Recce Troop Bren Gun Carrier – carrying a good deal more than a light machine gun – on return from reconnaissance, stop to check their information with the local population: Italy, September 1943

8. A *Sherman* of the Fifth Tanks pounds its way through the Italian village of Scafati after the bridge had been cleared, September 1943

9. Typical view of a typically-camouflaged typical 5RTR *Sherman Firefly* in typical Normandy bocage country with a typical crew member having a typical brew-up of typical char, June 1944

10. The crew of the leading Fifth Tanks' Cromwell pause to study the map. According to the Library picture caption, the tank was 'on its way to Aunay-sur-Odon'. If that caption is correct, they aren't going to get there heading down that road, August 1944

11. A line of 'C' squadron tanks wait in Holland for the road to be cleared of burnt-out enemy transport to allow the Regiment to move up into its support position for Operation 'Market Garden', September 1944

12. This Bryan de Grineau drawing from The Illustrated London News in fact depicts an action by VIII Hussars and Commandos against a German strong-point at Linne in Holland in January 1945. The attack was later re-enacted by 5RTR for the ILN war artist's benefit. The *Cromwell* in the foreground is the author's tank ESMERALDA

13. Waiting in the rain. 'A' Squadron tanks formed up ready for the 'Off' in a water-logged German field after the Rhine Crossing. The umbrella concealing the Troop Leader, as he returns from an O Group, gives a good idea of the weather in late March 1945

14. Tanks of the Regiment cross 'yet another boring old Bailey Bridge'. In this case, across the River Aller after the capture of Rethem in April 1945

15. Waiting in the sun. *Cromwells* à gogo. 'B' Squadron HQ tanks lined up for the final sprint across Lüneberg Heath which led them to within range of Hamburg, late April 1945

16. A war won and the washing done. Men of the Fifth Royal Tank Regiment hear the news that the War in Europe is finally over, Tuesday, 8th May 1945

stood on an anti-personnel mine, left behind as a booby trap. A lot of others were found in the same area. We were glad to get away next morning.'

Pete Petersen also had the unpleasant experience of losing a tank commander in action in Italy, 'After enjoying the swimming and sunbathing in the Med,' Pete wrote, 'we were all recuperated and fit to be on the march again and it wasn't long before we were embarked at Tripoli for the invasion of Italy. We arrived without incident in the Bay of Salerno with dog fights going on overhead and HMS *George the Fifth* hammering the hills beyond Salerno. We eventually landed on the beach without opposition: just a bit of sporadic shell-fire from the enemy. We had news that our infantry were making progress and dealt with a few guns. On Day Two we moved forward towards Sarno and later to Adversa. I think it was here in Adversa that we met some opposition and my tank commander, Sgt Thomas, was killed while endeavouring to direct my fire onto an enemy OP. A shell landed alongside the tank and a shell fragment struck him in the throat. It was an instantaneous death: he slumped into the turret and I supported him until such time as we could manoeuvre the tank into a safer position and remove Sgt Thomas from the tank. It was a shock to the crew but like good little soldiers we had to get on with the job.

'That night we were in leaguer in the town square and, while on patrol duty, one of the sergeants, Sgt Kitchen, lost a foot on an anti-personnel mine. Another nasty shock. But it was not all doom and gloom: we had our comical moments. One was when we had just ploughed through a mile or two of vineyards and came out into a village where the locals all came out to greet us with bunches of grapes, not knowing that we had just been smothered in the darn things. But the *signorinas* were quite attractive and the countryside was pleasant. All a bit of a change from the Desert. Well, we pressed on, running into sporadic opposition, leaving Vesuvius smoking behind us, until we came to the Volturno, where we met a bit of opposition, and on to Cassino. But we stopped short of Cassino and leaguered up in a field of tomatoes. It was here that we had the news that we were to be withdrawn, hand our tanks over to the Canadians and sent home.

'We all knew the reason we were being sent home but a sight of Blighty again was all we wanted.'

Titch Maple did not enjoy all the pleasures of Homs, being 'under the doctor' for much of the time but he did get back into harness in time to become WOp to Captain Crickmay, OC of the newly created Recce Section. Titch's first task was to train the other operators, as communication is second only to observation when it comes to reconnaissance. Like others, Titch had some doubts about Dingos and Bren Gun Carriers as suitable means of fighting armoured warfare but he soon found a partial solution. He converted his Carrier from a 0.303in Bren Gun Carrier into a 0.5in Browning Machine-gun Carrier to be on slightly more equal terms with the opposition. Titch recalls that, 'We landed at Salerno and after being pinned down for some time,

Captain Crickmay was called to a meeting one evening. On his return he told us, 'We are breaking out tomorrow morning.' I asked who was and he said, 'We are.' And so we did. It was a pitch black morning when we started off with the engine ticking over and we expected to be blown apart at any time. However, it seemed that the Germans had pulled out the night before but that didn't stop the butterflies in the stomach. At least we did finish up with a carrier full of grapes and there were many adventures like going out on patrol and coming back with a couple of Jerry prisoners or the unfortunate Italian who came out to greet us in his horse and trap, when the horse stood on a mine and killed them both.

'One disadvantage of the carrier was that it did not have much in the way of armour and we had to use our ingenuity to improve the situation. We covered the machine with sections of spare track, gash bogey wheels and as many sand bags as the suspension would bear. These sand bags came in handy on the occasion that we happened to find ourselves in a partly ruined jam factory which Jerry had been using as a quartermaster's store. There was more sugar than we had seen in years: sacks of it. Well, of course, we couldn't let anyone know that we had borrowed anything we found in the factory, so we emptied the sand and transferred the contents of the Wehrmacht sacks into the WD ones. That was all right until it rained! The civvies were very welcoming: they couldn't believe that we would help ourselves to their grapes, so they showered us with bunches of them whenever we stopped. Although we filled the carrier with grapes and spent our time treading them, we never made any wine. In between stirring buckshee sugar in our char and treading buckshee grapes, we did some recce work until, suddenly, we were told we were going home. That increased our chances of staying alive, so we didn't complain. After handing over our equipment, I was not feeling too good and went sick and woke up three days later in No 65 Hospital in Naples. Diagnosis: pneumonia. Cure: stay in dock until the ship sails for home!'

Bob Lay suffered first from flies, then from dysentery, then from the MO, then from being bombed or strafed while in hospital. Altogether not a happy arrival in Italy, as he wrote. 'We embarked on a Tank Landing Ship with the tanks inside on the lower deck and the lorries and guns on the upper one. I had dysentery: there was a constant battle with flies; they fell in the tea and mess tins, sat on the other end of the piece of melon you were eating: they were everywhere and we took what precautions we could to cover our food and drink but no system was perfect. We had no warning that we were about to beach: I was on the loo and fell off. More seriously, drivers and others were unshackling the tanks. One of them, Skeels, was crushed and killed and another man was injured. Lined up on the beach we were shelled. I was on the floor of the tank, tied in knots with dysentery, being showered with sand every time a shell fell near. Later we leaguered in a tomato field and the MO was called. He gave me a large dose of castor oil and arranged for an ambulance. I arrived at the CCS on the airfield, an unhealthy place to be as it was bombed and strafed three times a day with great regularity. Despite my protests, I was given yet another large dose of castor oil. I exploded during the night,

'Many of the people in the large single-storey building were badly wounded and awaiting evacuation. The strafing rattled the tiles on the roof. The infantry between us and the enemy were having a rough time and were in dire straits. On release from the CCS I was a skeleton. I dragged my kit out to the road – I couldn't carry it – and got a lift back to the battalion. I remained in the Echelon until I had enough flesh on me to get back to the crew. During this time I was guard commander. One night we had a flash flood and I was washed out of my bedroll. Back on the tank, I found we were in operations in hilly country, off road and into tomato fields, orange and lemon orchards, olive groves. The advance had to be along roads which was a tortuous business. We weren't best pleased while we were attempting to cross the Volturno to learn that the Americans had held a Victory Parade in Naples.

'The towns and villages contained a striking comparison between the haves and the have-nots. The have-nots were the most abject people I have met; children were naked and most of their heads were a mass of scabs. The Bedouins in the Desert were poor but they had a dignity and a culture which did not exist here. When we saw the haves, we smelt the Mafia. 'Baron' Witty had left us but, at Aversa, he managed to get artistes from Naples Opera to perform for us in the local theatre: a good performance but I wonder what it cost in terms of rations.

'The advance was directed towards the village of Sparanise: oranges and lemons dropped into the turret. At one point we gained some high ground near a farmhouse where the reception was good. Remembering the famous exchange I had once heard between our CO, 'Screaming Willy', and Paddy Doyle, now back as a Squadron Commander, I did a quick flip through the frequencies to hear what was going on and to get the latest news. I was more than a little surprised to learn that the Americans had taken Sparanise. I looked around for some and then remembered that we were part of the American Fifth Army. Even so ..

Referring to one particularly gruesome incident, Bob wrote, 'Slowly, some women with hand carts and children came up the road to the farmhouse from where they had taken cover. Suddenly there were shrieks and yells. The men had stayed behind and each had a German bullet in the back of his head.' Further advances to the Garigliano river and Cassino were on the cards, Bob added, but the order came instead, 'Home for Christmas.' He, for one, had no complaints.

Bob was one of the many who saw the humorous side of the far from comfortable conditions which The Fifth experienced while waiting for shipping. Shepherds going the rounds of the bars, playing their bagpipes. Very romantic . . . but they only knew two tunes. Men paid a visit to Vesuvius when it was in one of its more playful moods and speculated whether the sleeping giant inside it had taken umbrage at the Navy's bombardment of its slopes. Shopping expeditions played a major part in the lives of those who had money to spend – as who hadn't for there had been few opportunities for spending anything in the last four months. As Bob wrote, 'Kit bags were stuffed with presents: as many as possible and the crevices filled with nuts. Silk stockings and ladies' underwear were in demand. The shenanigans in explaining the sizes to the shop assistants were something to behold. Spaniels ears came into it somewhere. Christmas was near and it soon became clear that 'Home for Christmas' had been hot air.'

Bob was, of course, not in a position to know how critically short of sea transport the Allies were, any more than the Divisional Commander, who made the promise in good faith.

One of the most interesting and closely detailed parts of Jake Wardrop's Diary is that which covers the Fifth Tanks' actions between the Salerno Landings and the crossing of the River Volturno. It is not possible to give this account in full for Copyright reasons.

Jake was promoted Sergeant in Italy and, by the time the Regiment sailed for home, was one of the most experienced tank commanders in the unit. Jake's military responsibilities were taken very seriously but this did not deprive him of his enormous zest for life or scant respect for those who wielded officious power, rather than true authority, over him and his mates and his men. This part of the Diary contains a great deal of pure Jake as well as matter of great military interest.

Not surprisingly, the Italian chapter starts on a bitter note. Jake felt very keenly the loss, from a trivial and avoidable accident, of his great friend Stanley Skeels. A good few 'Squareheads' were going to have to pay for that. The other enemies in the Gulf of Salerno were the mosquitoes who were present in unprecedented numbers. Curiously enough, Jake noticed, the 'old drinking gang were immune'.

Sgt Wardrop was always a shrewd observer of, and interested in, the local, native population. It was evident to him that, although the Italian peasants were genuinely glad to see the Allies, they did not expect that soldiers in khaki would treat them much better than those in field grey. Their gratitude when the MO treated two of their number, who had been injured in the fighting, stayed in his mind for a long time. On a more mundane level, they were frequently surprised to be given cigarettes or tins of bully beef in exchange for the grapes or tomatoes or onions which was all they could offer for their *liberatori* .

When 'C' Squadron reached the jam-factory-cum-Wehrmacht-sugar store where the Recce Troop had refilled their sand-bags, Jake's crew were not so worried about restocking their larder. There was, after all, plenty left for the civilians.

Rain, the Moaning Minnies which they had not heard since the Mareth Line and the Queens night fighting patrols, dressed in shirts and slacks with black faces and armed with tommy guns and grenades, became as familiar sights to The Fifth as had the endless, trackless Desert. The retreating Boche often did no more than lay mines as they pulled back, but the Italians in many cases had watched them and warned the advancing tanks. As the winter advanced and the enemy got more desperate in retreating, they frequently turned on the local population, knowing they welcomed the Allies and favoured the Partisans. It was not uncommon to come across a herd of cows, ripped apart by machine-gun fire and, once, the dead body of a boy of no more than fourteen. But sometimes it was the live girls that caught Jake's eye. When he wrote up his Diary, he regretted that he could not remember the name of a village where he had seen two 'smashers'! Conversely, Jake did remember Cardito, because it was there he encountered Rosetta.

At this point in his Diary, Jake Wardrop recounts the incident of Lieut Haywood and the time-fuses in the ammunition dump. 'Rita', as Jake inevitably called him[6], was the Troop Officer and Jake 'was pleased with him' for this initiative. He was equally pleased with him for his willingness to get out of the tank and go off, like Daniel Boone, to scout out for himself what lay ahead.

Whether legitimately or not, Jake escaped into Naples more than once and visited the Cathedral and the Castel Nuovo. He was depressed by the dirt but not surprised: being occupied by an army and then fought over didn't do any city any good. Jake also shows a surprising side to his nature, lamenting that he could not get down to the front at Santa Lucia where Axel Munthe used to bathe and cool his head from the effects of cholera. Not unusually, Jake made friends in Naples as he did wherever he went: particularly when there was music to add to the pleasure of the wine and the company. While The Fifth was resting in Aversa, Jake got his third stripe . . . and rejoiced that this qualified him for 'a bottle of Vat 69 now and then' in the Sergeants' Mess. As a Sergeant crew commander, Jake followed 'Rita' Haywood into Number 9 Troop, where, with 'Rita' as a Troop Leader, life was never dull. Nor did all the action take place in the tanks, as Jake's 'Mr Haywood' had a penchant for stalking the enemy on foot when doing so in the tanks was not an option. Sometimes this produced rather more excitement than he and his two Troop Sergeants bargained on but, at least once, it brought personal congratulations from the Brigadier.

For anyone else, with the prospect of returning home, the quiet life would have been the good life but Jake was not made that way nor, be it said, were some of the other Fifth Tanks regulars. 'Never a dull moment' was more their motto than 'Anything for a quiet life' and, with no enemy to fight, Jake needed to enjoy 'swinging a few right hooks'. To his credit – or so he claimed – he never swung at a member of the Regiment: there were always a few Yanks around as suitable targets. Incredibly – well, perhaps not, considering Jake was at the back of it – they even had an all-ranks, mixed genders, party. This was accomplished with the assistance of one Toni, an Italian guitar-playing acquaintance of Jake's who brought along some musician friends. This turned out to be an all-ranks, all Regiments do with Nursing Sister from the nearby hospital numbered among the local girls.

Although the Regiment was virtually confined to barracks [barracks being pretty rough tentage] and certainly banned from going far afield, Jake decided that afternoon visits to his own particular signorina, living a short ten miles away, were to be the order of the day. With disarming naivety, Jake comments at the pleasure of the fair Rosetta at the progress he had made in learning Italian. Jake broke all the rules and told her that he was bound for home. Did Rosetta think that her *Giovanni* had forgotten his promise of a *presto ritorne* when the war was over or did she ever learn that her 'dashing Tank Sergeant' never lived to see peace in Europe again?

But, at heart and by training, Sergeant John Richard Wardrop was first and foremost an experienced soldier and a fighter: he concludes his Diary of the Italian Campaign by saying, 'The big job was finished and another one would be starting soon. We had done well enough in Italy and had the valuable experience of operating in continental conditions. That was the reason we did not come home after Tunis, we had to be introduced to the conditions on the continent, so different from the Desert. And we had done so. We had learned some new tricks and improved on the old ones and now we were going home.'

That concludes the *Italian Idyll*. The story of The Fifth's Mid-Winter Cruise forms a brief interlude before the Saga of Shakers Wood.

THE OTHER SIDE

It was obvious, even before the new ad hoc *Italian Government sued for an armistice, that Kesserling, as the Axis Commander-in-Chief in the Mediterranean, could not depend on his allies. The Italian Army's defence of Sicily had been less than whole-hearted. The Anglo-American forces would have been across the Straits of Messina in one quarter of the time it took them had he not been able to reinforce the island with the re-constituted 15th Panzer Division and the crack Herman Göring Division.*

When the defence of Sicily collapsed, Kesserling had to do some strategic guess-work. That the Allies would immediately cross the Straits was a foregone conclusion. The key question was what else they would do. As Kesserling saw it, there were three options: the allies might 'go for the throat' by going straight for Rome with an air-borne landing to coincide with an attack from the sea; they could make a sea-borne landing in – probably – the region of Naples; they could content themselves with trying to roll the Germans up the length and breadth of Italy until they had trapped them with their backs against the Alps.

These possibilities posed the question of where and how to conduct the defence of the Peninsula.

Rommel, now commanding Army Group 'B' in the north, was all in favour of shortening the lines of communication (lines of communication being a matter on which he had greater practical experience than Kesserling) and of making no serious defence south of the natural defensive line of the river Po.

Kesserling on the other hand, despite the immediate difficulties confronting his forces in the disarming and neutralising of the Italian Army and Air Force, believed in defence in depth – or, rather, since this was Italy – defence in length.

If (and he was realist enough to know that this was inevitable) there had to be any withdrawal, he would make the Allies fight every centimetre of the way. He did envisage a landing in the Bay of Salerno and was rather more ready for it than General Mark Clark liked.

Above all, his orders to his troops were to make the Allied advance as difficult as possible. No bridge was to be left to fall intact into the enemy's hands: it was to be destroyed. No roads were to be left passable: they were to be mined. All necessary resources were to be denied to the enemy: electricity and water supplies, railway lines, communications, all were to be rendered inoperative. If the civilian population was thereby inconvenienced, well, so be it: this was war.

In the late autumn and early winter of 1943, the position of Germany as the remaining western partner in the Axis was critical. In Russia, the Red Army had recaptured Smolensk and, in November, it had cut the Wehrmacht's line of retreat from the Crimea and retaken Kiev.

Kesserling had little prospect of reinforcement to halt the Allied advances in Italy. Only the most desperate resistance would succeed in slowing it.

THE WAR CHRONICLE

1943

September	21	Free French forces landed in Corsica
	22	German Battleship *Tirpitz* sunk in Norwegian fjord – With the Royal Navy, the Army and the Royal Air Force committed to action as never before, the UK was plagued by strikes in many key industries
	25	Smolensk recaptured by Russians
October	02	Australians captured Finschafen in New Guinea
	05	US Navy opened bombardment of Wake Island in Central Pacific
	06	US Marines landed on Kolombangara in Solomon Islands
	09	Red Army occupied Kuban Peninsula in Crimea
	13	Italy declared war on Germany
	20	Wavell installed as Viceroy of India
	26	Over 2,000 people died of cholera outbreak in Calcutta

		– British forced to evacuate Kos
	29	Thames dockers went on strike – Penicillin acknowledged to be a major 'war weapon' after proof of successful treatment of wounds – Not so successful was the Archbishops' call for moral awakening: VD still considered to be most serious enemy on the Home Front
November	01	Russian forces cut off Crimea – US Marines landed on Bougainville
	06	Red Army entered Kiev
	12	German forces invaded Leros in Dodecanese
	13	US forces assaulted Solomon Islands
	16	Anglo-Italian defences in Leros compelled to surrender
	18	RAF dropped 250 4,000lb bombs on Berlin
	20	US troops landed in Gilbert Islands . . . and suffered heavy losses
	23	US troops captured Tarawa in Gilbert Islands: all but 17 of Japanese garrison of 4,836 found dead
	26	Allied aircraft bombed Rangoon
	28	Teheran Conference began: Churchill and Roosevelt met Joseph Stalin
December	05	Japanese launched attack on Port of Calcutta, killing 350 civilians
	12	Feldmarschall Erwin Rommel appointed C-in-C of 'Fortress Europe'

NOTES

1 Salerno. The spelling of Italian place names is taken from the 1999 series of Michelin maps. The spelling in the official histories, the War Diary and the personal narratives varies very considerably

2 River Volturno. The bed of the Volturno meanders inland from its mouth at Castel Volturno in an east-north-easterly direction for some 30 miles and then swings north-north-west for a further 25 miles into the mountains almost due north of the mouth. As an obstacle, it was only the 30 mile stretch between the Apennines and the sea which held up the advance

3 Nebelwerfer. This is a common misconception and is actually a misnomer. A Nebelwerfer is a smoke-throwing mortar, *Nebel* being the German for 'fog'. See Note 8 to Chapter IX on 'Moaning Minnies' for the probable source of the mortar bombs

4 40RTR. There was a splendid irony attaching to this contact between 5RTR and 40RTR, as the latter Regiment was later to be commanded by Lieutenant Colonel WM Hutton DSO MC * – better known as 'Fearless Jim' to the men of The Fifth

5 Jupiter Pluvius. The Roman god of rain.
6 Rita. With a certain lack of subtlety, the nickname in the 1940s for anyone called Haywood (Jake Wardrop spells it Heywood) was inevitably 'Rita', which was as near as anyone was likely to get on the field of battle to the glamorous Hollywood film star, Rita Hayworth!

INTERLUDE

. . . *Mid-winter Cruise*

December 1943–January 1944

After the inescapable delays and disappointments, the hopes which were dupes and the fears which were liars, The Fifth finally embarked on the *Cameronia* in Naples on Monday, 20th December 1943. There are a number of versions of the journey but two aspects of the voyage predominate: the call at Oran and the OC Troops' fanatical insistence on lifeboat drill.

However, before going into the story of the Regiment's return to the UK, there is the 'Maunsell's Odyssey' to be recorded.

For the Italian Campaign, Bob Maunsell had the unenviable appointment of Second in Command of The Fifth to Dicker Wilson. Bob's misfortunes began when the ship carrying RHQ broke down and was eventually towed into the landing beaches several hours after the Regiment had got ashore and moved into its allotted position. The RHQ ship arrived in the middle of a naval bombardment which made it inadvisable, once landed, to leave the beach. When RHQ did get clear, they attempted to rejoin the Squadrons by going straight through no-man's-land. Fortunately it was dark and the Boche didn't see them before they realised their mistake and re-crossed no-man's-land to the comparative safety of the Regiment's leaguer.

Bob described the Italian Campaign as being 'very messy and often unpleasant': he was therefore not altogether sorry, if a little surprised, to be sent for by the Divisional Commander and told that he had been given 'a special assignment'. This was to take charge of a party, consisting of an officer and one or two ORs from each unit in the Division, to go back to Cairo and there to be responsible for getting all the Seventh Armoured's kit and equipment – all the *lares et penates* which they had not been able to carry with them into action – safely back to the UK.

First problem: how to get back to Cairo? Not easily overcome as there wasn't any noticeable direct service and Bob's party seemed to have grown daily. Second problem: on arrival in Cairo, how to find anyone who knew where the Seventh Armoured's worldly goods had been stored? Third problem: how to collect them? Fourth problem: where to take them? After solving problems one, two and three, Bob reported to Naval Movement Control and insisted on seeing someone with at least three rings on his sleeves. When asked by a hugely amused Commander RN what he wanted, Bob simply said, 'A ship'. 'And what for, may one ask?' said the Commander. To which there was a nice simple answer. 'To get the Seventh Armoured Division's bag and baggage back to the UK, Sir.' 'Very well: that seems reasonable. We'll see what can be done.' And a ship was duly provided.

The trouble was that no-one, least of all Naval Movement Control, knew when the ship would sail, whether it would take the short way through the Med or whether it would have to go the long way round the Cape. The date of its arrival was anyone's guess. Bob was not unduly troubled by this, as he felt that he had fulfilled his orders. Nevertheless, he considered he had a duty to get himself and his party back to the UK as soon as he possibly could.

Naval Movement Control was sympathetic but conveying individuals back to base was not their responsibility. 'Try the RAF,' they said. Bob did. No one batted an eyelid. 'Have your party on four hours' notice to report at such-and-such an airfield.' he was told. Two days later, Bob was reporting to the War Office in London.

On being told to go away and kick his heels, Bob did one better. He went away and got married!

Since the lifeboat drill hit The Fifth before the *Cameronia* hit Oran, accounts of this drill come first.

The men under him thought that the OC Troops had his eye on an OBE for his safety record and recalled how he used to sit in his office and guff over the intercom for hours about nothing. By good luck, however, the loud speakers had a plug and whenever the OC's voice came over with its, 'Attention, please, OC calling', out came the plug.

In Jake's opinion the *Cameronia*, with 1RTR, 4 CLY, XI Hussars and 1 RB to keep The Fifth company, had the best troops on board that ever took to the sea on one ship. They must have been good, another man recalled, since Lord Haw Haw prophesied that the convoy would be sunk by 'our brave U-boats'.

The convoy, in fact, had American escorts and had no trouble from below the surface.

Dennis Cockbaine provides some splendid details of what he described as the antics of the OC Troops. 'He was determined to have as many boat-drills as possible and would cordon off various passage-ways to make the task of reaching one's boat-station more difficult. These drills were started by five blasts on the ship's siren to denote 'practice drills' and we were so fed up with OC Troops' broadcasting the failure of the Desert Rats to reach their boat-stations in time, that we took longer and longer to get into position, until one day the ship's siren blasted an actual warning and the aforesaid Desert Rats beat all records!'

Syd Storer took a somewhat opposite view – at first. As he said, 'I had suffered from enemy action at sea before when we had had no preparation, so I didn't share the majority view that boat-drill was an unnecessary waste of time. However, I admit that, as the voyage proceeded, OC Troops selected some peculiar times and methods to make his point.'

Accounts differ as to whether the stop-over at Oran was scheduled or was caused by sudden and exceedingly rough weather. Whatever the reason, the Mediterranean blew up a real storm and the convoy put into Oran on 23rd December. Accounts of what happened when the *Cameronia* docked give a wide variety of comic experiences.

Syd afterwards wrote, 'We docked at noon and were given permission to walk along the mole. As we reached the end and were about to turn back, we were hailed by a group of American soldiers. They were keen to know where we'd come from and where we were going: they accepted our explanation that we were unable to tell them. Their chief interest turned out to be souvenirs. 'Have you guys got any German Lugers, cameras or Iron Crosses?' was the constant request. We told them we had none but that we would ask around .. and come back the next day if we had had any success.'

Although no-one knew how long the ship would stay in Oran, Syd and his friends did ask around as promised. The ship remained the following day but there didn't seem to be much prospect of trade. However, 'It was 'Pedlar' Palmer who came up with what turned out to be a brilliant suggestion – a truly Cockney idea. We had been issued with a small ration bag for our midday meal on the day we embarked. Pedlar proposed filling these bags with sand out of the ship's fire buckets. On Christmas Eve we were again allowed ashore on the mole, where we met our American friends. We told them the sad news that no-one wished to sell their Lugers etc but Trooper Palmer had an article that might interest them. 'A bag of sand collected at el Alamein,' said Palmer. I was astonished at the reaction. Poor old Palmer was nearly killed in the rush. The bag quickly changed hands [and, knowing Pedlar Palmer, it wouldn't have changed hands for peanuts] and we promised to bring more the next day if we could persuade any of the others to part with their souvenirs.

'The afternoon and evening were spent in collecting and filling several bags ready for our next meeting on Christmas Day. On our walk round the deck after breakfast we noticed much more activity around the ship. Fortunately for our scheme, we were ordered to fall in on the mole at 1500 hrs for a route march through the town. Our American friends followed us and, when we fell out for a break, the frenzied exchanges took place. The number of Americans interested in 'el Alamein sand' had doubled and business was very brisk. More was promised for the next day if we were still in harbour.

'The tale of 'el Alamein sand' was spreading round the ship and the other troops were beginning to demand money for their ration bags. The gen from the crew on Boxing Day was that we should shortly be sailing. This proved to be duff[1] as, straight after breakfast and an early boat-drill, we were then ordered to fall in on the mole for another route march. A new batch of 'souvenirs' had been prepared but we were too early for the Americans. We returned to the ship and, as soon as we boarded, it started to move away from the mole.'

Later in the voyage, the boat drills began to get on even Syd Storer's nerves but that didn't stop him having at least one laugh. 'The boat drills were now something to be seen to be believed. Their object was to familiarise everyone with the layout of the ship. OC Troops with his assistants spent most of the morning marking companion ways with coloured chalk to show that they were bombed and marking large bomb craters on the deck. If anyone was seen crossing a bomb crater instead of finding another way to the lifeboat, that person was in trouble. One Trooper was caught crossing such a crater: when charged, he explained that he had used an imaginary plank that lay nearby to cross the imaginary bomb crater.'

All the souvenirs were not, in fact, duff. Carlo Carlsson *did* have a couple of Lugers in his kit bag and sold them 'for a tidy bit on the side'.

Pete Petersen took advantage of the interest the US 'matelots' from the escort vessels showed in acquiring souvenirs. Pete didn't fancy going decorously on shore and strolling up and down the mole. He reckoned – and quite rightly – that Oran night life would be more amusing. He and his new-found Yankee friends had a neat answer. By a simple change of raiment, Pete became a US matelot and duly went on the town, returning somewhat the worse for wear and long past the time for good little Desert Rats to be tucked up in bed.

All good things come to an end and the *Cameronia* duly put out to sea and joined a convoy of five other ships all 'bound for old Blighty's shore'. The convoy headed west into the Atlantic to avoid the Condors[2]. They parted from the African shore in the dark. At first light it was no more and many men suddenly found themselves overcome by nostalgia. It hadn't been so bad: they had seen the pyramids, they had met the Senussi: above all, they had beaten the Afrika Korps.

They passed the Azores, they saw the occasional Coastal Command Hudson[3], they looked for signs that indicated a landfall for Avonmouth . . . for Liverpool. On 4th January they saw the Irish coast on the starboard bow. Jake knew where they were going: before nightfall he had seen the Mull of Kintyre. At first light on Thursday, 5th January 1944 the ship was at anchor in the Clyde. The last words in the Diary of Wardrop of The Fifth read, 'I was home.'

And so, for the first time since Friday, 1st November 1940, was the Fifth Royal Tank Regiment.

THE OTHER SIDE

There isn't much to be said about The Other Side during the short time between The Fifth's departure from Italy and its landing in the Clyde. Mussolini had been snatched from captivity and was once again 'restored' to his position as the Italian Dictator. In reality, he was no longer even Hitler's jackal: he was Hitler's poodle. All he achieved was to arraign the nineteen members of the Grand Council who had deposed him and try them for treason. Like the Mouse's Tail in Alice in Wonderland: *'I'll be judge I'll be jury, said the cunning old Fury: I'll try the whole cause and condemn you to death'. Mussolini did just that and included in their number, his own son-in-law, his one-time Foreign Minister, Count Ciano.*

THE WAR CHRONICLE

1943

December	24	General Dwight D Eisenhower nominated Supreme Commander, Allied Expeditionary Force
	26	German Battle Cruiser *Scharnhorst* sunk in Atlantic
	27	Red Army annihilated German forces in the Dnieper Bridgehead
	30	Main Allied invasion forces successfully landed in New Britain
	31	'Culturally', 1943 was memorable for the films *Casablanca* and *For whom the Bell Tolls* and for the arrival on the scene of a young singer by the name of Frank Sinatra or, for the highbrows, of Jean-Paul Sartre's 'Existentialism'

NOTES

1 Duff. Meaning 'of doubtful provenance' or 'downright false'. The RAF claim this from the 1930s but, in fact [and Jake Wardrop would have approved], earlier and originating in Glasgow

2 Condors. The Focke-Wulf Fw 200C 'Condor' was originally designed as a long-range civil airliner. Converted to military use, its phenomenally long range and considerable bomb-carrying capability made it a serious menace to shipping. Fortunately for the Allies, fewer than 300 were built

3 Hudson. RAF Coastal Command's general duty, land-based, eyes and ears for convoy escorting

CHAPTER XIII
. . . *Shakers Wood*

January–June 1944

There stands at the side of a country road, running through woodland near Thetford in Norfolk, a monument to the British Seventh Armoured Division – The Desert Rats. The monument consists of a *Cromwell* tank mounted on a plinth: on the side of this plinth is a plaque on which are inscribed the Desert Rats' Battle Honours. This site was chosen to commemorate the fact that the Division, on its return from North Africa and Italy in 1944, trained for the invasion of mainland Europe in the general area of Thetford Forest. Of course the Division never fought a battle there: at least, not against the King's Enemies. Nevertheless, there are many who think that the inclusion of Shakers Wood in the list of Battle Honours would be fully justified. The deprivations inflicted on the Division by the War Office were wanton and were bitterly resented. The lack of sympathy shown to all ranks was a disgrace. But for the knowledge that there was still a real enemy to be dealt with on the other side of the Channel, less trustworthy and experienced soldiers might well have become mutinous.

The reason for choosing Thetford Forest was that the vital training for the planned invasion of Europe could be carried on there under conditions of maximum possible secrecy. There was some justification for this. The War Office knew that German Intelligence knew that the Seventh Armoured Division was back in the UK: they certainly knew that Berlin knew that an invasion of the continent was scheduled for 1944. As far as possible, however, they wanted to keep secret the how and the where and the when of that invasion. And part of the 'how' was the equipping and training of an experienced armoured division for a semi-amphibious beach landing.

Granted all this, the treatment of the Divisions returning from Italy was shabby by any standards. The Desert Rats and the men of the 50th Northumbrian and the 51st Highland Divisions did not want to be treated like heroes. They simply felt they should have been treated like human beings.

Disillusion set in from the moment the ships tied up in the Clyde. A security black-out was clamped down. There was no chance to let families know of their men folks' return, although Lord Haw Haw from Radio Hamburg had been telling his listeners that the Desert Rats were at sea (and would undoubtedly be sunk) for the last two weeks. Instead the men were marched onto a railway platform – Jake Wardrop may have known where he was but there weren't all that many Glaswegians in the Division – entrained into blacked-out carriages and sent on their way. Where? No-one knew: not even the CO, and certainly not the officers who, by some whim of the RTO, were kept separate from their men. The only thing they were told was that they were, on no account, to tell anyone who they were or where they had come from. As Dennis Cockbaine remarked, 'Since we had Desert Rat Divisional flashes on our battle dress sleeves, this all seemed a bit stupid to us.' And, as well, they had the ribbon of their Africa Stars on their chests.

The War Diary for January 1944 is remarkably uninformative and would not, needless to say, have recorded the men's feeling. As it happens, a good number of men did express their feelings and the 'pulse' of The Fifth is pretty fully documented. Above all, The Fifth was not a happy Regiment and, for this, the Commanding Officer had a lot to answer.

The Fifth did not move directly to Shakers Wood. Some of those who have provided accounts are a bit uncertain of their geography of East Anglia [a common fault] but General Verney correctly places the 22nd Armoured Brigade in a concentration area 'round Brandon'. According to Carlo Carlsson the Regiment initially landed up near Mildenhall where their presence was much disapproved of by the RAF who felt that they had explored and opened up that part of England and could, therefore, claim it as their territory. What they really disapproved of was the vastly increased numbers of throats down which to pour very limited quantities of good – well, wartime good – English bitter beer. There were a number of punch-ups and it was a relief to everyone when leave started and the men were told to report back from that leave to Brandon.

Syd Storer, on a note of surprise as much as gratitude, recorded that on arrival at some [unknown] destination at 0330 hrs and before turning in, the men were given a full dinner in place of the Christmas Dinner they had missed. There were other surprises, like being directed to a canteen on some station platform where 'the ladies' served them tea and cakes and told them it was all free. The ladies were equally surprised when the men produced lemons from their kit bags and gave them each one. Surprises did not end there: Syd was greeted at home with a welcoming meal of Spam and was amazed when the article that caused most excitement when he turned out his kit bag was . . . a tin of bully beef.

Another return home is described by Harry Ireland. After describing how the strict security of the 'secret' return of the Desert Rats greatly enriched the GPO, as every man jack who could slip off-limits for a few moments was seen to be queuing outside a telephone kiosk to pass word of his return, Harry goes on to say, 'I had a marvellous homecoming, arriving at a very drab railway station [Lime Street, Liverpool], half bombed and the city centre torn to pieces, walking up my street I noticed the air raid shelter had a white-washed sign – WELCOME HOME HARRY. I had arrived and, to prove it, there I was.

'Leave was spent going around the town and visiting relatives. Very enjoyable: I noticed the change in England from the one I left a couple of years before. Rationing – 2oz butter: 2oz tea, – sugar, meat, all on ration. Drab clothes, unpainted houses, bomb-blast boarded-up windows, altogether indicating a rough time. However it was still good to be home. A few nights before leaving, I'd gone out with friends. Not being accustomed to the black-out, a friend of mine said he would guide me. He did: smack into a pillar box. (My first war wound: a very bad gash on my forehead) 'Welcome Home'! Stars: I saw the lot!'

Pete Petersen remarked on one aspect of absence from home that was by no means a unique experience for returning servicemen. How the kids had grown! In Pete's case, his little sister was now working in a factory, making – of all things – tanks, and his kid brother, last seen as a schoolboy, was now a young man and far too big to be bullied any more. In spite of that, Pete recalls that it was a joyous homecoming.

Dennis Cockbaine remembers those early days for the daily routine, not of 5RTR training but, in the mornings, of the Eighth US Air Force bombers gathering themselves together with clockwork regularity in mass formation for their daylight raids on Germany. And in the evenings on a visit to a public house (called something like the Ferryman's Inn) situated at the end of the runway at Mildenhall, being suitably impressed by the Lancasters taking off overhead to bomb Germany by night. Dennis added, 'Many of our RAF darts-playing friends were never seen again.'

If Dennis got a friendly welcome over his pint, he was luckier than Bob Lay. He wrote, 'Shortly after arriving at Shakers Wood, I aspired to a half pint in the local pub and I walked to Swaffham, a small market town with a large market place. No lights, of course; the doors of all the pubs were shut. I espied a solitary male go round the back of a pub and I followed him in. They did give me a drink but they froze me out. Others must have had similar experiences for, when [George] Stimpson passed through Swaffham in a liberty lorry on the way to Kings Lynn, he leant out of the back of the lorry with a hand bell, yelling, 'Bring out your Dead! Bring out your Dead!' I later recounted this story to the lady curator of the Swaffham Museum. She was not amused.'

From Brandon the men filtered through to Freckenham Camp and thence to Shakers Wood which General Verney aptly described as 'a low-lying sandy waste with groups of decaying Nissen huts clustered beneath tall pines.' It was not the War Office's fault that the weather was foul but it was the War Office's fault that only minimal arrangements had been made to render these 'decaying Nissen huts' proof against such weather.

All the men quite understood that the whole Regiment could not be sent off lock, stock and barrel on long disembarkation leave but they felt strongly that some creature comforts should have been provided for them while they waited their turn to go on the meagre two weeks' home leave which was all they were initially allowed.

Altogether, circumstances dictated that the officers and men of 22nd Armoured Brigade, fresh from the Desert and Italy, were not going to take kindly to being sent back to school and told how to fight a war. As well, of course, as familiarising themselves with the new *Cromwell* and *Firefly* tanks. For this reason, it took far longer than it need have done for the various Regiments to realise that they *did* have much new knowledge to acquire and many new skills to learn before they landed in . . . well, wherever it was they were going to land.

Before embarking on the various accounts of life in Shakers Wood, it is perhaps as well to look at some of these differences which faced, among others, the Fifth Royal Tank Regiment.

First and foremost was the new tank with which they had to come to terms. The *Cromwell*. Although a successor to the *Crusader* 'cruiser' tanks which many in the Regiment had known, it was alleged to be a vast improvement. The crews looked with dismay at the vertical sides of the turret, at the stepped glacis[1] at the front of the hull, at the thickness – or, rather, the thinness – of the side armour and at the same old 75mm pop-gun which it mounted. It seemed to have few advantages over the familiar *Shermans*: admittedly it was much faster (36mph road speed against the *Sherman's* 24mph), its suspension gave a far better cross-country ride and made it a more stable gun platform: at 8ft 2in it was 2ft 2in lower than a *Sherman*: it was difficult not to be impressed by the fact that the engine was derived from the Rolls-Royce Merlin which powered the Hurricanes and the Spitfires and the Lancasters. But – and it was a very big but – what good was it going to be against Panthers and Tigers and what about the 88s? They'd make colanders out of these *Cromwells*!

Few of the old hands were impressed. Acquaintance with the *Firefly* version of the *Sherman* did cheer up the crews who were assigned to them. They soon learnt that they were to be in the minority. For the invasion, each of the three squadrons was to have four Troops: each Troop was to have three *Cromwells* – the Troop Officer's, Sergeant's and Corporal's with five-men crews – and one *Firefly*, with a four-man crew, to be commanded by a second Sergeant and to have the task of making holes in any of the heavy German tanks which might be encountered. For this purpose, the *Firefly* was equipped with a new 17-pounder main gun[2]. As events proved, the 17-pounder could make holes in Panthers and Tigers but not always and not without considerable risk to the commander and crew of the *Firefly*.

Nor were the men of the 22nd Armd Bde convinced by the argument that the *Cromwells* were not expected to fight tank-v-tank battles with heavy Panzers but to exploit break-throughs. They'd heard that one before. The Wehrmacht – especially when the Desert Fox was around – had a habit of not paying attention to the British Army's Manuals on Theoretical Armoured Warfare. Anyway, how did you exploit a break-through with 36mph *Cromwells* and 24mph *Fireflies*? Had nobody ever told the Top Brass that the speed of the convoy is the speed of the slowest ship?

Next came the realisation that the free-and-easy manners of the Desert, carried across to Italy as a matter of course, were things of the past. As General Verney points out in THE DESERT RATS, rations were far from generous, stores had to be strictly accounted for, fuel was only issued on a set scale and – the final insult – 'barrack damages' were applied to those damnable, decaying Nissen huts. Then there were a number of administrative demands which, as far as the Desert Rats were concerned, served no warlike purpose whatsoever. Harassed Orderly Room clerks certainly shared that view and Adjutants suddenly found themselves treated as junior – very junior – Staff Officers instead of as essential members of a fighting unit. Even going on leave was no longer the simple business of climbing into the back of a three-tonner and shouting rude things at the driver: passes had to be applied for in due form: travel warrants had to be contended with and – worse still – one was seriously expected to be back at the time stated on the docket or 'into the Guard Room with you!'

Against this, as General Verney points out, there were difficulties for the Top Brass. With an invasion being prepared, planning had to be spot-on or it was useless . . . and plans were badly disrupted when an additional two infantry and one armoured division were brought back from Italy and had to be fitted into an already over-crowded schedule. Time on the ranges was at a premium and a complete armoured division's guns had to be fired-in before the tank gunners could start to put in target practice with new and unfamiliar weapons. Perhaps the hardest restraint for the Seventh Armoured to accept was the crippling lack of training areas. With nearly four million men under arms on the Island there were none of the wide open spaces the Division had been accustomed to in the Desert but there was still need for Battalion, Brigade, Division, even Corps, training exercises. However, some training really was unnecessary and, on occasion, Divisional Commanders dug their toes in and said so, as was the case when the order went out that all Padres from Seventh Armoured were to attend the Army Battle School. 'Why?' General Erskine is reputed to have asked, 'Are you short of experienced instructors?'

It was some comfort to officers and men alike that no-one was playing clever tricks with the composition of 22nd Armoured Brigade. It still consisted of 1RTR, 5RTR, 4 CLY and 1 RB. The supporting artillery and other services remained as before. There was a change in the composition of the infantry: the old Queens Brigade became 131 *Lorried* Infantry Brigade – reinforced by the First Battalion of the Royal Northumberland Fusiliers as a machine-gun and mortar support battalion – to enable them to work more closely with the tanks, as had been found advisable in Italy. Not so pleasing was the stealing of the Cherry Pickers by XXXth Corps. [This did not last long: it was very soon realised that a Light Reconnaissance Regiment was far more effective working with an armoured division on a relatively narrow front than with a Corps: the XI Hussars returned to 7th Armd Div in time for Normandy] An innovation was the introduction, at Divisional level, of VIII Hussars as an 'Armoured Reconnaissance Regiment'. The Fifth were not quite sure what this meant but were only too happy to welcome back old friends from the Desert days.

Throughout the Division there were extensive postings away of old hands and postings in of new ones. The main concern of the old hands was whether these new hands – often 'mere boys, unacquainted with the razor's blade' – would fit into the crews and learn their jobs by the time of the invasion. Little did the old hands realise how much this was exactly the worry felt by these self-same 'beardless youths'! In the event, there was time for the crews to settle in and work together: perhaps even more importantly, there was time for Squadron Commanders to shake out any crews which were not settling in.

Among the new hands was Denis Huett who arrived in Shakers Wood when most of the old hands were on leave. To him and his like fell the job of 'housekeeping' in the bleak Nissen huts. This included filling palliasses with straw – trust the War Office to ensure that men returning from the Mediterranean had every modern comfort – and scrounging wood and coal to try to get the huts' two combustion stoves to give out at least enough heat to dry them, if not to get them warm. As Denis commented, 'There was no trouble for us in spotting the old hands. They were older, deeply tanned and wearing their Africa Star ribbons.' And, although certainly not 'bearded like the pard', as was Shakespeare's soldier in the Seven Ages of Man, undoubtedly 'full of strange oaths' – of questionable Arabic origin – and totally incomprehensible to the new swaddies. 'They were a good crowd of chaps: a bit wary of the newcomers at first but we soon mingled in together and many friendships, formed then, have lasted to this day.' Denis concluded.

Despite the intensive preparations, some of the tanks were very late in arriving. Denis Huett was graded 'gunner-operator' and allocated to 'C' Squadron as crew for a *Firefly*. This was fine, except that he never saw a *Firefly* until about a week before he embarked and did not know, until the last minute, whether he was to be the 'gunner' or the 'loader-operator'. [In fact, he was the gunner] His crew got their tank with little or no time to spare to prepare it, waterproof it and join the queue for their LCT in Felixstowe harbour. Denis' dry comment on this was that he knew the *Fireflies* were meant to be 'secret weapons' but he did think the crews might have been let into the secret a little earlier, as they were the ones who had to fight in them.

One aspect of settling in, which the older hands knew to be important, was missing. For nearly all the time at Shakers Wood, messing was by Squadrons from a central cookhouse. What mattered was not whether this improved the men's diets or introduced them to new gastronomic delights but that it deprived the newcomers of experiencing one of the most important aspects of crew life – brewing-up, getting fed, doing the washing-up and generally 'mucking-in' as a team in the minimum of time and under the most adverse conditions. Frequently crews (and regrettably this was often the case with a new, young officer) which had the makings of efficient fighting units made very bad domestic ones. This could, and did, lead to a lot of ill-will and even open friction.

So much for generalities. Life began to settle into a pattern for The Fifth as the last of the men to go on leave returned to the fold and training began. However, it was not until February that the pattern for the Regiment began to develop and, even then, the War Diary for the first ten days of the month only records, 'Large proportion of personnel returning from disembarkation leave. Otherwise no events.' The 'one-liners' from the War Diary for the rest of February read as follows:

11	'C' Sqn move from Freckenham Camp to Shakers Wood Camp (Nr Thetford) GOC 7 Armd Div talks to all officers of the Div in 'Desert Rats' Theatre.
12	'A' and 'B' Sqns move from Freckenham Camp to Shakers Wood. HQ Sqn move from Freckenham Camp to Betts Covert Camp (Nr Thetford)
13–14	No Event
15	2/Lt RLC Dixon posted to this unit from 100 (Sandhurst) OCTU
16	No event
17	1130 hrs Visit to 22 Armd Brigade by Lt General Sir BL Montgomery at Didlington. Entire Brigade was formed up in a 'Hollow Square'
18–20	No event
21	Capt (QM) AE Thompson posted to this unit
22	1130 hrs Visit of HM The King. His Majesty inspected D&M, Wireless and Gunnery classes at the tank park, Shakers Wood Lt FJ Jansen returned from No 1 VRD, Guildford with greater proportion of our W/E B Vehicles Lt EJ Partridge posted to 17 PW Camp Major AA Biddell posted to 107 Regt RAC
23	No event
24	Major JR Paton posted to this unit from 107 RAC
25	No event
26	Lt GR Bingley returns from Castle Bromwich with eight *Cromwell* training tanks
27	Lt DI Grahame-Parker collected ten *Cromwell* training tanks from Brandon Station
28	2/Lt RLC Dixon returns from Slough with three *Centaur* training tanks Lt JH Ridley posted to this unit from 30th Rft Holding Unit

All these events, or non-events, in the first two months of 1944 were in a winter which was, as all the wartime winters seem to have been, extremely cold. The Nissen huts were little or no protection from the cold, and whatever damp there was seemed to collect on the roof immediately above the men's beds and drip down on the unfortunate inhabitants. Fuel for the stoves was rationed and the ration was totally inadequate for men who had spent the last three winters in the Mediterranean.

Something of this is given in the account provided by Roy Dixon [later Major General RLC Dixon CB, CVO, MC but then, as emerges from his account, still burdened by the weight of a solitary pip on each shoulder]. He wrote, 'I joined 5RTR in the middle of February 1944 immediately on commissioning from the RAC OCTU. I was picked up from Brandon railway station in a 15-cwt truck by a soldier who appeared to have come from another world: sun-tanned, monosyllabic and wearing scrubbed webbing. We set off through the frozen Norfolk Countryside at a speed that clearly exceeded any limit, civil or military, but instinct told me that it might be unwise to draw this to the attention of my evidently veteran companion. We eventually arrived at Shakers Wood, a desolate Nissen-hutted camp in a pine forest, that housed the Regiment. Or, at least part of it, for I was soon to discover that a large proportion was detached on various courses and a not insignificant number of soldiers were absent without leave.

'The latter calls for some explanation. 5RTR had fought in France in 1940 and in the Desert and in Italy: most of the officers and soldiers had been overseas for several years. They were not only highly experienced but also conscious that they had done at least their fair share. They were unimpressed to find that they had been dumped in a singularly remote and inhospitable environment when, for the first time in years, they might have had the opportunity of seeing something of their families: and even less enamoured later to discover that, in spite of their past sacrifices, they were to be in the first echelon of the invasion of mainland Europe. Despite the Regiment's obvious professionalism, the state of morale was therefore an unwelcome surprise to a keen, inexperienced and no doubt naïve, new arrival. My personal morale was not improved by my being for the first few weeks the only person (not merely the only officer) without campaign medals. It was interesting, incidentally, that once it became fairly obvious that the opening of the Second Front was imminent the absentees returned to duty – their indiscipline more or less excused in the light of more important priorities.'

Roy went on to give details of the *Cromwells* and *Fireflies* and the training exercises the Regiment undertook in the nearby Stamford Training Area. Roy found himself, as a 'Two Loot' at the age of nineteen, the Troop Leader of No 3 Troop in 'A' Squadron. Here he was fortunate enough to have the extremely experienced Sgt Cornish MM as his Troop Sergeant. In accordance with Regimental tradition, as Roy freely admits, Sgt Cornish was effectively the Troop Officer while he, 2/Lt Dixon, found his feet.

'Meanwhile life at Shakers Wood was fairly grim, with off-duty recreation limited to the odd pub visit (and then only when transport was available) and occasional ENSA shows. Most evenings were spent crouched round the fire in the Nissen hut mess, the conversation largely consisting of exchanges about experiences in the Desert or Italy, expressed in a language laced with Arabic expressions incomprehensible to a Sandhurst-trained novice. Food preparation for all ranks suffered from shortages of facilities and even coal, and the Orderly Officer virtually took his life in his hands when asking 'Any complaints?' in the soldiers' cookhouse.'

However, as appears later, things got better in May when the Regiment moved to a new staging area in Orwell Park.

Still in Shakers Wood, there was always a chance of relief from what Harry Ireland succinctly described as 'Nissen huts, winter, cold, rain'. This relief often came from being sent on a course. There was a Divisional policy of training the crews in other skills than the one(s) they had already acquired or practised. Harry was fortunate in this respect: in spite of having been the main gunner in both the Regiment's *Grant* and *Sherman* tanks in the Desert and Italy, he was sent to Catterick on a wireless operators' course. When he asked his Squadron Commander why he had been chosen, he was told that heavy casualties were expected and that scratch crews might well have to be made up out of job lots, new recruits or less experienced men. As a result it was necessary to have experienced men with more than one skill: one experienced man, although not practising his usual trade, might make the difference between a reasonably efficient crew and a shambles. Harry could see the force of the argument . . . but didn't find the reason behind it very reassuring!

Titch Maple was another man to be sent on a course. Even though he was probably the most expert and certainly one of the most experienced wireless operators in The Fifth, he was sent down to Bovington for a 'refresher' course. Wandering around the beehive of activity that was wartime Bovington, Titch felt little nostalgia for his first days' soldiering. He quickly realised that there was scope for a certain amount of amusement on the course. With perhaps one or two exceptions, all the men in his group had 'been there, done that, got the T-shirt'. Or, if not the T-shirt, at least an Africa Star. On the other hand, none of the instructors had seen any active service – but yet they knew it all. Titch and the other Desert types took a malicious delight in listening with mock respect and pretended deference to all they were told, particularly when they were introduced to some 'new' procedure that they had been practising for years. Titch (who had the ribbon of his Military Medal as well as his Africa star on his battle dress) would sit gazing solemnly at the instructors while he and his fellow Desert Rats would say, 'Is that so, Sergeant?' or 'Well, fancy that, Sergeant.' 'You don't say, Sergeant!' or, best of all, 'What a good idea, Sergeant. Who would have thought of that?'

(To some extent this technique was also used in the Regimental lines.

Whenever some duty made it possible, an OR or NCO, who had a decoration, made an appearance before Dicker Wilson who did not have any.)

Jimmy Nunn, who had been called up in May 1943 and posted, first to the Inniskilling Dragoon Guards and then to 5RTR, arrived in Shakers Wood in January 1944. He became a Scout Car driver/operator in HQ Squadron. Unlike most of the new arrivals, Jimmy didn't notice the rain. He had been with the 'Skins' in Yorkshire and had forgotten what life was like without it. His first – and lasting impression – of The Fifth was of the friendliness of the ex-Desert types to the new recruits. He probably didn't realise that the long chats which they had while on guard duty were a god-given opportunity for these old hands to grip the newcomers solid[3] and tell tales which all the other old hands had heard ad nauseam. His second impression, as someone fresh from training, was that the attitude of the veterans towards military discipline was a joke. 'They were used to working,' Jimmy wrote years later, 'and being together in crews, and rank made no difference; they knew their lives depended on one another and military 'bull' was thrown out of the window. This was a far different army from the one we were instructed in and, frankly, I liked it.

'The veterans, at this time, were very bitter with the treatment they were receiving. Many had been fighting in the Desert since [the Regiment left England] and had not seen their families for three years or more. They had been brought home to fight on the 'Second Front' and only got two weeks leave on arrival in this country. Pamphlets were thrown out of train carriages protesting but it didn't make any difference.

'Shakers Wood for me was a very useful location as my home was in Cambridge. Brandon railway station was but a short distance down the road from camp and non-corridor trains ran direct to Cambridge. The MPs on the platform had an impossible task trying to stop soldiers jumping on the train just as it was pulling out to get a free ride.'

Not everyone who joined The Fifth in Shakers Wood had joined the Royal Armoured Corps or gone directly into the RTR. At least one man had no intention of becoming a member of a tank crew and was quite content to be – literally – a Private in the Buffs. As a Private in the Buffs in 1941, Ron Poore had done rather too well in some aptitude tests and, for this sin, found himself in Catterick with an embarrassing choice of trades laid out before him. He chose one at random and was sent on a course for 'Gunner/Mechanics' When qualified, and Ron Poore developed a life-long fascination for the internal combustion engine, Ron was posted to one of 'Hobo's Funnies', the CDLs or 'Canal Defence Light' tanks. Liddell Hart has a lot to say about the CDLs but, one way or another, their practical use was judged to be limited, with the result that many of their crews became redundant. One such was 6353816 Trooper Poore R.

Somehow, Ron Poore never really felt that the CDLs were *tanks* so that, when he joined The Fifth in Shakers Wood, everything was rather new.

Particularly the 'tank suits' and the tommy guns (which he coveted and was disgusted when 'these pieces of beautifully engineered weaponry were exchanged for Sten guns which looked as if they had been made from Grandma's old iron bedstead').

George Johnson, who had been with The Fifth since October 1942 and had been, among other things, 'Pluto' Ellis' driver, had an unusual advantage on the train journey from Glasgow. His father was a railway signalman and George knew a thing or two about how trains got themselves round the country. He recounts that, 'Before we left on the train [from Glasgow] I got a message to my parents that we would be stopping in Doncaster for refreshments. We were about three hours late getting into Doncaster station but my mother was on the platform with a basket of bacon sandwiches. Food was rationed at that time but my father had killed a pig earlier in the winter. Those sandwiches did not last for very long. It wasn't difficult for my father to learn where we were bound for: on his stretch of the line towards Lincoln. As we left the station, I was standing at the window and the train pulled up close to the signal box. I was able to have a few words with my father before he pulled the signal and sent us on our way to Norfolk. Next time I saw him, he told me with a straight face that he had had to stop our train to let a coal train in front of us clear the station.'

That wasn't the only occasion when George managed to visit his family. 'We were at Shakers Wood and it was Easter 1944. A tank crew was required to collect a *Cromwell* tank with a 95mm howitzer from the Fowler's factory in Leeds. Bernard Holder sorted out the crew: I forget who the others were but the crew commander was Pluto Ellis and I was the driver. We set out in a 15-cwt truck and got to Leeds on the Thursday before Easter to find Fowler's closed for Easter (and this was wartime). Worked that one well, didn't we? We all went our separate ways until the following Wednesday when the 15-cwt driver collected us and we went to Leeds. We couldn't have the tank that day, the kit hadn't been checked. I think we stayed at the YMCA in Leeds. We collected the tank on Thursday morning and called home three miles south of Doncaster. I parked the tank on the grass verge of the old A1 road and then walked the odd 300 yards to where I lived to collect my kit. Couldn't have left the tank there now-a-days, someone would have nicked it! We only stopped once more on the way home and that was to tighten the tracks somewhere near Peterborough. This delay meant that we couldn't quite make Shakers Wood in daylight, so we stopped another night in Wisbech, getting back to camp on Friday. Not a bad week's work!'

George wasn't the only Johnson with memories of Shakers Wood. Bryan Johnson reported to 'a large sprawling camp at Shakers Wood in January and was posted to 'A' Sqn: here I was told that I would become a member of a tank crew . . . when there were some tanks. The first event I can remember was the visit of HM the King to the Rifle Brigade billeted next door. [Here Bryan's account differs wildly from the official version in the War Diary and Syd

Storer's account] We were supposed to have suddenly heard of the visit and to have rushed out from our non-existent training to see our sovereign. He sat bolt upright in his Daimler and looked to me to be rather elderly and his face seemed to me to be made up. One or two soldiers were quite resentful at this 'visit' and showed their displeasure.

'When the Regiment moved to Camp R5 at Orwell Park, I was forgotten by 'A' Sqn as I had been operating the telephone switchboard. I was then sent on my own to Yarmouth where I was put in charge of a *Cromwell* for waterproofing.' Bryan eventually got back to the Regiment in Orwell Park and found himself posted to the Recce Troop in Brian Beresford's crew. Here, as he well recollects, he was gripped solid by one Cpl Willie Dovey.

There are many others who remember Shakers Wood without affection but not all that number who knew just how deep-rooted the malaise in the Regiment was. This had been mentioned by, among others, Roy Dixon and I received a long account of it from Dai Mitchell who, as an old soldier and a 'regular' at that, watched with dismay the steady lowering of the Regiment's morale and the total lack of understanding of the men's problems shown by the CO.

It is ironical that, while morale was far from high in Shakers Wood, the GOC-in-C of 21st Army Group spent so much time in touring British and Canadian – even American – units with the sole purpose of building morale, speaking to the troops, as well as visiting factories, depots and just about anywhere that an audience could be found. Monty's avowed purpose was to reassure all and sundry that whatever it was that we were about to do, we were going to do it successfully. Nevertheless, it was said that Churchill eyed Monty's performance somewhat askance and commented drily on the need to revise the rules about public utterances by members of the higher command.

In many ways, of course, Monty was a magnificent showman. His practice of appearing in casual dress, the black beret with the two badges, the sheepskin jacket, the non-regulation slacks, was purely for PR purposes and in no way reflected the standards he exacted from his subordinates.

Nor did it make him popular with the US generals. General Bedell Smith, Eisenhower's Chief of Staff, became increasingly critical, an attitude that hardened progressively when Monty's more experienced views as a field commander clashed with those of the Supreme Commander.

To what extent it acted on General George S Patton (an avowed critic of Monty) is hard to say. There wasn't much that anyone could teach Georgie Patton about showmanship.

Probably the man least affected was General Omar Bradley. It may be, however, that Bradley's elevation (as Commander of the US 12th Army) to equal status with Monty – not well received in British Army circles – was intended to show the world that the Americans also had a popular figurehead.

However, life and training had to go on and some idea of this can be obtained from the War Diary for March and April.

For March, the Regimental HQ was at Betts [Covert] Camp. The War Diary reads:

1	6 tanks despatched to Kirkcudbright for range firing under Lt Haywood
2	7 tanks despatched to Kirkcudbright for range firing
3	TEWT. Object: to study handling of tank squadron in close country in the new establishment
4	No event
5	Capt Daniels joins unit; posted to 'C' Sqn
6	Advance party under Brigade arrangements leaves for Kirkcudbright under Major Adams
7	Major Maunsell relinquishes duties of 2 i/c and assumes command of 'C' Sqn Major RB Fleming posted to this unit, assumes duties of 2i/c. CO and 2i/c leave by road for Kirkcudbright
8	No event
9	Main party move to Kirkcudbright Ranges leaving Brandon Station at 1430 hrs under Major Maunsell. Party consists of 20 officers and 220 ORs
10	1230 hrs Main Party arrive at Kirkcudbright and are stationed at Howells Farm. Capt Beresford collects 9 Humber scout cars
11–15	Regt firing on ranges. 'C' Sqn troop wins competition shoot CO and 2i/c arrive back at Betts Camp 2355 hrs Main Party leaves Kirkcudbright by rail for Brandon
16	1140 hrs Main Party arrives at Brandon Station 1200 hrs Road Party leaves Howells Farm under Capt Messent 1400 hrs CO's Conference with Sqn Cmdrs
17	CO's Conference: General discussion
18	No event
19	0900 hrs Admin Party leaves for Boynton Ranges (Suffolk) under Lt Garnett. Capt Chesterfield posted to 104 Holding Unit, Skegness 6 A/A tanks arrive
20	1400 hrs Road Party arrive at Betts Covert 1400 hrs Major Fleming to Bognor Regis to attend RAF demo
21	Parties leave for Boynton Ranges under Squadron arrangements
22	No event
23	Boynton party returns 1400 hrs CO's Conference: 'Bn exercise No 1'
24–25	No event
26	1400 hrs Bn exercise No 1 starts. Bn moved to night leaguer
27	0630 hrs Regt leaves leaguer and continues exercise 1040 hrs Exercise ends. Regt returns to Betts Covert 1400 hrs CO's Conference

Capt Huxley, LAD, attached to this unit from 131 Brigade
28 Padre Dickson arrives and takes up duty as relinquished by Padre Harris
29 Lt Medland posted to this unit from Pre-OCTU Alma Barracks, Blackdown
30 No event
31 CO umpires exercise for 131 Brigade
Strength state: 39 officers & 776 Ors

Bob Lay, having narrowly escaped a Court Martial for too loudly expressing his views on (a) *Cromwell* tanks and (b) conditions at Shakers Wood, was even less impressed by (a) his *Centaur*[4] and (b) the arrangements made for firing on the ranges. He wrote, 'Tanks arrived from the manufacturers and I found myself in a *Centaur*. The bomb ammunition for this gun had imploding qualities as for a Piat[5]. The idea of ranging shots on a Panther or Tiger did not bear thinking about. There were exercises from time to time in growing crops which horrified me. Farmers had limed their fields: on one occasion this resulted in severe eye problems for some of the drivers.'

Like others, Syd Storer was not best pleased by the conditions at Shakers Wood. The lack of training facilities and equipment worried him as much as the appalling conditions. However, as is often found in the accounts written by men for the benefit of their families, it is the odd incident, completely unrelated to the war, which finds space. Such an occasion was recounted by Syd of his arrival at Kirkcudbright with a friend [by name Oscar, no surname being given] and having hours to spend in a NAAFI Canteen while waiting for a train. There was a piano in the Canteen: simply because he liked playing the piano, Oscar started to play some of his favourite Chopin. By the time the train arrived he was giving a full-scale concert to a very appreciative audience.

Syd duly managed his leave and arrived back to find the whole camp undergoing an orgy of cleaning. This was in preparation for a visit from Monty, by then Commanding 21st Army Group. 'The day Monty arrived was bitter cold with snow. We paraded in a large field: four squadrons in perfect formation, facing inwards, 300 yards apart. He did an extremely quick tour of the living quarters which we had carefully polished and then came directly to the specially-erected saluting platform in the middle of our square. Monty raised his voice and said, 'I want to talk to you all. If you think I'm going to shout to you right over there, you have another think coming. Come over here!' The troops were non-plussed: we were not allowed to break ranks without permission. The Colonel waved us across and we took our positions like a crowd at a boxing match. Monty spoke about the fighting in Africa and Italy and told us much harder fighting was to come but it could be done with the new tanks and aircraft support we were going to get. He ended, as was his custom, by saying we would be told our role in much greater detail nearer the day.

'Hardly had we recovered from this visit, and another leave party had left, than we were told another high personage was arriving three days later to look over the Division and its equipment. There were so few of us remaining in camp that a programme had to be made up to cover all the places this person was likely to visit. It turned out to be HM King George VI. The thirty of us that were in camp were inspected in the huts then, while he went to the Orderly Room, we took up positions doing maintenance on the tanks and, while he was being shown some other equipment, we ran through the pine trees to salute him as he drove round a corner: then there was a final sprint through the trees to give him the traditional Three Cheers as he left the camp. We were given the rest of the day off to recover.'

Not quite the same version of the King's visit as that given by Bryan Johnson but no two witnesses ever see the same thing and, *par excellence*, no two memories ever play back the same record.

Syd found himself allocated to Sgt Fearnside's *Firefly* crew, which pleased him, as the other members had also previously served together as his crew in one of The Fifth's *Shermans*.

For April, the War Diary records:

1	2 *Cromwell* command tanks arrive
2	CO goes on leave. Major RB Fleming assumes command of the Regiment
3	Capt Bellamy-Brown posted to RAC Depot, Catterick 18 *Cromwell* tanks arrive
4–5	No event
6	0830 hrs Party leaves Betts Covert under Lt Butler to collect 11 *Honey* tanks from Slough
7	1700 hrs Lt Butler returns from Slough with 11 *Honey* tanks
8	2/Lt Hargreaves posted to this unit
9	Lt Col Wilson returned re-assumes command of Regt
10	CO's orders for Exercise 'Springbok'
11	2/Lts Crocker, Allen, Abram and Clarke posted to this unit from OCTU 2/Lt Sabatini leaves to collect B vehicles from Oxford 1640 hrs Regt leave to take part in Exercise 'Springbok' and leaguers for the night
12	0800 hrs Regt leaves harbour and Exercise 'Springbok' begins 1020 hrs Cpl Whitehead, 'C' Sqn, killed by smoke shell 1620 hrs 'Springbok' ends. Regt harboured for night in Frogshill area 1700 hrs CO's Conference on Exercise 'Kangaroo'
13	0745 hrs Exercise 'Kangaroo' begins 1525 hrs 'Kangaroo' ends. Regiment returns to Betts Covert Visit of Lt Col Dinham Drew to Regt 2/Lt Sabatini returns to Regt with 6 B vehicles

CO on Div TEWT
2/Lt Hargreaves and 2/Lt Heynes posted to 'A' Sqn: 2/Lt Crocker posted to 'C' Sqn
2/Lt Allen posted to 'B' Sqn
14 Future address of Regt – 5RTR. APO. England
15 CO attends Div TEWT
7882672 AUL/Cpl Dolby posted to HQ Sqn [Presumably it was Dolby who had the job of typing up the War Diary!]
Transport holidays discontinued
16 1100 hrs Talk by CO to all officers in RHQ Mess. Subject: Future Operations
1800 hrs 'A' Sqn plus 2 'B' Sqn tanks leave by train for Wickham Market
17 0400 hrs 'B' Sqn leave by tank train for Wickham Market. One tank fell off flat during loading, causing delay
2100 hrs 'C' Sqn plus two RHQ tanks leave by tank train for Wickham Market
'A' Sqn fire T and A AP practice at Boyton Ranges
Lt Jansen posted to 'C' Sqn from HQ
Lt Medland posted from 'C' Sqn to HQ and assumed duties as Wireless Officer
18 'B' Sqn fire T & A practice at Boyton Ranges
0630 hrs 'A' Sqn leaves for Honeywell Camp by road
C[ourt] of I[nquiry] into death of Tpr [Cpl ?] Whitehead
'A' Sqn fire HE, also Troop shoot at Titchwell Range
'C' Sqn and RHQ fire T & A practice at Boyton Range
1700 hrs Bde Cmdr addresses all officers in the Desert Rat Theatre on Exercises 'Springbok' and 'Kangaroo'
19 *No entry*
20 0400 hrs 'B' Sqn leave by train for Dorking
Major Paton takes over duties of Officer i/c Sgts Mess Accounts
21 0800 hrs 'C' Sqn plus 2 RHQ tanks leave Wickham Market for Dorking
1400 hrs 'A' Sqn leaves Dorking by train for Brandon
'B' Sqn fires HE and troop shoot
'C' Sqn and 2 RHQ tanks fire HE and troop shoot
'B' Sqn returns by train to Brandon
22 0900 hrs 'C' Sqn plus 2 tanks RHQ return by train to Brandon
Promotions:
W/Sgt Lyons 'C' Sqn promoted to SQMS
AP/L/Sgt Fyffe 'C' Sqn promoted to AP/Sgt
AP/L/Sgt Robinson 'A' Sqn promoted to AP/Sgt
W/Cpl Cooper 'B' Sqn to AP/L/Sgt
W/Cpl Gordon HQ to AP/L/Sgt
W/Cpl Onions 'B' Sqn to AP/L/Sgt

23	1400 hrs Visitation {*sic*] by Maj Gen Sir Charles Broad KCB DSO Colonel Commandant RTR
24–26	No event
27	1430 hrs Regt visited by Div Cmdr who addresses the Regt formed up at Betts Covert
28	Officers inter-squadron postings: Lt Babbage 'B' Sqn to HQ; Lt Sabatini HQ Sqn to 'B' Sqn
29	Awards: MID – Sgt Campbell 'B' Sqn AP/L/Cpl Hay HQ Sqn
30	1030 hrs Regimental Church Parade Service in Desert Rats Theatre conducted by the Rev AH Dickson

Bob Lay gave his account of the unfortunate Whitehead's death. 'One of the last exercises involved advancing closely behind a rolling HE barrage. For some reason, one of the shells was Smoke and not HE. This hit the turret flap of the tank on our left, killing the operator. I reported this on our wireless: we went over to the tank but there was nothing anyone could do. That wasn't the end of our troubles. By the time we caught up with the squadron, our turret was filled with white smoke from one of the phosphorous grenades: this didn't fit into the rack properly and had fallen out, becoming mangled with the swash pump coupling. My greatcoat was riddle with smoking holes.'

There is a simple entry in the War Diary for April which is of enormous significance for The Fifth. This entry is for Thursday, 13th April and reads 'Visit of Lt Col Dinham Drew to Regt'. That visit was to change the fate of the Fifth Royal Tank Regiment. However, before we come to it, some background information is required.

Whatever qualifications Dicker Wilson may have had for holding the rank of Lieutenant Colonel in 1943 [he had been a Captain in the Third Battalion in the summer of 1939] they were not those required in the Commanding Officer of a Royal Tank Regiment on active service. It is very unlikely that Colonel Wilson was unaware of the sentiment in The Fifth and any doubts he might have felt about his grip on the Regiment cannot have been allayed by the extreme casualness which all ranks displayed towards regimental discipline. Nor can he have been unaware that the men of The Fifth thought they had been treated very badly on their return from Italy and were far from being happy about the role they would be called upon to play in the forthcoming Second Front. Colonel Wilson appears to have attributed this latter malaise erroneously and unforgivably to the men being 'shy'.

It is true that part of the casualness towards regimental discipline included the frequent absences from duty – and not infrequently from camp – of all ranks, not excluding some senior NCOs. To counteract this and to ensure that the men were not, in fact, shy but only somewhat disobedient,

Colonel Wilson very foolishly issued an order that no-one was to leave the camp, except on duty, without signing a chit affirming the man's readiness to fight in the forthcoming campaign. This aroused extreme indignation and, among other things, put Dicker Wilson's officers in a very invidious position. Many – probably most – were unhappy about the morale of the Regiment, although they can never have doubted its fighting spirit. Nevertheless, they were under an absolute obligation to support their Commanding Officer and could, therefore, show no sympathy to the discontents of their men.

For one man, however, enough was enough. This was Sergeant Emmin Hall, the holder of a Military Medal and a long serving regular soldier, who had been with the RTC in India in peace time. Not only was Sgt Hall one of the most experienced tank commanders in the Regiment, with service in France, the Desert and Italy, he was so highly regarded that, for months in North Africa, he had not merely commanded a tank, he had been trusted to command No 11 Troop in 'C' Squadron.

Sgt Hall refused to sign the chit and, for this act of indiscipline, was duly put on CO's Orders[6]. On being paraded before Colonel Wilson, Sgt Hall told him straightforwardly and honestly what he felt and why he had refused to be humiliated by signing a chit. This resulted in Sgt Hall being immediately placed under close arrest to await trial by Court Martial.

When Dinham Drew visited his old Regiment he not unnaturally asked to speak to some of the men that he had known and fought with. One of these was Sgt Emmin Hall. On hearing that one of The Fifth's finest NCOs was being held in close arrest, Dinham Drew not only wanted to know why, he wanted to hear the reason from Sgt Hall's own lips.

There has always been a great deal of speculation as to what was said in that interview between Sergeant and former Commanding Officer but the official record speaks for itself. The War Diary for Thursday, 4th May 1944, as will be seen, reads, 'Lt Col RN Wilson and Major RB Fleming leave the Regt.'[7]

The War Diary for May 1944 reads:

1	Brigade holiday – [in lieu of] Cambrai Day Celebrations
2	Brigade holiday
3	Lt G Firth posted to 30 RHU. Advance party leaves for Camp R5 under command Lt Peel
4	Lt Col RN Wilson and Major RB Fleming leave the Regt Major RE Maunsell MC assumes command of Regt Lt DE Cockbaine promoted A/Capt
5	1400 hrs CO's Conference
6	1030 hrs CO's Conference
7	The Regt prepares to move to new location
8	No event

9 0700 hrs Main party leaves Betts Covert for Camp R5 arriving there at 1200 hrs
0715 hrs Soft vehicles under command Lt GH Ridley leave for Camp R5 and arrive there at 1115 hrs
Residue left at Betts Covert under command Major JR Paton
10 Camp R5
Regiment commences waterproofing vehicles
11–14 No event
15 2/Lt Clarke posted to this unit from 61st Training Regt and is posted to 'A' Sqn
16 Echelon personnel leave Betts Covert for Camp T4.
2/Lt P Alexander posted to this unit from 100 OCTU and is posted to 'B' Sqn
17 Lt Col CA Holliman MC* posted to this unit and assumes comd of the Regt
Major RE Maunsell MC assumes duties of 2i/c
1200 hrs CO meets all officers of the Regt
18 1145 hrs Griff talk by CO to all ranks: Subject – Future operations
Lt BK Pearson posted to this unit and posted to 'C' Sqn
19 No event
20 Waterproofing complete
21 The Regt allowed day passes to London, allocated as follows:
'A', 'B' & 'C' Sqns – 9 men daily
HQ Sqn – 13 men daily
1230 hrs Brigade Conference for all officers i/c ships: Subject – Marshalling
22 Officers i/c Ships meet Ships' Cmdrs
23 Wading trials. On return to tank park vehicles formed up as per Craft allocation
24 No event
25 Regtl day passes cease and all personnel confined to camp as from 0001 hrs
26 No event
27 2/Lt Smith posted to this unit and posted to 'A' Sqn
2/Lt Feaver posted to this unit and posted to 'B' Sqn
2/Lt Pendrill posted to this unit and posted to HQ (Recce)
558560 Tpr Glynn L awarded 2 years hard labour for deserting His Majesty's Service by FGCM on May 20th
28 0800 hrs CO leaves to attend CIGS Conference at 21 Army Group HQ
1900 hrs CO addresses all NCOs of the rank of Cpl and above: Subject – Discipline
29 0845 hrs CO addresses the Regt on future operations and prospects
1230 hrs All officers cmdg Crafts attend Conference at Brigade
2330 hrs 2i/c lectures all Sqn Cmdrs and Sqn 2i/cs on beaches etc

30 Final briefings and details as to ship personnel which are to be known as Craft Groups
31 No event

Meanwhile 7th Armd Div's preparation for the Second Front had to go on, and go on apace, as time was running short. The Regiment had most of its complement of *Cromwells* and they were ready, hidden under the pine trees at Shakers Wood for the last stage of preparation and transfer to the Concentration Area. However, the *Fireflies* had yet to be collected, tested, taken on the ranges and given, so to speak, their pre-operation medication.

After explaining that he was again with Sgt Fearnside and was to be on a *Firefly*, Syd Storer recounts his experiences of collecting this. 'At midday on the 16th we were told to be ready to move by lorry at 1400 hrs to collect *Fireflies*. We arrived at Slough at 1930 hrs and were given space to sleep in the local cinema. By coincidence the officer in charge lived locally, so he took one of the lorries and went home for the night, saying he would meet us at the factory at 0900 hrs next morning. Sgt Fearnside now was in charge of the party. He told us to be on parade at 0830 hrs in order to march down to the factory at 0845 hrs. We had a cook with us and he provided early morning tea and a good breakfast: then at 0845 hrs we paraded outside the office of the tank factory. Ferny went into the factory, which had been doing a night shift and, by means known only to himself, persuaded the management that it would benefit us if the tanks were said not to be ready until the following morning. The officer arrived at 0900 hrs and was told the tanks were not quite ready. He made an effort to get things speeded up for the afternoon but, eventually, gave up, saying he was going home for the day and would see us the following morning.

'As soon as he had gone Ferny gave us passes and told us that, wherever we went, we had to be back on parade at 0900 hrs next day. The lorry took us down to Slough station where we filled out our passes while waiting for the London train. Ginger Tracey, whose home was in Manchester, insisted that he was going home to see his girl friend. We didn't think he'd make it in time and we thought we were right when we were all back for breakfast next morning except Ginger. We marched to the factory without him. Just as the officer arrived, Ginger came running after us and tagged on at the end of the line. The usual inspection took place and the officer stood in front of Ginger. 'And where,' he said, 'Did you get to yesterday, Tracey?' 'Home, Sir. Manchester,' Ginger replied and we all winced. 'You will have your little joke,' the officer said and went off to sign for the tanks which were all lined up for us in the yard.'

The journey back to the Regiment was broken by an overnight halt in Watford where they slept in a local school. Here the boys from the school watched fascinated as the fitters worked late to repair one of the tanks which had broken down and had been towed into Watford. This was Syd's first close-up sight of the new 17-pounder. He was impressed by the length of the barrel which was so long that, for ordinary journeys, it had to be traversed to the rear and held on a supporting stand over the engine cover. Syd hoped it would turn out to be as good as it looked

They returned to the Regiment in Orwell Park, via St Albans and Sudbury [Suffolk] just in time to get the gun into commission to test and adjust fire on the ranges. After Ginger, the gunner, had satisfied himself and Sgt Fearnside that all was in order. Syd had a shot . . . and split a telegraph pole at 2,000 yards. The gun, the crew concluded, promised well for what was to come.

The crew found that they had a lot of work to do to catch up with the *Cromwells* in their Troop. The special AP ammunition did not arrive until the end of May and the waterproofing was more elaborate – and infinitely better – than that for the Salerno landing: it was a dawn-to-dusk labour to get everything done.

'On Saturday, 27th May we had completed most of the work and were warned to stand-by to move. This turned out to be only a short move, still in the same park, but all squadrons were now separate and in individual troops. On the 29th we were called to a special lecture on the front lawn of the large house in the park. First we were given a warning that all the gates would be shut and the fence patrolled by Military Police, anyone found trying to leave the camp for any purpose would be put on a charge.' [Syd had previously commented on the high barbed wire fences all round the park and wondered if these were to keep the goodies in or baddies out. Neither: they were to keep the baddies *in*!]

In the event, several men did try to break out, two of them being caught. It was said that the infantry were either less disciplined or more successful at breaking bounds. It was reported that there were more PBI that night and the next in the pubs than there were in the camp!

Syd continued by saying that the Colonel then told everyone exactly where the Regiment would be landing in France, proceeding across the beach to the promenade and so on. He illustrated his instructions with large-scale maps and repeated them to make sure that all his listeners were quite clear as to what they had to do. Colonel Holliman said that, once the concentration area had been reached, all The Fifth had to do was to carry out its orders and fight the Germans.

Two new narrators join The Fifth at this point. Neither of them has been mentioned in the War Diary. One because, as the historian Anthony Bridge said, 'History is a snob' and the first narrator was only an OR reinforcement and, as such, did not merit individual mention. The other because, although an officer, being omitted from mention in the War Diary was the sort of thing that always happened to him throughout his career in The Fifth.

The first narrator is Norman Smith, not only a narrator for the purpose of this account but, in his own right, the author of a book, TANK SOLDIER. In fact, this book is not merely an account of Norman's sexual romps from Norfolk to Hamburg but is also a vivid account of the life of a very young man in a tank crew, told as a very young man saw it. I can vouch for the accuracy of much of the story – militarily speaking – as Norman was the wireless operator on my tank during our winter in the Low Countries and right through to the day we reached Hamburg.

The other narrator is Eric Stevenson.

Norman Smith has something of interest – some of it even military – to say about life in Shakers Wood. He beat his call-up by volunteering at the age of 18 and enjoyed the miseries of the Primary Training Wing at Bovington, having expressed a desire to fight Hitler in a tank. When trained, he had an abbreviated posting to the Skins [then still in reserve and not yet part of 22nd Armd Bde]. On being transferred to 5RTR he was posted to 'B' Sqn. Like many another new recruit he was, firstly, impressed by the professionalism of the ex-Desert and Italy men, NCOs and officers (a very different sort of professionalism from the spit-and-polish variety affected by the Training Wing instructors) and, secondly, by the informal and friendly relationship between all ranks and between old and new soldiers. He was, however, left wondering just what was going on when he heard some of the near mutinous mutterings against the CO and his 'Number Two'. Norman never experienced anything personally of the CO or 2i/c but he could not help noticing how the morale of the Regiment shot up like a rocket when Colonel Wilson and Major Fleming departed.

After retailing his account of the firing ranges in Scotland (and his defeats at the hands of the one-to-one ratio of chaperones to maidens at the weekly hops in Kirkcudbright), Norman goes on to describe life in Shakers Wood and Camp R5. He paints a rather more colourful picture of this than his fellow 'B' Sqn narrator, Syd Storer. He appears to attribute some of the wilder break-outs from 'Stalag-R-5' to men of 5RTR when, in truth, credit – if that is the word – really belongs to 1 RB or the Queens.

All bad things come to an end and, eventually, Norman's tank was backed, last of all, onto an LCT along with three others from 'B' Sqn and the CO's tank. Colonel Gus, Bob Maunsell, as 2i/c, the Adjutant and the IO were all on separate LCTs to minimise the risk of loss of command during the landing.

LCTs were very different from LSTs which, in the words of Churchill's Directive, were 'great ships which can cast up upon a beach, in any weather, large numbers of the heaviest tanks'. LCTs consisted of a flat bottom, flat sides, a flat stern and a flat bow which did double duty as a landing ramp. They had an engine compartment, minute crew quarters, a minuscule bridge-house and a (usually) insanitary latrine cupboard. Their purpose was to get their cargo of tanks as far and as quickly as possible up the beach and, having discharged their load, back out to make room for the next one.

Eric Stevenson, who had been commissioned out of Sandhurst in May 1944 at the relatively advanced age of 20, provided the following account of his arrival in The Fifth. 'As there had been fewer tank casualties than anticipated since the end of the war in North Africa, I was told to report, after a short leave, to the infamous and enormous RAC Holding Unit at Catterick. Most of my predecessors from Sandhurst, for many months, had been posted there and were still there. Anticipating that the Army would operate on a first-in, first-out basis, I planned on a long stay and had brought my tennis racquet and golf clubs!

'I was directed to a Nissen hut and started unpacking. Within half an hour an orderly appeared and told me the Adjutant wanted to see me urgently. I wondered what I could have done wrong in such a short time. However, the Adjutant told me there had been a mistake in my posting and I shouldn't have come to Catterick at all. I asked him where I should have gone. He said, 'I can't tell you that – security.' Within 20 minutes I had repacked and, armed with an envelope which the Adjutant had given me, reported to the RTO at the station. The RTO put me on a train and gave me another sealed envelope. This went on all through the night and until early evening the following day. At each stop there was another RTO and another sealed envelope. Without the RTOs I would have been even more lost than I was as, of course, there were no names on the stations. Eventually I reached my unknown destination and was met by a driver with an unmarked staff car. Between us we got my trunk on the roof of the car (I thought it might go right through the roof it was so heavy). We set off and I asked the driver where we were. 'Can't tell you that, Sir,' was his only reply. So I asked what Regiment he was from. Again came the reply, 'Can't tell you that, Sir.'

'At dusk we arrived at a unit of *Cromwell* and *Sherman Firefly* tanks in a field. The driver took me straight to the Officers Mess Tent and got hold of the Adjutant: he took me to the bar and introduced me to Colonel Gus Holliman who said, 'Welcome.' I said, 'Thank you, Sir, but would you mind telling me to which Regiment you are welcoming me?' He was taken aback: 'Don't you know?' So I told him the story of my journey and congratulated him on his security. It was the Fifth Royal Tank Regiment and it was stationed in [the Thetford area of] Norfolk. To this day, I don't know why I by-passed Catterick and was 'selected' for The Fifth.

'I was a potential battle replacement and was attached to B Echelon under Major Dickie Paton. Almost immediately we moved to West Ham Football Stadium. The camouflaged vehicles were on the pitch and we slept on the benches under the roof of the stand. There was tight security and no-one was allowed out but I had to get rid of my trunk and all my sports gear. I got over this difficulty by volunteering to be the motorcycle liaison officer with Brigade HQ. This enabled me to reach a phone and to arrange – no easy matter in those days – for my trunk to be returned to Scotland. A few days later I was in London Docks supervising the loading of our support vehicles onto the ships. I asked why the lorries had large rectangular red or yellow discs on their windscreens. I was told that they indicated different rates of danger money for the dock workers. The Dock Unions had a powerful grip even in the middle of a war!'

But most important of all is the introduction of Gus Holliman. To begin with, he wasn't 'Gus' at all [I have a certain sympathy there, as for many years I lived under the sobriquet of Gus] but Charles Alexander Holliman. He was born on 26th May 1917 (which meant that he was not quite 27 when he was promoted Lieutenant Colonel and given command of The Fifth). Colonel Gus was educated at Dulwich College where he covered himself in sporting glory: particularly cricket, playing for Buckinghamshire while still at school. He went to Sandhurst in 1935, collected his cricket colours and was commissioned into the RTC in 1937. He was posted to the First Battalion and was with it in Egypt at the outbreak of war. His promotions were rapid and predictable. For some two years he commanded the Rhodesian Patrol of the Long Range Desert Group. He won his first MC in the operations at Sirte in 1941 and his second outside Tunis in 1943. In May 1944 Colonel Gus was second in command of 1RTR to Mike Carver [they were very good friends: Mike Carver being godfather to the son whom Colonel Gus never knew] and was the obvious choice to take over The Fifth at such short notice before the Invasion.

There is something, but not much, still to be said before the Regiment set sail for France. The War Diary covers those last few days by noting:

1 2100 hrs Regt commenced marshalling on the main Felixstowe-Ipswich road (Trimly Heath area) prior to loading

2 0615 hrs Regt moved to 'The Hards' Felixstowe to commence loading operation onto respective LCTs
1040 hrs Loading completed: flotilla moved to take position in River Orwell
1145 hrs Crafts in position and at anchor

3 0900 hrs Craft Commanders brief their crews regarding operations both immediate and future: *ie* landing area: Objective – Bayeux

4 No event. Flotilla still at anchor awaiting favourable weather reports

5 0815 hrs Flotilla moves up and puts out to sea. Regt due to arrive in France at D-Day, second tide, after 50 Div have made the assault the morning of D-Day

6 At Sea. Sea choppy: few cases of slight sickness

The lasting impression gained by all those involved in this stage of the Invasion was of the ruthless efficiency of the arrangements. Everything was organised down to the start position of every vehicle: everything was organised so that human needs – meals, sleep, the calls of nature – were subordinated to the inexorable turning of the wheels of an enormous, relentless machine. It had to be like that. Wellington is supposed to have been unimpressed by the efficiency of his antagonist's planning, preferring a looser pattern which allowed for things to go wrong, for loose ends to be tied up, for harness to be mended and the march to continue. It is difficult to believe, however, that he would not have given his whole-hearted approval to the meticulous planning which had gone into Operation 'Overlord'. Like a giant river, collecting tributaries as it flowed, the tanks trickled onto the LSTs and LCTs, the ships and crafts poured into the stream, the stream became a river and flowed into the sea. Roy Dixon gives a picture of this at the beginning of the next chapter.

Other accounts describe the comfort – or more usually the discomfort – of the individual vessels in which the men found themselves: the relative luxury of the American ones, with their endless supply of coffee and donuts (with bowls of sugar, no sooner emptied by the tank crews than refilled by a smiling black sailor from the USN) or the wartime 'utility' aspects of the Royal Naval vessels. Sea-sickness was an anxiety not just to its victims but to Commanding Officers who knew that their men's lives would depend on their complete fitness when the battle was joined and who could see that fitness being vomited out of them. Fortunately the convoy which sailed from East Anglia did not suffer too badly: the men from the Regimental support groups that sailed from the Solent had rougher seas and rougher times.

Once loaded onto the LST or LCT, the second lasting impression was that of isolation. Everyone from the Colonel downwards had his orders: everyone knew what to do once the loading ramp touched down. What no-one really knew was what was happening between that loading and that unloading. 'How long?' was the main question: 'What can we do?' was the second. There was no official answer to either. And, of course, if an answer had been given to the first question, it would have been twenty-fours out. D-Day was not to be Monday, 5th June as planned but, because of adverse weather conditions, Tuesday, 6th June. As to the second question, some had brought books, some had brought playing cards or a pocket chess set, some had brought a note pad or writing paper and were writing what they felt – in some cases, correctly – might be their last letter to their families. Each vessel had become a world unto itself: there was no communication between one vessel and the next, except for the occasional blasphemous exchange when one skipper felt that his neighbour was getting too close for comfort. Whatever the occupation of the moment, there was nothing to do but wait.

THE OTHER SIDE

The Anglo-American Army's advance up the Italian Peninsula had ground to a halt in front of the Gustav Line which stretched from Minturno on the coast north to Monte Cassino. Italy, from the point of view of military operations, is better suited to defence than attack and the Gustav Line, although farther south than Rommel had suggested, proved almost impossible to breach.

To break this stalemate, the Allies launched the assault at Anzio in late January 1944.

Kesselring therefore found himself effectively fighting on three fronts, since the Appenines virtually divided his defences (and the Allied attack) into two separate theatres of war.

German resistance in Italy was stubborn: some military commentators claiming that the Wehrmacht never fought so well on any other front. Nevertheless, two days before the Allies landed on the Normandy coast, Allied forces entered Rome in triumph.

On the Eastern Front, the tide was turning against Germany. The extent of the Russian successes can be seen from 'The War Chronicle'. At sea, the Scharnhorst *had been sunk.*

One change which was to affect the future conduct of the war had taken place in the German High Command. Feldmarschall Erwin Rommel has been transferred from Italy to the command of Army Group 'B' with responsibility for the defence of the Channel coast.

What Rommel found appalled him. Many defensive positions had never been completed and those responsible had made little or no effort to make good the deficiencies: after years of inactivity and of being steadily drained of men and matériel for the Russian Front, the standard of training and discipline of the Army of Occupation was below anything that he could tolerate. Many area commanders simply did not believe in the possibility of a 'Second Front' and an Allied invasion.

Fortunately for the Allies, Rommel's appointment had come too late to remedy all the defects and to bring Army Group 'B' up to the fighting standard of the DAK. However, Rommel did what he could and, unlike his masters in Berlin, had a shrewd idea where the blow would fall. As was his invariable practice, he studied the problem from the enemy's point of view, studied the ground and concentrated his armour. He had three Panzer Divisions within three days march of the Invasion Beaches. However, only one of these – the 21st – was available to him. The other two could not be employed except on specific orders from Hitler. Again, the Allies were fortunate: Hitler did not give his permission for this reserve to be engaged until too late for it to be fully effective.

THE WAR CHRONICLE

1944

January	19	Russian Army recaptured Novgorod . . . and
	20	. . . surrounded the besiegers of Leningrad, which had been under siege since September 1941
	24	Luftwaffe sank clearly marked British Hospital Ship off Anzio

	26	Rome put under Martial Law by occupying German forces
	27	Siege of Leningrad broken
February	04	US forces consolidated their positions in Marshall Islands
	08	First use by RAF of 12,000 lb bombs
	17	Parliament told of plans to create the NHS to give free medical aid to all
	26–27	In the middle of armistice negotiations with Finland, Russian aircraft staged midnight raids on Helsinki
March	05	Chindit Brigades landed behind enemy lines in Burma
	06	Strategic bombing of military targets in France begun as preliminary to the 'Second Front'
	08	Miners in Wales and Durham went on strike for more pay – A million Italian workers went on strike against 'Nazi Occupation' of their country
	10	Red Army 'crushed' German defences in Ukraine
	18	German Army occupied Hungary
	22	Japanese troops crossed Indian border and reached Mainpur
	24	Major General Orde Wingate killed in plane crash
	28	Government defeated by one vote on Bill to introduce equal pay for women teachers
April	03	Further attack on German Battleship *Tirpitz* again disabled it after repairs – Mount Vesuvius erupted
	06	Japanese 'March on Delhi' stopped on Plain of Imphal
	08	Russian forces crossed border into Romania
	10	Soviet troops capture Odessa
	14	US ammunition ship exploded in Bombay harbour, wrecking 27 ships, 40,000 tons of food and killing 740 people. Worst disaster of this nature since Halifax, Nova Scotia in 1917
	16	Red Army captured Yalta
	28	Peace negotiations between Russia and Finland broke down
May	09	Sevastopol [Sebastopol of the Crimean War] back in Russian hands
	18	Monte Cassino, after four major battles, fell to Allies

	19	The 'Great Escape' massacre. Gestapo captured and murdered 50 Allied Prisoners of War who had broken out of Stalagluft III
	29	American tanks clashed with Japanese armour for the first time in an action on Beak Island
June	02	Indian troops forced Japanese withdrawal from Kohima
	04	Allied forces entered Rome

NOTES

1 Glacis. On a tank, the forward part of the hull. As the word 'glacis' means 'the gentle sloping forward part of a fortification' the use of the word was generally a misnomer, the forward part of tanks' hulls being all too often as series of vertical planes

2 17-pounder. For details of this gun, along with others, see Appendix 2

3 'grip the newcomers solid'. Analogous with 'to bind', the common use of the verb 'to grip' is to 'bore the pants off ' one's listener. In 5RTR, however, 'gripping sessions' or 'gripping someone solid' did not necessarily or always entail boring the listener. They were either sessions of mutual reminiscence or, as in these cases, the recounting of events which had happened when a particular listener was not with the Regiment

4 *Centaur*. A *Centaur* was, for all intents and purposes, a *Cromwell* with the 95mm howitzer mentioned by George Johnson. These howitzers were probably fired fewer times than any other tank main gun in the British Army. So great were their disadvantages that they were frequently removed and a dummy barrel was mounted externally, thus leaving more room in the turret for squadron or battalion commanders to operate

5 Piat. More correctly P.I.A.T. or 'Projector; Infantry; Anti Tank'. This was an extremely effective, short range British-designed member of the general 'Bazooka' family. The projector was light and easily managed by one man: it threw, over a range of 100 to 150 yards, a projectile designed on the 'beehive' explosion principle. This, if it hit armour plating, a concrete bunker etc at near right-angles, punched a hole on explosion. Piats registered an impressive number of 'kills': greatly to the credit of the operating infantry, when the short range is considered

6 CO's Orders. NCOs and ORs who had committed disciplinary offences, with which the Officer Commanding the unit could deal, were paraded in front of their CO for him to hear the charge and, if he considered it proved, to 'order' suitable punishment

7 Departure of 'Dicker' Wilson. There was an unhappy but inevitable sequel to this. As appears later in this Chapter, 'Gus' Holliman took over command of The Fifth on 17th May. It was left to him to clear up the mess that Dicker Wilson had got himself into. No-one, and that included Sgt Hall, could be allowed to think that an act of indiscipline – no matter how justified in the eyes of the men – could get rid of the CO. Sgt Hall *had* disobeyed an order and had to be disciplined for it. Rather than disgrace him in the Regiment he had served with such distinction, Colonel Gus arranged for Emmin Hall to be posted as a Troop Sergeant in the Staffordshire Yeomanry

CHAPTER XIV
. . . 'The Second Front'

June 1944

If the difficulty of writing about the Fifth Royal Tank Regiment in mainland Europe in 1940 was the paucity of information available, then the difficulty of writing about the Regiment in mainland Europe in 1944 and 1945 is its prodigality.

In addition to the War Diary and the narratives of individual members of the Regiment, there are whole shelves of books which cover this part of the war. Much of what is found in the 'official' accounts is necessarily repetitious; some of what is found in private accounts is amusingly contradictory. This 'plethora of narration' is doubly unfortunate: it makes it difficult to produce a balanced account and, more seriously, it makes it look as if the Second World War was fought between June 1944 and May 1945, with the rest of the actions in which the Allies were engaged between September 1939 and August 1945 being mere skirmishes.

Because of this richness of information, the chapters dealing with the 336 days between D-Day and VE-Day inevitably contain far more detail than any previous chapter. For this I can only apologise: the material is there; it would be wrong not to use at least some of it. Anyway, as the historian, AJP Taylor, said, 'History gets thicker as it approaches recent times.'

For the first time, the War Diary[1] for the North-west Europe Campaign includes the complete Regimental Casualty Return from 7th June 1944 to 8th May 1945. The information from this tragic record is included in this and the following chapters.

This 'thickening of history' makes tracing the trail of The Fifth a complicated business. What follows is inevitably just one of many intricately interwoven trails: I hope that it will, nevertheless, give a complete picture of the part played by the Fifth Tanks throughout the whole of the campaign.

For one thing, many of the places which became all too familiar to the men in the British Liberation Army, and which became household words to the public at home, turn out to be little more than hamlets only to be found on the most detailed maps. Villers-Bocage, for example, rates only two lines in the pre-war *Michelin Guides Rouges* (one line of which is the name and address of the local Michelin stockist) and is listed as having some 1,000 inhabitants. It is

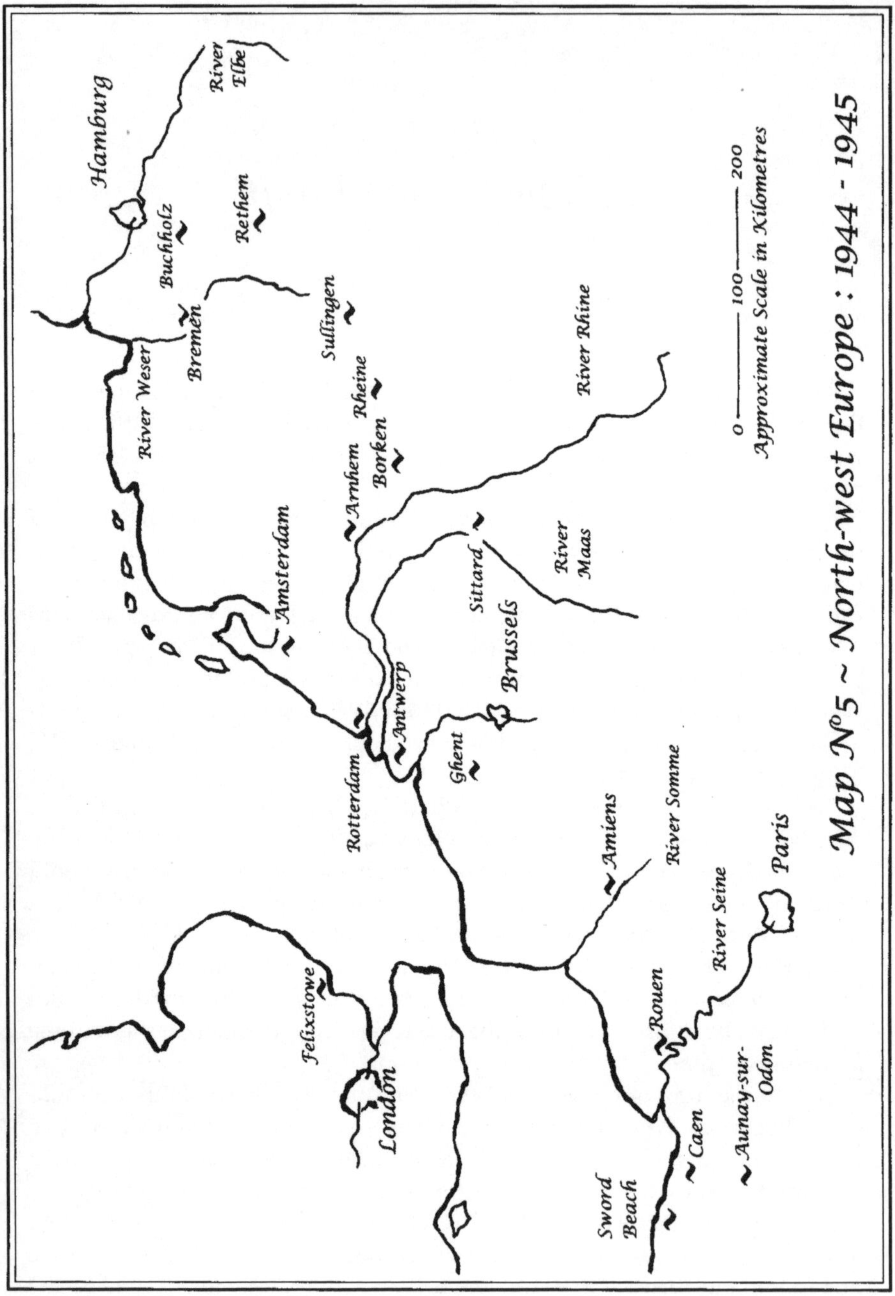

Map No5 ~ North-west Europe : 1944 - 1945

true that the 1946 Guide adds a third line but that only indicates that 'the village is almost completely destroyed'. Such familiar names as Bourguébus, Folliot and Grentheville get no mention at all in the Red Guides.

There are two aspects of the Battle for Normandy. One is the plan of campaign and the other is what actually happened. And they are very different stories.

Whatever the remit given to the Planners in the War Office was, the overriding political needs were two-fold: to liberate France and the Low Countries and to reach Berlin before the Russians did. There was a certain irony in this. Churchill and Roosevelt had tacitly agreed that, when peace broke out, the Soviet Union had to be made a partner in the new United Nations but they still recognised Stalin as a seriously disturbing factor in future world politics and a potential 'land-grabber' in Europe. Given these two needs, and the lessons learnt at Dieppe, the planners had to find a suitable landing place, a through route which led across the Seine and northern France, thence directly across Belgium into Holland: this then had to be followed by one which crossed the Rhine and the Central German Plain, over the Elbe and into Berlin.

There was no strategic significance in the liberation of Paris and, given de Gaulle's attitude to his Western Allies, not much political advantage either. It became, nevertheless, a major counter in the defeat of Hitler's Germany but whether it expedited the North-west Europe Campaign or not is another matter.

It was the unstated hope of the Western Allies that the cross-channel invasion of the Continent in June, coupled with the campaign in Italy and the intended landings in the south of France, would force Hitler to sue for peace by the end of the year. It appeared inconceivable to the Western Leaders that the Third Reich could continue to fight on four fronts – the aerial bombardment of Germany effectively making a fifth – for almost another year. Early capitulation might normally have been the case but Germany was not ruled by a normal man. If it was the Allies' intention to accept only unconditional surrender, it was Hitler's intention to concede only unconditional defeat.

In other words, the ideal scenario would have been for the Western Allies to have cleared the Axis forces out of the occupied territories and to have advanced across Germany before winter set in, forcing Hitler to see Germany occupied by his enemies in the West rather than his enemy in the East.

None of this happened and the writing was on the wall by D+3.

Except for the occasional surrender of non-German elements within it, the Wehrmacht fought with the same tenacity in Normandy as they were fighting in Italy: they proved to be, if not as well equipped, at least as skilful in warfare as ever, and they were tactically better disposed than had been anticipated.

Masterly though the selection of the Normandy beaches had been in terms of facilitating the actual landing, it was disastrous in terms of the terrain over which the invaders had to fight once the bridgehead was established. The War Diary and all the narratives and official histories say all that is necessary about the infamous 'bocage' and the skilful use made of it by the defending forces. Should it have been possible for the attacking forces to have made better use of it? According to one story, a captured officer from the Desert Rats' old enemies, the 21st Panzer Division, sent a message to the GOC telling him that 'it was about time the *Desert Mice* learnt that they were no longer in the Desert.' The proof of every pudding, however, is in the eating. Against almost impossible odds and with every advantage of terrain favouring the Germans, the attacking force *did* clear the defenders out of the bocage.

But it took time and time was not part of the strategic plan. For example, Caen, like Bayeux, was meant to have been captured by nightfall on D-Day. So rapid a capture would have meant that Caen, with its valuable communications, fell into the Allies' hands almost unscathed. In the event, the city was not finally cleared of the enemy until the 9th July, by which time more than half of it lay in ruins and over 5,000 civilians had died in the almost ceaseless bombardment. Another factor which made defence easier than attack was the favourable position of the defenders with regard to road communication. Behind the bocage, and as freely available as the RAF's frequent attentions allowed, was a network of roads along which the defenders could move to meet any new thrusts. By contrast, if the Allies wished to manoeuvre, only the cramped country lanes were available to them. These were bad enough in the dry; well nigh impossible – often impassable – in the rain.

Viewed largely, Monty's plan depended on two interconnected factors; the rapid advance of the assault forces and the regular arrival not merely of reinforcements to replace losses, but of fresh troops to take their place in the ever-widening front which would open up as the advance continued inland. Logically, as the advance continued, there would be ever more space for the build-up of the matériel necessary for the advance: space being at a premium in the bridgehead until the capture of at least one major Channel port made the beaches redundant.

Whatever may have been Monty's calculations for 'his men', after the endless slogging match in Normandy which seemed fated to go on for ever, by D+90 – in other words, 6th September 1944 – The Fifth were in the outskirts of Ghent! So far, so good but matters got worse when the British and Canadians reached Holland.

The Allied invasion plans were helped by the belief, held by both Rommel (in charge of anti-invasion measures) and Rundstedt (German Commander-in-Chief West) that the blow, when it fell, would be struck in the neighbourhood of Calais. Against this eventuality, the German Fifteenth Army was held in readiness in the Pas de Calais. It is noteworthy that Hitler did not abandon, until two months after D-Day, his firm belief that another major landing was planned in the neighbourhood of Calais. This was not altogether his fault. German Intelligence reports on the number of Divisions still held in readiness in England were wildly inaccurate

Under these conditions it was not surprising that the opposition encountered by both British and Canadians on the beaches was no heavier than it was. That the Americans met such strong resistance on Omaha Beach must be considered to be one of the misfortunes of war.

In the event, the very mixed Axis coastal defence troops were spread thinly in the Arromanches area and, of the three Panzer Divisions held in readiness, only 21st Panzer Division was available. Incredibly, the other two Panzer Divisions – 12th SS Panzer and Panzer 'Lehr' – were retained in the back area and could not be moved without Hitler's personal and express permission.

Nevertheless, the presence . . . the predictably active presence . . . of 21st Panzer was enough to block Monty's plan for the early surrounding and capture of both Bayeux and Caen and the seizing of Mont Pinçon, the feature 10 miles to the south-west of Caen which dominated the entire area.

Another part of the overall problem, and one which greatly influenced 7th Armd Div, was the delay (caused by deteriorating weather conditions in the Channel) in the arrival of 131 Brigade and a substantial part of the Division's back-up services. As a result of this, what should have been a major advance, if not quite a break-through, became a series of costly skirmishes in a sector of Normandy scarcely as large as Greater London.

The outcome of these frustrating and often bloody engagements was, however, far more decisive in the long term than anyone in The Fifth could have realised. Although the three Armoured Divisions – Seventh, Eleventh and Guards – did not achieve the advances they had attempted to make, they effectively prevented the Germans from driving wedges between the invading Armies and thus pushing the Allies back into the sea piecemeal.

During Operation 'Epsom' (in which the Desert Rats were not engaged) the Germans lost so heavily in both men and matériel that, although 'Epsom' was not the success Monty planned, they were unable effectively to resist when the break-out was launched. What is also of great significance during the Battle for Normandy is that the bulk of the eight Panzer Divisions available to Rundstedt was facing the British and Canadians, leaving only some six mixed and infantry divisions in all facing the Americans.

It was not only the eastern sector which experienced difficulties in terrain during those June days. Monty had ordered one Corps of the US Army to break out southwards and then swing south-east while the other US Corps struck west to liberate the Cotentin Peninsula and capture Cherbourg – which it did on 29th June. If the Anglo-Canadian contingent had had to contend with the bocage, the US contingent encountered the 'marais' – wide flooded or swampy areas of land, impassable to every kind of tracked or wheeled vehicle. What should have taken days had taken weeks.

Because, unlike in some of the earlier passages at arms, the War Diary gives a lucid account, it is used as the key to events and is elaborated by personal accounts. It will be noticed that many of these accounts overlap each other and the periods covered by the War Diary. This does not, however, interrupt the flow of the narrative

The War Diary for 7th June and for the rest of the month reads:

7 Regt landed on beaches at Hable-de-Heurat. One *Firefly* [but see below] and a CS *Cromwell* were lost by drowning. Owing to weather conditions and shipping congestion landing was not completed until 1500 hrs. Tanks still under the packet commanders proceeded to the concentration area, most of the dewaterproofing being done en route. Here could be seen the successful advance of 50 Div and Naval gun barrage. The Regt concentrated in the area just south of Sommervieu and was organised as fast as possible to meet expected enemy attack.
Casualties : None
Losses : 1 Honey [HQ] – drowned. 1 Cromwell [B] – drowned

8 'A' Sqn under comd of Major Macdonald were called upon to support 56 Brigade in clearing a pocket of enemy resistance in the Sully area who were situated in the Chateau there. The country proved to be very close in this area allowing Boche infantry to get very close to the tanks. On one occasion a tank under comd of Lt Garnett was boarded, prompt action by the officer using a Sten gun and his operator his revolver saved the situation. A lot of trouble was caused by enemy SP gun working its way into 'A' Sqn position in Sully village and succeeded in knocking out one *Firefly*. Even at this stage it was becoming very clear that fighting ranges would be extremely short: upward of 50 yards
'B' Sqn under command of Major Thompson was sent north to support the Commandos in their advance out of Port-en-Bessin and to consolidate positions. Here much sniping and close range tactics were encountered. 'B' Sqn returned to Regtl leaguer area at night. 'A' Sqn remained out in Vaux-sur-Ain area for one night. At this stage it is worth mentioning that a very good shoot was done against the Chateau in Sully, only marred by the fact that during the withdrawal for the night under cover of smoke, the only exit was a narrow bridge and the *Sherman* belonging to the OP of 5 RHA hit the bridge and fell over the side killing Capt Noble MC.
Casualties : [A] Tpr Lones H KIA
Cpl Fisher Wnd Tpr Davidson Wnd
[B] Cpl Davison H KIA Tpr Walker L KIA
Lt Wilde EAD Wnd Tpr Watters W Wnd
Tpr Moorey A Wnd
Losses : 1 Firefly [A] 1 Cromwell [B]
Enemy : 4 x 88mm, 1 x 75mm, 1 x 20mm SP, 1 Staff Car – destroyed
1 x 75mm SP – damaged

9 'A' Sqn return to Regt leaguer. 'C' Sqn leave to take up a position at Mornirel as close support to 50 Div in that area where they are

leaguered that night. The remainder of the Regt carried out maintenance during the day

1730 hrs CO attended conference at Brigade. Subject: Future operations

No Casualties or Losses

10 0630 hrs Brigade move forward with the intention of capturing the high ground between Hottot and Juguigny passing through FDL of 50 Div south of Bayeux, the Regt being on the right flank. Owing to close country the Regt moved one up with 'C' Sqn (Major Burt) leading. Progress was very slow. Lt Haywood at Folliot found himself near a small enemy leaguer where he put out of action a PzkKw IV before having to withdraw. 'B' Sqn were then ordered to try to find a gap on the right flank. The Village of Bernières Bocage was ultimately nearly surrounded but an SP gun, thought to be a Panther, knocked out 2 *Cromwells*. Meanwhile 4 CLY had reached Buceels on the CL and forward elements were reported in Tilly-sur-Seulles though this was thought doubtful. The Regt then leaguered in the Ellon [shown as Elion on Map 6] area for the night.

Casualties : [B] Tpr Langford E KIA Tpr Tutheridge KAW KIA
Tpr White N KIA
Tpr Harris C KIA
Sgt Cook C Wnd
[C] Lt Graham-Parker D KIA L/Cpl Perry HOL KIA
Tpr Walker WM KIA
Sgt Dixon Inj

Losses : 2 Cromwells

11 0430 hrs The Regt broke leaguer at first light and moved forward towards the Tilly – Balleroy main road in an attempt to cut the road and so push on to the original objectives. The village of Bernières Bocage was reported clear by Recce: this information proved to be incorrect as enemy infantry were still in nearby woods. Recce's leading tank was KO'd by an SP gun about a mile further on. Meanwhile one Coy of the Essex Regt occupied the village. The Regt then moved on across country, 'A' Sqn leading under command Major Macdonald. The large open space between Folliot and Langèvres was crossed by 'A' Sqn. On reaching the woods near Langèvres enemy tanks opened up and two *Cromwells* and a *Firefly* were KO'd. 'A' Sqn in co-operation with a Platoon of 'I' Coy 1 RB was ordered to proceed south through the woods to Langèvres. Good progress was made up to about 300 yards when the Rifle Sections who had got too far ahead of tank support were ambushed and suffered a few casualties. At this stage, 'A' Sqn halted, 'B' Sqn took up a position on the right, 'C' Sqn taking a position on high ground in the rear. It was impossible to get through the wood. Lt Heynes was on the right

flank of 'A' Sqn close to the road and was suddenly hit by a presumed Pzkw V which crept up along a sunken road unobserved. German Inf undoubtedly reported his position to the Pzkw V. Two members of his crew were killed, L/Cpl Day [? Hay] managed to escape although his leg was shattered. He was later picked up. The A[ble] tank of this Troop, commanded by Sgt Hill was also hit by the same gun almost immediately afterwards killing two of his crew. That evening the Essex put in an attack on the wood. The objective was taken and, although attacked by two Pzkw IV Flame-throwers, they succeeded in knocking one out with a PIAT and their position remained intact. That night the Regt leaguered in the area Folliot.

Casualties : [HQ] Tpr Richards F KIA Tpr Haw D KIA Tpr Carter J KIA
L/Cpl Hay Wnd
[A] Cpl Bridge WJ KIA L/Cpl Morrisey J KIA
Tpr Musson JF KIA
Tpr Holton A KIA
Tpr Hornsby L Msg
L/Cpl Johnson Wnd L/Cpl Day E Wnd
Tpr Branson Wnd
[B] Tpr Johnson G Wnd
[C] Sgt Whiting Law Wnd

Losses : 1 Honey 2 Cromwells

12 0430 hrs Regt took up defensive position on the high ground until the afternoon when the Brigade was ordered to carry out a flanking move and to capture the high ground SE of Villers-Bocage. Excellent progress made and the Regt leaguered at La Moulotière having met with no enemy opposition.

13 0500 hrs Advance resumed with 4 CLY leading and elements of 131 Brigade were left behind to form a firm base. All went well until one Sqn 4 CLY had passed through Villers-Bocage. Their HQ was then attacked by Pzkw VI [Tiger] tanks causing considerable damage. It now became clear that the 2nd SS Panzer Div was in the area and 5RTR immediately took up positions on the high ground east of the village Amaye-sur-Seulles. Again the country was very close and as the enemy attacked it was clear that his Inf were employed as eyes for the tanks. They advanced; drew our fire and then returned to point out our locations to the tank commanders who dealt with the targets. Fighting of this nature carried on throughout the day. The Regt leaguered for the night in 'Squadron Boxes'. 4 CLY, XI and VIII H[ussars] formed a close Brigade leaguer, 131 Brigade forming an outer perimeter.

Casualties : [C] SSM Ramage W KIA Tpr Harper H KIA
Tpr Hope P KIA
Tpr Whitby C DoW
Sgt Fishwick Wnd Tpr Larner R Wnd

L/Cpl Rawlings Inj
Tpr Chorley W Msg Tpr O'Callaghan Msg
Tpr Lynch Msg
Losses : 4 Cromwells
Enemy : 1 Pzkw IV

14 The day was quiet Regt being on the defensive and strengthened their positions all round. Towards evening a strong enemy attack was launched and this was thrown back with considerable losses to the enemy, official figures unknown but estimated losses were 8 tanks destroyed and approximately 500 infantry. RAF using rocket-bombs attack Villers-Bocage. At 2300 hrs the Brigade was ordered to withdraw to an area La Moulotière as the left flank was far too exposed, destroying all equipment which dropped out en route. This was done under cover of a heavy bombing attack on the enemy positions. Travelled all night, being the last unit to leave the area.
No Casualties or Losses

15 1430 hrs 'A' Sqn took up positions at La Paumerie. Remainder of Regt carried out maintenance
Casualties : [C] Tpr Johnson G Wnd
Losses: 1 Cromwell

16 1400 hrs The Brigade Commander addressed the men and thanked all ranks for the fine show which was put up at Villers-Bocage, this move being a tactical one had fulfilled its purposes
No Casualties or Losses

17 Lt Newton of the Westminster Dragoons posted to this unit
No Casualties or Losses

18–24 Squadrons still supporting 131 Brigade at La Paumerie
No event

18 *Casualties : [B] Cpl Attle J KIA*
Tpr Waterson H Wnd Tpr Thomson W Wnd

19 *Casualties : [B] L/Cpl Taylor AS KIA*
Sgt Onions G Wnd Tpr Waterson G Wnd
Tpr Spencely R Wnd
Tpr Sayell K Msg (POW?)
Losses : [B] 1 Cromwell

20–26 *No Casualties or Losses*

25 1000 hrs CO, Sqn Cmdrs and 2i/c attend Tank Busting demonstration near Balleroy by the US Army

26–27 No event

27 *Casualties : [C] L/Sgt Henry R DoW*
Major Burt P Wnd
No Losses

28 Major Adams rejoined unit and assumed command of 'C' Sqn
No Casualties or Losses

29 No event
No Casualties or Losses
30 Regt moved to Jerusalem area
Casualties : [HQ] Tpr Holland Wnd
No Losses

With the Commanding Officer of the Fifth Tanks on board, it is hardly surprising that the LCT which also carried Norman Smith was under orders to 'Press on Regardless'. Unfortunately, this is exactly what the Skipper did and, instead of making several soundings with his plumb-rod, he poked it down once, found what he thought was bottom, ordered the ramp to be lowered and gave the crew commander of Norman's tank the 'go-ahead'.

'We had the engine running already,' Norman wrote in TANK SOLDIER, 'and drove off and down into the drink: far too deep, far too deep. The first wave tore through all the ropes holding our bedding on the back of the tank; the second wave swamped the specially built air-intake chute on the back of the tank. We were drowned. The engine stopped and we had water over the whole hull and lashing around the turret. 'Knocker' Knight, our tank commander, leaped down into the water, opened up the flaps and pulled 'Ianto' Evans, our driver, and Billy Bilton, our co-driver out. It must have been one of those moments when the body provides extra strength because those flaps are very heavy and had the weight of the water on them as well. But he was down in the water and had them out and up on the turret before we realised what he was doing.

'We could hear our Colonel up on the craft shouting at the LCT commander that he was craven-hearted and had lost us a tank. The Colonel ordered him to back the LCT off and make another approach to the side of our tank; this time to run his craft in – never mind the mines – until he touched bottom. Meanwhile we were hanging onto the turret of our tank as the mountainous seas washed over us. One of the Pioneers – we had two with mine-clearing equipment on the back of the tank – decided to swim for it. He dived in but we never saw him again. Then, miraculously, a little Navy launch came alongside. We jumped in, the craft bumped its way to the beach and we scrambled ashore.'

After they got ashore, Sgt Knight led his crew to the comparative shelter of a deep German slit trench. Here they spent a cold, damp and miserable night, waiting for the dawn and the chance to get back to the Regiment. Here also, Norman encountered a phenomenon with which everyone who ever came in contact with the Wehrmacht sooner or later became familiar: the characteristic smell of the German soldier. None of us could define it: all of us could recognise it.

Titch Maple was luckier than Norman. In his case, the Skipper of the LCT stupidly cut the engine, with the result that the vessel was drifting back out to sea when Titch's tank came off the ramp. By inches, and in spite of half the

English Channel slopping into the turret, the Orwell Park waterproofing proved itself. Titch in the turret and two infantrymen hitching a ride on the back were soaked to the skin but the *Honey* made dry land. By way of explanation at this point, Titch Maple was in the Recce Section [or Troop] which was, for the rest of the war, equipped with an upgraded version of the *Honey* tanks first encountered years ago in the Desert.

A curious incident was – many years later – printed in a letter to TANK Magazine from a member of 'C' Sqn, Denis Huett. Denis wrote, 'In June 1944 I was the gun loader/radio operator of a *Firefly* tank in 5RTR. We arrive just off the Gold Beach at dusk on D-Day having left from Felixstowe on an LCT. Due to the huge numbers of boats of all kinds we were unable to land until the next day about 1100 hrs. Whilst waiting for a tractor ashore to hold us in position and keep the LCT steady for us to land, Sammy Hughes, the tank commander and I were looking over the side to see all the activities, when two Army officers came and stood by the side of us. One was wearing a khaki beret and Intelligence Corps shoulder badges and the other officer had a peaked cap with a red band, red [collar] flashes and had a small moustache. Sammy asked, 'How much bloody longer are we going to be?' There was no reply as they were too intent on seeing what was going on. The Intelligence Corps officer then called through a loudhailer something about 'Army Commander wants to come ashore.'

'Eventually our turn came to land. The front ramp was lowered and as the first tank of our Troop prepared to drive off, through about only four feet of water, these two officers climbed on and sat on the back. We thought nothing more of this incident, until a few weeks later, we saw a copy of *Picture Post* and on the front cover was the picture of an Army Officer, in a peaked cap with a red band, red collar flashes and a small moustache – the same officer we had seen on our LCT – General Dempsey, Commander of the British Second Army!

'I have never been able to solve the mystery of how General Dempsey came to be on our LCT. Did he come with us from Felixstowe? I didn't recall seeing any boats coming alongside or [anybody] coming aboard whilst we were waiting off-shore.'

Denis Huett never has found an answer to that one.

Bob Maunsell – having been separated from the rest of RHQ – found himself in part of a flotilla of LCTs that constituted a 'Deception Force'. While everyone else in 5RTR was heading for Gold Beach, Bob's flotilla was making a run towards the coast between Calais and Boulogne. As this run was made before the date for D-Day was delayed for 24 hours, when the flotilla changed direction and 'went for Gold', they were well ahead of schedule. Even running aground on a sand bank did not delay them: the skipper's efforts to get off the bank succeeded so well that they were still almost leading the Armada. Fortunately the error was detected in time and Bob finally landed when the Beach Master was expecting him. From there on, Bob described his role as

Second in Command as being a very mixed bag. Generally he was in charge of RHQ when the Colonel was off swanning – and Colonel Gus liked being at the sharp end: sometimes he acted as CO when the Colonel was at Brigade or Division: sometimes he was sent forward to see what was going on: sometimes he was left behind wondering what was going on.

The most unlikely story of The Fifth's arrival in Normandy was told by Arthur Crickmay – who swore that, however improbable, it did really happen to him. He had not been ashore very long but long enough to have some private business to attend to out of his tank. His attention was drawn by a nervous cough and an enquiry as to whether he was *un veritable officier britannique.* Arthur replied, in French, that he was indeed and had the speaker some useful information to impart to him about the enemy. The reply was negative but the speaker assured Arthur that he was the owner of a thoroughbred racehorse, which he would be ravished to sell to the gallant officer. With typical Crickmay *sang-froid*, Arthur replied that he would be enchanted to become the possessor of so noble an animal but that, regrettably, he had other affairs to attend to just at that moment.

Harry Ireland, now feeling very much the old soldier wrote afterwards of how, 'The young lads on the crew were all keyed up, just like I'd been in my early days. However, I wasn't going to spoil their interest and enthusiasm: I just kept mum. A marvellous sight awaited us on the other side of the Channel. The biggest concentration of ships ever seen: an Armada of every kind of naval vessel, also aircraft in their hundreds. What a sight! The landing on the beaches was a dry one, landing craft able to get up on the sands; not a wet foot. 'Good Show, Navy!' We had beach parties of all kinds: Engineers, Navy, Military Police, all doing their appropriate jobs in a fine manner. I'd noticed, going across the beaches, knocked-out tanks of a specialised type used for the early landings. Forty-eight hours ago we were all having drinks on Southampton dockside: now this. [Harry was in the replacement pool which sailed from Southampton two days before landing]

'Hearing, in the near distance, the gun fire brought it all back to me, so off we go to locate the Regiment. The beach-head was only a few miles deep and within the hour we joined the Regiment in action south-east of Caen. [Over the next few days] the fighting was very heavy and took its toll of the Regiment. Among the casualties was my best pal killed with all his crew (three months married: what a shame) and a lot of young soldiers first time in action. The Regiment had suffered heavily: just how right my Squadron Commander had been in his estimate. We were here to fill the gap but not enough; the Regiment was well below strength even after us joining them.'

Harry Ireland was both correct and incorrect in what he said about casualties. Every death is a tragedy, for 'no man is an island and each man's death diminishes us' and the Regiment's fatal casualties were twenty-two Killed in Action and two Died of Wounds. In addition there were twenty-two Wounded, two Injured and five men Missing. The Casualty List was, however, not nearly as bad as had been feared and the unit did not remain under strength for long.

'After a few days in action with very little progress, we were relieved and came out for maintenance and a rest. By now you could see the build-up on the bridgehead, tanks and troops occupying every field around. Although out of action, we were still within the range of the German guns and, from time to time, were heavily shelled, with casualties among the transport vehicles numerous. My tank commander was a sturdy chap like a little bulldog (tough). I'd been made up to Lance Corporal, the rest of the crew old hands. Bayeux had been taken on the first day's landing, so we baled in by truck and had a good look round.'

'Witnessed a thousand bomber daylight raid on German forward troops. 'What a sight: I'm glad they're ours.' The rest of June, news good, slight gains on all fronts.'

Lance Corporal Willie Dovey was still in Brian Beresford's crew but now in a *Honey*. A typical account of the conditions relates how the work of the Recce Section was almost impossible. Lines of advance were circumscribed by the character of the countryside. Detection of enemy positions was well-nigh impossible: Nature did the enemy's camouflaging for him. The Recce Troop was sniped at, blown up on mines, shot at by SP guns with a highly developed hit-and-run technique, frequently operating at a range of little more than 50 yards and commanding the only possible lines of approach. Recce units were not infrequently blamed for falling down on their job and failing to find an invisible enemy. This was grossly unjust: if the Boche wanted to remain invisible in the Normandy 'bocage' he could do so without difficulty until he had some bigger target in his sights than a Recce Section *Honey* or a LO's Dingo. It was the frequent practice of German FDPs deliberately to let Recce units through, expressly to save their guns for the tanks.

Normandy Veterans would probably not agree with the description of *bocage* given in pre-war editions of *Le Petit Dictionnaire Larousse* as 'pleasantly shaded woodland'! Post-war editions are more realistic and acknowledge that *bocage* describes the closely hedged fields, frequently of less than a hectare, the narrow, deep sunken lanes, the small farms with their scattered and often tumble-down outbuildings, the orchards with closely growing trees. What the dictionary does not say is that the lanes were scarcely wide enough for a tank and the dense foliage provided impenetrable cover for hostile artillery pieces. A type of country appropriated by *les Normands* to themselves in the name of such villages as Villers-Bocage.

Norman Smith, after a night in a second-hand slit trench near the beaches, was lucky in that someone had put two and two together and worked out where Knocker Knight and his crew were likely to be. In the middle of trying to persuade a Beach Master with a rapidly fraying temper to contact the Regiment, the crew saw to their surprise and delight one of the Echelon 15-

cwts drive down to the shore. Taking a last look at their tank which was then visible stranded 150 yards out to sea at low tide, they piled in and were soon re-united with 'B' Squadron. 'As soon as we got back to the Regiment I was put on George Onions' *Cromwell* as loader/operator. I was very fortunate in this as George Onions was a very fine man, as steady as the Rock of Gibraltar. 'B' Squadron had already been very much at the sharp end and my first day in combat was to be as testing as anyone could wish. We were operating immediately in the wooded bocage country which any tank man will tell you is just about the worst.'

Norman goes on to relate how his Troop was advancing down a typical Normandy lane: his tank acting as point tank, in other words, the one nearest the enemy in a part of the countryside which the enemy thought of as particularly belonging to him. They were crawling forward at about 10mph, 'hoping for the best but fearing the worst'. They eased round a corner and there, in front of them was the worst. A Tiger. Each saw the other at the same moment: each fired: each missed. George Onions was not the man to back off. He knew that it was no use firing AP from a low velocity *Cromwell* 75mm gun at a Tiger: it would scarcely scratch the surface but rapid fire HE might kill the commander or create enough damage to the gunner's sights to make the tank temporarily useless. Norman and the gunner got the 75 working like a Bofors while Sgt Onions gave the driver the order to reverse back round the corner. Sgt Onions was following laid-down procedure by manoeuvring his *Cromwell* out of the way and giving the Troop Leader a chance to bring the *Firefly* up in the hope of its being able to get a shot at the Tiger with its 17-pounder anti-tank gun.

What happened next was that Sgt Onions' tank fell victim to one of the hazards inherent in tracked vehicles which have the type of transmission used in the *Cromwells.* When reversing and turning, say, to the left, the left-hand track is locked so that, as the right-hand track runs, the tank pivots on the centre of the locked track and the front and rear ends in contact with the ground scrape across it. All too often on rough, stony or muddy ground, this scraping action collects spoil which either tears the track off the riding wheels or puts it under such strain that it snaps. In reversing round the bend, this latter is exactly what happened to Sgt Onions' tank . . . but not, luckily for them, until they were out of the Tiger's sights.

Now Norman and the crew learnt that that most hated of tank training exercises – repairing a track – was not just something that sadistic instructors inflicted on innocent new recruits. It was a matter of life and death. And, with a Tiger just round the corner, it was more likely to be a matter of death than life. While the *Cromwell* crew were at work, Pluto Ellis brought up a *Firefly* to try to get a shot at the Tiger. Unfortunately, it was the other way around and Pluto Ellis' tank was brewed up, killing all the crew members except the commander.

Although the rest of the Squadron stalked it, the Tiger got away.

Jimmy Nunn was the driver/operator on one of the Regiment's scout cars. Someone else on Jimmy's LCT benefited from the delay in launching the Invasion. He wheedled Jimmy into a card game and skinned him of the francs with which he had been issued . . . before they even set sail! Like everyone else, Jimmy was amazed by the size of the Armada, 'Ships of every description, fully laden with equipment and men, as far as the eye could see, left, right, in front, behind. There was little opposition. Our landing was good, the tide was out and a bridgehead had been formed. There were dead bodies lying on the beaches, some being lapped by the waves. It was then that I realised what war was all about. I was no longer a 19-year-old boy: in that short space of time, I had become a man.

'We then regrouped and were guided into a field for the rest of the night. SSM 'Knocker' Knight took over my scout car as he had lost his tank on landing in deep water. He was a veteran and I dare not repeat what he said about my first efforts at making a brew out of 'compo' tea. At least it was hot.

'I was used in the scout car as a general run-about until I was allocated to the Recce Troop with Sgt Tommy Marr [who is seen standing on the right in Illustration No 4] as my commander. In Recce we had both cars and *Honeys*, our role being the eyes and ears of the Regiment. Fortunately for us, the crews were not used by the Squadron Commander as cannon-fodder. We worked in pairs and reported back anything we found 'interesting' which had to be dealt with by the heavy armour. We were not meant to engage the enemy: only to defend ourselves if we had to.'

Alan Bashford, who joined The Fifth in Shakers Wood in February, should have been on the Normandy beaches with Nine Troop in 'C' Squadron as the front gunner on Sgt Harris' *Cromwell* but for a chance which may well have saved his life. A policy had been developed that each troop should, if possible, have a crew member who spoke German fluently. As this was not a very usual accomplishment, German-speakers were drafted in from *eg* the Polish, Dutch and Belgian forces and from other branches of the services. In addition, there were volunteers of exceptional courage, some of them being German-born Jewish refugees, who risked literally a fate worse than death if they were taken prisoner. Shortly before D-Day one such – a Pole, given by the Army the name of Paul Hope – was attached to 'C' Sqn and took Alan's place. On 13th June Paul Hope and the gunner, Jim Harper, were killed when their tank was brewed-up. Alan rejoined The Fifth on 22nd June..

In Normandy, Alan – like so many others – recalls the lack of sleep: five hours was a good night's rest. As soon as the tank was safely in the leaguer, the men realised how hungry they were but seeing to the tanks' needs took precedence over the crews'. One culinary short-cut was to put tins of whatever the 'Compo' pack provided on the tanks' exhausts: either the crew got a nice hot meal . . . or the tank got a nasty mess in the engine compartment when the tins got overheated and exploded.

Lack of sleep doesn't seem to have worried Pete Petersen whose whole attitude to the Invasion is commendably 'laid back'. 'The day came when we moved off to our port of embarkation which was Felixstowe. On 5th June 1944 we loaded the LCT but had to lay up for 24 hours because the weather had turned nasty. We eventually got underway and landed on the Normandy Beaches on D+1. Once we had landed in the face of very little opposition, we moved into a field and set about dewaterproofing the tank. [Telescoping history more than a little, Pete continues] 'We next pressed on down the road to Villers Bocage where we met some stiff opposition and my tank commander (can't remember his name) disappeared not to be seen again: the operator and I took command of the tank. That evening we had to disengage and withdraw to fresh positions. That night we withdrew further to allow a five hundred bomber raid to take place on enemy positions. We finally pulled far enough back where we were allowed to take a rest and, not forgetting the brew, we spent a couple of days here relaxing. We then moved to an area near Bayeux and experienced a bit of shelling. It was here we got our new tank commander, Lt Eric Stevenson. He came up to our expectations and gave a good account of himself. What more can a Trooper say?'

One 5RTR officer whose time in Normandy could be counted in hours was Eric Wilde, as it was here that he collected the second of his three Wound Stripes. He described his brief French 'short break' as follows. 'We landed without incident, dewaterproofed our tanks and moved to a concentration area a short distance inland. The following morning 'B' Sqn was ordered to move along a minor road a little inland, contact some Commando units which had landed on D-Day and then push on to the main road running south from Port-en-Bressin which was the boundary line between the British and American forces. I was leading the Squadron to the junction on the main road. I came under very heavy mortar fire but, with the high hedges, I could not engage any enemy and so needed to get across the road and into open country because I could not get off the road on our side of the boundary. Due to poor wireless reception, I could not get through to George Thompson, my Squadron Commander, although I was quite clear to the Colonel, Gus Holliman. I explained my problem to him and was asked to wait. He then told me he had been in contact with the Brigadier. He said I was to wait where I was and that I could not cross over into the American area, because they had not been able to contact the Americans and that, if I did so, there was a very real danger that they would think we were German and would fire at us or put us under air attack. So I waited. However, shortly after that, one of my tanks received a direct hit into the turret and brewed up and my tank was hit on the turret and I received a severe head wound and was evacuated to the UK.'

It was eight months before Eric rejoined The Fifth and he still had another Wound Stripe to collect. He doesn't mention it in his narrative but I shall, as I had, so to speak, a ring-side seat when he collected it!

Liddell Hart, who was not normally given to meiosis, described the first few days of The Fifth in Normandy as being of a very different nature from what the troops had been led to expect. As the War Diary recorded, the Regiment's initial contact with the enemy came not as part of a co-ordinated break-through but as support for infantry fighting limited-objective engagements. Events proved that this was typical of much of the fighting in Normandy. The break-through was still some way into the future.

THE HISTORY OF THE SEVENTH ARMOURED DIVISION: 7TH JUNE 1944 – 8TH MAY 1945 (originally published without credits in Berlin in 1945 and now re-issued by the Tank Museum) gives a clear description of the Seventh Armoured's North-west Europe campaign, being an amalgam of the Division, Brigade and Regimental War Diaries. It is therefore frequently worth drawing on.

According to this source, the build-up, largely because no unexpected enemy formations had put in an appearance (if one excepts two out-of-breath German reservist cycle battalions north-west of Bayeux), was sufficiently far advanced to launch the next strategic strike. This consisted of passing 22nd Armd Bde through 50 Div and pushing it south to test the strength of the defences. 5RTR led the advance and immediately ran into the difficulties of terrain and the enemy FDLs about which everyone has commented. The exception (as noted in the War Diary: the Troop Officer was 'Rita' Haywood) was the intrusion of a leading Troop into a German Panzer leaguer. The slow progress was due, 'once again to the infiltrating enemy infantry, snipers and strongly held road blocks'. Flanking moves were attempted but the plain truth was that there *were* no flanks and any tanks, attempting to work round a position, were met with exactly the same opposition as the main thrust on the Charlie Love. Occasionally, it is true, this typical opposition was varied by the presence of a well-sited, but well out-of-sight, Panther or Tiger or SP A/Tk gun.

At this stage a lesson, which really was learnt in Italy but seems to have been forgotten by the senior commanders, was learnt again at considerable cost. The lesson was simply that, in close country – and bocage is close country *par excellence* – tanks and infantry cannot operate in isolation. However, once the lesson was remembered and put into practice, 5RTR was able to renew the advance and the supporting infantry sustained fewer casualties.

When, at Ellon, Alan Bashford caught up with the Regiment he found himself as W/Op on Sgt George [Stimo] Stimpson's tank. This return of Trooper Bashford AH to 5RTR demonstrated one of the Army's more praiseworthy accomplishments: the almost uncanny way in which it was able to find, and return to their units, personnel of all ranks who had become detached. An efficiency only rivalled by the Army Post Office's achievements with the troops' incoming letters.

Another 'C' Sqn man was Stanley Bruce, the gunner in Sgt Wilcox's *Cromwell*. He recalled that, 'One night shortly after the landing a determined attack [was made] by the Jerries and the situation was saved by the murderous fire of 5 RHA firing over open sights. In spite of this fire, a couple of our tanks were hit. A rare 'baptism of fire' for a newcomer to the Regiment like myself. It was on the afternoon of 10th June that my Troop, now led by Lt Graham-Parker, attempted to take a cross roads in the Jerusalem area. The leading tank, which was Graham-Parker's, suffered a direct hit from a Pzkw IV and brewed up: Graham-Parker and his turret crew were killed. Only five minutes before this, my tank with Sgt Wilcox, had been leading the Troop, and had changed over just before our Troop Officer was killed.'

It was at this time that an unfortunate incident occurred, only mentioned in the Seventh Armoured Divisional history and hard to identify in the Regiment's War Diary. In the slow advance towards Ste Bazaire, about a mile north of Jerusalem, The Fifth had a brush with 8th Armd Bde. Eighth Armoured had not been informed of our presence[2] but was very well aware of the presence of German armour in their sector. Unfortunately it was easy to mistake the outline of a *Cromwell* for that of a PzKw IV, especially in bocage country and even more so, if the tanks were camouflaged. As a result, two 5RTR *Cromwells* were lost to 'friendly fire' before contact with 8th Armd Bde was established.

It was also about this time that the expression 'fighting at close quarters' became a reality for at least one 5RTR tank crew. Jackie Garnett, then a subaltern and a Troop Leader in 'A' Sqn, suddenly found his tank boarded by German infantry, intent on shooting him and dropping grenades inside the tank[3]. In this case, they had reckoned without their man: Jackie – like the goodies on the silver screen – was quicker on the draw than the baddies and, with the help of his W/Op, shot the invaders and saw the rest of the enemy off.

On 13th June an incident, recorded in a few laconic words, led to one of the most gruelling experiences of any members of The Fifth. Of that day, his twenty-third birthday, Bill Chorley, then the lap gunner in a *Cromwell*, wrote, 'We had to abandon the tank during the battle, due to engine failure. Frank [O'Callaghan, the W/Op], Bennie [Lynch, the driver] and I were taken prisoner.' Bill Chorley, many years later, wrote an account of his experiences as a POW and of the astonishing end to his captivity. This account is reproduced verbatim in Appendix 3.

Roy Dixon provided an account of an aspect of the Invasion which particularly appealed to him and, as things turned out when he attained senior rank, provided him with a lesson he never forgot in the way of planning and preparation.

He wrote, 'Each tank had been allotted a number so that, when we were lining up on the road to Felixstowe, we found a marker number (rather like a butcher's price label) had been planted at the road side. To me this was the first manifestation of the meticulous planning that subsequently evidenced itself in the whole embarkation process and which remains a vivid memory of the superb organisation and attention to detail. A less efficient preparation for action was the replacement at this eleventh hour of our Commanding Officer, despite the compelling need of a change having been clear ever since Italy. Nevertheless, the appointment of Lt Col 'Gus' Holliman was to prove a tremendous boost to morale in the form of an inspiring and much-loved leader: this, in spite of the fact that many in the Regiment did not even see him until we had crossed the Channel. On 2nd June the crews were ferried out to join the lined-up tanks and the slow movement down to the docks at Felixstowe began. As we passed through the town, people gave us cups of tea and biscuits and, just before embarkation, we were issued with some francs and a small brief case full of maps. This, incredible though it may seem now, was the first positive indication that we would be landing in France, rather than in Belgium or Holland. At some point in the early preparation, we had been told the serial numbers of the LCT in which each group of vehicles would be embarked but, in view of the hundreds of vehicles that were edging their way forward over a period of many hours, it was with amazement that, as my tank reached the 'hard', I saw an LCT bearing my allotted serial number come in. Yet another manifestation of immaculate planning and execution. Each LCT carried five tanks, so mine had my Troop of four and one from Squadron Headquarters. As soon as we were loaded the LCT moved out, sailed a short way up the River Orwell and anchored among the many other craft which assembled over the next two days. It is astonishing to reflect that these huge fleets were massing in ports all round the south coast without the enemy interfering – or apparently even receiving information of what was happening: largely due, of course, to our total air superiority. During this assembly phase Troop Leaders were brought together to receive our first battle orders, revealing that we were to land in the afternoon of D-Day in an area designated as 'Jig Green', part of Gold Beach, opposite Asnelles-sur-Mer [about one mile east along the coast from Arromanches]. The Division's mission was given as being to secure the Villers-Bocage area preparatory to an advance to capture Mont Pinçon and it was envisaged that this would take place at the end of the first week ashore. In the event, Mont Pinçon was not captured until the middle of August, two months after the landing.

'Though we did not know it at the time D-Day was postponed for 24 hours until 6th June on account of bad weather and we eventually set sail on 5th June on a course that took us past the Thames Estuary and Dover[4] before turning south across the Channel. The convoy was an amazing sight: a vast number of LCTs, many carrying barrage balloons for air defence, often so close together that there were occasional beam-to-beam collisions. The LCTs were mostly crewed by extremely inexperienced sailors[5] who were determined to stay together lest they got lost when darkness fell. The sea was still fairly rough and quite soon I was extremely sea-sick. There was no cover or accommodation of any kind, so I lay on a tarpaulin being periodically drenched with spray which dried as a salt compact on my face in the hot sun, praying for death by enemy or divine intervention. I later learnt that the

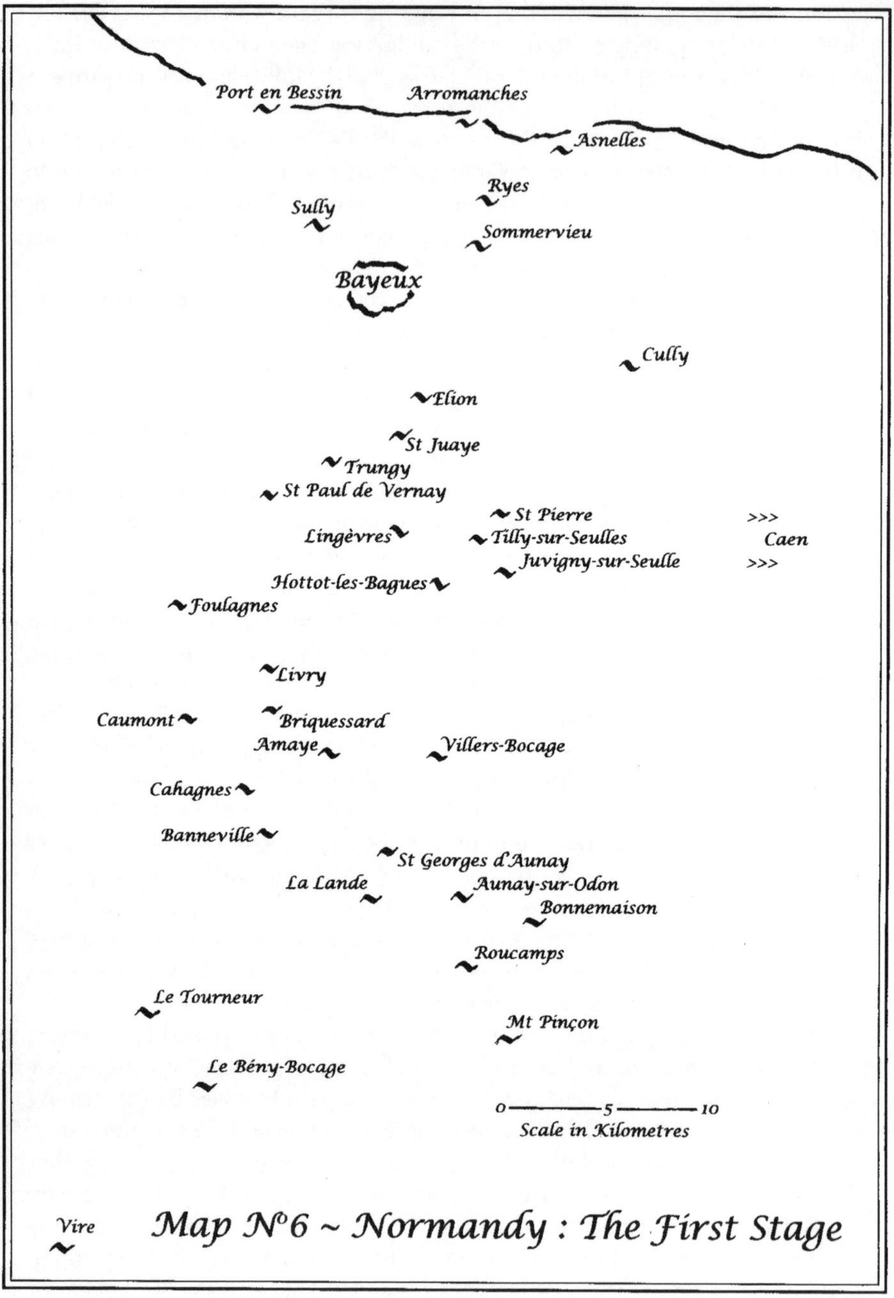
Port en Bessin
Arromanches
Asnelles
Ryes
Sully
Sommervieu
Bayeux
Cully
Elion
St Juaye
Trungy
St Paul de Vernay
St Pierre
Lingèvres
Tilly-sur-Seulles
Juvigny-sur-Seulle
>>>
Caen
>>>
Hottot-les-Bagues
Foulagnes
Livry
Caumont
Briquessard
Amaye
Villers-Bocage
Cahagnes
Banneville
St Georges d'Aunay
La Lande
Aunay-sur-Odon
Bonnemaison
Roucamps
Le Tourneur
Mt Pinçon
Le Bény-Bocage
0 5 10
Scale in Kilometres
Vire

Map N°6 ~ Normandy : The First Stage

members of my Troop found the condition of their Leader less than reassuring. Meanwhile, in the absence of any facilities on board, they had to prepare what food and drink they had on their petrol cookers beside the tanks.

'After two days and a night at sea we found ourselves hove-to off the French coast in darkness and it seemed that the weather had made us some 12 hours behind schedule and we were not likely to land until the following morning, 7th June. However, the sea was at least calm inshore and I was at last able to take some interest in events. The tracer of light anti-aircraft fire could be seen some distance inland and some aircraft seemed to be about but, as far as we could tell, the beach-head was secure, not under shell-fire, and a hive of activity. The next morning the LCTs carrying 5RTR began to move towards the beach. We saw one open its ramp too soon, so that the first tank out simply disappeared beneath the waves: from then on we were determined to get as far onto the beach as possible, though the Navy had other ideas, as they had to be able to get off the beach after disembarking us. In the case of my LCT we were able to achieve an almost dry landing. Once on dry land I well remember vowing that, if I survived the war, I would *never* return to Britain but would settle on the Continent rather than face another sea crossing – and, at the time, I really meant it!

'Now-a-days, people who were not there always seem to visualise the landing beaches as horrific sights with bodies everywhere but my recollection is that the beach organisation had done a magnificent job and that nearly all the bodies and most of the obstacles had already been removed. In fact the beach looked well under control, with Military Police marshalling the disembarking vehicles and directing them to the beach exits. We had been ordered to assemble at Sommervieu [a mile] east of Bayeux. Here we removed the waterproofing elements (that part of it that had not been removed by the explosives actuated from inside the tank) and generally got ourselves organised. I remember a few civilians watching us curiously from a distance, having been presumably sufficiently far inland to avoid the bombardment. The population had been evacuated [by the Germans] from the immediate coastal area but, in fact, throughout the whole of the Normandy battles we seldom saw much of any civilians either because they had fled or were hiding in cellars.

'After a peaceful night in leaguer, 'A' Sqn was given the task of clearing the chateau and hamlet of Sully just west of Bayeux which was still occupied by the enemy; although deeply bypassed. As I was the most inexperienced Troop Leader, 3 Troop was in reserve. It was, in the end, not much of a battle; the garrison (who seemed not to be Germans but probably Hungarian) surrendered quite quickly but not before two of the Squadron tanks had been knocked out, two 88mm guns destroyed and 2 Troop Leader, Lt Jackie Garnett, had had his tank boarded by some infantrymen. The following day, 9th June, the Regiment moved to the forward edge of the battle in the area of Juaye Mondaye.

'In leaguer that night, while we were replenishing, the commander of my *Firefly* tank, Cpl Bridges, came to see me and said that the day's events had proved to him that his nerve had gone (he was a veteran of the Desert and Italy) and that he could not face going into battle again. I told him that there was no way that he could be replaced in the remaining three or four hours of darkness and that he would have to carry on his duties at least for the next day, after which I would do my best to relieve him of tank crew duties. When dawn broke on 10th June the Squadron was directed southwards towards Lingèvres with two Troops 'up' [*ie* leading the advance], Jackie Garnett's 2 Troop on the left and my 3 Troop on the right. We had only advanced about a quarter of a mile when, while crossing some open ground around Verrières, I heard the loudest bang of my life and saw my *Firefly* tank career off into some woodland. We all took cover, as we were evidently under fire by some sort of anti-tank weapon: I ran over on foot to see what had happened to Cpl Bridges' tank. Having climbed onto the engine compartment and looked down into the turret, I nearly fell off again with shock at the sight that faced me. The shot had hit the cupola ring and Cpl Bridges' decapitated body had fallen down on top of the other two turret crew, pumping blood in all directions, where it dripped from the roof, periscopes, gun and everywhere. The gunner and wireless operator were lying on the floor of the turret, apparently wounded and soaked in Cpl Bridges' blood: there was no sign of the driver who had evidently baled out. Fortunately Jackie Garnett then appeared and reassuringly advised me to leave it to the others to deal with the situation and to return to my primary duty of leading the remainder of my Troop. This horrific incident on my very first day of my battle experience was etched more deeply on my consciousness by the sadness of Cpl Bridges' obviously having had a premonition of disaster and my inability to prevent it. In retrospect, it has remained something of a mystery to me that, while this incident (and many others that all of us experienced later) apparently had little if any effect on our morale or our ability to continue with our duties, far less horrific occurrences seemingly cause present-day soldiers to need psychological support. Somehow our generation apparently knew instinctively that war would mean death and injury and accepted them without undue emotion when they did occur.

'For the next two days we attempted to advance but were constantly hampered by the high tree-covered banks of the 'bocage' which divided the tiny fields and limited views and arcs of fire to a couple of hundred yards [or less]. They also constituted formidable anti-tank barriers. Although the Regiment got past Bernières Bocage, albeit with the loss of several tanks, no real progress was made towards Tilly-sur-Seulles and we began to feel the frustration of operating in such difficult tank country. However, an exciting new prospect emerged when we heard that the Americans had reached Caumont on the right flank of the British penetration and Seventh Armoured was to break off from its current activity and make a wide flanking move along the edge of the American sector, directed on Villers-Bocage. 4 CLY were in the lead and 5RTR followed. The night of 12th June was spent near Livry and in the morning of 13th June 4 CLY reached Villers-Bocage without opposition, having passed round the back of the enemy. Then, in what, in retrospect, seems incredible tactical incompetence, the leading squadron moved up to a point on the road leading north-east towards Caen but the Motor Company and RHQ halted in line-ahead along the road without taking any defensive precautions. It is not clear where the other two squadrons were initially deployed but it seems likely that they too did not at once take up positions to secure the town. However that may be, a group of five Tiger tanks (known to have been commanded by Obersturmführer Michael Wittmann[6]) now emerged from their location just east of the town and destroyed the whole of the leading squadron, the Motor Company and RHQ with no loss to themselves[7].

'When news of this disaster began to filter through to 5RTR, 'A' Sqn was ordered to take up a defensive position covering the road running west out of Villers-Bocage and my Troop was actually on the road at a point where it led down the hill into the town. It was now about midday and, during the afternoon, the remains of 4 CLY withdrew through us and our position was strengthened by the arrival of some of our infantry brigade. Probing attacks took place on a fairly small scale at first; these were repulsed but constant vigilance had to be maintained and we received orders to remain in our forward positions during the night – not a situation that tank crews relished. Apart from the gunners not being able to see anything through their gun sights in the dark, the whole tank crew were vulnerable to attack on foot and could not communicate, as the noise of their wireless sets would give away their position. During the whole of the next day the Division was under constant counter-attack by both tanks and infantry: this was mostly to the west of my Troop's position in the area around Tracy Bocage and Amaye-sur-Seulles and at one time the situation became so serious that our artillery were firing over open sights. As evening fell we received orders to withdraw during the night, the whole operation having apparently failed. While we were withdrawing we were able to observe a very heavy air attack by the RAF on Villers-Bocage. Our withdrawal entailed a long road march back to leaguer near Ellon.

'My abiding memory of Villers-Bocage is not so much of fierce and continuous fighting (though others certainly experienced plenty of that) but of enormous fatigue, in having to operate for days and nights without sleep and little chance of getting anything to eat . . . or even being able to get out of the tank for a few minutes. I do not recall losing any of my tanks or having any casualties in the Troop but we were continually under threat and frequently engaging enemy infantry. Because of this memory of intense tiredness, I now find it hard to accept that the whole action lasted only two days and nights. When we arrived at Ellon it was afternoon or evening and I remember the bliss of getting orders that there was no need to mount guards, no reveille and no wireless netting procedure next morning – just permission to sleep on. And we all did get down to sleep and, next morning, had a lazy start, cooking and chatting, before getting back into the routine of refuelling and maintenance.

'At my level, I did not register at the time what a catastrophic failure the operation had been – particularly as there had been no fault in our own Regiment's performance. But, in hindsight, it is extraordinary that the leading regiment allowed itself to be destroyed, that a whole armoured division could be dislodged from its defensive position by fairly weak elements of the 2nd Panzer Division which had only just arrived at the front: or that the Corps Commander did not rush forward more infantry formations to assist in maintaining Seventh Armoured's penetration. It is also interesting to note that, when we withdrew during the night of 14th June, our Squadron fitters' half-track was left behind because the exhausted crew had fallen asleep and, when they woke up next morning, they were entirely alone – no enemy to be seen. It seems likely therefore that the enemy was also exhausted and that, if the battle had been better handled at the highest level, it might have succeeded – which would have had an enormous effect on the subsequent campaign.'

Bob Lay, in discussing the writing of this book with me, has pointed out that the shambles at Villers-Bocage was not such a one-sided affair as was supposed at the time. This was another example of the British Army's poor record of PR. It is true that the Germans had a squad of photographers in Villers within hours and that it would not have been a healthy place for anyone from Fleet Street. But the truth of the battle never seems to have reached the British papers. Apart from knocking out five Tigers, the toll of PzKw IVs was impressive and the critical fact that the action prevented the Panzergruppe from breaking through and attacking the American flank was never reported at all.

Mention of these battles and an examination of the photographs taken shortly after them makes one wonder why, generations later, people still describe a scene of devastation as looking like a World War One battlefield. The devastation caused to the farms and villages and towns in Normandy in 1944 was frequently every bit as drastic . . . and was caused in a matter of days, not months or years of war.

This devastation produced its own phenomenon: the smell. Several men who were there commented on this. It was a mixture of cordite, high explosive, the peculiar smell of ruined buildings, of burning but, above all, of death. Sometimes, and nauseatingly so, that of dead animals. Humans were, sooner rather than later, given some sort of burial. Animals were left, sickeningly, to rot . . . and this was farming country where every farm, almost every family, had an animal or animals of sorts.

Like Eric Wilde, George Johnson only paid a brief visit to Normandy. Having driven a *Sherman* in Italy, George was converted to *Cromwells* [by training, not by allegiance: as did many others, he called them 'coffins on wheels']. What happened, in his own words, was that, 'On the Sunday after D-Day, I was sitting alone in the driver's seat when a Tiger came out of a wood and started to fire HE at us. I didn't dare reverse the tank: the rest of the crew might have been sheltering behind it, so I decided to get out myself. That was when I got a bit of shrapnel in the left side of my chest. I was sent back to Leeds General Hospital and, after a while, was moved to Leyburn, near Catterick to convalesce. One day, while I was there, I was seen kicking a football about by the MO. He sent for me and said, 'Johnson, if you're well enough to kick a football about, you're well enough to kick Jerry about' and I found myself on the way back to The Fifth!' Back with the Regiment, he found himself Pluto Ellis' gunner in a *Firefly* and stayed with Pluto until the war ended.

Being a member of a tank crew didn't mean that one necessarily had one's adventures in a tank. For Bryan Johnson, the landing was quite uneventful and so were the first few days in Normandy but, 'On the 10th June we moved off as a Regimental Group, consisting of a Company of the RBs and a Battery of 5 RHA. After a couple of days, we had an interesting job which was to go as Liaison Officer to the 2nd Essex who were held up in a wood near Bernières. A company of the infantry were dug in fairly close together. While Capt Beresford was trying to instruct the Coy Commander in the use of a '19 set' [the tank wireless] and report to our CO, Garry [the driver] and I decided to do a local foot patrol. After a bit of ribbing from the infantry, asking us where we'd been last night and so forth, we moved off and espied a wounded Panzer-Grenadier: we asked the infantry if they were going to bring him in and were told, 'Oh, no. We shot him.' Garry said to me, 'Come on, Johnny; we'll fetch him.' His leg had been smashed into a red pulp by Bren gun bullets. We did a bit of rough first aid and then wanted to give him a drink. Garry asked an infanteer for his water bottle but was curtly refused. I went back to the tank and got mine and gave him a drink. All he said was 'Du mit Panzer?' pointing to my badge. But, for our pains, we got sniped at going back to the *Honey*.

'The same day about 1800 hrs the Regiment disengaged from that sector and went to the western end of the front towards Caumont, leaguering for the night at Livry. The next two days were to prove momentous. The first battle for Villers-Bocage took place.' Bryan then briefly recounted what he had heard about the battle, going on to say, like Alan Bashford, 'During the war there were a number of German Jews who wanted to fight their countrymen by joining the British Army: at first, this was only allowed by joining the Pioneer Corps. However, in 1944 they were allowed to join tank units. They were all given good English names like Smith or Brown or Wilson [Thank you, Bryan!] which was the name of the one in RHQ, although his real name was Heinmann. Later he proved invaluable as interpreter to the CO at the surrender of Ghent. On this morning at Villers-Bocage he was brewing up, using an enamel iron jug, acquired from the mess tent at 'Stalag R-5'. Suddenly some concentrated shot from a mortar came down and we heard him muttering in German while the rest of us Recce chaps seized our weapons and rushed to see what had happened. What we found was Trooper Wilson holding all that was left of the of the jug – the handle – and cursing like fury!

'The following day, 14th June, every crew in The Fifth was waiting and watching for the expected counter-attack. I recall one junior officer sending a message on the regimental net to the effect that two enemy tanks had got round his position and were heading for RHQ. Whereupon Colonel Gus swiftly answered, 'They may have got past you: they won't get past me. Out!' He slipped into his *Cromwell* and traversed the gun onto the anticipated spot. That afternoon, although we didn't know it at the time, the decision had already been made to withdraw.

'In the evening, in the gathering gloom, the counter-attack arrived, led by the Panzer-Grenadier infantry. All the tanks in the Troop were lined up and every gun on them was firing defensively. The RHA guns, not far off, were firing at ranges of around 200 yards. The execution was fearful and the German losses heavy. On one of the guns, when the attack was broken, the special charges and projectiles were put back in the racks. The gun-layer chalked VILLERS on them: those chalk marks were not removed until the Victory Parade in Berlin! In the middle of the night the tanks were driven out. On approaching Caumont dawn broke. One *Sherman* had to be left on the road and was set alight. I think it belonged to Capt Butler but I know Capt Beresford said, 'Whenever you see him, offer him a box of matches.'

'The Regiment arrived back in the area of Foulognes some four miles north of Caumont. Everyone was very tired: I saw a DR in the ditch, the bike's engine still running, completely exhausted. We stayed in this area till almost the end of the month. One incident I do remember was when I had to report sick with a stomach upset. The MO seemed quite concerned and said he would send me to the MRS. While I was in the MRS tented area, laid out on a stretcher, a Frenchman brought his wife in for treatment. The wife, on seeing me, rushed over and embraced me, crying '*Oh, mon brave soldat*'!'

Ron Poore recorded his feelings as the LCT nosed its way into the surf. 'I viewed the situation I was in with mixed feelings. Some fear at going into the unknown, thinking 'Ronnie boy, this is no longer playing games. This exercise is for real.' It was nearly morning when we landed to the sound of distant gunfire. We drove through some villages. Our objective was Caen. Sitting in the turret with very little vision of where we were going, the mind races through a thousand thoughts. Have you sighted the gun correctly. You listen intently through your headset trying to hear what's happening to the rest of the Squadron. This is the initial tension that builds up when you realise you have entered the world of battle, with buildings destroyed all around. Although we had experienced being bombed night after night in the early years of the war, this was something different.

'Suddenly you are jolted back from your nervous thoughts. The voice in your headset, 'Seventy-five, traverse left'. That's you. You set the range. You take in the firing orders. Your loader has the HE shell loaded. A cold shiver seems to run through your body. You sight on the target. The moment comes as you fire your first shell in anger. The bang as the gun fires. You hear the metallic sound as the ejected shell-case falls into the canvas holder bag under the breech-block. A feeling of relief as you observe your first shell hit where it was aimed. We have arrived at war!'

Bert Reeves was one of the earliest reinforcements to be posted to the Regiment in Normandy. He started as the driver of a *Challenger* on Echelon Guard on D+6 which he found to be a surprisingly quiet occupation with a war going on. However this didn't last long and he was soon posted to 'B' Squadron as driver of a *Cromwell* in Michael van Gruisen's Troop where life was more varied.

Michael van Gruisen had landed on D+1 but not with 5RTR. He was in hospital on D+2 having had his foot run over when he misjudged the turning circle of the half-track he was directing. When he did join The Fifth, he was cut down to size (he stood well over six feet in his socks) by the men of his Troop whose combined years of battle experience added up to rather more than his years of life. It wasn't his fault that he had spent the first few months of his commissioned service in a cavalry regiment!

Syd Storer remembers with wry amusement that the last of Monty's famous messages before the troops landed in Normandy had read, 'Soldiers, Sailors and Airmen of the Allied Expeditionary Force', which included in the middle sentence the words 'your task will not be an easy one. Your enemy . . will fight savagely.' One night on French soil proved to him that Monty had got at least that one right! What impressed him, as it did others, was that, when the enemy were native Germans as opposed to members of one of Hitler's Empire countries, they did fight savagely right up to the moment when the alternative to death was surrender . . . and some of them beyond that point.

The first outside news which was picked up over the air was that 50 Division had captured Bayeux intact and advanced three miles farther inland. The Fifth soon found that its life was not going to be so easy. As Syd Storer recorded, progress, when there was any, was measured hedgerow by hedgerow down the road. It was in this type of fighting that The Fifth made its first real acquaintance with Panzerfausts[8]. On the main road from Sully to Port-en-Bessin, the Storer tank crew turned the tables on the Boche when the came upon a self-propelled gun that was firing at other Squadron tanks which were trying to advance down the main road. They caught it completely unawares and, with one shot, quickly disposed of it . . . then wisely retreated into cover. The choice of cover was a good one: from it they could see a cluster of three more 75mm A/Tk guns entrenched at a junction farther up the road. They couldn't get at these themselves but passed on the necessary information to the Gunners FOO, who laid a few ranging shots over the target. The Mortar

Support Group joined in the shoot, thus enabling the Squadron to continue its steady advance. From this point forward, the tanks had infantry on either side of the sunken road to support them and, after much hard fighting, succeeded in destroying four 88s and one 75mm gun. The twenty-eight prisoners whom they captured made a nice addition to the day's bag.

Shortly after this, an incident occurred which Syd would have preferred to forget but which he recounted because it was an 'incident of war' that he felt his family should know about. After several strenuous and nearly sleepless days and nights, Sgt Cook's tank was leading the Troop across a stretch of relatively open country . . . and doing so with extra caution, as they were advancing into the setting sun. He eased his tank round a corner and paused to see what was ahead. As so often happened in battle, everything seemed quiet: only the beat of the tank engines. There was a flash as an AP shell ripped apart the front of the tank. Jim Cook seemed to be thrown from the tank as it brewed up and exploded. He struggled down and stumbled towards the Troop Leader's tank: the crew ran to help him. He appeared to have no sense of direction. As they sat beside him in the shelter of the tank, to await the MO, they realised that he was blind.

Misfortunes seldom come singly. The next few days saw the loss of many more good men – and Syd Storer found this to be an example of the manner in which irrelevant thoughts often helped to mask more painful ones – whom he thought of not so much as good soldiers as good men in the Regimental football team. These were SSM 'Knocker' Knight, killed by a sniper, and a lad called 'Chalky' because his name was White and who was only eighteen years old.

On 11th June Syd had a near miraculous escape. In a lull in the fighting which had seen considerable success for the infantry, doing close-quarters work with PIATs and grenades, as well as some close-quarters work for the tanks when they caught some unsuspecting PzKws at a range of 100 yards or less, the crews decided to take advantage of a halt. They baled out and set about cooking a meal. Their cooking was rudely interrupted by a heavy mortar stonk. Cooking was abandoned amid the flying fragments, one of which hit Syd Storer on the thigh as he scrambled back into the tank. On examination, he found a most impressive bruise but no penetration – not even broken skin.

One thing that always horrified the older hands was the way in which new troops sometimes approached their first engagement. The old hands knew all the tricks. They would have been dead hands, not old hands, if they hadn't. Every now and then it seemed that the fresh troops hadn't been taught any tricks at all. On one occasion, the 'B' Squadron tanks crews watched in disbelief as a Company of the Essex Regt arrived and prepared to attack a wood. They appeared, to the watching crews, to be very new and too spick and span for the work in hand. On this particular occasion, the tank crews had seen what had happened to one lot of infantry who had put in an attack on this wood. They were horrified to see them lined up as if on Parade and, as the tanks began the covering fire, the men of the Essex started to walk slowly forward, upright, towards the wood with their rifles 'at the port'. In a few minutes the line was massacred; those who had not been hit fell back to the tanks. Again they formed up but, before they could repeat their advance, an officer came running up and shouted, 'Send them in on their bellies!' This time they made use of the waist-high corn as cover and took the enemy by surprise.

Syd then summarises the disastrous CLY debacle in Villers-Bocage, going on to say, 'When I had taken my turn on turret watch in the mid-afternoon, I had made a rough outline of the ground in front of us, and noted where the various haystacks were. To my surprise, when looking round a little later, I realised there was now a haystack in the middle of the field to our immediate front which had not been there previously. On taking a closer look, I could see the sprocket of a tank underneath the covering of hay and corn sheaves. I then counted 28 haystacks in front of us. I shook Ferny who was having a rest and pointed out what I had noticed. After checking he spoke to the Squadron Commander who instituted a quick check: this showed nearly a hundred camouflaged tanks approaching along our front. It was decided that it would be impossible to hold Villers-Bocage with the small garrison at present there and, with all these enemy tanks now in the area, it would certainly be cut off.'

Syd's Diary then records the withdrawal but points out that this was not accomplished without having to beat off a counter-attack. This was stopped chiefly by a 'Divisional shoot' by all the guns of 5 RHA and effective 'counter-counter-attack' by the Queens on the advancing German infantry. The next two weeks 'we had to settle down to the bocage fighting, but the movement of the tanks was very limited'. There was an interesting high-spot. The Fifth's front had been reinforced by the arrival of a Regiment of 6-pounder A/Tk Guns which took up position along their front. These were using the new special 'sabot' armour-piercing ammunition. At short range in the bocage country, these guns wreaked havoc on the enemy tanks before they came within range of the tank guns.

The end of the Regiment's long spell in action arrived when it was relieved by a United States Armoured Division which had been sharing the front. This did not mean peace and quiet. After moving on 30th June to St Honorine de Ducy the men were told to forget replenishment and get their heads down, an order which was carried out immediately. Hardly had they rolled into bed, when there was a shattering noise from the other side of the hedge. 5RTR had been sent to rest in a field next to a regiment of dug-in 105 Heavy Artillery. These friendly souls were busy shelling the enemy. It was impossible to sleep and, within an hour, orders were thankfully received to load up and stand by to move to another and more restful rest area.

Unfortunately [according to Syd Storer] the move brought tragedy. After a quick brew the Regiment moved off as the sun rose over the skyline. The roads were full of debris from the recent battles, with telegraph and electricity poles lying about everywhere. It was one of the wires from a broken telegraph pole which caused the casualty. As the tanks moved along the road in line ahead, each one passed over the trailing wires. Cpl French's tank passed over one of the broken wires attached to a partly broken concrete post: the extra tension broke the post off completely. It fell as the tank passed by and hit Cpl French in the head, killing him instantly as he stood in the turret[9].

THE OTHER SIDE

Whoever else was in Normandy on 6th June 1944 awaiting the invasion, it wasn't Feldmarschall Erwin Rommel. He was at home in Germany, celebrating his wife's birthday. This domestic footnote, although curious in view of Rommel's often expressed belief that invasion was imminent, had no effect on the outcome of the war.

What did have an important effect, although it would not have been immediately apparent to the troops on the ground, were the jealousies which existed between the different branches of the defending forces – the Kriegsmarine (who owed allegiance only to the Kriegsmarine), the SS troops (who owed allegiance only to Himmler), the Luftwaffe (who owed allegiance only to Göring). And, of course, the Wehrmacht who just did what someone in Berlin told them. This was a serious handicap to Rommel and one which he did not overcome until 1st July (D+25) when he contrived to bring them under unified control in the 'Sector West'.

Another factor which had an important effect in June 1944 was the dearth of matériel allowed for reinforcing the Atlantic Wall. Much of the concrete and steel, for example, that Rommel needed was allocated either to the development of the V-1 and V-2 weapons and their launching pads or to the belated development and building of Hitler's fabled 'super-U-boats'.

By contrast, one factor, soon to be felt by the troops on the ground, was Rommel's insistence on mine-laying. He contrived to have millions of mines laid: his ambition was have scores, even hundreds, of millions laid. He failed, partly because the mines weren't available, but largely because neither transport nor labour was available to him.

Apart from his tactical use of his forces, Rommel employed all the conventional ruses of defence in depth – dummy batteries and airfields, badly camouflaged (but really non-existent) defensive strong-points – but what he could not employ, because Berlin refused to allow it, were V-1 'flying bombs' against the invaders' steady stream of reinforcements and the shipping which brought them.

All these factors apart, Rommel was a realist. 'To stop the enemy,' he said, 'we must stop him in the water and destroy him while he is still afloat.' Once a beach-head was established and protected by the Allies' overwhelming air superiority, there would be no stopping him. A realist? Well, perhaps not altogether so, because there was a weakness in Rommel's reasoning. There were some 5,000 kilometres of water lapping at the foot of the Atlantic Wall and only 59 divisions to stop the enemy. And these divisions (forty nine infantry and ten armoured) were by no means all the stuff of the

DAK. Moreover, Rommel's strategic aim was over-ruled by his nominal superior, von Rundstedt, whose orthodox staff-college-trained mind convinced him that the landing would be in the orthodox place – the Pas de Calais – and, by holding the main reserves in that area against such an attack, deprived Rommel of any chance of 'throwing the British back to the fishes'.

By the end of June, both von Rundstedt and Rommel were certainly realists enough to acknowledge that the position was hopeless. Von Rundstedt, answering a question from Keitel in Berlin as to what the High Command should do, simply said, 'Make peace! What else can you do?': Rommel said openly that it would be better to end the war – even if that meant becoming another British Dominion – rather than fight on to see the Fatherland in ruins in the pursuit of a hopeless war.

In practical terms, Rommel and von Rundstedt realised that the Normandy bridgehead could not be contained and that an inner defensive line should be established – possibly even as far back as the Seine. This, however was a 'retreat' and brought a point-blank refusal from Hitler as an automatic reaction.

All of which lends spice to the comment of General (later Doctor of Philosophy and NATO-sponsored head of the Federal German Land Forces) Hans Speidel that the trouble with Germany stemmed from 'too many enemy soldiers and one too many German ones – Hitler.'

THE WAR CHRONICLE

1944

June	12	Chinese Nationalist and Communist Leaders reached agreement to co-operate – but only to fight the Japanese
	13	An experimental V-2 Rocket crashed landed and the wreckage was recovered by Swedish Military Engineers – First V-1 Flying Bomb landed on London
	16	HMS *Rodney* shelled targets 20 miles inland in Italy
	17	Allied troops captured Elba
	18	Assissi fell to the Allies
	19	Storms in the English Channel played havoc with 'Mulberry Harbour'
	28	Danes staged a General Strike in defiance of German orders
	30	Civilian casualties in UK – 1935 killed: 5906 injured since beginning of the month – Military casualties since D-Day – (British and Canadian) 2,836 killed: (American) 4,868 killed

NOTES

1 Casualties. The details of casualties given in the War Diary and in the Regimental Return do not always agree as to dates. In order to avoid confusion, the dates have been correlated from the best evidence available. They may not, therefore, always agree precisely with one document or the other

2 '... informed of our presence' This was due to the fact that – after nearly five years of war – all the scout cars being used by Seventh Armoured still did not have wireless sets and were, therefore, useless for liaison purposes

3 Infantry-v-tanks. The 'boarding' method of anti-tank warfare was occasionally practised with success. Never regarded by the infantry as more than a very risky daylight way of dealing with tanks, one such successful attack was made in Abyssinia by Nigel Leakey – the elder brother of Rea Leakey who later commanded The Fifth. Nigel Leakey used this method to knock out two Italian tanks which had overrun his unit's position: he was awarded a posthumous Victoria Cross

4 Dover. Roy Dixon's home town

5 Inexperienced sailors. One such was a man I knew as a schoolboy: he was already minus a leg when he was only nine. When he volunteered, he was told that he wouldn't have a quarter deck to pace, so the absent leg didn't matter. His whole war was a series of cross-Channel runs: he said that just one run in an LCT would have been quite enough!

6 Wittmann. See Note in Appendix 3. For a full, graphic not to say grisly, account of this battle, see Daniel Taylor's VILLERS BOCAGE THROUGH THE LENS. The lens is that of a German War Photographer

7 German losses. Again according to Taylor, this statement is not correct. It is reasonably certain that Wittmann's N° 1 Kompanie did not lose any tanks but that N° 2 Kompanie lost five of their Tigers

8 Panzerfaust. Literally 'armour fist'. The German member of the Bazooka/PIAT family

9 Cpl French. There is some confusion about the date of this accident. According to the Regimental Roll, Corporal French was killed at Breuil, near Aunay-sur-Odon, on Friday, 4th August and not when Syd Storer reports the event

CHAPTER XV

. . . Goodwood – A Day at the Races

July 1944

Some explanation will help to understand the events reported in the War Diary or recounted in the individual narratives in this chapter.

It is easy to forget that what was happening in the British Sector was only part of the struggle to break out of the bridgehead. By the beginning of July a near-stalemate situation had developed in Normandy. The American forces under General Bradley had not – to Bradley's despair – achieved their expected break-out south and the battle for Caen had dragged on from days into weeks.

The solution Monty adopted was intended to roll the concentrated German armour back towards Falaise, the main British armour being 'required to dominate the area Bourguébus– Vimont–Bretteville and to fight and destroy the enemy .. but armoured cars should push far to the south towards Falaise and spread alarm and despondency and discover 'the form.' That, believe it or not, is a quotation from VIIIth Corps' original 'Battle Plan'.

The 'main British armour' in this case was a novelty. General Sir Richard O'Connor, lately escaped from being a prisoner in Italy, was back with the Army and commanding a Corps in BLA. His command was VIIIth Corps which, for Monty's next stroke, consisted of the Seventh (well-known to Dick O'Connor from Desert days), the Eleventh and the Guards Armoured Divisions.

Monty's plan – Operation 'Goodwood' – was that the three armoured divisions should concentrate north of Caen, cross the Orne River and Canal and then advance on a semi-circular CL clockwise at a distance of some five miles from the centre of Caen. Infantry support on the right flank was to come from the Second and Third Canadian Infantry Divisions who were to clear the Fauberg de Vaucelles south-eastern suburb of Caen with Ist Corps on the left flank. However, the plan had two built-in complications and one major fault. Crossing the Orne was only possible one division at a time, almost in single file and always at a snail's pace: the corridor down the east side of Caen, although better tank country than the bocage, was only about 2,000 yards wide, thus severely restricting manoeuvre. Those were the complications: the fault was that of Second Army Intelligence who had grossly underestimated the strength of the Boche defences.

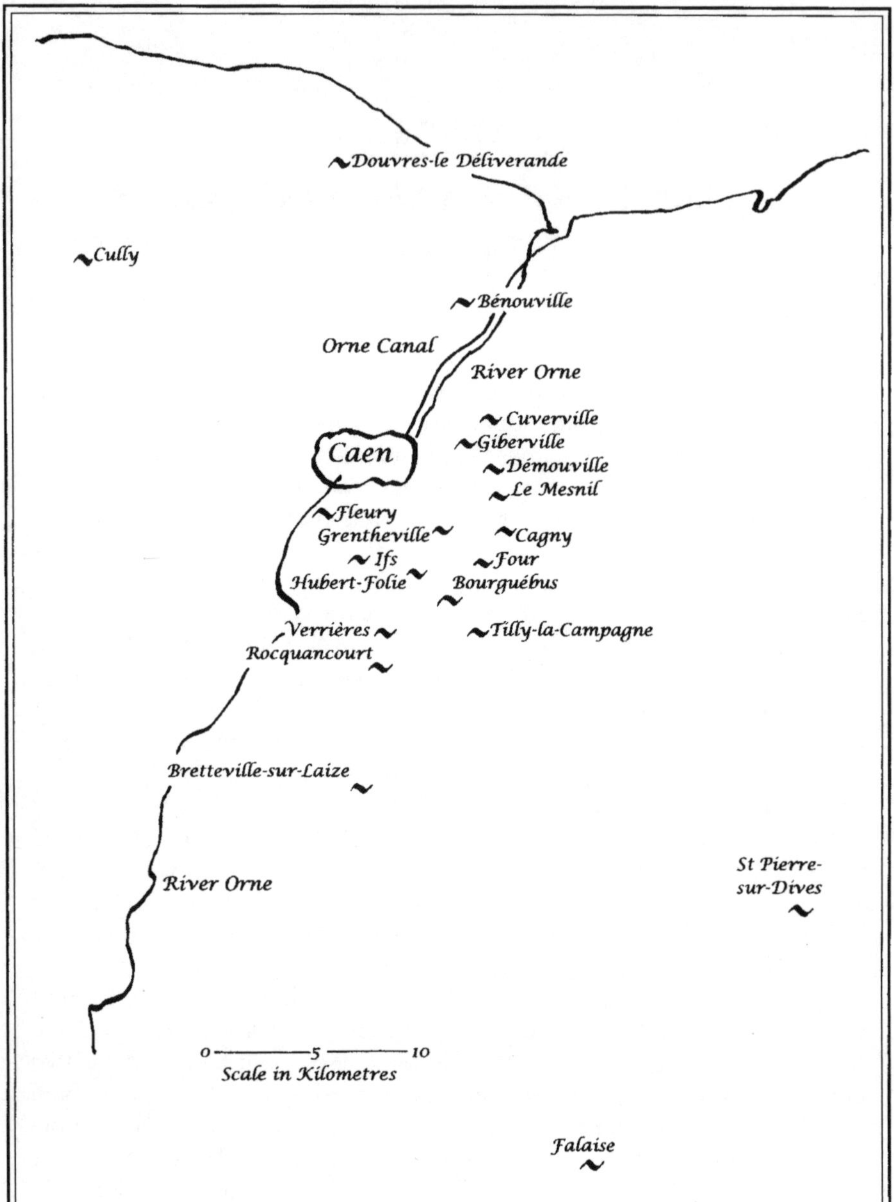
Douvres-le Déliverande
Cully
Bénouville
Orne Canal
River Orne
Cuverville
Giberville
Démouville
Le Mesnil
Caen
Fleury
Grentheville
Cagny
Ifs
Four
Hubert-Folie
Bourguébus
Verrières
Tilly-la-Campagne
Rocquancourt
Bretteville-sur-Laize
St Pierre-sur-Dives
River Orne
0 5 10
Scale in Kilometres
Falaise

Map N°7 ~ Normandy : The Second Stage

They should have known better. Their adversary was Rommel and the Desert Fox had anticipated just such a move as his old Desert sparring partner had planned. Rommel's defence lines were not just four miles deep, as Intelligence reported, with only one Panzer Division in reserve, but ten miles deep. There were five layers: in front were two infantry divisions with, close behind, the first armoured reserve (21st Panzers – under strength but still formidable – 503rd Heavy Tank Battalion, equipped with Tigers, and Panzer IV Battalion from 1st SS Panzer Division). Next came a defensive line of villages and farms near the main railway line, manned by infantry and A/Tk guns. Fourthly came some four score 88s on the crest of the Bourguébus Ridge, bolstered by twice that number of field guns and three times that number of Minenwerfers. Last came a mobile reserve which included Panthers and PzKw IVs.

Any advantage to the British in tank numbers [there were something in the order of 700 of them] was outweighed by the lack of room to manoeuvre. Any loss of advantage which the Germans suffered by not being able to bring up mines to sow on the line of advance was outweighed by their almost overwhelming A/Tk gun strength. The dominating factor which should have made 'Goodwood' the success that it wasn't was the crushing Allied air superiority, a mixed bag of over 2,000 bombers being involved.

In the end, it might be best to say of 'Goodwood', as of so many other sporting events from time immemorial, that 'Rain Stopped Play'.

Those wise men – critics who see things only in the clear light of wisdom after the event – have put much of the blame for the failure of 'Goodwood' on the slowness of 22nd Armd Bde to cross the Orne and follow in the wake of Guards Armoured, coupled with their reluctance to press on regardless in the face of opposition which the high command ought to have, but had not, foreseen. There is only one answer to that. Those wise men did not take part in 'Goodwood': The Fifth, along with the others in 22nd Armd Bde, did.

The War Diary for July 1944 reads:

1-3 Regt moved to Ellon. Formed open leaguer. Maintenance
Casualties : [HQ] Tpr Holland G Wnd

4 1000 hrs Visit from GOC 7 Armd Div. Maj Gen GWEJ Erskine CB DSO

5-6 Tank crews re-organised and made up to strength from a very small reserve
Casualties : [HQ] L/Cpl Hearne J KIA

7 Regtl courses; wireless, D&M and Gunnery commenced in tank area

8-16 Recce carried out for defensive positions in area St Leger, Ducy Ste Marguerite and southwards to Folliot
Casualties : [HQ] L/Cpl Goodman Wnd L/Cpl Lambert Wnd
Sgm Williams Wnd

17 Leaguer shelled in early hours of the morning thought to be SP guns shelling newly constructed airfield close to Regt's location.

Reg. Moved to Cully where Brigade concentrated for big attack E of Caen in which the Guards Armd Div, 11 Armd Div and 7 Armd Div were all taking part

Casualties : [LAD] Cfn Davie N KIA
S/Sgt Turner Wnd Cpl Lynn Wnd L/Cpl Giles Wnd
[HQ] Tpr Harrison Wnd Tpr Bramley Wnd

18 930 hrs Regt moved over London Bridge and immediately behind Northants Yeo, the last regiment in 29 Armd Brigade. CL took shape over open going to Suverville and then to Demouville where the leading Sqn – 'B' – was ordered to deploy and move up abreast of Northants Yeo. The first incident was an enemy tank 800 yards east of Demouville opened up and knocked out a *Firefly* of 'B' Sqn reserve troop and a *Honey* from Recce. Fire was immediately returned and the enemy brewed up. The CL was directed to Grentheville and advance continued to Mesnil Frêmentel where several British tanks were brewing including one from 'B' Sqn. Meanwhile POWs had been coming in to the number of 80. It was soon established that there were 4 Panthers in [the village of] Four. 'A' Sqn were accordingly directed against Grentheville 1200 yards NW of Four and 'C' Sqn came into position where they could watch and shoot into Four if necessary. 'B' Sqn came into reserve: 'A' Sqn reached Grentheville and after a short action against enemy Inf, established themselves in the southern outskirts. The enemy reacted strongly and attacked from Four with 2 Panthers and 2 Pzkw IVs. 'A' Sqn lost 2 tanks and 'C' Sqn KO'd 2 enemy tanks. The remainder withdrawing. 'A' Sqn remained in Grentheville and the Regt leaguered after dark in area Mesnil Frêmentel. Some shelling during the night.

Casualties : [HQ] L/Cpl Garratt TA KIA
Sgt Hill Wnd Cpl Bell TS Wnd Tpr Rooke Wnd
[A] L/Cpl Needham F KIA
Lt Garnett J Wnd[1] *L/Cpl Summer J Wnd*
[C] 2/Lt Clarke DJ Wnd 2/Lt Crocker KRT Wnd
L/Cpl Ferguson T Wnd L/Cpl Fry Wnd
Tpr Evans Wnd
Tpr Lewis L Wnd
[N/S] Cpl Attle J KIA
Tpr Thompson Wnd Tpr Trent Wnd Tpr Watson Wnd

19 'B' Sqn plus 2 platoons of 'I' Coy 1 RB passed through 'A' Sqn who had formed a firm base at Grentheville and pushed into Soliers, clearing minor Inf. opposition on the way, which they then made firm. Spasmodic AP fire came from the direction of the left flank (direction of Four) but nothing was seen of the tanks or SPs. 'B' Sqn was ordered to put 2 troops in Bourguébus which arrived in the outskirts after carefully working their way there, a few minutes before

3 Tigers and 2 Panthers came into the village. In the ensuing fight 2 Tigers and 1 Panther were brewed up for the loss of 1 *Cromwell*. The enemy then withdrew and at first light the 2 troops of 'B' Sqn returned to Soliers where the Sqn leaguered for the night.

Casualties : [A] Tpr Baudry TA DoW
Lt Roberts JP Wnd Sgt Squires H Wnd
L/Cpl Barker J Wnd
Tpr Parris Wnd Tpr Hayes Wnd
[B] 2/Lt Alexander P KIA
Sgt Onions GR Wnd
[C] Cpl Stainton G Wnd Tpr Pearce Wnd
Tpr Wood J Wnd
[NK] L/Cpl Taylor AS KIA
Tpr Dodd Wnd Tpr Spenceley Wnd
Tpr Waterson Wnd Tpr Sayell Msg

Losses : 1 Firefly 2 Cromwells
Bag : 2 Tigers 1 Panther

20 'B' Sqn at first light moved into Bourguébus and after a short fight in the outskirts a Tiger was brewed up. There was no other enemy in the village except 2 abandoned Panthers, one of which was brewed up and the other towed back to Brigade Workshops, also 4 abandoned Nebelwerfers[2]. The enemy continued to shell heavily in Bourguébus, Soliers and Grentheville. The Guards Armd Div by now had established themselves in Four. Later in the day a 'B' Sqn *Firefly* succeeded in stalking a Panther and brewed it up 800 yards SE of Bourguébus. 1700 hrs VIII Hussars relieved the Regt and open leaguer was formed near Démouville. It was under observation and very heavily shelled.

Casualties : [HQ] Sgt Bennett [REME] Wnd
[NK] L/Cpl Donald Wnd L/Cpl Fry Wnd

Losses : Nil
Bag : 1 Tiger 3 Panthers (I intact) 4 Nebelwerfers

21 Sqn locations were adjusted and an attempt made to maintain and reorganise. A1 Echelon moved to the factory area of Caen where the fitters were able to work without interruption.

Casualties : [HQ] Lt Peel Wnd Sgt Kershaw Wnd L/Sgt Tatum Wnd
Cpl Topp Wnd Cpl Lynn Wnd Tpr Manning Wnd
[A] Cpl Adamson R Wnd Tpr Lewis C Wnd

Losses : 2 soft vehicles in A2 Echelon

22–24 The Regt in reserve, maintenance carried out though there was a certain amount of shelling during the day and fairly heavy Anti-Personnel air raids at night.

Casualties : [HQ] Tpr Moulton Wnd
[N/S] Sgt Harbin HR KIA
Cpl Bell Wnd L/Cpl Booth Wnd Tpr Bayer Wnd

25 0515 hrs Brigade moved in support [new area]. The Brigade was 2-up with the Regt in reserve behind 1 RTR and 4 CLY. No progress was made and positions prepared against what seemed a very probable counter-attack.
Casualties : [B] Tpr Morris G KIA Tpr Palmer A KIA
L/Cpl Slater A L DoW
Lt Abram Wnd Cpl Pollard Wnd Tpr Wright A Wnd
[C] Tpr Sayers W Inj
[N/S] Tpr Clarke J Wnd
Losses : 1 Humber Scout Car

26 Regt took up position of 1RTR and a Sqn was sent into Verriers in support of Royal Hamilton Light Infantry[3]. Verriers was shelled very badly and enemy attempted to infiltrate back into village. Both tanks and infantry had several good shoots.
Casualties : [HQ] Tpr Tinkin Wnd
[N/S] Tpr Gowan Wnd

27–29 Regt moved to area half mile NE of Ifs and remained in reserve. The Sqns in Verriers being changed daily. There were several good shoots.
Casualties : [A] Tpr Lawrence T Wnd
[N/S] Tpr Manning Wnd
Bag : Mixed bag of MT, 1 SP

30 1600 hrs Regt moved back to Ellon and leaguered, their positions being taken over by a Canadian Armoured Brigade.

31 Regt placed under command of 131 Brigade and at night made an approach march to Caumont area.

Eric Stevenson, whom Pete Petersen had voted to be 'all right' but who, according to Norman Smith, had a lot to learn about domestic duties when he did arrive in a Troop, had moved up from the B Echelon to 'B' Squadron and became a tank Commander in 7 Troop under the watchful eye of Sgt West. Roy Dixon has already commented on this practice of breaking in new officers: it was followed in one form or another, right up to the end of the war and probably saved the lives of many junior subalterns . . . and, more importantly, many experienced tank crews. Eric's first run-in with the enemy as a Troop Officer was in the hapless role of spectator during Operation 'Goodwood', watching the tanks of the leading Armoured Divisions being picked off one by one by those 88s on Bouguébus Ridge.

Years after the war I commented on his 'laid back' attitude to Pete Petersen. His answer summed up his whole – and commendable – philosophy: 'You died if you worried: you died if you didn't. So why worry? Anyway,' he added, 'in those days it helped to be a bit mad.' Here he is again on the subject of 'Goodwood'. 'We eventually moved and made our push on Caen and, in the open plains around Caen, we met our opposition in the form of Panthers and Tigers. My friend, Harry Ireland, who was manning a 17-pounder on a

Firefly had the proud boast of bagging two Panthers before breakfast.' Harry Ireland (see later in this chapter), who should know, protests that the bag was not two Panthers but two Tigers . . . and there was another Tiger later in the day! 'This battle for Caen continued for a number of days until the Canadians, while the Guards Armoured and the Seventh Armoured Divisions were keeping the enemy busy in the surrounding country, finally overcame the enemy resistance in Caen and the enemy was in retreat. He got a bit naughty at times and gave us a taste of his multi-barrelled mortars. We would advance through the cornfields in which the Germans had taken cover until a few rounds of 75mm airburst and a few sprays of machine-gun fire made them change their minds and beat a hasty exit. In these situations you never know how many you might have killed or wounded: sometimes it was best not to know. We knew that Jerry was there to do his duty and we had to do our duty . . . before Jerry could do his to us!

'However, our adrenaline was up and we were in high spirits and survived again. That was the name of the game: survival. There was one little encounter we had when my 75mm decided to go on strike. An enemy gun about 500 yards away was stonking our infantry, so we engaged it and, much to our dismay, the gun failed. I let loose with machine-gun fire instead and hit their ammunition which exploded. The little Nazis made a run for it but it wasn't all over for us. An infantry officer, with his arm all shot-up appeared. Apparently he had just had an argument with a Panther and reported that it was coming our way. That did make us sweat: we had no gun to deal with it, so we decided to sit it out. Much to our relief, that Panther must have changed direction for we never saw it and it never saw us, so we survived once again. Next day we had to stay behind to get our gun fixed. Our crew commander changed to take command of another tank and was killed in action later that day. That's the way it went.'

When Bernard Holder was part of the Tobruk Garrison he had an amusing encounter with a land-mine. Perhaps a 'lucky escape from' would be a better way of putting it. His second encounter was also a lucky escape but it was far from being amusing. Just outside Caen, Bernard was indulging in a well-earned rest, lying at the side of a cornfield waiting for orders to move. Opening his eyes as he turned over to get more comfortable, he saw something black floating down. He closed his eyes again, thinking that it wasn't his worry and someone else would take care of it. A few seconds later, he recalls. 'There was one hell of a bang. It was a land-mine. The cornfield was just stubble and you could have got two three-ton lorries in the crater that land-mine made. Fortunately for me, the field was on a slope and the blast went up and over me.' One way or another, Bernard seems to have made a speciality of big bangs. A few days after the land-mine incident, he was watching a flight of three Flying Fortresses going on their way through some light flak. As he watched there was an almighty flash in the sky and two Flying Fortresses were going on their way through some light flak.

Bryan Johnson has provided a detailed account of Operation 'Goodwood' from the point of view of a member of the Recce Troop. He writes as follows. 'About the beginning of July we moved again to the area around Ellon where we had been on 10th June. This was for rest and training. In the early morning the leaguer was shelled while the crews were all asleep. Later in the morning we were to move to the area of Cully about halfway between Bayeux and Caen. Most of 22nd Armd Bde's vehicles were spread out in open rolling country, a complete change from the bocage that we had got accustomed to since landing. The next day we moved off; we soon encountered clouds of dust caused by the mass movement of a whole armoured division. After crossing a rickety bridge over the River Orne we emerged into a wide expanse of meadow-land. On our right was the embanked railway line: as we turned south the shelling was becoming more intense. Garry [L/Cpl Garratt T] and I were riding with our heads out. The noise seemed to me to be getting nearer which prompted me to shout to the driver to close down. Garry made a derisory wave with his hand. The next second we heard – or rather there was – a terrific explosion. I had my hand on the seat release [lever] and, somehow or other, the periscope block came loose and fell down with me and knocked me out. Not for long but, when I recovered, the tank was careering onwards out of control. Garry was seriously wounded and his blood and tissue had sprayed onto me. Somehow someone stopped the tank and the first thing I did was to give Garry a shot of morphine. We got him out and the MO took him away in his half-track. We knew he wasn't long for this world. Unaccountably the front of the *Honey* was almost undamaged.

'We changed over in the crew, Willie Dovey became the driver and I was the wireless operator and helper to Capt Beresford in the turret. We soon caught up with the rest of the Troop and spent the rest of the day on the high ground just off the village of Grentheville. The next day we moved further south to somewhere around Soliers: the day after that we prepared to move in the direction of Bourguébus when a squadron of VIII Hussars appeared and we were withdrawn into reserve. This was in the area of Giberville, about three-quarters of a mile from where we had started. The combination of shelling and very wet weather made life rather unrestful. On 25th July we moved off through the suburbs of Caen to a point south of Fleury-sur-Orne quite near the hamlet of Ifs, within shouting distance of the main Caen–Falaise road which was the scene of some vicious fighting. We were not there very long when our vehicle was sent off to contact the Canadian Brigade HQ. The 'Canucks' we met seemed very inexperienced and it wasn't long before Willie had gathered a small knot of them to communicate his war experiences. By now we had a new driver, Tinklin by name; he was rather quiet but when he spoke he sounded like a BBC announcer. [Tpr Tinklin had been one of the crew of the 'HQ' Sqn *Honey* which was 'drowned' on the beaches]

'The following day we returned to RHQ and were immediately sent out to the Royal Hamilton Light Infantry who were pinned down on the ridge near

Verrières. We came to a track crossing a main road. A Jeep had been blown up and the dead Canadian driver was still lying near-by. We moved up to Sgt Stimpson's *Firefly*; he was actually doing his 'morning exercises'! Suddenly there was a bang which seemed to be right under my feet. The engine stopped and I was waiting for the driver to say something. After a pause, Tinklin said, 'I think we should get out.' I nipped out with alacrity but the driver needed help, as his leg was injured. Captain 'Bessy' and Willie had run off at speed but turned and shouted, 'Come on.' When they came back we found that the base plate of the floor of the *Honey* had split. The tank had to be abandoned and, early in the afternoon, we were picked up by an ARV from the LAD and slept out in the open. The driver had been taken to the MRS and we never saw him again.'

Ironically, in spite of this incident, Willie Dovey maintains that he was always glad to be in the Recce Troop, rather than in the 'heavy tanks, as a lot of the casualties were sustained there'. There is no accounting for tastes.

'The next day,' Bryan continued, 'we went to the Echelon to await the arrival of a new tank. The peace and quiet was almost boring. The following day the new *Honey* arrived with one of the Regiment's most battle-hardened drivers, L/Cpl 'Woggy' Worrall. On 29th July we met up with the column moving back to the Ellon area again. The day after, in this area, we heard that the CLY were to leave the Brigade. This was sad as 4 CLY had been in 22nd Armd Bde since August 1942. They were replaced by the [Fifth] Inniskilling Dragoon Guards. On the last day of July we moved over towards Caumont and leaguered about 1,000 yards north of the town by the morning of 1st August. Later that day we bypassed the ruins of Caumont and leaguered. some distance south.'

Harry Ireland's account is shorter but every bit as much to the point. 'In mid-July all ranks were briefed by the CO on the coming offensive which was code-named 'Goodwood'. It had been a tremendous strain on all the troops in the bridgehead, incessant night bombing raids, shelling, mortaring, the intensity of which I'd never before encountered. Now was the time to enlarge the area and give us more breathing space. Three armoured divisions were used in this attack, which meant hundreds of tanks, all plentiful but with very small reserve of tank crews. Our target was to be a large concentration of enemy armour and guns east of Caen and our objective was to be 'to contain and destroy' with limited gains of territory.

'The Regiment had a field day: although we incurred losses, our gains cancelled them out. My tank alone [a *Firefly*] knocked out three Tigers in the first day. I, being the gunner, and the rest of the crew were very pleased with our day's work. More success to come for the rest of the Regiment in the next few days: move to Bourguébus, our most forward objective.' Harry went on to say, with more loyalty to the Regiment than military truth, that it was a very successful operation for the whole Army. He then recorded his horror at the shambles which occurred after the Canadians took over the Brigade area, when the combined Allied Air Forces dropped their bombs short of the target and concentrated on the forward Allied lines. Harry concluded by saying, 'We pressed on regardless. Then in late July when the Regiment was in the Caumont area, we did a night march and our tank commander had an unlucky accident. An overhanging telephone wire caught the turret flap as we drove under it. The flap crashed on his arm and broke his wrist. He retired injured and the next commander we had was a very meek and mild chap but did his best under very difficult times. I'd learnt from other commanders: you don't just sit still and hope for your target to go away; you have a bash and hope for good results.'

Denis Huett remembers isolated incidents: things that shouldn't happen but did, like the barrel on the Browning machine-gun in his *Firefly* getting so hot that it went on firing after he released the trigger; or the time that the crew commander told him to traverse onto a new target, and how he did so and how he was about to press down on the foot trigger when he realised that the tank he was sighted on was the *Firefly* from the next Troop which had just broken cover in the bocage. Or thinking inconsequential thoughts, like the hot Sunday morning when they were driving past the burning remains of a supply convoy and all he could think about was the neighbours at home getting out their mowers to cut their lawns. Or not such inconsequential thoughts such as his hatred of the wailing noise made by the Minenwerfers on their way to their targets . . . which could, just possibly, be him.

'It was during 'Goodwood',' writes Stanley Bruce, 'that my tank hit a mine in a wheat field but fortunately none of us suffered any serious injury. We clambered off the back of the tank under heavy shell-fire and wended our way to the rear by walking in the tank tracks in the field we had just crossed. All this 'Goodwood' territory was very different country from what we had been used to in the early part of the campaign. It was mostly agricultural land with open fields and a few villages with attendant orchards. The incident with the mine was the end of my stay with 'C' Squadron as the whole crew was dispersed. I don't know what happened to the others but I was remustered as a tank driver in 'A' Squadron. My first experience there was a Squadron parade addressed by Major Macdonald on the occasion of his award of an MC. What he had to say was that the honour did not belong to him but to the whole Squadron. I must confess that most of my other memories of the battles in Normandy are pretty vague.'

After the luxury of the rest period at Ellon, ' .. in beautiful surroundings, regular meals, much conversation [gripping would probably be a more accurate word!], visits to the Mobile Bath Unit and so on, our next operation was in part of 'Goodwood'. Although 5RTR's part was relatively small,' Roy Dixon wrote, 'it was both an interesting and very nasty experience. As is well-known, the attack was launched from the very restricted and crowded bridgehead over the River Orne secured by 6th Airborne Division on D-Day [the famous Pegasus Bridge landing]: by now this concentration area also contained the 3rd Infantry and 51st Highland Divisions. The only bridge [by which tanks could cross] over the river was at Benouville, four miles north-east of Caen, so we had a long road march around the north of Caen, a dusty and unenjoyable performance. The battle plan was for 11th Armd Div to move over the bridge first during the night of 17th July in order to cross the Start Line at 0745 hrs on the 18th after a gigantic bombing attack by the RAF and USAAF and following a rolling artillery barrage. The second division to cross was the Guards Armoured, then the Seventh. Even after the inevitable delay in crossing the bridge in what seemed like a colossal traffic jam, there was only a narrow corridor between minefields through which the Guards had to move before they could deploy. The result of all this was that 5RTR, in the lead of Seventh Armoured, only arrived in the battle area at 1900 hrs. My troop was the leading one and we had a brief battle at Grentheville but, once it got dark, we leaguered in a cornfield. A curious incident here was that in the leaguer we found the body of a Luftwaffe officer who, despite not being in flying overalls or attached to a parachute, appeared to have fallen from an aircraft.

'The following morning, 19th July, 'A' Squadron was directed to Soliers which my Troop reached without opposition. The Division's objective was Bourguébus, 11th Armoured having Bras and Hubert Folie and Guards Armoured having Cagny as their objectives. However, the scene I was presented with was extremely confusing. We knew by now that the Eleventh had suffered a severe reverse on the previous day with enormous tank casualties and, although the Guards were supposed to be in Cagny, we were still receiving anti-tank fire from its vicinity and, indeed, one of my tanks was hit. All around were tanks, mostly *Shermans*, some still burning and it was hard to tell which were knocked-out and which were still alive, let alone which formation or regiment they belonged to. There was a lot of enemy artillery fire, particularly those most unpleasant Minenwerfers with their unnerving moaning sound and any movement out of cover seemed to attract anti-tank fire both from the ridge and from Four. Soliers itself was simply a ruin after the air and artillery attacks and there were bodies and fragments of bodies everywhere. This repellent atmosphere suddenly became even more so for me when, while I was sitting on the cupola to get a better view through my binoculars, an airburst overhead caused a shell fragment to pass between my legs and into the back of my gunner, Tpr Baldrey[4], severely wounding him. It was a difficult task to extract him from the turret and it may be that our efforts to do so hastened his death. All of us in the crew were left with our overalls heavily stained with his blood and I could hardly believe how lucky I had been to avoid death.

'My recollection is that during the whole of 19th July we really made no progress, although 'B' Squadron managed to get into Bourguébus but then had to withdraw for the night because of lack of infantry support. On 20th July, with Bourguébus finally taken by 'B' Squadron, my Troop was ordered to move over to the west and support the Canadians who had attacked from the west and were now held up and vulnerable in the area of Verrières. This sector proved equally uninviting – open and with (surprisingly) unburied Canadian dead – but fairly soon torrential rain brought the whole 'Goodwood' operation to a halt.'

Syd Storer has vivid memories of the aerial activity: heavy bombers approaching from the north-west, escorted by both Spitfires and American fighters. The sheer numbers left no doubt in anyone's mind what the effect on the ground would be: a whole village – Villers-Bocage – wiped out, along with the Germans who were occupying it. With no enemy aircraft within miles, the men of The Fifth were horrified to see that, as the American fighters passed over them and they could see their markings quite clearly, the nearby American Ack-Ack gunners opened fire and shot one down.

An impressive aspect of attacks by the Typhoons of Tactical Air Force was the way they swept overhead and then suddenly zoned in and blasted enemy positions or columns which had, until the moment the Typhoons opened up with machine-guns and rockets, been invisible to the troops on the ground. Once a target had been located in this way, the tanks immediately joined in with HE and MG fire. This was the signal for the Gunners to bring their 25-pounders to bear on the ground behind the attack to prevent reinforcements coming forward and for the infantry to move in and consolidate. This close co-operation between TAF and the advancing armoured divisions was soon to be carried a step farther forward. An RAF spotter officer in a scout car (sometimes an armoured car, if he was lucky) was attached to the leading Squadron HQs and directed the Typhoon pilots where to seek for targets, or where – to use RAF language – to prang those that the tanks had found.

As Syd Storer reported, the strain was beginning to tell: on one replenishing halt, carried out under enemy shelling, some crews refused to get out of the tanks. They were not regarded as mutineers (as their fathers in WW I would have been) but were more sympathetically treated, being relegated to the echelons or returned to base if the MO could do nothing for them.

While the Regiment was resting in the middle of July, Syd's crew lost their veteran and well-liked commander, Sgt Fearnside. Not as a victim of enemy action but through a knee injury received in a football match with The Fifth's traditional rivals, the First Battalion! However, the old saying about ill winds came true: the replacement was Pluto Ellis.

Syd Storer provided the readers of his Diary with a long description of 'Goodwood' but it adds little to the accounts already included. It must, nevertheless, have held his family spellbound when they read it. He mentions one minor point that I have not found recorded anywhere else. When Eleventh Armoured Division was held up – and being cut up – by the batteries of 88s, a Polish Armoured Brigade worked their way round to the rear and, despite considerable losses, cleared the ridge of all the remaining guns.

Carlo Carlsson was one of the crew on Jake Wardrop's tank who had a lucky escape. On 19th July their *Firefly* had the misfortune to receive a direct hit in the engine compartment from an A/Tk gun whose position they had over-run but whose crew had manhandled it far enough round to catch them. Luckily one of the *Cromwells* in the Troop saw what had happened and was able to get close to the burning tank and rescue them. The tank brewed but only Tpr Wood was wounded. Among Peter's worst memories of the Normandy battles was the appalling slaughter of animals – the farm horses and the cattle, whose carcasses were left to rot in the fields, generating a stench which the men hardly ever were able to get out of their nostrils.

Rather surprisingly it is Norman Smith (whose usual line of reportage is, to say the least, lurid) who provides one of the best picture of the domestic life of a tank crew in Normandy. Fully to understand what Norman has to say, it is necessary to point out that the World War Two tanks one sees in a Museum – even a military one like that at Bovington or Duxford – do not look like the tanks that actually took part in 'Hitler's War'. For one thing, they are much too clean and tidy; for another, they do not carry all the ancillary equipment which was so essential to (and beloved by) the crews. As has been pointed out earlier, tank crews had to be self-sufficient for most of their time in action. Although the Echelons brought up ammunition, fuel and rations only the guns and the engines were able to consume their fodder in the raw state. As careful culinary preparation was not a luxury in which the crews could normally indulge, the Army devised what one can now consider to be a primitive form of 'convenience food'. But some of this still needed, at least, heating and, at most, cooking.

This meant that, in addition to the crew's bedrolls, the spare jerricans of water and such odds and ends as spare track links, the tanks were decorated with the crew's cooking equipment, essentially the ubiquitous 'tank cookers'. Tank cookers were to the tank crews what an Aga is to the house-proud *mater familias*. It is true that most tanks came equipped with a portable cookers of the 'Primus' type but these had a strictly limited capacity. More of them later. The standard tank cooker has already been described but, because the territory through which the Army was now passing offered more opportunity of 'acquiring' cooking utensils than did the Desert, the variety of such utensils was very much larger. All these were strung on the tanks (or on the Bren Gun Carriers of the RBs) in a most un-military manner. Some tanks with a skilled *chef de cuisine* on board had a quite remarkable assortment of cooking utensils attached to it somewhere. Sophisticated or not, a little ingenuity went a long way to ameliorating an otherwise unpalatable (if dietetically nourishing) Army menu.

And what was the 'often otherwise unpalatable menu'? For most of the time that the crews were in action or on the move in North-west Europe, the rations came in the form of the boxed 'Compo' [short for composite] Pack. These contained rations, as the Regimental Quartermasters told the troops, for fourteen men for one day or one man for fourteen days. The composition of these boxes did, in fact, include everything that was essential for feeding the troops through to dealing with the consequences of the troops being fed. The trouble was the monotony of the ingredients. They may have been carefully selected with the troops' health in mind, to say nothing of the limited resources of the nation's larder after five years of war, but tins of meat and vegetable stew varied by tins of vegetable and meat soup, with sausage links – no-one ever discovered what the sausages were supposed to be linked to – or desiccated bacon rashers or tins of beans or of uncooked but ready peeled potatoes as a side dish, coupled with unvaried and invariable Army Hard Tack Biscuit, did tend to be monotonous week-in-week-out. The only compensation – apart from the chocolate and the cigarettes [which were occasionally made out of real Virginian tobacco] – was the fact that the packs came up with splendid regularity and with a frequency which defied the logistical problem of dividing fourteen men packs between four or five man tank crews. There was, it must be said, one unforgivable aspect of the Compo Pack and that was the 'instant' mix of tea, sugar and dried milk. This tasted not of tea, not of sugar and not of milk and made the appearance of real tea leaves, real sugar and good old-fashioned tinned milk more than ever welcome.

As Norman points out for his readers what everyone in the crews knew, namely that, 'Eating and drinking in action (like washing and shaving) were things you did when you could. Sometimes you had to wait a long time for a meal and, if it was a very long time, one of the crew would nip out and grab whatever came to hand from the lockers on the outside of the tank.' Experienced crews very quickly learnt to have their private 'emergency rations' stored *inside* the tank. However, as he explained, the crews did like to cook hot food when they could. In theory, each member of the crew was available to take his turn at cooking but there was often one member of the crew more ready to do so than the others. This was not usually the tank commander, who might have to disappear at any moment to get his orders, nor the W/Op who frequently had to remain on wireless watch. Of the three remaining members of a *Cromwell* crew, the lap gunner usually had the least to do in the way of maintenance and was consequently the man who found that he was the 'volunteer' cook.

This was the theory: sometimes things turned out differently and the lap gunner had other things to think about besides the cooking. 'Once, in leaguer, we were going about the business of replenishing when, suddenly, the whole sky lit up. We could see and hear the German aircraft that had dropped the flares above us. It was light enough to see *everything* and we knew we had been spotted. Bert Diwell, the W/Op, swung the water cans up onto the top of the turret and Bert dropped inside. I passed the cans to him and shouted to the Echelon driver to come and join us: he needed no persuading and I felt his feet coming down on my shoulders as I slid onto the gunner's seat. Meanwhile

Maurice [Bonnet, the driver] and Tony [Webber, the lap gunner] had emptied the open petrol cans and slung the full ones as far away from the tank as possible and scrambled into their seats. Pretty smartly, too, came our tank commander's boots, followed by the rest of him through the turret cupola. We felt safe but very crowded, as four into the space designed for three doesn't go very comfortably.

'As we guessed, the real purpose of the visitor from the Luftwaffe was not so much to drop his bombs as to spot for the German artillery. As soon as he droned away, Tony and Maurice resumed the petrol pouring (illumination still by courtesy of our aerial visitor) while Bert and I started to load the boxes of machine-gun belts and the 75mm ammo. Bert's eyesight was not his greatest asset so he got into the turret while the Echelon driver threw the rounds up to me to catch. I passed them in to Bert who stacked them in the ammo bins. Not the method of handling high explosives which would recommend itself to the Health and Safety Executive! We were about half way through when the Jerry gunners began to find us with HE. This time it was the ammo wagon driver that we had with us in the tank.'

There wasn't much time left for sleeping that night, Norman went on to say but, at least Tony Webber did find time to cook up some tinned sausages and beans. Not *haute cuisine* but nevertheless welcome.

THE OTHER SIDE

The main events in July 1944, so far as the other side was concerned, were the attempt to assassinate Hitler and Rommel's serious wounding when his staff car was strafed by the RAF. Chronologically, the latter event occurred first: historically, the former event had much earlier roots.

Until his recall from North Africa, Rommel still had some faith in Hitler as his patron and as head of the Armed Forces. Once disillusion started, it did not take long for him to realise that Hitler was not worth his loyalty: was a man without honour, without humanity, without scruples.

Even if Rommel had realised that the Führer was blindly driving his country to destruction, it is unlikely that he would have initiated a plot to murder him. In fact, Rommel was against the assassination: it would, he argued, only make a martyr of Hitler, whereas his arrest by the Army would show who was in command.

In the event, Rommel had no need to plot: murder was already afoot and had been at least since February 1943. In February 1944, however, Rommel put the problem of saving Germany from Hitler on one side and attended to the problem of saving Germany from the Anglo-Saxon Invaders. But, unknown to him, there were others who kept Rommel well in mind. Two of the principal plotters, Dr Gördeler, the Mayor of Leipzig, and Colonel-General Ludwig Beck, a former Chief of General Staff, were aware that merely to eliminate der Führer would be of no advantage: his place would simply be taken by another of the leaders of the Nazi pack – who might, indeed, prove to be a bigger menace than his late master.

Gördeler and Beck realised that a man who commanded the respect of the people and of the Army would have to be produced, ready and able to take over. There was only one such man. Rommel was a national hero: except in the minds of a few die-hards in the High Command, his reputation in the Army was outstanding: he had the respect of the British – with whom he would shortly have to negotiate an armistice. If.

If Rommel could be persuaded to plot against his Commander-in-Chief.

He could and the story of the plot is as complicated and as intricate – and as unlikely –as anything in fiction. Apart from Gördeler and Beck, it involved Frau Rommel, Rommel's Chief of Staff, the head of the Military Counter Intelligence Service and the Military Governors of both France and Belgium.

It included, in written form, the complete details of the armistice terms to be negotiated with Eisenhower and Montgomery. Terms which, unknown to the plotters, would never have been accepted by the Western Allies, since they included the freedom of Germany to continue to wage war on the Communists on the Eastern Front: any cease-fire, which did not include Russia, was specifically excluded under the terms of the Casablanca Agreement.

Although Rommel played no active part in the machinations of the plotters and probably knew nothing of the two previous, abortive, bomb attempts, he must have been aware of the elaborate plans drawn up for taking over control once Hitler was eliminated. To that extent he must be considered a guilty party and privy to the activities of the plotters.

The activities of the plotters centred on one Colonel Count Claus von Stauffenberg who had been badly wounded in North Africa but whose zeal for assassination had not been diminished by the loss of an arm, an eye and two of his remaining fingers. However, for the Count, as for the other conspirators, there remained three questions. How? Where? When?

The answer to these questions came in a form which reads like the script of a bad Hollywood 'B' movie. Colonel von Stauffenberg was given an appointment – by someone totally unconnected with the plot – which brought him into official and almost daily contact with Hitler.

On three occasions in early July 1944 von Stauffenberg was in Hitler's presence with a powerful bomb in his brief case but refrained from planting it because one or more of the other targets – Göbels or Göring or Himmler – was absent.

But on 20th July, even though Hitler was alone, von Stauffenberg decided to act. He planted the bomb, left the meeting, heard the bomb explode and sent the success signal to his contact with the conspirators.

It is true that the bomb did explode but it had been designed to be effective only in the confined space of the concrete bunker where Hitler always held his meetings. Always . . . except on this one occasion. On 20th July the meeting was held in a temporary timber hut while some work was being carried out in the command bunker. When the bomb exploded, the hut disintegrated and the force of the explosion was dissipated. Those present, including Hitler, escaped with very minor injuries.

The success message set in motion the arrangements for the takeover of power but these were immediately nullified when the news of Hitler's escape became known.

What happened to the other conspirators is part of history. Exactly what happened to Feldmarschall Erwin Rommel is an unsolved mystery, although there is little doubt that his death was encompassed on the 13th October 1944 by the Schutzstaffel.

THE WAR CHRONICLE

1944

July	03	Algerian troops from the Free French entered Siena
	07	Soviet forces entered Vilnia in Lithuania
	16	British troops captured Arezzo
	20	Plot to assassinate Hitler misfired – V-bomb attacks on London caused mass evacuation on a scale which rivalled 'the Blitz'

NOTES

1. Lt Garnett. Although wounded, Jackie Garnett remained on duty with his crew
2. Nebelwerfers. As previously noted, these were the 'Moaning Minnie' type of Minenwerfers
3. Royal Hamiltons. The Royal Hamilton Light Infantry was a Canadian Militia (*ie* Territorial) Regiment, originally raised in the town of Hamilton, Ontario
4. Tpr Baldrey. This name is given as Trooper Baudry in the Regimental Casualty List

CHAPTER XVI
. . . *The Falaise Gap*

August 1944

Operation 'Goodwood' slid imperceptibly into the actions which led to the capture of Mont Pinçon, the closing of the Falaise Gap and the eventual break-out from Normandy.

These events cannot be taken in isolation: they were part of the general scheme of things. It is true that the impetus of the Invasion had been lost early on, with the failure to capture Caen as Monty had promised on D-Day, or D+1 at the latest. According to Alanbrooke, at this stage of the war Churchill reviled Monty whenever his name was mentioned. 'Brookie' defended his protégé but could not hide his anxiety that matters were moving so slowly. The truth was that Monty's plans *were* succeeding, if not as fast as he hoped – and had been unwise enough to trumpet from the housetops. He had, as he intended, drawn the weight of the German armour into the British Sector, thus freeing the Americans for their break-out. In fact, US General Omar Bradley seems to have been the only Senior Officer in the High Command who appreciated just how sound Monty's strategy was or how hard-pressed the British and Canadians were.

While the Germans were congratulating themselves on halting 'Goodwood', they soon found that their celebrations were premature. Monty *had* drawn the bulk of their armour into the British Sector and, as a result, had left the Americans confronted by only two Panzer Divisions, with fewer than a hundred tanks between them, and six tatterdemalion Infantry Divisions.

Weather delayed the US Operation 'Cobra' from the 21st to 25th July. What delayed it even more effectively during its initial stages was less the weather or the enemy opposition than the devastation of the roads, and the terrain generally, created by bombing on an even heavier scale than that which preceded 'Goodwood'. But, once launched, it gained momentum and by the end of the month had broken through the Avranches bottleneck and had split, as planned, into spearheads. One spearhead was commanded by US General 'Georgie' Patton who now had yet another chance to carve his name in history: his spear was aimed south and south-west and is, therefore, not relevant to the history of The Fifth.

What is relevant is Monty's plan to drive south and south-east from the area of Caumont, where 5RTR was at the end of July, thereby depriving the Boche of the chance of regrouping to cope with the American break-out. Again the British and Canadians had overwhelming armour superiority – something like 1,000 AFVs and replacements which were easy to come by. By contrast, the Panzer Divisions were lucky if they got as many as one in ten replacements and they had, by mid-August, lost some 250 tanks.

What followed was Operation 'Bluecoat' and it was preceded by a 'bomb carpet' laid by over 1,100 bombers. Initially, according to Liddell Hart, the Seventh Armoured had made very slow progress down the main Caumont–Aunay-sur-Odon road, the principal defensive works being mines covered by well-placed screens of small arms fire. It is probable that this is one of the incidents which generated the clear-light-of-wisdom-after-the-event criticism that the Desert Rats had lost their former desire and ability to press on. It was certainly a criticism which Miles Dempsey levelled at their GOC and it is unfortunately true that the slow progress allowed the enemy to reinforce many of their strong points instead of withdrawing from them.

At this juncture, and doubtless not unconnected with the Seventh Armoured's somewhat cautious advance, there was a major shake-up in command. The Commander of XXXth Corps (Lt General Bucknall), the Divisional Commander of the Seventh Armoured (Bobbie Erskine) and the Brigade Commander of the Twenty-second Armoured (Loonie Hinde) were all 'blown out' and Lt Gen Brian Horrocks, now recovered from the serious wounds he sustained in Tunisia, Major General GL Verney, from 6th Guards Tank Brigade, and Brigadier H Mackeson, from the Royal Scots Greys, were 'blown in' to take their places.

These changes produced little or no immediate results on the ground, as the German resistance was still well organised and incredibly stubborn. What did bring about a change was not Monty's orders for an advance on the Seine but Hitler's orders to the unfortunate Feldmarschall Günther Hans von Kluge who had been appointed the 'Supremo West' on 7th July in place of von Rundstedt. On 3rd August von Kluge, going one stage further than his predecessor had dared to go, had proposed a strategic withdrawal from Normandy, principally to enable him to contain the American break-out but incidentally to enable him to halt the British advance and thereby to meet it on ground of his own choosing. Hitler, now Supreme Tactical Commander as well as Commander-in-Chief, decreed otherwise and, with all the wisdom of a man who fights his battles on maps and reckons up his divisions by their nominal strength, ordered a massive Panzer counterstroke from the German left flank near Mortain, directed at Avranches. In theory – and if the Germans had had the strength on the ground and the control of the air – this counterstroke could have been a master-stroke. It might well have boxed the combined British and Canadian forces up in the Caen salient and it might well have completely cut Patton's Third American Army off from its base and its supplies.

Whatever Hitler might have fooled himself into believing about the strength of his nine paper Panzer Divisions the truth was that, between them, they mustered fewer tanks than one British armoured division. He appears also to have forgotten that the Luftwaffe had lost control of the air and the Allies knew how to use it.

Obedient to Hitler's orders, von Kluge[1] launched his attack, directing his forces west to cut through the British Sector and head for Avranches. Simultaneously, on 7th August, the forty-one year old Canadian Corps Commander, Guy Simmonds, launched the 2nd Canadian Infantry Division and the 51st Highland Division counter-stroke down the line of *Route Nationale N^{r} 158* which runs from Caen to Falaise. As von Kluge's offensive faltered, he realised that he had put his head in a noose. The offensive became defensive. The noose was drawn tighter and tighter during the ten days that followed but the complete strangle-hold was not obtained until 19th August by which time a great many of the German defenders had escaped.

Even so, the bag exceeded 50,000 prisoners and vast quantities of matériel which was gratifying. What was not welcome were the 10,000 or so dead members of the German forces and the countless thousand carcasses of dead and decomposing transport horses.

The War Diary for August which, for the crucial days at the beginning of the month, takes on full narrative form reads:

1 Caumont. 'B' Sqn was placed under comd of 1/6 Queens and 'C' Sqn under 1/5 Queens. 'A' Sqn being in reserve.

0900 hrs Bde attacked from area Benneville, 1/5 Queens Group left directed on Breuil, 1/6 Queens Group right directed on Monpied. All went well but 1/5 Queens found themselves unable to establish themselves on the Breuil feature. It was decided to pass 1RTR through who, although suffering casualties, succeeded in forcing the enemy to withdraw

Casualties : [HQ] Tpr Harwood JH KIA
Sgt Gordon Wnd Tpr Richardson Wnd

2 Regt switched to comd 22 Armd Bde and a further plan made to attack the Breuil feature with 1/6 Queens and then to pass the Regt through directed on to Aunay-sur-Odon. RHQ was one mile south of Cahagnes and after a quick exchange of fire from 'A' Sqn, 37 POWs were collected from hedgerows

Casualties : [LAD] Cfn Tedder Wnd
[B] Tpr Reid P Wnd

Bag : 37 POWs

3 Cahagnes. At first light the Regt left the area and passing through the 1/6 Queens made for the high ground which overlooked the Aunay–Villers road. 'A' Sqn almost immediately overran 40 POWs. A fairly heavy mist which had persisted, lifted (0830 hrs) and when it

had been hoped that it would be a cover from the high ground in the south, none existed and the Regt was under observation the rest of the day. 'A' Sqn made very good progress as far as La Lande and Courcelles.
'C' Sqn was protecting the left flank and were stationary in a position 400 yds S of St Georges d'Aunay. Both squadrons having contacted the enemy, 3 Tp in 'A' Sqn in La Lande got the better of a head-on encounter with a Mk IV, but enemy inf forced them to withdraw from the rlwy bridge. 4 Tp reached 'Pt 138' where they commenced shelling the road. The enemy reacted quickly by heavy and accurate shelling on 4 Tp's position. AP was also reported.
1130 hrs 'B' Sqn passed through 'A' with the intention of recapturing 'Pt 138' and deal with any opposition there.
1300 hrs Enemy opposition in La Lande had increased considerably and several tks were seen and engaged. 3 Tp 'A' Sqn KO'd 2 Mk IVs for the loss of 2 *Cromwells*, despite the fact that one tk had a broken cocking lever[2] on the 75mm at a range of 200 yds.
2 Tp followed with an action against 3 Mk IVs and 1 Mk V at a range of 1000 yds. 1 *Cromwell* was lost, also a *Challenger*[3] which, through lack of opportunity, had not been able to T&A sights with the result that all three shots fired missed.
RHQ stayed with 1/6 Queens with whom no supporting plans had been made as this was considered a firm base and it appeared to be a case of Armour looking after itself and getting established 1½ miles E of the Queens FDLs. As all moves were under enemy observation, the effect of a sudden attack with concentrated gun and mortar fire against the A/Tk screen of 1/6 Queens was to KO 50% of them.
Following the bombardment, a sudden counter-attack by the enemy Bn strength supported by 6 tanks from Bassieux had the effect of overrunning two Coys and cutting off 'A' and 'B' Sqns from RHQ
Meanwhile 2 or 3 enemy tks together with infantry opened up on 'C' Sqn from the area of St Georges and 5 more tks attacked 'A' and 'B' Sqns inflicting casualties who then made for the only cover available with the intention of making one complete squadron of the two. Meanwhile 'C' Sqn and RHQ got into position to support 1/6 Queens RHQ and so prevent them being overrun, at the same time covering the area S of St Georges. The attack was stopped 800–1500 yds short of the 1/6 RHQ and a strong point made out of the tks and inf.
A Sqn of VIII Hussars came up and took over the front S of St Georges. The enemy now had reinforced the ring around 'A' and 'B' Sqns, though one Tp had been extricated by means of a smoke screen and rejoined RHQ.
Several attempts to break out were frustrated before dark, but during darkness after leaguer had been attacked by bazookas, Maj

Macdonald [OC 'A' Sqn] gave the order to break out W. 9 tks out of the 12 succeeded in rejoining RHQ, Maj Thomson [OC 'B' Sqn] being wounded.

Casualties : [A] Lt Heynes R KIA Sgt Cornish AR KIA
Tpr Butler FJ KIA
SSM Grenslade Wnd Sgt Soloman Wnd
Cpl Hydes A Wnd
L/Cpl Pett Wnd Tpr MacIntyre Wnd
Tpr Marshall W Wnd
Tpr Beatties R Wnd Tpr Trewick E Wnd
Tpr Harland J Wnd
2/Lt Smith D Wnd & POW Tpr Hewins O POW
Tpr Bruce D POW Tpr Pocock E POW
Cpl Greenhalgh Msg Tpr Wood J Msg
Tpr Browne D Msg Tpr Hewson B Msg
[B] Sgt Nuttal C KIA
L/Cpl French A/D
Major Thompson G Wnd 2/Lt Feaver Wnd
[C] Lt Pearson Wnd
Losses : 7 Cromwells
Enemy : 3 Pzkw IVs destroyed
40 POWs and much other unconfirmed 'bag'

4 VIII Hussars relieved the Regt which went into reserve on the Breuil feature
Casualties : [C] Capt Messent JC Wnd

5–6 Regt moved to Courvadon and spent the time in re-organising
Casualties : [HQ] Sgt Lissiemore Wnd

7 Regtl Gp was ordered to advance via Le Val–Aunay and establish itself at Prosty [? Le Postit?]. This was completed by 1700 hrs, 'C' Sqn leading.

8 Regt moved to Comd 131 Bde; CL changed to road Roucamps–le Plessis Grimoult. A Sqn VIII Hussars were placed under Regtl control: 'A' and 'B' Sqns amalgamated and called 'A' Sqn. VIII Hussars led and became involved in area le Plessis Grimoult, losing 3 tks. Orders were received to make good the ground and 'A' Sqn took up defensive positions on the eastern flank of Mt Pinçon.

9 A plan was made to extend the Bde area and 'C' Sqn was ordered to co-operate with 1/6 Queens and to do an advance from Mt Pinçon to a group of houses in a forward area. The area was taken after some good co-operation between tks and inf.
Casualties : [C] Sgt Fyffe PD KIA
Tpr Davies J Wnd Tpr Williams A Wnd
Losses : Nil
Enemy : 20 POWs

10 'C' Sqn were withdrawn and the Regt moved to the area Bonnemaison 0650 hrs for rest and re-organisation

11–14 Maintenance. Talk by Lt Gen Horrocks XXXth Corps Comd to all full-rank NCOs.
Brig WRN Hinde leaves 22 Armd Bde and new Comd appointed, Brig H Mackeson.

15 7 Armd Div under comd of 1 Cdn Corps

16 1225 hrs Regt moved to Caen sector; leaguered at Robert Mesnil

17 40 fresh reinforcements arrive to replace personnel unsuitable in the unit.
1530 hrs Regt moved to area Favières

18 1000 hrs Regt moved to Pt 70, passing through St Pierre sur Dives

19 Regt remained in open leaguer in Bde area, subjected to night bombing attacks.
A2 Echelon suffering particularly in the loss of vehicles
Casualties : [HQ] Tpr Turner RF KIA
Capt Dickson AH (Padre) Wnd
Tpr Stafford P Wnd Tpr Smeaton Wnd
[LAD] Cpl Cutts Wnd Cfn Brocks Wnd
Losses : 10 x A2 Echelon vehicles

20 0900 hrs Regt moved to Boissey
1300 hrs Regt ordered to proceed via St Michel de Livet to Livarot and thence to Fervaques. After a slow start due to narrow roads, 'C' Sqn deployed ½ mile beyond Livarot and reached a cross-roads, where a 'Volkswagon' was caught and brewed up. As the bridge at Fervaques was essential, a base was formed and 'B' Sqn with 2 Mortar Platoons of 'I' Coy 1 RB moved in and attacked a small outpost in the neighbourhood of the bridge where the RB quickly established themselves.
Casualties : Nil
Enemy : 1 half-track, 4 x Staff Cars, 2 x lorries – destroyed
40 POWs

21 At first light 'A' Sqn was ordered to pass through Fervaques with intention of reaching St Cyr du Roncerai. After a short advance, 3 Tp was attacked by enemy inf using bazookas and grenades: the opposition became stiffer. 'A' Sqn was therefore ordered to hold Fervaques with 2 Coys ('A' and 'I') of RBs. The village was shelled by about four enemy tks, so 'C' Sqn, who were supporting 'A' Sqn, opened up from the high ground to the west of Fervaques on suspected enemy positions, thus disclosing their own locations. Very accurate fire was returned and one *Cromwell* was KO at a range of 2,500 yds.
1800 hrs An attack was put in by the enemy which had been suspected to be materialising for most of the day and it was successfully beaten

off. Mortar and 25-pdr fire to the rear of the retreating Germans having good effect, according to a POW statement.

Casualties : [HQ] L/Sgt Tatum Wnd
[B] Tpr Pettit GW DoW Tpr Dean L DoW
Sgt Ackroyd J Wnd
[C] Tpr Inwards B DoW
Lt Newton WF Wnd [4] Tpr Freeman W Wnd

Losses : 1 Cromwell
Enemy: 3 POWs

22–23 Canadians now took over position in the village and the Regt leaguered in area 1½ miles W of Fervaques

24 0700 hrs Regt was moved forward to Lisieux, Bde CL was main road Lisieux– Thiberville but the Regt was ordered to proceed to Moyaux and find a route running parallel to the Bde CL. Recce reported that the bridge at Hermival was suitable for crossing: 'B' Sqn went forward as an advance guard for the Regt Gp, now consisting of 'G' Bty 5 RHA and 'C' Sqn Lothian and Border Yeomanry (Flails[5]), a Scissors Bridge Coy RE and 'I' Coy RB. A few enemy infantry were met just E of Moyaux: these withdrew after a few shots.

1600 hrs 'B' Sqn pushed on and reached the bridge at Bailleu and reported it blown, whereupon the 'Scissors' was brought quickly into use and the Regt crossed. 'B' Sqn was ordered to move into Fresne-Cauverville. It was now getting dark and the Regt was ordered to continue the advance, 'B' Sqn pulling into the area at last light to form outposts as there was a danger from Lieurey where a Bn of German inf supported by tks had previously been reported. The remainder of the Regt formed a leaguer by 2100 hrs.

Postings of Officers to Unit:
A/Capt Grimstone J 2/Lts Bentley, Gwilliam J, Zoeftig E.

25 At first light open leaguer was formed until midday when the Regt was ordered to move via St Georges du Vièvre to St Georges

Meanwhile the 5 DGs had crossed the R Risle at La Romançon and the Regt was then ordered to cross the river and take Pt 162 but, owing to the traffic congestion, were only able to get across before dark and formed a leaguer to the left of 5 DG.

26 Carrier Plns of 1 RB doing close recce for 'C' Sqn moved to Aptot and then to Monbuisson without opposition until reaching the station at St Léger du Gennetey where there was a half-hearted attempt by the enemy armed with bazookas to stop the advance. This was quickly moved by 'C' Sqn firing HE and Besa into the area. 25 POWs were taken.

Immediately after the station came a thick wood through which the CL passed. A foot patrol of RB was soon in contact with the enemy.

However orders were received from Bde Gp to move from the Appot area and onto the main road Montfort sur Risle – Appeville to Brestot. At night a scattered leaguer was formed along this road and a strict guard kept.

27 0900 hrs Regiment ordered to return to St Léger du Gennetey, the only CL available being Touville to Bois Inger as VIII Hussars were operating on the Regiment's east with the intention of cutting the east–west road. A Coy of 1/7 Queens came under comd and were ordered to attack the area La Mesilière. 'C' Sqn cleared the area Bois Inger where a few enemy had been seen and 1/7 Queens formed up. After a stonk by Mediums and 'G' Bty 5 RHA, the Queens moved into La Mesilière, 'C' Sqn supporting, and the main road was cut. One POW reported that 30 men from his unit had baled-out taking 2 x 50mm guns.

Enemy – 1 POW

28 'C' Sqn made La Mesilière firm and 'B' Sqn passed through and cut the main road Routout–Bourg Achard without opposition, 2 Tps being sent to Viquesnil.

1000 hrs There was no sign of the enemy and the Regt was ordered to concentrate and move to Lieurey via St Georges du Vièvre.

Officer postings to this unit:

2/Lts Bayly L, Darbyshire H, Lambert O.

29 Regt moved to Semerville where 22 Armd Bde concentrated.

1800 hrs Bde conference called and the new objective made known – Ghent – over 200 miles away!

30 No event

31 0430 hrs Advance begins under 'peace' march conditions. The route to the River Seine being via Le Neubourg – Louviers and the River crossed at St Pierre du Vauvray. The route then ran: Houville en Vexin–le Tronquay–La Feuille, the Regt leaguering a mile S of Gaillefontaine.

Officer postings to this unit:

Lts Swain and Rhodes, 2/Lts Chacksfield C, MacIntyre.

Successful or not in terms of achieving what the High Command intended – Monty is reputed to have told Dempsey, the Army Commander, to throw caution to the wind and to pay any price necessary – 'Bluecoat' must deserve a place in the GUINNESS BOOK OF RECORDS for fast planning. Between initial order and Zero Hour, less than 40 hours elapsed. As the War Diary shows, progress on the ground was not quite so rapid.

The Fifth's engagement in the first few days was reminiscent of the ferocity of Sidi Rezegh, the confusion of The Cauldron and the close-quarters slogging of Alam Halfa. Once again, the actions took place in an area where distances on the map were not much larger than an English Parish, where there was no scope for manoeuvring and all the advantages for terrain, as in the bocage, were with the defence. The sole advantage which lay with the Allies was the lesson learnt on close co-operation between armour and infantry and on close support from the Gunners and Sappers.

For the Division as a whole, it was a bad time: there were tales (unfortunately true) of infantry surrendering in pockets where resistance was by no means useless. There was a general feeling that the efforts being put into the actions by the men in the tanks should have produced better results if the men at the top knew their job: a feeling reinforced by the almost daily news of the successful advance of the Americans.

For The Fifth, as the Regimental Casualty List shows, the worst day came on 3rd August and the worst to suffer was 'A' Squadron. The men who fought in those battles retained vivid, albeit sometimes conflicting, memories The conflict is hardly surprising for nothing in those first three days of August was clear. Advance, attack, counter-attack, flanking and out-flanking manoeuvres until the reduced 'A' and 'B' Squadrons were completely ringed by tanks, anti-tank guns and infantry armed with – and eager to use – their Panzerfausts.

As Dennis Cockbaine, then 2i/c of 'B' Squadron, wrote, 'By 1st August the Caen bridgehead was just starting to enlarge after nearly two months' very hard and unpleasant fighting. We had been bombed and shelled day and night and, despite tremendous air and land power, we had not been able to achieve a major break-through. The two stages of the 'Goodwood' operation, for example, had been preceded by thousand-bomber attacks, the first by the USAAF, the second by the RAF. We reckoned that more damage was inflicted on our own troops than on the enemy. Certainly a lot of Germans survived to fight again. We were all very tired but spirits were uplifted when the front seemed to be getting a little less populated by the enemy.

'We reached the area of Aunay-sur-Odon on 1st August and 'A' and 'B' Squadrons were ordered to push forward at day-break on the 3rd. A heavy mist made observation almost impossible and the inevitable happened when we had advanced about a mile and the mist suddenly lifted. We were on a forward slope with little cover and were faced by a large number of Pzkw IVs and Panthers who were well place in hull-down positions. They picked us off throughout the day, although during this action we were able to knock out a Panther and about a dozen Pzkw IVs but, by dusk, we were all but surrounded. It was decided to form a defensive leaguer and this was done. However the 'B' Squadron Commander, George Thomson, somehow wandered outside the leaguer[6] and did not answer a challenge from an 'A' Squadron sergeant who thereupon fired at him, wounding him severely in the stomach.

'I took command of the Squadron and arranged for Jackie Garnett to put George in the turret of his tank and go like the clappers on a compass bearing, hoping to find HQ. He did it and George survived, although he was too badly wounded ever to return to 5RTR. It was then obvious that we would be finished off if we stayed where we were. There was some confusion between the two Squadrons as to command, so I took charge and decided to order what was left of us to make a break for it towards a cross roads that we had passed in the morning mist. Twelve tanks were left from thirty-two starters in 'A' and 'B' Squadrons and we were to lose three more on the break-out.. It was a mad rush through the orchards, going as hard as we could – only stopping to pick up Roy Dixon[7] on the way and cramming him down in the bottom of the turret – until we reached the cross roads where a building was on fire. I got out to make sure that we headed down the right way when 'Butch' Lovell yelled from my tank for me to get down, whereupon he fired over my head at two or three Boches who were lining me up in their sights. I scrambled back on board and we reached the HQ outpost and safety. For most of that eventful day we had had the badly burned body of a fellow tankman on the engine cover at the back of my tank and I was very relieved to be able to bring him back to the Regiment and to a decent burial.

'So ended an eventful and thoroughly unpleasant day.'

Roy Dixon said that his next memory of any note after 'Goodwood' was also of 3rd August when his troop was the leading one in 'A' Squadron. His account is rather more graphic than that given in the War Diary and reads, 'As we reached a railway bridge over the road at La Lande just west of Aunay, I got out of my tank to have a look through this opening and heard any enemy tracked vehicle approaching. I just had time to get back into the turret and to give orders to my gunner when a Pzkw IV appeared. We both fired simultaneously but at such short range that both gunners fired over the top of their targets and the Pzkw IV withdrew behind the railway embankment. Some infantry looked over at me and, as I tried to manoeuvre to take up a better position, my tank threw a track. After a hasty change of tank, we knocked out the original Pzkw IV but, in the subsequent action, my veteran Troop Sergeant [A Cornish MM] was killed and my fourth tank – a *Challenger* – was also knocked out. It was commanded by 2/Lt Douglas Smith, who was supposed to be gaining experience under me but who ended up wounded and a prisoner of war[8]. Later we knocked out a second Pzkw IV but, during the late afternoon, we heard that an enemy counter-attack from the south had more or less cut us off, together with 'B' Squadron. At about this time my own tank was knocked out but I was lucky enough to be able to bale out unhurt and transfer to my one remaining tank. As darkness fell we received orders to break out from the leaguer which the remainder of the 'A' and 'B' Squadron tanks had formed and head westwards to join the rest of the Regiment. However, my tank was suddenly hit by something – possibly a Panzerfaust – in the gloom: it was just one big flash and bang and it was difficult to tell what had happened. In any event, it seemed prudent to make another hasty exit. It was by now a scene of some confusion, with tanks withdrawing and crews on their feet. I managed to flag down a tank that turned out to be Dennis Cockbaine's. It was crouching room only and I made the journey to safety like that at the bottom of the turret of Dennis' tank.

'Having got out of three tanks, lost four together with an officer, a sergeant and most of the crew members, it was certainly not a day to be proud of or easily forgotten. After these somewhat disastrous events I had a couple of days in A2 Echelon while four more tanks and their crews were assembled to form a new 3 Troop. A number of the new men, including the whole of my own crew came from 2nd Northants Yeomanry which had been disbanded after 'Goodwood'. They proved to be an excellent crew.'

Harry Ireland's account of that day's affray in August ties in with Roy Dixon's and Dennis Cockbaine's but is told from a different point of view: that of a *Firefly* gunner. It begins on 3rd August on the Breuil feature, after the counter-attack which over-ran the infantry positions and left the two squadrons completely encircled and cut off from the rest of the Regiment. 'We slogged away all day trying to break out but the enemy had complete observation of every move we made and, by night-fall, had a tight grip on the remaining tanks. What a feeling, hearing the CO coming on the air and saying, 'I've tried everything possible to get you out. You must form your own defence and we'll try again in the morning.' We had been forced into a small field so that the remaining tanks were in close touch. The order was passed round, 'Wireless silence. Everything that moves is enemy, so shoot to kill. When the OC's tank starts up, all tanks start up. When he moves, follow him.' A tricky situation but better than doing nothing; just waiting our doom. Which had started, as the Boche infantry had crept up on us with their bazookas.

'When the time came to go and the Squadron Commander's tank started up, we all started up. Maximum revs: go like hell. But not far. There was a blinding flash in the turret. We'd been hit and my tank commander, Sgt Nuttal, had fallen across my back, dead. The driver shouted, 'What's happened?' I didn't take time off to explain. I picked up the mike and shouted 'Go like bloody hell!' I was in charge but I couldn't see where the others had gone. We hit a country road and I ordered the driver to turn left. We zig-zagged down the road at top speed, crashing through a make-shift road block. No good: I knew we were lost. I called a halt. It was time for more than one to make a decision. We halted near a small wood. We laid Sgt Nuttal on the back of the tank and covered him with our great coats. We decided to pull off the road and hide up in the wood. Ten minutes later we were shelled by our own guns: not nice; air-burst all around the tank. We closed down and tried to contact RHQ on the air. No joy: the aerial had been shot away. As I went to close down again, I saw a German soldier standing in front of the tank. He shouted 'Kamerad! Kamerad!'. For me this was too much. I slammed the turret flaps shut, calling to the others, 'There's a blood Jerry outside!'

'We had been fairly calm up to now but, I must admit, panic was beginning to take over. We decided the tank was not the place for us and we'd be better off if we baled out. I took the firing pin out of the 17-pdr and a half bottle of whisky that had belonged to poor Sgt Nuttal and out we got. We crawled across the road, through a hedgerow and found some abandoned German slit-trenches, with equipment lying all over the place, as if the owners had left in a hurry. Exhausted, we drank the whisky. The silence was soon broken by shouting and the noise of running feet. German voices. We sat tight and they passed us not ten yards away. An hour later our own guns opened up again. We crouched at the bottom of the slit-trench and waited until it began to get light. As luck would have it, the W/Op had brought a small compass out of the tank. We all agreed north was the way to go. We hadn't crawled 500 yards through the mist which had come up with the dawn, when I spotted a couple of British steel helmets. I stood up (foolish of me) and waved my beret, shouting as loud as I could. It was an infantry FOP and the lads welcomed us but, they wanted to know, 'What the bloody hell were you doing out there, Tankies. We're putting in an attack on those woods as soon as the mist clears.'

'After explaining to the infantry officer what we'd been up to and telling him that Jerry had pulled out during the night, the driver and I felt confident enough to go back with a small section of infantry to give us covering fire and bring the tank out. Starting the tank up brought a German soldier out into the open. Arms held high, he gave himself up with a big grin. Back at the infantry position, the officer, who spoke German, told me the prisoner was Polish, forced into the German Army. He was the lad who tried to surrender to us last night. The infantry officer gave us directions and we motored back to the Regiment, where the CO gave us a warm welcome. Later that day the Padre conducted the service for our crew commander and I climbed back into the tank utterly exhausted. The Regiment had suffered badly and the next few days were no picnic either but by the middle of the month it was a different story. The Falaise Pocket was closed. After a few days rest, the break-out from the bridgehead began.'

Since Harry was an old Desert hand and an example of The Fifth's well-know sartorial individualism he was probably one of the men who gave William Jackson a nasty shock when he was posted to 'C' Squadron on 10th August. Bill Jackson had, in fact, landed in Normandy on D-Day but with XXIV Lancers. When they were disbanded, he was sent to The Fifth as a reinforcement. 'It was quite a shock to someone who'd been expected always to be properly dressed to see this rag-time outfit,' Bill recalls. 'The first man I saw when I reached 9 Troop was wearing a top hat and a monocle on a piece of string. He turned out to be the Troop Corporal.' As his new crew commander was Sgt Snowy Harris and the other Troop Sergeant was Jake Wardrop, the former 'Donkey Walloper' Jackson soon learnt that negative smartness off parade didn't mean negative efficiency in action. Nor did it mean lack of initiative: one of Bill's early tasks was to restow the ammunition so that the racks could be made available to house the wine which Snowy had, somehow or other, managed to acquire.

Bryan Johnson's many memories of August 1944 include some from those first ferocious days. He recalled that on 3rd August the Regiment moved off in the early morning in a heavy mist which covered the whole countryside. By mid-morning the shelling had become pretty heavy and the tank crews were all closed down: all right for them but not so funny for those in the 'sawn-offs' and dingos. The day was hot and the unwelcome whine of the Minenwerfer stonks added to the unpleasantness. The men in the Recce Troop listened on the wireless to the reports coming in from 'A' and 'B' Squadrons but there was nothing that they could do. They were unaware of the success or failure of the intended break-out and were themselves ordered to withdraw to a defensive position where they stayed overnight and most of the following day. On the 5th, Recce moved out to new positions at Courvaudon, east of Aunay, where they stayed for 48 hours before withdrawing through the rubble which was all that was left of Aunay[9]. Bryan's account reads, 'On 8th August at midday we were sent up to the summit of Mont Pinçon, the highest point on Normandy. The view down the valley was superb, the weather was hot and the sun bright. All we had to do was to observe the road to the east. Suddenly, while Capt Beresford was glued to his binoculars, a shell landed quite close to the tank. For some quite unexplained reason I shouted to him, 'Move, Sir. Move!' 'Bessy' seemed surprised at my vehemence, replying, 'Yes. We'd better move.' The driver needed no telling and pulled back to a new position. No sooner had he done so than we heard the crump of an exploding shell. When the dust had settled, Capt Beresford looked at the ground and said, 'My God! That's just where we were!' No-one spoke. There wasn't anything to say. Don't ask me how but one did get those premonitions.'

Bryan's narrative continues with some interesting sidelights on life in the Regiment. When the Division was pulled out for 'rest and reorganisation' between 9th and the 19th August, the Recce Troop was reorganised. Brian Beresford left to become 2i/c of 'B' Squadron and his place was taken by Captain Stiddard [who had won an MC with 6RTR]. Willie Dovey went with 'Bessy' but Bryan Johnson refused the offer. Bryan's first impression of Jack Stiddard was of his returning from some conference in a flaming temper. The reason was that 'some damned Brass Hat' had given Colonel Gus a dressing down in public. 'What bloody right has that man with his damn Coronation Medal[10] to speak to *our* Colonel like that?' One way or another, Jack Stiddard, in the contemporary idiom, did have a short fuse. Bryan recounts an experience which occurred during a visit to the Mobile Laundry. Steve Barton [Sgt Barton DCM] was in the party in a battle dress jacket with no insignia and was unceremoniously ordered by one of the laundry wallahs to operate the pump. Bryan was horrified and started to protest: Steve simply said, 'Don't worry; lad, I know what to do and it's for the blokes.'

On 10th August, Bryan was one of many from the Regiment who watched an impromptu field concert given by George Formby. At least that was the idea: when the men arrived there was no George, only the redoubtable Beryl who explained that George was still doing his stuff for some paratroopers. This didn't go down very well but, fortunately, George – plus ukulele – turned up eventually and the show ended with cheers instead of catcalls. Less amusing for Bryan than George Formby were the abandoned farms with the cattle lowing to be milked. Bryan was quite prepared to milk them to the ground but they refused to be caught.

Gilbert Cresswell, a pre-war Territorial, was called up in September 1939 and posted to the 1st Royal Gloucester Hussars, with whom he stayed until August 1944, by which time he was a W/S Sergeant. On Monday 14th August he was posted, complete with his tank crew, to an unknown – but easily guessed – overseas destination. The next day they sailed from Southampton on an LCT and were dumped on 'Sword' Beach to be collected by a wagon from 5RTR. In the process of taking over a *Cromwell* to take forward to the Regiment, he met a man whom he knew in Civvy Street and so was able to learn a bit about what was in store for him. He also found out a bit more of that on the night of the 19th when the Echelon was bombed: his first regimental duty the next morning was burying Trooper Turner. According to Gilbert, the attack by Stukas was sheer misfortune: their real target was probably a battery of 'Long Tom' Heavy Artillery in a wood 200 yards away. After being shuttled from 'A' Squadron to HQ, he became a Troop Sergeant in 'C' Squadron.

Another man who followed much the same route to arrive with The Fifth was John Gwilliam. John had spent fifteen months with 1 RGH who had, in John's words, 'being doing their best to teach us how to cope with *Cromwells.* We often thought that they were fanatical in their training until we realised that their Second Battalion had been sent out hurriedly to the Desert without proper training or equipment and had been decimated by Rommel. We left Newhaven and arrived in the extraordinary Mulberry Harbour and were immediately shepherded into a 3-ton lorry. As far as we knew the journey could not be long because progress had been quite slow in the Caen area and off we rode into the unknown . . . which is exactly what it turned out to be. We rumbled on with plenty of stops and starts: eventually we decided that the very thought of our arrival had caused the entire German Army to retreat in alarm and our next stop would be Berlin. At last we came to a halt and clambered out of the lorry to be met with a line of tanks and two very impressive-looking officers. One was Colonel 'Gus' Holliman, CO of 5RTR and the other was Captain Jackie Garnett. [John then gave a description of these two and their records] Even though we were unaware at the time of their distinction, it did strike us as a little odd that such a distinguished reception committee had turned out to welcome a 'Dad's Army' complement of raw recruits. Gradually we realised the truth: the driver had got hopelessly lost and had spent some hours wandering around the area which was later to become all too well-known as the Falaise Gap. We were informed that we were the first reinforcements to arrive at The Fifth from the wrong end. It took us a long time to live down this little experience, especially when the driver had embellished the story by describing the difficulty he had had negotiating all the minefields!'

John continued by saying that he then had the good fortune to be posted to 'B' Squadron: commenting on the coincidence that it was then being commanded by Captain Cockbaine, late of the RGH. As John also remarked, he had the good fortune to become Troop Leader of the Troop which had Sgt Cyril 'Taff' Rees MM as its Troop Sergeant. John Gwilliam adds an interesting note on another of the of the German-speakers who were drafted into the front-line units. In his case it was one Trooper IM Glynn whose family had escaped from Germany in the 1930s and who had gained himself an Economics Degree at Oxford. One did not enquire too closely what the men like Tpr Glynn had been called before they left their native Germany: one just thanked Providence for their presence. Not the most endearing of Glynn's foibles were his habit of wearing carpet slippers at all times and in all places, and his frankness: he didn't think much of the school-boy German produced by John Gwilliam, adding that it would be a waste of time to try to improve his accent. Undoubtedly one of his more endearing foibles was the use to which he put the co-driver's seat in the Gwilliam *Cromwell*. Glynn ran a licensed delikatessen stall, handing out bully beef sandwiches and tots of rum – the latter from a very large jar of proof spirit which he had contrived to liberate – whenever the crew most needed them. However, Trooper Glynn really comes into his own at a later stage in the 5RTR history.

THE OTHER SIDE

Once again, a governing factor in the war from the point of view of the Axis was Hitler's fanaticism. His decision to fight until 'the clock struck thirteen'. At this crucial point in the war, it is arguable that Hitler's diktat *of 'No Surrender' guaranteed that, sooner or later somewhere on the Central German Plain, the Western and Eastern Allied armies would meet.*

Curiously, there is another factor which was, at this time, not fully appreciated by the British population at home. The continued mass bombing of Axis territory, with devastation ten-fold that of anything London or other British cities had experienced, produced in mainland Germany something remarkably like the 'Dunkirk Spirit'. Not that Hitler cared what the civil population thought or did, it nevertheless meant that Germany's war effort was also maintained on a 'No Surrender' basis through 1944 and well into 1945.

In the early weeks of the Normandy landings, Hitler's diktat *had been not merely 'No Surrender' but 'No Withdrawal'. Despite the evidence of his eyes and ears, Hitler maintained his fixed belief that France could be held or, better still, that the Invaders could be pushed back into the sea. However, the combination of the sealing of the Falaise Pocket and Operation 'Anvil' – the Franco-American landing in the south of France on 15th August – meant that withdrawal became inevitable. It was meant to be limited to the line of the River Seine but, on 25th August, General Le Clerc's Second French Armoured Division was in Paris and the British Second Army was across the Seine.*

THE WAR CHRONICLE

AUGUST 1944

August	04	South African forces reached Florence – Anne Frank, the 14-year-old Jewish girl, in hiding in Amsterdam since July 1942, betrayed to the Gestapo
	10	General strike declared in Paris and region – American forces cleared Japanese from Guam
	11	Russian Army attacked Pskov
	12	PLUTO [Pipe Line Under The Ocean] between Isle of Wight and Cherbourg completed
	15	'Second' Second Front opened on French Riviera
	16	Stalin refused to allow Red Army to support Warsaw Uprising
	17	Russian ground forces reached Germany's Prussian frontier
	20	Russian forces entered Romania
	22	Fleet Air Arm attacked German Battleship *Tirpitz* in Altenfijord in Norway
	23	Romania capitulated and sued for separate peace
	25	Liberation of Paris. Hitler had declared that it was to be razed to the ground. It wasn't but there were nevertheless some 3,000 civilian casualties
	26	Bulgarian Government declared that Bulgaria had 'withdrawn from the war'
	27	Last of the Chindits withdrawn to India
	28	Marseilles and Toulon fell to the Free French
	29	Allied forces captured Pinkaw in Burma
	31	Eighth Army began assault on Gothic Line in Italy – UK civilian casualties for August were 1,103 killed and 2,921 injured by enemy action

NOTES

1 von Kluge. Von Kluge committed suicide on 18th August, the day after he was replaced by Feldmarschall Model
2 Cocking lever. A device by means of which either the gunner opened the breach to eject the spent shell-case and to insert a new round or the breach opened automatically on recoil. The closing of the breach either way then 'cocked' the firing mechanism
3 *Challenger*. An experimental tank. Basically a *Cromwell* with an enlarged turret to mount the 17-pdr gun. Intended as a replacement for the *Firefly*, it never came into general use in WW II
4 Lt Newton. Although wounded, remained on duty
5 Flails. These were mine-destroying tanks
6 Major Thomson. The sad and simple truth was that he had 'taken the shovel for a walk'
7 Roy Dixon. It was not until I recounted Roy Dixon's story to him 58years later, that Dennis Cockbaine learnt the identity of his passenger!
8 Douglas Smith. As a wounded officer, Douglas Smith was evacuated by the Germans, treated by a Danish doctor and ended up in hospital in France. Douglas was released by the Americans at Challons-sur-Marne and flown back to the UK by them. He returned to the Regiment later in 1944 and 'lost' another tank in Vreden (Holland) at the end of March 1945.
9 Aunay. The 1946 *Guide Rouge Michelin* simply states that 'The town has been razed to the ground'
10 Coronation Medal. The reference was probably to General Verney's not-necessarily-military MVO. As a Guardsman, Verney had a good deal of prejudice to overcome in Seventh Armoured. He had, however, also been awarded a DSO

CHAPTER XVII

. . . *The Great Swan*

September 1944

For once, the crews in the *Cromwells* were happy men. Well, more or less. They had tanks which were designed for swanning. Fast, reliable, comfortable even, if comfort is a relative term. Above all, fewer of those bad men with big guns in the hedgerows. Not quite so comfortable were the crews of the slower *Fireflies* with their harsh suspension and tendency to snap their tracks after bouts of high-speed motoring. 'Maleesh[1]. Colonel Gus has said next stop Ghent. So let's get cracking!' was the general attitude. The War Diary may have called it an advance 'under peace march conditions': for the men it started more like a holiday. And, after the bocage and the orchards of Normandy and the ruined towns and villages, it was almost incredible to be moving through open country, through towns and villages, past houses and shops with glass in their windows and their doors open to the streets. The only problem: could the Echelons keep up? Tanks, as well as their crews, are very thirsty things.

Of course it wasn't quite the picnic that introductory paragraph makes it out to be. As the War Diary and the personal accounts show, Brother Boche was not about to surrender all the French territory he had been occupying for the last four years without taking a few last swipes at the 'usurpers' – or 'liberators', as the French preferred to call us.

The September War Diary for the Great Swan reads:

1 Gaillefontaine. Advance continues, the route being Gaillefontaine–Aumale. Regt leaguered till dark. Regt now came under command 131 Bde in order to cross River Somme half mile north of Amiens and to concentrate in the area of St Vaast, in preparation for an attack northwards the following day.

2200 hrs. The Regiment moved, reaching Molliens Vidame at midnight

2 Regt formed Group, with 1/6 Queens under command, with as objective the village of Ernaille. 0715 hrs. A Sqn led the Regtl Gp with nothing to report except an abandoned 170mm in the village of Vignacourt and continued to advance to St Léger. Meanwhile one

troop of C Sqn had been sent to St Ouen. On reaching the outskirts of Dommart, A Sqn came under mortar and machine-gun fire: also St Léger was mortared, scattering the cheering locals. A Coy of Queens came forward in PCVs and occupied defensive positions. B Sqn engaged all likely places in Dommart and soon moved on again. As they approached Berneuil, a regiment from 4 Armd Bde also arrived from the east, thus putting 400 POWs in the bag. Berneuil proved to be a Flying Bomb site. B Sqn pushed on half way to Bernaville and were engaged by 4 x 105mm guns, apparently firing over open sights. They were immediately engaged and, after a few casualties had been inflicted, the guns were abandoned and the crews made prisoner. B Sqn pushed ahead meeting minor opposition in Boisbergues and Outrebois but crossed the river successfully. The woods in this area contained about 50 enemy and fighting began. The Regt was then ordered to form a firm base with 1/6 Queens. A Sqn withdrew from the bridge at last light.

Enemy Losses: 30 POWs. 4 x 105mm guns

3 Regt reverted to command 22 Armd Bde

0800 hrs. Orders received to move to new area via Gandas and Doullens. The move was continued to main road St Pol–Arras, via Frévent, Bonneville–Ternas. The Dragoon Guards had already passed this point and the Regt caught up the tail of the column at Mazingarbe, having taken the following route: Aubigny–Hersin–Mazingarbe.

4 Advance continued. Regt leading Brigade Group. Route: Lens–Carvin–Seclin–Mesquin–Toufflers–Néchlin and a leaguer was formed at last light at Kirkhove.

5–6 Orders received to form firm base at Kruishoutem[2]. By 0900 hrs this had been accomplished having passed through Oudenaarde.

0915 hrs. Regt ordered to original Centre Line and advance on Ghent. C Sqn moved off and established themselves on cross-roads and the whole Regt moved up behind them. One SP gun encountered and A Sqn immediately ordered to Nazereth on a parallel route one mile from the CL. Meanwhile the SP gun moved in that direction and was brewed up together with a 20mm SP gun. Enemy infantry then withdrew and A Sqn rejoined the CL at Eeke. C Sqn moved to Hutepot, where they overran some enemy infantry. They were ordered to move to Zwijnaarde and then north into the city. At the same time, A Sqn were ordered to establish themselves at the cross roads so that all approaches SW of Ghent were cut off. B Sqn remained in Eeke to watch the cross-roads. Enemy reported by civilians to be in St Martens Latem and were anxious to surrender. Two Troops despatched there and 300 POWs taken. C Sqn had by now found the way into the suburbs of the city. It became apparent there were a large number of enemy in Ghent and a plan was made to order C Sqn and a Coy of the Queens under command to start at 1800 hrs. At this moment a civilian indicated to Major Crickmay, Officer Commanding C Sqn, that the enemy wished to surrender. He therefore went forward and saw the officer at the German barrier where he was joined by the Commanding Officer. Major Crickmay was blindfolded and led to see the German General, returning to report that the General was prepared to come outside his barricade and discuss surrender with the British General. The Colonel was hastily promoted but it was obvious that the German was playing for time. Brigadier Mackeson then appeared but no terms were agreed upon. The party broke up at 0300 hrs.

Casualties : [HQ] Tpr Parrott C Wnd
[C] Tpr Taylor E Wnd Tpr Ryder R Wnd
Tpr Smith J Msg Tpr de Bourcier Msg (both believed POW)

Enemy Losses : 300 POWs. 1 x 88mm gun, 1 x 20mm gun

7 Following civilian reports that enemy had withdrawn to the northern part of the city and were not south of the main east–west canal on the northern edge, part of A Sqn and C Sqn with a Coy of Queens entered the city. The remainder of A Sqn stayed in Latem and collected further POWs. There was no provision by Bde for disposal and by 2200 hrs a very restive and hungry collection of 400 POWs were evacuated under escort of tanks to Ootenhaus* POW cage.

Casualties : [A] Tpr Friend GW DoW
[B] Sgt Bull C KIA[3]

Losses Enemy : 450 POWs

8 Due to civilian representation that numerous enemy pockets were in the area, the Regt was ordered into Ghent to eliminate any chance of the enemy re-occupying the city. B Sqn now under command of 131 Bde remained at the cross-roads. 1/6 Queens were holding the bridge at Gavere. The remainder of the Regt leaguered near the railway station for the night, less B Sqn. HQ was leaguered in the Cathedral Square for close co-operation with Bn HQ of 1st Queens. During the night B Sqn left a Troop on the cross roads with 1/6 Queens. Unfortunately, an enemy force came out from Nazereth and brewed up one *Cromwell* but retired after a second Troop opened fire. B Sqn passed under command of 15 Scottish Division.

The Regiment was ordered to leave C Sqn under command 131 Bde and concentrate at Massemen and, on arrival, A Sqn patrolled Wetteren area. B Sqn put in reserve and concentrated at Oosterzele.

Loss : 1 Cromwell[3]

9 C Sqn took part in some hard fighting on enemy positions which necessitated crossing a swing bridge put into position by Sappers and

1/6 Queens. More tanks were needed and A Sqn moved into the area and came into support of Glasgow Highlanders of 15 Scottish Division.
Casualties : [C] Capt Butler BL DoW

10 B Sqn moved from Oosterzele to join Tactical HQ and went into the area Oostakker and patrols were carried out further to the north. The enemy had concentrated west of the main canal and possessed several field guns and three railway guns. 2 Troops of B Sqn were established on the canal bank and managed to get range and bearing for the guns. B Bty of 5 RHA opened up and silenced the guns for the rest of the day but they opened up again at night on Ghent and counter-battery fire was unable to be carried out as close leaguer had been formed.
Meanwhile C Sqn was completely across the swing bridge and 1/6 Queens had cleared the factory area. Two Troops of A Sqn moved across the same bridge, this being the only means of crossing to the north part of the town.. In moving east, continued to support 15 Scottish Div. The Boche fought hard, thus necessitating knocking down houses one by one with 75mm gunfire. The enemy pulled out from the north and POWs were taken.
Casualties : [A] SSM Hill R Wnd
Tpr Ogden K Wnd Tpr Sinden C Wnd
[C] Sgt Watkins L Wnd
Enemy Losses : 40 POWs (many others being killed)

11 Quiet day for A and C Sqn. B Sqn started in counter-battery work against the guns which remained silenced. Typhoons shot-up the railway guns. It was anticipated that the guns would open up again at night, an 88mm firing at 2100 hrs. Stonking was carried out all night to the tune of 150 rounds per gun. Civilians in Ghent reported that it was the quietest night they had since the Occupation

12 Regiment pulled out and concentrated at Messemen and maintenance was carried out.

13 1100 hrs. Regiment moved to an area 1½ miles NE of Malines on the Tirlemont road.

14 Maintenance, re-organisation and rest. Major S P Wood posted to this unit

15–20 No entries recorded

21 Regt placed under command of 15 Scottish Division and moved to Westerloo via Heist-op-den-Bers and remained in open leaguer.

22 Regiment moved, crossing Dutch border. Moved Gheel–Moll–Lonnel–Luykgest–Westerhoven–Eersel–Veldhoven–Eindhoven.
Leaguer formed in the Philips factory car park ½ mile west of Eindhoven.

23 Visit from GOC 15 Scottish Division. Otherwise no event.

24 Regiment now back under command of 22 Armd Bde.

25 Regt advanced to Sint Oedenrode via Best, the western half still in enemy hands and defensive positions taken up in conjunction with 501st American Airborne Regiment. Meanwhile 5 Dragoon Guards had moved forward to clear the enemy who had cut the 30 Corps; centre line. At the same time the Regt with more Americans was able to advance from Veghel. Regt ordered to pass through 5 DGs and in conjunction with US Airborne troops took up defensive positions in Veghel.

26 Exercise completed by 1500 hrs. Regiment received orders to proceed to Nistelrode via Uden.

27 C Sqn contacted a Sqn of the Gds Armd Div and accompanying the Grenadier Guards and arrived NNW of the village. A Sqn were directed south and found a crossing which was unfortunately unsuitable for tanks so were directed to Loosbroek. From here Troops were sent out 1½ miles west and south-west. Regt leaguered at Nistelrode.

28 Regt moved to take position at Loosbroek. B Sqn moved into the village and covered the installation of RHQ and G Bty 5 RHA. A Sqn proceeded to area Rukven and established a position covering the area SW. 5 Troop under Capt Babbage organised a foot patrol of six men from the crews and covered a distance of 200 yards in a NW direction. Two enemy infantry were seen and in the pursuit which followed the patrol, in reaching a further fording point, found themselves in a company position. They killed 3 Boche and one NCO was taken prisoner. The enemy reacted and started moving to this area. The patrol withdrew to Coy HQ which was heavily stonked.

1600 hrs. 8 Troop B Sqn contacted the enemy, killing four.

Casualties: [B] Sgt Greenwood Msg (later confirmed POW)

Enemy Losses: At least 7 killed, 1 POW

29 Regt had orders to cut the road Heesch–s'Hertogenbosch in area Erpendijk*. Difficulty was experienced in crossing the Barrier-Wettering Canal* but, after careful reconnaissance, two Troops of B Sqn crossed the bridge and moved northwards towards the road. C Sqn received orders to return to Nistelrode and deal with the enemy making a nuisance of them selves in Lagewirést and Groes*. The plan being to drive them onto B Sqn's two Troops.

1430 hrs. B Sqn was very near main road with a third troop on the right side at Eart. No 7 Tp on the left flank had knocked out a 75mm gun and disorganised some enemy infantry and the Troop on the right also took on and inflicted casualties on further infantry. Meanwhile C Sqn were a little slow and the enemy pushed northwards. At last light the road from Battenburg east was cleared and the road north for about 1 mile. Lagewirst and Groes were also cleared. Regiment leaguered at Loosbroek

Enemy Losses: 1 x 75mm gun, at least 10 killed

30 At first light, C Sqn returned to Nistelrode area. B Sqn in Katehoven* taking 2 POW. A Sqn in position SW of Loosbroek.

Following civilian reports, a German patrol was captured near Neikel*. 5 Troop ordered to main road in conjunction with 11 Hussars captured further 9 POWs.

1100 hrs. Regt was ordered to return and concentrate in Loosbroek and stand down

The War Diary for mid- to late-September requires some explanation: the topography alone is far from clear and the Charlie Love looks as if it had been drawn by an inebriated spider with a wooden leg. Briefly, therefore, the story for September 1944 is this. Having crossed the Seine at St Pierre du Vauvray on 31st August the Divisional Charlie Love took a north-easterly direction until reaching the town of Poix some 15 or 16 miles south west of Amiens. The Fifth crossed the Somme at Picquigny on 1st September, whereupon the CL changed direction to north-north-east until it reached the River Calanches at St Pol-sur-Ternoise which is a town about 25 miles to the west of Arras. From St Pol the CL switched north-east again, wriggling – in the case of 5RTR – back towards the north to allow 'C' Squadron to liberate Ghent, having crossed the Belgian border between Toufflers and Néchlin on 4th September.

What is significant, although no-one would have been thinking about it at the time, is that, in the space of these two World War Two September days, the Fifth Royal Tank Regiment drove through an area of northern France and southern Belgium which the Allied Armies fought for four World War One years to free from the invading German horde.

So far, so good. Matters then became a bit more complicated. From Ghent in the middle of September the Regiment went almost due east to allow 'B' Squadron to liberate Malines (Mechelen). The complication was that, in moving rapidly east from Ghent, Seventh Armoured had swung across the northern flank of the German Fifteenth Army, commanded by General von Zangen and comprising eleven battered and battle-weary divisions. Still, however, a force to be reckoned with, particularly as von Zangen was in a position to cut the lines of communication of both the Seventh and Eleventh Armoured Divisions. This threat did not, in the event, materialise but, with one thing and another, Seventh Armoured was stretched from Béthune in the west to Malines in the east.

For ten days from 14th September there was little serious tank action but no shortage of shelling and mortaring from the scattered enemy positions. Nor was there any shortage of patrolling by both sides. In the words of more than one disgruntled tank crew member, who found himself doing foot patrols, 'This ain't what I joined the flippin' Tanks for!'

On 22nd September the Regiment crossed the Dutch border and reached Eindhoven, leaguering by courtesy of Philips Electrical Enterprises. The countryside in that part of the world was yet another change for The Fifth. It might have seemed familiar to someone born and brought up in the Fens but the flat, marshy wastes, intersected by canals and drainage ditches, with roads raised high above the surrounding land did not appeal aesthetically. Nor did it appeal tactically. Movement for all vehicles was only possible on these roads: escape from them was impossible and one's presence on those raised embankments made sitting targets of the vehicles.

During this lull, activity centred on Operation 'Market Garden', the magnificent, if abortive, attempt by the Airborne Forces to seize the Rhine crossing at Arnhem. Seventh Armoured played no active part in 'Market Garden', being positioned to guard the west flank of the corridor leading up to Nijmegen.

By the end of the month The Fifth was finding its feet – rather more than its tracks – in a part of Holland it was to know well before the winter was out.

By far the most important and certainly the most dramatic event in September was the liberation of Ghent. However, before The Fifth got there, they had covered more than the 200 miles which Colonel Gus had promised them. At the end of August they were poised to cross the Somme: on 3rd September they crossed the Belgian frontier. From then on, the Great Swan was over: it has to be measured in distance covered, not in the time it lasted. By the end of the first week in September German resistance, although not on the scale experienced in Normandy, was stiffening and becoming more organised. Worse from the point of view of the liberating forces, it was unpredictable.

Bill Jackson recalls the speed of the advance as being so great that, for the crews, 'everything was a bit of a blur.' One stop on the way to Ghent was in a mining town. The retreating Germans hadn't left much for the locals to offer the liberators but there were the pit-head baths and they were very much appreciated. Bill's tank broke down in Oudenaarde [where Winston Churchill's ancestor, the Duke of Marlborough, won a notable victory in 1708] cleverly timing its misdemeanour so that the crew had to spend the night there, having been befriended by the Chief of Police. This delay meant that they missed the liberation of Ghent but went straight into action in the Canal area.

Another man who made an overnight stop in Oudenaarde was Harry Ireland only, in his case, something went amiss with the replenishing. Not only was the tank filled to the brim with petrol by the Echelon, the crew was filled to the brim with champagne by the locals. . . and put to bed in their boots by the Mayor's family!

As the War Diary states, the liberation of Ghent was not entirely straightforward nor does the Diary tell the complete story. For this we must rely on Major Maunsell. As recounted to me by Bob, the details are, 'With the rapid advance through France and into Belgium, it was obvious that big cities like Ghent could only hold out at the cost of near-total destruction. Seventh

Armoured had seen enough of that in Normandy and didn't want to see any more. Arthur Crickmay's 'C' Squadron had probed the outskirts and found them only lightly defended. Arhtur's experience and instincts (he had commanded the Recce Section) made him suspect, nevertheless, that there were more substantial defences within the city. Various versions of what happened next have been recorded – including the one in the War Diary. My recollection is that it was not a civilian but a German officer who contacted Arthur and indicated that a surrender might be arranged. Belgian civilian or German officer is not important, what happened next is that Arthur suggested that 5RTR should try to negotiate. Colonel Gus agreed and taking me and Albert Hillen, a Belgian interpreter (who, like some other of these splendid characters, had attached themselves to the Regiment) with him, we set off in a scout car under a flag of truce. Incidentally, a comic aspect of these negotiations was that Gus and I were both carrying our side-arms and the German soldiers escorting the party all had something far more lethal. Hardly the correct protocol!

'The negotiations were not very promising, as the German Commander insisted that it was 'No surrender[4]', adding as an afterthought, 'Without negotiations with your General': the implication being that we were mere riff-raff with whom no General in the Wehrmacht could be expected to deal. Word was sent back over the air and a message relayed to the Brigade Commander. I am not sure, but I don't think that Brigadier Mackeson knew of Colonel Gus' initiative or what the state of play was. He must, however, been a bit surprised when Gus and I addressed him as 'General' when explaining the situation. Whether the German General smelt a rat or whether he was just playing for time and trying to weigh up our intentions, I don't know. The latter, I suspect. Anyway, he brought the negotiations to an abrupt stop by saying that his orders were 'to hold the city against all attacks'. 'So be it,' Brigadier Mackeson replied. 'But you must know very well what my orders are!''

Bob continued his tale with the entry of 'C' Squadron into the city and then handed the story over to some of the men in the tanks. One of these was Harry Beacon. His tank was edging its way into the city, the advance being somewhat slow and the time being when the morning brew was beginning to work its way through Harry's system. It's one thing to nip out of the turret and 'wet the ground at one's feet' from the back of the tank but it's quite another when the ground at one's feet is crowded with deliriously happy Belgians trying to climb on the tank and embrace their liberators. The crew commander spotted that they were about to enter the square outside the main railway station. 'OK', he told Harry. 'We'll stop over there. You can pop into the Gents.' Which is what Harry did. Now it was standard practice, if one was wearing a cumbersome access-inhibiting tank suit, to leave one's webbing belt and pistol holster in the tank when ground-wetting was in mind. Harry was, therefore, unarmed and rather longer than usual at his stall and only vaguely noticed that someone had come to stand beside him. As he backed out 'to adjust his dress' [as gentlemen used to be reminded to do on these occasions] he realised to his horror that his neighbour was not another 'Tommy' but a large sub-machine-gun-toting member of the opposition. Harry nipped out fast, shouted an explanation to his crew commander and then stepped behind the German infantryman when he came out into the street. 'Hans' was a realist and readily agreed that his war was over. Harry kept Hans' sub-machine-gun on the tank for the rest of the war.

That wasn't the end of Harry's connections with Ghent. 'C' Squadron remained in the city for several days and Harry's tank was parked outside a Café-Bar. Rather than sit out his spells on wireless watch on top of the tank, Harry slung a remote control lead from the turret to a comfortable stool by the bar. While sitting there he was approached by another customer – a very friendly and rather attractive young woman. They got talking and shared several glasses of whatever the barman was able to offer. When the Regiment moved on, Harry was sorry to have to say good-bye, so he got his companion's address. He wrote but never received a reply. On revisiting Ghent on leave later on, Harry made tracks for the bar and asked the barman if he knew what had happened to his 'girl friend'. The barman pointed to her picture on a poster . . . asking for information about 'wanted collaborators'! Harry acquired another girl friend in Ghent. She was a safer bet: she was the Mayor's daughter.

Alan Bashford missed the entry into Ghent for the most trivial but embarrassing reason. He sprained his ankle when jumping off the tank. Embarrassing but well-timed, as Alan was sent back to the UK and was not re-posted until after spending Christmas at home.

As far as Carlo Carlsson was concerned the entry into Ghent had its tricky moments. Jake Wardrop's tank, with Carlo as driver, and that of Sgt White had been sent to probe the approaches to the river when they came under mortar fire, followed by well-directed rifle fire. They were able to deal with the infantry (no doubt, Jake would have said that 'we duffed them up a bit') but only just got back across the bridge before the first sighting shots of AP started to whistle round them.

Roy Dixon's chief memory of Ghent was the contrast between two officers he encountered. One was an arrogant German who scorned to give his name, rank and number on being taken prisoner, saying only in best *''Allo, 'Allo.'* fashion, 'Ve vill be back . . .' The other could not have been more different. His name was Fromont, nicknamed 'From', and he had been an officer in the Belgian Army. So determined was he to re-join in the war that he attached himself to 'A' Squadron, accepted the honorary rank of Sergeant and remained cheerfully with The Fifth until the end of the war, acting as interpreter, general liaison officer and link with the civil population in Belgium, Holland and Germany.

Pete Petersen had reason to remember the run up to Ghent, as he very nearly didn't get there. 'We went,' he wrote, 'across the Belgian border, cheered on by the civilian population, and on towards Ghent but we did meet some resistance at Oost [probably Ooosterzele]. Just before Ghent on a canal we shot up some pill boxes, brewed up a house by the lock where the Jerries were dug in. One of them tried to escape by swimming the canal and climbing onto a barge but he was put to rest, never to see the Fatherland again. My Commander, Eric Stevenson, and I did a reconnaissance to see what was behind the house by crossing the blown-up lock, only to come face to face with some Germans. They were as surprised as we were and scarpered. We did likewise, only being armed with side arms we were at a disadvantage. We made our way back to what we thought was the safety of the tank but, as I got onto the back of the tank, a burst of machine-gun fire whipped above me and I laid possum for a minute before daring to dive into the turret. If that wasn't enough excitement, when it came to starting the tank, it wouldn't: the batteries were flat. A Belgian Resistance Group came to our assistance and stood guard on the tank overnight. We were withdrawn but the tank was recovered and restarted the next morning, allowing us to join the all-night celebration parties in Ghent.'

All the excitement of the Great Swan did not centre on Ghent, however. Apart from being given a dressing down, rather than a clinical dressing, by Doc Sproull[5] for complaining of something as trivial as a pain in his foot, Bryan Johnson had quite an adventurous life. [The fact that the piece of shrapnel in his foot did not work its way out until the following May is not part of the story] This was not surprising since he was with Jack Stiddard in the Recce Section and Jack used to treat his Section pretty well like Popski's Private Army[6]. Before crossing into Belgium, Bryan's tank, a sawn-off *Honey*, was given the special task of recceing Béthune and the canal to the north. 'We set off,' Bryan recorded, 'to cover the five miles about mid-morning. We passed through the Queens' FDL and moved towards the built-up area. It soon became obvious that the main difficulty would be the growing crowds of the town's inhabitants. When we stopped between some high buildings, a Frenchman with three days growth of stubble, leapt onto the front of the vehicle and gave me a huge sweaty embrace and a smacking kiss on either cheek! We finally came to a stop in the main square alongside the belfry tower. Flowers and champagne were pressed on us. The smell, a queer mixture of flowers, champagne, unwashed humanity and petrol, stayed with us for days.

'Captain Stiddard left us and strode off in the direction of the canal. Among the crowd of men, who all seemed to be dressed in a 'uniform' of black arm-bands and berets, a little man appeared and told us he was from Peckham and had 'stayed on after the last war'. After about an hour, Captain Stiddard returned and told us that we had to get back jildi[7] as the Regiment was on the move. We pulled out and the town was taken over by 1RTR.'

Belgium had one surprise for Bryan and that was the sight of formally-habited nuns dancing for joy round the tanks and showing their ankles for all the world to see. Outside Ghent, a quiet night leaguer was enlivened by a band of students who turned the tank park into a carnival. After being moved around various parts of Ghent, the Recce Section ended up bivouacking in Citadel Park and soon began to realise what the animals in the zoo must feel like at feeding time. Every mouthful they ate was watched by crowds of happy Ghentois, every action started a ripple of speculative gesticulation and comment. If all the exchanged addresses had been followed by exchanges of letters, the Post Offices in the UK and Belgium would have collapsed under the strain.

Bob Lay, like Roy Dixon, found the reception given to their liberators by the Belgians was much more enthusiastic than that given by the northern French. Enthusiastic but not always honest. One tank was brought to a halt and overwhelmed by a crowd of youngsters. When they were eventually cleared off and the tank got underway again, the W/Op found that someone had 'liberated' his revolver! But if the Belgians were friendly towards the liberators they were brutal towards the collaborators. Girls who had granted their favours to the occupiers were lucky if nothing worse befell them than having their hair cut off in public. Bob had mixed feelings when Ghent was liberated. In the relaxation after the liberation, many crews were temporarily billeted in houses near the tank park. Bob didn't like that: he felt naked outside his tank.

As already recorded, the liberation of Ghent was a spasmodic affair and the Boche were not cleared out of the city for some days. The result was that parts of the city were subjected to intermittent sniping and mortar fire, even after the canal was crossed and the northern industrial area nominally free from enemy. One victim of this mortar fire was a long-serving officer, Captain Butler, the 2i/c of 'C' Squadron and formerly Bob Lay's crew commander. As noted in the War Diary, Capt Butler died of the wounds he received. Another victim, this time of machine-gun fire, was a man with a curious record: Len Watkins. Len had been commissioned earlier in the war but had been, so to speak, de-commissioned and was serving in The Fifth as a Sergeant crew commander in 'C' Squadron in Ghent. After recovering from a serious leg wound, Len was re-commissioned and later returned to 5RTR as Welfare Officer.

Jimmy Nunn, who had joined The Fifth in Shakers Wood as a scout car driver/operator, was a man with as many lives as a cat. How he nearly lost one of his nine lives is told in detail in Norman Smith's TANK SOLDIER. Jimmy must be one of the few men who won an engagement between a Daimler Dingo and a Tiger. Jimmy didn't actually brew the Tiger up but he got out of its claws with a whole skin which counts as a victory on any terms. Another life was almost taken from him in the s'Hertogenbosch area when the Regiment was doing what can loosely be described as 'holding the line'. This entailed moving into forward observation positions by day and retreating to over-night leaguer. Jimmy's particular role was to sneak out at sparrow fart in his Dingo and make sure that there was no-one in a farmhouse, it being generally known that the Boche had been using it as *their* FOP overnight. Once Jimmy gave the all-clear, the Troop Leader on duty would bring his Troop forward and take up the day-time position. One morning the Troop Leader told Jimmy not to bother doing the recce as the Boche always baled out before dawn. Off went the Troop Corporal's tank and off went the mine which the night-time occupiers of the farmhouse had sown. The driver of the *Cromwell* was injured. If Jimmy's scout car had hit that mine all Jimmy's remaining eight lives would have been forfeited.

Another man to have lucky escapes was Ron Poore. After having been brewed up earlier by an 88, his tank was hit again on the run-up to Ghent. Ron wrote years later, 'There was another time when being on the receiving end of an 88 was not a tragic event for the crew at all. I was looking through the telescopic sights, hand resting on the traverse [control handle], when a blinding white flash and an ear-piercing bang occurred, causing the turret traverse control to spin a couple of times as the turret moved. We made a quick check to be sure that all the crew were OK and no-one was hurt. 'What the hell was that?' said the crew commander, followed by his cry of, 'Look at that!' We did. Our gun barrel was split open just like a peeled banana. The shell that had struck our gun barrel must have been a complete fluke shot. We duly reported in and were told to report to the TDS in the northern outskirts of Brussels. Driving back, sitting outside the tank, was a great experience as, along the way, we were showered with flowers and cheered by the Belgian civilians. It was three or four days before we got a new tank and reported back to the unit so we had an enjoyable break as well as a lucky escape.'

Eric Stevenson, like so many others, remembers more of the comic incidents of the Great Swan than the nasty bits. In fact, the worst he suffered was indigestion. Once one of his crew liberated a large dark bird which appeared to be a cross between a duck and a crow. The bird, duly plucked, went into the pot and onto a desert cooker where it boiled happily for a good three hours without having any noticeable effect on the toughness of its sinews. Orders came to move; the cooker was dowsed, the pot drained and the bird hung on the back of the turret. Next halt, the cooking recommenced and continued for another couple of hours until the crew's duty cook announced that it was cooked. It may have been cooked but it was still as tough as ever and induced the severest indigestion which the crew had ever experienced.

Another bird in Eric's life was a chicken which was caught by Sgt Allen, commanding the Troop *Firefly*. Sgt Allen wrung the chicken's neck, tied string round its neck and secured it to the back of the turret. Where it dangled, lifeless, for the next five hours. When the halt for the night was called and the tank's needs had been attended to, Norman Allen cut the string, laid the body on the top of the turret, turned to put his penknife back in his pocket and watched with disbelief as the chicken fluttered squawking onto the back of the tank, onto the ground and into some sheltering bushes. Bully beef again for supper!

The question of the crew's domestic duties was, from the Troop Leader's point of view, sometimes a delicate one. The driver checked engine and tracks and dealt with re-fuelling: the W/Op had to stay by the set to get the 'gen' for the next day's net: the gunner had to check his weapons, load and restow the ammunition, in which he was generally helped by the lap gunner, who then turned his attention to the evening meal. The Troop Leader had to get himself and his maps organised, then report to the Squadron Commander for the day's de-briefing and the next day's briefing. By the time he got back to his tank, the housework had been done and he was (with certain exceptions which have been noted) handed his dinner on a plate. It happened once that Eric Stevenson found himself back with his crew before the cooking had started: in a moment of rashness he volunteered to do it. There wasn't much scope, so it was fortunate that the men liked bully beef fritters. At the back of Eric's mind was the idea that the fritters would be better if he could make them with self-raising flour. Impossible, of course, but what about adding some Andrews Little Liver Salts of which he just happened to have a tin? The fritters were superb – light, fluffy and tasty. But the shovel got taken for an awful lot of walks during the night!

There were times when life was grimmer and more earnest. 'The most extraordinary and exciting night of my life occurred shortly after we crossed the border into Belgium. We had been in an extensively wooded area all day, mopping up a few German stragglers who had lost their units.' Eric recalled. 'They gave themselves up readily enough and we sent them back to be dealt with. A young Belgian member of the Resistance had attached himself to my Troop. There being no room in the tank, he sat happily on the engine compartment, nursing the Sten gun which I gave him.

'Our Squadron was ordered to pull back to a village and I followed the other three troops along a track until we reached a main road where I was ordered to halt and take up position there overnight. I posted the tanks to guard each of the approaches, my own tank being alongside a two-storey house. Just as we pulled in, a civilian ran out of the house and headed for the woods where we knew that there were still some Germans. I was tempted to shoot him but decided he was probably just frightened by the presence of our tanks near his house. Nevertheless, my sixth sense told me something was going to happen, so I gave orders that everyone was to remain in the tanks and close watch was to be kept all night. I then reported to Squadron HQ and asked for orders in the event of an attack. I was told not to worry but, if anything did happen, to pull back to the bridge at the other end of the village. Darkness came and with it the rain so visibility was very poor. Even so, I spotted a tiny glimmer of light up the road. I asked the young Resistance fighter to work his way down the ditch and see if he could spot anything. He came back after a couple of minutes to say that there were some Germans about 30 metres down the road. Before I could take any action, a flare was sent up and a gun opened fire. The first shell hit the house beside me, bringing the wall down on my tank. I gave the immediate order to start up and get back down the road to the bridge.

'That wall must have fallen on the young Belgian for we never saw him again. I called-in to OC Squadron and was told to halt at the bridge and locate the Queens infantry and take up position with them. Easier said than done. There were only a few houses but no sign of the Queens, so Sgt Bull and I dismounted to do a recce on foot. We couldn't find anything. While we were out on foot, the gunner on my tank opened fire with his Besa. I raced back and my operator told me that a column of enemy had appeared about a hundred yards down the road. They scattered and returned our fire. I decided that we had to find the Queens, also that it would be easier to defend the bridge from the other side, as there was plenty of cover for the tanks there. I reported in again and was told to recross the bridge and take up positions facing up the road. As we moved to do this, poor Sgt Bull was hit by a stray bullet.

'I told Sgt Bull's crew to take him back into the village and got the other three tanks into defensive positions. By this time all our wireless equipment had gone dis because of the rain and I could not risk sending anyone out as a runner while we were still in the sights of any snipers. I had time during the night vigil to work out that the Germans must have been fully motorised to have been able to follow us up so quickly. I was right. As dawn broke and visibility improved, I saw down the road a column of SPs, half-tracks and soft vehicles. To my amazement, they were turning round and heading away from us as fast as they could. We gave chase, firing as we went all the way back to the cross roads, where we were told to halt. (I learnt later that they were the spear point of an armoured column, attempting to break out to the east . . . and had been stopped by two *Cromwells* and a solitary *Firefly*!)

'I went into the house which had been hit and found there was a family still taking refuge there. The first round must have been AP, for I was shown the place where the shot had passed clean under the cot in which a baby had been sleeping. The villagers placed a plaque on the bridge in memory of Sgt Bull. Fifty years later when I revisited the village, the plaque had been transferred to the new bridge but fresh flowers were laid under it every day.

'On another occasion in Belgium we were again ordered to stop where we were for the night and found ourselves on a long, straight, tree-lined road outside a village. I got the tanks parked up on the verges under the trees and the crews got down to maintenance, when three or four villagers came along and asked for the officer in charge. When I was pointed out to them, they asked if we were staying for the night and I said I expected so. The spokesman then invited me to join them for the night in the local pub, hot bath, dinner, bed and breakfast. I was tempted but felt guilty about accepting. I suggested we should draw lots for the honour but the villagers wanted 'the officer' and the chaps urged me to accept, saying, 'Go on: make a pig of yourself.' I don't think I made a pig of myself but I certainly appreciated the hospitality. In the morning as I came down to breakfast, I heard a baby crying. The daughter of the house had given birth during the night. It was a boy and they called him Eric. Many members of The Fifth claim to have fathered children during those long war years but I don't think many of them have had babies named after them. Sadly I lost the address and was never able to locate my namesake: I should have liked to have been his godfather.'

Eric's own godparents would doubtless have liked to be in Mechelen (or Malines), which 'B' Squadron had just liberated, on 19th September 1944 as that was Eric's twenty-first birthday. The Regiment was resting and the Squadron officers managed to organise a suitable celebration for the 'baby' in their midst.

Eric ended his account of this part of The Fifth's war with a sad little postscript to Pete Petersen's account of the action at the canal lock. During the exchange of fire, the tracer in the machine-gun ammunition set fire to the lock-keeper's little house. When the shooting was over, the owner, an elderly women, came back and broke down when she saw the smouldering remains of her home. Eric did his best to console her but she could not be reconciled to the cruelty and futility of war. And who shall blame her?

One man whose war did not quite follow the usual pattern was Edward Zoeftig. To begin with, Ted's name had originally been Zöftig and his ancestry German. His loathing of what the land of his fathers was doing on the mainland of Europe, as well as his pride in his British citizenship, was such that he was wearing a British Army uniform by October 1939. He was commissioned in the RGH and posted from their First Battalion to 5RTR in late July 1944 as a Troop Leader. Within three weeks he was in a field hospital, luckily with nothing worse than abrasions from mortar fragments. Back with the Regiment in time to cross the Seine on 27th August, Ted found one incident in the advance very far from the 'peace-time conditions' mentioned in the War Diary. The regiment was widely spread out and Ted's troop was following a country lane, parallel to but far removed from the unit's Charlie Love. They came round a corner and found the lane blocked by a group of 'obviously agricultural folk.' Ted's story continues in his own words, 'In the midst of this group was a pale blotchy head. I gave the order, 'Driver. Halt.' and my tank stopped. None of my crew was over 21 years of age: they stared in disbelief. A girl, or young woman, practically naked – what rags she had were in tatters – head shaved (or hair torn out), screaming and fighting, was being thrown to us. So that we could take revenge and enjoy her as she had let the Germans enjoy her? I waved the group aside and ordered the driver to advance, leaving this little group of human misery behind but not, I think, out of our memories.

'The following day, the Squadron moved through Lens. I was, I estimated, about three hours behind, as the *Cromwell's* normally reliable Rolls-Royce engine had earlier developed valve trouble. Anyway, we were on our own and batting along at a good 35mph through village after village, still coming to terms with the idea of liberation but not yet indulging the frenzy which realisation brought, until we came to one where realisation was reality and the main street was a mad house. Perforce, we had to halt. Among the bottle-waving revellers was one stout but very, very happy character who was, I suddenly realised, speaking English. A Tommy from The Great War who had stayed behind to marry the miner's daughter whom he had met when stationed there twenty-seven years ago. Suddenly he drew out from the crowd a blushing, beautiful girl of seventeen or thereabouts and presented her to me as, 'Your sweetheart for tonight!' Jolly laughter – or was it ribald? – and slaps on the back followed.'

Ted continues his story, after a bit of suitable moralising on being ruthlessly parted from this promised treat by orders over the air from his Squadron Commander, with an interesting statistic. The rate of advance on the Great Swan had been such that the Echelons were scarcely able to keep up the daily supply of 70,000 gallons of 100 octane petrol which Seventh Armoured's tanks were burning.

Nevertheless, the advance had to be continued and the objective was still Ghent. By the time that The Fifth reached within striking distance, only a handful of tanks were left in 'A' Squadron. Ted's was one of them and the orders were still to 'Press on. Press on.' The British Army was expected; some Ghentois had come more than five miles out of the city to greet them. This caused a problem, as Ted explained. 'About 1230 hrs an 88 SP appeared from the direction of Coutrai. As I was covering that road, I naturally gave my gunner the necessary orders but, when it came to telling him to 'Fire', I realised that this was quite impossible without doing untold harm to innocent civilians. I reported the position to the CO. Colonel Gus was not at all pleased. Fortunately that 88 SP disappeared and we were able to deal with another one, although its crew escaped. Early next morning I heard from a chap in the Resistance about the join-up of German forces at St Martens Latem and I thought I ought to go and investigate. I called 'Big Sunray' for permission but he refused somewhat sharpish. I've no doubt he had a dozen other things to think about, because he shortly got round to my request and told me to go ahead . . . but on my own! Five young men in one *Cromwell* tank off to the Convent of Sint Martens Latem with no reconnaissance and no infantry cover but with pockets of enemy on the look out for just such a target as us. We got within about 100 yards of the buildings I took to be the Convent when I was waved to a halt by a character who introduced himself as Major Ham of the Belgian Army. In English he explained that there was a group of German officers in the courtyard. Unsaid was the clear hope that I would 'Go and get 'em!' It might well have been a trap but I told the driver to let the tank trickle forward until we had a command of the courtyard. Then, the epitome of the scruffy Fifth Tanks officer, I unslung my pistol belt and clambered off the tank. I reckoned if I looked belligerent not only E Zoeftig but one *Cromwell* crew would have 'bought it'. The crew did their best: they covered my advance with an HE 'up the spout' and both Besas at the ready – my W/Op even covered my advance with the Verey pistol! I walked – no marched – resolutely forward with Major Ham for company and found myself confronted by half-a-dozen immaculately-dressed officers of the Wehrmacht. Armed. The senior officer – he was a colonel – shouted. My heart missed a beat (I thought it was going to be its last one, anyway). The machine-pistols were lowered and the colonel saluted. I replied in my best Sandhurst manner then found my hand being shaken by the colonel. My eyes must have nearly popped out of my head at what I saw next. The surrender of six officers became the surrender of some 300 Other Ranks. Half a battalion bagged by one tank's crew. Their small arms were snapped up by the Resistance and they 'got fell in' and were marched smartly off back down the road we had come in on.

'That wasn't the end of the story by any means. Stuart Jones, the Squadron 2i/c, met us in a Dingo after two or three miles and told me that the CO had organised a POW stockade and I was to shepherd my bag there. News of what had happened must have spread, because a crowd came surging out of a nearby village. You can imagine the reaction when they saw the column.. I told the German colonel to descend and got off the tank beside him. From out of the jeering, baying mob a small man, seething with rage and spitting invective, dashed across the road with another, younger man following. They were onto my captive in a flash, kicking, biting, stamping. The Geneva Convention came to mind, so I tried to defend him. I was dashed against the tank and got my share of fists, teeth and feet until the assailants were hauled off by my crew. I was told that the man's daughter had been taken off by the garrison 'to entertain the troops'. The younger man was the girl's fiancé. Not, in retrospect, commendable but, even in retrospect, understandable.'

Ted, along with 'A' Squadron's remaining six tanks, followed 'C' Squadron into Ghent. With more poetry than usually graces a soldier's recollections, Ted described the scene. 'The bells were ringing. The stream of people moved forward like a stream of silver sound which surged and swirled with a single note of happiness and joy, a chorus of exaltation which centred on us, around us and, now it seemed, above us. With our begrimed hands and faces, in our sorry oil-stained clothing, in tanks that looked only fit for the knacker's yard, we were 'The Liberators'!'

THE OTHER SIDE

If the British and Canadian advance through France and into the Low Countries had been rather less than meticulously planned at times, the German retreat had been chaotic. Lacking almost all forms of transport and short of fuel for what mechanised transport they did have, most of their resources were allocated to their armour, their self-propelled artillery and their anti-tank guns. The Luftwaffe could offer very little protection and seldom had an opportunity for offensive action.

On 4th September Hitler re-imposed on von Rundstedt the unenviable appointment as C-in-C West, in spite of having previously relieved him of this responsibility for having dared to suggest a strategic withdrawal from Normandy. As his deputy he was given the in-post C-in-C, Feldmarschall Model, famous for his efficiency . . . and for his ruthlessness. Von Rundstedt decided to hold a line consisting of the Albertkanal and the River Meuse down to the French border with Luxembourg. The Albertkanal runs east-south-east from Antwerp – in Allied hands since 4th September – to Maastricht (north of which the Meuse becomes the Maas) and then following the line of the Meuse, south to Liège: from here the Meuse runs south-west towards Charleroi.

Von Rundstedt's line was, therefore, a salient into which the Allies had penetrated deeply. It is, however, one thing to decree what a defensive line is to be: it is quite another thing to man it. This was particularly true as von Zangen's Fifteenth Army was cut off on the far side of the Scheldt Estuary. From a barrel, the bottom of which had already been scraped pretty thoroughly, Hitler conjured up men from hospitals, officer cadet schools, training units and staff establishments. Added to these, by virtue of the fact that the German Parachute Regiments were part of the Luftwaffe and not part of the Wehrmacht, Göring produced a force of 5,000 partly-trained but keen and confident paratroop infantry and also, by virtue of the fact that they had neither planes nor fuel, nearly 20,000 Luftwaffe air- and ground-crews.

Von Rundstedt did not succeed in holding his defensive line. Among other units, 5RTR was across the Albertkanal and in Eindhoven by 22nd September.

Hitler may have been losing the battles which men were fighting on sea, land and air but he was becoming perilously near to winning another battle: that of the 'V' weapons. The V-1 Flying Bombs or Doodle Bugs were unquestionably a menace and capable of causing loss of life and damage to property but they did not have the effect on either matériel or morale which their inventors had intended. The V-2 rockets were quite a different proposition. Their effect on impact was devastating, their unheralded arrival out of a clear sky was even more so. Used indiscriminately against targets in southern England and the liberated areas of Belgium and Holland, they caused heavy casualties and got near to achieving what the Blitz had failed to achieve, namely breaking the indomitable spirit of the London population.

THE WAR CHRONICLE

1944

September	02	Finns and Russians agreed an armistice – Canadians captured Dieppe – General Eisenhower assumed direct control of Allied land forces in Europe
	04	Germans evacuated Brussels
	06	The Home Guard stood down

08 First V-2 landed on London
10 US Army entered German territory at Aachen
15 German Battle ship *Tirpitz* hit by 12,000lb bombs
21 Allies captured Rimini
22 Red Army captured Estonian capital, Tallinn

NOTES

1 Maleesh. From the Arabic, introduced in the Army during WWI but popularised in the Desert in WWII. Expresses indifference: 'So what?', 'Not to worry!', 'Never mind'

2 Kruishoutem. This is one of several places in Belgium and Holland which, from the War Diary spelling, it is not possible to identify on a modern map. The locality can be verified from neighbouring place names but the exact town, village or hamlet remains uncertain. Such places are indicated by an * the first time the name appears in this text

3 Sgt Bull. There is a discrepancy here. According to the certified correct Regimental Casualty List, Sgt Bull was killed and buried on 7th September. The same source, referring to the same incident, states that Sgt Bull was killed by bazooka fire *while he was out of his tank, which was unharmed.* Another source states that he was killed by sniper fire. This is repeated by Stevenson. According to Joe Cannon, the gunner of the tank at the time of the incident, it was a fragment from an exploding Panzerfaust striking his tank, without doing it any material damage, that killed Charlie Bull

4 No surrender. The Garrison Commander (General Daser) was, as it happens, obeying Hitler's orders. He could not only have brought dire penalties on himself but also on his family if he had surrendered the city without a fight. This bears out Major Maunsell's belief that Daser was only playing for time

5 Doc Sproull. One of several Medical Officers who served with 5RTR. To many, Doc Sproull could have doubled as 'Grumpy' in any version of *Snow White*. In fact, a selfless and very brave man, he used to operate from a White half-track, invariably accompanied by Padre Dickson. They both deserved, and were awarded, Military Crosses

6 Popski was the nickname of Lt Col Vladimir Peniakoff, the Polish-ancestored, Belgian-born British Army officer who was not content with being a member of the LRDG in North Africa but, with official sanction, formed his own operational sub-group in Italy

7 Jildi. The word is Hindustani (although it also appears in Romany). Probably the best translation is the slang word 'sharpish' but the general sense is that of the original word which means 'quickness'.

CHAPTER XVIII

. . . *'When the year to Autumn comes ..'*

The Low Countries: October and November 1944

All good things come to an end and that was true of the Great Swan. The use of the word 'parked' in the first line of the War Diary for October 1944 makes that quite clear.

It was unfortunate that, at the time the Allies' thrust was slowing down, relations between Monty and 'Ike' Eisenhower were steadily deteriorating. Those between Monty and Beddell Smith, Ike's Chief of Staff, had never been anything but acrimonious but Monty might have had some cause for irritation with his Supremo. It is hard for a Field Commander to believe that a man, with his two main Armies penetrating deeply into enemy-held territory, who could take time off to play golf with his (female) staff car driver, really had a grip on the military situation. Firm direction was lacking. Ike had become like the girl who can't say 'No', with the result that neither Bradley, driving to the German border to try to cross the Rhine there, nor Montgomery, striving to cross the Rhine at Arnhem, was given the decisive support their operations required at the planning or build-up stages.

This, in part, explains the events recorded in the October War Diary, which reads as follows:

1 Nistelrode. The Bde for an indefinite period was to be parked in a watching role in protection of 30 Corps centre line. It was therefore decided to give the Regiment as much opportunity of re-organisation and maintenance as possible. One squadron only was to be actively employed at a time. C Sqn being the Sqn on duty. The Regiment moved to Nistelrode. The Regt right and left boundaries were the Barrier-Wettering Canal and the Heesch–s'Hertogenbosch road respectively. The enemy was known to hold positions roughly along a position to the east. 'I' Coy 1 Rifle Bde was placed under command and formed together with C Sqn a strong point in Hunnigen Wijnkel*. Infantry patrols were sent forward to investigate enemy positions by night and reported enemy patrols in the area. Major Wood assumed command of B Sqn.

2 B Sqn relieved C Sqn otherwise no event.

3 Regimental HQ joined B Sqn who were relieved by C and the Recce Troop moved to Venghel to take over defence of the town and safeguard the area between the canal and the river. 4th Field Sqn RE placed under command to act as infantry and later took over the American Paratroop positions along the railway.

4 The Canal, running east and west, prevented Reconnaissance from going further NW. Recce patrols went out but no sign of enemy. However, enemy confirmed to be in nearby wood. Indirect shoots were carried out by B Sqn.

5 In conjunction with 131 Bde, feint attack was carried out and B Sqn sent two Troops east down the canal bank and destroyed enemy held houses on the southern bank.

6 8 Hussars took over positions and Regimental Group returned to Nistelrode. A Sqn reverted to Regimental command and also returned to Nistelrode.

7 C Sqn relieved by B Sqn who are billeted in Nistelrode. The remainder of the Regiment carrying out maintenance and training.

8 Tpr Colson of C Sqn[1] killed on a miniature range erected by C Sqn

9 A Sqn relieved B Sqn. Enemy patrols active. Mortar fire reported,

10 No event on Regtl front, except stand-to at 2300 hrs due to enemy activity.

11 A Sqn relieved by C Sqn: otherwise no activity.

12 0600 hrs Recce Troop took over the responsibility of 'I' Coy 1st RB Carrier Platoon for 3 days

13–14 No event other than patrols.

15 B Sqn relieved C Sqn. Otherwise no event.

16 'I' Coy 1 RB took over positions from Recce Tp, during which a Boche patrol was captured and passed back to RHQ

Casualties : Nil

Enemy losses : 7 POW

17 0300 hrs 'I' Coy 1 RB clashed with enemy patrols laying mines on RB's front. Enemy patrol withdrew. Unfortunately it was not noticed that the patrol had laid mines, the result being that one Cromwell, moving up on the usual patrol was badly damaged. There were no casualties in personnel. A further incident during the day was a very concentrated stonk directed at HQ at Mannekens Winkel*. Firing was from 3 separated gun areas: a concentration landed 200 – 300 yds east of HQ. Enemy guns could have found our location through the medium of a civilian

Casulties : [B] Tpr Chitty A Wnd

18 A vigorous counter-battery shoot was carried out during which HQ Coy and 'I' Coy moved forward 1,000 yds.

19 No event other than A Sqn relieving B

20 Regt less Recce Troop and two Sqns – B and C – came under command

of 53 Welsh Div prior to attack on s'Hertogenbosch. No event on the A Sqn front.

1420 hrs CO, Lt Col C A Holliman, addressed all ranks on the forthcoming operations in the Catholic Hall.

21 Final arrangements made by liaison with 71 Bde for attack on s'Hertogenbosch. Quiet day on A Sqn front, but towards evening the enemy manhandled an 88mm anti-tank gun into position and brewed up one Cromwell. This gun, however, was knocked out the following day.

During the evening B Echelon was subjected to enemy air attack using anti-personnel bombs.

Casualties : [HQ] Capt QM Thompson AE Wnd Tpr Harty Wnd
Pte Williams (ACCorps) Wnd
[A] 2/Lt Derbyshire HF KIA Tpr Jackman JE KIA
Tpr Lewis TH KIA
Tpr Perkins AJ KIA Tpr Taylor R KIA

Losses : 1 Cromwell

Enemy losses : Nil

22 The first phase of the main s'Hertogenbosch action began at 0630 hrs. A Sqn after careful and detailed planning with 4 Royal Welch Fusiliers, moved forward across the start-line in support of them. Progress along this line of advance was good, having been preceded by heavy artillery barrage. The country in this area towards the final objective was extremely thick and contained a considerable number of enemy snipers. The upshot of this situation was that one Coy of RWF lost all their officers and a few ORs. Also an officer tank commander of A Sqn was shot through the head. A Sqn fired a great deal of ammunition into the suspected areas and, at last light, infantry had inflicted casualties, making it possible for the infantry to take over the whole area.

Casualties : [A] Lt Collinge J KIA

Losses : Nil

Enemy losses : 1 x 75mm A/Tk gun: 1 x 20mm A/Tk gun: 1 x 21mm mortar

23 A Sqn and RHQ back under command of 22 Armd Bde and concentrated as Regiment at Nistelrode.

24 1600 hrs Regiment moved to new area and leaguered for night.

25 1100 hrs It was anticipated that the Regt might have to cross the canal by one of the two bridges that were available or a bridge near Helvoirt-Udenhout[2] would have to be made. A Section of 4 Field Sqn RE under command of the Regiment put up a scissors bridge and secured a crossing but opposition a 1,000 yds further on was too strong for the Regt to effect a crossing. The Regiment leaguered for the night at Sint Michielsgestel.

26 51 Highland Div having secured the bridgehead, the Regiment was

ordered to cross and proceed to Helvoit [Helvoirt] via Molenstraat. C Sqn leading reached Molenstraat without opposition. At this point the leading troops were fired on by an SP gun but no damage was done. The SP was thought to be in an area 1,000 yds due west of Molenstraat and C Sqn set about stalking it. At this stage B Sqn had passed through C Sqn to make a strong-point at the cross roads and to exploit to the next cross roads. The 1st Royal Tanks was then passed through B Sqn and C Sqn and directed to Udenhout. B and C Sqns changed direction and advanced SW. B Sqn made some advance before being fired on with armour-piercing shot. C Sqn met no opposition and reached Holeinde*. Good progress was maintained until nightfall when the Regiment leaguered in s'Hertogenbosch

Enemy losses: 6 killed and 20 POWs

27 The Regiment now placed under command 131 Bde. B and C Sqns ordered to proceed in support of 1/6 Queens who were protecting Divisional centre-line. The centre-line was the main road Helvoirt–Nemelaer. The right and left boundaries were the roads Guildenberg* to Helvoirt. During the afternoon A Sqn reported some mortaring and enemy infantry were seen on their front. At night RHQ leaguered in Helvoirt. A Sqn in defensive position plus a Coy 1 RB, with B Sqn and C Sqn at Guildenberg. 51 Division Reconnaissance reported possibility of enemy cutting the centre-line.

28 1/6 Queens and a squadron of 11 Hussars, now under command of the Regtl Gp who in turn were placed under direct command of 7 Armd Div, still carrying out the role of centre-line protection. 1/6 Queens took up positions in support. B Sqn was in reserve. C Sqn was in Guildenberg. Night patrols reported enemy in strength of approx one Company in Eind*, also mortar and Spandau fire from the area.

29 Plan was made to clear enemy from the area and to establish B Coy 1/6 Queens and B Sqn on this front. The operation was successfully complete in 1½ hrs. B Sqn having to destroy a number of houses containing enemy infantry and inflicting heavy casualties. Country extremely thick and difficult. An A/Tk gun located on the front led to an exchange of fire enabling C Sqn to proceed through the village of Guildenberg. The outskirts proved to be heavily mined. One corporal being lost. A tank being commanded by Lt Jones became a casualty. He escaped being wounded.

Casulaties : [C] L/Cpl Carter R KIA Tpr Makinson A KIA

Losses : I Cromwell

Enemy losses : 6 killed: 32 POWs.

30 At first light, the area having been completely cleared, the Regt concentrated and moved to take over positions held by 4 Arm Bde in the vicinity of Rijen. The route being from Helvoirt to Tilburg and then to Rijen. 1/6 Queens remained under command and with the

Recce Troop carried out extensive reconnaissance. The area 2 mile out to the west seemed to be clear of enemy. Royal Netherlands Bde now under our command. 1st Polish Armd Division was also contacted, their HQ being at Gilze.

31 Regiment now under command of 22 Armd Bde. Regt was established at 1400 hrs at Horst

The War Diary paints, as usual, only a fragmented sketch of November's activities but, before drawing in details from individual narratives to complete the picture, I shall digress for a moment to introduce two further characters into the story.

The first of these is myself.

The other newcomer who arrived in October was André Kemps, a young Dutchman from Oss. What happened, in his own words, was that, ' .. at the end of September, Oss was liberated. On 3rd October my eldest sister, a member of the Dutch Resistance Movement, came home and said to me, 'I have been asked by a British Intelligence Officer whether I could find someone who speaks English, French and German (as well as his native Dutch/ Flemish) and is willing to join a Tank Division. Maybe something for you, eh, André?' I was 22 years-old then and had several years of High School language studies behind me. Besides that, I was only too ready to fight the Nazi occupiers of my country. So I said, 'I'll do that.' My father was standing nearby and he said, 'Are you mad, boy? You can't even handle a gun!' My reply was, 'Never mind that. The fighting will be done by my colleagues.'

'The next day, George Roberts picked me up in Oss (later I got the nickname 'The Wizard of Oss') and took me to Nistelrode where I was given the necessary uniform and equipment. At dinner time, I was invited into the Officers Mess[3] for introduction to the Commanding Officer. Here I learnt that I was to be a member of 'B' Squadron, the Fifth Royal Tank Regiment in the famous Desert Rats, of whom everyone in Holland had heard. I very nearly disgraced myself on that occasion. The officers were so friendly and generous that they plied me with more cigarettes and drink than I had been accustomed to. I fainted! Luckily, they managed to bring me round before the CO arrived and I was able to be formally introduced to and made welcome by him.

'In the beginning I was given a small armoured car [in fact, a Dingo scout car] with the code name DOGDOGDOG and a driver who taught me the phonetic alphabet – Able, Baker, Charlie, Dog and so on – and the meaning of such Army expressions as 'the Charlie Love', 'The Blue' and generally helped me to settle in to this strange new way of life. My first job, I remember, was finding billets for the officers and men in the Squadron in the various villages and towns where we were based.'

André soon became a popular member of the Squadron, both in the Officers Mess, for his cheerful good humour, and, with the men, for his willingness to help and to do his share of the dirty jobs as well as his own work.

Sometimes the memories of the war which come to mind have nothing to do with the material aspects – comic or not so funny – of the conflict but are recollections of one's feelings. For Ted Zoeftig the time the Regiment was halted in Holland in October brought to mind that, ' .. the very close physical contact with so many of the enemy at this time – not simply the eye-ball-to-eye-ball, gun-muzzle-to-gun-muzzle confrontation of the usual kind – gave me, for the first time, an opportunity to see the enemy as young men of my own age. They were obviously highly disciplined, intelligent and keeping to a tight personal regimen. Thus I saw them as individuals, each holding himself from degenerating into a morass of defeated self-pity, subservient and beaten, cringing, all of which I had anticipated. We showed them no leniency; they were stripped of watches, money, wallets and the officers even lost their boots if they were any good. I am certain that, by and large, we did *not* manage to strip them of their self-respect. One small incident comes to mind. A party of four, one of whom was quietly crying, approached me. The unhappy man had been in the DAK in the early days and had carried his father's watch with him until that very day: it was his only memory of his father. I ferreted through the bags. It was a battered old silver watch. I gave it back.

'My curiosity as to my relatives (remote) in NW Germany had been rekindled outside Ghent by these soldiers. I was undeniably, at least partially, of North German/Scandinavian stock. I made discreet enquiries about Holstein. Hamburg and Lubeck were 'getting it'. Further west, Bremen of course but the hamlets in between were not too badly hit.' Ted went on to reflect on the disappointment that was felt as the 'Home for Christmas' spirit which had pervaded the Army on the Great Swan gradually evaporated when the BLA reached the Dutch frontier. This was revived – all too briefly – when the Airborne forces made their assault on Arnhem and died finally and definitively in Brabant. For The Fifth, this meant Nistelrode, where there had been [and here Ted quotes] 'Hard but monotonous fighting; not very bitter because the enemy always seemed to withdraw when pressed, having no great reinforcement strength.' Ted continues, 'The terrain was extremely difficult for tanks and the *Cromwells* were never able to use their speed. Polders and narrow, wooded lanes took their toll and it was also a happy hunting-ground for snipers. We had casualties and, consequently, reinforcements of officers and men. One of these officers was Harold Derbyshire, a 21-year-old, third-generation Argentinian, who had volunteered to fight for his beleaguered home country. He was a cheerful, God-fearing soul with a gentle nature.

'High Command had made us, through force of circumstances commit the cardinal military sin of returning to the same set positions every day for a week. We could – and did – camouflage our tanks but we could not dig them into fox holes. The terrain made turret-down and even hull-down positions impracticable. We were sitting ducks. It seems that, with great stealth, the Boche had moved a Jagdpanzer[4] or some heavy artillery piece close to us and that this had not been spotted by the normally very alert Dutch Resistance. One morning at first light we took up our positions and waited on the alert. After two hours or so it came. There was a crack and a thump but no flash. Harold, who was commanding a tank in my Troop, came on the air to report. All crews strained to see the next flash – anything to fire at, for, of course, there was no question of random fire which would have given away our tank positions. About ten seconds later came the next crack and thump. Harold had not yet fired because he had not been able to identify the target. The third crack was followed not by a thump but by the sound of a great gong being struck. The gong was Harold's tank and it exploded with an evil mushroom cloud rising high above the trees where his tank had been. Where Harold and his crew had died.'

As was not uncommon, besides the formal letter which the Commanding Officer invariably wrote to the next of kin of anyone in his unit who had died on active service, the friends of the casualty also wrote, offering their sympathy and paying a tribute to the dead man. Ted wrote to Harold's mother. She wrote back to thank him: the letter followed Ted half way round the world and did not reach him until a year after her son had died.

A day later, tragedy struck again for Ted. It so happened that The Fifth was involved – albeit anonymously – in an action which attracted much press and radio notice in the UK. This was by reason of the exceptionally heavy artillery barrage that preceded the attack on s'Hertogenbosch on 22nd October. The Fifth was in support of the Fourth Battalion of the RWF and Ted's Troop was in support of the Company which, as the War Diary reported, lost all its officers. Before the action, the crew commanders met the Platoon Commanders and the Troop Leaders carefully explained what part the tanks were going to play. This was often a mutually unpopular role. The PBI did not relish the close proximity of tanks, because it drew fire down on their unprotected heads and tank crews did not relish having to move at infantry pace across open country, because so doing brought fire down on *them*. This much-publicised artillery barrage did not clear the area of its chief menace. Snipers. These retreated into their fox holes only to emerge when the barrage had rolled on. In spite of the tanks drenching the woods – and the advance was through closely-wooded country – with steady machine-gun fire and random HE, the snipers took their toll. Generally, the tanks were immune from snipers' fire. It was always possible to close down completely, even if that meant loss of observation. However, as any crew commander will tell you, loss of observation was better than loss of life. Nevertheless, crew commanders were particularly vulnerable – being normally head and shoulders, if not from the waist upwards, out of the turret – to this type of sniping. And, of course, so were members of the crew, if they had to leave the tank for some reason.

As Ted was clearing up round one side of a wood, another of his friends was clearing up round the other side. This was Lieutenant Collinge, who had been with The Fifth in the Desert, who had been taken prisoner, who had made his way back from captivity in Italy to England, who had there been married, who had volunteered to rejoin his old Regiment although in no way bound to do so, who had left a pregnant wife behind him. For some reason, Collinge had gone over to the OC Squadron's tank to point out some target or obstacle to him. He never got back to his own tank. A sniper picked him off just before he reached its safety.

Other have recollections of episodes rather than events. Eric Stevenson once found himself point tank in the leading Troop, sent forward to watch at a cross roads where it was suspected that there might be enemy armour on the prowl somewhere up front. Positioning himself carefully where he could see without being seen, he sat back to look and listen. The last thing he expected was to hear tanks coming up behind him but, sure enough, a line of *Cromwells* was fast approaching from the rear. He leapt off his tank and flagged them down, noting as he did so that the leading tank was flying some sort of pennant. As it slowed to a halt, Eric scaled the front in the typical insouciant manner of all *Cromwell* crews . . . to find himself confronted by the Brigade Commander! After remembering to salute, he explained tactfully that further advance up that particular Charlie Love might be inadvisable. The Brigadier consulted his map, made some remark to the officer occupying the W/Op's place, casually thanked Eric and gave the order to his driver to turn round and go back the way he had come.

Roy Dixon also had some unexpected visitors. He tells the story against himself in the following words. 'I remember one episode (which I often quote, because it shows how easy it is, when reporting an incident, to cover up one's mistakes or to make it sound praiseworthy when, in fact, it was quite the opposite). One day my Troop was guarding a flank where not much had been happening and no enemy seemed to be about. My tank was in position covering a track and I was sitting in the turret idly studying my map, when I looked up and saw two German infantrymen standing a few feet in front of the tank, evidently having mistaken it for one of their own. They reacted to my surprise by making a dash for it, so my gunner fired a burst of Besa at them but they dropped flat on the ground and were not hit. We signalled them to come in and took them prisoner. In reporting the contact on the wireless I didn't reveal my carelessness but made it sound as if we had achieved a successful capture. I think many of us practised this little deceit at some stage.'

Bob Lay remembers the rain not as an incident but as a permanent feature of life. This is a slight exaggeration but it certainly coloured some of the incidents he recalls. Escorting Echelon vehicles . . . in the rain. Being dragged off by a young Dutch lass to join her family's liberation celebrations . . . in the rain. Watching for newly laid mines in the track marks down the lanes . . . in the rain. More precisely, he recalls the triumph of practice over theory. Bob was, at that time, the Squadron Operator – *ie* the W/Op on the Rear Link tank.

He was told to ensure that all crew members were familiar with the operation of the tanks' Number 19 wireless sets. This he did by the practical expedient of showing them how to tune in to the BBC to get the Six O'clock News. Unfortunately, the Royal Corps of Signals Officer attached to the Regiment decided to test Bob's pupils and, not altogether surprisingly, found that they did not meet the Signal Corps' exacting standards. Bob was hauled up before the Signals Officer and asked what his qualifications were. He produced his AB 64[5] and proudly showed it. No courses since 1941! He was manifestly incompetent . . . but he still went on being the Squadron Operator and the crews went on tuning in to the BBC.

Carlo Carlsson was one of the men who tuned in to the BBC. He remembers doing so with indignation. The announcer was telling the listening world that 'the men' were all being given leave to go to Eindhoven to relax and be entertained by the still-rejoicing Dutch. One man wasn't: Carlo was stuck in leaguer. He had, however, had one unexpected bonanza. Along with Jake Wardrop, he had found himself being made welcome in a monastery. Worldly delights – a hot bath, a chance to shave, a chance to wash their clothes, a warm meal – were offered them . . . but only if, like good sons of Rome, they confessed their sins. Jake, God rest his soul, must, one feels, have taken rather a long time to do that!

For more cohesive accounts of October, when the year was coming to autumn, both Bryan Johnson and Syd Storer have something to say. Bryan Johnson recalls that, on 1st October his vehicle was used as a 'step-up' – that is a wireless link between two stations which were too far apart for direct communication: in this case between RHQ and 'A' Squadron. This was an exacting task as it meant being on watch the whole time. After two days of this, he was pulled back to Nistelrode and told by Jack Stiddard that he had been promoted to HQ Troop. Bryan protested in vain. Although life as a member of the Colonel's tank crew carried fewer hazards than being in the Recce Section, Bryan felt that the devil he had known all these months was better than an unknown devil. However, the worst in store for him was in the Nistelrode Town Hall, where in a damp basement cell, lit and aired only by a small grill, he found a wizened old lady. Just the place for her: she was known to have betrayed members of the Resistance to the Gestapo.

The population was by and large friendly but they had little or nothing to offer except friendship; their own supplies were still extremely short and their delivery was restricted by the Allied military transport on the roads . . . and the transport, like the population, was vulnerable to air attack or long-range shelling. Cigarettes, as always, were the common currency but a great Dutch virtue was their ability and willingness to turn dull Army rations into imaginative and tasty meals. It became the accepted if strictly illegal thing, when the Regiment was more rather than less settled in one place, for rations to be issued for men to take to their billets for cooking by the woman of the house. In this way, everyone benefited: the families got some extra food and the men got tastier meals.

An additional benefit was the use of the Resistance Movement's Intelligence network. This was generally connected to parts of Holland which were still in German hands and much useful information filtered through. There was a certain amount of two-way trade here, as there was a strong pro-German element among the Dutch. To the shame of their compatriots, there even existed a Dutch SS Division: admittedly recruited to 'fight the Communist Menace' and thus on the Russian Front. However, some of the Dutch who stayed in Holland preferred the occupying Germans to the liberating Allies: these passed information about Allied positions and movements on to the Wehrmacht and the Luftwaffe.

Of what happened in the third week of October, Bryan wrote, 'It became obvious that some activity was proposed. Colonels of infantry battalions and 'elderly' gentlemen trooped into the mobile Orderly Room. It transpired that 53rd Welsh Division was to make an attack on s'Hertogenbosch, supported by the Regiment. It was thought that this would not be very easy as there were some 88s along the embankment of the canal. Accordingly, in the misty light of dawn, we set off down the main road in support. The infantry attack was reported to have gone well and I learnt over the air that one of the spoils of war was a bevy of German Army nurses. By last light on the 23rd a message came from Colonel Gus that we were 'to return to the place where we have been so comfortable'. Nothing more had to be said. We went back to Nistelrode.

'Next morning we were all keyed up for an early move but we didn't in fact shove off until 1640 hrs. This move took us westwards and entailed spending a night in the open en route. At 1100 hrs on the 25th we moved off through Sint Michielsgestel to Esch where we settled down for the night in a private house. The following morning we moved back through Sint Michielsgestel and crossed the River Aa and leaguered in the vicinity of Helvoirt. 19th October was spent in the same vicinity but the night was spent in St Joseph's College. This was still in use and some classes were being held there. The Signal Corps officer's driver thought that he would be helpful and give the children some lessons in English. These proved very useful – for the driver, who ended up being instructed in his mother tongue by the gleeful children.

'On 30th October we moved off through Tilburg, newly liberated and still reasonably intact. On the last day of the month we moved back through Tilburg, crossing the river by a big railway bridge and ending up near Dongen for the night.'

A point which is not mentioned in the Diary or in the personal narratives is that the attack on s'Hertogenbosch was accompanied by 79 Armd Div *Crocodile* flame-throwers. Devastating though these machines were from the opposition point of view, they were uncomfortable neighbours for the crews of tanks carrying highly inflammable high-octane fuel.

Syd Storer remembers being surprised at the ages of the prisoners they took. In the tank crews there was very little difference in age: the average was in the early twenties. The captives taken in Holland were found to be anything from mid-teenagers to middle-aged or even older men. Some of these were glad to give themselves up. 'But,' Syd wrote, 'we had to be on our guard against SS officers and NCOs who would deliberately send men forward to surrender in the hope of catching us unawares when they mounted a sudden attack. We continued our sweeps each day in an effort to stop any infiltration back across the Maas. We were now patrolling the area round Oss each night and our HQ had moved to Nistelrode. Here the tanks were parked between the buildings to conceal them from the air and the crews were billeted in the houses. This was welcome as our bedding was soaked from nights of sleeping out in the rain. There was an unfortunate incident one night when a tank hit a house and brought down the side wall, revealing the family all tucked up in their beds.

'Once we parked our tank in a barn beside a farmhouse where the family gave us a large room for the crew and another for the Squadron Commander. The family had two young daughters which interested the crew considerably. They had a piano which we used for a sing-song the first evening. We hoped this would become a daily event but were disappointed when we were called out urgently the second day to support some infantry in the area of Vinkel. The enemy had crossed the river and had cut the Heesch to s'Hertogenbosch road. It took most of the day to remove them, as they continually disappeared into the woods only to re-appear elsewhere. Eventually, before nightfall, our forces coming down from Oss took them in the rear: many surrendered but not before many others were killed. We stayed in position near the river for the rest of the night but no further effort was made to cross it. The morning of the 9th we made our way back to the farm where Bill, Trooper Bilton our second driver, was given a very warm welcome by the elder daughter.

'We stayed in Nistelrode for the next few days, carrying out maintenance with visits being arranged to Eindhoven. There was occasional shelling but, on the whole, things were very quiet until the morning of October 20th when we were told to net the wireless sets in preparation for a move.'

Syd records that the next objective was Antwerp. This reveals a curious situation in top-level planning. What happened perhaps shows that Monty, like his boss, did not always have a crystal clear grasp of the 'big picture'. Up to this point, the main British and Canadian fuel supplies still had to be brought forward from the PLUTO feeder point in Cherbourg. This was an unsustainable burden which could only become worse as winter approached. The use of Antwerp was therefore crucial. However, and this should have been obvious to Monty, capturing the city did not ensure the use of the harbour. So long as the Germans remained in control of either bank of the Schelde estuary, shipping could not reach the port facilities. It is true that clearing the approaches required mounting a major operation whereas capturing the city meant only an advance on a narrow front but the two should have been co-ordinated . . . and they were not, in spite of Eisenhower's pressure on Monty not merely to *capture* Antwerp but to *use* it.

Syd's narrative continues by summarising this and then explains. 'Attacking from our Nijmegen corridor, we were to exploit a bridgehead that the infantry would make over the rivers Dommel and Aa. The terrain would be similar to what we had just cleared round Vinkel and Nistelrode. We moved down to the village of Middelrode and supported an attack by the infantry through the wooded areas. Over 400 prisoners were taken, chiefly due to good, well-planned shooting by the artillery. Later in the evening we were transferred southwards and crossed the Dommel but were held up at Esch due to very heavy mortar and gun fire on the bridge which we hoped to cross. During the night the enemy succeeded in destroying the bridge. Once more the Engineers found a suitable place and we crossed on the new bridge after the infantry had established a firm bridgehead. Our particular task was, first, to block all the roads leading north and north-east out of Tilburg. Going was very slow due to small but well-sighted rearguards with SP guns.

'By evening we had reached a point just north of Oisterwijk. That night the Boche fell back as our infantry entered Tilburg. All the roads in the district were heavily mined. Two tanks, attempting to avoid some swampy ground, found the mines when they lost their tracks. In continuing rain the infantry made an attack of Udenhout, some 40 prisoners being taken. We had a very disturbed night there, as we were shelled continuously. An early attack by the infantry through the woods relieved the situation and, as our friends attacked Loon-op-Zand, we by-passed it and pushed on towards Dongen. The following morning we were ordered to avoid Dongen, so by-passed it to the south-west. We crossed the Wilhelmina Canal without much opposition and moved quickly towards Breda. Before we reached the town we contacted the Polish Armoured Division who had cleared the town. They were on their way north to the Maas on the west side of the Canal. We turned north on the east side towards Oosterhout as the enemy fell back towards the Schelde. Our infantry – the 51st Highland Division – cleaned up the area west of the town. It was a cold and rainy day: we kept wireless watch all night but slept in a house. The following morning, continual rain and bad roads meant only slow progress. There was a problem of finding routes solid enough to take the weight of the tanks. Towards evening we reached a deserted monastery. We leaguered and spent the night, one each in the monks' cells. We had a good night's sleep while the Highlanders were attacking Ramsdonkveer.'

The change of date from October to November 1944 may have been real on the calendar but it was not apparent to The Fifth on the ground. The War Diary for November shows this:

1 B Sqn placed under command of 1 Rifle Bde and moved to Ramsdonkveer. Geertrudenberg on the west bank of the Wilhelmina Canal was still in enemy hands but, on the east of the Canal, the

enemy had withdrawn north to the River Maas. 1RB responsibility was the area around Ramsdonkveer to the River Maas west. 1st British Armd Division at the same time was moving slowly in the direction of Geertrudenberg, and a Liaison Officer from Recce Troop was despatched to their HQ for a period of four days. The remainder of the Regiment carried out maintenance

2 1350 hrs. Regt less B Sqn formed up and moved to Oosterhout. No event except shelling and mortaring on B Sqn front.

No event

Casualties : [B] Trooper Bilton R KIA

4 No event

5 With the removal of 51st Highland Division from the area, 7th Armd Div had to take over a much larger front extending from Geertrudenberg to the west, to the bend in the Canal. Consequently the various regiments were moved forward.

1330 hrs. B Sqn back under command and the Regt moved to new area Heistraat*. The Regimental front line was extended to s'Kapelle* to Lavegaat*. This front was held by two tanks in both s'Kapelle and Lavegaat with dismounted troops in addition each night

6 C Sqn remained in detached defensive position. The rest of the Regt, less HQ, in Heistraat. A recreational centre was established in Tilburg

7–8 C Sqn still in position. Otherwise nothing to report

9–10 A Sqn relieved C Sqn

11 Position now taken over by Canadian Armd Div

1600 hrs Regiment formed up and moved to a concentration area around Dongen

12–15 No operational events

16 0715 hrs. Regiment formed up and moved to Kinrooi. Regtl Party removed via Tilburg to Turnhout and Geel and was established in Kinrooi by 1700 hrs. 7th Armd Div now under command of 12 Corps

17–19 This period was utilised for re-organisation and training, including courses in wireless, driving and maintenance, and gunnery: also a target course run under supervision of RSM

20 Battalion Holiday. Cambrai celebrations. Inter-squadron football competition won by A Sqn

1830 hrs ENSA entertainment at Bree Theatre

21–25 No events. Regimental training

Casualties : [C] Tpr Carter J Natural Causes

26 1000 hrs. Visit to the Regiment by the new Divisional Commander, Major General LO Lyne[s] DSO

27 No event

28 1100 hrs. Investiture by Field Marshal Sir Bernard Montgomery at Bree at which the Colonel, Lt Col CA Holliman MC & BAR, was awarded the DSO. The FM also decorated the Adjutant, Captain

Garnett, with the MC; Major Macdonald and Lieut Dixon were similarly awarded the MC and L/Cpl Dove the MM

29–30 Training and Regimental sports

What the War Diary doesn't say is that, during most of November, we were billeted in sundry farms. Very 'sundry', as some were reasonably prosperous and others were, quite frankly, primitive. One such farm had several small children and at least one of these young innocents had mumps. Mumps takes a certain time to develop, so I cannot say exactly when or from which child I contracted the disease but catch it I did and duly reported sick to the MO shortly after we reached Kinrooi. The MO, Doc Sproull, only needed one look at my neck and the 102° F on the thermometer to convince him I was a hospital case. For self-evident reasons, infectious diseases were not popular in the front-line hospital system. Nevertheless, to hospital I had to go and I was, accordingly, bundled into the back of a 15-cwt truck and dumped without ceremony on my stretcher in a cold, dark room in the local school which was being used for the Divisional CCS. After what seemed like hours, I had a visitor. A Padre. He squatted by my stretcher and asked sympathetically if 'it' hurt and where I'd copped 'it'. By 'it' he meant a wound: by 'it' I meant mumps. I said 'yes' to his first question and 'in the throat' to his second. How, he asked, did I get 'it'? 'From one of the damned kids at the farm,' I replied. The Padre looked puzzled and had a shufti at the label which had been tied on me. To my astonishment and, I must add, indignation, he burst out laughing. I protested it was no laughing matter. 'Oh yes it is,' he replied. 'D'you know why you've been brought in here?' 'To keep me away from the wounded, I suppose.' 'Oh no. This is where they bring the men who're too badly wounded to live to get to the Field Hospital. I thought you were a goner and you've only got mumps!' he stood up, adding, 'Hang on. I know what you need.' He disappeared, to return a few moments later with two bottles of Bass. He propped me into a sitting position while I consumed one bottle and he the other.

That wasn't the end of the story. I was feeling rather under the weather, so I have no idea how I was transported but I do remember the journey seemed endless. Anyway, I ended up in a special unit that had been established in a former nunnery near Reims in France. The unit was a pukka Army hospital and the nurses were pukka Army Nursing Sisters, not the original nuns. That didn't mean it wasn't comfortable. It was: after the Dutch farmhouses, it was positively a Five Star Hotel. The significance of being near Reims emerged after I'd been there about a week and was on the mend. A local producer provided free champagne *pour les braves officiers anglais, si gravement blessés.* One bottle per day for each ward. Although I had room to myself, there were two other officers in the 'ward'. One had a stomach wound and couldn't digest, the other had a throat wound and couldn't swallow.

It worked out, therefore, that the duty Nursing Sister and I had a daily bottle of bubbly to share between us. Somehow, it was always the same Sister and we used to get more than a little merry. I rather think that that Sister was even committing that most deadly of all hospital sins; sitting on the patient's bed. One evening nemesis caught up with us. Halfway down the bottle, the door opened and in walked . . . Matron. She took the situation in at a glance and swept out of the room. Gone, Sister and I told each other, to summon the Firing Squad. But no, she returned a moment later with a glass in her hand and calmly announced that there was quite enough in a bottle of champagne for three people. From then, until the end of my stay, the bottle *was* shared by three people!

There is a postscript to this story which shows how well The Fifth looked after its own, even if 'its own' was only a newly-joined subaltern. When I was signed off, the hospital sent a message through to the Regiment that I was fit. I didn't have to go through the usual channels – with the risk of being posted to another unit. The Fifth sent a truck to collect me. I may have missed the Cambrai Celebrations and the Investiture but I did have a free Champagne Holiday.

Some of the children in those farms may have been young but not all were innocent. The crews of two of my tanks were billeted in the byre end of a typical Dutch farm – byre at one end, hay store in the middle, farmhouse at the other end. There were two teenage daughters in the family and Friday night was bath night and the hay store was the bathroom. The wall between the byre and the hay store had several holes in it. As my informant – no names no pack drill – said, 'Those two bints knew bloody well we were watching and they made damn sure we saw everything there was to be seen!' And to think that one used to pay for stalls in *The Windmill*.

However, the main reason The Fifth was in Holland was to fight a war and there was a war going on. Syd Storer described one reminder of this. 'Fresh vegetables had been issued in the morning of the 3rd and we decided to make a decent meal while the Squadron Commander was at an RHQ conference. Another of the crew, Mo Geliher, and I were standing in front of a window and peeling potatoes; Bill [Tpr Bilton] said he would take the peelings out to dispose of them. As he opened the door, a shell landed slap in front of the house and blew the window in. Mo and I dived under the table and listened as two more shells landed. We got up, badly shaken, and I said to Mo, 'Where's Bill?' We dashed outside and saw a body lying in the road. Bill's body, although he had been hit in the head and it was difficult to recognise him. We carried him to the Regimental First Aid Station which had been set up nearby but the MO just looked and shook his head.

'The Padre came up and we buried Bill along with three infantrymen who had also been hit by the shells. We finished cooking that meal but none of us could eat it. The next day I collected Bill's things together for them to be sent home. Among them was a letter to Mij Guerts, the daughter from the farm at

Nistelrode. Bill had told me that he intended to return and marry her.

'By this time the Poles had succeeded in clearing Geertrudenberg so, on the morning of the 5th, we moved along the s'Hertogenbosch road and took up a position in Kaatsheuvel [not surprisingly known as 'Cat shovel'] still in the area of the River Maas which had been earlier cleared by the infantry. We remained on partial stand-by as the enemy were still in strength over the river, so each morning the W/Ops had to rise early and 'net' the sets until we were told to stand-down. That meant that while the W/Op hung around the tank with his ear-phones round his neck, he was the one who made breakfast while the others were still in bed!

'There was very little to do in the area, so we played several of the local football teams, who generally beat us because of our many sleepless nights. On 11th November we moved to Dongen where we were billeted in the local 'public house': here the locals arranged very popular dances for us. It was eventually realised that constant wireless watch was an unnecessary drain on the batteries, so we were issued with field telephones, for which we had to lay the wires. The whole of the armoured brigade was concentrated in the Dongen area, so we enjoyed inter-unit football matches, beating the 'Skins' and 1RTR. A return match on the 15th was suddenly cancelled and we were put on immediate stand-by. Immediate meant 0630 hrs the next morning. We passed through Tilburg and reached Bree on the other side of the Divisional front.'

Syd commented – adversely – on the quality of the billets but had nothing but praise for the hospitality and generosity of the householders on whom they were billeted. For everything that the men provided – such as cups of Ovaltine from a tin that the Storer family had sent to Syd – the woman of the house always managed to provide some treat in return. A bonus for Syd was playing the organ in Masseik church for a Church Parade on Sunday, 26th November.

Apart from Tpr Bilton, there was only one other fatality in the Regiment in November and this was Trooper George Carter who died of heart failure. In many ways his friends found this more disturbing than if he had been killed in action. Natural death was not natural to them.

There were, inevitably, some minor casualties to report to the MO. One of these was sustained while 'B' Sqn was billeted in 'Cat's Shovel'. Someone – again, no names no pack drill – in 'B' Sqn had liberated a Packard motorcar on the grounds that it was painted field grey and, therefore, must have belonged to the 'Moffe'. André Kemps, being Dutch, was invited to a Liberation Celebration in Tilburg along with a 5RTR officer. The officer chosen was 'Babs'. Babs was the nickname of one of The Fifth's finest types. A commissioned regular with more service behind him than almost all of the Regiment's other officers, Alfred Gilbert Babbage was, at the time, acting as Second Captain in 'B' Squadron. Babs took André to the Celebrations and started to bring him back. The reason for what happened next must have been the poor mechanical state of the Packard and its limited 'black-out' lighting: it cannot possibly have had anything to do with the Celebrations themselves. Be that as it may, the car left the road and ran into a tree. The Packard was a write-off. The tree and Babs suffered cuts and bruises but André flew through the windscreen. He nobly turned up for breakfast in the Mess next morning but was immediately paraded before Doc Sproull. On being admitted to hospital, he was diagnosed as having a double fracture of the jaw, multiple glass fragments in his face and concussion. On being discharged from hospital, the Dutch Authorities caught up with André, put him through an official Interpreters Course and enlisted him in the Royal Netherlands Army. Those formalities attended to, he rejoined us in 'B' Squadron before the end of the year.

Of incidents there were plenty and, in 'B' Squadron, many of these could be described as getting on the wrong side of Pat Wood. An easy thing to do. Probably the officers suffered most but he inspired so little confidence in the men that the Sergeants (in spite of the fate of Emmin Hall in Shakers Wood) risked dire consequences by petitioning the CO for his removal and the re-instatement of Dennis Cockbaine as Squadron Commander. Already a Captain with some seniority in 1939, Pat Wood had never, despite reaching the temporary rank of half-colonel, seen wartime soldiering until he was posted to The Fifth. He had had a fairly tough time, however, having made several journeys to Russia, delivering tanks to our ungrateful allies. Nevertheless, the unwritten rule was that, if Regular Officers looked for post-war promotion, they had to have active service experience even if it meant coming down in rank. It wasn't Major Wood's fault that he arrived when the active service wasn't very active, so that he never learnt what the sharp end was really like, but it was his fault that he simply could – or would – not adapt to commanding a very battle-experienced Squadron, made up largely of non-regular troops and officered entirely by non-regular officers. Leave it that: during the winter of 1944/45, 'B' Squadron was not a happy Squadron. Colonel Gus, incidentally, dismissed the Sergeants' petition by the simple expedient of taking no notice of it but he did tell Dennis Cockbaine in no uncertain terms what would have happened to him if he, Colonel Holliman, thought Dennis was behind it. Serious ructions, in the event, did not occur for some weeks.

The business of patrolling on foot, albeit with occasional spells of static tank vigil, militated against high morale. It was a dreary business: probably the only people who got any amusement from our efforts were those ebullient Cockneys in 'I' Company of the First Battalion, The Rifle Brigade. Patrolling was meat and drink to them: they gave us advice on the subject but one could see that they felt it would be easier to turn elephants into ballerinas. Our efforts sometimes puzzled our own side. We used to share one particular stretch of what was theoretically the front line with the RBs, taking four days' turn-and-turn-about with them and with the other Troops in the Squadron. To alleviate the boredom of these stints, one of the Troop Officers decided one lovely moonless night to play Boy Scouts. In due course, he told the Platoon Commander from the RBs what had been done. However, the RB subaltern didn't think it was worth mentioning it to Michael van Gruisen who had the next tour of duty from The Fifth. The moon had meanwhile waxed and the frost had set in, so the nights were cold and bright. Michael decided to investigate what was causing the mysterious noise on his particular section of 'the front line'. In the words of Bert Reeves who had only just arrived in 'B' Squadron from the Echelons, 'Our Troop Officer asked for some men to check up on possible booby traps just inside No Man's Land. Thinking that I should show my mettle, I volunteered and, when the time came, found I was the only one and the other lads thought that I wanted my head looked at. The occasion was on a bright, moonlit night with crackling frost under foot. Mr van Gruisen and I set off: he walked upright as if he was on a ramble. I followed behind in a crouching stance with the Sten gun from the tank as our armoury. When we reached our objective, it turned out to be a line of wire with old bean cans hanging with some stones inside so that, should the Germans touch the wire, the cans would rattle and their presence be known.'

When Michael solemnly reported this intrepid reconnaissance operation on his return, he couldn't understand why his report was greeted with laughter. Bert Reeves didn't learn the truth for another fifty years.

By the end of November it was no use pretending that it was still autumn. Winter had set in with a vengeance.

THE OTHER SIDE

The situation in Germany in the autumn of 1944 was a peculiar one. In many ways, that of the German Armed Services was becoming desperate and more than one of the High Command must have wished that Rommel's advice had been followed, namely that the Army should overthrow Hitler and sue for peace with the Western Allies. As far as the public was concerned – not that Hitler would have thought of consulting them – Der Führer was still able to work marvels and morale remained high. Despite the Allied bombing, this was also true of munitions production. The 'V' weapons were beginning to prove their value. Perhaps not the case with the V-1s which were too erratic to be as successful as had been hoped but, as terror weapons – as weapons of mass destruction – the V-2s were turning up trumps.

By this time the Western Allies were effectively fighting on four separate fronts in Europe alone: the Low Countries (British and Canadian, with Polish and Dutch support), the German border (American and French), Italy (British and American) and the Eastern Mediterranean (British). It is true that Germany was fighting on the same four fronts as well as on the vast length of the Eastern Front against the Russians but they were doing so from a single, central base and they were being directed by one man. However megalomaniacal that man may have been, this did make co-ordination of affairs simpler and it also gave more scope to a man who –like Hitler – believed in the 'master stroke'.

Although there is reason to believe that Hitler had not, initially and unlike his Generals, taken the Western Allies' attack on Fortress Europe seriously, he could not by the autumn of 1944 ignore reality. The U-boat war, from the Kriegsmarine viewpoint, represented a defeat and sea-borne supplies had almost completely dried up. Shortage of fuel was critical and there was savage inter-Service competition for what supplies there were. Arguably in so far as the land war was concerned, the decision to make greater allocations to the Wehrmacht than to the Luftwaffe was the right one. Tanks and self-propelled guns could do more damage than aircraft and, in any event, so far as protecting the Fatherland went, the Luftwaffe had ceased to be a serious factor.

With General Alfred Jodl, the Chief of his Operations Staff, Hitler made an appraisal of the situation in the West. He appears to have been misled by the loss of momentum in Holland, the immense casualties (over 30,000 US Army losses in dead and wounded on the German border in two months) and the slow progress up the Italian Peninsula, into thinking that the Allies lacked strategic reserves and could not, therefore, offer serious resistance to a sudden, strong and well-directed counter-offensive.

If Hitler did take account of the negative factors, he did not allow them to block his desire for a master stroke. This – it was subsequently known as the 'Ardennes Offensive' (or, more colloquially, as the 'Battle of the Bulge') – was confidently expected to throw the Western Allies so far off balance that they (or certainly the war-weary British) would be open to negotiate a separate armistice, thus allowing a victorious Germany to gird its loins and trounce the invading Bolsheviks.

THE WAR CHRONICLE

1944

October	01	Brazilian Army Units joined drive on Bologna
	02	Allies landed in Crete
	03	Warsaw uprising ended when ammunition and food ran out
	06	Soviet troops entered Czechoslovakia
	12	British Commandos landed on Corfu
	14	Erwin Rommel, suspected of complicity in the '20th July Plot', committed suicide – Athens liberated

	19	Russian Army reached German soil in East Prussia
	20	In Yugoslavia, Marshal Tito's partisans entered Belgrade
November	01	Japanese launched 9,000 'balloon' bombs, designed to float across the Pacific and land on the US and Canadian coast
	05	US bombers, based on Calcutta, bombed Singapore
	08	Franklin D Roosevelt elected President of the USA for a fourth term
	10	V-2 attacks on London intensified
	12	German Battleship *Tirpitz* finally sunk
	20	'The lights go up in London'. Piccadilly and The Strand lit up after 5 years and 2 month of 'black-out'
	23	Finnish troops, fighting *with* Russian, drove German forces out of Lapland
	24	USAAF planes bombed Tokyo
	29	Red Army entered Hungary

NOTES

1 Trooper Colson. There is no record of this unfortunate accident in the Regimental Casualty List

2 Helvoirt-Udenhout. This probably should read 'between' rather than 'near' as the two villages are about 5km apart

3 Officers Mess. This was a curious piece of class distinction. The Interpreters on official attachment to Army units held the rank of Sergeant. Fromont, the Interpreter attached to 'A' Squadron, and Albert Hillen, attached to 'C ' Squadrons had their being in the Sergeants Mess. For some unknown reason, André Kemps was made a member of the 'B' Squadron Officers Mess

4 Jagdpanzer. Literally 'hunting tank'. These were self propelled A/Tk guns. There were various types with guns of various calibre: the most deadly were the 88s but the 75mm high-velocity guns were well able to penetrate any Allied tanks

5 AB 64. The Other Ranks' Record of Training and Qualifications

CHAPTER XIX

. . . *'The Winter of our Discontent'*

The Low Countries: December 1944 to March 1945

The Winter of our Discontent. Those five words by Shakespeare, if enunciated openly (and in uniform) in the winter of 1944/45, would undoubtedly have been deemed to be 'spreading alarm and despondency' and would have had dire consequences for the speaker. Nevertheless, there cannot have been many serving in North-West Europe during those months who were anything but dis-chuffed[1].

The weather was appalling: the routine of service was dreary: with fortunate exceptions, seldom found among the rank and file in the notional front line, the accommodation was indifferent: rations may have been adequate but the meals were repetitively unimaginative: entertainment was limited. Almost universally, officers and men felt 'Fed up . . . and Far From home' (with the other ... bit in the middle).

There wasn't anything anyone could do about it, so things just went on . . . and on . . . and on. The War Diary for December 1944 shows this:

1	No event. Regimental training
2	No event. Regimental training
3	1030 Visit by 30 Corps Commander, Lt-Gen Horrocks. Otherwise no event
4	No event
5	Regiment forms two Infantry Companies, B and C Sqns, with a view to holding the line as such during the coming operation to be carried out by 43rd Div
6	0800 Regiment formed up and moved to new area, Sittard, following route Maaseik– Elen–Double Dutch Bridge–Born–Sittard 1200 Regt established in new area. Regtl HQ, Recce Tp, B and C Sqns grouped in one area. A Sqn location NW of the town. The tanks of B and C Sqns being left in A2 Echelon.
7	Infantry positions occupied in area Tüddern by B and C Sqns and Recce Tp
8–13	No events

14	1400 All ranks present for talk by CO: subject 'Present situation on the Western Front and forthcoming operations'
15–18	No events
19	Regiment now placed under command of 53 (Welsh) Div. B and C Sqns reverting to their tanks
20	Regiment reverts to command 22 Armoured Bde. Enemy aircraft active during night, dropping a number of anti-personnel bombs
21	1200 Regiment less A Sqn moved to Limbricht. Otherwise no event
22	No event. At night A Sqn subjected to heavy stonk from enemy guns. Strong suspicion of civilian information in this area passing to the enemy *Casualties : [A] Cpl Cant RDC KIA* *Tpr Gilroy H DoW Tpr Ibbotson CJ DoW* *Cpl Hovells J Wnd L/Cpl Preston J Wnd* *Tpr Stokes J Wnd*
23–24	No events
25	Christmas Day. Extra rations forthcoming
26	B Sqn placed under command of 1st Rifle Bde and took their positions in line at Holtum. A Sqn had one troop in Nieuwstadt. Defensive positions for tanks previously prepared by bull-dozers
27–28	No events
29	B Sqn leaves command of 1 RB and returns to Limbricht
30–31	No events

Looking back over the years, there aren't many people who can now tell the difference between 'No event' and 'Regt Training'. A nothing day is a nothing day whatever it is called and December 1944 was full of nothing days. There is much greater significance in the entry for 7th December than the words indicate. Tüdern is in Germany. The Fifth, for the first time since it had formed part of the Army of Occupation in 1920, was back on German soil.

As the War Diary shows, there were no engagements with the enemy, although he frequently made his presence felt. It was rare that the Squadron Duty Officer (an unofficial title for an unofficial function) did not turn out to take bearings and report that 'Those chaps making all that noise are on bearing whatever-it-was-degrees from you-knowwhere-I-am' when the Squadron's rest was disturbed by a night-time stonk. Luckily, few such stonks were directed at us. That unlucky Friday, the 22nd, produced the last casualties of the year.

The business of 'forming two Infantry Companies' was nothing like as drastic as being turned into the Mobile Infantry Companies of April and May 1941 in Tobruk. We did acquire some rifles and a few extra Bren guns and we did go clumping around on foot but it is doubtful if any of us really knew what we were supposed to do if Brother Boche turned nasty and we all felt horribly naked with nothing else between ourselves and angry men with guns than our

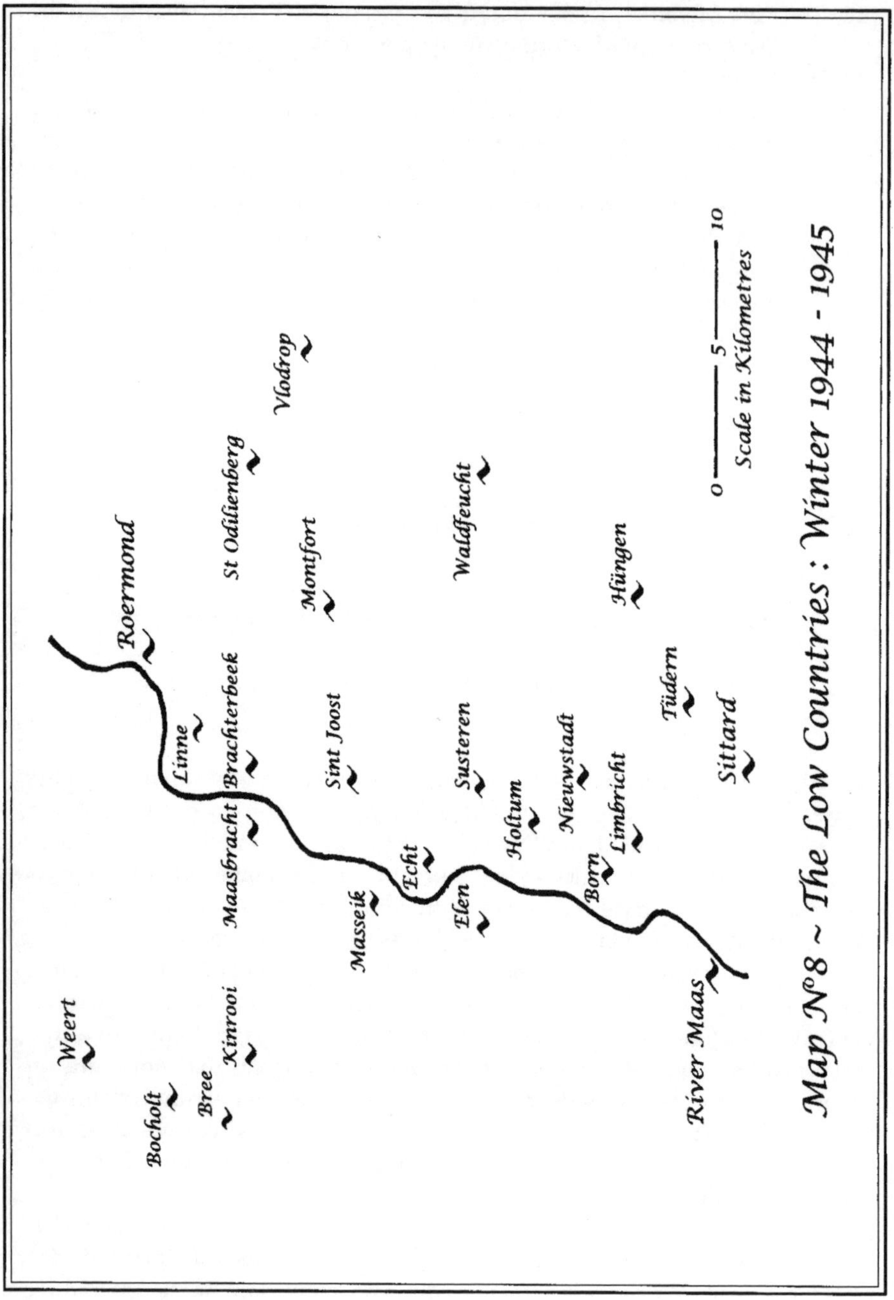

Map N°8 ~ The Low Countries : Winter 1944 - 1945

grubby battle dresses. Fortunately our quality as PBI was never tested. Equally fortunate was that our white paint cloak of invisibility was never closely examined. A tank still looks like a tank even when painted white.

In spite of moving to Sittard and being notionally in the front line, our main concern was keeping ourselves warm and our main consolation was the friendliness of the inhabitants of Sittard and the surrounding villages on whom we were billeted.

At one period the cold became so intense that the tanks had to be started every four hours, night and day, to ensure that they would start if we had suddenly to stand-to. Mostly, with a good priming from the Ki-gass pump which injected neat fuel into the inlet manifolds and a few words of endearment from the driver, the Meteor engines in the *Cromwells* would splutter into life. Often they simply died when the fuel sloshing around in the manifolds was burnt up and the mixture from the carburettor was too weak. The driver's words would then be of malediction rather than endearment: the whole process having to be repeated again and again – punctuated by Gargantuan backfires – until the engine rumbled into life. The radial engines in the *Fireflies* were a different matter. In any case, every time a radial engine had stood for any length of time it had to be cranked over by hand before starting it. This was a precaution to ensure that no oil or liquid fuel had drained into the bottom cylinder – the engines being mounted vertically. This did not frequently happen but when it did, the engine locked solid when the piston tried to compress the liquid against the cylinder-head. If this test was omitted and the engine fired up with a flooded bottom cylinder, it quite literally blew the engine up. The hand crank was geared down and cranking the engine over could entail several score turns of the crank. Then and only then could the Ki-gass procedure be followed.

One particularly cold night, one of John Gwilliam's *Cromwells* refused all efforts to start it. It happened that the OC Squadron was around to observe this. Pat Wood suggested that the Russian method should be tried. What, John asked, was the Russian method? Lighting some straw under the engine compartment to warm it up, was the reply. John demurred at this suggestion, rightly thinking that Russian T-34 diesel-engined tanks used something a little less volatile than the Meteor's 100 octane aero-engine spirit. John quickly learnt that what the Major had said was not a suggestion but an order. John scrounged some straw from a near-by barn, stuffed it under the tank and, on Pat Wood's order, poured petrol on the straw and threw a match under the tank. There was a loud whoomph and a cloud of thick white smoke, through which showed some enthusiastic flames. 'Go on, man!' Pat Wood shouted at the driver. 'Get in and start it.' With the air of a Christian martyr being thrown to some particularly hungry lions the driver got in. He didn't dare use the Ki-gass yet again for fear of liquid petrol flooding out; he prayed to whatever gods occurred to him at that moment; pressed the starter button and nearly fainted with relief when the engine roared into life.

Starting engines up was done by twos or threes. Firing up all a Squadron's twenty tanks at the same time would have undoubtedly attracted unfriendly attention from the German artillery.

Eric Stevenson's experience of 'firing-up' a *Cromwell* was rather different. His Troop had been parked overnight in a field and, when he gave the morning order to start the tanks, he saw the crew of one of his *Cromwells* baling out at a rate of knots. He went to see what was wrong and was told the tank was on fire. Eric could see no signs of flames or smoke, so he climbed on board and had a look in the turret. The bottom of the tank was bathed in flickering blue flame. As the Technical Adjutant explained later, there must have been some spillage when the tank was refuelled but the extreme cold had prevented any vaporisation. The inert petrol had lain there until ignited by a spark from the starter motor and then simply burnt itself out.

It *was* cold and the roads were often icy . . . as Eric Stevenson discovered in a disconcerting manner. Halted in a column on a typical, raised, heavily-cambered road, the crew got out for a leg-stretch and a smoke. Noticing how unsteady the rest of the crew were on their feet, the driver leant against the side of the tank. Which promptly slid off sideways into a field!

It was about this time that André Kemps found there were disadvantages to becoming a member of the Dutch Army instead of being a civilian interpreter attached to the British Army. He was now a combatant and, one cold and frosty night, found that, rather than spending the evening with the family on whom he was billeted and climbing into a nice warm bed, he had to spend the night lying in the snow behind a Bren gun, festooned with hand grenades, waiting to greet a Jerry patrol which, fortunately, never turned up.

Bob Lay made light of what must have been a very painful accident. 'It is winter (he writes) and bitterly cold. Waiting orders to move, we are in an empty cottage. Well below zero. Several people try to light the stove using petrol. I push a petrol-soaked rag into the stove with my petrol-soaked hand. There must be an ember in there, for –Whoosh! – the stove is alight and so is my hand. I try to stifle the flames putting my hand between my legs. It is very, very painful so I am taken off to the CCS in a scout car. Intense cold and petrol burns don't mix. Next I am in a Red Cross train, destination Abbeville. A massive hospital: I am in a very large ward. So are many badly injured men. Then I am in the operating theatre and a medic lass is trying to put me out with an injection. 'Count ten,' she says. 'I'm still here,' I say. When she says count ten she means count the number of tries she needs before her needle finds the vein. At last I am seeing all the stars in the universe and I wake up with a huge dolly for a hand. I am issued with hospital blues which fit where they touch. I can't tie my tie.

'That night a young lad with a bullet in his spine is in noisy agony as the morphine wears off. I am elected to go to get help. Because of the excess of knock-out drops in my system, I cannot control my legs. I ricochet down the corridor and knock on the door and the nurse jumps out of her skin. I explain the situation and a doctor arrives to administer to the patient. Next morning: Matron's Rounds. She makes a bee-line for me. To congratulate me for my Good Samaritan act? No way: I am not wearing a tie and get lambasted for it. I am past caring for petty-fogging and I enjoy seeing her retinue's scarcely concealed mirth.' Bob rejoined the Regiment in Sittard.

Rather more frequently than usual in December, the Regiment or bits of it came under command of some organisation other than our parent 22nd Armoured Brigade. These references in the War Diary reflected responsibilities which had no immediate effect on the tank crews. There was, in fact, no reason why they should have been aware of them. The importance, so far as the CO was concerned, could be enormous, particularly if there was a cock-up somewhere along the line. It might be vital for him to be able to show from whom he received his orders. There were never any problems when The Fifth came under command of the Rifle Brigade. Everyone in Fifth Tanks had complete confidence in First RB's Colonel, Victor Paley. His men adored him and, although they called him 'Colonel Nuff-Nuff' because of his cleft pallet, would nearly murder anyone from outside their ranks who dared to mock him for it. There was a peculiar bond between 5RTR and 1 RB. We both took a pride in the unconventionality of our dress and the scruffiness of our vehicles on active service and in our smartness when parade ground 'bull' was called for. It was to prove an advantage that we worked with the Welsh Division in those winter months. Later, in Germany, there was to come a time when our lives depended on each other. With the Highland Division, the Desert Rats always felt at home. They had known one another for a very long time.

A proposed attack had been abandoned, much to everyone's relief, as the continuous wet weather had made the roads – little more than tracks really – unsuitable for the tanks. This, as Syd Storer found, did not stop the Boche from shelling any town or village where the Fifth Tanks had found billets. 'On the night of 16th December,' Syd wrote, 'Sittard came under heavy fire and we were ordered to stand-to; the infantry had reported sounds of tracked vehicles from behind the enemy lines. Just as we were settling down and looking forward to Christmas we were moved again. This time nearer the front and into inferior billets: only a short move but much nearer the enemy who showed it by shelling us continually. On 22nd December we were again dismounted from our tanks and ordered to man the line, as the infantry was being moved to assist in holding the Ardennes offensive. The shelling continued at night and there were increased sounds of movement. A deserter later told us that this was 'canned music'[2] and that there were no tanks in the area!'

Christmas Day came and went with Syd playing the organ in the severely damaged church in Limbricht (where The Fifth was billeted) for the

Regimental Church Parade. What followed sounds like a story from *'Boys' Own'* or even *'Tiger Tim's'* but is gospel truth.

'It had been very quiet during the Service (Syd recalled) but, as we made our way back to the village through the snow, the German guns opened up and we threw ourselves on the ground. Instead of the expected shells, down fell balls of paper which, when unravelled, turned out to be Christmas Cards with a small piece of holly and some stars and the words, 'Hello there'. Inside, we read:

'You thought you would be home for Christmas:
Well boys – take it easy – you have been promised many things –
It's not your first and certainly not your last disappointment.
Cheer up – console yourself with Jerry.
He wishes you a very Merry Christmas and
The best of luck in the New Year.'

Jerry must have had a good laugh over the other side of the valley when they saw us dive into the snow.'

Bryan Johnson was having a pretty cushy time at the beginning of December. Life on the CO's tank suited him and he felt confident in his job. He also struck lucky over the matter of short leave in Brussels but not so lucky as the Orderly Room Corporal who had managed to take a girl from his billet on leave with him. Although being RHQ meant that Bryan did not get involved in infantry patrols, he did come in for some route marches. He felt pretty hard done by on this account until one of their outings took them into Guards Armoured territory and they marched slap into a drill parade!.

Apart from the Christmas Dinner – and there were, indeed, extra rations – the high spot for some in the Division was a Children's Party organised by two Staff Officers, Major Jo Grimmond, later Leader of the Liberal Party and a Watford Solicitor named Wilson [again no relation]. An anonymous description of this party, dictated I believe in the 1990s, follows. I can vouch for its accuracy: I was the 'Lieut who got himself volunteered' from 5RTR.

'Christmas was over and there wasn't much doing until three volunteers ha-ha were called for from every regiment in the Division. A Lieut, a Sarge and one of the blokes. I was the one of the blokes being an Echelon driver it saved transport didn't it? We were wanted sharpish after dinner as a Tea Party was being arranged for these local kids I think it was in Sittard in some hall that didn't have black-out so they had to be out before it got dark We got dolled up and I trolleyed us there in my 15-cwt and dumped us outside where there were some others all dolled up like us. I went and had a gander at what wasn't a hall but a sodding great empty warehouse with nothing in it but some tables and benches all as bare as the bride groom's arse if you'll pardon my French. After a bit a staff car arrived followed by three 3-tonners and out got two officers and a whole bevy of poncey types from the Catering Corps. With baskets and hampers and gawd knows what else which they said would we please to help and carry them in thank you ever so much. I had a shuftie inside one of the hampers and blimey . . . well wait for it!

'These Catering Corps types set about spreading cloths everywhere and told us to get 'em laid. 'What with?' we asked. Their Sarge pointed to a crate and said we'd find crockery – crockery, I ask you – in it. He was right. These kids weren't about to have their char and a wad off tinware. This was real china and real noshing irons. We laid the tables like our grandmas taught us and stood back to see what came next.

'It was the kids came next. Hundreds of the little bleeders from about three to nine or ten I reckon with their Mums and a few older sisters and the odd nun. We got 'em organised and sat down. Some of the older ones tried their English out on us so we told 'em to sit still and be good and wait and see. The Catering Corps ponces got us organised and we started loading up the tables. The kids couldn't believe their eyes. Nor us neither. There was sandwiches and buns and scones and there was cakes and there was jellies and creams and gawd knows what else. For all I can remember there could have been oranges and lemons and even bananas I don't know. There was orange squash and milk and tea. The kids went for the orange squash. Most of 'em had never seen it before.

'Could those kids eat! There was one table that didn't have any Mums looking after them just these two or three nuns. I asked a Mum who spoke English where their Mums were and she just looked at me. I felt a right fool. Of course, they hadn't Mums. They were from the orphanage weren't they? We kept fetching plates of more cakes and things and they kept on eating what we put in front of 'em. Why none of them weren't sick I don't know. Perhaps their Mums got them out in time. When the kids finally ground to a halt, we told the Mums to tuck in and they knew how alright. It was beginning to get dark and I could see the officers in charge were getting a bit worried. Someone brought in yet another chest and the one of the nuns banged on the table for quiet and set the kids to singing Dutch Christmas carols. We thought we were hardened Desert Rats but we found ourselves blowing our noses and wiping our eyes. And that other chest. We were told to come and collect the presents from it and they meant it. There was something for all of them. I can't remember what. Any ways something for girls and something for boys. Enough for all of them.

'Well that was that and it was time to say good bye. At first the kids just shook our hands and said their thank-yous politely but then one of the girls threw her arms round our Sarge's neck and kissed him like he was her long lost Dad and they were all at it. I've never been kissed by so many or such sticky kids in all my life. And by some of the Mums only they weren't sticky and they got kissed proper right back. I may be getting soft in my old age but, honest, I believe those were among the happiest hours in my whole five years in the Army.'

*

That was one side of life but there was a war going on and The Fifth was involved in it. For many, December brought a bitter disappointment – the cancellation of home leave arrangements for the longer serving men.

The reason for this was the situation developing in the American Sector.

The rationale behind what was developing belongs in *The Other Side* but it will make better sense of 5RTR's activities in December 1944 and January 1945 if the details of the Ardennes Offensive . . . the Battle of the Bulge . . . are explained here.

General Bradley and his Field Commanders had considered that the territory guarded by the thinly-spread-out US VIIIth Corps was unsuitable for a counter-offensive, impossible for an attack by heavy armour. On 15th December they had a rude awakening. On 14th December the Allies' front line had followed, more rather than less, the curves of the Siegfried Line just inside the German frontier. There was a small breach in this, made after much bloody fighting when the Americans took Aachen. Less than a week later the front could no longer be described as a 'line'. Defensive sectors were to be found between Monschau and Stavelot, 20 miles inside Belgium: around St Vith, 10 miles inside Belgium and south of Stavelot, with a third around Bastogne, 30 miles north-west of Luxembourg City.

However, and this is what caused near-panic in high places, the First SS Panzer Division had broken through the front south of Stavelot and, heading north-west, had nearly reached a crucial Allied fuel depot: two Panzer Divisions, 116 and 2 SS, had broken through north of Bastogne, and the Second Panzer Division and Panzer Lehr had broken through in the southern sector and had almost reached Dinant by Christmas Eve.

It is not surprising that 2nd Army leave plans were abandoned. It did not otherwise affect The Fifth.

The one consistent comment, in the Fifth Tanks' accounts and the official histories, concerns the intense cold. It was during this period that the 'Zoot suits[3]' appeared officially. Some accounts claim that they were in use at the beginning of autumn but either memories are playing tricks or some suits were obtained in advance of official issue. Zoot suits were tank overalls of an intelligent design and robust construction. They could be worn comfortably over battle-dress, were waterproofed and interlined with something that could almost have been wool. Their faults were minor ones: they were inevitably bulky which made getting in and out of the tanks more difficult and everything that opened and shut did so by means of zip-fasteners which were tricky to deal with in the dark or with near-frozen fingers. For a while after they appeared, we all felt slightly self-conscious. We were clean! Their issue was not confined to tank crews, both the Gunners and the RB carrier crews happily wore them.

1945

As a general rule, no-one took much account of days of the week or could say with any certainty what the date was. We might, if we'd thought, have been able to say, 'Oh yes, next Monday will be 1st January 1945 which means the war will be stretching out into its seventh year' but we were given to understand that no-one was to make a party of the arrival of this particular New Year. Fortunately for our Sector, the RAF had been given strict instructions that Sunday, 31st December was 'early to bed' and Monday, 1st January was to be 'early to rise'. The Luftwaffe had gambled on the Allies being seriously overhung, particularly the RAF, and had therefore planned a major air offensive with the intention of wiping out Tactical Air Force on the ground and properly duffing up the ground forces in the front line. Despite the 'clear heads' instructions, the RAF was caught, if not exactly napping, then at least by surprise. The Luftwaffe had mustered every available Me 262 *Schwalbe*[4] fighter and very effective they proved to be, with the RAF losing 157 planes on the ground or in the air. The balance, nevertheless, was in the RAF's favour: total Luftwaffe losses were 277. If Göring claimed it was a victory, it was a pyrrhic one, as the Luftwaffe could afford neither the planes nor the pilots. Certainly Limbricht, where the Regiment was, got a glancing blow (which did no damage but added immensely to the excitement of watching the dog-fights). Why nobody was killed or even injured goes down as being the working of Providence, because half the Regiment was in the streets literally yelling support for the pilots in the slower but numerically superior RAF planes. Calm reigned again by the middle of the morning and, as far as the War Diary was concerned, the Luftwaffe's 'Great New Year's Day Air Show' was a non-event.

The War Diary for the first three weeks of January1945 is a masterpiece of non-information and reads:

1	Regt location at LIMBRICHT.
2	No event
3	'C' Sqn relieved 'B' Sqn at HOLTUM and occupy inf posns there.
4	No event
5	'A' Sqn with part of Recce Tp under comd take over from 'C' Sqn
6	N.T.R.
7	'A' Sqn relieved by 8H.
8–13	N.T.R.
14	1300 Regt moves to new area at GELEEN making a direct change over with Main HQ 7 Armd Div. Route – via SITTARD
15	GELEEN N.T.R.
16	1200 The CO addresses all ranks in the Cinema on the forthcoming operation 'BLACKCOCK' the object of which is to clear the pocket of

enemy resistance between the Rivers MAAS and ROER. Fms taking part 7 Armd Div 8 Armd Bde 52(L) Div and 43 Div

17 All ranks dance held in cinema

18 No event

19 Regt at 1 hrs Notice to move as from 1100hrs

20 1330 Regt leaves for operations. 'C' Sqn leading and approach march made to BUCHTEN

21 C.O. Lt. Col. C. A. Holliman DSO MC killed by enemy shell-fire at SCHILBURG X-rds whilst on the way to 22 Arms Bde. Maj D. N. Macdonald assumes comd of the Regt. 'C' Sqn moved to HOLTUM
Casualties : [HQ] Lt Col C A Holliman DSO MC *KIA*

That last entry records the bitterest blow suffered by The Fifth since Fearless Jim was relieved of his command of the Regiment at Homs. Colonel Gus, like Colonel Hutton, had rapidly earned the respect, then the admiration and soon the devotion of all ranks. An unexpected characteristic was his light-heartedness. Even when we thought we were getting to know him, we could still be taken aback, for example, by his starting an O Group with a tap dance to the tune 'My Blue Heaven' This was most appropriate, as Mrs Holliman's nickname was 'Molly' and young Jeremy had not long arrived to complete the ' .. Molly and me and baby makes three .. ' which he sang as he danced.

Colonel Gus was on his way to 1RTR HQ for an informal conference with Colonel Hobart[5] when he was killed. He had taken his usual driver – the faithful Cpl Grey – and had asked Stuart Jones to come with him in the Dingo.

I know what the War Diary says and I am sure that it is the version that was reported to Mrs Holliman when the official letters followed the ghastly telegram, 'DEEPLY REGRET TO INFORM YOU THAT YOUR HUSBAND LT COL CHARLES ALEXANDER HOLLIMAN DSO MC WAS KILLED IN ACTION WITH THE BRITISH LIBERATION ARMY ON THE 21ST INSTANT.' The point of that comment is that, so far as anyone then serving in The Fifth was concerned, there was *no* enemy shelling over Schillburg at the time but the Royal Artillery heavies were doing a long-range shoot over the village. We all believed – and it added to the pointless tragedy of losing so fine a man and splendid a leader – that our CO had been killed accidentally by the premature air-burst of one of our own shells. I know that 'friendly fire' or 'blue on blue' were never given officially as the cause of death and I can well understand the reason. Nevertheless, I believe that the foregoing account is the true one.

'His passing cast a dark shadow over the Regiment,' Bryan Johnson wrote, 'and to me he was unlike any officer I had ever known. He treated me, a callow youth, more like a father than a Commanding Officer. The day after he was killed three of us from the Troop dug a shallow grave near Buchten and laid the Colonel to rest. A Padre from the 52nd Lowland Division read the service. To me he didn't seem to appreciate sufficiently the splendid officer he was interring.'

With 'Blackcock' looming, it must have been more than usually imperative for the Divisional Commander immediately to replace Colonel Gus with someone of the right calibre. It was decided that the man for the job was Rea Leakey, then Lieutenant Colonel Commanding 7RTR. Rea Leakey, with the assistance (and doubtless restraining hand) of George Forty, wrote a brief autobiography which was published shortly before he died and which – with complete justification – he called LEAKEY'S LUCK. He came to The Fifth with a reputation for outstanding courage (it was rumoured that one of his two MCs was awarded on the strength of a recommendation for a Victoria Cross). That was fine by The Fifth. One man apart, the Regiment had been accustomed to courageous leadership. What was not so welcome was Rea's reputation for being 'barbary[6]'. Nor were we altogether delighted when we found that he was much more inclined to do things, and have things done, by the rule book than Colonels Drew and Hutton and Holliman had been. The change in form of the War Diary between the entries for the 22nd and the 23rd January 1945 is not a coincidence.

The best character study of Rea [pronounced Ray] Leakey is undoubtedly LEAKEY'S LUCK. Some official histories – and the Fifth Tanks War Diary – do not agree with all he has to say, so it should be read as much as a rousing adventure story as serious military history. For the record, Colonel Leakey was one of several Fifth Tanks Officers who retired from the Army with the rank of General, in his case, Major General CB DSO MC*.

The War Diary for January continues:

22 1430 Regt moved to ECHT

23 'C' Sqn come under comd 2 Devons[7] 131Bde and passed through St JOOST. 9 and 12 Tps supported 2 Devons in night attack on AANDENBERG*. Attack successful and remainder of night spent mopping up – 18 PoW taken incl 1 Offr were taken and approx 100 Inf routed and observed making off in an easterly direction. During the early hours of the morning both tps were subjected to heavy and accurate shell-fire.

The new C.O. Lt. Col. A. R. Leakey MC arrives and takes over comd of the Regt

Casualties : [C] L/Cpl Billett JL KIA

Losses : Enemy 18 POW including 1 Officer

24 'C' Sqn consolidate AANDENBERG, both 9 Troop and 12 Tp moved to new posns where they remained in observation.

'B' Sqn moved to ECHT to new posn at a farm. 7 Tp opened fire at some Bosch [sic] digging in around the station setting fire to the waiting room. 5 Tp brewed up a house where some enemy had been seen

Casualties : [C] Tpr Wallace Wnd

25 'A' Sqn left ECHT and spent the night outside MONTFORT.

'B' Sqn remained in the same posns around the woods where 5 Tp were subjected to a certain amount of shell-fire

'C' Sqn changed over tps No 10 and 11 taking over from 9 and 12 tps. The latter two in the afternoon with 2 Carrier sections and 2 Inf pls of the 2 Devons continued to advance eastwards. 9 Tp reached MR with an Inf patrol at MR. 12 Tp reached MUNINGSBOSCHHOF*. In the evening 'C' Sqn withdrew to ECHT

26 0900 'A' Sqn moved off to support 1 Cdo Bde. No1Tp was placed at MR supporting 6 Cdo, remainder of Sqn at MR

1400 Nos 1 and 2 Tps went out with 6 Cdo to do a patrol in area wood HEIDE* Enemy seen in wood – Spandau fire from house. After firing Besa and HE at the house Patrol returned. 'B' Sqn did recce forward to try and find out where or what the enemy were doing. One *Honey* tank from Recce Tp was hit by a Bazooka. Apart from unpleasant stonking on Sqn HQ and 5 Tp bothered by snipers, all objectives were reached without enemy interference.

'C' Sqn remained in ECHT

Casualties : [HQ] Tpr Jenkins Wnd Tpr Nicol Wnd

27 1000 No. 1 Tp 'A' Sqn relieved No. 3

1300 2, 3 and 4 Tps supported 6 Cdo in a recce in force with the intention of safe-guarding the left flank of the 5 DGs and 1 RB who were clearing up St Odilienberg. Some enemy shot up but apart from shelling and mortar fire all objectives were reached without cas[ualties].

'B' Sqn remained in posn as before with NTR.

'C' Sqn in ECHT

28 1 and 4 Tps 'A' Sqn patrolled in same area as before and were heavily mortared, causing cas among Cdo. Cdo took 4 PoWs. 'C' Sqn moved up and took over from 'B' Sqn with two Tps remainder in observation all day. 'C' Sqn moved to MAASBRACHT and also RHQ

29 'A' Sqn HQ went to HEIDE oc[cupie]d with 2 Troops of Recce Dingoes and Cdos to investigate BOSCHBERG* and surrounding area. Maj D. N. Macdonald MC OC 'A' Sqn went over a mine in a Dingo, but was later recovered by 3 troop. A few enemy were seen but no enemy offensive action taken.

30 Nos. 1 and 2 Tps 'A' Sqn patrolled same area. Cdos entered wood and intended to clear it but lost two officers killed and several men wounded.

One dingo was lost on a mine and the driver wounded. The patrol eventually returned after an unsuccessful attempt to rescue the dingo during which a second mine exploded, killing Capt J. C. Messent of the Recce Tp.

Casualties : [HQ] Capt Messent JC KIA
Unknown Trooper Wnd

31 B Sqn relieved 'A' Sqn of its commitments – otherwise NTR

The business, recorded on several days, of working with the Commandos was one of the more bizarre aspects of January. The patrols in themselves were not too bad: cold, damp, dark and often dangerous – fatal, even – but our experience over the preceding weeks had taught us a lot. What was strange was the life we led. The Commandos, being rather more permanently on the job than us, had established themselves in whatever they could find by way of buildings in this singularly bleak and open corner of Holland. Here they had established almost 'ship-board' discipline and always appeared horribly smart and alert. We often had no quarters during our spells on duty. Our tanks were our homes and 'scruff order' was second nature to us. The Troop Officers had frequently to make night-time journeys on foot from the outposts to Squadron HQ and back. More than one of us was scared nearly out of our wits by a figure looming up out of nowhere and commanding us to 'Halt!' and asking 'Who goes there?' After the formal exchange of 'Friend.' 'Advance friend and be recognised' 'Lieutenant Buggins: Fifth Royal Tanks' 'Pass friend. All's well!' it was frequently a case of 'You haven't got a cigarette to spare, have you, Sir?' (which, smokers and non-smokers alike, we generally had) and a chat about life in general and soldiering in Holland in mid-winter in particular. When we tottered off to where we hoped we'd find our tanks, it was with the sentry's, 'Good night, Sir. Good luck.' in our ears.

Nowadays Governments spend a lot of the money they get from tobacco tax telling us how bad smoking is for us. Smoking may have been bad for our health but it was good for our nerves, our morale, our comfort . . . and a fag was often the last solace a dying man knew. Somehow, in spite of smoking, we seem to have survived.

The entry for 30th January is especially poignant for me, as it records the loss of my original contact with The Fifth. Colin Messent died in particularly tragic circumstances. He had gone out to deal with the routine matter of collecting the Humber Scout Car in which Deryk Macdonald had had a narrow escape earlier in the day. Colin was out of his Dingo, directing it back to a point where a tow-rope could be hitched to the damaged vehicle, when it hit a mine, killing Colin instantly. Another tragic aspect of the accident was that the third man in the party was Stuart Jones who, only nine days earlier, had been with Colonel Gus when he was killed.

Operation 'Blackcock' was postponed for 24 hours due to thick fog. The ground ahead of 22nd Armd Bde had been well prepared by 131 Bde, assault units of the REs using purpose-built ladders to cross the dikes and 'Flail' tanks from 79 Armd Div which had successfully ploughed through the numerous minefields. The attack was so successful that the Boche packed in their opposition and pulled out during the second night. The follow-up was not so easy and, as the third tank unit in the advance, The Fifth spent more time waiting than advancing. The final objective was taken before 5RTR reached it and the Regiment was ordered westward to join the attack on Sustern. During the pause while the infantry consolidated their position in Sustern, it started to snow seriously and a day was spent painting the tanks white. This would not have been an easy or pleasant job with clean tanks on a mild spring morning. In freezing snow with wet, dirty tanks it was hideous . . . and not overly successful. The once olive drab but now patchy white Fifth Tanks moved on through Hingen in the direction of St Joost where the enemy was putting up stiff resistance in an attempt to maintain a toe-hold west of the Roer.

Here 22nd Armd Bde encountered an old familiar, but still unwelcome, situation: small pockets of enemy infantry ensconced in the woods. The tactic north-east of St Joost was to take parties from the Devons on the backs of the tanks and makes 'sweeps' through the woods. This had varying success: sometimes producing prisoners, sometimes casualties. At the end of the day, The Fifth and the Devons were five miles nearer the Roer. While this was going on, the RAF put in a devastating attack on Montfort to the Regiment's immediate front, as this was where the Germans were concentrating. This brought in yet more POWs and enabled the 'Skins' to clear Montfort, while 5RTR reached the river and turned towards St Odilienberg.

In his account of the approach to St Odilienberg, Bryan Johnson records that one of the leading tanks in the attack was that commanded by the newly-arrived CO . . . who wanted to get some personal experience of what war was like in *Cromwells*!

What followed was less a counter-attack than an infiltration by the Germans into the area immediately north of Sustern. It was at this stage that our operations with the Commandos began. They had also been clearing wooded areas and The Fifth found their methods to be alarming but extremely effective. Unlike some infantrymen, the Commandos had no qualms about working with tanks. Some of them thought that we are a bit soft, because we stopped firing to give Jerry a chance to surrender: the Commandos went on firing to make very sure he did . . . or died in the attempt! As much as their aggressiveness, Rea Leakey appreciated the smartness of the Commandos but probably even he was surprised by the Adjutant of 45 Commando – a man with a patch over one eye and a disabled arm – who stood smartly at the salute as his CO drove off in the 5RTR Command *Cromwell* and remained like that until the tank was almost out of sight.

Which comes back to the arrival of Rea Leakey. With respect to his shade, his arrival did *not* happen as he described it in LEAKEY'S LUCK. To begin with, the date is wrong and, as Jackie Garnett was expecting his arrival, Jackie, at least, cannot have been on leave at the time. Rea's description of the weather is certainly accurate but his claim that, in the weeks after his arrival, The Fifth lost several tanks on enemy mines is not borne out by the War Diary or any other record. Colonel Leakey's description of his somewhat cavalier dismissal of Jackie Garnett as Adjutant is out of place by several weeks. Roy Dixon – not, in fact, the only one of The Fifth's subalterns to have had an education as Rea implies – did not replace Jackie until just before the Rhine Crossing. One thing all can agree upon is Rea's disapproval of our scruffiness and his attempts to remedy it. For a short while he almost succeeded but we soon beat him and it was not until the War in Europe was over that he won the Parade Ground Battle.

January merged unnoticed into February, about which the War Diary has the following to say:

1 Reg. under Comd. 1 Commando Bde, 'C' Sqn. being employed in an observation role with Sqn HQ at Maasbracht and troops in position at MRs. Apart from spasmodic gunfire NTR

2 'C' Sqn troops moved out at first light to positions of previous day, being preceded by an infantry patrol of 2 Devons for each troop, who in turn searched wooded area and tracks for mines. During this day Heide Wood was shot up with HE and Besa: a certain amount of mortar fire was returned. Towards evening enemy were observed at MR apparently digging in. These were promptly shot up; it was however difficult to observe the damage inflicted but the enemy disappeared. At last light troops were withdrawn

3 'A' Sqn relieved 'C' who returned to Brachterbeek. During the day 'A' Sqn T&A'd sights from their positions, practising both Direct and Indirect firing into Heide Wood, also Spielmanshof* and the factory area at MR

4–5 'A' Sqn continue to T&A. Remainder of Regt. continue maintenance

6 'C' Sqn took over 'B' Sqn's positions at Maasbracht. One troop was out at MR. This troop was placed under command of 6 Commando Brigade.
Casualties : [N/S] Tpr Smith M Wnd

7 1 Troop of 'C' Sqn supported by Commandos moved to MR and shelled the island in the R Maas SW of Linne. At least 12 enemy killed and wounded. Also destroying what was thought to be the only W/T set on the island being used by the enemy, killing the operator. Towards nightfall one scout car accompanied the Commandos who broadcast to the enemy resulting in the surrender of 12 more Boche
Casualties : [A] Tpr Newman P DoW
Enemy : 24 Killed, wounded or POW

8 'B' Sqn took over 'A' Sqn positions, otherwise NTR

9 An enemy patrol of 6 men attacked a tank with a Bazooka, these however were seen off by [men from] 6 Commandos

10 Div. Comds. talk in the cinema to all officers and full-rank NCOs, subject – Exercise Blackcock

11 'C' Sqn took over positions from 'B' Sqn

	0830 hrs. Recce parties left for next area Bocholt, otherwise NTR
12–13	NTR. 'C' Sqn carry out shooting practice
14	'A' Sqn took over from 'C' Sqn. Otherwise NTR
15–17	Shooting practice continued, but there was a reply from an enemy gun of large calibre although no casualty was sustained
18	NTR
19	0715 hrs. Regt. less 'A' Sqn. moved back into Belgium for a rest period, position being taken over by 8 US Armd. Div.
	1100 hrs. Regt arrived in Bocholt having taken the following route – Schillberg– Susteren–Maaseik–Kinrooi–Bree.
	1500 hrs. 'A' Sqn arrived in Bocholt
20	CO's Sqn Leaders conference
21	1430 hrs CO inspected HQ Sqn
	1530 hrs CO inspected Recce troop
22	0930 hrs CO inspected 'A' Sqn
	1030 hrs CO inspected 'A2' Echelon
23	CO inspected 'B' and 'C' Sqns
24	Firing on Lommel ranges
	1000 hrs. Lecture by Brigadier Wingfield D.S.O. to all tank Comds.
25	Firing on Lommel ranges
26	Cloth model exercise[8] at 22 Armd. Brigade in Bree attended by all officers.
	1000 hrs Visit by Field Marshal B.L. Montgomery D.S.O. who stopped for a brief period in the regimental area. Later he also visited the Cloth model exercise.
27-28	NTR.

'NTR'; one Squadron relieving another; testing and adjusting guns that had already seen considerable service; shooting practice continuing. It hardly sounds like a serious war . . . and it wasn't. This was not the fault of the Fifth Royal Tank Regiment or the Brigade or the Division or the Corps or the British Liberation Army. If it had been, February might have been less frustrating for the GOC-in-C down to the humble *Cromwell* lap gunners. We felt we might have been able to do something – get on with the war and get home – if we knew what was – or rather wasn't – happening and why. The Winter of Discontent had set in with a vengeance: the only consolation was that February produced only two bad casualties, the lowest rate per month since D+1.

Fortunately this period of relative inactivity enabled us to get to know our new CO and gave him a chance to assess us before we were called on to make the final push. There were still quite a few of the genuine Desert Rats spread through the Regiment at all levels, although there were by now very few of the real 'old sweat' pre-war 5RTC regulars left in the ranks and none in the Officers Mess. In fact, there were very few Regular Officers on the strength.

Ironically, one of these, Pat Wood, commanding 'B' Squadron, was considerably senior to Rea Leakey in years and commissioned service. Deryk Macdonald, who was commanding 'A' Squadron and whom Rea Leakey knew, did most of his regular soldiering after the war, as did Arthur Crickmay, commanding 'C' Squadron. Among the commissioned rankers from pre-war days were Captain 'Babs' Babbage in 'B' Squadron and Captain Jackie Garnett (a Corporal with several years' service in 4RTC when 2/Lt Leakey AR was posted to that Regiment) whom Colonel Gus had appointed as Adjutant in Shakers Wood in succession to Arthur Crickmay. With the additional exception of the QM, Lieut Jim Meehan, all the Captains and Subalterns in the Fighting Squadrons were 'War Only' officers.

The War Diary cannot be expected to give a picture of what was really going on and most of us have pretty confused recollections of those days, because they followed no coherent or cohesive pattern. When we were not living very rough indeed . . . as we were, when in one of those 'positions' waiting for another Squadron to come and take over from us . . . we were billeted on the local population and made welcome by them. For several glorious days – or rather nights – when the weather was at its worst, I slept in an enormous double feather bed. I retired less only my boots and my battle dress, gradually shedding garments until, warm at last, I was down to my Canadian Army issue genuine pure wool vest and underpants. If I say that I was not alone in this respect, I do not mean that there was anyone sharing my bed: no such luck. I mean that others, elsewhere, were as fortunate as I was! The main trouble for the men was the lack of purpose or pattern in our existence. 'Monty', they felt, 'said we should be told what was happening and what we were supposed to be doing. We haven't heard much from him about this lot.' Even the odd encounter which we had with Brother Boche was patternless and generally pointless. We were not having a proper go at the enemy nor he at us and yet we couldn't settle down to do anything useful. Even the shooting practices were designed more to keep up our morale than inflict damage on the Wehrmacht.

There is a persistent myth in The Fifth that we were directly concerned in 'rescuing the Yanks in the Ardennes'. This is only a myth. General Verney is positive, saying only that 21st Army Group moved a number of Divisions down to act as a covering force but *the 7th Armoured Division was not involved.* Liddell Hart mentions three RTR units which were peripherally involved: 5RTR was *not* one of them. In the face of these facts, one can only shrug one's shoulders at the supposed reminiscences . . . mostly unflattering to our American Allies.

Where we *were* involved with US Forces was on 19th February, as briefly mentioned in the War Diary. The Fifth was holding positions which were technically in the Front Line and might theoretically have been in range of arms and ammunition capable of doing us harm. It was at this juncture that, rather than our 'rescuing our American cousins', they came to relieve us! Our proximity to the enemy, when a fleet of *Shermans* arrived from the 8th US Armored Division arrived, had not worried us. We therefore saw with some amusement the look in the American Tank Company Commander's eyes which said quite clearly that he was going to order a bit of 'reconnaissance by fire' on likely targets the moment our backs were turned. Even so, it would be apocryphal to claim we heard gunfire as we drove away.

The next time we heard of 'rescuing the Yanks in the Ardennes' was on 26th February when Monty visited 7th Armoured. At an unsocial hour on that Monday morning, all the Division's available officers were herded into 3-tonners and driven to a village-hall-without-a-village in some god-forsaken spot in the wilds. Mere two- and three-pippers were herded out of sight round the back while the high-priced help got themselves lined-up on the approach road. We had been told that Monty was coming and would be addressing us. Monty did turn up. We were suddenly aware of an immaculate Rolls-Royce limousine with an enormous flag on the bonnet, bumping along the track which led to the goods entrance. It stopped and out got Monty. He looked around and then approached our lot. Someone had the wit to murmur, 'Watch it, chaps!' and we sprang to attention and saluted. Monty returned our collective salute and said, 'How do I get into this place?' (If he hadn't known, his ADC was due for the sack) We fell over each other to be the one to usher him to the front of the hall, Monty stopping every few paces to chat with those around him. If Monty wanted to catch the senior officers by surprise as well as to show us lesser breeds that he was hail-fellow-well-met with us as well as with the rank and file, he certainly succeeded . . . and he gave us junior officers a good laugh at the consternation he created.

Inside, Monty addressed us and told us what 'My American Army' had done. He said this jokingly, not boastfully, but quite accurately. For practical reasons, as the GOC-in-C of the main force north of 'the Bulge' he had been given temporary command of *all* the Allied forces in that sector: this included General Hodges' US First Army. As usual, Monty gave one of his crystal-clear and concise resumés, explaining how the situation had developed, what measures had been taken to deal with it and what the resulting situation was. Monty left, visiting the Regimental area on the way, and we got down to the 'Cloth model exercise': an exercise designed to explain the nature of the final operations leading up to the Rhine Crossing.

As many remember fondly, there was one bright spot in February: this was our good fortune in being allocated Bree and Bocholt as our bases for the next few weeks. The Bocholt in question was a large village just inside Belgium, about 20 miles west of Roermond and *not* the Bocholt in Germany on the other side of the Rhine. Apart from a friendly population and a number of pretty girls, Bocholt possessed a brewery. It was, obviously, a matter of critical importance to get supplies for the brewery and to get it functioning again – for local population as well as for The Fifth. This was quickly, if mysteriously, accomplished and nothing was too good for all ranks in the Regiment. We depended on the brewery and the brewery depended on us[9]. It was surprising how many crates of beer could be carried in or on the Squadron's Dingo!

Most of the reminiscences about these weeks concern our contacts with the civilian population rather than the enemy. No doubt the Belgians were asking themselves the same questions as we were – 'When is something going to happen?' 'When will this war be over?' – but there was never any suggestion that we should be out fighting rather than tinkering with our tanks and spending the evenings with our feet under their tables.

The War Diary for the first three weeks of March occupies only three lines:

1–5 Regt. at rest in Bocholt
6–20 Regt. at rest in Nederweert
21 Sqns on ranges at Lommel
The entry for the next day reads:
22 Sqns. on ranges. Brigadier A.D.R. Wingfield, D.S.O., visited CO Lt.Col.A.R.Leakey M.C. Maj. D.N. Macdonald left with recce party to recce conc. area for operation 'Plunder' – area Westbroek

And this may have been connected with an incident which followed at that time.

As mentioned earlier, Pat Wood was not a popular nor a particularly successful Squadron Commander. With a young newly joined Subaltern (who also left the Regiment shortly thereafter) Major Wood had drawn attention to himself in an unfortunate manner. Rea Leakey was holding an informal O Group for all officers outside the mess after lunch when a stray airburst went off near enough to be heard but not near enough to hurt. Two officers dived for cover: the rest of us went on listening to what the CO had to say.

Sacking a Subaltern is all in the day's work for a Regimental Commander and the Subaltern duly departed. Pat Wood did not go so easily. During what cannot have been an easy encounter for either man, Pat Wood was unwise enough to tell the CO that he, Major SP Wood, was far senior to Lt Col AR Leakey and was not going to be thrown out on his ear. Events proved him wrong and that evening Rea Leakey sent for Dennis Cockbaine and told him to resume command of 'B' Squadron . . . and hope soon to replace his three pips with a crown. What moderated our relief was that Pat Wood departed in 'B' Squadron's unofficial staff car: we never saw either again.

THE OTHER SIDE

Probably the only man in the Armed Forces of The Third Reich who still believed, in the winter of 1944/45, that Germany could win the war was the Commander-in-Chief – Adolf Hitler. He based his belief on the conviction that, by pushing the 'Anglo-

Saxons' back into the Channel, he would so discourage them that they would sue for peace. This he would accept on his own (unspecified) terms and then deal with the real enemy – the Union of Soviet Socialist Republics.

To accomplish this, Hitler conceived yet another 'master stroke'. In many ways it was to be a repeat of von Manstein's 'Sickle Plan' of 1940. This is an aspect of the situation which the Allied Supreme Command seems completely to have left out of account. There was, either coincidentally or because Hitler was more acute than his General Staff, another reason for copying von Manstein's strategy. Whereas Allied aerial reconnaissance was not a factor in 1940, it would have been in 1944: however the weather forecasts for November and December 1944 made it practically certain that the Allied Air Forces would not be able to fly reconnaissance sorties over the concentration area, even if (which was not the case) Allied Intelligence had cause to suspect unusual activity in the Ardennes.

In fairness, it would have been difficult for Allied Intelligence to get advance warning that anything unusual was planned, as the strictest secrecy was observed. Even the Generals whose Divisions were involved were given no inkling of why changes were being made in their troop dispositions. The need for secrecy was one reason – the other being the 20th July Plot – why Hitler barely trusted even so able a man as von Rundstedt whom he had put in charge. In the event, practical considerations – such as shortage of supplies, particularly fuel for the tanks and transport, and the administrative difficulties of regrouping Wehrmacht Divisions under SS command – forced him to delay the launch of Operation 'Wacht am Rhein' *from October to November and eventually to mid-December.*

The main difference between the Sickle Plan and Wacht am Rhein *was the objective. The Sickle Plan had been aimed at the French Channel ports:* Wacht am Rhein *was aimed at Antwerp.*

A study of the military situation had shown Hitler that the Allied line from the town of Monschau (just inside the German frontier and some 35 miles east-by-south-east of Liège) running south to a point on the frontier halfway between the City of Luxembourg and the German town of Trier, was relatively lightly held. He calculated – rightly – that the force opposite him on this front had one man where the forces on the rest of the front had three. What he didn't know, but what proved a bonus for him as the result of delaying the attack until mid-December, was that among this force there were many taken out of the line for a rest after the fighting round Aachen.

For Wacht am Rhein, *Feldmarschall Model had command of Army Group 'B' which consisted of the Sixth SS Panzer Army with nine Divisions (four Panzer; four Volksgrenadier; one Parachute): the Fifth Panzer Army, also with nine Divisions (four Panzer – including the 2nd and the* Lehr; *four Volksgrenadier; one Panzer Grenadier): the Seventh Army with seven Divisions (four Volksgrenadier; one Panzer Grenadier; one Infantry; one Parachute): sundry assorted support troops. This was a formidable force, even though none of the Divisions had as many fit, trained, men on the ground as they had on paper.*

Initially everything went according to plan. Surprise was complete; success seemed assured. Unlike the Sickle Plan, however, the momentum was lost: the Luftwaffe did not have control of the skies and, ultimately, logistics played their part. The Allies, particularly the US Army, could demand – and get – whatever supplies they called for: the Germans could not. Once the initiative was lost, the battle was lost.

THE WAR CHRONICLE

1944

December	05	British tanks, involved in Greek Civil War, ordered to fire on Communists 'rebels' in Athens
	08	Assault on Iwo Jima began
	10	World's longest Bailey Bridge (1,154 ft) built across the Chindwin
	16	American 'Big Band' leader, Glenn Miller, lost when his plane went missing
	29	Soviet tanks entered Budapest – On the cultural front there had been David Niven in *The Way Ahead* and Laurence Olivier's *Henry V*: the introduction of The Old Vic Company: Sir Henry Wood and the 50th Anniversary 'Prom' Concert – It was also the year, as *Punch* remarked, that LDV no longer meant 'Local Defence Volunteers' but 'Lokaler Deutsche Volksturm'

1945

January	02	Admiral Bertram Ramsey, organiser of the Evacuation from Dunkirk and the D-Day Flotilla, killed in an air crash
	03	Mini-mutiny by Canadian Army conscripts, objecting to compulsory overseas service
	14	General Slim's forces crossed the Irrawaddy
	17	Warsaw liberated by Russian Army – who then started to round up 'pro-democracy' Poles
	24	Colonel-General Heinz Guderian, Hitler's Panzer Suptremo, told von Ribbentrop, German Foreign Minister, that the war was lost and he should sue for peace
	27	Russian advance guard reached Auschwitz
	31	Red Army got within 100 miles of Berlin – Russian submarine torpedoed German liner,

		unaware that it was carrying refugees: 7,000 feared lost
February	02	Singapore heavily bombed
	05	Russian forces crossed River Oder
	06	Manila, capital of the Philippines, surrounded
	13	Budapest captured after 50 day siege
	14	Controversial air attack on Dresden
	21	Kamikaze pilots added USS *Bismarck Sea* to their ever-growing list of sinkings
	28	Red Army soldiers accused (rightly as events proved) of mass murder, rape and looting on German soil
		– After 66 months of war, casualty figures put at 307,201 members of the British, Empire and Commonwealth Armed Forces killed and 60,585 civilians killed by enemy bombing
March	03	Manila fell to General MacArthur's forces
	04	Finland declared its change of sides by declaring war on Germany
	06	US Army units captured Cologne
	07	Germany launched major counter-attack in Hungary
	10	US Air Force carried out mass incendiary bomb raid on Tokyo
	14	RAF dropped its 'biggest and best bomb': 22,000 lbs of high explosive landed on Bielefeld viaduct
	17	V-2 offensive on London intensified
	20	Mandalay recaptured by Indian Army units
	24	War in Italy re-activated after three depressing months of stalemate

NOTES

1 Dis-chuffed. This may have been Fifth Tanks slang or it may have had wider use: the meaning being 'not chuffed' or 'far from pleased with life in general. 'Browned off' was, of course, the more usual expression

2 Canned music. This account was denied, counter-denied and rebutted. One, light-hearted, version has it that the wrong record was once played and the listening out-posts distinctly heard trumpets sounding for a cavalry charge!

3 Zoot suits. Americanese for a change. According to Brewer, *zoot* [?from the Dutch word *zoet* = sweet or special] suits were the 'in' wear of a class of sharp-dressing American youths in the 1930s. Zoot suits were OTT – appropriately, as Tank Suits went over the top of everything else

4 Me 262 *Schwalbe* or 'Swallow'. These were twin-engined, jet-powered, Messerschmitt fighters. Not only were they the first aircraft, flown in combat, to be powered by jet engines – BMW designed and developed – they had a

novel wing design which made them superbly manoeuvrable. The Allies had Hitler to thank for the fact that so few of them ever came into action: for some reason, he interfered in their development, with the result that relatively few were ever built

5 Colonel Hobart. Nephew of 'Hobo' (Major General Sir Percy Hobart, then Commanding his 'funnies' in 79th Armoured Division). Colonel Hobart took over 1RTR when Mike Carver was promoted

6 Barbary. Can also be spelt 'barbery'. Means 'tough' as of a hard-nosed officer or NCO and was common in WWII. Also used of the enemy when he became too active for one's liking. The special Fifth Tanks sense was to imply that someone in authority was a bit too anxious to get on with the 'shooting war'

7 Devons. The 2nd Battalion The Devonshire Regiment and the 9th Battalion The Durham Light Infantry had been brought into 131 Brigade to replace 1st/6th and 1st/7th Queens who were deemed to be 'battle weary' after the Normandy break-out

8 Cloth model exercise. First cousin to a sand table exercise, serving the same purpose. Monty's visit was not a coincidence: the whole operation was carefully prepared and stage-managed. Monty, incidentally, by this time had more initials after his name than DSO

9 Bocholt. The interdependence was long-lasting. Certainly at Christmas 1945, the Assistant Adjutant (the present 'historian') signed a Work Ticket authorising a 3-tonner to make an essential journey from Wilster on the Kiel Canal to Bocholt to supplement the men's 'beer ration'

CHAPTER XX

. . . *Into the Home Stretch*

March and early April 1945 – the Rhine Crossing

Whatever was behind naming the Rhine Crossing Operation 'Plunder', the authorities were careful to point out that this did not mean we were about to go on a looting spree. Just because we were in Germany, we were told, was not *carte blanche* to do as the Germans had done in the countries they had occupied. Above all, there was to be no fraternisation. This was decreed in part for political reasons but also because no-one knew exactly what the reaction of the civilian population was going to be when the Allies entered and occupied *Das Vaterland.*

Except for the incorrigible few, 'looting and loving' were not in our minds: all we wanted to do was to get across the Rhine alive and still be that way at the end of the road. Operation 'Plunder' presented a good chance of achieving both those ambitions: everything was planned on a grand scale.

Resuming where Chapter XIX left off, the War Diary for March 1945 reads:

23 Scheme with 'I' Coy 1 RB
CO to Divisional Comd's Conference

24 The Regt. still in the area of Nederweert [Holland]. The CO briefed Sqn Leaders and explained the operation 'Plunder' which was the crossing of the Rhine. This attack started before dawn and was led by 15 (S) Div. and 51 (HD). The role of 7 Armd. Div was to break out of the bridgehead as soon as possible and the first objective was given as Borken. 5RTR were to move from Brünen to Borken by subsidiary roads doing left flank protection to the Division. [The original Operation Order was attached to the War Diary but is now missing]

25 The Regt moved off in the late afternoon and reached conc area at Westerbroek (Germany) at 1930 hrs. CO attended conference at 22 Armd Brigade and was told the route and timings for the move across the Rhine. By this time a firm bridgehead had been established by 15 (S) Div and 6 Airborne Div on our Corps (12 Corps) front. By 2300 hrs Regt grouping was complete and the following came under command 5RTR: 'I' Coy 1 RB. 'G' Battery 5 RHA, Tp WD (Flails), detachment 4 Fwd [*sic*: should be Field] Sqn RE.

26 The day was spent in working out the detailed plans for our coming role. Recce parties proceeded ahead and crossed the Rhine to recce conc areas in the Bridgehead.

27 By 0100 hrs a Class 40 Bridge[1] was across the Rhine and it was possible to pass the armour through a day earlier than was anticipated. The Regt moved off at 0400 hrs.

28 By last light 'C' Sqn had reached the outskirts of Borken and joined up with the remainder of the Brigade group who had come up the main road from Brünen

Casualties : [B] Tpr Cheesman F KIA Tpr Baines WH KIA
Sgt Sharrocks Wnd Tpr Osborne Wnd
[C] Cpl Riley Wnd

29 0600 hrs Regt passed under command of 131 Brigade and took up positions of observation

The enemy had received a good loosening up the previous day and all morning POWs were collected, a mixed bag including members of Battle Groups *Karst* and *Becker.* 3 members of a 75mm SP from Battle Group *Becker* stated that their gun had been KO'd the previous day and also that Col Becker had been seriously wounded.

0855 hrs Orders were received for the Regt to go to an area Borken with the exception of 'C' Sqn who remained in position north of the River Aa. It was later confirmed that all bridges across had been blown. 'A' Sqn went to support 1/5 Queens. Two troops were employed in a sweep of the area north of Heiden*. An unknown gun had opened up on 22 Armd Brigade TAC HQ from this area. Quite a few enemy infantry with MGs came to light and the sweep yielded about 30 POWs, also KO'd 88mm already destroyed

Casualties : [A] Cpl Shute Wnd Tpr Whitely Wnd Tpr Roe Wnd
Tpr Bowstead Wnd

Losses – Enemy : 81 POWs; 3 Ammunition trailers: 2 Staff cars.

At the time of the initial crossing on the night of 23rd March The Fifth, along with the rest of the Division, was deliberately held some miles away to the west of the Rhine. With the necessity of forging six crossing points over which six infantry divisions and an armoured division, with an additional armoured brigade in support, had to pass, the biggest danger was that of confusion on the west bank.

'At 1000 hrs on 24th March [Bryan Johnson writes] a massive fleet of aircraft flew overhead with the Airborne Division destined for the other side of the Rhine. The sun had suddenly appeared, making the aircraft glitter in its rays. And – to our immense surprise – the heat from those rays and the heavy ground traffic produced something we hadn't seen for months: dust instead of mud! On Sunday 25th March we moved further east at 1500 hrs across the Maas and leaguered at a place called Westerbroek. Although we were back in Germany, the names still sounded Dutch.'

By midnight at Westerbroek the Regiment settled down to wait. All of us in the tanks, as I very well remember, waited throughout the whole of the next day, mostly wandering from one tank to another and chatting with the crews. There was still no possibility of final plans being made until the number of bridges across the Rhine and the progress of the forward troops were known. We were told our objectives and all had our maps marked and, I suspect, all Troop Leaders were privately rejoicing it was the Recce Section's task to lead the Regiment across!

Under cover of darkness on the 26th the Engineers worked to get a 'double-Bailey' pontoon bridge across the river and in the very early hours were able to give the go-ahead for the tanks to start crossing. The Brigade had moved up to its start point under cover of an artillery barrage. This was both to do damage to the Boche and to cover the noise of the tanks' approach. As soon as we reached the start point, we switched off and maintained listening watch on the wireless. Just before 'zero hour' as we sat waiting for the signal to move, the stillness of the night was rent by the opening notes of a solitary piper playing 'Scotland the Brave'. This may have left the Sassenachs in the waiting tanks cold but, talking afterwards to such staunch Scots as Jake Wardrop and 'Bangle' Bowman, I knew that it certainly stirred our blood.

Our turn to move came almost immediately and the sound of the pipes was drowned by the noise of the tanks being fired-up. Within minutes the *Cromwells* and *Fireflies* were being nosed forward by drivers anxious to pick up the markers which would lead them onto the bridge. The anxiety would have been greater for the *Cromwell* drivers than for the men holding the steering levers in the *Fireflies*. The *Cromwells* would be in third, or probably second, gear as they approached and crossed. In these gears, the steering ratio of the *Fireflies* was not affected: in the *Cromwells* anything other than the most delicate touch would have caused the tank to veer abruptly and hit a side member of the bridge.

As we made our approach to the Rhine, we had another reminder of the cost of war. The town of Xanten had virtually ceased to exist. On a happier note, we were able to do an RAF Sergeant Pilot a good turn. He had been shot down over northern France some days previously and had been following his nose in the hope of finding a forward airfield. He had no idea where he was and was surprised to find himself in the middle of a battle. The leading tank picked him up and he was soon on his way back to the Echelons.

Across the Rhine we had another reminder of the cost of war. Although the airborne assault had been successful, it had not been lightly achieved and the toll of planes and gliders had been a heavy one – and one all too clearly visible to us as we moved forward to take up position. As it happened, not only were we across a day earlier than planned, the resistance we had expected to meet on the eastern banks of the Rhine did not materialise. 'A' and 'B' Squadrons swung north while 'C' Squadron pushed up the Brigade Centre Line. Again life had a lighter moment. In situations like this, unless the Regiment was actually engaged with the enemy, any movement on the roads involved fighting for space with a mixture of traffic from other units. The men in RHQ were startled to observe a battle-stained Sergeant from 6th Airborne Division weaving his Jeep between the tanks . . . nonchalantly wearing a top hat.

Bryan Johnson's narrative mentions something that the War Diary omits. Practically the whole of the time the Regiment was manoeuvring around Borken, we were being heavily shelled as well as losing a *Cromwell* to a Panzerfaust. For once in a way, however, the War Dairy for 29th March gives a clear picture of what was going on. Certainly more explicit than General Verney's account which implies that the advance was uneventful. For those Troop Leaders and tank commanders who had only recently joined the Regiment or been promoted, these days were their first real taste of war. Much of the movement was done in hours of darkness, nearly all the nights were spent in anticipation of counter-attacks or, at least, tank-hunting expeditions by small bands armed with deadly Panzerfausts. Sleep, once again, became a major factor in our lives. We began to realise that getting home and dry was not – to borrow RAF slang – going to be a 'piece of cake'. Even the veteran Syd Storer noted that 'nerves were beginning to stretch a bit.' (also that the reinforcements who were being sent up were 'nothing but mere boys')

The War Diary for the last two days in March and the early days of April reads:

30 0735 hrs 2 POWs were picked up by a troop of 'C' Sqn who were in an observation role in this area. The remainder of the unit were resting and ready to move along the main centre line. The V [Inniskilling] DG together with 9 DLI had moved on well and reached as far as Stadtlohn. The 4th Armd Brigade on the left had connected with the VIII Hussars and on the right the Airborne troops were keeping well up with the Div advance.

1400 hrs The Regt was ordered to Gemen in order to be in a position for an advance with 131 Brigade the following day.

2115 hrs Regt returned to Comd 22 Armd Brigade and ordered to conc in area Sudlohn MR and be prepared to night march along the route Sudlohn–Vreden and then turn NNE along Brown Route. 'A' Coy 2nd Devons were placed under command to be carried on the tanks

31 0100 hrs A start was made in bright moonlight. All went well despite the difficult track until a road block was encountered. The infantry dismounted and removed the block and then the advance continued.

0400 hrs The leading tanks were bazookaed, one KO'd and the commander, Lt Zoeftig wounded and taken prisoner. The tank then blocked the road which was just short of the first objective – Vreden. This made things difficult as there was no room to pass. A plan was made to clear the enemy out – after the leading tank had given the infantry supporting fire, the Inf were to go forward. This attempt was unsuccessful. At first light the enemy withdrew blowing the bridge behind them. Any further advance was therefore jeopardised and the Regt was ordered to return to the Brigade centre line. The route was then through Stadlohn and then to turn westward to Ottenstein and Wessum. The advance went very successfully and by last light Wessum had been recced.

Casualties : [A] Lt Zoeftig EM Wnd & POW L/Cpl Jones Wnd & POW
Tpr Topham Wnd

Losses : I Cromwell [A]

Enemy : 2 POWs: 1 x 75mm (gun)

And into the first days of April:

1 [Nienburg and Wessum] The Regt passed under command 131 Brigade and was ordered to remain in the area Ottenstein–Wessum until relieved by a Bn of 155 Bde. The Coy of 2 Devons reverted to comd of 2 Devons.

B Sqn continued to probe the defences covering Wessum, but the enemy were still holding this well-dug line. At 1130 hrs, however, a 95mm gun [howitzer] shoot by 4 tks was carried out on all known enemy posns. The results were excellent and 30 enemy surrendered. By 1300 hrs Wessum was entered and a further 15 POWs were taken. Once again the Regt passed back to comd 22 Armd Bde and was ordered to move to Nienburg which had been cleared by 1RTR.

131 Bde had now taken the lead and were directed to Rheine moving through Metelen. 22 Armd Bde were ordered to open up a second CL through Ochtrup and thence NE to Rheine, The action at Wessum was hardly completed before the Regt was once again on the move, moving through Ahaus and thence on to Nienburg. On the way 'I' Coy 1 RB and 'G' Bty RHA joined the Regtl Gp and by 1500 hrs the advance was started on Ochtrup. The Regt was led by 2 S[cout] C[ars] of Recce Tp followed by 'B' Sqn. As the leading car entered the wood at MR it was hit by a Panzerfaust and set on fire. The Comd, Lt Rhodes and his driver were killed. The leading Tp of 'B' Sqn was deployed and engaged the enemy in the area, much Spandau fire was encountered.. A plan was laid for one platoon of 'I' Coy 1 RB to clear the wood, supported by the tks. After the area had been shelled, the inf entered the wood and cleared the part to the east of the road without difficulty, taking 6 POWs.

On crossing the road a certain amount of opposition was met but a tp of tks which had worked round to the N was able to bring fire to bear and the enemy withdrew to a farm in the NW of the wood. A carrier belonging to 'I' Coy 1 RB was blown up on the road in the wood and it was discovered that the area was heavily mined with R mines. By last light the wood had still not been completely cleared although the tks and the pl of 'I' Coy estimated that they had killed at least 45 of the enemy and had taken a further 12 prisoners.. A section of Recce tp working round to the east of the main road and found a second line strongly held by the enemy. It was considered impossible to continue the adv that night and orders were given to stop the enemy advancing on the main Div CL.

During the night the Recce Tp captured a patrol of 6 men who were out tank-hunting with panzerfausts.

Casualties : [HQ] Lt Rhodes GL KIA Tpr Riddle CA KIA

Losses : 1 Scout Car [HQ]

Enemy : 63 POW

2 [Wettingen] The Regt moved to a new area where it was considered there would be a chance of a few days rest before the next phase of ops started. By the afternoon 7 AD led by 131 Bde was closing in on Rheine but the northern flank of the CL was none too secure. At 1700 hrs XIIth Corps received information that a counter-attack was coming from the north and they duly took measures to deal with it.

1800 hrs 5RTR were moved to cover the roads N of Wettingen MR. Thus instead of being able to enjoy a night's rest and do maintenance, an unpleasantly wet night was spent guarding the approaches from the N of the Div CL. 15 POWs were taken during the night but these were not aggressive members of the German Army. The counter-attack did not develop and at 1600 hrs the following day the Regiment was relieved of its commitments and returned to rest.

Enemy losses : 15 POWs

3 Rest and maint

Going back to the end of March and picking up an individual history means explaining how one Fifth Tanks officer made rather closer acquaintance with his remote cousins than he found altogether pleasant: Ted Zoeftig. On the night of 30th/31st March, as the War Diary states, The Fifth was doing a night approach into territory, known to be defended, in the hope of capturing a bridge at Vreden which the Cherry Pickers had reported as being intact.

Night-navigation – as any former crew commander will tell you – is synonymous with night-mare. Your vehicle has no lights, the driver cannot see where he is going and relies on you to tell him. Not only have you got to keep him – and the tank – out of the ditch, you have to identify landmarks which you cannot see. It is not only landmarks which you cannot see; it is the enemy. He has an unfair advantage: you can't see him because he has taken care that you cannot do so. You are in a large, conspicuous, noisy object which he can see all too easily. Your only comfort is that night-sighting is also a night-mare and he may give away his position by firing and missing you. Then, of course, you can see where he is but night-sighting is a night-mare for you and your gunner as well.

In Ted Zoeftig's case, the enemy could see him, did see him and had his tank plainly in the sights of his Panzerfaust. 'My troop was leading. (Ted wrote some years later) We had some Canadian infantry[2] with us on the tanks: I arranged verey light signals with their platoon commander. A fellow subaltern, Doug Smith was in my 'Baker' tank. My 'Charlie' tank (a *Firefly*) had shed a track some miles back. Wireless communication was a bit 'blabby' but that was of no immediate consequence. We were contacted by an XI Hussar armoured car, whose officer told me that the road was clear up to a small road block. He volunteered to lead me up to the obstacle and clear it for us if I would give him covering fire if the need arose. We cleared the road block and I sent Doug ahead in the 'Baker' tank. We got through the wood and saw about 1,200 yards of open ground. I asked my 'Sunray' for permission to drop the infantry but was told 'No. You are already late: speed up if you can.' I get on the air and tell Doug that I'll take the lead again. I can see the blur of some buildings on my right front. Head down for a second to look at the map. Torch a bit dim but then we are about 300 yards from the river. 'Driver, slow down.' Don't want to go head-first into 'the blue'! Another shuftie at the map. Head out again. Yes, that looks like the bridge.

'Then a massive vibration of thick, light and dark grey lines. I feel very heavy and find that I am being pressed down to the bottom of the turret. It is as if I am swimming under water. In strange slow motion I start to move up. No, no-one is near me. The tank seems to be pointing up in the air. A high-pitched screaming whistle persists in my ears. I find myself sliding over the back of the engine deck to fall and roll over onto the road. There is a spitting, crackling sound – rather sharp but not loud – round me. One pace and I flop into a shallow ditch. A grey lump is level with my right eye. I have just tripped over someone. Sticky feeling in my mouth. My nose is bleeding or something. I feel all right. A sizzling sound is in front of me about nine inches from my head. A realisation that this is tracer, seemingly aimed directly at me, rapidly clears my sleepy thinking. But something is definitely wrong with my hearing. That machine-gun is doing nothing but *squeak*!

'Now I realise that my tank has been heavily fired on, The [infantry] who had clung so eagerly to the turret have scattered: one or two, probably many more, are lying in the road: my protection from death. What had happened to my crew? Have I failed them? Where was Doug? God! He must have got it as well. What was to have been the first, firm, speedy sure-footed thrust to the Elbe had been tripped. The machine-gun stopped. I was becoming alert. I must do something – what a bloody mess. Can I get back into the tank to use the wireless? I turn my head slowly sideways. The nose of the tank and turret seemed to be mountainously high against the dark skyline. Must be careful or they'll see me (No need to ask who 'they' are). Where were my crew? Still in the tank– wounded; smashed? 'Do something!' I told myself. 'At least you're not dead. Think clearly, Zoeftig! This is easy. Make a dash for it!' Straight into the arms of a group of about eight Jerry paratroopers – all young. Their marksmanship was appalling. They'd missed me at point bank range. But I was moving, straight into them: that's what spoiled their aim! Then the kicking, struggling, shouting started but that was nothing: *anything* was better than the dreadful sense of failure. What was the waiting regiment going to do? The bitter taste of defeat and the chagrin of fallen pride remains with me today.

'They dragged me off – over the bridge and then blew it up. Later, shortly after, I got away'

Neither that last sentence nor the Regimental entry which simply states 'Lt Zoeftig wounded and PW: RTU 7 Apr 45. Evac.' tell the whole story. Ted was more than a little roughed-up by his captors as well as being rendered almost completely deaf but, as he said, he did get away from them . . . only temporarily, as the next thing he remembers was being dumped in a German hospital in Lingen. There were, he recalls, some prisoners who had been taken at Arnhem and for whom there were no medical resources and only 'one ancient doctor'. They all looked pretty frail but they were clean and well cared-for. Soon after, Lingen was captured by the Guards Armoured Division who marked their approach by shelling the town: as soon as they captured it, the Germans shelled it in their turn. Ted had had enough of that: he got out and flagged down a Jeep which 'was whizzing by driven by a major with red hair'. The red-haired major dropped Ted off at the nearest British hospital which patched him up enough for him to get back to The Fifth. Here, the MO didn't think he 'looked all that clever' and put him back into the hospital system.

As to Ted's crew, the Casualty List shows that Tpr Topham was wounded and that L/Cpl Jones was also wounded, taken POW and RTU. There is no mention of the other two crew members who were, presumably, unhurt.

Telling the story of Ted Zoeftig's encounter at Vreden from the 'B' Squadron point of view, Syd wrote, 'Vreden stood on the River Berkel where the bridge was reported to be still intact. We were despatched immediately to capture the bridge. The Devons piled onto the backs of the tanks and we took some very poor cross-country tracks until we reached the main Vreden road where we were held up by what turned out to be an unmanned road block. The infantry cleared this and we moved on to be met with small arms fire from the woods. The first tank was hit' – and here, the Storer account complements the Zoeftig one – 'by a bazooka and the second, in an attempt to avoid it, turned over in the ditch. Enemy infantry suddenly appeared out of the woods [capturing Ted Zoeftig and L/Cpl Jones] but our infantry managed to fight them off. All the infantry now dismounted and prepared to attack this strong-point but, before they could put their plan into effect, the Squadron Commander took a side turning which avoided the strong-point and eventually brought us out onto the road where the bridge was. Too late, however: as we approached, the bridge was blown. We opened fire and then worked round to attack the strong-point in the rear.'

As the War Diary indicates, All Fools Day 1945 was an energetic one for The

Fifth, heavy opposition being met, particularly from infantry with Panzerfausts in positions well protected by mines. Both of these took their toll on Fifth Tanks and the patrols of the XI Hussars and, indeed, on the Air OP's temporary airstrip where they destroyed four spotter planes. On the 2nd, when the Regiment moved up to cross the bridge over the Ems, we came under extremely heavy artillery fire. Under cover of this fire, enemy infantry attempted to rush the bridge, taking advantage of our restricted ability to manoeuvre and consequently to defend ourselves. We received very effective help from an unexpected quarter. The Ack-ack gunners who were positioned to protect the bridge from aerial attack turned their Bofors onto the charging infantry and rapidly saw them off.

At long last, on 3rd April, the Regiment got its promised day of rest.

THE OTHER SIDE

There is really very little that can be said about 'the other side' at this stage in the war. In accordance with Hitler's decrees, each possible line was ordered to be held, even if this meant giving away tactical or strategic advantages. The German position on the Western Front had been irrevocably weakened by the failure of Wacht am Rhein *and the Red Army had commenced its irresistible descent on Berlin from the east. At sea, the U-boat campaign had ceased to be any serious threat and the new Super-U-boats which Hitler had ordered were still 'on the drawing board'. In the air, only isolated units of the Luftwaffe (lucky enough to have fuel for their planes and manned by the few remaining pilots with combat experience) represented any sort of threat to the Allies' advance. For every Luftwaffe aircraft in the skies over Western Germany, there were scores with the markings of the RAF and the USAAF.*

Matériel of nearly every description was lacking – except possibly ammunition for the artillery, tanks and infantry which remained in uncomfortably long supply right until the end of hostilities. Substitute material was used for the bullets of rifle and machine-gun ammunition: plastic and even compressed wood being employed . . . the latter shattering on impact with unpleasant consequences for its victims. Inevitably, the High Command's main problems lay in attempting to co-ordinate any defences and in moving the necessary supplies.

In the absence of any plans, much of the defence was left to local commanders who simply fought while and where they could and then either surrendered or withdrew farther eastwards.

Another feature of the Allies advance into Germany was the complete absence of any strong-points or prepared fortifications to provide 'defence in depth'. Whatever contingencies Hitler had taken into consideration, war on German soil was not one of them.

Hitler still maintained some degree of control over himself and the Army – mostly command by threatening, and often exacting, ruthless penalties on those who did not or could not obey his orders.

Probably the most remarkable aspect of the war at this stage was the belief of the German population that they could still win it.

THE WAR CHRONICLE

1945

April	01	The lights went on again in Paris with the floodlighting of the Arc de Triomphe

NOTES

1 Class 40 Bridge. One capable of bearing the all-up weight of a single vehicle or of a combination of vehicles with gross laden weight not exceeding forty tons

2 Canadian infantry. Ted has gone a bit too far west here. They weren't Canadians: they were the Second Devons

CHAPTER XXI

. . . *The Central German Plain*

April 1945 – East to the Elbe

The story continues after our long-hoped-for day of rest with the War Diary for Wednesday, 4th April:

4 Orders were given for the next thrust by the div and the objectives were given as the crossing over the river Wessel[1] to the SE of Bremen. The Regt were to lead the advance and the Gp included I Coy 1 RBs, G Bty 5 RHA, and moved off at 1130 hrs. The route was Burgsteinfort –Emsdetten–MR to Mesum and thence onto the 11 AD CL through Tecklenburg to Lotte. From here the Regt had to open the CL for 7 A Div and speed was essential in order to clear the 11 AD CL. The br over the Ems–Wesser canal was intact and B Sqn who were leading crossed at 1930 hrs. Another br was reported intact and the Regt was ordered to secure this by last light. The distance to be covered was 15 miles. By 1810 hrs[2] the leading tks were across the bridge, no opposition was met and the column covered the distance almost as fast as the vehicles could travel.

5 At dawn the advance continued directed at Diepholz. In the village of Hunteburg a few enemy were seen but did not put up a fight and were rapidly swept into the bag by a pl of I Coy 1 RBs; 22 POWs were taken

A rd block held by about 20 inf was encountered. After shooting it up for about 10 mins, the enemy withdrew and the crew of the leading tank were able to deal with 5 brave Bazooka men who made a last stand.

Two more road blocks were encountered at Deilingen but were rapidly dealt with. As the leading Tp were approaching Lembruch[3] two 88 mm guns opened up. One was immediately engaged by the troop and KO'd. Two more were located by G Bty 5 RHA who helped in their destruction. Two more 20 mm guns came to life but did not live long. It was evident that the enemy was in this area in a certain amount of strength. However, after accurate shelling by G Bty, smoke was put down and what remained of the enemy withdrew. The leading tp entered the village closely followed by a pl of I Coy who mopped up the remaining stragglers

From 1430 hrs the Luftwaffe was most active and the column was heavily strafed, 2 aircraft were shot down and I Coy claimed a third. At last light the Regt was held up by a defended rd block. However, after being shot up by the tanks, the enemy withdrew and the rly br was reached. This br was fully prepared for demolition, a guard was left on [it] throughout the night. At Lembruch two tps of C Sqn branched E and by last light had entered Wagenfeld against light opposition; with one tp of 11 H they held this village which was to be the axis for 1RTR the next day

Casualties: [C] Tpr Carlsson P Wnd
[NS] Cpl Clowes Wnd
RTU [A] Lt Zoeftig E M – liberated POW
Enemy losses: 20 dead: 25 POWs
4 x 88mm guns: 1 x 75 mm gun: 2 x 20 mm guns:
5 x rly engines: 10 x lorries
2 m/gs: large quantity of ammunition

6 [Diepholz] 0330 hrs A German officer walked down the road from Diepholz and contacted the guard on the br and asked if he and his men and 100 Luftwaffe personnel could surrender. He was sent back to bring in his men but evidently in his absence they had decided on a few more days of liberty for, at 0500 hrs I Coy 1 RB entered Diepholz and there was no sign of the braves. 15 stragglers were rounded up and the town was considered 'liberated'.

The Regt was now directed at Sulingen and B Sqn adv E from Diepholz. A rd block was soon taken and 3 POWs taken. At Rehden another rd block was found to be held but a few rounds of HE induced the enemy to come in and 20 POWs were taken

Between this village and the rd junct a further 6 rd blocks were cleared and 23 POWs taken. The telephone wires to Sulingen were found to be intact and a call was put through to the Burgomaster. He was told to surrender the village unless he wanted to be truly liberated. He replied that he was only too willing, but there was one tk which was manned and he could not induce the crew to retire. However, he informed us of the exact location of this lone tk and we were able to brew it up. As the leading tp entered the village an A/Tk gun to the N fired 5 shots but all missed. An accurate conc of shells from G Bty on this gun put it out of action.

[Sulingen] Shortly after the Regt entered Sulingen, 1RTR entered it from the S. Whilst they advanced E, the Regt was ordered to adv N, the objective being Wilsen: moving on two roads, B Sqn continue the advance. At MR the leading troop was engaged by a 75 mm A/Tk gun and several Spandaus opened up. At the same time the tp on the route

to Schwaforden was engaged by AP coming from a wood. The leading tank was hit and put out of action and two Tigers were observed. They were engaged but the light was fading and the action was broken off. At night the Regt halted N of Sulingen guarding the approaches to this important centre.
Casualties : [B] Tpr Tompkins Wnd
Enemy losses : 46 POWs

At the beginning of the section dealing with North-West Europe, I remarked that there was an *embarras de richesse* of material covering the campaign. This is particularly true about these last few weeks – days, almost – of the war. Much of the material covers the same ground: I have, therefore, selected one version of each of the various incidents mentioned in the War Diary. Like the War Diary, they reflect the more light-hearted atmosphere that prevailed in The Fifth but, like the War Diary, they record the tragedies which occurred in those last few weeks.

On 4th April we heard that our main objective was to cross the Weser at a point south-east of Bremen. Our first reaction was one of relief, since Part Three Orders held that our job was to 'liberate' the defended city of Bremen – a task to which we were not looking forward. Our next reaction was one of disbelief. Some quick map-reader worked out that such a point for the river crossing meant the town of Verden . . . and Verden was 95 straight-line miles from where we stood! Not since the heady days of the 'Great Swan' had we been set such a target.

The order must have been meat and drink to Rea Leakey. We were all convinced that he was the man who had persuaded Brigadier Wingfield to persuade General Lyne that this objective could be achieved by giving the lead regiment – Fifth Tanks – the order to press on regardless and use the speed of the *Cromwells* for just this purpose.

Whether this is true or not, released from the ponderous *Churchills* which he had known in 7RTR, Colonel Rea must have been happy to 'let slip the dogs of war.' However, he was not able to give the order as soon as he wanted because 22nd Armd Bde had encountered unexpectedly stiff opposition in clearing the town of Ibbenbüren. The approaches to the town were protected by a ridge and both the town and the high ground had highly skilled, determined and ably led defenders. These came from an NCOs' and officers' tactical training school in the neighbourhood and they sold the ground they fought on and their lives very dearly. Ibbenbüren did not finally fall to the 7th Armd Div assault but to the combined onslaught of the 52nd and 53rd Infantry Divisions.

But, when we dogs of war were let slip on the 4th, we covered some 50 miles in 6 hours. In 2003 that may not seem much. However, readers who weren't there, must just believe that it was 'some bash'. Particularly, as one Diarist recalls but the War Diary doesn't mention, it poured with rain nearly all the way.

The weather changed on 5th April and some idea of the speed of our advance can be gauged by what happened when The Fifth reached Lembruch. 'The sun was shining [wrote Syd Storer] as we approached the town of Lembruch. Here we were met by young couples, German soldiers with their girls out for a stroll in the sunshine. They waved quite happily at us and we continued into the town. Again the population stood in the streets and waved. The Squadron Commander [Dennis Cockbaine] said to me, 'They don't know who we are; put up the flag.' We had a Union Jack with us and, as we moved along, I fixed it to the wireless aerial. The streets cleared as if by magic!' In fact, there was no opposition in Lembruch; such troops as had any organisation left were withdrawing towards Bremen, some 40 miles to the north-east. Syd continued by recording how the Regiment resumed the advance as rapidly as possible – a method of swanning which appealed to everyone . . . until, suddenly, a tank was hit from a concealed road block and, in a few seconds, everyone's peace of mind was shattered and nerves were once more on edge. The end of the war was drawing near and we were all relaxing: it took something like this to make us concentrate on the job in hand.

The 5th was marked – or marred, rather – by the Luftwaffe's attack. It was a particularly well-co-ordinated and concentrated one. I suppose we were lucky only to suffer one serious casualty from such an attack. The casualty was Tpr Peter Carlsson – the 'Carlo' of Jake Wardrop's Diary: one of The Fifth's longest-serving men. A 20 mm cannon shell shattered Carlo's arm and left him partially crippled for life.

The official records state that the attack was by both Focke Wulf and 'jet-engined' planes. If there were FWs they were probably190Ds but it was certainly a flock of Messerschmidt 262 *Schwalbe* ['Swallow' being the inappropriately pacific name given to these extremely warlike birds] that made their presence felt. We were not only beaten up by cannon fire, we were strafed by low-level bombing. As at least one veteran remarked, there had been nothing like it since the days in the Desert before the RAF got the mastery. The Regiment was strung out along a road when the attack started. This road led through a wood and, as fast as we could, we got the tanks off the road and under cover of the trees. The attacks came in waves and, between attacks, some of the crew commanders tried to move into less vulnerable positions. It was in the middle of one such move, while attempting to get his tank into the shelter of some buildings that Eric Wilde was caught in the open. A bomb hit the house he was manoeuvring round and the front wall collapsed on top of Eric's tank. The impact either stunned Eric's driver or caused him to stall but, whatever the reason, the tank was stuck in the middle of the road and a punch-drunk Eric was stuck in the turret. We soon learnt that these 'Swallows' had not migrated and all too soon they were on their way back. With Bill Holmes from my Troop and Harry Ashman, my Troop Sergeant, we ran across to do what we could to help. This turned out not to be much. Every time we got Eric halfway out of the turret, a flock of Swallows put in another appearance and we had to stuff him back inside and take cover ourselves. It may be all right if you are *Cigarette*, the no-better-than-she-should-be heroine of UNDER TWO FLAGS, to throw yourself in front of the hero and save him from the undeserved firing-squad by collecting a shapely breastful of musket balls but it is plain downright foolish to try that trick with 20mm cannon shells, leaving the muzzle with a velocity in excess of 2,000 feet per second and mounted on an aircraft flying at well over 500 knots. Such shells would have gone straight through Harry Ashman, Edward Wilson, Bill Holmes, Eric Wilde, Old Uncle Tom Cobley and All and still have done a mischief to the tank! Thus the three of us spent the next few minutes alternately pulling the unfortunate Eric half out of or pushing him wholly back into the turret, until the driver got the tank underway again and pulled it off the road. Here we got the bemused victim out of the tank and into the Squadron Dingo – which the Luftwaffe took particular delight in trying to beat up all the way back to the Regimental FAP. When the MO asked Eric what was wrong with him he simply answered that a house fell on him. The MO was a wise man: a stiff drink and twenty-four hours in the Echelons restored Eric to his normal self.

Having got out of the tank, Bill Holmes stayed out, sitting on the front of his tank and loosing off with a Bren gun every time a plane swept by. Perhaps he shot down one of the ones that the War Diary claimed. The Luftwaffe, incidentally, nearly bagged a far more senior victim than Carlo or Eric Wilde. During an interval between sorties, a couple of Dingos rolled up and stopped in the middle of the road opposite the leading tanks. Out got the Divisional GOC and some red-tabbed staff officer, both complete with binoculars, map cases and immaculately pressed battle dress. Before they could ask why we had decided to halt instead of racing for the Elbe, the Swallows came back and they did not stop for any bird-watching. Astonishing how quickly even Brass Hats can move!

It was when 1RTR was attacking Diepholz and The Fifth was redirected onto Sullingen that the famous telephone conversation with the Burgomaster took place. The War Diary tells [and not quite correctly at that] only what it is proper for such a document to record. The full story is best told by John Gwilliam, whose Troop it was that made the contact but even John's account stops short of the punch-line. The true story reads:

'We reached a small town called Sullingen where the whole of the Second Army was held up. Hundreds of tanks and vehicles seemed to be lined up on the road approaching this small town. Because of the difficult terrain, they could not get off the road and this is the kind of situation which caused senior officers to become frantic. The Recce Troop had announced that they could not proceed because there were German tanks in the centre of the town. At this stage of the war everyone thought of Tigers with their heavy armour and deadly guns as being still at large when anyone mentioned 'tanks' and decided that discretion was needed. So, despite the anguished demands from all the colonels, brigadiers and generals, we remained quietly on the road approaching Sullingen for some hours.

'At this stage, Trooper Glynn appeared from his co-driver's berth in his carpet slippers and spotted a Gasthaus at the side of the road. No doubt with a view to replenishing his jar of rum he disappeared inside. When he reappeared he had to admit failure in his search for rum but happened to mention that the telephone in the pub was still working. Someone had a bright idea [his friends attributed the idea to John himself] and told him to go back and try to ring the Burgomaster of Sullingen. To our surprise he did this and had a long talk with that worthy. Glynn cunningly told the Burgomaster that he had become separated from his Panzer Division and was near Sullingen and anxious to help to defend the Fatherland to the bitter end. The Burgomaster replied that he had better go somewhere else as there was only one tank in Sullingen and that was the one in the middle of the town square and that was broken down. Glynn rushed back to relay this good news to our operator, Cpl Winter, who passed the information over the air that the whole of Second Army was being held up by one broken down tank. Big Sunray (Colonel Leakey) was not at all pleased and his reaction to the information was decidedly frosty.'

The cream of the jest was this: before the CO could issue his orders, the resourceful Trooper Glynn – who later in life had a no-doubt highly successful career with Hambros, the Merchant Bankers – took hold of Cpl Winter's microphone and asked if he should take advantage of the contact he had established to try to gain some additional information and was there anything he ought to ask? Before Rea Leakey could reply, a voice – which belonged, as no-one doubted, to Arthur Crickmay – piped up, 'Ask him what's on at the pictures?'

From the information given by the Burgomaster – about the location of the tank, not the programme at the Odeon – it was possible to put in a good shoot and, broken down or ready to fight, the tank was duly brewed up. After that, Sullingen was 'liberated' without any problems.

The War Diary for the next four days show that the war, far from being a 'piece of cake' with no serious opposition to worry about, had turned very nasty again.

The entries for those days read:

7 [Wilsen] The remainder of the Regt moved E and NE capturing Hoya and later Wilsen. The Regiment was told to clear the villages of Scholen and Schwaforden and remain in this area until further orders.
1030 hrs Task completed against only slight opposition. One 75 mm A/Tk gun was KO'd and one Tiger tank was found abandoned and 12 POWs taken
1500 hrs The Regt moved to Wilsen and were given the task of holding this place, also the village of Heiligenfelde to the N. A Sqn

carried out the latter task. At last light the Regt was ordered to clear the village of Syke the next day.
Enemy losses : 12 POWs

8 [Barrien] 0430 hrs I Coy 1 RB moved out to recce towards Syke with C Sqn supporting them. By 0530 hrs they reached the outskirts of the village and here they were fired on by Spandau and small arms from the houses. A tp of tks soon silenced the Spandaus but sniping continued mainly by civilians. It was only after the tks had 'liberated' several houses and the church that the usual array of sheets appeared and the firing ceased. 24 POWs were taken and several German staff cars were captured.

As the main Bde effort was directed towards another br, the Regt was ordered not to advance any further. However, one tp pushed N and captured the village of Barrien. Although this place was held by about 40 inf with Panzerfausts they mostly came in when ordered by one of our German speakers who called them up on a military line.

1600 hrs The other br was reported blown and the Bde effort directed W to Delmenhorst and Bremen, B Sqn going NW towards Sud while C Sqn adv towards Brinkum. Recce Tp pushed W and after stiff fighting got into the outskirts of Ristedt whilst one car patrol moved N along a very poor track and by last light had reached the outskirts of Brinkum. The nearby wood was found to be held and the leading tk of C Sqn was hit and set on fire by a Pzfaust. C Sqn deployed round the wood and a way was found but as this rd was the main axis it was decided to mop up the enemy.

1930 hrs I Coy 1 RBs put in an attack on the edge of the wood but soon found that the enemy was dug in and in much greater strength than anticipated. It was soon realised that this strength was too much for one Coy so the tps were withdrawn.

I Coy suffered 10 cas but estimate that 20 enemy were killed and 12 POWs were taken. The enemy was identified as SS.

By this time it was dark and C Sqn and I Coy 1 RBs withdrew to area Barrien. In the meantime, B Sqn had reached the outskirts of Leeste against stiff opposition; 35 SS POWs being taken: at last light the Sqn withdrew for the night. During the night I Coy patrolled the wood which had held up the adv and found it still occupied by the enemy.

Casualties : [B] Sgt Allen ND KIA
[C] Sgt Harris VHJ KIA
Tpr Edis CE DoW
Tpr Foreman Wnd Tpr Spendelow Wnd
Tpr Sykes Wnd

Losses : 1 Cromwell
Enemy : 83 POWs

9 [Barrien] At first light B and C Sqns took up positions of observation

vacated the previous evening. C Sqn reported a wood on the approach line still held and the Brig ordered the 2 Devons to move up and attack in the afternoon.
0830 hrs B Sqn were ordered to move N of the wood and by 1000 hrs they were on the road. From here they moved and one tp reached the outskirts of Brinkum
The Recce Tp operating in the area Ristedt encountered enemy strong points and in clearing the first of these took 15 POWs.
Unfortunately the enemy succeeded in killing Lt Newton[4] when he went forward to collect 2 Germans with their hands up.
At this stage the Germans put in a counter-attack on Syke from W. Two tks, several SPs and 100 inf were reported moving E through the wood. 1 RBs were holding Syke and were very thin on the ground and it was anticipated that they would require assistance. A Sqn were ordered up into the high ground in the area Leefssen and from this they were able to engage the N flank of the enemy. B Sqn were ordered to conc back in the area Barrien ready to move to Syke if required.
1530 hrs The attack had been broken up and it only remained to clear and hold the high ground immediately W of Syke. This was carried out by the 2 Devons supp by B Sqn. Little opposition was met and the regt remained in the area Syke–Barrien in reserve.
Casualties : [HQ] Lt Newton WF KIA
Enemy losses : 15 POWs

10 Eystrup 1000 hrs Regt now u/c 53 Welsh Div who were at this time engaged in enlarging across the R Weser E of Hoya. A Sqn moved from Syke at 1200 hrs.
1400 hrs Remainder of Regt leaves Syke crossing the br at Hoya. A Sqn made contact with 4 Welch Regt at Hessel, at 1630 hrs were busily engaged in assisting this Bn to clear the villages of Borverden and Westen. This completed by last light. A Sqn remained in the area with the 4 Welch
1700 hrs Remainder of Regt conc in the area Hessel. C Sqn moved off immediately to support 6 RWF. One tp was allotted to each Coy and were sent off to clear the rds leading E and SE from Eystrup. Three of the tp/coy cols reached this objective with little trouble, the fourth, however, was most successfully ambushed at a rd junction. The tp was carrying a pl on the tanks and was told to move down the road without wasting time. The tp ldr objected to the Coy Comd at moving through the thick woods without some sort of foot recce but it was considered that there would be no opposition and speed was essential. The enemy, about 50 strong, had lined the road at this particular pt and had erected a rd block about 200 yds ahead. The leading tk stopped to work at the block and immediately the enemy

showered Pzfausts at the 4 tks. 2 were badly hit and put out of action, the 3rd was hit but was able to get back and the 4th had the operator killed by a sniper. The inf pl who were riding on the tks suffered very heavily, and in fact, only 3 members got back and they were all wounded. The remainder of the Coy came up and after a short fight supported by one tk left in action were able to force the enemy to withdraw. By last light the 6 RWF and C Sqn conc in the area MR.

Casualties : [C] Sgt Wardrop JR KIA Tpr Colton KIA
Tpr Forrest WA KIA
Tpr Skidmore D KIA
Tpr Hennessey T DoW
Cpl Richardson Msg Tpr Butler Msg Tpr Kinvig Msg
Tpr Wood Msg Tpr Wilson H Msg

Comparatively speaking 7th April was a quiet day. As the War Diary states, clearing the villages of Scholen and Schwaforden was accomplished with only slight opposition and there were no casualties with a score of 12 POWs and an A/Tk gun. The abandoned Tiger was not such a rarity as it may sound. These tanks, due to their heavy weight (56 tons), were hard on their transmissions and were not, as a result, very reliable if worked too hard or if not carefully maintained. With a road speed of only just over 20 mph, rapid and continuous retreating took its toll. There were also a number of occasions when the crews thought it prudent to continue their retreat by some other means and their Tigers were captured intact.

On the 7th, Bryan Johnson was involved in one of those incidents which really did happen in war but sound more like something in *Boys' Own Paper* or *Modern Boy* or whatever it was one read in those days. 'On this particular night [wrote Bryan] instead of the usual stint on wireless watch, I was put on patrol up and down the main street [of Wilsen]. At 0430 hrs an armoured truck appeared, out jumped a major of the RE's. I noticed the truck had 21st Army Group insignia on it. From the back of the truck there followed five perfectly uniformed Germans complete with their kit and bicycles. The major told me that this was a special operation and I was not to say a word. One of the Germans was quite nervous and was cursing, in German, over his kit. My mate on patrol thought it was a huge joke but I didn't. I eventually persuaded the major to see the Adjutant (Captain Dixon) who was woken from his slumbers. Everything appeared to be genuine and he said the 'Germans' would have to hurry if they wanted to catch the enemy in their guise as stragglers.'

The 8th April was a very different story for all the Squadrons. 'C' Squadron suffered heavily with the loss of Sgt Harris [Jake Wardrop's friend, 'Snowy'] who was killed by machine-gun fire he baled out of his *Cromwell* after it was hit and immobilised by a Panzerfaust. The rest of his crew were wounded, Tpr Edis subsequently dying of his wounds.

Word soon got round the Regiment that civilians (or perhaps soldiers who had managed to get into civvies as the first move to avoid capture) were engaged in sniping and we were all very much on the alert. Perhaps because of Trooper Glynn's success with the Burgomaster of Sullingen, a number of the Troop Leaders had formed the habit, on approaching a village, of sorting out what we thought was a responsible looking citizen and questioning him as to the presence or absence of the military in his village. Treachery was always uppermost in our minds and we made it clear that the penalty for lying would be swift and irreversible. We enforced this by sitting the citizen on the front of the tank with the muzzle of the Besa pressing uncomfortably into his spine. As far as I know, the penalty was never exacted but, by watching the citizen's reactions, we could generally tell what the score was.

Approaching the village of Leeste as the light was failing, I had one such citizen on the front of my tank, which was following Cpl Irvine in my Baker tank, in the lead for the Squadron. As we reached the first of the houses, my involuntary guide – despite his years, which were many – leapt off the tank and scuttled for the shelter of a house. The indication was clear: enemy in the village. I took over Cpl Irvine's tank, since it was not possible for me to get my tank past his in the narrow street. We moved forward cautiously until we came to a sort of village green on the right of the road. Here we halted: the silence was suspicious but I could see no sign of the enemy. At this point, the commander of my Charlie tank – the Troop *Firefly* – did something very foolish which cost him his life. Sgt Allen was not, as the War Diary says, sniped while collecting prisoners: he left his tank without orders and started to walk across the open ground. It was here that he was shot. We were still unaware that we were in the middle of the ambush which had been prepared for us. Two of his crew and I went forward to collect his body. As we reached it, the 34 SS men . . . well, boys, really . . . decided to surrender and suddenly rose out of the ground about 30 yards away. They were led by a veteran NCO waving a very grubby white handkerchief.

I reported what had happened and Dennis Cockbaine came up and took charge of the prisoners and ordered the *Firefly* with Norman Allen's body to the rear.

My orders were to continue into the village to try to clear it by last light. Now back in my own tank and in the lead, I crept forward past the end of the 'village green' until we were between the houses. Here we were met with mortar fire instead of the expected sniping. In street fighting, tanks were at a disadvantage when attacked by mortars. Mortars could lob their bombs over the houses without giving away their position but the tanks couldn't fire back. The way to deal with them was to call on the Gunners and this was what I did. However, just as the 5 RHA 25-pounders put down their sighting shots, we came under heavy machine-gun fire. This, and the fact that the RHA shot was landing among the houses, meant that I could not see where it was falling and consequently could not give the FOO any information. Instead of giving the expected corrections, therefore, I asked the FOO to call off the shoot. Before he could answer, Rea Leakey came storming on the air and told me – just as if we were on a peace-time exercise on Salisbury Plain – that I had 'called up fifteen[5]' and I was to blank, blank, blank well see the shoot through.

The entertainment was not, however, over yet. The first of a shower of Panzerfaust projectiles landed in the road uncomfortably near the front of my tank and I spotted their operators creeping up on us. It struck me then (and I still think I was right) that dealing with these gentry was more important than giving orders to the Gunners by remote control. I replied by repeating that I could not see the fall of the shot and concluded by saying 'Out.'

We did deal with the interlopers by firing off a belt or two of Besa and some well-aimed HE. It was a comfort to read many years later that the War Diary recorded our approach as being 'against stiff opposition.'

But there is a postscript. A few days later, the Colonel was with the Squadron and giving us a briefing. At the end, he turned to me – 'on me' probably better describes Colonel Rea's manner of dealing with disrespectful subalterns – saying, 'And, young Wilson, just remember that you do *not, repeat not* sign off the air by saying 'Out' when your CO is giving you orders!' When I replied that you did when your tank was being liberally sprayed by Spandaus and stalked by unfriendly men with nasty weapons, Rea Leakey was the first to laugh.

Worse was to happen the next day, with the treacherous killing of the unfortunate Newton who *was* going forward to collect prisoners and who had no reason to expect that the men with their hands in the air were, in reality, covering other men with guns which they fully intended to use.

The opening of John Donne's famous lines '.. *never send to know for whom the bell tolls: it tolls for thee*' reads, '*Any man's death diminishes me, because I am involved in mankind*'. This was and always will be true in war. It was particularly true in cases where the Regiment lost a member whom everyone knew and respected, such as Colonel Robbie Uniacke or Colonel Gus Holliman, or one lost a particular friend. In many ways, nonetheless, the death on 10th April of Jake Wardrop diminished us more than almost any other. Jake was an immortal: he had to be to have survived all he had gone through. The War Diary strikes a bitter note in reporting the circumstances in which Jake was killed. We felt it never should have happened: that Jake was deliberately sent to his death by being forced to do something which every good tank man – and few came better than Jake or were more competent than Keith Crocker, his Troop Officer – knew was sheer folly. Jake, typically, lost his life trying to save others. His crew had baled out when their tank was ambushed. They were being fired on as they did so: some were hit. Jake went to their rescue . . . and paid the price.

It is true that he was not alone in this: others in Keith's Troop lost their lives but, by Jake's death – so near to what must surely have been the end of the war – we all felt diminished.

The War Diary continues in full narrative form. On 11th March we were still in Eystrup:

11 A Sqn remained in support of 4 Welch Regt throughout the day and assisted them in clearing small pockets of enemy opposition in the area N of Westen.

0830 hrs C Sqn moved in support of 6 RWF in an attack on Stöcken and by 1600 hrs this village was reported clear

1030 hrs Recce Tp take the village of Rethemer capturing 15 POWs but in trying to advance E and N they met heavy opposition inc AP fire.

The next objective of the 53 W Div was to be Rethem which was strongly held. The 5 Welch Regt had attempted to take the town on the night 10/11 April but the opposition was too strong. 2 Monmouths supported by 2 Sqns of 5RTR were ordered to attack Rethem from the S.

Owing to the nature of the ground it was decided to use only one Sqn as there was little room for tks to deploy. B Sqn were to move up to the area, Stöcken, and at 1600 hrs supported the attack by the 2 Monmouths. All went well until the leading inf were about 400 yds short of the rly embankment just S of the town. The embankment was very strongly held with well dug-in MG positions. On the rly were 8 x 105 mm guns which were being manned when the tks came up. However they made excellent targets and were soon KO'd. 2 x 75 mm A/Tk guns to the E gave a certain amount of trouble and these too had to be KO'd before more damage was done.

Several times the Monmouths tried to close in on the enemy but owing to the open nature of the ground their cas[ualties] were very heavy. One tp of tks got onto the embankment and were met with a shower of Pzfausts and had to withdraw. After two hours fighting the 2 leading tps had run out of ammo; these were in turn relieved by two tps of C Sqn. But despite the maximum fire support from the tks the inf could make no progress and at last light they withdrew 2000 yds

Enemy losses : 15 POWs: 8 x 105mm guns: 2 x 75mm guns

12 Eystrup 53 W Div considered it vital that Rethem be taken and accordingly they asked for flame throwers and very strong air support. An attack was to be put in on 13 April and constant bombing throughout the day 12 April,

0900 hrs One tp of C Sqn moved N from Stöcken to cover the recovery of a tk which was bogged 500 yds short of the rly embankment. At the same time the Recce Tp operating from Rethemer had entered Hedern and then adv NW to the outskirts of Rethem. Several Pzfausts were fired at the leading tk but the enemy was in no strength and by 0950 hrs the Recce Tp were half way into the village of Rethem. C Sqn were rapidly moving up and by 1230 hrs the town of Rethem was cleared and 120 POWs were taken and more dead were seen. The most difficult part of this small operation was cancelling the big air programme that 53 Div had arranged for the benefit of the Rethem garrison.

Throughout the day A Sqn was engaged in assisting 4 RWF in clearing rds leading N to Verden. At Barnstedt considerable opposition was met from A/Tk guns and Spandau teams in the houses. One was KO'd and in trying to move across country, two more got badly bogged. A second tp came up and carried out a most successful shoot on the A/Tk guns. As these were located on the E of the River Aller it was impossible to say how many were KO'd.

1400 hrs A Coy of the 4 RWF supported by the tks attacked the village and by 1500 hrs it was reported clear. Geestefeld was cleared by last light and one tp of A Sqn remained with the inf Coy in this area.

Casualties : [A] Lt Hargreaves D Wnd Sgt Mills Wnd L/Cpl Dawes Wnd
L/Cpl Jeffcut Wnd
[B] Tpr Cadman Wnd
Losses : 1 Cromwell
Enemy : 120 POWs
Unrecorded A/Tk guns

The action during which the village of Rethem (pre-war population 1,586) was 'liberated' has been described as The Fifth's last major engagement in World War Two. Major engagement or not, it is certainly the one which got the Regiment a major write-up.

John Russell wrote NO TRIUMPHANT PROCESSION: THE FORGOTTEN BATTLES OF APRIL 1945 with Roderick de Norman. While I was researching this book, I was told Russell's described the action at Rethem[6] – particularly the part played by John Gwilliam. Accordingly, I acquired a copy and looked in the index and saw 'Gwilliam, Lt: 134'. The pages turned themselves over and I found myself looking at 'Wilson, Edward: 118, 124, 239'! This evidently went back to correspondence which Eric Wilde (*vide op cit* 'Wilde, Capt: 122, 136') and I had with Roderick de Norman in 1986 when de Norman wanted some information about the Monmouths. The information which Eric and I supplied is incidental but the part played by John is quoted in full.

The size or importance of an engagement cannot be judged by the number of words written about it. General Verney dismisses the 'liberation' of Rethem in ten not very accurate lines. Likewise the 'official' history of the Division and Liddell Hart allocate it but a paragraph. Norman Smith in his book gives a detailed description but exaggerates when he claims that his tank – mine, because he was my W/Op – knocked-out all the heavy calibre weaponry on the embankment.

Interestingly, Norman Smith quotes a German source which confirms that the defenders belonged to detachment of Marines out of Hamburg reinforced by SS Recruits. There is a splendidly racy account of one aspect of the Battle of Rethem in Rea Leakey's autobiography. His story, which comes later, is about the cancellation of the massive air strike planned to reduce the strong-point.

But, before that, the battle itself.

The significance of Rethem was that it contained, and therefore commanded, a key crossing over the River Aller and, for once in a way, there was a co-ordinated plan of defence. It was the task of 53rd Welsh Division to capture and secure the crossing. As Colonel Leakey said in his book, the Welsh Division had had a long hard war and no-one was looking for medals. Caution and firepower were the twin watchwords. In part, 'B' Squadron 5RTR supplied the fire power, being detached from the Regiment and coming under command of the 2nd Monmouths. This caused an amusing situation. Although we were officially under the command of 2nd Monmouths, their CO thought it would be better for him to be under command of OC 'B' Squadron. Dennis Cockbaine hurriedly removed the pips from his tank suit and silently prayed that nobody would address him as 'Captain Cockbaine' – instead of the usual 'Sir' or 'Dennis' – thereby betraying the fact that he was much the junior member.

As John Russell explains, the difficulty facing the attackers was two-fold. The defenders had, firstly, well-sited and concealed fox holes liberally supplied with machine-guns, to oppose the infantry and, secondly, a railway embankment bristling with artillery, to oppose the tanks. The approach to these defences was across about 1,200 or 1,500 yards of completely open ground. We could deal with the defenders in the fox holes only if we could first eliminate the anti-tank guns: the Monmouths could do little or nothing – except suffer casualties – until we dealt with the fox holes. In the event we were able to deal with both lines of defence but not until both Michael van Gruisen's Troop and mine had completely exhausted our ammunition. After this, the other two 'B' Squadron Troops [*not*, as the War Diary states, two Troops from 'C' Squadron] moved forward and took over our 'front line' until last light when both the tanks and the infantry withdrew.

As the War Diary records, the unfortunate infantry suffered heavy casualties while, by contrast, Fifth Tanks suffered none.

Unsurprisingly the GOC Welsh Division decided that only a serious preliminary softening-up would justify his ordering his men to launch another frontal attack. For this he asked for support from flame-throwers (*Crocodiles* from 79th Armoured Division) and a saturation aerial assault. There is some doubt about the intended scale of the latter. Most probably it was generously planned for a number of reasons. TAF was running out of targets; the pilots were getting bored; a major assault would be an object lesson to German force commanders that further resistance was useless. Nevertheless, the popularly quoted figure of '500 bombers' seems more suitable for roughing up a town the size of Reading than a village the size of Rethem. Be that as it may, a major aerial onslaught was planned to make life uncomfortable for those on the ground beneath it. The trouble was that, some 36 hours after the call for air support went out, those on the ground beneath it would have been the Second Battalion the Monmouthshire Regiment and the Fifth Royal Tank Regiment!

What happened was that, on 12th April, the defenders withdrew and abandoned their strong point, as the Recce Troop and, shortly afterwards, 'C' Squadron discovered. However, the village was not quite so completely cleared of the Boche as was thought and it was while the 'B' Squadron tanks were edging their way into the place that John Gwilliam, the largest but the most gentle of the Squadron's subalterns, made his capture. Whatever else one did in a tank in enemy territory, one did not drive round blind corners. At least, not more than once. John was leading his troop and came to a junction where the houses obscured visibility down the side turnings: John got down to have his shufti to discover what horrors were waiting for his approach. Nothing was to be seen but a sniper's bullet zipped past his nose at a distance of millimetres. Instead of calling up his tank and blitzing everything in sight, John set off on foot in the direction of the shot. He returned a minute or two later almost carrying a very small, very young and very scared figure in field grey.

It happened that the CO had arrived while John was making his reconnaissance and had heard the shot. Rea Leakey asked John if his captive was the man who had shot at him. John said he thought so. 'Why didn't you shoot the . . . (at this point, Rea would normally have used a rude word but even he never used one when talking to John) . . . ?' John held the boy at arm's length and inspected him, 'Oh, he's not worth the powder and shot, Sir,' was his reply.

Shortly after this Colonel Leakey was alerted as to what TAF had in store for Rethem and he set off on the life-saving and luckily successful mission of persuading first the Brigadier, then the Divisional Commander and heaven only knows whom in the Royal Air Force to call off the attack. Meanwhile, Fifth Tanks was clearing out some 120 old men and young boys who had been left behind (with uncounted dead) when the gallant Marines and SS recruits baled out. They also released a few British POWs who had been left behind and who were badly shaken by the assault their friends had launched on the place.

The subject of POWs proved to be one of major disaster for a most respected London magazine and a serious blow to the credibility of the Allies' propaganda machine. Rumour had spread during the attack on the village that the Germans – the SS, of course – were not taking prisoners but shooting any men who fell into their hands. So widely was this rumour circulated and believed that the *Illustrated London News* ran a double-page spread . . . 'drawn from an eye-witness account by our Special Correspondent, the War Artist, Captain Bryan de Grineau'. . . of men of the Monmouths being gunned down by a helmeted Hun with a Mauser or shot in the back of the head by an SS officer. What caused this rumour is believed to have been a mysterious outburst of Spandau firing, during a lull in the fighting and not aimed at any discernible target. There was absolutely no truth in the rumour and no British prisoners were shot. Fortunately no German ones were shot in retaliation.

Number Five Troop 'B' Squadron, while investigating buildings in Rethem believed to contain either stragglers or injured British POWs, came upon the local HQ of the Volksturm. This, naturally, had to be carefully investigated but all it revealed of interest was a very neat, and brand-new, portable typewriter and a heavily padlocked strong box. This latter was removed for further examination. That evening, when it was opened, it proved to contain a generous collection of photographs, whose sheer eroticism would have made even the most hardened Cairo purveyor of pornography blush to the soles of his feet. I was considered too young and innocent to see any – well, many – of these but I did use the typewriter for the next thirty years!

One of the differences between the UK-designed *Cromwells* and the American *Shermans* was the way in which the hulls were slung inside the tracks of the *Cromwells* (see Illustrations 10, 12 and 15), whereas the hulls were built up over the tracks of the *Shermans* (*see* Illustrations 8 and 9). There was, and still may be for all I know, a saying that 'What is good for General Motors is good for America'. I don't know about that but, since General Motors designed and built the *Shermans*, what was good for General Motors was certainly, on one occasion, good for me.

As can be clearly seen in Illustration 9. The full-width, slab-sided hull of a *Sherman Firefly* goes up at least as high as a man's shoulders. It was this feature which enabled me, in a manner of speaking, to record this brief autobiographical sketch. Had I been standing on the back of my *Cromwell* instead of the Troop *Firefly*, the 'friendly fire' mortar bomb which exploded alongside me would have meant that someone else would have had to write this book

While an assault was being prepared on Ibbenbüren, it was decided to clear a strong force of enemy infantry out of their positions in a wood and into a 'killing field' for our infantry to mop up. This was to be done by the Divisional Mortar Support Group saturating the wood with mortar fire. Our task in The Fifth was to sit between the mortars and the wood in order to pick off any enemy who made a bolt for safety towards their front instead of retiring to their rear. When the stonk started I realised that my Charlie tank had moved far too near the wood. I couldn't use the wireless to call him back as there was blanket silence on the air. I therefore walked over to the *Firefly*, climbed aboard and leant into the turret to attract the attention of the crew commander.

Just as I straightened up there was an almighty bang and large chunks of Germany and flame and the acrid fumes of high explosive erupted into the air at my elbow. Someone on our side, in all innocence, had loosed off a mortar bomb with an inadequate propellant charge and the bomb had landed about a hundred yards short of target and six inches short of the tank I was standing on. If it had travelled three feet less, the explosion would have left only my legs to be buried. If it had travelled three feet more, there wouldn't have been enough of me left to bother about burying. If I had been standing on a *Cromwell* and the bomb had landed where it did, well, 'you pays your money and you takes your choice' as to what the Padre would have had left to bury.

Curiously, all the bits of the Fatherland that went up into the air came straight down again: we received only a powdering of dust.

Human reaction being the illogical thing it is, I was totally oblivious of just how close to me the Grim Reaper had swung his scythe and I went on instructing the *Firefly* commander to pull his tank back nearer the rest of the Troop. In fact, I rode back with him and then walked back to ESMERALDA. Only when Cpl Hewitt, my gunner, said something to me about 'lucky escapes' and I failed to respond, did I realise that I was completely deaf. Some of my hearing came back quite quickly: the rest never has come back.

The man who was most shaken by the incident was Dennis Cockbaine. He had apparently watched me walking over to the *Firefly* and no doubt had wondered what that idiot Wilson was up to this time. He saw me climb onto the tank just before the explosion and his immediate reaction, knowing that my brother had already been killed in Normandy, was 'My God. Edward's poor parents, losing both their sons.' For once in a way, he told me afterwards, he was quite relieved to see that I was still on the Squadron strength!

Before last light on the 12th the Regiment was on the move again on its way north to the crossing over the Weser at Verden. This was, in fact, Guards Armoured Division territory, so the Charlie Love was switched back in an easterly direction.

The War Diary entries for the next few days are much shorter and read:

13 Geestefeld 0400 hrs An enemy patrol 50 strong entered the village of Geestefeld and succeeded in surrounding the coy HQ ['D' Company 4th Battalion, the Welch Regiment] and entered the house where two crews of the tk tp were sleeping. Hand to hand fighting took place and Lt Jones successfully resisted, killing the German officer leading the patrol, this restoring the situation around coy HQ.

0700 hrs The Regt reverted to 22 Armd Bde and conc in area Eystrup MR.

Casualties : [N/S] Tpr Murray Wnd

14 Eystrup The Regt remained in its present location at 2 hrs notice to move. The br at Rethem which the Div was to cross the River Aller was not ready until 1130 hrs. The 4 Armd Bde began to cross at 1200

hrs and had 2 Sqns of 44RTR across during the afternoon. At 2000 hrs the Regt came at one hour's notice from first light
Casualties : [A] L/Cpl Lewis Wnd

15 No move, except the Regt came u/c 131 Bde for movement purposes. 22 Armd Bde commenced to cross the river and started the adv to Soltau.
Casualties : [N/S] Cpl Dovey Wnd

16 Walsrode During the night enemy aircraft attacked the Rethem br causing damage so that the move was held up until 1600 hrs. After the crossing the regt conc near Walsrode. The POW Camps XI B and 237 at Fallingbostel were liberated by 8 H and 4 of the men of C Sqn captured a few days ago were retaken. They were Cpl Richardson, L/Cpl Wilson, Tprs Kinvig and Butler. They reported bad treatment and Tpr Wood who had been wounded was in hospital. This accounted for all crews of C Sqn's action on the 10th.

17 Meinern The Regt moved to Meinern still with no task. In the meantime 22 Armd Bde had bypassed Soltau which was strongly held and had adv to area Neuenkirchen.

18 Meningen By 0900 hrs Soltau had been cleaned and 131 Bde was ordered to proceed through Soltau to Heber and thence along tracks through woods E of the main road as far as Bucholz, doing right protection for 22 Armd Bde.
The Regt with I Coy 1 RBs u/c and 9 DLI in support led the Bde. Soon after turning E from Heber opposition was met at rd junct but, after being shelled, the enemy withdrew and a pl of I Coy cleared the area, taking 15 SS POWs.
From here C Sqn with one Coy of 9 DLI were left to clear the route to Behringen whilst the rest turned N and moving through very thick wooded country reached Wesel by last light
C Sqn met considerable opposition in their task but by last light had reached Behringen, taking 45 POWs and KO'd three 75mm A/Tk guns.
During the night B Sqn at Wesel were twice attacked by enemy patrols with Pzfausts but suffered no casualties and killed a number of the enemy.
Casualties : [N/S] Tpr Evans Wnd Tpr Youds Wnd
Enemy losses : 45 POWs
3 x 75mm A/Tk guns

Once clear of Rethem, the Regiment expected to start rolling again but it seemed that the Boche had anticipated our line of advance and decided to do his best to obstruct our *Drang nach Osten.* Certainly we met more than just casual opposition. In fact, the incident on 13th April caused serious worry in high places that it might be a foretaste of the 'Werewolf'[7] packs which (it was rumoured) were designed, in the event of Germany being over-run, to operate against Allied military installations. There is no evidence that it was so and the patrol which tried to do some hell-raising at Geestefeld got more than it bargained for. The War Diary, in giving Lou Jones all the credit (he was later awarded an MC for his share in the fracas). does not tell the whole story. The enemy patrol was composed of Marines and their target was actually Stedorf. The 'two crews of the tk tp' who were sleeping in a house were from 'A' Squadron and had every right to anticipate a night's quiet kip. They were surrounded by men from the Welch Regiment who were supposed to be doing guard duty. When the Marines got into the house, the crews were all sound asleep and were woken to face the muzzles of sundry hand guns which brooked no argument. 'Whilst we were being led out of the house as prisoners-of-war [Stanley Bruce, one of the sleeping tank crews, was later to write] with me the last man in the column and some weapon dug in my back by the officer in charge of the patrol, L/Cpl Thomas – the wireless operator on my tank – who had concealed himself behind a door in the house, shot the officer dead, whereupon all hell was let loose and Mr Jones, along with others, jumped their captors. The Marines started firing and this brought the infantry into the action. Those of us who were unarmed made a run for it. My run felt like five miles long and brought me to Squadron HQ where I alerted Major MacDonald as to what was going on. By the time the Major and I got back to the scene of activity, all there was to show for it was several dead Germans.'

Syd Storer's crew were able to do some wandering refugees a good turn. On the outskirts of Walsrode, 'B' Squadron had investigated a large and rather surprisingly undamaged building by the side of the road. On having a shufti inside, they found it was a warehouse stacked with leather goods of all descriptions, from Army boots to snake and crocodile skins. Finding these refugees in sad need of footwear, the crews directed them to the warehouse.

One of the reasons why Soltau was bypassed was that the approaches were all guarded by road blocks, not in themselves insuperable tank obstacles but heavily booby-trapped and best left to the Royal Engineers to deal with. It was some satisfaction, on the 18th, to the men of The Fifth when they looked back to the west and saw Soltau in flames after the attack by 131 Infantry Brigade.

About this time, Bryan Johnson had another of the bizarre experiences in which he seemed to specialise. He had been sent back to the Forward TDS [to collect a replacement tank as his own had broken down] and landed up with the Echelons, with incidental instructions from the CO to 'remind the Echelon Commander of the necessity to get supplies up *urgently*'. With the new tank, driven by 'Slip' Baker from 'C' Squadron, he set off, mapless but relying on route-memory, to rejoin the Regiment. He shortly arrived at a landmark he didn't recognise and, on going to investigate, found it was a large mansion, thickly peopled with strapping blonde females . . . whose task [already in train perhaps?] was to perpetuate the Master Race and who were not, repeat not, interested in British swaddies!

There is a difference of opinion between the War Diary entry for 18th April and the recollections of several members of the Regiment. It is true that the VIII Hussars were the first on the spot at Fallingbostel and that the camps lay on their Charlie Love and not on ours but there is no doubt that some tanks from The Fifth were also there soon after the liberation. The most probable explanation for this discrepancy is that the tanks from the Regiment had no official business to be where they were but had had unofficial word from the Hussars that there were blue and red shoulder tabs to be seen around the place and the crews had acted on their own initiative. According to Bill Chorley's account, The Fifth played a part in freeing him from his years in captivity and there are some who will never forget the sight of those men at the gates. It was, as the Divisional History states, a sight of ordered chaos. Men were milling everywhere but the British Army was already in charge, under the command of the redoubtable RSM Lord of the Grenadier Guards. In spite of RSM Lord's discipline, some men did decide to make their own way back to their units. One such was L/Cpl 'Topper' Brown from 'A' Squadron who had been taken prisoner in France and who made himself known to the crew of Bryan Johnson's tank amid general rejoicing.

Similarly, no-one from The Fifth had any right or reason to be near the notorious death camp at Belsen but there are two accounts of individual contacts with the Camp. An effort had been made by the Germans to steer the approaching British away from the camp on the pretext that typhus was rampant but, in reality, to hide as long as possible the true state of affairs and to allow those responsible to get away. Discovery was inevitable but the shock to those who made the discovery was a life-long nightmare. Bernard Holder, 'B' Squadron's Man Friday, was, or should have been, with the Echelons on another Centre Line but nevertheless managed to get almost to the gates of the Camp. Here he saw men who were just skin and bone, 'as near to a skeleton as you will ever get'. He was told not to go into the camp by an RAMC chap who gave him the impression that typhus was prevalent. It is not impossible that I, too, was on the wrong Charlie Love when I nosed my tank round a bend in the road, expecting to meet enemy fire at any moment but saw, instead, several British staff cars grouped round the well-wired entrance to what I thought must be yet another POW or 'slave labour' camp. I was flagged down by one of the many people in uniform far too smart to be in what I believed was the front line and asked where I was going. I explained and was told that I had better get off that road and tell my superiors to keep well away from it. I could not understand how this chap or any of the rest of them had got where they were but it was made quite clear to me that if I wanted to play soldiers I had better go and do so elsewhere. I suppose I reported what had happened to Dennis Cockbaine but as I no doubt gave him a wrong map reference for my position, it was not until much later that he, or any of us, became aware of what we had just passed.

*

The War Diary for the rest of April is a tale of steadily diminishing activity, though not of lessening ferocity in the actions and not, unfortunately, a tale without casualties:

19 Bucholz The Regt continued the advance towards Bucholz with B Sqn leading. By 0950 hrs Lullau was liberated and 20 POWs taken. A Sqn had in the meantime moved E of Bde CL and were held up by a rd block. One Coy of 9 DLI attacked the enemy in this area and by 1130 hrs the route was clear. 25 POWs were taken. Continuing N, A Sqn entered Hanstedt taking a further 15 POWs

C Sqn, who had spent the night at Behringen, decided on trying to open up the road to Soltau, but met with strong opposition and lost 1 tk to an SP. At 1130 hrs orders were given for them to rejoin the unit Lullau.

Having drawn level with 22 Armd Bde, 131 Bde was ordered to make firm but to patrol to the N. The Recce Tp cleared Jesteburg, taking POWs, and a carrier section of 9 DLI entered Bucholz without difficulty. At 1600 hrs orders were given to occupy Bucholz and Jesteburg. The Regt, less A Sqn and 9 DLI, occupied the former place whilst A Sqn and I Coy 1 RBs occupied Jesteburg.

Patrolling N and W from Bucholz B Sqn reached Steinbeck where they were able to welcome the leading tp of 1RTR who were adv up rd from S-SW. another tp of B Sqn entered the village where 30 POWs were taken and at least 10 [enemy] killed.

Casualties : [C] Tpr Evans R Wnd Tpr Scott Wnd Tpr Upward Wnd

Losses : 1 Firefly

Enemy : 10 Killed: 90 POWs

20 Hittfeld At 0330 hrs I Coy 1 RBs set out from Jesteburg with Harburg as the objective, moving N through Harmstorf MR. By 0600 hrs the leading pl had reached Helmstorf and had taken 30 POWs. A Sqn and the Recce Tp were moving in close support. Moving E and W from Harmstorf, the Recce Tp took 35 POWs and a further 12 from Ramelslon. Now A Sqn took on the lead going N and crossing the autobahn entered Hittfeld and was only stopped when the br was blown up just before the leading tank reached it.

C Sqn with one coy of 9 DLI moved from Harmsdorf to Ramelslon and were thence directed to Maschen. However, in the woods N of Horst, an A/Tk gun supported by inf held the rd. An attack was put in and 15 POWs were taken whilst the A/Tk gun was destroyed. Maschen was entered without opposition and the Recce Tp moving E liberated Stelle.

Advancing N from Hittfeld, A Sqn soon encountered the main def line covering Harburg and further progress was impossible. The afternoon was spent in consolidating the posns reached and in closing to the main line of defence. In the evening 2 enemy SP guns moved up to E of the wood and hit 2 tks before they could be engaged. They

withdrew rapidly when a second tp opened fire on them and caused no further trouble.
Casualties : [C] Tpr Brady Wnd (remained on duty) Tpr Parker Wnd
Enemy : 62 POWs

21 Hittfeld At first light posns reached the previous night were taken up. The Regt had been ordered to maintain contact only and not to attempt to break into the enemy lines. B Sqn had tps in posn. Recce held posns at Jehrden and patrolled to Glusingen. A Spandau and Pzfaust post in the area was engaged and 4 POWs taken. 2 prisoners who passed through Harburg last night stated that the autobahn br had been hit by our aircraft and was not in use but the rly br and the rd br in the same area were intact but ready for blowing.
C Sqn tps at Maschen had tps [*sic* ? tks ?]on the outskirts of the town. Enemy movement was engaged in the area of the blown br.
At 1800 hrs, 1 x 88mm opened fire and hit one of the tks: Shelldrake[8] opened up and the gun stopped firing.
Enemy losses : 6 POWs

22 Hittfeld Posns remained the same except that A Sqn relieved C Sqn at Maschen and pushed out tps to Stelle and Winsen – here friends were contacted from the right. The Recce Tp working with a section of C Coy DLI patrolled fwd in the Glusingen area. It was estimated that about a coy of enemy inf were in the area. POWs comprising Volksturm and 3 officers who claimed to be in the legal section of the Wehrmacht were collected. Also 5 German WAAFs were found in Maschen and handed over to the Burgomeister of Hittfeld.
Bearings were take on enemy guns firing and they were thought to be 105mm rly guns.
At 1900 hrs, C Sqn moved out to the W in the village of Eddelsen.
Enemy losses : 9 POWs

23 Hittfeld All the previous evening's posns were resumed at first light and A Sqn collected 2 POWs. They stated that they were part of a patrol 30 strong which left Harburg the previous evening and got lost while looking for food.
One deserter came in to Recce. He said he belonged to a regt with HQ AT Glusingen. A number of enemy up to 8 were observed nearby and these were thought to be a section posn.
Enemy guns were active most of the day and bearings taken which were passed on to 3 RHA for their attention.
Enemy losses : 10 POWs: 1 German ATS Private

24 Hittfeld At first light Recce tp were moving out to their posns at Jehrden but, as they were advancing, the leading tk was fired on by a Pzfaust: failed to KO the tk but the Comd was wounded. However he managed to shoot the firer with his revolver and another Boche similarly armed was killed. The Tp withdrew 100 yds and then began

the adv again with inf support, capturing 4 more enemy. They were part of a patrol to find out the tk posns and numbers: this was based on civilian reports. 2 of the patrol were killed, 1 wounded and 4 captured out of 10.

B and A Sqns took up their usual posns and owing to 3 RHA being limited to their ammo expenditure, carried out a series of tp shoots. A Sqn KO'd 1 x 88mm gun in its area, while B Sqn engaged some dug-in enemy inf along the line to their front. The accuracy of this induced 1 Boche to surrender and he was told to go back and tell the others to come in. However, he was greeted with rifle fire and reckoned he had had enough. He gave us the exact locations and said there about 60 inf there. They were shot up at intervals during the day and approx 500 rds of HE were fired – also 15 rds of 95mm were fired into Harburg.

All civilians were evacuated from the fwd areas as a safety precaution.

Enemy losses : 2 killed: 2 wounded: 6 POWs
1 x 88mm gun

25 Hittfeld At last light the previous evening the impression was that the enemy had withdrawn his line further back. At 0800 hrs tentative patrols moved out and contact was made with the enemy at three points. 2 POWs were taken by Recce at Glusingen. B Sqn engaged dug-in inf in their area.

A Dutch civilian gave infm to C Sqn as to an enemy posn and so a dismounted patrol of 1 officer and 6 men were sent out to investigate. They met opposition 2 were wounded and the patrol withdrew. One tp of tks were then sent out and contacted an enemy patrol of 12 – 2 of these were killed, 2 wounded and the rest got away. The tp went further on and stonked the area thoroughly. This was an old AA site and it was discovered that the telephone comm had been maintained from here to Harburg. One German officer in civilian clothes was arrested and with him 3 German WRENS.

At last light, all tps pulled back to their own posns.

Casualties : [C] Tpr Hadley Wnd, taken POW, escaped and evacuated
Tpr Palfrey Inj

Enemy losses : 6 POWs

26 Dibbersen At first light C Sqn moved out to the area Sottorf to support 2 Devons who had been counter-attacked during the night. The situation was however soon dealt with, with some assistance from the tks and by 1300 hrs tps were in new posns.

At 0900 hrs 1RTR took over from the Regt and, after a little delay, moved into Dibbersen

C Sqn remained behind

Casualties : [C] Tpr Saunders Wnd

Enemy losses : 6 POWs

The actions in which the Regiment was involved were generally short and sharp with the tank crews being pretty prodigal with ammunition. And why not? Further resistance was futile, the ammo had already been manufactured and couldn't be 'returned to store'. Might as well use it: it was the people on the receiving end who were going to get hurt!

Those short sharp engagements inevitably caused casualties and it was one of Fate's cruel ironies that all the casualties in the last few days of the war occurred in C Squadron.

By contrast, there were some surprising incidents. At this risk of turning this account of the Fifth Tanks into an autobiography, I shall recount a further two of them. First: I had an unexpected night of luxury. We had pulled back at some stage during those last few days and were definitely out of the line but in something more than a conventional April shower. It seemed reasonable to me, therefore, to investigate the fairly substantial buildings only a few yards from our designated area. I found them to be a large house and a row of farm outbuildings. Walking round the house, I saw a sliver of light from a ground floor window. I found the front door and, revolver in hand, rang the bell. If there were people indoors, they must have known something was going on: you can't drive four tanks into the back yard without someone noticing it.

The door was pulled cautiously open and I saw two women standing in the hallway. I started to explain my presence in school-boy German but was interrupted: one of the women said, 'If you are British, we can speak English.' I agreed that I was British and explained that, as it was such a foul night, I would like to get my men under cover. I was invited into the house, the door was shut and a light turned on. I returned my revolver to its holster but ostentatiously rested my hand on the butt. However, there were only the two women, one middle-aged, one much my own age. I was invited to come through to the kitchen where, the older woman explained, there was no-one but the old servant and plenty of room for the men. I thanked her, fetched the men in and set up a roster of guard duty to ensure that everyone would get some sleep in the dry but that neither the tanks nor the men in the house would be caught napping.

I asked someone to bring my bedroll in but the older woman immediately said that it was not fitting for me, as an officer, to sleep in the kitchen. With their eyes on the younger of the pair, my crew encouraged me to take my chance in the front of the house. My 'hostesses' then led me into what was obviously the master's study. 'Will our Army be coming back?' the younger woman asked. I said I thought that was most improbable. 'Can we make up a bed for you here, then? You will be quite comfortable on the couch.' I looked round: it wasn't a style of interior decoration which I admired but it all spelt money and the couch was large and looked comfortable. The elder woman said something to the younger, who left the room and came back shortly with her arms full of sheets and pillows and eiderdowns. She made up a bed on the couch while the other woman showed me where the downstairs cloakroom was, apologising for the quality of the soap, adding that I probably had some much better of my own.

I had arranged to be woken at 0600 hrs, unless anything happened during the night. I slipped my revolver under the pillow and, in doing so, noticed that not just the pillow cases but the sheets and eiderdown cover were all real linen, the likes of which I hadn't seen in years. Shortly after being woken by the Troop Sergeant, there was a knock on the door and the old servant came in, with a basin and an immense jug of steaming hot water. 'Is the war going to end soon?' she asked. 'I hope so,' I replied. 'War is terrible,' she said. 'Why do young men have to kill each other?' The question was rhetorical so I had no need of a reply. 'My man was a soldier. Twenty nine or perhaps it was only twenty eight years ago, he went to the war. I never saw him again,' '*Mein Mann*', I realised, meant 'My husband'. 'How sad,' was all I could think of saying. The old woman shrugged and said she would make me some breakfast.

It seems that she made breakfast for all the troop as well: boiled eggs, bread and butter. In return they made a brew-up . . . and left her with a month's ration of tea. I got my breakfast with profound apologies that the coffee was only *ersatz*. It might have been but it wasn't all that much worse than some of the station canteen variety. This was all, of course, a flagrant violation of the ban on fraternisation but one didn't turn away fresh home-made bread and butter from the farm and three boiled eggs for a mere technicality like that. As I had expected, the women protested that they had always been against the Nazi regime: I had expected that but was inclined to believe them: possibly I was right since they came from Hamburg, a Hanseatic city with a reputation for internationalism and independence.

Another, but perhaps not so flagrant, breach of the 'no-fratting' ban also occurred in my own Troop. Again we were out of the line, somewhere on Lüneberg Heath, and were, consequently, more than a little alarmed when there was a burst of firing from close to, followed by a shout of 'Got him!' I went to investigate and found that one of the men had shot a good-sized deer. The German-speaking member of my troop said his uncle had been a furrier and he knew how to skin it. Fine, but nobody had any idea how to cook it and we didn't really relish the idea of grilling gobbets of fresh-killed meat over a desert fire. 'Leave it to me,' said our hero, wiping the blood off his hands. 'They'll cook it for us quickly enough in the farm over there, if we offer to give them half of it. And they'll have the carrots and onions and potatoes to make a really good stew.' He put a ground sheet round his neck and slung the bullet-ridden carcass over his shoulder and staggered off. He came back grinning. 'Dinner will be ready in a couple of hours,' he reported. It was and it was a really good stew.

THE OTHER SIDE

The war had reached the stage at which 'the other side' had almost ceased to exist. Germany was like the proverbial chicken with its head cut off: still able to function without any brain to control the function.

At the time, it was thought that the Service Chiefs, who had earlier advocated suing for a cease-fire with the Western Allies, would make an attempt to do so with the Russians at the gates of Berlin. In some ways this would have been reasonable but there were two probable reasons why it did not happen.

Centralised control of the armed services had become impossible: it is by no means certain that there was immediate agreement as to who was in command of the Armed Forces once Hitler had withdrawn himself from all operational control of – or even interest in – the conduct of the war.

Hitler may have ceased to control events but the most sinister of his henchmen – Himmler – had become, at least in theory, Commander-in Chief as well as being the head of the Schutzstaffel and the Gestapo. None of the Generals knew his intentions and all mistrusted his powers.

In the last weeks of April, Hitler had withdrawn to his 'bunker' – a massive shelter under the Berlin Chancellery – in company with his mistress, Eva Braun.

THE WAR CHRONICLE

1945

April	06	Red Army invested Vienna
	07	World's largest battleship, the Japanese *Yamoto*, sunk
	10	Allies launched 'make-or-break' offensive in Italy
	12	Franklin Delano Roosvelt, four times elected President of the United States of America, died at the age of 63, having been the 32nd holder of that Office – Buchenwald survivors freed by the US Army
	13	Vienna passed from Nazi German control to Communist Russian control
	15	Arnhem captured: end of effective German Army resistance in Holland
	16	Colditz POW Camp liberated by American forces – Germany's last 'Pocket Battleship', *Lutzow*, sunk
	18	American Army units reached Czechoslovakia

NOTES

1 River Wessel. There is a consistent error in the War Diary. The only river 'to the SE of Bremen' to which this order could refer is the Weser (*'The River Weser deep and wide ..'* in Browning's PIED PIPER OF HAMELIN) and not the Wessel. (Future references to *Wessel* have been corrected to read *Weser)*

2 1810 hrs. This is another error. If The Fifth crossed the Ems–Wsser Canal at 1930 hrs, we could not possibly have crossed another bridge 15 miles away, 70 minutes earlier . . . no matter how fast we could travel

3 Lembruch. This is wrongly shown as *Lembusch* on the map between pages 436 and 437 in VOL 2 of THE TANKS

4 Lt W F Newton. For some unknown reason, Newton's death is not recorded in the Regimental Casualty List. It is, however, rightly described as an act of treachery in General Verney's THE DESERT RATS

5 'called up fifteen'. 'Fifteen' was the wireless code number of the Gunner's FOO who travelled with the Regiment. By 'calling fifteen', Troop or Squadron Commanders were in direct contact with the supporting RHA Battery

6 Rethem. NO TRIUMPHANT PROCESSION also quotes an incident in which I was involved. The night of 11/12th April was a filthy one and the 2 Monmouths were cut off from their echelon. The tank crews had the PBI into the tanks, a few at a time, and gave them a brew or some hot soup. While their Platoon Officer and two or three men were in my tank, the A1 Echelon arrived and we loaded up our quota. The Platoon Commander asked me who was in charge of the Forward Echelon and I replied that it was the RSM. An awed voice, which could only have come from the Principality, was heard in the bottom of the tank saying, 'The RSM? You'd never see our Friar Tuck this near the sharp end!'

7 Werewolf Packs. The threat of 'Werewolf Packs', never substantially realised, was expected to come from groups of fanatical Nazis (particularly from the SS and Hitlerjugend), pledged to attack and kill members of the Army of Occupation. They claimed that they would have been like the French Resistance Fighters, whose activities were designed to tie down the German occupying forces and disrupt communications,: they would, in reality, have been more like modern-style terrorists

8 Shelldrake. The general code name used when referring to the supporting artillery

CHAPTER XXII

. . . *The Chequered Flag – Hamburg*

April–May 1945

There isn't very much more to be said. The War Diary records that on 27th April the Regiment was at Dibbersen, the only item being reported was that 'B' Squadron relieved 'C' Squadron. What the War Diary does not record but the Regimental Casualty List does, is that the unfortunate 'C' Squadron suffered two most unlucky casualties. One was the last fatal casualty during the war years. Cpl Richardson was seriously wounded in the head and stomach when a demolition charge exploded while he was supervising the destruction of enemy weapons by German POWs. He died from the wounds received on 13th May. Cpl Warris, also of 'C' Squadron, was injured in the same explosion.

On the 28th there was NTR.

On the 29th there was still NTR . . . except that "B' Squadron engaged some enemy movement. At 1700 'A' Squadron took over from 'B' Squadron'.

'B' Squadron had a lovely time. Enemy movement having been detected and a target passed on to the Troops, all those with any excuse to shoot at or near the target area did so with gay abandon. The more enterprising crew commanders decided that there were signs of enemy movement in other, and not always adjacent, areas. The only appropriate way to deal with this threat to our safety was to loose off with anything handy in the ammo racks. What good we did – or harm for that matter – is nowhere recorded but we liked to think that any member of the Hamburg City Council who had doubts about persuading the military to surrender the place would have had second thoughts after our little *feu de joie*. Of course, we stopped as soon as our Sunray told us to!

On 30th April rumours of the imminent surrender of Hamburg were rife. The War Diary records this, adding that the Regiment was at rest. Rumours that the war was about to end were equally rife but the ways in which this was to happen were by no means clear.

All that happened, according to the War Diary, in the first two days of May was that 'A' Squadron rejoined the fold. This is not the full story: one curious little incident is not officially recorded; again it is autobiographical. We were fairly thinly spread out on our approach to Hamburg and still fairly alert. We had been told to take the *Werewolf* threat seriously. If it were to come, we assumed it would be from the Hamburg area and so, at night, put tanks across the roads leading to Hamburg and guards on those tanks. I was doing my spell on watch on my Troop's guard tank when I heard the sound of vehicle movement. I looked around and saw the lights of two vehicles approaching from our rear. Rather bright lights. I collected my pet ex-Wehrmacht sub-machine-gun and got down to investigate. Two scout cars approached and halted. I was told, in very Staff College tones, to get my tank out of the way as the speaker had business to attend to. Before I could point out that any business on the far side of the guard tank was likely to be a bit dangerous, I was called back to the tank to speak to 'Big Sunray'. Big Sunray told me that I was to pass out *and back* two scout cars who would identify themselves as having business to do. Obediently, I ordered the driver to pull the tank to the side of the road. A Daimler Dingo and a Humber Scout Car passed through.

By chance I was on duty again when I saw distant lights approaching from the direction of Hamburg. I woke the crew and we sat and watched to see what would happen. There was by then enough dawn light to identify the approaching vehicle as the Dingo. The driver started the tank and I climbed down. The same voice again told me to move the tank. I asked where the other scout car was, thinking it might be in trouble and need our help. 'Oh, he's still talking!' was the cheerful reply. This time the tones were those of a happy man and not a Staff College graduate. As the Dingo drove past, I saw that the speaker had a Union Jack draped across his shoulders.

The momentous days which followed are thus recorded in the War Diary:
May 1945

3 1600 hrs Regt moved forward to occupy the centre of Hamburg, 1RTR having already seized the bridges crossing the R Elbe, passing through a much bombed area to the Adolf Hitler Platz. RHQ plus1/5 Queens was established in Streits Hotel.

4 Recce carried out patrols in the western outskirts of the town: otherwise NTR.

5 Orders were received during the early morning for the Regt to proceed to the Danish-German border.
0830 hrs the Regt was formed up ready for this operation by 0830 hrs when this order was cancelled
1100 hrs Regt now ordered to move to an area N of Hamburg between the village of Hutte and Garstedt.

6 Regt awaiting orders
1015 hrs CO Lt Col A R Leakey M.C., addressed all ranks making clear the present war situation in the area.

7 1520 hrs Regt now ordered to move to Kiel Canal area. Route:- Pinneberg–Elmshorn–Steinberg – then west to Itzehoe – and to Gribbohm
At last light Regt came under command of 22 Armd Bde.

Considering that the War Diary described the Great Swan as being almost under peace-time conditions, it is surprising that there is no hint in these entries that the few days we spent in Hamburg were also under 'almost peace-time conditions'. From the moment that we got the orders to move into Hamburg we knew what that meant. Hitler was *kaput*! Anything else which happened would be incidental. The move into Hamburg would, therefore, be the Fifth Royal Tank Regiment's last – but greatest – Triumphal Entry.

In the libraries of war films – Pathé Gazette, Gaumont British News, Army Film Unit or whatever – there is a lot of footage of completely anonymous *Cromwell* tanks roaring across bridges, through bombed streets, past gaunt ruins, occasionally with small groups of apathetic and silent spectators watching from what once had been pavements. Those tanks may appear anonymous to the ordinary viewer but, to those in the know, those tanks belonged to The Fifth.

First into Hamburg, as was right and proper, were the Cherry Pickers – the Eleventh Hussars – who, with only a short break, had been the Seventh Armoured Division's Reconnaissance Regiment ever since the Desert Rats came into being in 1940. By chance, the Divisional Order of March was for the First Tanks to 'seize' the bridges and take up positions to guard them, then for the Fifth Tanks to pass through and take up positions in the city centre. As to the Regimental Order of March, its being 'B' Squadron's turn to lead the Regiment, the Squadron Order of March was for Five Troop to lead the Squadron and thereby have the honour of being the first of the occupying (as opposed to reconnoitring) troops in the city. An honour which I, as Troop Officer of Number Five Troop, did not enjoy. I lost my way among the rubble.

The result was that Major DE Cockbaine, OC 'B' Squadron, was the man who had this honour . . . an honour in no way diminished because, as he pulled into his allotted position outside the Hamburg General Post Office, his *Cromwell* shed a track and came to an abrupt halt. That particular tank had made the journey – on its tracks – from the beaches in Normandy to the centre of Hamburg, one of the very few tanks to have made it right through from D+1 to VE Day – 5. As Tom Bowsfield, Dennis' veteran driver, said, 'Well, Sir. That's that.' It was indeed.

The War Diary records that RHQ established itself in Streits Hotel[1]. According to Bob Maunsell, 'established' was an understatement. We had rolled into Hamburg in the early evening and, when Bob and a couple of officers from The Queens went into the hotel, they found that dinner was already being served. What a waste: all that delicious food going down the throats of those stout Hamburgers! It was only a matter of minutes to pass the word to the others in the HQ tanks that 'grub up' was the order of the day, for tables to be cleared of the intending diners and for the waiters, without batting an eyelid, to provide their new masters with the best served meal that anyone in The Fifth had had since Shepherd's Hotel in Cairo!

'Bully for the elite of RHQ!' one might say but it was a case of 'bully for us' in another sense. The raff and scaff of the Regiment – in other words, those of us in the 'Fighting Squadrons' – had to make do with bully-beef or whatever else the Compo Packs had in store!

'B' Squadron drew the General Post Office for their quarters and I dare say that quite a lot of secondary parcel sorting was carried out by the troops over the next day or two.

Life in those first two days was completely artificial. Norman Smith described how he and some of his pals found where to look for Hamburg's forbidden delights[2]. He was also honest enough to admit that, when the order to move was finally given, he and his cronies were in no position to answer the call of military duty. 'B' Squadron looked as if it was going to move off several bodies short but all was well that ended well and there were full, if somewhat exhausted, crews in all the tanks.

There was now a decidedly holiday atmosphere and, when Rea Leakey 'made clear the present war situation in the area', it has to be admitted that he was listened to with scant interest. Everyone's thoughts were revolving round just one question, 'How soon will I get home?'

And, when peace did eventually break out on Tuesday, 8th May 1945 . . . well, let the War Diary have the last word:

Regt resting – VE Day was celebrated in the usual way – Bonfires and shooting Verey lights.

THE OTHER SIDE

At the end, Hitler appears to have lived a fantasy life. Although he had no effective control over the Armed Forces, he imagined that he had, and that those forces were limitless and invincible.

Towards the end of April Hitler left Berchtesgaden for 'the Berlin Bunker'.

On 28th April he went through a form of marriage with his mistress, Eva Braun, choosing as witnesses Hermann Göring and his family. The newly married couple did not enjoy a honeymoon: instead they committed suicide; the bridegroom by shooting himself and the bride by taking poison.

Had they but known it, they might have had more numerous and less welcome witnesses to their marriage. The advance guard of the Russian Army was only a few hundred yards from the bunker.

Hitler's suicide, although simplifying matters for the Allies in the immediate post-war days, had no effect on the last phase of the war.

Most histories agree that, with Hitler's death, Grand Admiral Karl Dönitz was charged with making what peace terms he could with the Allies. Some historians say that Dönitz was made Führer by Hitler himself and, if so, it was Hitler's last rational act. Whatever the truth, Dönitz ordered Field Marshal Keitel, the Commander-in-Chief of the Army, to sue for an armistice with the Western Allies. Having done this, he was replaced by Admiral von Friedeburg.

What happened next must have gladdened Monty's heart. The deputation which was sent to General Dempsey was told that if they 'wanted out', they would have to talk to the Field Marshal. They did, so they did . . . and had little choice but to accept what he, Monty, and not the Supreme Commander told them.

During the preliminary discussions (they were scarcely negotiations), the German delegation made two serious mistakes: these had no effect on the conclusion of hostilities but they did on Monty. The delegation pleaded that the Western Allies would do what they could to restrain the Russians from – in short – doing to the German population what the Germans had done to the Russians. Monty, somewhat light-heartedly, suggested that they should have thought of that in 1941 before invading Russia. However, when the delegation asked for Monty's assurance that the civil population would not be 'brutalised' by the Allies, Monty lost his temper. He had, only a few days before, visited Belsen and was not in a mood to listen to any Germans talking about suffering brutality.

In the end, the terms offered to Keitel's negotiators were those of unconditional surrender. In the end they were accepted.

THE WAR CHRONICLE

1945

April	27	Mussolini, rescued on Hitler's orders, again captured by Italian Partisans – American and Russian troops linked up at Torgau
	28	Mussolini 'executed' by Italian Partisans
	29	Dachau liberated by US Army
	30	Red Army invested Berlin
May	01	Tito's Partisans captured Trieste, only hours before the arrival of British forces
	02	Berlin surrendered to Marshal Zhukov – German Army surrendered in Italy
	03	Allied forces captured Rangoon
	05	British Paratroops landed in Denmark 'to protect the Germans from the fury of the Danes'
	08	VE-Day . . . and Jane of *Daily Mirror* fame – never the most-dressed figure in Fleet Street – finally put 'strip' into the strip cartoon

NOTES

1 Streits Hotel. This incident may sound improbable in a city which had suffered the devastation experienced by Hamburg. It so happened, however, that the area round the Alster where the Regiment leaguered was substantially intact

2 Forbidden delights. These were to be found in the Rieper Bahn – if not with the cosmopolitan glitz of later years, certainly forbidden enough for Dennis Cockbaine, in whose zone of responsibility this notorious red-light district lay, to order that its gates be closed at the end where The Fifth was to be found

APPENDIX 1
Phonetic Alphabets

Two phonetic alphabets were used in WW II. One had been in use since 1938: the other was adopted in 1941. They read as shown (the NATO alphabet is given for comparison):

1938	1941	NATO
ACK	ABLE	ALPHA
BEER	BAKER	BRAVO
CHARLIE	CHARLIE	CHARLIE
DON	DOG	DELTA
EDWARD	EASY	ECHO
FREDDIE	FOX	FOXTROT
GEORGE	GEORGE	GOLF
HARRY	HOW	HOTEL
INK	ITEM	INDIA
JOHNNIE	JIG	JULIET
KING	KING	KILO
LONDON	LOVE	LIMA
MONKEY	MIKE	MIKE
NUTS	NAN	NOVEMBER
ORANGE	OBOE	OSCAR
PIP	PETER	PAPA
QUEEN	QUEEN	QUEBEC
ROBERT	ROGER	ROMEO
SUGAR	SUGAR	SIERRA
TOC	TARE	TANGO
UNCLE	UNCLE	UNIFORM
VIC	VICTOR	VICTOR
WILLIAM	WILLIAM	WHISKEY
X-RAY	X-RAY	XRAY
YORKER	YORK	YANKEE
ZEBRA	ZEBRA	ZULU

Source: Royal Signals Museum, Blandford Forum

APPENDIX 2
Tanks and Guns

This Appendix contains brief information about the tanks, and their guns, that The Fifth fought with and against between September 1939 and May 1945.

NB. The mileage given under 'Range' represents the distance travelled on road. In the case of the General Stuart (Honey) *for example, Mike Carver calculated that their range, manoeuvring across open desert, was only 40 miles.*

Part One: ALLIES

MARK VI LIGHT
Various Models: Mark VI: VIA: VIB: VIC
Crew: 3
Weight: 5.2tons ~ *Length*: 13ft ~ *Width*: 6ft 9in ~ *Height*: 7ft 4in
Armour: Max – 14mm: Min – 4mm
Armament: 1 x Vickers .303in (Water-cooled) MG
1 x Vickers .50in — ditto —
[Mk VIC: 1 Besa 7.92mm (Air-cooled) MG
1 Besa 15mm — ditto —]
Engine: Meadows 4.5litre – 85bhp – 6 cyl – petrol ~ *Speed*: 35mph ~ *Range*: 130 miles
Suspension: Box bogies

First produced: 1936. Used in France (1939/40) and Western Desert (1940/41)

CRUISER TANK MARK 1: *A9*
Crew: 6
Weight: 12tons ~ *Length*: 19ft 3in ~ *Width*: 8ft 4in ~ *Height*: 8ft 4in
Armour: Max – 14mm: Min – 6mm
Armament: 1 x 2pdr Gun
3 x Vickers .303in MG (1 coaxially-mounted in turret: 2 hull-mounted)
Engine: AEC – 150bhp – 6cyl – petrol ~ *Speed*: 25mph ~ *Range*: 100 miles
Suspension: 'Newton' type shock-absorbers on sprung bogies

Produced as a 'cheap' 'Medium' tank, the A9 became – for Service policy reasons – a 'Cruiser'. Initial, unsatisfactory, development work dates from 1934: production limited to 125 units: used in France (1939/40) and North Africa (1941). First British tank with powered turret traverse.

CRUISER TANK MARK II: *A10*
Crew: 4 [5 in Mk IIA]
Weight: 13.75tons ~ *Length*: 18ft 1in ~ *Width*: 8ft 4in ~ *Height*: 8ft 6in
Armour: Max – 30mm
Armament: 1 x 2pdr gun or 3.7in mortar
1 x Vickers .303in MG or 7.92mm Besa MG (coaxially-mounted in turret)
Engine: As A9 ~ *Speed*: 16mph ~ *Range*: 100 miles
Suspension: As A9

The A10 was partly a revision of the Army's idea of a 'Medium' tank. Vickers-Armstrong, having completed the design of the A9, was asked by the War Office to design a 'heavier tank to work with infantry'. Like Topsy, the A10 'just growed'. Extra thickness of armour was achieved by bolting armour plating onto the existing 14mm shell: the extra weight being dealt with by reducing the gear ratios. Production was limited due to the development of the later 'Cruiser' tanks and more powerful engines. A10s were used in France (1940) and North Africa (1940/1941)

CRUISER TANK MARK III: *A13*
Crew: 4
Weight: 14tons ~ *Length*: 19ft 9in ~ *Width*: 8ft 4in ~ *Height*: 8ft 6in
Armour: Max – 14mm: Min – 6mm
Armament: 1 x 2pdr gun
1 x .303in Vickers MG (coaxially-mounted in turret)
Engine: Nuffield 'Liberty' – 340bhp – V12cyl – petrol ~ *Speed:* 30mph ~ *Range*: 90 miles
Suspension: Christie – 4-wheel

Paradoxically, the A13 design came to Britain from America, via Russia, neither US nor British War Offices being interested in J Walter Christie's large riding-wheel, torsion-bar suspension. The Russian were, building the T28 in 1936. Whitehall reluctantly allowed Nuffields to develop prototypes which were sufficiently far advanced for the first production A13s to be delivered by Morris Motors in September 1939. A13s saw limited service in France (1939/40) and more extensive service in the Western Desert (1940/41)

CRUISER TANK MARK IV: *(A13 MK II)*
Three-quarters of a ton heavier than the Mark I but otherwise built to the same specification, the Mark II had 30mm frontal armour. The extra 16mm plating was not bolted on but 'spaced'. 'Spaced' armour became a feature of German tank design later in the war.

Some 650 A13s Mark II were produced and used in North Africa.

CRUISER TANK MARK V: *Covenanter*
Crew: 4
Weight: 18tons ~ *Length*: 19ft ~ *Width*: 8ft 7in ~ *Height*: 7ft 4in
Armour: Max – 40mm: Min – 7mm
Armament: 1 x 2pdr gun or 3in howitzer
1 x 7.92mm Besa MG (coaxially-mounted in turret)
Engine: Meadows – 300bhp – 'flat' 12cyl – Petrol ~ *Speed*: 31mph ~ *Range*: 100 miles
Suspension: Christie – 4-wheel

Covenanters were a design hotch-potch. They used Christie suspension, a purpose-built Meadows horizontally-opposed 12 cylinder engine (*cf* that designed by Vauxhalls for the *Churchill*) with a Wilson compound epicyclic gearbox. Despite production of 1,770 tanks, few *Covenanters* saw operational service, except as the basis for 79th Armoured Division 'funnies'.

The *Covenanter* was the first British tank with the 'C' initial model name: a practice continued to this day.

CRUISER TANK MARK VI: *Crusader*
Crew: 4 [only 3 for the Mk III version]
Weight: 19tons [19.75tons for the Mk III] ~ *Length*: 19ft 8in ~ *Width*: 8ft 8in ~ *Height*: 7ft 4in
Armour: Max – 40mm [51mm for Mk III]: Min – 7mm
Armament: 1 x 2pdr gun [1 x 6pdr gun for Mk III]
2 x 7.92mm Besa MG (1 coaxially-mounted in turret: 1 hull-mounted)
Engine: Nuffield 'Liberty' – 340bhp – V12cyl – petrol ~ *Speed*: 27mph ~ *Range*: 100 miles
Suspension: Christie – 5-wheel

A logical – if slower – development of previous 'Cruiser' designs, the *Crusader* was a product of collaboration between Nuffields and the Mechanisation Directorate of the War Office. 200 were originally commissioned and delivered by May 1940: this order was increased to 1,000 and then to 5,300 by 1943. Although necessity made the *Crusader* the main cruiser tank in North Africa, it was never as reliable or competitive an AFV (even when up-graded to Mk III with the 6pdr) as circumstances required
Some *Crusaders* were also converted as 'Hobo's funnies'.

CRUISER TANKS MK VII (A24): *Cavalier* and CRUISER TANK MARK VIII (A27L): *Centaur*

Neither of these developments of the *Crusader* saw service with Seventh Armoured Division. In many ways they were fore-runners of the *Cromwell*: in other ways, their development delayed the production of the *Cromwell*. Both the *Cavalier* and the *Centaur* had improved Christie suspension, the A27L being fitted with an up-graded 410bhp 'Liberty' engine – hence the 'L' – and a Merritt-Brown epicyclic gearbox.

CRUISER TANK MARK VIII (A27M): *Cromwell*
Crew: 5
Weight: 27.5 tons ~ *Length*: 20ft 10in ~ *Width*: 9ft 7in ~ *Height:* 8ft 2in
Armour: Max – 76mm: Min – 8mm [Max – 101mm: Min – 10mm with welded-on additional plating]
Armament: 1 x 75mm dual-purpose gun or 95mm howitzer
2 x 7.92mm Besa MG (1 coaxially-mounted in turret: 1 hull-mounted)
Engine: Rolls-Royce 'Meteor' – 600bhp – V12cyl – petrol ~ *Speed*: 32 – 40mph, depending on Mark
Range: 175 miles
Suspension: Full 5-wheel Christie

The *Cromwell* underwent its first trials in 1942 but suffered every kind of bureaucratic growing pain, partly because of time taken for information to filter back from North Africa; partly because of need to keep *Crusaders* in production and supplied with spares. Additional complications arose from dithering over choice of main armament (Mks I, II and III were fitted with 6pdrs) and misconception that speed was as good protection as armour.
Ironically, this lightly-armed and vulnerable AFV became known as 'the main British battle tank' in North-West Europe.

INFANTRY TANK MARK II: *Matilda*
Crew: 4
Weight: 26.5tons ~ *Length*: 18ft 5in ~ *Width*: 8ft 6in ~ *Height*: 8ft
Armour: Max – 78mm: Min – 20mm
Armament: 1 x 2pdr gun
1 x .303in Vickers MG [later models: 1 x 7.92mm Besa MG] (coaxially-mounted in turret)
Engine(s): 2 x AEC – 87bhp – diesel ~ *Speed*: 15mph ~ *Range*: 70 miles

First saw service in small numbers in France in 1939/40 and, later, throughout the Desert Campaign. One time 'Queen of the Desert': when obsolete for its main infantry support role, modified for a variety of other uses.

US LIGHT TANK M3: *General Stuart* [A1 to A3 Series]
Crew: 4
Weight: 12.25tons up to 14.17tons for A3 Series ~ *Length*: 14ft 11in up to 16ft 6in for A3 Series
Width: 7ft 4in up to 8ft 3in for A3 Series ~ *Height*: 8ft 3in reduced to 7ft 7in for A3 Series
Armour: Max – 51mm: Min – 10mm

Armament: 1 x 37mm gun
2 x .30in Browning MG (1 coaxially-mounted in turret: 1 hull-mounted)
Engine: Continental – Radial 7cyl – petrol or Guiberson – Radial 9cyl – diesel
Speed: 34 – 36mph ~ *Range*: 70 – 100 miles
Suspension: Vertical volute

Stuarts (universally called *Honeys*) were developed by US Army in 1940 as a result of observation of the war in Europe and, later, in North Africa. *Honeys* underwent numerous model modifications which improved them without curing all their inherent faults. Nevertheless, they were welcomed when they arrived in the Western Desert in 1941.

US LIGHT TANK M5: *General Stuart*
Crew: 4
Weight: 14.75tons ~ *Length*: 14ft 3in ~ *Width*: 7ft 5in ~ *Height*: 7ft 7in
Armour: Max – 67mm: Min – 12mm
Armament: 1 x 37mm
2 x .30in Browning MG (1 coaxially-mounted in turret: 1 hull-mounted)
Engine(s): Twin Cadillac – 220bhp – V8cyl – petrol ~ *Transmission*: GM Hydramatic
Speed: 36mph ~ *Range*: 100 miles
Suspension: Vertical volute

A rationalised development of the M3 *Stuarts*, which they gradually replaced, when neither Continental nor Guiberson could increase production to match demand. The first tank to have an automatic gearbox. In service with US, British and Canadian forces from 1943.

US MEDIUM TANK M3: *General Grant*
Crew: 6
Weight: 26.8tons ~ *Length*: 18ft 6in ~ *Width*: 8ft 11in ~ *Height*: 10ft 3in
Armour: Max – 37mm: Min – 12mm
Armament: 1 x 75mm gun mounted in right-side hull sponson with limited traverse
1 x 37mm gun in full-traverse (upper) turret
1 x .30in Browning MG (coaxially-mounted in upper turret)
2 x .30in Browning MG hull-mounted
Engine combinations – see below ~ *Speeds*: according to engine type in 25 – 28mph ~ *Range*: 125 miles
Suspension: vertical volute

Although classified as a 'Medium' tank, it was conceived 'by the infantry for the infantry'. The maxim 'What's good for General Motors is good for America' applied, as *Grants* were designed by GM and produced using automobile mass-production techniques. A serious disadvantage was the hull-mounting of the main armament.

The *Grant* was essentially the US Army *General Lee.*

Engine combinations: Wright – radial 9cyl – petrol
Continental – radial 9cyl – petrol
Guiberson – radial 9cyl – diesel
Chrysler – 5 x A57 – 370bhp – multi-bank – petrol

US MEDIUM TANK M4: *Sherman*

Crew: 5

Weight: 29.7tons – 30.6tons ~ *Length*: 19ft 4in ~ *Width*: 8ft 7in ~ *Height*: 9ft

Armour: Max – 75mm: Min – 12mm [hull thickness, + or – 25mm, varied with model]

Armament: 1 x 75mm gun
2 x .39in Browning MG (1 coaxially-mounted in turret: 1 hull-mounted)

Engine(s): as for *Grants* ~ *Speed*: 25 – 29mph, depending on engine type

Range: 110 – 150 miles, depending on engine type

Suspension: Vertical volute

A mutation of the *Grant* design to eliminate its short-comings, *Shermans* became, in practice, the Western Allies' main battle tank, some 40,000 being produced in tank form, with only slight modifications, between 1942 and 1945. Saw service in all theatres of war: the ability to produce *Shermans* in large quantities was regarded as outweighing the need for major improvement. A further 19,000 were produced and modified for a wide variety of uses.

US MEDIUM TANK M4: *Firefly*

A *Firefly* was an M4 *Sherman* with a British designed turret mounting the British 17-pounder high-velocity anti-tank gun. In order to stow more ammunition, *Fireflies* did not have a front gunner.

All other details are those given for *Shermans*.

Technical details of the main armament carried by these tanks are given below:

British

Gun	Calibre	Muzzle Velocity	Projectile	Mounted in
2-pounder	40.0mm	2,600 ft/sec	AP	A9: A10: A13: Matilda: Covenanter: Crusader
6-pounder	57.0mm	2,340 ft/sec	AP	Crusader Mk III
75 mm	75.0mm	2,050 ft/sec	AP or HE	Cromwell
17-pounder	76.2mm	2,980 ft/sec	AP *	Firefly

* Muzzle velocity is given for the standard ammunition (a figure which, for the 17pdr, equates to 2,032mph)

U S

37 mm	37.0mm	2,600 or 2,900 ft/sec	AP	Stuart
75 mm [M2]	75.0mm	1,850 ft/sec	AP or HE	Grant
75 mm [M3]	75.0mm	2,050 ft/sec	AP or HE	Sherman

Ranged against these tanks and guns, were five basic design of German tanks, with a number of Czechoslovakian tanks and an even larger quantity of Italian tanks.

Part Two: AXIS

MEDIUM TANK PZ KPF WG III
Crew: 5
Weight: 19.1tons ~ *Length*: 17ft 8in ~ *Width:* 9ft 6in ~ *Height*: 8ft
Armour: Max – 30mm: Min – 10mm
Armament: 1 x 37mm gun [later models: 1 x 50mm gun]
2 x 7.92mm MG (1 coaxially-mounted in turret: 1 hull-mounted)
Engine: Maybach – 300bhp – V12cyl – petrol ~ *Speed*: 25mph ~ *Range*: 110 miles

Designed to be the main battle tank for the new Wehrmacht in the late 1930s, the PzKw III was a radical advance on the earlier PzKw I and PzKw II which were relegated as 'training tanks' after the invasion of France. Total production between 4,000 and 5,000: more than a dozen major modifications incorporated by 1941.

MEDIUM TANK PZ KPF WG IV [Specification given for Model D]
Crew: 5
Weight: 18.5tons ~ *Length*: 19ft 4in ~ *Width*: 9ft 7in ~ *Height*: 8ft 6in
Armour: Max – 30mm: Min – 10mm
Armament: 1 x 75mm gun
2 x 7.92mm MG (1 coaxially-mounted: 1 hull-mounted)
Engine: Norddeutsche Motorenbau – 280bhp – V12cyl – petrol ~ *Speed*: 30mph ~ *Range:* 130 miles

The PzKw IV dates from 1936 and went through seven model changes before being considered not worth further development in early 1942. The PzKw IV was surprisingly lightly armoured, although very well armed. Used in all theatres of operations, it was a familiar sight in the Desert.

MEDIUM TANK PZ KPF WG V: Panther
Crew: 5
Weight: 44.1tons ~ *Length*: 22ft 6in ~ *Width*: 10ft 10in ~ *Height*: 9ft 8in
Armour: Max 120mm – Min: 20mm
Armament: 1 x 75mm 'L70' gun
2 x 7,92mm MG (1 coaxially-mounted in turret: 1 hull-mounted)

Engine: Maybach – 700bhp – 23litre – V12cyl – petrol ~ *Speed*: 29mph ~ *Range*: 120 miles

After teething troubles, the first batch of 200 or 300 emerged in the winter of 1942/43. The Panther gave a new meaning to the designation 'Medium', as it weighed nearly two-and-a-half times as much as a PzKw IV. With frontal armour impenetrable by all Western Allied tank guns, its 'Long 70' gun made it master of the *Sherman* and equal of the Russian T34, both of whose performance it could equal. Total production of Panthers was 5,500 units.

BATTLE TANK PZ KPF WG MARK VI: Tiger I
Crew: 5
Weight: 50.25tons dry weight (55.5tons in full battle order)
Length: 20ft 9in ~ *Width:* 12ft 3in [see below] ~ *Height*: 9ft 5in
Armour: Max – 102mm: Min – 26mm
Armament: 1 x 88mm 'L56' gun
2 x 7,92mm MG (1 coaxially-mounted in turret: 1 hull-mounted)
Engine: Maybach – 640bhp – 21.5litres – V12cyl – petrol ~ *Speed:* 16mph ~ *Range:* 90 miles

As noted below, the concept of such a tank as the Tiger dates back to 1939. When it did arrive, the Tiger was, nevertheless, an entirely new animal in the AFV Zoo: more of a mammoth really than a tiger or, at least, a rhinoceros. Serious practical disadvantages were its weight and width: the weight for bridge-crossing; the width for transportation. When transported by train, modifications were carried out to the suspension *ie* removing the outer riding wheels and fitting narrower tracks. Its main tactical and practical disadvantages were engine and transmission frailty and its ability only to move on roads or hard ground. Generally, its enormous killing power and invulnerability were considered by its victims to outweigh all such shortcomings. Principally intended for the Russian front, prototypes emerged in September 1942 and were used, disastrously, in the attack on Leningrad.

BATTLE TANK PZ KPF WG VI [MODEL B]: Royal or King Tiger or Tiger II
Crew: 5
Weight: 66tons ~ *Length*: 24ft 8in ~ *Width*: 11ft 10in ~ *Height*: 10ft 2in
Armour: Max 150mm: Min – 25mm
Armament: 1 x 88mm 'L71' gun
2 x 7.92mm MG (1 coaxially-mounted in turret: I hull-mounted)
Engine: Maybach – 690bhp – 23litre – fuel-injected – V12cyl – petrol ~ *Speed:* 24mph ~ *Range*:100 miles

The ultimate Axis tank of WW II, designed primarily as a 'tank-destroyer', rather than as a battle tank. Suffering from the same drawbacks as the standard Tiger, it had the advantages of sloped armour and an even more deadly 88mm main gun. Fortunately for the Allies, only some 500 Tiger IIs were produced and the need to distribute these between the Eastern and Western Fronts (and the length of those Fronts) meant that Tiger IIs were seldom encountered in strategically significant numbers – probably not more than 100 in North-West Europe. However, 'When met, best avoided' was the universal maxim.

It is worth noting that the Panther/Tiger concept was seriously considered in Potsdam as early as 1939 but was shelved by reason of cost and manufacturing limitations.

LIGHT TANK PZ KPF WG 38(t) [Czechoslovakia]
Crew: 4
Weight: 9.15tons ~ *Length*: 15ft 3in ~ *Width*: 7ft ~ *Height*: 7ft 2in
Armour: Max – 30mm: Min – 8mm
Armament: 1 x 37mm gun
2 x Besa-type 7.92mm MG (1 coaxially mounted: 1 hull-mounted)
Engine: EPA – 125bhp – 7.75litre – 6cyl – petrol ~ *Speed:* 25mph ~ *Range*: 140 miles
Suspension: Christie-type

The PzKw 38(t) tanks used by the Wehrmacht were originally those captured from the Czechoslovak Army in 1939 and, subsequently with a German 37mm gun, those manufactured in Czechoslovakia for the Wehrmacht. PzKw 38(t)s made up nearly a quarter of the Panzer strength in 1940/41. From 1942, hulls continued in large scale production as the basis of an SP gun.

LIGHT/MEDIUM TANK M14.41 [Italy]
Crew: 4
Weight: 13.8tons ~ *Length*: 16ft 2 in ~ *Width*: 7ft 3in ~ *Height*: 7ft 10in
Armour: Max – 40mm: Min – 14mm
Armament: 1 x 47mm gun
3 x 8.8mm MG (1 coaxially-mounted in turret: 2 hull-mounted)
Engine: 145bhp – V8cyl – diesel ~ *Speed*: 20mph ~ *Range*: 125 miles

Developed from the M13/40, it shared with that tank the distinction of being widely and simultaneously used by the three armies engaged in the Western Desert. Almost directly comparable to British AFVs in armour and fire-power in 1941, captured M13/40s and M14.41s – of which there were many – were pressed into service by the British, as well as simply commandeered by the DAK.

Technical details of the main armament carried by the German tanks are given below:

Gun	Calibre	Muzzle Velocity	Projectile	Mounted in
3,7cm	37mm	2,445 ft/sec	AP or HE	Early PzKw III
5cm L/42	50mm	2,250 ft/sec	AP or HE	PzKw III
5cm L/60	50mm	2,700 ft/sec	AP or HE	Late PzKw III
7.5cm L/24	75mm	1,265 ft/sec	HE	Early PzKw IV
7.5cm L/43	75mm	2,425 ft/sec	AP or HE	PzKw IV
7.5cm L/48	75mm	2,460 ft/sec	AP or HE	Late PzKw IV
7.5cm L/70	75mm	3,070 ft/sec	AP or HE	Panther
8.8cm L/56	88mm	2,660 ft/sec	AP or HE	Tiger I
8.8cm L/71	88mm	3,340 ft/sec	AP or HE	Tiger II

APPENDIX 3
A Long Walk Home

being an account of his time as a POW: June 1944 to April 1945
by 7943359 Trooper CHORLEY W

On 13th June, a Tuesday, there was a heavy battle to capture a large wooded area where the Boche were putting up a strong defence from prepared positions. During a lull in the fighting we were ordered to camouflage our tanks with branches. We got out to do so and our commander, Sgt 'Digger' Whitinglaw, was injured and taken away. He had been wounded with me in Italy, at Scafati, near Pompeii. He recovered from both wounds. The Germans moved out and we moved into leaguer but got no sleep because of shelling. We moved up again the following morning, now with a crew of only four. It seemed that our objective was the village of Jerusalem. The advance had continued for several days but slowly, due to lack of infantry support.

Between the British and Canadian lines on the one hand and the Americans on the other, a gap was found and the Division was moved through this behind our own and the German lines towards Villers Bocage, to prevent a Panzer Division reaching the American sector. Meanwhile, Cpl George Stainton had taken over the tank and I had moved into the turret as main gunner. We stopped on a hillside overlooking Villers and were probably the most forward tank. We could see some action taking place on the main road through the town. The Boche then started to counter-attack us; some of our tank crews were running to our right rear, shouting, 'Tigers!' I don't know if their tanks had been knocked out or not. Our Corporal Commander had baled out too, so that left us with a crew of three and I was virtually in charge of the tank.

Luckily we did not panic: the wireless had remained open so I knew what was going on. I heard tank engines to our right front: they did not seem to be ours so I reported on the link to the OC. He asked me how I knew them to be 'hornets[1]'. 'Only by the sound of their engines,' I replied because I could see nothing through the hedges. We decided to pull back but the engine would not start. I learnt later from our driver that the night before he had mistakenly put water in the fuel tank, using the wrong jerrican: it had been dark and we were very tired. The three of us had a short discussion and decided to abandon the tank.

I had got the impression from listening to the wireless that 4 CLY had taken Villers Bocage so, instead of going back among all the commotion and perhaps meeting enemy tanks, I decided we should go forward towards the CLY. We crept through the hedgerows, which took a long time, until we came to the main road. It seemed all quiet so I got up and suddenly heard, 'Hände hoch, Engländer!', followed by a burst of machine-gun fire. We had no weapons, so we had to surrender: we were marched to a farmhouse which hid the German tanks. A tank commander showed us his Tiger tank which had six inches of reinforced concrete added to the front of it. He was proud of that tank. He pointed out our tanks burning on the opposite hill and also the CLY tanks burning in the main road through Villers Bocage. He asked me where I had fought and my age. I told him and added that I was twenty-three that very day – a fact which I had forgotten. He went into the farmhouse, came back with a bottle: he knocked the top off and gave me a drink of the famous Normandy cider.

During this battle, a German tank knocked out 28 British tanks and armoured vehicles. Its commander was Obersturmführer Michael Wittmann[2] who was himself killed three weeks later, being credited with 117 kills and likened to the WW I legendary air ace, Baron Richthofen.

We were taken to their rear to be interrogated. We would only give them our names, ranks and numbers: the interrogators seemed to know a lot about our Division and tanks; the dates we left Africa, Naples etc but they put no physical pressure on us. We were then sent by lorry to a holding centre in a French village where there were a few other prisoners, mostly infantry: one fellow had a graze on his cheek and a bullet hole through his ear lobe. We were reasonably well treated: we talked to the French people living next door to the compound. Frank, O'Callaghan, our wireless-operator and an ex-seminarian, even went to Mass with two German soldiers.

Now our 'adventures' began. We had been given some sugar cubes by the French for our ersatz coffee. One of the Queens managed to put a few of them in the petrol tank of a truck in which about six of us were to set out for Chartres.

It was well-known that Allied planes had air supremacy during the day and shot up any moving vehicles, except French farm carts. We saw a Boche despatch rider's body, bike and side-car at the side of the road. We did not get very far before the engine of the truck conked out and we had to push the lorry. A couple of times the fighter planes came over and I stood waving a white sheet to warn them off: they came so close that they could recognise our uniforms. They veered off but it was a frightening experience. We pushed that truck to Chartres where we were held in a huge building. We had nothing but straw to sleep on: there were no ablution facilities and, although there must have been a couple of hundred men, there were only two large cut-down barrels for use as latrines . . . and there was no privacy in the privy.

This building was close to the famous Cathedral. One day we were all ordered out into the courtyard and told to leave everything, except what we were wearing, behind. When we went back into the building there were uniforms – British, Canadian, American, French – missing. (After the war, learning about the Ardennes Offensive, it became obvious to me how the Germans obtained Allied uniforms).

We were sent by rail from Chartres to a holding camp in Trier [in Germany] for a short time. We passed through Paris and talked to a few French people at the station. We could only tell them we thought the war would soon be over. I can't remember much about Trier except that we did not get much food and became weaker and weaker each day. Dates have slipped from my memory: all I can recall is that we only had the clothes we stood up in. We were sent on from Trier to Sagan Camp 8c, south of Berlin, in freight cars similar to the ones used to send Jews and others to the Concentration Camps: the journey took two days. There was barely enough room to sit down and only one bucket for a latrine. Conditions were horrible; it is now hard to comprehend that such conditions could be allowed. There were several different camps at Sagan, including the infamous Stalag Luft 3 from which the 'Great Escape[3]' was made. The Germans let it be known that a similar fate awaited anyone else who tried to escape. The Russian prisoners were the worst treated, just living skeletons – which is what we became by the end of our captivity. I think all the prisoners in our compound were British, except for a few Free French Paratroopers captured during the Invasion.

The living conditions in the camp were spartan; three-tier bunks, a blanket and a pillow. We were clean and not too cold; there was just enough food, some of which we had to cook for ourselves on an electric stove. We received a Red Cross parcel every two weeks or so. Life was very boring but we occasionally obtained books. Once some prisoners put on a stage show. We got the news: a wireless was concealed somewhere; the Germans knew but could not find it, in spite of lining us all up outside and then searching the buildings.

Eventually our group was sent to work in a sugar factory near Breslau [now Wroclaw in Poland]. I think the small town was called something like Neumarkt – a German name, because the Germans had occupied the area for some time. We had a couple of sergeants with us to maintain military standards as best they could. There were barracks attached to the factory. Many of the workers were women: I don't know where they were housed but they were virtually prisoners like us. Some of these women were well educated and those of us who could speak French or German could talk to them, although this was, of course, forbidden. Some of these women were made to do heavy work like unloading the sugar beet from the railway wagons. The weather by the time we reached Neumarkt was bitterly cold but it was warm in the factory, as a lot of heat was used in the processing. We were not allowed to move around much, because the Germans were aware that the plant could be sabotaged. This did happen once, when the dryer for the beet residue was slowed down so that it caught on fire. There was a great panic but it was soon repaired and work went on.

We had a twelve hour working day, except when we changed shifts and then we worked either six or eighteen hours. We didn't have much fun but at least there were people around. Frank and I were working under the automatic furnaces with thick sacks over our heads and shoulders to protect us from the fall of ash and still-burning embers. This ash was put into barrows and then sent by conveyor to a slag heap similar to those at coal mines. The supervisor was an old man who talked a lot: he was a civilian and unarmed. He instructed us on the jobs: we bore him no malice or ill-will. Once, shortly before we left, he showed me his lunch: cold cabbage and a rabbit leg. He was confident that Germany had enough to eat and would win the war. On one occasion we refused to work because the sacking protection had become useless. He advised a German officer, who had an Iron Cross but only one arm, having lost the other in Russia. The officer drew his Luger, pointed it at us and ordered us back to work. We went.

We had two British Commandos with us; a sergeant and a private. The latter was a young Jewish lad from London. His Jewishness was obvious; his features were similar to the caricatures used by the Germans in their anti-semitic propaganda. The Germans questioned us about this, hoping we would agree, but we all insisted that he was a typical Londoner. He could have been in trouble, because Hitler had wanted all Commandos to be executed. I'm sure that lad would not have survived the march.

Every few days a party had to go to the local bakery to collect our bread ration, usually one loaf of black bread for four or five men. The bakers were French POWs. Frank and I were usually included in the ration party because we could communicate with them. They would trade extra bread for sugar: we could have been punished severely for these transactions but, obviously, the guards were in on the racket. We had a simple system: we used to put our greatcoats over our shoulders with sugar in the sleeves on the way out, and bread in the sleeves on the way back. Our guards were either old men or soldiers who had been badly wounded on the Russian front.

One day I had a serious situation develop with a German officer. I had passed him in the yard without recognising his rank. He made me walk back past him again so that I could salute him. I didn't want to because of the way the Germans treated the women and other forced labour. Any way, I wasn't wearing my beret: nevertheless, he insisted that I walk past him, giving the 'eyes right' a number of times.

We received a couple of Red Cross parcels at the factory and many of us shared the tit-bits with the women workers; chocolate etc. They told us horrific stories of what had happened to their families. Many of them had children but did not know where they were. They knew all about the crematoria and the extermination camps. At that time we could hardly believe what we were told. In retrospect, however, I now realise that the sugar beet factory was not far from Auschwitz.

By mid-December 1944 everybody realised that the Russians were not far away and would reach us soon. We saw large numbers of Junkers transport planes flying supplies to the front, very low in very bad weather. We spent several nights in the air-raid shelters without hearing any bombing. Work in the factory carried on as usual. There was a nice ironic touch about that factory: the power was generated by an old gas engine – MADE IN ENGLAND! The supervisor was very proud of it and its condition.

The Germans gave us a little extra soup for our Christmas meal and we sang a few carols

The guards seemed to be ignorant of, or indifferent to, what was going to happen to them: they knew that the Russians were close but still thought they were going to win the war. Propaganda about the V1 and V2 bombs helped this complacency. We knew more of what was happening on their home ground than they did.

On New Year's Day 1945, we were lined up and marched out into the snow. I've no idea what happened to the other workers in the factory. Frank and I had always worn sabots with cloth wrapped round our feet when at work. This was why we still had our good army boots for the Long March. Some men only had light footwear: I've no idea of how or if they survived. We marched through the day and, for the first two nights, we slept in the deep snow, huddled together for warmth. The traffic on the roads was composed of horse-drawn farm carts driven by Germans who had settled in the area years ago. I admit I had no sympathy for them because of our condition: it seemed to be retribution for the atrocities which Germany had committed. I really thought they were getting their due punishment.

It must have been the third or fourth day of the March that we met up with some German troops who had been in action only two days before. Some had Panzerfausts but were in a very nervous state. Again, we had no sympathy for them: we had nothing to eat.

Time passed and we marched: southwards at first but we could only guess that. Usually at night we slept in farm buildings, barns etc, sometimes at the roadside. The warmest place was in the barns next the cows. Sometimes we would get a loaf of black bread for four or five men: sometimes nothing. Many men became ill – I don't know what happened to them. Some with dysentery walked with a blanket around their middles, no trousers, so that they could squat whenever necessary. There were thousands of us: our column was led by the one-armed officer from the sugar factory. Occasionally German women gave us hot drinks of ersatz coffee: I've no idea who they were; they may have been from the Red Cross but they had no identification on them.

There was a general consensus that we were heading for Czechoslovakia. We crossed a large river, presumably the Elbe: the bridge was already mined ready to be blown up. We could see the charges on the piers. The bridge was in a large town: I can only assume that it was Dresden. We were always kept isolated and just marched, marched, marched: we had no way of knowing where we were. There were some Australians with us by now. They had somehow acquired a light farm cart and pushed it with some sick men inside with their belongings. They must have been in the bag since the Desert or Greece or Crete some years before.

We saw many large formations of Allied planes, mainly Flying Fortresses. The Luftwaffe attacked them often with their jet fighters. I remember seeing vapour trails of fast planes over Sagan but did not know what they were but they brought down many bombers. Some crews escaped by parachute. It was not a pleasant sight. We were close to a target once, the bombs rained down and we went flat on our faces. The earth shook like an enormous earthquake. We learnt later that this was what was known as 'carpet bombing'.

We marched through the late winter snow with very little to eat. I can't remember ever having a hot meal: just bread. One time Frank and I had saved a little bread as a reserve. I slept with that bread under my head but someone stole it just the same. I must have been really exhausted. Finally to our surprise we arrived back at Sagan 8c. Sagan! We had walked a long way round to get there. Most of the camp had been evacuated, abandoned. It was still very cold but once again we had a roof over our heads. But not for long.

Suddenly one night there was a great panic: the guards disappeared and, on going outside, we could see a town burning. Many of us tried to find a hiding place; I know some French Paratroopers got away. The Germans then sent in their regular troops and some SS to round us up and we were marched away. The troops quickly took over the Red Cross Depot: we saw the parcels being loaded onto trucks and tanks. We had nothing.

We stopped for a few days at another deserted camp, then we carried on, sleeping in barns and other evacuated buildings, until we reached Fallingbostel, Stalag 11B. By now we were so thin and weak that it was difficult to carry on. We had a roof over our heads and a bed again. The weather was warmer but we became infected with lice – a very itchy and miserable state as, under those conditions, it was impossible to get rid of them. We had had neither bath nor shower for over three months.

It was here that the German guards perpetrated one of the most malicious acts that I have ever known. There were many French prisoners who had reached Fallingbostel about the same time as us, some of them women. The Germans paraded them but told them to leave their belongings on the ground, then marched them away. These possession had been patiently hoarded during their long captivity and were precious to them. With nobody around, their packs were ransacked by other prisoners, mostly British: some complete packs were stolen. When the French came back there was a huge brawl and the French recovered what they could. The Germans did it deliberately: the rest of the prisoners were at their wits end and were literally starving and had no possessions.

Two days before we were released I saw a well dressed 'tankie' walking around with the red and blue markings of 5RTR on his epaulets. He was 'Taffy' Evans from 'C' Squadron whom I knew from the Desert days. His tank had been knocked out a few miles away and he had been brought to the camp that day. He assured us that we would soon be freed.

So, on Monday, 16th April 1945 the Fifth Royal Tank Regiment arrived at the gates and we were reunited with our comrades and learned how many had gone. At last we had some food and, the following day, the Salvation Army turned up with their canteens.

What a remarkable coincidence – to be freed by your own Regiment

We were free to move around the huge camp. There were warehouses full of goods from the occupied territories. I still have a well-made notebook which I used as an address book for 30 years: it was made in Czechoslovakia. I ventured into the officers mess where the cutlery was all stainless steel . . . a rarity in those days. I took a large serving tray, engraved *Offiziersheim Fallingbostel* for my mother and then filled a pack with fountain pens and pipes and other things which had been unobtainable at home even before I left. I still have the tray here[4] with me: it was returned when my mother paid us a visit in 1962.

On being freed our clothes were burnt, we were showered and scrubbed clean and liberally sprayed with insecticide all over to kill the lice which could quickly have caused many and unpleasant diseases.

Fallingbostel is near Bergen Belsen, the concentration camp on a par with Auschwitz as far as the people who perished in the gas chambers were concerned.

There was an aerodrome at Celle, near the camp: we were flown home from there in DC3s, stopping at Brussels to refuel. We were sent on leave for ten weeks on double rations. I weighed less than seven stone when I got home to Manchester. Luckily we had a good family doctor who managed to obtained some special body-building medicine for me. I did a lot of swimming at the local pool, so recovered quickly.

Frank and I met once before going back into the Army: he into the Signals in Germany and I into the Engineers in Italy, as there was no call for tanks crews.

To sum up, what can I say? The conditions were so bad on that march that we had no way of knowing where we were or, after a time, what day it was. We were oblivious to many things but we still had the will to survive for three and a half months. It is impossible to calculate how far we walked. I have not embellished this story in any way. The sad part is that, from the memory point of view, many facts have been forgotten after all these years: the glad part is that I am still alive to tell the tale!

NOTES

1. Hornets. Code word used in wireless transmission for enemy tanks and their like
2. Wittmann. Obersturmführer Michael Wittmann of the 501st SS Heavy Tank Battalion was born in 1914 and served briefly in the Reichswehr in the 1930s. Recalled, he served in Poland and on the Russian Front, being award the Iron Cross (2nd Class but later promoted to 1st Class), before being transferred to France. Credited by Major KJ Macksey MC with being ' the most celebrated example of German tank commander' in his GUINNESS BOOK OF TANK FACTS AND FEATS. Wittmann was almost certainly killed in action on 8th August 1944 and *not* 'three weeks later' as Bill Chorley states
3. The Great Escape. Some fifty RAF officers achieved a mass break-out from Stalag Luft 3. Those – and they were in the majority – who were rounded up were shot in cold blood by their captors
4. 'here' is Woolgoolga, New South Wales, Australia

Bibliography

BATTLE FOR NORMANDY, THE: E Belfield and H Essame. *Severn House*
BATTLE OF THE BULGE: John Pimlott. *Bison Group*
CAEN: Henry Maule. *David & Charles*
CHURCHILL'S DESERT RATS (NW EUROPE): Patrick Delaforce. *Alan Sutton*
DESERT RATS, THE: Maj Gen G L Verney. *Greenhill Books*
DILEMMAS OF THE DESERT WAR: Field Marshal Lord Carver. *Spellmount*
EYE WITNESS – D-DAY: [Edited by] Jon E Lewis. *Robinson*
GUINNESS BOOK OF TANK FACTS AND FEATS, THE: Kenneth Macksey. *Guinness Superlatives*
HISTORY OF THE 7TH ARMOURED DIVISION: No Author or Publisher originally stated but reprinted by *The Tank Museum*
HITLER'S GENERALS: [Edited by] Shelford Bidwell. *Salamander*
IKE & MONTY: Norman Gelb. *Constable*
LEAKEY'S LUCK: Maj Gen A R Leakey with G Forty. *Sutton Publishing*
NO TRIUMPHANT PROCESSION: John Russell with R de Norman. *Arms and Armour*
NORMANDY 1944: Stephen Badsey. *Osprey Publishing*
NORMANDY LANDINGS, THE: Derek Blizard. *Reed International Books*
PANZER BATTLÉS: Maj Gen E W von Mellenthin. *Futura*
PICTORIAL HISTORY OF THE ROYAL TANK REGIMENT: George Forty. *Halsgrove*
PICTORIAL HISTORY OF WORLD WAR II, THE: Charles Messenger. *Bison Books*
PRISONER FROM ALAMEIN: Brian Stone. *H F & G Witherby*
ROMMEL: Desmond Young. *Collins*
SIX ARMIES IN NORMANDY: John Keegan. *Pimlico*
STRUGGLE FOR EUROPE, THE: Chester Wilmot. *The Reprint Society*
TANK SOLDIER: Norman Smith. *Book Guild*
TANK VERSUS TANK: Kenneth Macksey. *Guild Publishing*
TANKS: Eric Morris. *Octopus*
TANKS ACROSS THE DESERT: George Forty. *See Note Below*
TANKS, THE: VOLUMES 1 & 2: Basil Liddell Hart. *Cassell*
TOBRUK: Frank Harrison. *Brockhampton Press*
VICTORY IN EUROPE: Julian Thompson. *Imperial War Museum*

VILLERS BOCAGE THROUGH THE LENS: Daniel Taylor. *Battle of Britain International*
WAR ON LAND 1939-1940, THE: [Edited by] Ronald Lewin. *Pimlico*
WARDROP OF THE FIFTH: [Edited by] J Garnett. *Printed and issued privately*

NOTE

George Forty edited and annotated WARDROP OF THE FIFTH (the personal diary of Sergeant 'Jake' Wardrop of 5RTR) with the title TANKS ACROSS THE DESERT. This was originally published by *William Kimber*. It is shortly to be republished by *Sutton Publishing*.

Principal Index

Aus = Australian
C = Canadian
F = French
G = German
I = Italian
SA = South African
US = American
Gen = General (of what ever rank)
Mar = Marshal (G or I)

Index of Service Units

Note: References to military Units and Formations (both Allied and Axis) will be found in the following Chapters

9th Bn Rifle Brigade	VI
1st Bn King's Royal Rifle Corps	VI, VII
7AD Infantry Regiments	
2nd Bn Devonshire Regiment	XIX, XX
9th Bn Durham Light Infantry	IX, XXI
Queens Royal Regiment	IX, X, XI, XIV, XVII
1/5th Bn Queens Royal Regt	VIII, VII, XXII
1/6th Bn Queens Royal Regt	VIII, XII, XVI, XVII
1/7th Bn Queens Royal Regt	XI, XII, XVI
Other Infantry Regiments	
The Essex Regiment	XIV
Glasgow Highlanders	XVII
Gordon Highlanders	IX
2nd Bn Monmouthshire Regiment	XXI
4th Bn Royal Welsh Fusiliers	XVIII
Tower Hamlets Regiment	III
The Welch Regiment	XXI
Royal Horse Artillery	
1st Regt RHA	III, VI, VII
2nd Regt RHA	V
3rd Regt RHA	III, IV
4th Regt RHA	VI
5th Regt RHA	X, XI, XIV, XVI, XVII, XX, XXI
102nd Regt RHA	VI
Other Royal Artillery Regiments	
4th Field Regt RA	VII
97th Field Regt RA	VII, VIII
15th Light AA Regt RA	VI
'H' Tp 259 A/T Bty 65 A/T Regt RA	VIII
Armoured & Motorised Brigades	
2nd Armd Bde	VI
3rd Armd Bde	I, III
4th Armd Bde	IV, V, VI, VIII, XVII, XVIII, XXI
7th Armd Bde	V
8th Armd Bde	IX, XIV
22nd Armd Bde	V, VI, VII, VIII, IX, XI, XII, XIII, XIV, XV, XVII, XIX, XX, XXI, XXII
23rd Armd Bde	VII
26th Armd Bde	X
29th Armd Bde	XV
7th Motorised Bde	VI
7AD Divisional Infantry and Lorried Infantry Brigades	
131 Brigade	XII, XIII, XIV, XVI, XX, XXI
141 Lorried Infantry Bde	VIII

COMMONWEALTH UNITS	
Australian (Tobruk Garrison)	IV
Royal Hamilton Light Infantry	XV
2nd Canadian Inf Div	XV
3rd Canadian Inf Div	XV
5th Canadian Armd Div	XII
Ist Canadian Corps	XVI
Gurkhas	X
3rd Indian Inf Bde	VI
4th Indian Inf Div	IX, X
New Zealand Forces	V, VII, VIII, IX
South African Forces	VI
ALLIED UNITS	
Free French	VI, VIII
Polish Armd Bde/Div	XV, XVIII
Spahis	X
UNITED STATES UNITS	
Armed Forces	XIV
501st Airborne Div	XVII
US 8th Armd Div	XIX
US 8 Corps	XIX
US 12 Corps	XIII
US 5th Army	XI, XII
AIR FORCES	
RAF	I, V, VII, IX, Int, XIV, XV, XIX
TAF	XV, XIX, XXI
USAAF	XV
AXIS FORCES	
DAK	III, VI, VII, VIII, IX, X
Panzerarmee	IX
5th Tank Regiment	III
593 Heavy Tank Bn	XV
Panzer Div 'Lehr'	XIV, XIX
1st SS Panzer Div	XV
2nd SS Panzer Div	XIX
7th [Ghost] Panzer Div	I
12th SS Panzer Div	XIV, XV
15th Light Panzer Div	V, VI, VIII
16th Panzer Div	IX
21st Panzer Div	V, VI, VIII, XIII, XIV, XV
116th Panzer Div	XIX
Panzergruppe	X
164 Inf Div	X
Italian Ariete Div	VI